The
U-Boat War
in the Caribbean

THE
U-BOAT WAR
IN THE
CARIBBEAN

Gaylord T. M. Kelshall

Naval Institute Press
Annapolis, Maryland

© 1988, 1994 by Gaylord T. M. Kelshall

Foreword © 1994
by the United States Naval Institute
Annapolis, Maryland

Originally published in 1988 by Paria Publishing Co. Ltd., Port-of-Spain, Trinidad and
Tobago.

Library of Congress Cataloging-in-Publication Data
Kelshall, Gaylord.
    The U-boat war in the Caribbean / Gaylord T. M. Kelshall.
        p.   cm.
    Originally published: Port of Spain, Trinidad, West Indies : Paria
Pub. Co., 1988.
    Includes bibliographical references and indexes.
    ISBN 1-55750-452-0
    1. World War, 1939–1945—Naval operations—Submarine.   2. World
War, 1939–1945—Naval operations, German.   3. World War, 1939–1945—
Campaigns—Caribbean Area.   I. Title.
D781.K45   1994   94-3130
940.54′51—dc20   CIP

Printed in the United States of America on acid-free paper ∞

9   8   7   6   5   4   3   2
First printing

In Dedication

To the memory of all those brave men who lost their lives in the Caribbean U-Boat War and in tribute to all those who took part.

Contents

List of Figures

Foreword

During World War II seventeen U-boats were sunk in the Caribbean—2 percent of the total U-boat losses for the entire war. But for each U-boat sunk in the Caribbean, the Allies lost 23.5 merchant ships. For the German navy, the Caribbean U-boat campaign was the most cost-effective campaign fought by Germany anywhere during World War II.

But the Caribbean campaign has been virtually overlooked by postwar authors. Most of the books written about this aspect of the war deal exclusively with attacks on shipping off the coast of the United States. The other two theaters that made up the Caribbean operations area have been ignored. *The U-Boat War in the Caribbean* tells the whole story.

Gaylord T. M. Kelshall has done more than simply recount the exploits of the U-boats that fought in the three Caribbean theaters. Drawing on Allied and German documents, interviews with participants, and the available published material, as well as his professional expertise in antisubmarine warfare, Kelshall has skillfully and authoritatively written the definitive history of this savagely fought war within a war. This book will appeal to readers and historians who are looking for complete details and little-known facts about the Caribbean U-boat campaign.

His account is placed in the context of the United States' sometimes abrasive relations with its Caribbean allies, the arguments (often heated) between the U.S. Navy and the Royal Navy over mining the entrance to the Gulf of Paria, the role of radio intelligence, and the U.S. Navy's steadily growing superiority in antisubmarine warfare technology.

Kelshall does not overstate the importance of the Caribbean campaign. It was, however, an important peripheral campaign in which, by the end of 1942, 36 percent of all shipping losses worldwide had occurred. Peripheral or not, such military success is notable. Kelshall carefully analyzes that success in light of the Germans' logistical problems, their solutions to those problems, and their strategic errors. He also shows how the individual U-boat commanders adapted to the Allies' growing antisubmarine warfare capabilities. This well-written, fast-paced book will be a valuable research tool for anyone interested in strategies for fighting a submarine war, both from the conning tower and aboard the antisubmarine unit.

Dwight R. Messimer

Preface

The history of the War in the Caribbean has been written to fill an important gap in the story of World War Two. It has often been alluded to, but historians have not noted its critical importance. In fact, in World War Two and today, the Caribbean is the outer defence ring covering the soft underbelly of the United States, as well as being the lynch pin for control of the central Atlantic. How did this vital struggle between the Allies and the German U-Boats come to be neglected?

Throughout the Second World War, the bulk of the United States Navy operated in the Pacific Ocean and the dramatic battles which took place in that theatre tended to overshadow the more critical naval War in the Atlantic. The action-packed Pacific campaign also threw up a lobby of powerful carrier admirals, whose influence shaped the public perception of the War and the role of the US Navy. Historians tended to follow the lead of the war correspondents and concentrated on the Pacific, because this was easily the most exciting and dramatic combat theatre of the US Navy.

However, the west coast of the United States was never seriously threatened either militarily or economically by the Japanese. The Pacific war was fought over territory and freedom of the adjacent seas and could almost be termed a foreign policy war. On the other hand, the German Atlantic threat impinged directly on America's industrial potential to wage war. But in the Atlantic, against the Germans the US Navy were never as successful as they were in the Pacific against the Japanese. This tended to reinforce the view that the US Navy's story was the Pacific story.

American historians tended to leave the Atlantic story to the British, who naturally concentrated on their titanic struggle in the North Atlantic, to the exclusion of the lesser known, but just as important peripheral theatres. Such a theatre was the Caribbean. When American historians did deal with the Atlantic, they tended to concentrate on British criticism of their handling of the U-Boat threat to their east coast shipping lanes. By extension, they included the coastline of the Americas as part of their east coast, lumping into one what took place in three distinct theatres.

The Germans were the defeated nation and for a considerable period of time, the public did not want to hear their side of the story. When in time the German records became available for research, the few German historians who emerged were forced to concentrate on the questions posed by Allied historians and write to a public who had been conditioned into the Allied view of the war. Naturally, the Allied version of events was still heavily spiced with the very necessary war winning propaganda, and this meant that anyone writing about the Battle of the Atlantic was forced to consider everything that took place in the western ocean as part of the U-Boat offensive off the American east coast.

But in fact, the war in the west took place in three distinct theatres and time frames. The first operation Paukenschlag, began in mid-January 1942 and ushered in the offensive off the American east coast. By mid 1942, this offensive had virtually run out of steam and only continued as a minor campaign to the end of the war.

One month after the start of Paukenschlag, operation Neuland commenced as a separate offensive. This was a distinctly Caribbean operation which lasted for the rest of 1942. The U-Boats which took part in operation Neuland did not come south from the American east coast, but direct to the Caribbean. By the end of the year, thirty-six percent of all world wide merchant shipping losses had occured in the Caribbean theatre. For the first few months of 1943, the Caribbean theatre was relegated to the status of a secondary operation, but in mid-1943, the Germans once again launched another massive Caribbean offensive. This was decisively defeated by the US Navy and for the rest of the War the Germans kept the Caribbean operation going purely for its nuisance value.

The third offensive in the west, was against Brazilian coastal traffic and this continued at varying levels of intensity for the rest of the war. Both the important Caribbean theatre and the associated Brazilian theatre have been largely neglected by historians of the post-war Battle of the Atlantic.

After 1942 with the exception of the July 1943 offensive in the Caribbean, the principal German objective in the west, was the tying down of Allied anti-submarine forces, which they managed to achieve. From northern Canada to the southern boundary of Brazil, the Allies had to keep a vast anti-submarine network in operation and the Germans kept up the threat by ensuring that there were always U-Boats operating in the west.

From the Allied point of view the war in the west was a very frustrating experience. Nowhere did the U-Boat kills equate with the vast resources deployed. Pilots spent days, weeks, and even years quartering the open wastes, sometimes without ever sighting a U-Boat, far less carrying out an attack. Yet they had to be ready at all times to roll straight into an attack, which would in later years be thoroughly criticized.

For some, the boredom was intersperced with periods of sheer terror, as they faced the formidable U-Boat anti-aircraft armament. Some never pulled out of their attack dive. Others succumbed to early aviation's temperamental aero engines and machines, which at times caused a loss rate many times greater than combat losses.

For the crews of the surface escorts, it was also a very frustrating experience. There were never enough escorts, or even adequate escort vessels in the Caribbean, with the result that convoy escorts relied heavily on the air component. Surface escorts only sank three of the seventeen U-Boats lost in the area, despite hundreds of contacts and depth-charge attacks.

For the U-Boat crews, the Caribbean initially represented the true Golden West. During 1942, they rampaged almost unchecked and a trip to the area was considered a gift. But as the war ground on and the US Navy built up its awesome power, the Caribbean became a very dangerous place for U-Boats. Yet, the morale of the U-Boatmen never cracked. Even in the days when no U-Boat left the Caribbean without being heavily damaged, the magnificent fighting spirit of the crews remained high.

The Caribbean was a theatre where both the Allies and the Germans made critical mistakes. The defenders always seemed to be reacting to German moves, and at times they were hopelessly outclassed. On the other hand, the German command seemed mesmerised by the great distance that separated the Caribbean from Europe and they never attempted close control and co-ordination of their Caribbean U-Boats in the manner in which they operated in the Atlantic. As a result they missed some golden opportunities. This was particularly true in 1943, when they challenged American airpower to do battle in the chokepoints, instead of going for the merchant shipping in the more vulnerable open spaces.

With good reasons, both sides chose to let the Caribbean story almost die and to concentrate their histories on the areas where they could capture the imagination of the reading public. Despite this the men who fought in the Caribbean did not forget the area.

Perhaps the only participants who never forgot the Caribbean were the merchant seamen, who were its principal victims. For them, the sunny Caribbean became a place of horror. They died in their thousands from the effects of torpedo explosions, of heat stroke, of thirst, of despair, or simply by drowning and by the ever present sharks. They alone kept the Caribbean story alive in the years when the military men were glorying in their gallant deeds in other, more successful and glamorous battles.

The real cost to the Caribbean cannot be measured so much by the events of the Second World War, but rather in the damage that has been done by trying to forget what took place. Because it was downgraded as an historical event, the military potential of the Caribbean was lost on the succeeding generations of military and civilians.

The residents of the Caribbean islands know little of what took place in 1942. Throughout the conflict they were kept in the dark and with the end of the war all records were classified as secret. This has led to a generation of military men who through lack of knowledge of the past, cannot conceive of the military threat that the Caribbean can pose in the future, and Caribbean politicians who believe that the area has no military significance. It has allowed the politicians to believe that they can remain neutral in world power politics because as far as they know the islands of the beautiful Caribbean Sea are of no tactical or strategic importance. This makes the subsequent neglect of the Caribbean story during the last four decades a dangerous precedent for the future.

GAYLORD T.M. KELSHALL
St. Augustine, Trinidad, W.I.
August 1987

Acknowledgments

In compiling any history such as this, the author needs to rely on a large number of sources for his material and this is particularly important when dealing with the largely untold story of the Caribbean in World War Two. It would not have been possible without the sterling assitance that I received from a large number of knowledgeable people.

Firstly, the book "Axis Submarine Successes" written by the leading U-Boat historian Dr. Jurgen Rohwer, was virtually the dictionary for this work. In addition, Dr. Rohwer took time off on many occasions to answer my many and varied querries on the U-Boat war. Also from West Germany the former U-Boatmen Klaus Erhardt and Alfred Hiller contributed greatly to my knowledge of U-Boat warfare, while Horst Bredow and Axel Niestle of the U-Boat Association were a great source of help, often guiding me in the right direction.

From the United States Mr. D.C. Allard of the US Navy Historical Centre, along with Colonel W. Stanick and Major Lester Sliter of the USAF Historical Centre, proved to be an unending source of encouragement, while making volumes of records available to me.

From Great Britain Mr. R.M. Coppock of the Ministry of Defence, Mr. F.J. Kemp of the Imperial War Museum, Mr. T.R. Padfield of the Public Records office and author Geoffrey Jones provided a great deal of assistance and data.

From Canada Mr. Hal Lawrence and Mr. W. Douglas provided much information on the Royal Canadian Navy and its role in the Caribbean during World War Two.

To all those people, as well as the many others too numerous to mention by name goes the credit for providing the volumes of information that I needed to begin writing. With the unstinting help that they gave and the inspiration from my father who first awoke a love of books and history in me, I was able to put together a manuscript.

But a manuscript is not a book and to a dedicated group of good people in Trinidad, I owe a debt of gratitude. Mrs. Juliet Roopnarinesingh and her daughter Beth, Judy and David Law, Paula and William Lucie-Smith, Thomas Harding and Joyce Basanta. They typed and did the proof reading in record time, while providing invaluable advice and encouragement. Lawrence Goldstraw put his hard won knowledge of German at my disposal and translated much data into English, while to Margaret Power and her brother Geoffrey must go the credit for the planned publication of this book in Europe and America.

My thanks also go to Loren McIntyre, who read this book and decided that it was worth republication. He contacted the Naval Institute Press, and as a result of his efforts the book will reach a much wider audience. To him I owe a tremendous debt of gratitude.

But behind every project there is a power source and in the case of this book, it was the tireless work, influence and encouragement of Mrs. Olga Mavrogordato. She was the person who read the original manuscript and decided that this was a story worth the telling. She mobilised support and became the driving force who made all things possible. She above all others must get the credit for this work and I will be eternally in her debt. She made this book possible.

G.T.M.K.

Publisher's Note

Owing to economic constraints the Naval Institute Press is unable to give full editorial treatment to *The U-Boat War in the Caribbean,* one thousand copies of which were originally published by the author in 1988 in his native Trinidad and Tobago. Rather than forgo publication of this important historical record, the Press presents this work in a facsimile edition, with minor corrections, some different photographs, the addition of notes, and a new foreword.

The
U-Boat War
in the Caribbean

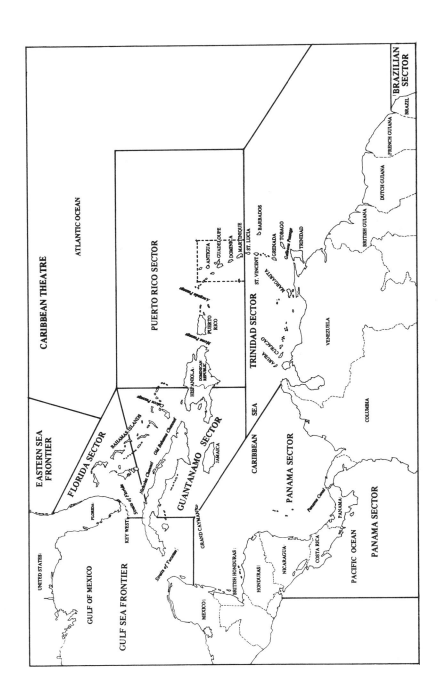

CHAPTER

1

If you want Peace, prepare for War

The declaration of war in 1939 was a signal for the Germans to unleash their submarine fleet to prey on the vital shipping that plied the waters around the British Isles. This initial thrust later developed into the famous Battle of the Atlantic. Reminiscent of the First World War, when German submarines had almost brought Britain to her knees, Hitler's Kriegsmarine set out to emulate and better their forebears. The British, once again under siege, resorted to the formula that had frustrated the Germans in 1917 and established the convoy system. By October 1940, the German U-Boats answered with the wolf pack concept and the battle at sea entered a new and grimmer phase. The end of 1940 marked a period when more than one thousand ships had been sunk, despite the valiant effort that had been put into protecting them. The problem for the British revolved around the availability of purpose-built convoy escorts.

The type of vessel required needed to be able to steam slowly at convoy speed, with the endurance necessary to stay with the North Atlantic convoys and still be capable of hunting and killing submarines along the way.

The lack of such vessels in sufficient numbers meant that destroyers had to be used for escort. Designed as a fast dashing naval vessel for killing surface ships and escorting the great battle fleets, the destroyer had also been adapted to the anti-submarine role. They lacked the endurance to stay with the slow plodding merchant ships, and at best they could perform as escort leaders, but in 1940, destroyers were the only naval vessels available for convoy escort, and therefore they had to be relied on almost exclusively.

In September of that year, Britain possessed one hundred and seventy-one destroyers to handle all her commitments worldwide. However, half of this number were undergoing repairs for battle damage, yet this was not the major problem. The critical factor was that during 1940, Britain had added twenty-one new destroyers to her fleet, but she had lost thirty-four during the same period. Sheer attrition would eventually reduce the number of destroyers to the point where fleet requirements would leave the convoys exposed, without escorts. Something had to be acquired quickly to bridge the gap between the losses and new production, if they were not to lose the battle of the Atlantic. Mid-1940 also saw the fall of France, which opened up the French channel ports to the U-Boats, thus vastly increasing their effectiveness.

At the start of the conflict, Roosevelt had told the American people to judge for themselves who was right, while remaining neutral as a nation. This well-meaning statement was based on the American President's personal view of the war. As far as he was concerned, Britain was the champion, fighting against world domination by an offensive tyranny, but unfortunately, not everyone in America thought that way. There was a strong lobby that favoured contined American neutrality, based on the soon to be discredited nineteenth century isolationist foreign policy. They felt that the United States should keep well clear of European politics and go her own independent way.

Events were to prove them very wrong, because World War Two had started and would continue to escalate, almost exclusively based on the acquisition of territory. The reasons for the war were not as complex as the tangled politics which had led to the First World War. The mid-twentieth century did not tolerate neutral giants. In addition to the isolationists, there was a strong lobby of Americans of German extraction, particularly in big business circles, who felt a stronger kinship with Germany than with Britain. The President's well-meaning call for individual judging of the situation opened the door for some of the German-Americans to help Germany. It has even been said that while the British navy hunted the Bismark, there were four American tankers waiting in the Atlantic to refuel her.

Roosevelt however, with the backing of the majority of the American people remained firmly committed to Britain. He was an astute judge of the world situation, if not of people. He realised that sooner or later America would not be able to continue her neutrality without being isolated and eventually overwhelmed by world power politics. In the furtherance of his ideals, he took a keen interest in how Britain was faring against the might of Germany and Italy. In this atmosphere, he developed a close friendship with the British Prime Minister, which led in its turn to America slowly joining the conflict, without the average American being aware of it.

In May 1940, when the losses in the Atlantic began to reach the critical stage, Churchill looked around for help. Russia had made a separate peace with Germany, having shared in the dismemberment of Poland, and Italy was firmly in the Axis camp. Only America could help and on the fifteenth of that month, Churchill approached Roosevelt. Using his new-found friendship with the American President and taking the line that German domination was their common enemy, he asked the President for an outright gift of fifty destroyers, with which he could stem the tide of losses in the Atlantic.

Roosevelt, conscious of the need for solidarity among the English-speaking peoples, looked very favourably on the request, and put the question to his people. He was trying to get Americans to realise the grave danger that would threaten them if Britain fell, but he ran up against immediate opposition. The isolationists opposed the idea on the grounds that handing over the destroyers was tantamount to joining the British in their war. The view was also expressed that handing over the destroyers as a gift would prejudice America's relationship with Germany, and at this stage it looked very much as if Germany would be the winning team. Dunkirk, and the fall of France convinced many Americans that the end was near for Britain. The Battle of Britain was soon to be fought and this would be followed by a German invasion of England. America would be hanging onto the losing team and stood to lose everything.

Argument over the question of the fifty destroyers continued, but Roosevelt was determined to find a way. The destroyers were available. The US Navy had a large number of old flush-decked, four-funnelled destroyers, mothballed in her reserve fleet. The problem was how to transfer them to the British and still satisfy the politics of the thing. Finally, an influential lobby of Americans, called the Century Group, came up with a solution for the President. They harked back to a First World War proposal, that Britain hand over all her military bases in the western hemisphere as payment for her war debt. The idea was refurbished and brought up to date. It was impossible to ask a nation at war to relinquish her military bases to a neutral country. Instead, the idea was put forward that American bases could be positioned alongside British bases in the British colonies, in exchange for the destroyers. That way it almost amounted to a sale and Germany should not be quite so offended. Actually the Germans never considered the bases agreement as anything other than an attempt by America to bolster Britain, and they made full use of it in their wartime propaganda. The deal was put to Churchill and he, facing the prospect of his Atlantic lifeline being severed by the U-Boats, had no option but to agree.

The destroyers were handed over, — forty-four of them to the Royal Navy, and six to the Royal Canadian Navy. Old they may have been, but they arrived just in time and made an immediate impact on the battle. They bridged the gap while specialist convoy escorts were being built and helped to keep the Atlantic route open. The breathing space had been gained but now the price had to be paid. In August Churchill announced the deal in the House of Commons, to be followed in September by Roosevelt telling Congress. But where were these American bases to be located?

By this stage American survey teams had already done preliminary work and they knew precisely what they wanted. Land was granted for army and navy installations on Great Exuma Island in the Bahamas and in Jamaica. On the eastern side of the Caribbean, the islands of Antigua and St. Lucia were chosen, while Trinidad and British Guiana completed the circle of bases ringing the Caribbean. Bases on Bermuda and in Newfoundland came later and technically were not a part of the Agreement. Final discussions were held in October of 1940 and it was here that the ultimate harsh terms were agreed on. The land for the bases in the various countries was to be leased to America for ninety-nine years. The isolationists had got their pound of flesh and more.

In March 1941, the formal signing of the bases agreement took place in London, but by this stage work had already started on many of the sites. The British Governors in the various islands took the news of the American incursion according to the individual needs of the islands. Most accepted the fact that it had all been agreed on before they became involved, but not so the Governor of Trinidad Sir Hubert Young. He took up the fight although few of the native Trinidadians understood what it was all about. He objected to the siting of the bases, particularly the naval base at Chaguaramas, because it took the best part of the island. He even travelled to the United States to argue his case. He fought vehemently but to no avail and his relations with the Americans were so difficult, that early in the war he was recalled to England.

It is ironic that the bases agreement should have generated so much controversy both before and after the war, because events were shortly to dictate that they had to be there anyway. Whether the British, the Americans or the local people wanted the bases or not, the war was going to dictate that they had to be built, bases agreement or not.

The chief bone of contention was the length of the projected lease. To the people involved in 1941, ninety-nine years seemed like eternity. In reality the last base was closed twenty-five years later and the agreement could easily have given this figure and thus not generated the level of opposition which it did. Churchill had been primarily concerned with ensuring that Britain was able to survive and thus preserve western civilisation, and it is unlikely that he gave much thought to the anomaly that the whole idea presented, both from a military and political point of view. All the territories concerned were part of the British Empire and as such, at war with Germany. America was neutral, yet her military bases sat on the islands that were all on a war footing. It presented a serious problem to the defenders of the territories when they thought in terms of what would happen in the event of a German raid.

With the anomaly in mind, a conference was held on 9th July 1941 that had as its theme the joint Anglo American defence of the Caribbean. Coming out of the conference was a declaration by the neutral Americans, that they would resist any change in the sovereignty of the territories. Whether it was made public or not, it was virtually an American declaration of war on Germany. It was obvious that Roosevelt considered America at war in all but a formal declaration. The planners in Washington obviously were quite firm in their intention to fight, but the British commanders on the islands can be forgiven for viewing the whole thing with a certain degree of scepticism. In Trinidad for example, British and American forces pursued their own aims quite independently of each other and it was not until America had actually been at war for three weeks that they sat down together to draw up a joint defence plan, and this plan was not complete until June 1942.

Another American plan which had confused the issue earlier was the announcement in 1939 of the Pan American neutrality agreement, which had been signed in Panama. This established a neutral zone extending three hundred miles from the coast of the Americas! The fact that the zone encompassed British and Dutch territories at war with Germany, as well as Vichy French islands, does not seem to have worried the signatories to the document. Eighty US destroyers were assigned to this neutrality patrol and on paper it looked as if the United States could back up its commitment.

Unfortunately, nearly all of these destroyers operated in the western reaches of the Atlantic on quite another mission. Within this official neutrality zone these destroyers were seldom if ever seen, and it was within this zone that the heaviest blow fell when war came. No wonder the British commanders in the islands put little faith in the Washington declaration.

Great Exuma and Antigua ended up with military aviation facilities, while Jamaica ended up with a small US Army presence. Jamaica was a special case because it had always been a British military base and indeed there was always a full battalion of infantry deployed there. In addition, Jamaica lay close to the large US Navy installations at Guantanamo Bay in Cuba and extensive Jamaican facilities would only have been a duplication of effort. St. Lucia however, had a large facility constructed suitable for housing an entire infantry division, although the island never received such a large garrison. Within St. Lucia's army camp an extensive air base was constructed, that like its infantry counterpart, spent the war with only a fraction of its intended complement. Nevertheless, St. Lucia proved to be an excellent refuelling stop for patrol bombers and it also served as an ideal base for keeping the Vichy French islands under surveillance.

British Guiana ended up with a small US Army detachment guarding the airport, which became a front line airbase in the fight against the U.Boats. Trinidad on the other hand, appeared to be the major acquisition of the bases agreement. A large army base was constructed in the north-east of the island and named Fort Reid, after Major General Reid, an American First World War hero. This extensive facility was designed to accommodate a garrison of three divisions, although its strength never exceeded twenty thousand.

Geographically, the United States of America has always been at a severe strategic disadvantage, having to defend two oceans without a connecting sea link. From a naval point of view, this means that the transfer from one coast to another of even a minor naval vessel, involved a sea journey of more than twelve thousand miles. Not only was this a very long journey that could use up precious time, but in wartime it could also be very hazardous. In this respect, the Panama Canal became and continues to be vital to American strategic interests. The Canal made possible the transfer of naval resources between the two oceans and its defence became a major issue. It was so sensitive that it distorted American strategy during World War Two in the Caribbean.

Historians have traditionally pointed to the destruction of the US Navy's battle line at Pearl Harbour as the spur which forced American reliance on the aircraft carrier. This in turn is said to have dictated how the

Pacific war was fought. This view does the American Armed forces less than credit. They were heavily air-oriented before Pearl Harbour and nowhere was this more apparent than in the defence of the Panama Canal.

Before the Germans struck in the Caribbean, American defence planning revolved around defending the Panama Canal against two primary threats. The first of these was the possibility of a Pacific carrier strike by the Japanese and the second was the possibility of a German air strike against the Canal from airbases in the broad expanse of the Amazon plain. This is borne out by the periodic reports of defence inspections of the area carried out before America was involved in World War Two and the disposition of the forces in the area. They were fully aware of Japanese carrier potential and the possible Luftwaffe threat. What shocked the Americans and caused the almost paralytic trauma was not what airpower could do, but the fact that they had been struck without warning. Pearl Harbour only strengthened the threat to the Canal and dictated what sort of continued defensive stance the forces in the Caribbean should adopt.

This is dramatically borne out by the placement of the bases in the Caribbean and the equipment which they were provided. There was an outer defence ring anchored at Trinidad and running in an arc through Puerto Rico to Cuba in the northwest and these bases were all airpower-oriented. Prior to the German thrust into the area, the United States air resources in the theatre were composed of one hundred and eighty-nine bombers and two hundred and two fighters. The bombers were tasked with an anti-shipping role, to hit German aircraft carriers, as well as the threatened air bases in the wide Amazon Valley. The fighters were for defence against these air threats and in some cases bomber escort. The infantry garrisons and coast defences were sited to defend these airfields. The US Navy had attached a similar priority to the area, but with a purely offensive capability. There was a submarine base in St. Croix for the outer ring and another on the Caribbean side of the Panama Canal. These submarines would operate offensively alongside the Army Air Corps in strikes against attacking aircraft carriers. Later, when the Vichy fleet became a threat, these same forces were expected to deal with them.

This was not the sort of organisation which could handle a German U-Boat threat, because the US Navy in the Caribbean was almost exclusively offensive-oriented. The tragedy was that the shock of Pearl Harbour could not be shaken off. The defensive posture was not flexible enough to switch to an anti-submarine oriented stance when the U-Boats appeared. The result was that for most of 1942 the heavy emphasis on air defence persisted and accounted for the large number of fighter aircraft stationed in the theatre.

In fact, long after the U-Boat offensive had begun to die out, there were still large numbers of fighters stationed in the area.

Early in 1942, the British scientist Watson Watt was invited to inspect the area and make recommendations for handling the U-Boat threat. His report detailed surface search radar equipment in all the passages primarily to detect U-Boats as they entered the Caribbean. By 1943, radar was installed in all the passages, but air search sets to guard against the air threat. To the end of the war these air search sets remained and the U-Boats profited greatly by the refusal to set aside the possibility of air attack on the canal.

In June 1941, the US Navy established the Caribbean Sea Frontier. The new command extended from the Yucatan Peninsula to the area west of the island of Grand Cayman, then northwards to Cuba and out through the Bahamas, before stretching eastwards into the Atlantic. In the southeast corner, the limit of the Caribbean Sea Frontier was defined by a line running eastwards from the French Guiana/Brazil border. Later in the war, the area to the south of this line became the Brazilian theatre.

Initially, the Caribbean Sea Frontier was divided into three sectors, controlled from Panama, Trinidad and Puerto Rico. Panama controlled the area from the Venezuelan/Colombian border, northwest to Grand Cayman, thence to the Yacatan Peninsula. The demarcation line between the northern Puerto Rican Sector and the Trinidad Sector ran east/west across the Caribbean, passing between St. Lucia and Martinique. To the eastwards, the Sea Frontier extended out to the extreme range of the aircraft based in the area. In 1942, this gave a practical eastwards limit of five hundred miles but this kept increasing as longer ranged aircraft became available. This meant that even in its initial form, the Caribbean Sea Frontier was one of the largest anti-submarine commands in the world. From its northwest corner to the far southeast, it stretched for two thousand five hundred miles. From the Venezuelan coast northwards, the command was a thousand miles wide. This gave it an area of two and a half million square miles, with thousands of miles of coastline. The war was to force many amendments.

The Trinidad Sector had bases with airfields running along its length from Aruba in the west to Dutch Guiana in the southeast. This meant that from the very beginning Trinidad was geographically able to handle adequately its area of responsibility. The Panama Sector, however, was desperately short of space to base its aircraft. Most of the Caribbean airpower was clustered in Panama, near to the Canal, but until the Central American countries declared war on Germany and bases could be constructed on their territories, most of this airpower was wasted. In any case, the majority of aviation units in Panama were committed to the Pacific side of the Canal and carrying out reconnaissance flights over the Amazon Valley. Among them were twenty-five B17s and a number of PBYs that never operated over the Caribbean waters. This meant that from the start of the conflict, the aircraft of the Trinidad command based in Aruba, had to work westwards well into the Panama Sector; and in fact for most of the war, Trinidad carried responsibility for keeping aircraft on the Atlantic side of Panama. In the long term a subsidiary sector was established at Curacao, which handled the eastern part of the Panama Sector.

From the start of the German thrust into the Caribbean, it became apparent that the Puerto Rico Sector was too large. Aircraft based in Puerto Rico were always primarily concerned with the threat to the north and east of the islands. Very much like the Panama Sector, the US defences were initially clustered on American soil and as such, unable to cover the whole sector. As a result, in practice Trinidad assumed the responsibility for the island chain, but the major problem did not lie in the east.

The island of Hispaniola lay between Puerto Rico and the Windward Passage and this forced the creation of a completely different command sector, based on the naval base at Guantanamo Bay. From this area, aircraft were able to operate westwards to Grand Cayman and the strategically important Straits of Yucatan. As bases were completed in Cuba, this task was more easily accomplished. Much the same situation existed to the north of the Windward Passage and in practice Guantanamo controlled the Bahamas. These changes effectively divided the Caribbean Sea Frontier into four command sectors.

The Gulf of Mexico was established as the Gulf Sea Frontier, with its bases on American soil. This area came under the command of the Eastern Sea Frontier which was responsible for the American coast. In peacetime, the Gulf Sea Frontier had responsibility for the whole Gulf, but once war was declared the situation changed dramatically. Half of the land area surrounding the Gulf was Mexican territory, including the Yucatan Peninsula guarding the Straits of Yucatan; and until Mexico declared war and allowed American bases on her soil, the Americans were unable to patrol the Gulf effectively. In theory, the Gulf Sea Frontier had control of a portion of the Caribbean which extended almost to Grand Cayman, but in practice this area had to be handled by the Guantanamo Sector. The Gulf Sea Frontier was independent of the Caribbean, but this was not how the Germans viewed the area.

Initially, the German U-Boats operated off Florida and Key West as part of the offensive against shipping on the east coast of the United States.

The Florida Sector was part of this Eastern Sea Frontier and was reinforced long before the Caribbean, with the result that the Straits of Florida became a dangerous place for U-Boat operations. This forced the U-Boats enroute to and from the Gulf of Mexico to use the wider and deeper Yucatan Straits. To do this they had to pass through the Caribbean, which automatically made the Caribbean Sea Frontier largely responsible for what went on in the Gulf. As the campaign developed the Germans considered the Gulf of Mexico as an extension of the Caribbean campaign. When a U-Boat received orders for the Caribbean, it could find itself assigned to the Gulf of Mexico, the Straits of Florida, the Bahamas, within the Caribbean proper, or off the South American coast, as far as French Guiana. This meant that the Caribbean theatre stretched from the furthest corners of the Gulf of Mexico right down to the French Guiana/Brazil border. This did not conform to the American command boundaries, but it was the German offensive area and as such, the defence of the whole area needed to be considered as one. This was particularly important when U-Boats began slipping into the Gulf of Mexico and out again, several times on a single patrol.

Later, when Brazil entered the war, the Germans considered the war in the west as being three distinct operating theatres. These were, the American east coast as far as Florida, the Caribbean including the Gulf of Mexico and associated areas, and the Brazilian theatre. All three theatres grew eastwards as the war progressed, until by 1944, the Caribbean theatre controlled half of the Atlantic east of the islands.

As far back as July 1940, an American Senator had proposed that the United States be encircled by a steel ring of defences, but December 1941 found this ring to be largely a paper organization. The Panama Sector never received the anti-submarine resources that it needed and the Germans took full advantage of this in 1942. However, as the Caribbean campaign slowed up, the Germans found themselves increasingly tied down trying to break the American hold on the merchant shipping chokepoints and in so doing, they missed many opportunities in the Panama Sector. The Puerto Rico Sector evolved into the guardian of the Mona Passage and the lesser Anegada Passage, which were primarily U-Boat transitting areas. The Puerto Rico based forces were constantly tracking boats as they came in from the Atlantic and hastening their retreat on the way out from the battle areas.

The main Caribbean battle areas were off the mouth of the Mississippi in the Gulf of Mexico, around the Windward Passage and the Trinidad area. The battle off the Mississippi did not last more than three months, because the American reaction was fast and furious. It was too close to the American oil ports and the water was shallow, making it easier to detect the U-Boats.

The Windward Passage however, was a merchant shipping chokepoint. All convoys had to pass through this passage and the Germans made a serious attempt to cut the shipping lane. Although the water in the Passage was deep, it was a confined area and the advantage lay with the defenders. The U-Boats operating in the Windward Passage fought hard and sank a number of ships, but by the end of 1942 they had virtually been driven out of the area.

The Trinidad area however, was fiercely fought over right up to the end of the war. During 1941 when the Americans were building their bases and preparing for war, they were not concentrating on a U-Boat threat. Within the compound of the Army base, a twin parallel runway aviation complex was constructed for the US Army Air Corps, and this with its outlying auxiliary airfields proved to be the only useful component of the Army bases in the coming conflict.

The idea behind these bases, particularly the one in Trinidad, was to guard against a German move, either around Britain to West Africa, or across North Africa to West Africa and then across the Atlantic to the Caribbean from which area, the soft underbelly of the United States would be exposed, as well as the sensitive Panama Canal.

The idea that there was a land threat to the United States through the Caribbean was never taken seriously by the British, but it does not seem quite so farfetched when the South American situation is taken into account. There were one million Germans living in Brazil and a greater number in Argentina, and this German element carried considerable political and business influence in the South American countries. A little later in the war, Venezuela had five thousand Germans interned in concentration camps. Curacao had three hundred detained, and Dutch Guiana had a hundred and fifty-one, against only three Germans detained in Trinidad. The American idea was that if all these South American Germans were to influence the Vichy French in Martinique to join them and provide the naval component, they could with very little support from Germany, pose a significant threat to the United States.

Throughout the war, all the Caribbean countries boasted a complex civil defence organization geared to handling air raids by German aircraft. This may seem laughable when it is considered that the Luftwaffe was at least five thousand miles away, – but there was a good reason. On the outbreak of the Second World War, a surprising number of Lufthansa aircraft had been trapped in South America and these machines were considered capable of being used as bombers. When the fleet with its aircraft carrier in Martinique was considered as a part of the potential enemy capability, the

American worry about Caribbean security gains considerable credence. It must be remembered that at this time, children in certain schools in Martinique were being taught the NAZI salute and the most casual remark about Britain surviving was grounds enough for a Vichy French Magistrate to jail the offender. Had anything gone wrong in the region, the US Army would have been commended for being in the right place, at the right time. But the Caribbean war became an almost exclusively naval event, with the result that the US Army garrisons were destined to spend a very frustrating war in the region and the scale of US Army involvement has often been criticised.

All the treaties, promises real and nebulous commitments and anomolies died on 7th December 1941, when the aircraft of the Japanese carrier fleet devastated Pearl Harbour, and American innocence. The bloodbath shocked the American people to the core and relegated the isolationist view to the scrapheap of history. But the trauma of Pearl Harbour was such that it tended to overshadow what took place shortly afterwards off the American east coast. The phase of the Battle of the Atlantic which was ushered in was to make the losses to the American Pacific fleet at Pearl Harbour appear miniscule.

The American declaration of war on December 8th, opened up an entirely new field of operations for the hard pressed German U-Boats, and they took full advantage of it. The U-Boats traditionally operated in the least defended areas in use by their targets and survival in the North Atlantic was becoming more difficult. The British escort vessels were becoming much more prevalent and the battles between the wolf packs and the escort groups were causing losses, without the high return in merchant ships sunk which the Germans needed. Air power and escorts had rendered the early hunting grounds around the British coasts untenable and the savagery of the fight out in mid-Atlantic was causing the German Command to look elsewhere for easy targets. They were on the threshold of discovering "The Golden West".

On December 29th 1941, British code analysts detected the first wave of five U-Boats heading westwards to the American coast. They advised the Americans of the coming onslaught, but it was rather late to make up for the neglect of the previous two years.

Grand Admiral Carl Doenitz, in command of Germany's U-Boat arm, despatched five U-Boats to the American Coast on the basis of a hunch that conditions there might be more profitable than continuing the killing match in the wastes of the North Atlantic. The full force of the intended blow was stunted by Hitler, who insisted that there was a British threat to Norway.

He ordered that twenty U-Boats be held in reserve to counter any British move on the northern flank. Thus, instead of twenty-five, Doenitz was only able to despatch five boats. This order from Hitler reduced the scale of the blow to one fifth of its potential power and the decision has been much criticised.

Ironically, Churchill was at this time considering a diversionary invasion of Norway to take the pressure off other areas. Churchill's advisers successfully defeated the Norway proposal, but Hitler's intuition was correct. Nevertheless, the five U-Boats which could be spared ploughed across the Atlantic to a new hunting ground, full of hope that their experience would make the difference when they ran into the American escort groups, – who no doubt would take some time to learn their trade. They were not aware that the American escort groups did not exist.

The offensive by the U-Boats off the American coast was code named, Paukenschlag, freely translated to mean, "roll of the drums". It was scheduled to begin on January 14th when all the boats were in position and thus spread the anti-submarine reaction. However, Kapitanleutnant Reinhard Hardegen in command of U123 was in position on 12th January and astonished to find brightly lit up merchant ships sailing without any protection, as though in peace-time. Grabbing the undreamed of opportunity, he began Paukenschlag that same day by sending the freighter Cyclops to the bottom, with the loss of eighty-seven lives. The Golden West had been discovered. The U-Boat commanders had difficulty believing that they were operating off the coasts of a nation at war. Independently sailing merchant ships, silhouetted against a brightly lit coastline proved to be ideal targets for the U-Boats and they sent twenty-five to the bottom in the first ten days. The U-Boats adopted the tactic of lying on the bottom in daylight in relatively deep water, surfacing and moving into very shallow water at night, to continue the slaughter. In the nineteen days of January, thirty-nine ships were sunk, sixteen of them tankers. During this period, not a single U-Boat was even detected.

Despite having had two years to observe the development of U-Boat warfare and prepare, the US Navy was caught totally unprepared. The much publicised neutrality patrol along the Americas, simply did not exist. To cover the three thousand mile American coastline, the navy had only twenty escort vessels and not one of them could outrun a U-Boat on the surface. Of the one hundred and eight aircraft assigned to the east coast, half were trainers. There were no convoys, there was no coastal blackout, navigation aids remained on and shipping broadcasts continued as in peace-time. The few destroyers which operated in the area, did so in hunting groups and on fixed schedules, making them easy to avoid.

Early in the war, the British had tried hunting groups and found that they failed. The U-Boats were primarily after merchant ships, therefore they could be more easily located in proximity to these vessels. But the hunting group idea always appeals to the naval officer and fits in much more readily with his ideas of a dashing agressive war, than the slow tedious job of protecting merchant shipping. The tragedy of the situation was that the US Navy were insisting on their right to make mistakes which had been made much earlier in the conflict. The day of the hunting group would come, but 1942 needed a different solution.

This astonishing unpreparedness for war also extended to the civilians ashore and afloat. It appeared at first to be very difficult to get people to understand that by leaving their lights burning ashore, they were silhouetting the merchant ships for the prowling U-Boats. In the south a glaring example was highlighted when the Chamber of Commerce declined to turn off their neon–lighted waterfrontage. A blackout of this area would keep the tourists away. The incongruous situation then existed of the tourists sitting in their brightly lit bars and beachfront hotels, relaxing while they watched the U-Boats at work offshore.

This attitude had a parallel in the Caribbean, when the war reached that theatre. They were thousands of miles away from the nearest German soldiers and found it very difficult to identify with the shocked merchant seamen survivors who came ashore. Officially, secrecy forbade the military men from telling anyone what was going on a few miles offshore and a barrier came up between the combatants and the general population of the islands, to the point where the islanders carried on as if the war didn't exist.

In some territories the civilians took the situation seriously and played their part in the civil defence measures, while in others the level of preparedness was extremely poor. In all the islands there was almost total ignorance of the seriousness of the Caribbean conflict during and after the war, with the result that all they could remember was the restrictions that this so-called war had imposed on their lives.

But the difficulty of getting a realisation of the importance of going onto a war footing, was not restricted to the civilians ashore. Surprisingly the merchant seamen took a long time to realise that the death struggle in mid-Atlantic had now moved westward to the shores of the Americas. The merchant men chatted away to each other on the radio, often giving their positions and where they were going. The U-Boats naturally just listened to the radio conversations and acted accordingly. They were also extremely gullible, as is evidenced by one case where a U-Boat pretended to be a light vessel and transmitted to his intended victim, the information that he was standing into danger and directed the ship into a course towards the waiting torpedoes. The ship obeyed and was sunk with the loss of twenty lives.

There were no Port Directors to brief the merchantmen on the discipline and stealth needed to survive in what had become hostile waters. When this total lack of appreciation of the situation was combined with regular shipping broadcasts which told the U-Boats where the ships were, the result was chaos. But the real failure lay in not having planned for war, aggravated by the unwillingness to employ the convoy system.

In the First World War, the lesson had been learned the hard way, that the only real answer to the U-Boat was the convoy. In the second conflict, the British had lost no time in implementing the system, while trying other solutions on a limited scale to see what would happen. Trial and error had ruled out everything but the convoy system and purpose-built escorts. Somewhere along the line, the US Government had got the idea that convoy escorts could be quickly constructed, when the need arose, despite the fact that they had been the principal spectators and intimate confidants of the British crisis over lack of escorts. Now that the escorts were desperately needed, they would take time to build and the US Navy desperately looked elsewhere for solutions.

The newly appointed commander of the US Navy, Admiral Ernest J. King, is reputed to have said that he preferred no convoys to inadequately escorted convoys. It has been suggested that this was a reaction against following the British lead and accepting their solution as the American solution. The traditional American independence of thought and deed came to the fore and they obstinately refused to listen to the voice of experience. The result could be seen in the rising daily toll of merchant ships lost.

Historians have derided the time the US Navy took in evaluating the innumerable solutions as a total waste, and branded consideration of these schemes as a deliberate attempt to avoid the obvious solution. Events were to prove that this was only partly true. A judgement that ignores the impact of Pearl Harbour on the American mind cannot be considered final. The fact of the matter was that the shock and indignation over the attack caused all Americans to consider Japan as the arch enemy. Long before the Japanese attack, American leaders had planned to tackle Germany first and it is to their credit that they were able to hold to this doctrine and persevere with a European solution.

However, emotion dictated that Japan had to be stopped and taught a lesson, before tackling the major problem of Germany. Doctrine stated that

Germany was the most powerful adversary and a great deal of lip service was paid to this concept, but it was never fully implemented. In real terms this meant that instead of a massive transfusion of destroyers to the Atlantic seaboard, the opposite took place. Livermore Class destroyers were scheduled to serve off the coast where they were built, while the more powerful Benson and Fletcher class destroyers were to serve in the Pacific, regardless of on which coast they were built.

This policy put out early in the war shows clearly a bias to the Pacific, but as the war progressed the Germans were to force amendments. When the situation became grim enough, Fletcher class destroyers would find their way to the Caribbean, but this was still some time off. The start of the Paukenschlag offensive found nearly all the American Atlantic Fleet destroyers concentrated off the western end of the North Atlantic convoy route. It is undoubtedly true that American troops began crossing the Atlantic shortly after the commencement of hostilities and they needed protection, but this strategy left the routes over which the raw material flowed toward America, almost totally unprotected.

There were flaws in the American strategy, and these dictated what took place. In the meantime, the U-Boat commanders rejoiced, not really believing that their freedom off the American coast could be true, nor could it last.

It has often been suggested that America had no strategy for handling the U-Boats. This is also true, although the strategy could not be released to the mass of the American people. Doenitz estimated that if his U-Boats could sink seven hundred thousand tons of shipping each month, he would win the battle of the Atlantic. For the U-Boats it was a tonnage war, but it was also a tonnage war in reverse for the Americans. The strategy was simply to build more merchant ships than the U-Boat could sink. No one dared to put into writing such a strategy which took no cognizance of the cost in human lives, but it explains the lack of initial concern over the convoying of the ships and the heavy emphasis on merchant ship construction. American industry would win the battle with material. On 19th February 1942, Roosevelt inaugurated the largest ship building programme in history. Twenty-four million tons of shipping were to be built in 1942. This raised the ship building rate from one, to three a day. In 1943, they were to double the 1942 levels and so on, – but what was going to happen while this mammoth task was getting underway?

On 3rd February, Admiral King turned down a suggestion from his staff that limited convoys should be initiated, holding fast to his doctrine that no convoys were better than inadequately escorted convoys. However, the scale of merchant shipping losses was rising so fast that by the end of February, the US Navy were forced to swallow their pride and accept proffered help from the Royal Navy. Even then there was an element of pride. They accepted the offer of escort vessels, but adamantly refused the experienced personnel that the British offered to help set up a defensive system.

Once again events were moving too fast. March saw the losses reach crisis proportions and Admiral King was forced to appoint a Board to advise on the implementing of a convoy system. The Board came back from their deliberations with the answer that full convoys would not be possible before August 1942. This assessment was based on the planned availability of escort vessels and not on the urgency of the situation. By this stage, the US Navy had collected one hundred and twenty-two vessels capable of escort duty, but the full convoy system would require five hundred and ninety. Based on the shortfall, the assumption was drawn that convoying was not possible, but the Royal Navy was holding its own, although it was short of three hundred and forty-two escorts! Sometimes, improvisation is the most difficult art that a nation at war is forced to learn and this is doubly true for a nation that believes in material. It was with this in mind that Roosevelt urged Admiral Andrews in command of the east coast to – improvise, invent and do things that no one had done before. Eventually, the U-Boats forced the US Navy to improvise and partial convoys began in April. It is significant that the US Navy sank their first U-Boat in April.

The Battle of the Atlantic was vital to the Allies; it was the survival link for both Britain and America. It is well documented that if the Atlantic lifeline had been severed, Britain would have gone under, or been fought to a standstill, but less well considered is the impact of such a severing on America. In these circumstances, Russia might have made a separate peace with Germany, as she had done in 1939, or at the very least, stood on the defensive for many years. In this event, Germany triumphant in Europe, would almost certainly have influenced the giant South American republics to join her camp.

American influence in South America began only during the closing years of the war, when Germany was on the retreat. Most of Africa, formerly British or European, would have been in the Axis camp and who knows where India and China might have ended up. This would have pitted America alone against the combined might of the Axis powers and their Allies.

American military might in the closing years of the war has tended to overshadow how unprepared she was in 1942. Her navy was not the equal of a small portion of Germany's submarine fleet, far less had it been pitted against the full might of all three Axis powers, possibly augmented by captured British and French vessels. Her navy was a pale shadow of the world-girdling giant that would roam the oceans unchallenged in 1945. Her Army Air Corps hardly existed in 1942 and it would take at least a year before American aircraft made a significant contribution and two years before they took command of the air, while the best example of her unpreparedness on land comes from the Trinidad Sector.

In January 1942, forty replacements arrived in Trinidad to join the 434th infantry regiment, stationed at Fort Reid. These soldiers had been in uniform for just one week before being shipped overseas.

Had these relative children been pitted against the German combat veterans, at that time lying in the snow outside Moscow, the result would have been very predictable. It is probable that with Britain out of the picture, combined with the changes in world politics and allegiances that would have ensued, America would have had to face Germany, Italy and their Allies on the east coast, with Japan hammering at her west coast, while the German dominated South Americans nudged into the soft underbelly. America could have been defeated, or at the very least been forced into a humiliating peace, to buy time. America needed time to mobilise for war, and Britain defying Germany provided that time. The Battle of the Atlantic was the key. It was probably the only battle in World War Two that could not be lost.

At this stage of the war, Britain needed four tankers arriving at her oil terminals each day, in order to keep her war machine functioning. Most of this oil came from the fields in Trinidad and Venezuela, through the refinery at Point-a-Pierre in the Gulf of Paria, or through the world's largest refinery on the island of Aruba. Britain was also dependent on virtually every commodity in daily use, via the Atlantic lifeline. Many of the cargoes lost off the American coast in the first few months of the Paukenschlag offensive were destined for Britain, and this explains the British Admiralty's mounting impatience with the situation. A large percentage of these cargoes had originated, or passed through the Caribbean on their way north.

Less well known is American dependence on merchant shipping from South America. Bauxite from the Guianas was vital to the expanding American aircraft industry, while sugar, coffee, fruits, leather and beef were imported in considerable quantities. Nearly all the shipping carrying these American destined cargoes had to pass through the Caribbean, or the zone under its control. Thus the security of the Caribbean shipping lanes was just as important to America, as it was to the British. This meant that the Caribbean was a merchant shipping chokepoint for both the Allies, and the Germans knew it.

The Paukenschlag offensive had begun off the great ports on the northern part of the American coastline, in the areas where shipping had to concentrate. However, the profusion of targets and the ease with which they were sunk, prompted the Germans to extend their offensive southward, first off the New England coastline, then the Carolinas and finally Florida. Seven more U-Boats were despatched to the American theatre to cover this southward shift. This was followed by a fresh wave of five U-Boats whose task it was to interdict the Caribbean chokepoint. It seemed a reasonable bet that if the United States coastline was undefended, so too the Caribbean would provide a fertile hunting ground.

The new Caribbean offensive, scheduled to begin in mid-February 1942, was code named, "Neuland" and indeed, the area was to some extent even worse off than the American coast. During the First World War German U-Boats had reached the American coast, so at least there was a precedent for Paukenschlag, but no one believed that a U-Boat had the range to reach the Caribbean. Indeed, in pre-war Caribbean defence planning, the South American threat combined with the French fleet from Martinique had been the major consideration. At no time was a U-Boat threat to the Caribbean mentioned in their documents. The U-Boat thrust into the Caribbean came as a complete surprise to the American military authorities. It appears that the British naval authorities may have been a little more aware that there was a threat because they actually had token anti-submarine defences installed in Trinidad, although not on a scale that could defeat a determined enemy. Nevertheless, the Caribbean was too remote for the British to spare substantial naval forces for its protection and the Caribbean defence problem became and remained a largely American responsibility.

The Caribbean theatre of operations encompassed nearly two and a half million square miles of sea, an area as big as the American east coast defensive zone. Yet, between the Yucatan peninsula in the west and the island chain in the east, the American fleet was composed of two old destroyers and a few tugs and yard craft. The fleet was supposed to defend the three Caribbean Sectors, but because Trinidad was the most important, most of the vessels were based there. Also based in Trinidad was a Royal Naval Volunteer Force called the TRNVR, which operated a patrol base with a number of anti-submarine yachts and minesweepers, but they were only a coastal force. Passing through the area were the merchant ships for America and Britain, and to this vital area, the five Neuland boats were heading.

In December 1941, when the United States officially joined World War Two, they began a major diplomatic offensive to encourage the many neutral countries of Central America and the Caribbean to join the conflict. The Americans needed to base aircraft right round the Caribbean Sea, so that they could cover the extensive dead areas that their aircraft could not reach.

Thus the original bases agreement, with modifications as regards the length of the lease, had to be hurriedly implemented throughout the area. This initiative succeeded to a remarkable degree and led to extensive construction activity throughout the theatre. The result was that by the end of the war nearly all the land area surrounding the Caribbean was hostile to the U-Boats and there was no part of the area that was not regularly patrolled. However, at the start of the German offensive, only the bases agreed to between Churchill and Roosevelt were available and the facilities in these territories had to suffice.

Trinidad, being the focal point of the new acquisitions, was the first to receive troops and on the eleventh of May 1941, the US 11th Infantry regiment, along with elements of the 252nd Coast Artillery regiment landed on the island. They were to be the first garrison of Fort Reid. The Waller Field runways were commissioned in October of that year and work began on the outlying auxillary fields.

The island of Trinidad lies off the South American coast opposite Venezuela, with its northern and southern peninsulas extending westwards almost to the Venezuelan coast. The two thousand square miles of water within the peninsula is called the Gulf of Paria. When the entrances to this area were properly protected, it became the finest natural harbour in the western hemisphere. In time it became one of the largest naval bases in the world and a major convoy center. It was later to be used as a US Navy training area of considerable importance as well as the major tactical base for the prosecution of the war against the U-Boats in the Caribbean.

The northern gap between the Venezuelan coast and the peninsula is called the Dragon's Mouth. It consists of four entrances, three of them very narrow and the fourth, six miles across. The entrances to the Gulf were known as Bocas and named Boca de Monos, Boca de Heuvos, Boca de Navios and the largest, Boca Grande. The four Bocas were also called the first, second, third and Grand, running westward. They are all deep, in most cases up to a hundred fathoms, and all subject to strong tidal flows. The three smaller Bocas call for a degree of caution and seamanship on the part of ships entering or leaving, but the Grand Boca is a considerable piece of water, difficult to defend. The three islands separating the Bocas are Monos,

Heuvos and the most westerly, Chacachacare. All the islands are steep-sided and easily defended, providing ideal sites for coast defence guns.

The TRNVR manned the anti-submarine defences which consisted of seven magnetic detection loops laid on the sea bed, which would give indications ashore of the passage of submarines. Patrol craft would then deal with the intruder, or so the plan specified. Slightly to the southeast of the Bocas lies the island of Gaspar Grande on which was mounted two World War One four point seven inch coast defence guns, sighted to cover the shipping inspection area inside the Bocas.

When the bases agreement was signed, the Americans chose the area along the northern peninsula adjacent to the Bocas as their Chaguaramas naval installation. They dredged the bays and turned the area into a major fleet anchorage and repair base, but initially, the accent was on getting a naval air station operational with flying boats. To protect this installation, the US Army based a battalion of coastal artillery guns on the island of Chacachacare. By mid 1942, the defences of the Dragon's Mouth were quite formidable, but at the start of operation Neuland, only the guns on Chaca-chacare and Gaspar Grande and the anti-submarine detection loops were operational. At this stage the two destroyers which comprised the main portion of the Caribbean Fleet were based at the Chaguaramas Naval Station.

Eastwards of Chaguaramas, lay the city of Port of Spain with its capacious harbour and outer anchorage. The British naval base, HMS Benbow was located on the docks in Port of Spain and a Unit of the TRNVR patrol craft was based there.

Further along the coast to the south lay the largest oil refinery of the British Empire, at Point-a-Pierre. These installations were protected by a pair of six inch coast defence guns manned by a force of the Royal Artillery and local volunteers. The second oil loading installation was further south at Point Fortin and this was also protected by a pair of six inch guns.

The southern entrance to the Gulf of Paria, called the Serpent's Mouth, is quite unlike the north. Silt from the Orinoco Delta on the mainland had filled up this seven mile gap, leaving only a shallow navigable channel which was treacherous with rocks and a very strong in-flowing tidal race. This entrance was seldom used except by small coasters. The British laid three anti-submarine detection cables across this channel to be backed up by patrol craft. When the Americans arrived in 1941, they mounted four 155mm coast defence guns on a prominence known as Green Hill and the Serpent's Mouth needed no additional protection.

In the field of military aviation, Trinidad was perhaps best prepared to face the coming onslaught, although much was still in the planning phase. In Chaguaramas, the facilities for long range patrol squadrons were being prepared, but at this stage, the squadrons didn't exist. In fact American disorganization was so complete that it would take seven months before the patrol planes moved in and commenced operations against the U-Boats. This meant that for a large part of 1942, anti-submarine work had to be handled by the US Army Air Corps.

Within the Fort Reid complex, the Waller Field airbase was operational and capable of considerable expansion. Its outlying auxillary fields would be built in 1942, eventually giving Trinidad a considerable aviation punch. However, February 1942 was when the U-Boats struck and the question must be asked, where were the aircraft? The US Army Air Corps 1st Bombardment squadron with B18 bombers was based at Waller Field, but the squadron was neither trained nor equipped for anti-submarine warfare. In fact, at the start of the Paukenschlag offensive, there were only six PBYs with crews trained in anti-submarine warfare. These six aircraft were the only machines capable of effectively attacking a U-Boat between the American/Canadian border and the southern tip of the Trinidad Sector. It would take a long time before the United States was ready.

Piarco airfield, some six miles away from Waller Field was the island's original airport. In 1940, the Fleet Air Arm had moved their Observer and Air gunner training school to Piarco. They had picked a quiet area away from the wartime atmosphere in Britain to set up the training school, never realising that the skies over Trinidad would eventually become almost as crowded as those over Britain. Their quiet backwater was to be thrust into the center of the conflict. They extended Piarco airport and numbers 749, 750, 752 and 793 squadron moved in with a facility at Golden Grove to accommodate eight hundred students. However, among the instructors there were a number of experienced pilots with over water and anti-submarine experience and at the start of operation Neuland they would have to forget about training anyone for a while. Although most of their aircraft were short ranged and incapable of carrying a serious war load, they could provide surveillance, which they did.

Five hundred miles to the west of Trinidad lay the three Dutch islands of Curacao, Aruba and Bonaire. Both Curacao and Aruba had extensive oil refineries. The one located on Aruba was the largest in the world, with a monthly production of seven million, one hundred thousand barrels. Aruba's installation was located at the eastern tip of the island, near the town of San Nicholas, but the island had no Gulf of Paria and the refinery was on the coast, clearly visible from seaward. The only protection was a coral reef that encircled the island, but beyond the reef there was deep water, allowing submarine operations close inshore.

Forty miles eastward lay the island of Curacao, which also boasted a considerable oil storage capability as well as a smaller refinery. Unlike Aruba however, Curacao's facility lay some distance from the coast on the shore of what could be called a small inland lake.

Entry to this almost landlocked area was via a wide ship canal that passed through the center of the capital city of Willemstadt. The oil installation did not appear to be threatened other than by an invasion force. The ship canal could be protected, but the only disadvantage was the deep water which surrounded the island, allowing submarine operations close inshore, similar to Aruba.

These oil refining and storage facilities on the Dutch islands had been developed primarily to get Venezuelan crude oil out of the turmoil of South American politics and process it in a stable offshore environment. The oil was drilled in the very shallow almost landlocked Lake Maracaibo, from whence it was transported to the refineries, but the depth of water imposed a penalty.

The Gulf of Venezuela which is connected to Lake Maracaibo, is not deep enough to accommodate ocean-going tankers and this necessitated the development of special shallow draft vessels. These specialist tankers were able to traverse the shallow waters to the refineries, which on Aruba lay only fifteen miles offshore. After processing, the ocean-going tankers loaded the refined products at the Dutch islands and took them on the long haul to Europe, but the weak link lay with the shallow draft vessels. There were only a limited number of these specialist vessels and losses could not be replaced other than by new construction.

The importance of these Dutch refineries was not lost on the British and they moved quickly to secure the installations. As soon as the Germans invaded Holland, a British infantry force was despatched from Jamaica, with orders to secure the islands, if necessary by force. Two days before all of Holland was completely over-run, the British infantry landed on the Dutch islands and using considerable tact, took control of their defences.

There was no problem with the Dutch because they intended to remain at war with Germany, and acting immediately and with typical Dutch efficiency, they detained all German and Italian nationals on the islands. This joint British Dutch defence force on the island worked well, but it was primarily an anti-sabotage force, which could not protect the tankers, which were in effect the Achilles heel of the Caribbean.

Throughout the rest of 1940 and into 1941, as the situation deteriorated for Britain, the garrison in the Dutch islands became almost a luxury which they could ill afford. The need for trained soldiers was so pressing elsewhere, that the search was on for an alternative, when Pearl Harbour presented the answer.

America's entry into the war allowed them to negotiate for the release of their forces. On 11th February, the switch took place and US Infantry with coast defence artillery took their place. The US Infantry went into barracks and the artillery was emplaced near to each refinery. None of the American troops realized that within a week, they would be in action. More than a month before, the US 59th Bombardment Squadron had moved in with A20 aircraft. They were based initially on Curacao's small grass flying field, but work started almost immediately on the construction of an extensive airbase to be called Hato field. Work also began to a slightly smaller installation on Aruba that would become known as Dakota field. The 59th squadron was destined to make the first air attack on a U-Boat in the Caribbean, as well as later the first kill of a U-Boat in the Caribbean.

Aruba had what was called "an air raid lights on". This was probably unique in World War Two. British pilots found that when the air raid alert was sounded and the island plunged into darkness in the conventional manner, the refinery stood out, its position being given away by the glow from its furnaces. Trials indicated that if the lights in the city were left on, it created a dazzle effect on a pilot and made it difficult for him to differentiate the refinery from the city. To help this effect, the lights were augmented so that pilots of attacking aircraft would confuse the city with the refinery and Aruba went through the war, with its curious "lights on", black out. The feelings of the townspeople about being made a target are not recorded, but it is obvious that no one was thinking in terms of a submarine.

Both Aruba and Curacao lay within the Trinidad Sector and came under the headquarters in Trinidad.

Because these islands lay so close to the Venezuelan oil fields, the presence of American troops was kept as quiet as possible so as not to upset the South Americans who were maintaining a strict neutrality. Actually all of this deception was quite unnecessary because within a year American troops would be in Venezuela.

The islands of the Caribbean had always been associated with holidays and quiet carefree living. Coconut palms, friendly natives, stable British administration and golden beaches. Peaceful turquoise coloured seas, disturbed only by the occasional hurricane, were the destination of the five

German and two Italian submarines ploughing across the Atlantic. Within a short while people would fear these seas and what danger lurked out there. There would always be wreckage being circled by sharks and shocked oil-covered survivors telling tales of horror. The war had reached the Caribbean and it was destined to change the area for ever.

CHAPTER

2

Operation Neuland Begins

On 15th January 1942, a meeting took place in the French channel port of Lorient that was to have a great influence on how World War Two was going to affect the Caribbean. The decision had already been made that the U-Boats were going to try to cut the shipping routes through the region and this meeting was a tactical conference involving the men who were actually going to do the job.

Sitting in the room was Kapitanleutnant Werner Hartenstein, the thirty-four year old commander of the Type IXC boat, U156. He was the senior officer of the Neuland group and around him sat the other four captains, Jurgen Von Rosensteil of U502, Gunther Muller-Stockheim of U67, Albrecht Achilles of U161 and Nicoli Clausen of U129.

Across the table the Flotilla commander Kapitanleutnant Khunke and his Operations Officer faced the group of keen hunters and detailed the tactical dispositions of the boats and their command and control arrangements. Later in the meeting, the Grand Admiral himself would give a pep talk on the operation, but before that, the U-Boat officers listened to two men who would greatly assist them in their venture. Captain Striewing and Captain Kregoll had both sailed the waters of the Caribbean for a great many years in command of Hamburg America line merchant ships. They spoke at length on sea conditions, reefs, rocks, harbour organisations, lights, currents, shipping routes and the habits of the area's merchant ships. The U-Boat captains listened intently to the briefing given by these two doyens of the sea and took copious notes of what was said. In this company Achilles was at home because he had been a cadet officer with the same steamship line before the war, and he also knew Trinidad well.

Sunday 15th of February 1942, in the Dutch island of Aruba was as unchanging as it had been for centuries. The local people attended their usual church services in the morning and then prepared to spend the day in the traditional Caribbean manner. The middle of the dry season meant clear blue skies and brilliant sunshine, ideal for beach picnics. There was the minor inconvenience of beach defences being erected and curious American soldiers, but the war was far away and they had learned to live with soldiers. For the Americans it was quite an experience because the twin islands of Aruba and Curacao were quite unlike any other Caribbean territory. Dry bare islands with little high ground, they had been converted into little pieces of Holland, with quaint houses, tiny streets and a very conservative people. Language was a problem and the soldiers felt cut off from the populace, as though they were seeing it all from a distance. There was very little in the islands other than the oil installations and indeed, most of the population were employed at the refinery. In fact the Dutch islands had been populated almost exclusively by immigrants seeking work in oil.

The evening of February 15 found the U-Boat captains far away from Lorient, on the eve of launching one of the most dramatic submarine campaigns in history. While the American soldiers marvelled at the quaint, seemingly out of place Dutch surroundings of Aruba, and the coast defence gunners lounged lazily in their barracks, – eyes were watching.

U156 was submerged off the harbour, with only the tip of its periscope above the surface of the sea. Werner Hartenstein, eyes glued to the eye piece, stood in the boat's control room and watched the tranquil scene ashore. He was taking note of the position of the ships in the harbour and calculating. When he had seen enough, down came the periscope and U156 turned and slipped silently out to sea, to await the night. To the east Muller-Stockheim was similarly engaged in surveillance of Willemstad harbour in Curacao. Away to the west, near the uninhabited islands called Los Monjie, "The Monks", Von Hartenstein relaxed on the conning tower of U502 and also waited. He was north of the Gulf of Venezuela and he also was waiting for the night. The three boats had been ordered to commence operations after midnight and planning was now at an end, the operation was about to begin. Ashore, no one suspected that there were U-Boats within thousands of miles, far less in the Caribbean, off the principal oil ports.

Away to the east, Trinidadians were sweltering in the heat as they gathered for their traditional Sunday lunch of crab and callaloo, a local concoction that almost signified the day of rest. But only a few were resting. Events off the American eastern seaboard had caused a dramatic increase in the speed with which the bases were being constructed and the majority of the working men were on the job. Not that they minded, because American salaries were well above the previous income of the average man and there was strong competition for the work. None of the labourers, the supervisors or the American civilian contractors knew why the American military were pushing them so hard and few cared, because there was money to be made. Even in military circles there were few who knew why there was this sense of tremendous urgency about everything. The activities of the U-Boats way up north were not common knowledge. Senior Americans on the island had a good idea of what was going on, but none of them had any inkling of the scale of the tragedy being enacted off the US east coast. Their motivational motto of "Time is Short" had very quickly taken on a completely different aspect. Time was indeed short, — indeed it had run out.

At midnight, U156 surfaced and began threading her way towards the harbour at San Nicholas, with Hartenstein on the conning tower, binoculars glued to his eyes. As expected the shore was brilliantly lit up and so were all the ships in the harbour. The U-Boat was trimmed down to avoid detection, but this was hardly necessary because no one was really looking for a German submarine. The hour had come. Inside San Nicholas harbour, the ship's watches changed at midnight and the new men settled down to four hours of what they confidently expected to be sheer boredom.

At one minute past two o'clock in the morning, the four thousand ton tanker Pedernales shuddered as a torpedo penetrated her side, to be followed almost immediately by a shattering explosion that lifted the ship. The dazed survivors had hardly got to their feet, before another tanker the Oranjestad, heaved to the twin blasts of two torpedoes tearing her apart. Columns of water climbed upwards alongside the ships as the tremendous concussion of the explosion startled nearly all the inhabitants of the island. Burning oil flowed out of the great holes torn in the sides of the two ships and soon spread over the surface of the entire harbour. Ashore, men tumbled out of their bunks, not knowing what had happened, — to be greeted by the appalling sight of the harbour in flames.

But at least one man was thinking clearly and Corporal Bruce Park of the 116th Infantry regiment, became the first bugler in the western hemisphere, to blow a genuine call to arms. While his bugle call was floating above the roaring sound of the flames in the harbour, men ran in all directions trying to find out what had happened, while others died in the flames in the harbour. Sailors ran to the PCs tied up in the harbour and soon the tiny patrol vessels were moving out, not to hunt U-Boats, because they had no idea that a U-Boat was responsible, they were simply trying to get their wooden vessels out of the flames in the harbour.

On the conning tower of the U156, Hartenstein watched with satisfaction as the lurid flames lit up the harbour and the area for miles around. Neuland had been started in fine style, but the very flames in the area made another torpedo shot impossible, because the entire harbour was soon covered in thick black smoke. Hartenstein was a daring commander and he could easily have left the area having caused enough confusion, but instead he stood on the conning tower and stayed surfaced. He let as many of his crew as possible come up on deck to see the confusion. But this was not the wisest move because the excitement affected them, with tragic results. U-Boatmen always heard from their commander, or a few bridge personnel what had happened during an attack, they seldom saw the results.

Ashore the flames danced on the water while the tanker Oranjestad rolled on her side and settled into the mud on the floor of the harbour, still afire from end to end. She had been ripped open from her keel to the maindeck and was beyond salvage. The Pedernales was fortunate because she was in shallower water and soon settled on the bottom. Despite the enormous hole in her side, she would one day be salvaged. The other ships in the harbour spent the next hour with their crews fighting the fires.

Oil on fire in an oil port creates an extremely hazardous environment and nearly all the available men were engaged in combatting the situation. Realization was beginning to dawn on the men ashore that only an enemy submarine, which had come inside the reef, could have wrought such havoc. And indeed, U156 was inside the reef.

As the oil on the water burnt off, Hartenstein was able to see the results of his attack, and while the crew below struggled to reload the bow tubes, he eased U156 back in, closer to the harbour. Ashore they marvelled at the destruction wrought by the suspected enemy submarine. The Oranjestad had rolled over and sunk in only forty-eight seconds and there were many casualties. The submarine, if that was what it was, would now be long gone, because more than an hour had elapsed since the attack, but no one could possibly relax. The garrison troops were all at their combat stations, still wondering what had happened, while the coast defence gunners peered into the darkness, fully awake now. If only they could see a target. Then the harbour was rocked again.

The two torpedoes hit the six thousand, four hundred ton tanker Arkansas almost simultaneously. The great ship was ripped open and once again burning oil flowed out into the harbour. Incredulously, the worn out fire fighters stared at the impossible. The Arkansas, owned by the Eagle Oil Company, settled onto the bottom almost immediately, but oil continued to flow out of the great gashes in her hull, fuelling the raging inferno in the harbour. Once again the harbour was covered by an ever increasing pall of smoke as the weary oil company fire fighters moved back in. U156 had torpedoed the Arkansas at forty-three minutes past three in the morning, nearly three hours after Hartenstein had eased his craft through the gap in the reef. This time he could not wait for the smoke to clear for a third attack, because by then it would be daylight, but there was still work to be done.

The U156 eased eastwards inside the reef to get away from the cloud of smoke and there ashore, lay the refinery. It was still lit up and from the bridge they could see the furnaces glowing. The orders had stated that if the opportunity arose, both the refinery in Aruba and the one at Curacao were to be attacked. The opportunity was too good to miss. Hartenstein ordered his gun crew to bring the big 105 mm on target. Down below on the foredeck, the excited gunners swung their cannon round onto the tempting target, and as the aimer called out the range, the wheels spun and the long barrel lifted. A clang announced that a shell had been loaded. All was now set. The excitement on the U-Boat was at fever pitch, this was a golden opportunity, the destruction of the refinery would equal the sinking of dozens of tankers, although it was optimistic to think that a single 105 mm could destroy the refinery. However, some well placed shells could have done considerable damage and seriously cut down the refinery's production. Hartenstein was aware of all this as he leaned over the conning tower and gave the order to open fire.

On shore the coast defence gunners had their big 155 mm guns loaded and ready. They were scanning the darkness for something to shoot at, when to their intense surprise a tremendous flash was observed to seaward; The flash appeared to come from what looked like a vessel offshore and the gunners quickly swung their cannons round to the bearing of the explosion and the big guns roared. On board the U156 tragedy had struck. The excitement had been too great and the sailor responsible had forgotten to remove the heavy tompion from the muzzle of the gun. The 105 mm shell had raced up the barrel and detonated inside the muzzle. The explosion opened up the muzzle like a flower. Red hot pieces of shell and burst barrel swept the deck around the gun and two men went down. When Hartenstein looked over the edge of the conning tower, two bodies were lying in spreading pools of blood and there was absolute confusion on the submarine's casing. He could hear the great rush as two 155 mm shells flashed over the boat, hitting the water beyond. As the towers of water from the exploding shells cascaded back down, Hartenstein realised that his boat was now in grave danger. The U156 raced for the cover of the spreading smoke cloud from the harbour, as two more shells flashed over.

Once U156 was back in the smoke, the gunners of the 252nd Garrison artillery lost their target and the great guns fell silent. They had almost had a chance to even the score. On the U-Boat, the sailor whose job it had been to remove the heavy watertight tompion lay mortally wounded, while on the other side of the mounting, the gun captain lay seriously injured. Hartenstein ordered the men carried below and called for his Engineer. They held a quick discussion about the gun and decided to cut the damaged end off. While the boat hid in the smoke cloud, the engineers using hacksaws worked away at the barrel, in this highly unorthodox procedure. It took quite a while and many hacksaw blades to finally cut through the wire wound gun barrel and dump the useless end overboard. All this time Hartenstein fumed with impatience.

Finally, the U156 was ready. Her deck gun was now forty centimetres short, but Hartenstein wanted to try again. Once more the U-Boat turned towards the refinery. Ashore, the report that the gunners had fired at a submarine reached the headquarters and the defences were now fully prepared. As the U156 came out of the pall of smoke, the big guns opened up. A shell splinter from one of those 155 mm cannon could put U156 totally out of commission and Hartenstein wisely swung away, as a searchlight probed the area, looking for the offending U-Boat. Nevertheless, the considerably shortened U-Boat gun had managed to get off two rounds, both of which surprisingly landed in the refinery compound. Dawn was coming, and if he was going to escape Hartenstein had to retire. Bitterly disappointed, he eased the U156 out of the gap in the reef and into deep water. The retirement was none too soon, because there were now two PCs and an aircraft hunting for him. For all concerned, it had been a night to remember.

Morning found San Nicholas harbour in a state of utter confusion. There were heavily armed soldiers everywhere, and virtually every officer was on the telephone to someone else, while the oil company officials stared at the mess in the harbour with disbelief. Everything was fire blackened, including many of the small craft which had been caught in the fires on the water. Even now, although the fire had been put out, there was oil all over the water, on the jetties and loading piers and on the people. The Pedernales sat on the bottom, a burnt out wreck, while the Arkansas, also sitting on the mud, continued to pour oil out of the gashes in her side. All that was left of the Oranjestad was an oil blackened hulk, the greater part of which was underwater. The confusion in military circles was even greater because they reported directly to the command in Curacao, but during the night sentries had reported a glow in the east, over Curacao, and indeed, Curacao also had had a rough night.

Muller-Stockheim, the commander of U67 had not had quite as good a night as U156 but he had done his job. At four thirty-five, while U156 had been hiding, the U67 had struck. The boat gently eased its way in through the reef and crept towards the harbour at Willemstad. Within the inner harbour were a large number of tankers, but these were unreachable, so Muller-Stockheim concentrated on those anchored offshore. U67 lined up its bows on a tanker and loosed two torpedoes, then swung onto another tanker and fired two more. On the conning tower, the bridge watch all stared at the targets and waited. Long after the elapsed time for the torpedoes to have struck, there was silence. On the ships in question, men were scampering about because all four torpedoes had hit their targets, but they were duds. Each had caused the ships' hulls to ring like bells when they struck and some had actually penetrated the outer hulls, but none of the torpedoes had gone off.

In exasperation Muller-Stockheim turned U67 until her stern was pointing at a third tanker and emptied the stern tubes. A minute later, the thirty-one hundred ton tanker Rafaela shuddered to the impact of the torpedoes. As in Aruba, burning oil immediately issued forth, but this was a mile offshore so it did not create the inferno which had been caused in the smaller island. Nevertheless, Rafaela burned and the glow lit up the shore and the U-Boat to seaward. For more than an hour reports had been coming in from Aruba, so the defences in Curacao had been fully alert. Almost immediately shells began falling around U67 and her hydrophone operators were able to pick up the sound of approaching propellers. With all six torpedo tubes empty, Muller-Stockheim had very sensibly turned and raced out of the reef to safety. Inshore, the glow from the burning Rafaela now balanced the glow on the horizon in the direction of Aruba and the defences were fully aroused.

While U156 and U67 had been busily at work in Curacao and Aruba,

Von Rosenstiel took U502 down into the Gulf of Venezuela and arrived astride the tanker route from Maracaibo to Aruba. At three forty-four in the morning, torpedoes had stopped the tanker Tia Juana, twenty-five miles southwest of Point Macolla. The bridge stared fascinated, as the tanker slowly sank from view. U502 moved on slowly going deeper into the Gulf. At five fifteen, the tanker San Nicholas, ignorant of the fate of Tia Juana, appeared out of the darkness, heading for Aruba. Fifteen minutes later Von Rosensteil was in position and two more torpedoes sped towards their target. Sheets of flame engulfed the San Nicholas, as the torpedoes detonated in her cargo. The ship didn't burn for long because the explosive had opened up her hull to the sea and in a short while she was no more. Having dispatched the two tankers, Von Rosenteil turned his boat and started heading out of the restricted waters of the Gulf; dawn was not far away.

At this stage there appears to have been some confusion in the orders which the U-Boats received before the operation. With U156 and U67 racing away from the islands of Curacao and Aruba, where the garrisons were now throughly awake and ready, U502 was going in the opposite direction towards Aruba, intending to attempt to shell the refinery. Von Rosensteil had no hope of achieving this objective because by the time he was off Aruba, the aircraft of the 59th Bombardment squadron were airborne and there were three PCs on an anti-submarine hunt outside the reef.

Surprisingly, later in the morning when U156 reported her night's adventure, U-Boat headquarters censured Hartenstein for wasting time and endangering his boat in the attempt to shell the refinery on Aruba. This was followed, after U502 had reported that she was unable to get close enough to the refinery, by an order from U-Boat headquarters rescinding the orders to bombard the refinery. All three boats were surfaced between the islands and the Venezuelan coast while this exchange of radio signals took place. In this they were lucky because the pilots of the 59th squadron had no prior experience of anti-submarine operations and the three attacks made on them were easily avoided. Lt. West flying an A20 attacked U67 only eight miles offshore, but the aircraft didn't carry a sufficient weapon load to harm the boat and the attack was not even reported by the U-Boat. After lunch U156 was attacked with similar results, southwest of Aruba and in the evening U502 was to be attacked by Lt. Lazenby, without any damage being caused. It would be some time before the 59th Squadron aircraft were equipped with the powerful MK44 depth bombs which would be able to puncture the pressure hulls of the U-Boats from as far away as twenty feet.

U156 had been given permission to proceed to the Vichy French island of Martinique to land its wounded gun captain. The other sailor who had been wounded by the barrel explosion had died and was buried at sea. Late on Monday evening, other funerals were being held in Curacao and Aruba, where the first fifty-six casualties of the Caribbean conflict were being buried. The first stanza of the Caribbean war had been played and the killing had begun.

At the headquarters of the Trinidad Sector, news of the attacks in Aruba and Curacao were greeted with consternation. Doubt was expressed among top commanders that U-Boats could have been responsible. The belief was still prevalent that the boats could not operate as far from the French coast, as the Caribbean. In fact, the Type IXC U-Boats now in the Caribbean were capable of not only making it that far, but of operating in the area for up to three weeks. These twelve hundred ton boats had a range of more than sixteen thousand miles, with a war load of nineteen torpedoes. They carried a formidable armament and in the early days of the Caribbean conflict, their time in the area was only limited by the availability of torpedoes.

Trinidad was in a state of military command chaos. The British Governor who had always opposed the siting of the naval base was determined that command of the island would remain in his hands. This caused many a bitter dispute between the Americans and the British. Trinidad was the headquarters of the Trinidad Sector, not just the island. The commander of this sector was Major General Pratt, US Army, with Captain S.P. Oineder USN in command of the Naval Air Station and Lt. Col. Waddington in command of the Air Corps. Ranged on the other side were the Governor, who in fact outranked everyone, and Admiral Sir Michael Hodges, RN, who also outranked all the American officers.

Disagreement had started over the previous American commander, who had wanted to erect anti-parachute devices in the savannah. British authorities always belittled the American fear of an invasion and in this they were backed by the local officials. In an atmosphere where each side had completely different views of the threat, they all went their own independent way, with the result that at this stage of the war there was no such thing as a combined defensive plan. None of them expected a U-Boat offensive and even when the U-Boats struck in Aruba and Curacao, they still felt that because of range constraints, the threat was only transitory. The U161 was to change all this and teach Trinidad a lesson.

It was obvious from the timing of the attacks that there were two U-Boats involved. Two tankers were also missing in the Gulf of Venezuela. All day the discussions continued on what sort of threat they were facing. It was agreed that as a precautionary measure, all oil shipments from Maracaibo to Aruba and Curacao should be stopped. Unfortunately, this decision was passed to the Associated Press and broadcast. This information was picked up immediately by the Germans, who promptly ordered U502 to moved away from the Gulf and concentrate on the east-west traffic along the Venezuelan coast.

If the broadcast had not been made U502 would have been tied up waiting for shipping that would not arrive. Throughout the day reports kept coming in of aircraft attacking U-Boats and in fact the 59th Bombardment Squadron was busy. So far they had claimed three U-Boats sunk; If there was a remote possibility that the pilots were right, then Trinidad had to do something. In the evening the only major surface vessels, the US destroyers Barney and Blakely were dispatched to Curacao. At the moment there was no threat to Trinidad and it did not appear that there would be one. Ironically, when the Barney and Blakely steamed out of the Bocas and worked up to full speed, quite unknowingly they swept past U156, which at that time was having a look at the Trinidad area. While the destroyers were disappearing westwards, U156 signaled to U-Boat headquarters the information that there was a lot of shipping in the Trinidad area. Only the Germans knew that at that time U161 was nearing the Galleon's passage, north of Trinidad.

In April 1941, Kapitanleutnant Hans Witt, was appointed to command of the Type IXC boat U161 being built by Seebeck Werft at Bremerhaven. Shortly afterwards, the First Lieutenant Oberleutnant Bender and chief engineer Oberleutnant Erhardt joined. They stood by the boat while it was launched and tested until December, when Hans Witt broke his leg in an accident. By chance, the chief engineer Erhardt was also transferred to become the Flotilla Engineer of the 7th Flotilla in St. Naziere at the same time. Thus at one stroke, the boat had lost its captain and chief engineer.

Fate sometimes takes a hand in the affairs of men and the next U-Boat first Lieutenant who had passed his commander's course and was waiting for a boat happened to be the Brunswick born Albrecht Achilles. This combined Achilles and Bender, both of whom had served with the Hamburg America line in the West Indies, on the same boat. They were naturals for Operation Neuland. Early in January 1942, shortly after they had left on their first patrol, the decision to attack in the Caribbean was made. They were recalled from the north of Scotland in time for the conference on the Caribbean offensive.

February 17th saw U161 off the north coast of Trinidad. The crew had found some difficulty in adapting from the European winter to the heat of the Caribbean in the dry season, but U161 was one of the great U-Boats and even the sight of patrolling American aircraft before they sighted the first island, did not deter them. It is obvious that the aircraft crew did not see them because the defenders ashore were quite aware of the presence of a U-Boat near Trinidad.

The night of February 17th was spent off the north coast of Trinidad with Achilles and Bender studying the Bocas through binoculars. Achilles had not only entered the Bocas many times, but had also done quite a lot of sailing in the harbour and among the islands. Prior to the war local residents had always watched the Hamburg America ships with awe, because of the speed at which they always transited the Bocas. Most vessels took great care when slowly penetrating the rock strewn area, but the German ships had been known as the only ones which seemed not to care for a slow careful entry. Now a former Hamburg America man was going to enter the heavily guarded Bocas on a mission to destroy.

A continuous threat with no action, tends to generate a feeling of complacency and so it was with many of Trinidad's forces in February 1942. They had been on the alert since the formation of the TRNVR in 1940 and nothing had happened to disturb the quiet backwater of the war that Trinidad had become. In fact, most of the activities of the military had been rather amusing to the local residents, who considered the war to be a European affair. The last alert had been in August 1941, when British Intelligence warned that there was a German surface raider near Trinidad. Once again, there was great excitement and tension, but nothing had happened and when at 9.30 a.m. on the morning of February 18th, the receiving station at Staubles Bay reported an unidentified crossing of number three anti-submarine loop in the Bocas, the report was taken too casually. HMS Benbow reported the incident to the American headquarters and they in turn ordered aircraft from No. 1 Bombardment Squadron at Waller Field to carry out an anti-submarine search. It appears that the resulting investigation was considered routine. Only the senior officers knew anything of the events in the Dutch islands and as such there was no great cause for alarm among the men actually patrolling the area.

Achilles had taken U161 through the Boca in daylight. He banked on the fact that during daylight the defenders would not be as vigilant as they might be at night. While some miles off the Grand Boca, U161 had submerged and crept through at periscope depth. Neither the gunners on Chacachacare island, nor the pilots of the patrolling aircraft had seen the tip of the periscope cutting through the water in the Boca. There was ample room because the water was over a hundred fathoms deep, but it was still an extremely daring thing to do.

Once inside, Achilles had taken U161 into relatively shallow water southeast of Chaguaramas and grounded the U-Boat. Thus while the aircraft searched in vain, U161 had been lying quietly on the seabed in thirty fathoms. It was a nerve wracking experience for the crew because all day they could hear propellers going over and the scratching sound of the probing Asdic fingers against their hull. Inside the U-Boat, there was absolute silence as the men lay on their bunks and waited. Finally at three o' clock in the afternoon the defenders cancelled the alert and recalled the anti-submarine vessels and aircraft. Both the British and Americans agreed that the alleged loop crossing had been caused by one of the patrolling vessels out of station. Incredibly, the offending vessel was not identified, but the matter was dropped.

Inside the U-Boat, the tension eased a little, but they had no idea when they would start looking for them again. It was hot in the boat and the air was foul, but they had to remain quiet and move around as little as possible. Ashore, the defenders released from their alert, once again cursed the boredom of their war. The B18 bombers at Waller Field went back to their regular patrol routine and the majority of the patrol vessels were back alongside. For the sailors it had been a waste of time because they were required to patrol all night anyway, so the time spent chasing a U-Boat that wasn't there was using up the precious hours that they could have spent sleeping.

As the sun set, the patrol boats left the docks for their night's work, another night in an unending war. When it was properly dark on the surface, movement started in the U-Boat. Achilles brought U161 up to periscope depth and swept the horizon; no sign of the patrols, so he brought the boat to the surface. No one saw the sinister hull of the U-Boat break the surface. When the hatch was opened, a draught of cool fresh air swept through the boat and men breathed deeply. On the conning tower, Achilles and Bender, swept the shore with binoculars. Achilles was in his own private playground.

To the north, the naval station was well lit up, while to the northwest searchlights swept the horizon, as the defenders of the Gulf tried to detect intruders. Ahead, the city of Port of Spain was brilliantly lit up, as in peacetime. The U-Boat's diesels coughed into life and Achilles brought her slowly round towards the distant harbour. Trimmed down and moving very slowly, U161 crept towards the harbour. Soon they began passing small fishing boats, each with a tiny lantern held up on a stick. The fishermen in their open boats, either didn't see or didn't recognise the long dark shape of the U-Boat sliding past them. Leaving very little wake, the boat with the white horse of the 2nd U-Boat Flotilla painted on the sides of the conning tower edged closer to the anchorage, while Achilles, eyes glued to binoculars, chose his intended targets. Painted on the front of the conning tower was the U-Boats personal emblem, a Viking ship on a shield. The four conning tower lookouts swept their quadrants, guarding against surprise, as Achilles and Bender discussed the inner reaches of the harbour they knew so well. By eleven o'clock, U161 was south of Nelson Island in thirty-six feet of water, gliding ever closer. Eleven thirty, found the boat in firing position and Achilles lined her up on a freighter.

The night was very dark, with a calm sea, and very little wind, so the ships rode easily to their anchors two miles out in the stream. On board the American registered freighter Mokihana, the anchor and cargo lights were all burning, with only two sailors on gangway watch. The Mokihana had picked up a cargo of lend-lease material in Baltimore, Maryland, and sailed to the Caribbean for a stop in Port of Spain, to unload some of the cargo, destined for the Americans ashore, before proceeding to the Middle East. With all her lights on and the lights of Port of Spain silhouetting her, she presented a beautiful target for the U-Boat.

At eleven thirty-five, U161 gave a slight lurch, as the torpedo left the tube and romped away towards the freighter. Achilles ordered starboard rudder and the bow of the U161 began swinging towards the second target. Another lurch and the second torpedo was on its way. Achilles called down for full right rudder and full speed as the boat began swinging round. Within a short while this same peaceful-looking harbour would be a hive of activity and the U-Boat's sole mission now, was to get away. Achilles stared at his targets as the boat swung away, willing the torpedoes on their journey, on this his first torpedo attack as a U-Boat Commander.

It seemed like an age before the watchers on the U-Boat saw the tower of water climbing upwards alongside their first target. The Mokihana shuddered as the torpedo penetrated her side plates and detonated. The seven thousand, four hundred ton ship whipped to the explosion and seemed to rise out of the water. She immediately heeled over to starboard and began to settle, with a hole thirty-five feet by forty-five feet torn in her side. As the tremendous noise of the first explosion rolled over the city, the second torpedo plunged into the side of the tanker, British Consul. The twin blasts rolled like thunder across the city as the two ships began to settle onto the mud of the harbour. On board the British Consul the explosion had started a fire and the shocked crew fought their way to the fire hoses. They would save their ship on this occasion and in time the Mokihana would sail again, but for the moment, they both rested on the mud of the harbour with gaping holes in them.

Achilles knew survival now demanded that U161 act quickly and as soon as he was sure that both torpedoes had hit, he ordered the conning tower cleared and U161 dived. The boat had hardly dipped below the surface, before it buried its bow in the soft mud of the harbour floor; the water was far too shallow for a submerged escape. Working his engines Achilles, managed to pull the U-Boat's bow out of the mud and immediately gave the order to surface. The lookouts lost no time in scrambling out of the hatch behind Achilles as he called for full speed on the diesels, which both roared into life. U161 was going to make her run on the surface.

Ashore, chaos reigned, the war had reached Trinidad. Alarm bells were ringing, telephones were buzzing and military officers were dashing all over the place. Messages flashed to all the various bases and outposts. At the Trinidad Sector headquarters and at HMS Benbow, they began to evaluate the situation. There were three possibilities. Whatever had hit the harbour could be waiting out there and planning further attacks against the other ships, or the enemy could be trying to escape across the Gulf, or heading for the Point-a-Pierre refinery. Throughout the island, the coastal defence gunners loaded their guns and began scanning the darkness for a target. Infantry began moving out for their defensive positions around the island. In the absolute confusion, it took nearly an hour for the defence system to get organised, and far too late, the air raid sirens sounded.

At twenty past twelve, the wailing of the sirens galvanised the civil defence organisations in Port of Spain, Point-a-Pierre, San Fernando and Point Fortin. Then the power was cut and the island plunged into darkness. This was the first real alert and the shortcomings became immediately evident. The power cut also killed the lights in the various military head-quarters and the anti-submarine operations room at Benbow found them-selves working by flashlight. The total power cut also affected many of the vital radio communications so that the telephone was all that was available.

Many young, inexperienced American officers started telephoning their headquarters to find out what happened, instead of waiting for orders. The antiquated, inadequate telephone system, unable to handle the load, simply broke down completely. In the chaos of careering military vehicles roaring about without lights, the air raid Wardens had a difficult time on their bicycles, as they worked all over the island to ensure that no lights were showing anywhere. Many of them expected German bombers to appear in the sky at any moment.

The naval side of things was only slightly less confused. Immediately after the two explosions, crash boats roared away from the docks and out into the harbour to find out what had happened. Before the power cut killed communications, Benbow had ordered and assigned its patrol craft to concentrate in three groups, off the Point-a-Pierre refinery, inside the main

Dragon's Mouth and inside the Serpent's Mouth. Chaguaramas ordered its PCs and other craft to sea, whether they had an anti-submarine capability or not. Messages were flashed to the ships in the harbour and they all turned off their lights. Out in the Gulf of Paria, the anti-submarine patrol craft swept the harbour bottom with their Asdic sets, confident that the offending U-Boat, if that was what it was, would be hiding somewhere underwater. Achilles's objective had been to cause alarm and confusion and in this he succeeded admirably.

Achilles raced towards the shelter of Diego Island before putting his plan into effect. He had noted the continual traffic in launches running east/west along the south shore of the naval base at Chaguaramas, while he had been on his way into the harbour and now he planned to use this knowledge to get out. He adjusted his speed to coincide with that of the traffic that he had noted earlier and then trimmed U161 down until her decks were awash. He switched on his running lights and began crossing the entrance to Chaguaramas Bay, right among the many US Navy and RN small craft plying that route. Few of the men manning those small boats, launches and tugs had ever seen a U-Boat and to them, the U161's running lights looked like just another launch. He had little to fear from those boats, the real test lay ahead, where the shore batteries and patrol vessels waited.

The island of Gaspar Grande is an elongated hump, rising to just over three hundred feet above sea level. The guns were sited almost at the top of the long ridge that runs along the island, the sides of which are cliffs. Deep water extends right up to the cliffs and small craft usually used the close inshore route. The guns were sighted to command the sea approaches to the westward and not the area close inshore. Achilles took U161 close inshore and right under the guns. The Royal Artillery and Trinidadians manning those guns, probably saw U161, but no one was expecting a German U-Boat to be passing within a hundred feet of the shore, a scant two hundred yards below the guns, with its lights on. Someone probably glanced at the lights going by below and assumed that they belonged to a US Navy launch. The gunners were concentrating their attention out to sea, no doubt expecting to see a surfaced submarine racing for the Bocas, or the white feather of a periscope. On the conning tower of the U-Boat, the tension must have been unbearable.

To the south, the old converted yacht, Dorothy Duke plodded northwards, towards the Bocas. She had seen the fire in the harbour and received a warning signal that a German submarine may have caused it. Her crew were at action stations, with her depth charge party closed up, when they must have spotted the red port light of the U161 going westward. Discussion probably followed on her bridge as they tried to figure out what was crossing ahead of them and it is more than likely that they identified it as a US Navy vessel on the small boat route. Actually, if the Dorothy Duke had known that the U-Boat was crossing ahead of her, they still could not have done anything to stop her. The vessel's ancient machinery could never have pushed her fast enough to catch a surfaced Type IX U-Boat. Under normal circumstances, the Dorothy Duke had difficulty escaping the blast of her own depth charges.

Clear of Gaspar Grande island, Achilles continued his westward movement past Monos. In theory he was not at the most dangerous point because if he was identified the guns on Gaspar Grande and the eight 155 mm coastal defence guns on Chacachacare could blow him out of the water. He was in their killing zone. For three miles he ran westward still carrying on the deception, but he knew that he now had a chance because the water under his keel was now roughly fifty fathoms and if anything had gone wrong U161 could have dived. South of the island of Huevos, Achilles ordered the running lights turned off, turned sharply to starboard and called for full power.

U161 had three miles to run. With water foaming over her decks and leaving a wide turbulent wake, U161 ran those three miles right under the gunners' noses, without being seen. Behind them there were two four point sevens, and on their port side eight of the big 155 mm cannons, but no one saw the U-Boat. The US Army gunners were looking southward down into the Gulf, not virtually at their feet.

Once again, Staubles Bay provided the only reliable source of information. At twenty-four minutes past twelve midnight, four minutes after the air raid sirens had sounded, and forty-nine minutes after the attack in the harbour, Staubles Bay detected the passage of a submarine over the anti-submarine loops. This was U161 on her way out. Just before submerging, the bridge lookouts and officers on U161's conning tower were able to note the searchlights sweeping the water within the Gulf for them. U161 had pulled off an impossible feat.

Once again, the information from Staubles Bay was ignored. The B18 bombers from Waller Field had been ordered into the air shortly after the attack had taken place and they were now quartering the Gulf of Paria. Every anti-submarine vessel that Trinidad possessed was out, looking for the U161, but all the searches were being conducted within the Gulf. Taken seriously, the detection of U161 by Staubles, was literally a fix on the U-Boat's position, and had the aircraft and ships been directed outside the Bocas, they could have given the U-Boat a rough time.

At three o'clock in the morning the aircraft were all recalled, so that they could be refueled and ready to launch a massive anti-submarine search at dawn. A recall signal was sent to the Barney and Blakely, only just getting to Curacao. The threat was now in Trinidad. Captain Burton RN., the officer commanding the Fleet Air Arm school at Piarco was called in to the deliberations and it was decided that all training would be suspended. Every aircraft was required for the morning's hunt, but U161 had long gone.

U156 had received clearance from U-Boat headquarters to enter Martinique harbour and land their wounded gun captain. On 18th February, on her way north from Trinidad, the U-Boat entered Fort de France harbour and the wounded sailor had been duly transferred. Without a doubt, crewmen from the submarine went ashore and they probably reprovisioned U156 with fruits and vegetables, while it is also possible that the French navy may have entertained Hartenstein for a short while. But no documents exist which give any indication of the U-Boat being refueled. The problem was that no one believed this.

America's entry into the war confused the issue for the Vichy French in Martinique and in French Guiana, where they were also entrenched. The result was that they cut themselves off from all but the Vichy Government in France. The Germans didn't completely trust the Vichy French either, with the result that both the Germans and the Americans found themselves blockading Martinique at the same time. The Americans to ensure that the U-Boats did not call at Martinique for fuel or provisions, and the Germans to ensure that the Vichy French ships did not break out and join the Allies. No one trusted the Vichy French. Churchill had been right, and the proof of this was the fact that the Vichy French navy, handed over a number of their surviving vessels to Italy, while Italy was one of the Axis partners.

Throughout the war in the Caribbean, the unfortunate inhabitants of the French island walked a tight-rope between the Vichy French military and political figures and the Germans and Allies on the other side. On the fall of France in 1940, the pro German Vichy Government had been formed with the head of the French navy as a Cabinet member. Prior to the formation of the Government, elements of the French Fleet including the aircraft carrier Berne, some cruisers and destroyers had sailed to Martinique, carrying the French gold reserves.

The French Navy, unlike their Army, had not been defeated by the Germans and had always been a closely knit organization, fiercely loyal to its commander. The commander in turn was fiercely loyal to Vichy, leaving many French naval officers in a quandry as regards what they should do. Some escaped to England to join the Free French, but the majority just obeyed orders. Churchill on the other hand, could not tolerate the existence in a form of limbo, of the world's fourth largest navy and quite correctly ordered those ships which would not desert the Vichy cause destroyed. The Royal Navy was ordered to carry out this odious task, which was accomplished without loss to themselves. The resultant anger of the French, fueled by German propaganda, ensured that there would be no accommodation between the Vichy French, particularly the remains of their navy, and the British.

The French ships in Martinique were under the Command of Admiral Robert, who proved to be a staunch opponent of anything British, with the result that the orders to the French military in Martinique were to shoot on sight, any British vessels. Ironically, the orders were modified in the case of American vessels to shoot only if they showed hostile intentions. At this stage the Vichy French felt the traditional kinship with Americans that harked back to the American war of Independence when Frenchmen had assisted Americans against the British. They had no way of knowing that it was Churchill's firmness in dealing with the problem of the French Fleet at Oran, which had convinced Roosevelt that Britain really intended to fight Germany, and not surrender or sue for peace, as some of his advisers were predicting. The demonstration of British resolve at Oran convinced Roosevelt that he should help, and lend-lease resulted.

Hartenstein's visit to Martinique and Achilles's escape from the Gulf of Paria signalled a short lull in the Neuland offensive. For the next thirty hours, no U-Boat struck in the Caribbean, − they did not need to. The major ports in the Caribbean had been virtually paralysed. Only four tankers had been sunk and a further three tankers and a freighter seriously damaged, but it was enough to bring all shipping in the area to a halt.

This was particularly important in respect of oil shipments. Ten percent of the shallow draft tankers ferrying the crude oil from Venezuela had either been sunk, or put out of action and the shock had been so severe that the crews of the remaining vessels mutinied. They refused to take their vessels to sea, unless the Allies could find naval forces to escort them.

The Dutch authorities had no hesitation when dealing with the mutiny and the crews of the vessels ended up in jail, but this action did not solve the problem. Venezuela was basically a producing area with numerous oil wells and pumping facilities, but little or no storage capacity. The fact that the tankers were no longer running, meant that production in the Maracaibo area had to cease. On the other hand, without crude oil coming out of the Gulf of Venezuela via the shallow draft tankers, the refineries in the Dutch islands were forced to cease operations. Britain's major supply of oil was cut off at its source.

Traffic in both the Gulf of Venezuela and the Gulf of Paria had been brought to a standstill and all available aircraft and vessels which the Allies had based in the Caribbean were engaged on a massive anti-submarine search. However, they were looking for U-Boats that were no longer there. U67 had moved westwards from Aruba and was now off the coast of Colombia. U502 had sailed north, away from the Dutch islands. U161 was heading northwest, out into the wastes of the central Caribbean and U156 was moving into the Puerto Rican Sector. The U-Boats were pulling back to give the traffic a chance to get moving again, before they moved in for the kill.

The psychological impact of the opening round of operation Neuland had been tremendous. The offensive had not started quietly, or in a piece-meal manner. All the U-Boats concerned had acted together and very aggressively. Each boat had carried out an audacious operation under very difficult circumstances and in areas where the Allies had had good reason to feel relatively secure.

The shocked defenders were not to know that very shortly, three more submarines were to make their presence felt in the Caribbean theatre. When the U-Boats moved back in, they concentrated on the ocean going tankers and freighters leaving the Dutch islands and the Gulf of Paria and began to take a serious toll of this shipping, but for some unexplained reason, they never again interrupted the flow of oil from Venezuela to Aruba.

If the renewed offensive had been directed against the shallow draft tankers, they could have been totally destroyed, which might well have cut off oil from the Caribbean permanently. It is possible that the Germans were not aware of the vulnerability of this one weak link. Had they moved against these few specialist tankers, the whole course of World War Two might well have been altered. They neglected to take advantage of this critical weak link and thereby gave the Allies the opportunity to act decisively.

On March first, Rear Admiral Jesse B. Oldendorf was rushed to Curacao and with the agreement of the Dutch Government in exile, he was appointed Commander of all Forces in the Aruba Curacao area. This very able seaman soon ensured that the U-Boats never got the opportunity to threaten the weak link again. However, that event was still ten days in the future and the U-Boats were to create absolute chaos in that period of time. The Allies did not really know what was going on, how many U-Boats were involved, or how long this threat to the Caribbean would last. In fact, all they knew was that something was very wrong in the Caribbean.

CHAPTER

3

The second half of Neuland

The first of the second wave of Neuland boats to find a target was the Italian submarine Luigi Torelli. This boat's operational area coincided with the eastern extremity of the Trinidad Sector's area of responsibility, which meant that she was on the shipping lane from Brazil to New York.

Late on Thursday 19th February, the unsuspecting British freighter Scottish Star came up over the horizon. She was on her way to New York and by staying well to the eastward, her captain was hoping to avoid the submarine killing ground along the US coast. Two torpedoes sent the seven thousand two hundred ton ship to the bottom. Her last SSS signal was picked up in Trinidad, but there was absolutely nothing that the command could do about it. They had problems of their own, much closer to home.

The Marconi class submarine Torelli had an interesting service history. Built in 1940, it operated in the central Atlantic throughout most of 1942, under the command of de Giacomo. At this stage, he was not to know that his submarine was the only one of the Neuland boats that would survive the war. Early in 1943, the boat was withdrawn from operational service and converted into a large transport, primarily to link the Japanese with their European Axis partners. Italy's surrender in 1943, found the Torelli in Singapore, where the Japanese immediately seized the ship and handed it over to the Germans. The Germans renamed the boat the UIT 25 and it remained in the Far East for a couple of months under German command. Difficulties in keeping it fully manned caused the Germans to transfer the submarine to the Imperial Japanese Navy. They renamed it first R504, then later I504 and operated it against the American Pacific fleet, up to Japan's surrender in 1945. The boat's end came in 1946 when the US Navy scuttled it in the central Pacific.

While speculation continued on the identity of the boat that had sunk the Scottish Star, a sinister shape slid through the seas towards Trinidad's Galera Point, – the U129 had arrived. This was a U-Boat that was to make no less than four Caribbean patrols. Only one U-Boat was to beat this record and only one other to equal it.

On the conning tower of the Bremen-built Type IXC U-Boat, stood the veteran Nicoli Clausen, holder of the Iron Cross. He stared into the blood red sunset and probably pondered on what sort of hunting this Caribbean operation would realise. At age thirty-one, he was the second oldest commander of the Neuland boats and although not as senior as Hartenstein, he was easily the most experienced of the Group. He had graduated with the 1929 naval officers' class and served as second in command of a U-Boat during the first year of the war. During this time he had been present at the sinking of eighteen ships, before rising to command of first U37 and then U142. As a commander, he had sunk thirteen ships in the North Atlantic, before his appointment to the ocean going U129 and the Caribbean offensive.

His assigned hunting ground was the stretch of water between Trinidad and the Guianas, and his targets were to be the bauxite ships. Painted in black on the front of the conning tower of the U129 was the legend "Westward Ho", symbolising the hopes of the U-Boat commanders who began the offensive in the Americas. On either side of the conning tower the U129 displayed a set of playing cards which were the boat's personal emblem. Clausen had spent all his service career battling his way into heavily defended convoys and back out after the attack. Now he was going to sink undefended merchant ships under ideal conditions.

As night fell on the 19th, U129 arrived off Galera Point and it was not long before the first target appeared. The Norwegian tanker, SS Nordvangen was ploughing along Trinidad's north coast. While many Merchant captains kept their vessels bottled up in the Gulf of Paria, waiting for the navy to tell them when the submarine menace had been dealt with, the captain of the Nordvangen thought otherwise. He felt that alone, he could make it more safely than the others who were trying to get together in an unofficial unescorted convoy. Clausen's lookouts spotted the tanker and he put his boat in a position from which he could hit the vessel, whichever course she came onto. At ten o'clock at night, the Nordvangen rounded the turbulent Galera Point and steadied on her course, south south east. Two torpedoes destroyed the tanker. The small ship simply exploded and the pieces went straight to bottom in a hundred and forty feet of water. The destruction of the Nordvangen was so fast and violent that no SOS went out, no wreckage remained and no trace of her crew was ever found.

The result was as if the Nordvangen had sailed off the edge of the world. At the end of the war she was not even listed as having been sunk, although the spot where she perished was only two miles from the Point. The only indication of the passing of the Nordvangen was the dull thunder that rolled across the village of Toco, about four miles away. Because the authorities were not aware of her sinking, no one sought to question the villagers and in time they became so used to hearing the same thunder to seaward, that they all but forgot the first one. The Nordvangen was the first of the many ships to go down in what was to become known as Torpedo Junction.

Three hundred miles to the northward, Hartenstein had left Martinique and travelled westward to cover the inner side of the Dominica Channel. He was chafing at the bit. It was four days since he had attacked anything and he needed desperately to sink ships to forestall problems on his return. He was almost certain of a reprimand on his arrival in Lorient. The incident with the tompion on the gun and the resultant loss of two men, would not be forgotten. It would not help if he arrived back home without an impressive tally. There was no way he could know that Hartenstein and the U156 was to be the most successful team in the whole Caribbean war, because that was far in the future.

Dawn on the 20th found the U156 sixty miles west of the Dominica Channel and on the horizon was the first answer to Hartenstein's dilemma. The five thousand ton freighter Delplata knew nothing of the U-Boats in the Caribbean. She was sailing peacefully southwards, confident that she had survived the hazardous waters off the American coast and was now safely in the peaceful Caribbean. Routine had been relaxed, with the result that there were very few on her bridge, and they were not looking for torpedo tracks. U156 took up the chase until the boat was in position abeam of the American vessel. Hartenstein made his calculations and sent two torpedoes on their way, but his aim had been faulty, the torpedoes raced past the freighter and onwards. On the conning tower, they waited for the detonations that never came. The Delplata sailed on, oblivious to the twin machines of destruction that had missed her. Exasperated, Hartenstein turned his boat and gave chase. Slowly, he drew level and once again turned towards the ship. This time he took more care and the second set of torpedoes found their mark. The vessel began to settle almost immediately, but while the mad scramble for lifeboats took place, the radio operator got off his SSS.

The Delplata was the first vessel to be sunk in the Puerto Rico Sector, and the receipt of the vessel's dying signal added considerably to the Admiral's problem. He now suspected U-Boats in two of his three Caribbean sectors, and very little in the way of effective defensive units with which to counter the threat. Nevertheless, the message was flashed to Borinquen Field, adjacent to the Mona Passage and the 45th Bombardment squadron dispatched its first operational anti-submarine mission. The morning of the 20th saw all the Caribbean squadrons hard at work, because No. 59 in Aruba and No. 1 in Trinidad had been searching ceaselessly for the suspected U-Boats, since the beginning of the offensive. The U-Boats were to report about them, that they were adequate, but very inexperienced. Time would change this assessment.

Another twenty-four hours were to go by before another U-Boat struck. U67 had been having a lean time. Since its four dud torpedoes in Willemstad, the boat had moved westward along the Colombian coast, without finding any targets. Muller-Stockheim was not to know at this stage that this was not going to be a very successful cruise, but that there would come a time when he simply would not have enough torpedoes. In fact the combination of Muller-Stockheim and U67 were to make no less than four successful Caribbean patrols, rivalling U129 and beating her, because all of the U67's Caribbean ventures were to be with the same team on board. However, the morning of the 20th was to provide the U67 with a choice target.

Like the Delplata, the American tanker J.N. Pew had no knowledge of U-Boats in the Caribbean and she was cruising along the Colombian coast towards Aruba, when she ran straight into the U67. Two well placed torpedoes that worked, stopped the nine thousand ton tanker and she began to go down. The SSS message relayed to Puerto Rico, told the Admiral in command of the Caribbean Sea Frontier that he now had U-Boats operating in all three Caribbean Sectors. At this stage, the Panama Sector had no anti-submarine defences at all and Aruba had to depatch its A20s westwards into the adjacent sector.

The J.N. Pew was the largest vessel to have been hit so far in Operation Neuland and the sight of the big tanker breaking up and going down in twelve hundred feet of water was a cheering sight to the U-Boat's crew.

Watching a large tanker die at ten o'clock in the morning was good fun, but it was disturbed by the appearance of another target. After days of seeing no targets at all, U67 was now being swamped. A freighter had chanced on the scene, but it appears that this captain had heard the rumours about U-Boats, because he wasted no time. The scene before him was all too clear. The freighter decided to make a run for it to the eastwards, back the way it had come. Muller-Stockheim was not to be outdone and the U-Boat raced off at its maximum surface speed after the freighter, leaving the J.N. Pew to sink alone. After an hour, Muller-Stockheim had to concede defeat, for not only had the plucky freighter outrun him, but it was saved because aircraft were on the horizon. The U-Boat lost no time in disappearing beneath the waves. The aircraft were from 59th squadron, on their way to the scene of the J.N. Pew tragedy.

As the long day wore on, the Ace of the opening round of Neuland, Achilles in the U161, was to strike again. Achilles had taken the boat northwest from Trinidad after his exploit in the harbour, to escape the ceaseless air activity. The suspension of training activity at Piarco had added eighty aircraft to the massive hunt taking place off the coast of the island. It was now three days since he had stirred up the hornet's nest and it was time to go back in. Midday on the 21st found him once again off Trinidad, a little to the northwest of the Boca Grande.

The eight thousand ton tanker, SS Circle Shell had left the river Clyde in Scotland in ballast for Aruba, where she was to collect a cargo of precious oil. Obviously they had been warned of U-Boat activity, because the Circle Shell was playing it as safe as she could. Four hundred miles east of Barbados, the tanker had detached from its central Atlantic convoy and sailed southwest for Trinidad, at its best speed. Her master no doubt felt that it would be safer to hug the coastline where he might expect a measure of protection. Achilles spotted the vessel heading towards the coast and shallower water, thirty miles off the Boca Grande. The U161 was slightly to the west of the tanker's course and Achilles eased her into an attacking position and waited for the tanker to sail across his bow.

On board the Circle Shell, the four lookouts scanned the sea, as the tanker cut through the slight swell. They must have wondered how come they were the only vessel off Trinidad's normally busy north coast. At three fifteen in the afternoon, without any warning torpedo wakes or periscope sightings, the vessel shuddered to the impact of a torpedo, which entered number three tank. The explosion as the warhead detonated, blew out the plates on the starboard side. Ripping through the inner bulkheads, the blast carried right across the ship and also opened up the plates on the port side. Seconds later, the second torpedo slammed into the starboard side, aft of the engines. The second explosion seemed greater than the first and it blew off the stern portion of the ship, taking the propeller and rudder clean off. The dazed crew of the vessel scrambled for the lifeboats, as the abandon ship signal blared from her siren. There was no point in manning the four inch gun, because the horizon was clear in all directions. The two lifeboats splashed into the sea with fifty-seven of her crew. One man had been killed in the stern of the ship, when the second torpedo hit her.

The Circle Shell had been abandoned and her confidential books thrown overboard, but the tanker still floated, although low in the water. Her wireless operator had managed to send out the code SSS, to signify a submarine attack and the signal had been acknowledged by Trinidad, so it was more than likely that help would soon arrive, – which it did.

A Royal Navy aircraft from Piarco appeared on the scene and after circling the stricken tanker, a light flashed from its rear cockpit signalling, "help coming". Up above, the RN instructor pilot circled the stricken vessel and on one of his passes, noticed the darker shadow underwater that signalled the presence of the offending submarine. Down dived the Albacore and two bombs left the racks. The survivors in their lifeboat watched the two black objects detach from the aircraft to the north of them and detonate on the sea. Great colums of water were thrown upwards as the bombs exploded. Down below, Achilles and his crew heard the bombs explode, but the effect was negligible. The hundred pound anti-submarine bombs that the aircraft dropped would have had to detonate directly on the submarine to do any damage at all. Up above, the master of the Circle Shell could now feel a measure of satisfaction. The submarine had been attacked and might even have been sunk and now, two more aircraft appeared. These were B18 bombers of No. 1 squadron from Waller Field. The Circle Shell was badly damaged, but it was not sinking and it was obvious that help was on the way.

In the meantime U161 had cruised underwater around the stricken tanker, ignoring the aircraft which appeared to be seeing her shadow under the water. When the boat was east of the damaged vessel, Achilles had a look at it through his periscope. He realised immediately that the tanker could easily be towed into Port of Spain and saved if he didn't finish her off. Braving the circling aircraft in the knowledge that a torpedo wake would give away his position, he fired.

With the appearance of the aircraft, the captain of the Circle Shell had collected his lifeboats and they tied a line to what was left of the vessel's stern. At three-fifty, the third torpedo slammed into the great ship, about six feet underwater on her port side. The explosion was of such intensity that it ripped the bottom out of the tanker and she sank immediately. She went so fast that the survivors had difficulty getting the two lifeboats clear of the fast disappearing stern. The Circle Shell had gone and all that was left was a forlorn group of survivors sitting in their lifeboats, twenty miles northwest of the Boca Grande.

Soon the aircraft appeared to lose interest and left the scene. The tanker's crew began to feel that now their ship was gone, they were of no importance. The clear skies of February gave way to a golden sunset and still there was no sign of the promised help. Then the moon rose and the sea was bathed in its faint silver glow, lighting up the unhappy groups of survivors, whose mood soon changed from apathy to terror.

Close by, with a great splashing of water, a submarine appeared from the depths. The U161 had come to pay them a call. They could see the U-Boat silhouetted in the moonlight as it circled them. They could see the white cap of the commander, as he scanned them with binoculars. Merchant seamen frequently abandoned lifeboats on the appearance of a U-Boat, because of the legends that surrounded these predators of the deep. The nature of unrestricted submarine warfare was such that rumour soon took hold and the U-Boats were hated with an intensity that did not end, even after the war was over. Merchant seamen lived in terror of them and the Circle Shell crew were no different. They watched the U161 fascinated, but terrified of the apparition from the deep, as it inspected them. They were prepared to face the sharks, rather than come into contact with the menace that the U-Boat represented. After a while, to the considerable relief of the survivors, the U-Boat moved away and with a final wave from the man in the white hat, was soon lost in the darkness. Time dragged, and the current carried them westwards, away from the position of the sinking. When they began to despair of ever being rescued, help arrived. With a flourish reminiscent of a cavalry charge, the shape of His Majesty's TRNVR Tug, Busy, came charging across the moonlit water to their rescue.

The sinking of the Anglo Saxon Petroleum Company owned, Circle Shell, did absolutely nothing to help lessen the tension in Trinidad. The defensive system was in complete disarray. When the military realised that U161 had escaped out of the Gulf of Paria, the "all clear" had been blown in the military camps. The troops were still in their defensive positions around the coasts and there was still a lot of military traffic on the roads, but they had forgotten the sound the civilian "All clear"! The result was that the Civil Defence organisation was still in top gear. Wartime censorship, combined with a distrust of the population as a whole, meant that very little of what was taking place around the coast of Trinidad was passed on to the news media.

In fact, local residents knew more about the goings on in North Africa and Britain, than they did about the situation around their own island. This withholding of information was the cause of a number of bitter clashes during the war. The situation remained the same throughout the war and was not confined to Trinidad. All the islands of the Caribbean were in the same boat. On the 21st when the Circle Shell went down, the Trinidad Air Raid Wardens were still on duty and as far as they were concerned, the island either had been already invaded or would shortly experience a holocaust.

Just as the Circle Shell's survivors were being rescued, the U502 struck again in the Curacao area. The boat had patrolled away from Aruba up into the Puerto Rican Sector, to give Curacao a break and allow the traffic to move again, now she was back. At one minute to nine o'clock that night, the nine thousand four hundred ton Norwegian tanker SS Kongsgaard, making a run from Curacao for the Windward Passage, rounded the island's northern point and set course northwest. Von Rosensteil had brought U502 close inshore off the north coast of the island and all he had to do was wait for the tanker to cross his bow. Seven miles off the Point, two torpedoes slammed into the large vessel blowing out her engine room and setting her cargo on fire. The Kongsgaard was the largest ship to be caught since the offensive commenced and she presented the all too familiar and appalling catastrophe of a tanker on fire. The glow from the burning vessel lit up the sky and watchers on the coast remained mesmerised by the spectacle.

Once again, aircraft and patrol vessels swarmed into the area and concentrated their anti-submarine hunt near the site of the sinking. Ashore, the planners were trying to produce an up-to-date plot of the sinkings from which to estimate the number of U-Boats in the Caribbean. It was now painfully obvious, that the same U-Boat could not have sunk the Scottish Star, well to the east, the Delplata well to the north, the Circle Shell off Trinidad, the J.N. Pew off Colombia and now the Kongsgaard. The five locations were too widely separated and this indicated the presence of five U-Boats, yet the Caribbean still had only two destroyers.

Admiral Hoover, in command of the Caribbean now began sending his appreciation of the situation to Washington, pleading for immediate reinforcement. As yet U129 had not been detected and no one in the Caribbean was aware that another U-Boat, the U126 under Kapitanleutnant Ernst Bauer was plodding its way across the Atlantic, for the Caribbean.

East of Trinidad, the veteran Clausen had taken U129 southeast from Galera Point and now sat astride the bauxite route. At four o'clock in the afternoon of the twenty-second, the seventeen hundred ton freighter George

L. Torrain hove into view. The U129 was ideally placed and just waited for the ship to cross its sights. At four-thirty, one torpedo hissed out of its tube and raced across the intervening distance. The detonation of the warhead broke the back of the little ship and almost immediately the vessel began to go down. Within minutes the vessel had gone and only the forlorn group of survivors in their single lifeboat were left. The U129 stayed on the surface throughout the attack and now approached the horrified group.

Still in shock, they watched the predator approach their lifeboat. The man on the bridge with the battered white cap and the old experienced-looking eyes, wanted to know the name of their ship, its cargo, and its destination. Surprisingly, he did not look like the baby-eating, dedicated Nazi they had been led to believe all Germans were. In fact, although they didn't know it, few U-Boat men were fanatical Nazis,—theirs was far too hazardous a world for politics. The U-Boat captain told them that Trinidad was a hundred and twenty miles to the northwest and handed over food and water, before the U-Boat drew away. The surprised crew of the little freighter set sail on a journey which hundreds of sailors were to take in the next two years. They would end up on Trinidad's east coast, which by the end of the war would be littered with the wreckage and flotsam of the many merchant ships. The George L. Torrain had gone down so fast that they had not got a chance to send off an SSS. Trinidad still knew nothing of the U129, to the east.

The U-Boat didn't have very far to go in its search for targets. Clausen knew that he was sitting astride the shipping route and they would come to him. At eleven o'clock that night, along came the American registered freighter West Zeda. In the faint moonlight the freighter was a sitting target and the two torpedoes that hissed out of the forward tubes found their mark. The five thousand ton bulk of the freighter shuddered to the twin explosions. The ship's side was ripped open and the sea poured in, while bauxite dust slid out of the giant hole and spread across the sea. Once again the ship went too quickly for the radio operator to send out his final signal and another ship disappeared, with Trinidad still ignorant of the presence of the U-Boat. As with the crew of the George L. Torrain, who were still close enough to hear the explosions, the U129 visited the shocked crew of the West Zeda in their lifeboats. They also had a hundred and twenty miles to traverse to the sanctuary of Trinidad.

Midnight found U129 cruising slowly southeast and U161 cruising northwest. Achilles had taken the U161 away from the coast of Trinidad knowing that the area would become extremely unhealthy. All day on the twenty-second, the boat sped northwest, until at midnight he was two hundred miles west off Martinique. Forty-five minutes later, the seven thousand ton American freighter Lihue appeared on the horizon. Achilles brought his boat into firing position and one torpedo raced away towards the freighter. The torpedo slammed into the bulk of the freighter, but she didn't stop. She was badly damaged, but her master intended to put up a fight. The radio operator was sending out his position and the information about the U-Boat, while her gun crew ran to their four inch gun. Achilles brought U161 in again and another torpedo raced away.

In the moonlight, the master was able to see the torpedo coming towards him and the Lihue turned in time. The deadly fish passed down the side of the vessel and the captain brought her back on course for the islands to the eastward. Almost immediately, the freighter's deck gun banged out and a shell sped on its way to the general area of the U-Boat. Achilles couldn't waste another torpedo, he had only eight left. He was also well aware that he had time on his side. The U161's gun crew were ordered up and they commenced to reduce the Lihue to a blazing wreck. When the freighter was alight from end to end, the U161 broke off the action and turned east towards the islands. She left the Lihue going down, but in fact the freighter took more than two days to sink.

Later on the morning of the eighth day of Operation Neuland, Von Rosensteil in the U502 sent another big tanker to the bottom. The eight thousand ton American registered Thalia went down eighty miles off the island of Aruba. Later the same morning, Clausen sent the two thousand ton freighter Lennox to the bottom, only twenty miles away from his previous double sinkings of the night before. Once again the sea to the southeast of Trinidad was covered with bauxite dust, but this time the radio operator managed to get off a signal and finally Trinidad was alerted to the fact that a U-Boat was operating on the bauxite route.

Midday on the twenty-third saw U502 carry out its final attack of the patrol on the nine thousand ton American tanker, Sun. The torpedo hit the Sun about midships but the impact didn't stop the vessel. Heavily damaged, the ship held its course for Aruba. Von Rosensteil could do nothing about it. In broad daylight, the bombers would be overhead in a short while and he was now out of torpedoes. The Sun lived, for a while. She was to be caught in the month of May and sunk by the U506, in the Gulf of Mexico.

U502 was finished with Neuland. She had played her part magnificently. All her targets had been tankers and she had sunk five of them and damaged the last. She had sunk twenty-five thousand, two hundred tons of shipping in the Caribbean. Von Rosensteil turned his boat northwards to leave the Caribbean via the Windward Passage.

For a full day the Caribbean was quiet. The U502 was on its way home, while the U156 was also on its way home, although she was still to play a part. The U129 cruised southeast of Trinidad finding the bauxite route strangely quiet. In fact it was paralysed. The sinking of the Lennox had caused the shipments of bauxite to be stopped and the arrival of survivors on Trinidad's east coast had confirmed that a wolf was among the fold, east of Trinidad.

Torelli was well east of the islands and U67 was in the central Caribbean. U161 was cruising eastwards towards the island chains, with Achilles and Bender planning another spectacular exploit. It was obvious to the planners ashore, that they were not facing a minor U-Boat raid, there were too many sinkings, too widely spaced for the spate of lost ships to be anything other than a full scale assault. Ships were tied up in many of the harbours, not daring to sail and the pilots of the Caribbean's three bomber squadrons were becoming worn out. For almost nine days they had been dancing to the tune being played by the U-Boats, and the area's destroyers had stopped only long enough to refuel before racing off again on fruitless searches. Inexperience ruled the planners and they made a major mistake.

Having virtually cleared the normal shipping lanes, the U-Boats were hunting for targets that weren't there. The planners had to get shipping moving again. They cleared the ships to leave harbours all over the zone, in the hope that their masters would be able to evade the predators, but then spoilt the whole thing with an unnecessary broadcast that gave the game away. The broadcast was picked up in Germany by the B'dienst and rebroadcast to the Caribbean boats. It warned of the presence of U-Boats in the Zone, cautioned the merchant vessels to exercise extreme care, then suggested a route for them to take. The broadcast advised the merchant vessels to keep close inshore on the eastern side of the island chain, presumably because they felt that the U-Boats were concentrated within the Caribbean. The merchant ships accepted this advice and so did the U-Boats.

Late on Tuesday night U156 was cruising south of the Mona Passage when the British tanker La Carriere hove into sight. Hartenstein was still chafing at the bit and the appearance of the tanker running the gauntlet was a gift. He lined up the U156 and two deadly torpedoes left their tubes. Once again, luck was not with him. One torpedo missed and the other hit the tanker just aft of the bow. Although the great ship shuddered to the impact, she kept going. An hour later, U156 was in a firing position again and one torpedo went romping away. Once again, a miss. By this time the tanker was moving as fast as its engines could push it, because in the faint moonlight the bridge watch could see the U-Boat silhouetted on the horizon. At three o'clock in the morning, Hartenstein was once again in a firing position and this time two torpedoes crossed the intervening sea.

Both hit the La Carriere. The tanker came to a stop with flames leaping, as her cargo went up. The radio operator had been giving the listening station in Puerto Rico a running commentary on their plight and Hartenstein knew this. The B18 bombers of No. 45 Squadron were only sixty miles away and it was a matter of time before one appeared overhead. The La Carriere had almost made it, but now she was aflame from stem to stern and slowly settling. Hartenstein had to leave, but the tanker wouldn't sink. It took a full day for the vessel to go down. The wreck settled into the very deep Muertos Trough, nearly two and a half miles below.

While U156 had vainly tried to make the La Carriere die quickly, two of the three Italian submarines which took part in Operation Neuland were at work. The Torelli caught the nine thousand ton Panamanian tanker Esso Copenhagen, four hundred and eighty miles east of Trinidad. Two torpedoes stopped the ship and set it on fire. De Giacomo then brought his submarine close in and finished off the tanker. Unlike Hartenstein, he had all the time in the world to pound the tanker slowly, until she went down.

While the Torelli was thus engaged, her sister ship the Marconi class submarine, Da Vinci, was also busy. Under the command of Longanes-Cattani, she sank the Brazilian freighter Cabedelo. This was the third Brazilian vessel to be sunk. Brazil was neutral and U-Boats were forbidden to attack ships of that registry. The Cabedelo went down with the loss of all fifty-seven lives, the first in the Caribbean zone. Not surprisingly, the Italian commander did not name the ship he had sunk, because it was the continued sinking of neutral Brazilian ships by the U-Boats, that finally, in August 1942, brought Brazil into the war, with dire consequences for the U-Boats.

In fairness to the U-Boats, there were occasions during the war, when it was very difficult to identify neutral ships. They were supposed to sail well lit up, but many a neutral captain turned off his lights and tried to sneak through threatened areas, although the survivors would never admit that their ship had been darkened. In addition to this, many of the so-called neutrals were actively helping one side or the other, with the result that for each side, there were vessels which were more neutral than others.

On Friday twenty-seventh of February, the U156 sank the twenty-five hundred ton freighter Macgregor by gunfire alone. U156 had used up all of her torpedoes on the tanker. She was now operating outside of the Caribbean proper, having slipped through the Mona Passage on the twenty-sixth. The Macgregor went down twenty-five miles off the north coast of Hispaniola, on the edge of the very deep Puerto Rico Trench. U156 used her highly unorthodox, shortened main deck gun, to pulverise the little freighter.

Almost a thousand miles to the southeast, the U129 caught the small freighter, Bayou off the coast of Dutch Guiana. Having frightened nearly all the shipping in the area to a standstill, the U129 was now having difficulty finding targets.

The last day of February 1942, saw two more ships die. The Italian boat Da Vinci sent the thirty-six hundred ton freighter Everasma down to the sea bed, right out on the eastern edge of the Puerto Rican Sector. Further to the north Hartenstein ended his first Caribbean adventure in fine style, sinking the seven thousand ton American tanker Oregon by gunfire alone. He was one hundred miles north of the Mona Passage and the wreck of the Oregon settled into the four and a half mile deep Puerto Rico Trench. It was a daredevil act because the bombers in Puerto Rico could have arrived on the scene at any moment and it took a considerable time to sink the large tanker. After this, the U156 turned for home. She had the impressive tally of five ships sunk and two damaged, for a total tonnage in the Neuland Operation of twenty-two thousand, seven hundred and twenty-three. Five of the seven ships hit by U156 were tankers.

The end of February 1942, saw the end of ten days of intensive submarine warfare in the Caribbean. The scale of the attack can be judged by the fact that forty-five ships were sunk by the U-Boats operating in the western hemisphere throughout the whole month. Of this total, twenty-two had been in the Caribbean zone in ten days. Neuland had outstripped Paukenschlag, but Neuland was not over yet. The Caribbean was screaming for urgent reinforcement and it was far too late. Of the twenty-two ships sunk and six ships damaged in the Caribbean, seventeen had been the precious tankers.

March began with the new boat U126 opening its contribution by sinking the Norwegian freighter Gunny, northeast of the Bahamas. The U126 was heading for the Bahamas, an area which was to prove a good hunting ground for many U-Boats.

On Tuesday third of March, U129 scored again by sending the five thousand ton American freighter, Mary to the bottom. Once again Clausen had covered the sea off the Guianas in bauxite dust.

On the same day, U161 operating two hundred miles northwest of Trinidad, attacked a freighter and missed. Before she could get into position for another shot, a B18 from Waller Field attacked her. The boat was badly shaken up by the explosions and all the lights went out. She complained to

U-Boat headquarters about the moonlight. And indeed the Caribbean full moon was not the friend of the U-Boats. It lit up the sea in a silver glow which allowed the merchant ships to see the silhouette of the attacking U-Boats, before the U-Boat's lookouts low down on the water, could see the targets. Additionally, strong moonlight showed up the torpedo tracks, giving the merchant ships more time to evade them. The pilots of the Caribbean based squadrons blessed the moonlight because operating as they were without radar, it was the only time they could hunt the U-Boats at night. In time when there were enough aircraft, U-Boats would have to move out of the Caribbean during the full moon periods. U161 was the first Caribbean U-Boat to experience a night attack by moonlight, and it shook them up. Achilles retired immediately away from the island to reload his torpedo tubes and escape the attentions of the aircraft, for a while.

The next boat to strike was the Italian Calvi class submarine Guiseppe Finzi under the command of Guidice. The Finzi torpedoed the British seven thousand ton tanker, Melpomere, three hundred and thirty miles north of the island of St. Maarten. These sinkings to the north of Puerto Rico were beginning to stretch the island's defensive resources very thin indeed. Later that day Clausen in U129 sent his last ship of the patrol, the American freighter Steel Age to the bottom, sixty miles off Vichy French Guiana. On seventh of March, the Finzi struck again and using both torpedoes and her deck gun, sent the neutral Swedish freighter Skane, to the bottom, one hundred and eighty miles north of Antigua. The second neutral had now been sunk in the Caribbean zone.

Saturday seventh of March belonged to Ernst Bauer in U126. Bauer worked U126 through the Bahama islands and into the very sensitive gateway to the Caribbean, the Windward Passage. This was the route from the Dutch islands and Trinidad, for the heavily laden tankers that would go north to New York and thence across the Atlantic to Britain. Guarding the passage was the US Naval station at Guantanamo Bay, but all they had available were some wooden hulled PCs and part of a squadron of light floatplanes. The twin blows which Bauer was about to strike would do far more than just sink two ships. It meant literally that the lifeline had been cut. U-Boats could not be allowed to operate in the Windward Passage. This more than anything else galvanised the American command to the danger of the U-Boats' Caribbean offensive and caused reinforcement of the entire Caribbean, even if it was slow.

At three thirty-five in the morning, Bauer sent the four thousand six hundred ton Barbara to the bottom, just off the northwest tip of Haiti. The freighter went down in almost eight thousand feet of water and another valuable cargo of imports for the United States, was lost. Three hours later in the same area, he hit the American freighter Cardona with a torpedo and finished off the vessel with gunfire. The five thousand ton freighter's scream for help was picked up in far off Germany. U126 not only operated in the Passage, she did so at dawn, on the surface; — taking time off to shell a freighter into a blazing hulk, a mere hundred miles from Guantanamo Bay.

Later in the morning, Achilles in U161 caught the large Canadian tanker Uniwaleco forty-five miles west of the island of St. Vincent. This, the second largest tanker to be sunk in the Neuland offensive, gave Achilles and his crew a severe shaking. The nine thousand, seven hundred and fifty-five ton tanker had left Trinidad the previous day and was running the gauntlet up the islands, probably intending to get out of the Caribbean via the Anegada Passage. The tanker was carrying gasolene but the crew of the U-Boat swore that it had to be ammunition. Achilles' two torpedoes found their mark on the Uniwaleco and the vessel promptly exploded.

The U161 had made a submerged attack because they were in dangerous water close to the island chain. The force of the explosion shook the boat even though they were a good two miles away. As the wreckage of the great ship slid underwater on its journey to the seabed, Achilles watched fascinated at the total destruction of such a ship. Long after the wreck had disappeared from the surface, explosions continued. The U-Boat's crew could literally hear the wreck of the Uniwaleco on its journey to the seabed, because it kept exploding all the way. Each explosion rocked the boat so violently that most of the U-Boat's crew thought that they were being bombed by an unseen aircraft. The boat left the area as quickly and as deeply as it could. There were no survivors from the Uniwaleco.

U67 continued to have a lean time around Curacao and Aruba; The Dutch merchant vessel Brastegi reported that two torpedoes had missed her. In fact U67 had fired six torpedoes, three at the Brastegi and three at another vessel. All six torpedoes missed. Utterly frustrated, Muller-Stockheim turned for home. His score was two ships sunk and one damaged. Compared to the other U-Boats, the U67's score was pretty dismal, but the boat would be back. The Caribbean was to be her operational home.

On the northern side of the Caribbean, Bauer in U126 was beginning to rival Achilles in U161. As dawn was breaking on eighth of March, Bauer fired two torpedoes at the ten thousand four hundred ton Panamanian tanker Esso Bolivar. The great vessel, the largest attacked during Neuland, shuddered as one of the two torpedoes ripped into her plates, blowing a large hole in her side. The second torpedo missed the tanker by a few feet and the vessel's master immediately altered course to the northwest, not away from the U-Boat, but towards the safety of Guantanamo Bay, which was only twenty miles away. Bauer gave chase and the deck gun was brought into action, hitting the fleeing tanker several times, until at last, Bauer decided that he could take impudence only so far and broke off the attack. It was full daylight and he was in sight of the US Naval Base at Guantanamo. As U126 slid beneath the waves, the aircraft were taxiing out and the PCs leaving the dock.

On the following day, Monday ninth of March, U126 caught the eight thousand two hundred ton Panamanian tanker Hanseat, a scant ten miles off the eastern tip of Cuba. This time two torpedoes found their mark and once again he came in on the surface and in broad daylight finished off the burning tanker with his deck gun. Bauer was acting as though he owned the Windward Passage. What reigned ashore at the naval base could easily be described as a major flap.

The tenth of March was to see another never-to-be-forgotten exploit by Achilles in the U161. The day started three hundred and sixty miles north of Antigua where Giudice in the Guiseppe Finzi put three well placed torpedoes into the big tanker, Charles Racine. The nine thousand, nine hundred and fifty-seven ton vessel had its back broken and went down quickly, leaving burning fuel on the sea. The largest tanker sunk during Operation Neuland left no survivors.

Albrecht Achilles and his First Lieutenant Werner Bender stood on the conning tower of U161 as she cruised along on the surface, about a hundred miles west of the Windward Islands. They were discussing what course of action U161 should pursue. She did not have a great deal of fuel to play around with and very shortly, they would have to start for home. Ahead, a four thousand mile journey awaited them.

The U161 had given a good account of itself, starting off the Caribbean adventure with the daring raid on Port of Spain harbour and following up this with an impressive tally of ships sunk. Achilles was complaining about the lack of targets. They had three torpedoes left and he didn't want to carry them home. Waiting around for targets to appear would use up precious fuel and they could easily end up carrying the torpedoes back. The idea that he should bring torpedoes all the way to the Caribbean and then carry them home was abhorrent to Achilles. He wanted to do something positive. Eventually, Bender suggested a raid on St. Lucia. The idea of another Trinidad-style exploit appealed immensely to Achilles and both men hurried below to study the chart of the island and the main harbour at Castries. It was impossible, — so they would try it.

The island of St. Lucia is kidney shaped, with very high ground around the old volcano of Soufriere in the southern half. The cliffs come down to the sea around most of the island, providing deep water close inshore to the island. The old Vieux Fort area at the southern end of the island had been chosen as the site of the military base with the coming of the Americans.

Beane Field, the gigantic runway complex had been completed and named after Lieutenant James D. Beane, who had achieved five kills in the air battles of the First World War, before being awarded the Croix de Guerre and then being killed in action. However, Beane Field was a long way from the island's only harbour at Castries in the north. This meant that the Americans had to also take over several defensive locations around the capital to guard the harbour. The port of Castries was the only entry point for American war material. Guarding Castries harbour was not a very difficult job because the tiny harbour was almost land-locked by two headlands and surrounded by high ground. Additionally, once past the headlands, the bay, only one mile wide, curled around to the right with the water never deeper than thirty feet. It was definitely not a submarine operating area.

After the discussion, Achilles set course for St. Lucia and adjusted his speed so that he would arrive off the harbour in daylight. As the sun set on that Tuesday evening U161 was at periscope depth five miles off the harbour mouth, with Achilles studying the entrance. Bender had entered Castries harbour before and as such he was to be the technical expert for this venture. The harbour was far too shallow and confined for anything other than a straightforward cavalry charge on the surface. The navigable channel also twisted and turned around rocks and sandbars and was no more than a quarter of a mile wide. In fact the crew of the U161 were to call Castries harbour "Devils Bay".

Ten o'clock was to see U161 slowly nosing its way past the outer headlands of D'Estrees Point on the left and La Toc Point on the right. The moon was on the wane but it still provided enough light for the officers on the conning tower to make out the various features. It was now too shallow for U161 to dive, so Achilles had four lookouts on the conning tower, as well as his gun's crew closed up. The harbour authorities had not considered their anchorage to be in danger and had left the inner navigational beacons on, as well as all the lights on the docks. In fact two ships had come into the harbour that day loaded with equipment for Beane Field, and the Americans anxious to get their stores ashore had called for unloading to take place right through the night. The result was that both vessels were against the wharves and brilliantly lit up.

U161 came to the first turn in the channel and with Bender pointing out the navigable areas to Achilles, the long sinister shape of the U-Boat turned to head up to the anchorage. There was no turning back now, because the channel was too narrow. U161 was committed to the venture, she would have to go right into the harbour in order to turn.

On the right, the American troops in defensive positions were probably playing cards, secure in the knowledge that they were not in danger. On the left, the spit of land on which the Castries landing field and an American camp stood, glided by. No one saw the U-Boat as she slid through the water in the faint moonlight. The sentries must have been asleep, because it was almost impossible not to see the U-Boat's bow-wave and wake in a one mile wide stretch of water.

At eleven forty-five U161 was in the anchorage. The Canadian steamship Lady Nelson was tied up ahead of the British freighter Umtata. Achilles brought the U161 round until she was pointing at the Lady Nelson; a command and the long steel cylinder flashed out of the torpedo tube. The U-Boat's bow continued to swing and another deadly engine of destruction hissed out of its tube and raced away. Achilles' shout for "full power" and "hard left rudder", was almost drowned out by the shattering explosion that rocked the harbour as the first torpedo found its mark on the Lady Nelson. The U-Boat's diesels were building up to full revolutions, emitting a cloud of blue smoke as the bow swung faster, when the second torpedo crashed into the eight thousand ton bulk of the Umtata. A tower of water rose alongside the Lady Nelson and the rolling thunder of the explosion shattered windows far and wide. The following detonation alongside the Umtata, finished off the remaining windows.

In Castries the houses of the town come right down to the water's edge and nearly all were damaged by the blast. By the time U161 had turned to face the channel, both the Lady Nelson and the Umtata were on fire. St. Lucia had been awakened in a most dramatic fashion. With white water boiling at its stern, the U-Boat began its dash back out of the harbour. This time they would be going out at full speed. There was no room for error and both Achilles and Bender were on the bridge staring into the darkness ahead. Behind, the two eight thousand ton ships, each with great holes torn in their sides, had begun to settle onto the mud of the harbour floor, but neither of the officers could spare a moment to glance back.

To the lookouts, the scene must have been out of "Dante's Inferno" as the town was bathed in the glow from the burning ships. The dockyard workers had scampered to safety, as dazed residents dared to peep out of their windows at the appalling scene on the waterfront. On the surrounding ridges, the soldiers tumbled out of their barracks, dazed and uncertain of what to do. Few were sure whether the twin explosions were caused by an accident on the docks, or enemy action. But a U-Boat inside that tiny harbour, was unthinkable.

U161 raced down the channel with the after-end of the conning tower bathed in the light from the fires ashore and the boat's wake tossing silver in the moonlight. U161 came to port as the channel wound its way out of the bay. The tension on the boat was at its highest.

Achilles had briefed his crew on what they were going to do and they all knew that the dangerous part was to get out of the harbour. A final turn and the inferno behind them was out of sight, the open sea was just ahead, although there were sandbanks on either side. Achilles ordered his gun crew below so that he could submerge quickly when he got out of the channel.

Tracer bullets began crossing the conning tower. At last one of the defenders had woken up. but just as the stream of tracer from the machine guns had started, it stopped. No doubt a confused gunner who could see the U-Boat's shape racing by, but was unsure of what it was, or whether he should be firing without orders from a superior officer. Before the startled gunner could make up his mind, the U-Boat was gone. U161 had reached the open sea. A great shout went up among the U-Boat's crew when Achilles passed the word down the hatch that they were out. U161 had pulled off another daredevil attack, under what had previously been considered impossible conditions. The team of Achilles and Bender were unbeatable!

The Lady Nelson and the Umtata settled at their moorings and eventually the crews put out the fires, but the long term effects of the raid were much more important. St. Lucia had become a front-line base. The Umtata was eventually repaired, but in July she was sunk off the Florida Keys by the U571. The Lady Nelson was repaired and survived the war to become well known in the Caribbean.

The morning of March eleventh, saw the military in the Caribbean attempting to digest the news from St. Lucia. The first priority was the mammoth task of salvaging the two ships in the harbour, because until that was complete the harbour was useless and this in effect, meant that the US garrison was cut off.

One of the reasons for the escape of the U161 was the uncertainty of the raw recruits about when to fire and at what. The same could be said for the Trinidad operation. To correct this situation, the fire orders had to be changed both for Trinidad and St. Lucia. What was required was a greater awareness of the capabilities of the U-Boats and the determination of the German crews. What resulted, in many ways, was just the opposite to the previous defensive posture. The enemy showed that they could operate with impunity right inside the defended harbours and bring the war to the heavily garrisoned islands. The enquiries and recriminations which followed the two attacks made the soldiers very jumpy and trigger-happy. They shot at anything − Their own vessels, friendly aircraft, and with tragic results at each other, and at the residents of the islands. Achilles' legacy was to last long after he was dead.

Besides the psychological effects of the attacks, the Caribbean Sea Frontier now had to increase dramatically the protection which Trinidad and St. Lucia had. Almost immediately, St. Lucia had to have an anti-submarine net installed across the harbour mouth, and a complete battalion of 155 mm coastal artillery moved in to defend the approaches to the harbour. If a U-Boat could get into the harbour and do so much damage, then Beane Field, sitting on the coast within sight of the sea, was very vulnerable. Another battalion of coast-defence-guns had to be moved in to defend the base.

In Trinidad, a new sense of urgency took hold and on the morning after the St. Lucia attack, a submarine was assigned to the Chaguaramas Naval Station. The first to be posted, the USS S11 had a three-fold job. Firstly, everyone concerned could now have a look at a submarine so that they could recognise one in future. Secondly, she was to be used as a target boat to allow the anti-submarine forces to practice their trade, and thirdly, she was to defend the Bocas. Every night for the rest of the war, a US submarine sat inside the Bocas on listening watch. Prior to the arrival of the SS 11 all submarines were hostile, − now highly secret submarine sanctuaries had to be established, both inside the Gulf and outside, of the north coast. The Germans knew nothing of submarine sanctuaries but benefitted because unknowingly they used the sanctuary to attack shipping, while anti-submarine forces had to hesitate before being cleared to attack.

Trinidad's coast defences were also considerably strengthened. The building of emplacements for a battalion of 155 mm coastal-artillery-guns started on the island of Monos. Within a month or so a complete regiment of 90 mm anti-aircraft guns were moved in, most of them defending the inner reaches of the harbour, with the remainder emplaced on Trinidad's east coast. Additionally, the British started construction of heavy emplacements for long-range nine point two inch coastal guns, on disappearing mountings, at Claxton Bay and Point Ligoure, where they could command the approaches to the refinery at Point-a-Pierre and Point Fortin. The base and barracks were completed, but the U-Boats got the guns before they could reach Trinidad. Work also started on the controversial mining of all the Bocas, and an anti-submarine net had to be placed right around the anchorage.

This scheme of enhanced protection had to be duplicated in all the major harbours of the Caribbean, with the related lookout points, communication facilities and enhanced garrisons. Achilles caused the deployment of considerable military resources in the Caribbean. On his return to France, the Germans broadcasted a commentary of his Caribbean exploits and on reading a transcript of it, a senior American army officer commented that "he (Achilles) was a bit of a liar". In fact it was one of those rare occasions when German propaganda coincided with fact. If, as often has been said, war is purely economic, then Achilles and the U161 had paid their way over and over again.

As Achilles raced westwards from St. Lucia to escape the expected hostile, anti-submarine reaction, the commander in Trinidad had no way of knowing that Operation Neuland was over for the Trinidad Sector. It would be a month before another ship was sunk in this part of the Caribbean, but now that the U-Boats had gone, the tension ashore was at its peak. For twenty days the U-Boats had pulverised shipping in this Sector and the toll was appalling. Nineteen ships had been sunk and eight others damaged in the sector. Operation Neuland only had another six days to run and all the action was to be in the northern Caribbean within the Puerto Rico Sector.

The eleventh of March saw Bauer working his way up the north coast of Cuba via the Old Bahama Channel. Early in the morning he damaged the American tanker, Halo. Later that night, he sank the seven thousand ton freighter, Texan, with a combination of torpedoes and fire from his deck gun. Once again, he was operating on the surface, only fifteen miles from the coast and the flames from the burning vessel were easily visible from the shore.

Early the next morning he sent the small American freighter Olga, to the bottom, twenty miles off the north coast of Cuba. The thirteenth of March saw Bauer fire his last torpedoes and damage the American freighter, Colabee. The damaged ship was only ten miles from the coast and when U126 surfaced to use her deck gun, the freighter made it to safety. Bauer had now used all his torpedoes and their was nothing left for him to do but take U126 out through the Bahamas and go home. It had been a good cruise, in fact the best for operation Neuland. The U-Boat had sunk eight ships and damaged three others, with a total tonnage sunk of thirty-two thousand, nine hundred and fifty-five. He would be back.

Five Italian submarines participated in Operation Neuland. None of them came into the Caribbean proper but they operated within the zone and each accounted for one or two ships. On the eleventh of March, the fourth and fifth boats made their appearance on the northern flank. The Enrico Tazzoli, a sister ship of the Finzi, under the command of Fecia di

Cossato came right in among the northern Bahamas islands and late in the evening sank the American thirty-six hundred ton freighter, Cygnet, five miles off the shore of San Salvador. Late that night the Marcello class Italian boat Morsini, under the command of Fraternali, sank the British six thousand ton freighter Stangarth, two hundred miles north of the Virgin Islands.

Saturday 14th of March turned out to be a lucky day for the luckless U67. Muller-Stockheim had decided to take the boat home via the Dominica Channel. Either his firing table had been out of alignment, or his aim had been bad because he had missed with a large number of torpedoes and fired a few duds as well. But on this day, his luck held. The eight thousand four hundred ton Panamanian tanker, Penelope crossed his bow and he brought U67 into a firing position and sent two torpedoes racing to intercept it. The first torpedo crashed into the tanker's engine room and detonated, and almost immediately the second opened up the ship's bottom to the sea. He watched, satisfied as the big tanker settled and finally disappeared, one hundred and eighty miles from the Dominica Channel. He felt much better about the cruise, so far, despite all the ill luck, his three ships totalled over seventeen thousand tons.

The rest of that day belonged to Achilles. He had decided to take the U161 home, via the Mona Passage, in the hope that he would find a target for his last torpedo. Two hundred miles west of the island of Guadeloupe he came upon the nineteen hundred ton Canadian freighter, Sarniadoc, and decided that this would be the target for his eel. The torpedo raced across the intervening space and entered the Sarniadoc. A tremendous explosion ensued, as if the ship had been carrying something very volatile. Thirty seconds later there was no trace of the freighter. Twenty-four hours later, U161 was south of Hispaniola, preparing to make the transit through the Mona Passage, when the USS Accacia, a twelve hundred ton lighthouse-tender came up over the horizon. He had no torpedoes left, but this still left the main deck gun, and Achilles promptly ordered up the gun crew.

An hour later, the first US Navy vessel to be attacked in the Caribbean was going down. That night, the boat finally left the Caribbean on its way home. A happy crew who had achieved considerable success, toasted their commander, who had done wonders on his first patrol. The tally was five ships sunk for a total tonnage of twenty-seven thousand, nine hundred and ninety-seven, as well as four ships damaged. His exploits in Trinidad were to win him acclaim and the nickname of "The Trinidad Well-Borer", while St. Lucia would never forget him. Although he didn't sink as much as some of

Footnote – *Eel, German nickname for a torpedo.*

the other boats, his was to be the most famous Caribbean cruise of the war, and he would be back.

The rest of Operation Neuland was almost an anti-climax. The Italian boat Morsini used torpedoes and gunfire to sink the last ship of Neuland accredited to the boats orginally allocated to the operation. The Dutch six thousand ton tanker Oscilla was sent to the seabed, a scant hundred miles north of the island of Barbuda on the sixteenth of March. Later that day the U504 under Poske, sank the twenty-eight hundred ton freighter, Manaqui, forty miles east of Antigua. The Manaqui was the last ship of operation Neuland. The U504 had been on a Paukenschlag patrol, coming southward along the American coast and had decided to go home via the Bahamas and the northern side of the Caribbean. Poske couldn't help but hear the sinking reports of the Neuland boats and he was rewarded with a small one.

Neuland was over. U502 arrived in Lorient on the day it ended and U156 was due in the following day. U161 was coming home feeling very pleased with themselves, while U67 was also enroute. U129 had left the Guianas on March eleventh, having sunk seven ships totalling twenty-five thousand tons. The veteran, Clausen had completed his first and only Caribbean patrol. On his return to Lorient he was promoted to Korvettankapitan and awarded the Knight's Cross.

Then came an appointment as commander of the new long range Type IXD boat U182. He lost his life, along with all his crew when U182 exploded underwater, after a depth-charge attack by USS Mckenzie. At his death, he had sunk twenty-five ships as a commander. U129's next commander was to be Kapitanleutnant Hans Witt, the first commander of U161, who was also to win the Kinght's Cross in it, on its next patrol to the Caribbean. Bauer was bringing U126 across the Atlantic, also well pleased with himself, after a very successful patrol. The last of the German U-Boats, the U504 was also enroute to Lorient. All five Italian submarines were enroute to their base. No submarine had been lost, or even seriously damaged.

Operation Neuland had been an outstanding success. It had lasted for twenty-eight days and during that time, the U-Boats had despatched forty-one ships, of which eighteen were tankers. They had sunk two hundred and twenty-two thousand, six hundred and fifty-one tons of merchant shipping. During this same period eleven ships, seven of them tankers, had been damaged. The experimental deployment of U-Boats to the Caribbean during the Operation, would now develop into the U-Boats' Caribbean campaign.

Operation Neuland had one final tragic victim. In June 1940, the French submarine Surcouf, arrived in a British port, her officers and men preferring the safety of England, to the uncertainty of a tottering France.

The Surcouf had been taken over by the Royal Navy, at the same time as the Vichy French fleet had been destroyed in Oran. In 1941, the Surcouf was handed over to the Free-French navy under De Gaulle. She was the world's largest submarine, displacing two thousand eight hundred tons surfaced, carrying two eight inch guns on her deck and ten torpedo tubes. She also carried a small seaplane in a hanger aft of her conning tower. In January 1942, the Surcouf began a journey from England to Tahati in the Pacific. The submarine was sailing across the Atlantic to Bermuda and thence to the Panama Canal to reach the Pacific. On February eighteenth, two days after the start of operation Neuland, while U161 was in the Gulf of Paria, the Surcouf was approaching the Panama Canal Zone.

That morning, the US registered freighter, Thompson Lykes, had left Cristobal Colon in the Canal zone, loaded with war material for the naval base at Guantanamo. The US freighter and the Free-French submarine approached each other, with the crew of the freighter quite unaware of the presence of a friendly submarine in the area, but aware that German submarines had opened an offensive in the Caribbean. That night, the Thompson Lykes and the Surcouf inadvertently met. Neither vessel was showing lights and neither carried radar or any such location device.

It was an exceptionally dark night and the captain of the Thompson Lykes had left his bridge for a few minutes to read a signal, when his vessel shuddered and he heard an enormous crash. Rushing back to the outer bridge, he was in time to see the bow of what appeared to be a giant submarine, sticking straight out of the water and sliding downwards fast. Faint cries were heard and someone reported seeing a light in the water, as the freighter forged ahead, but the merchantmen were of the opinion that they had rammed a German U-Boat. Merchant ships never stopped to pick up U-Boat survivors and the vessel soon disappeared. A signal was sent off to Panama describing the incident, while the merchant ship continued on her way to Guantanamo Bay.

The Surcouf went down in nine thousand feet of water, somewhere north of Galinas island in the Panama zone. There were no survivors from her two hundred and seven man crew and to this day her sinking is still shrouded in mystery. She lies alongside four other submarines, who all found their graves in the Panama zone. In fact, one of the five, the US Navy S-26 had been sunk in January that year, when she was rammed by an escort vessel.

CHAPTER

4

The merry month of May

Operation Neuland was over and by the third week of March, the exhausted Allied military forces in the Caribbean were aware that the U-Boats had pulled back. They were also fully aware that the lull in the area could only be temporary. The U-Boat offensive had been far too successful for the Germans not to take advantage of the golden opportunities that existed in the region. The commander of the Caribbean Sea Frontier realised that even though the U-Boats had gone, the period of grace thus granted had to be used to rebuild the confidence of the military and the merchantmen, who looked to them for protection. But where was this reinforcement to come from?

Winston Churchill considered the battle against the U-Boats to be of such importance that he personally chaired the British anti-submarine committee. He encouraged and badgered his navel staff to find ways to reinforce the Americas, so that this German move against another vulnerable link in the chain could be blocked.

While the U-Boats had been off the American coast and in the Caribbean, the British had managed to get four hundred and fifty merchant ships across the Atlantic in nineteen unopposed convoys, but Churchill realised that this was a double-edged sword. While these ships scuttled across the North Atlantic, the U-Boats had virtually enforced a stranglehold in the west, which stopped the flow of raw material to the great American ports. In the long run an open Atlantic lifeline with nothing to carry across, would be the same as if the lifeline had been cut. What was taking place off the Americas was of vital importance.

By the middle of March the US Navy was becoming seriously alarmed and the Royal Navy impatient, over the success of the U-Boats in the coastal waters and adjacent Caribbean. The situation had reached the stage where national pride had to be subordinated to the urgent demands of the situation and a joint approach to the problem was imperative. It was in this near crisis atmosphere that the Americans finally accepted the transfer of British warships to their waters.

Twenty-four experienced anti-submarine trawlers were dispatched to the US coast. Eventually after the American situation had been stabilised, these vessels would find their way to the Caribbean. The second major step was the reduction of the North Atlantic convoy frequency from five to seven days. This change immediately released two British and Canadian escort groups, as well as ten US Navy destroyers. The North Atlantic escort groups usually averaged eight or nine vessels a piece, and consisted of a mix of destroyers and corvettes. These forces could be put to work along US coastal waters, where with the anti-submarine trawlers, they allowed the first tentative steps to be made in the formation of a coastal convoy system.

The immediate gain for the Caribbean was the transfer to the area of a few of the older four-stackers, one of which was the USS Upshur, a neutrality patrol destroyer with an experienced crew, which had taken part in the North Atlantic convoy clashes. By the end of April, the US Authorities were also able to transfer sixteen Coast Guard cutters, five more PCs two minesweepers and twelve Yard patrol craft. May was also to see the US destroyer Landsdowne, arrive in the Caribbean.

The British contribution to the Caribbean consisted of the transfer of the 19th Motor Torpedo Boat Flotilla to Trinidad. This formation with ten Vosper Type III MTBs were not capable of hunting submerged submarines, but each boat carried four depth charges and could keep a U-Boat down. Together with the coastal patrol vessels of the TRNVR, they helped to strengthen the defences of the Gulf of Paria and carry out limited escorting of inter-island vessels. There was a danger of the islands of the Leeward and Windward groups being totally cut off from each other and goods from Trinidad. The U-Boat assault in February and March had virtually brought the inter-island trade to a standstill.

The Caribbean had one month to prepare for the next full onslaught but it simply wasn't enough time. The naval resources were not enough to make any impression on the U-Boats and would not be so for nearly a year, but aviation was beginning to pick up. The naval air-stations were being prepared very quickly, but unfortunately the naval aircraft were not available. By the end of May, Chaguaramas was ready and capable of operating five squadrons of flying boats, but the first squadron would not be deployed until September. In the interim a squadron of single engine float planes arrived for observation and surveillance duties. The Naval Air-Station at Isla Grande in Puerto Rico received a detachment of the precious PBYs, which virtually had the whole Caribbean to patrol. Guantanamo Bay was in a similar position to Chaguaramas, and they received only the OS2N float planes.

Army aviation seemed to be moving much more quickly to meet the crisis in the Caribbean. This might possibly be a reflection of General Marshall's greater sense of commitment to ending the European conflict before tackling the Pacific, as opposed to Admiral King who was always Pacific orientated.

In the first five months of the Caribbean offensive the U-Boats' only worry in the area, was the threat of air attack by Air Corps aircraft. Although they were inexperienced, they were all that was available. They were the ones who made the first tentative steps towards turning the Caribbean into a U-Boat operating area where they would always be in a totally hostile aviation environment.

A good example of Air Corps preparedness concerns the operations of the U129. Clausen exposed the bauxite route by bringing shipping to a standstill. The first indication that Clausen had cut the bauxite route was the sinking of the Lennox on the twenty-third of February. On the tenth of March fifteen days later, Number 99 Bombardment squadron left the United States for the Pan Am airfield of Zandery in Dutch Guiana. Two days later their B 18 Bombers were operating along the bauxite route. Army Air Corps' reaction time was measured in days rather than months.

The Neuland boats began arriving in Lorient on sixteenth March, when U502 came alongside. The following day U156 came in and predictably, Hartenstein had to face his enquiry over the accident with the deck gun. Then Bauer brought U126 in on the twenty-ninth and U-Boat command heard at first hand, how poorly defended was the vital Windward Passage. Achilles came home to a well deserved hero's welcome on the second of April and Clausen, the man who cut the bauxite route, arrived on the fifth of the month. U67 continued to have problems, even on the way home. On the twentieth of March Muller-Stockheim signalled his base to say that he had discovered an unexplained hole in the boat's pressure hull, which restricted his diving capability. The returning captains told of a completely undefended Caribbean, where targets abounded and detailed debriefings indicated the choke-points, where U-Boats could do most damage. But the Grand Admiral had not waited for the returning boats to brief him before deciding on continuing the Caribbean campaign.

Five days before the first boat came in, Korvettenkapitan Walter Kolle took the Bremen built Type IXC boat U154 out of Lorient, bound for the Caribbean. His orders indicated that the Mona Passage and the vital Windward Passage were to be his operating areas, Doenitz had not waited for Bauer's briefing. The U154 was to operate in the Caribbean on six patrols, a record that no other boat was to equal.

The next U-Boat out was the U66 under the command of Korvettenkapitan Richard Zapp, holder of the Knight's Cross. The U66 had completed two North Atlantic patrols and taken part in the Paukenschlag attacks off the US coast in February. As Zapp took the U-Boat with the two red devil figures on the front of the conning tower, out of the dock at Lorient on the twenty-first, the bearded commander had not had the opportunity to talk to either Achilles or Clausen, both of whom were still at sea, but he was bound for Trinidad and a very successful patrol.

Three days later another Type IXC boat, U130 commanded by Ernst Kals, slipped out of Lorient on his way to Curacao. The thirtieth day of March saw the U108 under the command of Kapitanleutnant Klaus Scholtz destined for the Bahamas, but also to take part in one of the really important aspects of the Caribbean campaign, − a rendezvous with a U Tanker.

On the twelfth of April U108 made a mid-Atlantic link-up with the first of the U Tankers, U459 commanded by Von Wilamowitz Mollendorf, a veteran First World War U-Boat commander. The U Tankers displaced seventeen hundred tons and other than anti-aircraft weapons, they carried no offensive weapons. Their role was basically to refuel operational boats, with the seven hundred tons of fuel which they carried. They could refuel twelve medium sized U-Boats or five of the Type IXCs. The additional fuel which they handed over allowed the smaller more numerous Type VIIC boats to reach the Caribbean and gave the larger boats the ability to operate to the furthest reaches of the area and Gulf of Mexico for extended periods of time. The U Tankers became critical to the Caribbean campaign and up to ninety percent of the many boats which operated in the area were refuelled by U459 and the U Tankers to follow. So critical was the role played by the U Tankers that when they were defeated, it sealed the fate of the Caribbean boats. U108 became the first of the Caribbean boats to refuel when she hooked up to U459 prior to penetrating the Caribbean. On this occasion, U459 refuelled twelve boats in ten days.

The temporary peace of the Caribbean area was disturbed on the last day of March, when an SSS was received from the tanker T.C. Mc Cobb. Actually the seven thousand five hundred ton American vessel was sunk by the Italian submarine Calvi, at longitude forty-five west, well outside the range of the Trinidad based aircraft. Nevertheless, its sinking was logged and served to prematurely bring the still very inadequate defences to a state of alert, four days too early.

While the four boats were enroute to the Caribbean a remarkable entry was made in the U-Boat command War Diary and broadcast to the Caribbean bound boats. They were warned that the entrances to the Gulf of Paria in Trinidad were mined. The Germans had broken the Allied Naval Code, just as the Allies had done to the Germans, but it still does not explain how the U-Boat command got hold of this information.

The US Navy decided that the only safe way to secure the Dragon's and Serpent's Mouth entrances to the Gulf of Paria was with a mine field. It was to be a source of considerable friction between the Royal Navy and the US Navy. Three hundred and fifty mines were laid in the fast-flowing current of the entrances, on extra long cables. The British contended that the current was too strong, it had been measured at up to seven knots, and would cause the mines to lie at an angle to their moorings, which would keep them too far underwater to be useful. They proceeded to prove this by passing several vessels drawing up to twenty-two feet, safely across the minefield. In fact, within three months the mines began breaking off and drifting, sometimes with tragic results.

The third Boca was the only unmined entry/exit point, and in time the Germans were also to try closing it with mines. However, the important thing about this mining operation was that the existence of the minefield was supposed to be a closely guarded secret. Many of the captains of the patrol vessels who operated around the area throughout the war, were unaware that there was a minefield in the Boca. That was an area which was out of bounds to all vessels and there the matter rested. Yet, before the mining operation was complete, the Germans were aware of it. Fifth column work, an educated guess, or was it a colossal security blunder?

U154 started its first Caribbean cruise auspiciously. On the fourth and fifth of April she sank two five thousand ton American tankers, the Comol

Rico and Catahoula. The first was one hundred and forty miles north of Puerto Rico, while the second was thirty miles north of the Mona Passage. Both wrecks slid down into the Puerto Rico Trench. On the sixth U154 attempted to sail through the Mona Passage on the surface, but 45 Squadron at Borinquen would have none of it. The boat had to wait for nightfall and complete part of the journey submerged. However, once south of the Passage, there was very little air activity.

While U154 was finding 45 Squadron very active in the passage, two more U-Boats left Lorient for the Caribbean. U125 under the command of Ulrich Folkers and U507 under Harro Schacht. Both Type IXC boats were destined to make only one Caribbean cruise. U125 was heading for the Jamaica, Yucatan region and U507 was destined to be the first U-Boat to operate in the Gulf of Mexico.

The eleventh of April saw Kals in U130 open his scoring on his only Caribbean cruise, by sinking the five thousand ton freighter Grenager with torpedoes and gunfire, northeast of Antigua. The following day Kolle in U154 sank the American freighter Delvale, seventy-five miles southwest of Cabo Beata in Haiti. It was not just another lost cargo. The Delvale was heading for Trinidad loaded with equipment for the military bases.

When the wreck slid down into fourteen thousand feet of water, it came to rest to the west of the underwater Beata Ridge, carrying the parts for the second large flying-boat hangar at Chaguaramas Naval Air Station. By the time another hangar was available, the war was almost over and Chaguaramas had been reduced to only one patrol squadron. The decision was made to leave the base with only one hangar. The sinking of the Delvale, may well have adversely affected the operation of the same flying-boats which were in the future to become the chief tormentors of the U-Boats in the Trinidad Sector.

Later that day Kals woke up the 12th Infantry regiment based in Antigua, when he attacked the seven thousand seven hundred ton tanker Esso Boston, with torpedoes and his deck gun. The tanker kept going at its best speed towards the distant islands while shells slammed into its burning hull. By the time U130 turned away the tanker was burning from end to end, but still pounding through the seas. Eventually the burning tanker beached itself on Barbuda in a most dramatic fashion and became a total loss. The following day Kolle kept up the tempo by sinking the eight thousand ton tanker Empire Amethyst, forty miles south of Haiti's western tip, in the area considered to be the inner approaches to the Windward Passage.

The U-Boats eventually concentrated on three main areas of the

Caribbean, where merchant ships passed through choke-points. These were the Windward Passage, the Curacao-Aruba area and the Trinidad area. The Windward Passage area concerned the stretch of water between Jamaica, Cuba and Haiti, with fans on both sides. The first boat to interdict this area had been Bauer in U126 and it would develop into a merchant shipping killing ground as the campaign got underway.

Many of the Caribbean convoy battles would be fought in this choke-point. The second choke-point around the Dutch islands revolved around a two hundred mile radius half circle with its base running southeast, north-west across the islands. Primarily, a tanker killing ground, it had been opened up by U67, U156 and U502 during Neuland. The area would be fiercely fought over, but in the long run it was dominated by the aircraft and escorts, with the result that the U-Boats did not do as well as they could have done. They never concentrated their strength in this vital area.

The third choke-point was Trinidad. Much more complex and much more dangerous for merchant shipping, the area proved to be the most fiercely fought over. There were four main hunting areas. The first was a fan shaped area of sea with its sides running from the Dragons's Mouth, westwards to the island of Margarita and northwards past Grenada for a hundred and fifty miles. This western fan was to account for about forty ships.

The second killing ground ran from the Dragon's Mouth northwards to Grenada, then in a half circle around Tobago to Galera Point. This was the north coast killing ground and was to become the graveyard for roughly twenty-five ships, and be called Torpedo Junction by the Merchantmen.

The third zone concerned shipping routes that came in from the central Atlantic. In the north its boundary ran from Grenada through Bar-bados and outwards for five hundred miles, then in a quarter circle until it met the bauxite route. This Atlantic fan was to account for more than a hundred merchant ships and three U-Boats.

The fourth killing ground concerned the bauxite route. This was a strip from Trinidad to the Brazilian border and had been opened up by Clausen in the U129. It was to take at least seventy-five ships before the war ended.

As the month of April wore on, the U-Boats seemed to have been concentrating on the Puerto Rico Sector and this only increased the tension in the Trinidad Sector, because the planners knew that the blow had to come and indeed U66 was on the way. On Tuesday fourteenth of April Zapp announced his presence by sinking the small freighter Korthion, south east of St. Vincent. Every available aircraft was out, vainly trying to stem the onslaught they knew was coming. The sinking of this small vessel announced the beginning of the campaign around Trinidad.

Two days later Zapp sank the seven thousand four hundred ton tanker Amsterdam, sixty miles from Grenada. This Dutch vessel was the first to go to the bottom in the western fan. The following day Zapp torpedoed the eleven thousand ton tanker Heinrich Von Riedemann, thirty miles north of Margarita. This Panamanian vessel was the largest sunk in the Caribbean up to this time and turned out to be the fourth largest vessel sunk by the Caribbean U-Boats during the war.

Two days later Kals in U130, announced his presence in the Trinidad Sector by attempting to shell the refinery at Bullen Point in Curacao. Reinforcements in the form of the 243rd Garrison Artillery regiment had arrived in the Caribbean only a short time before. One battalion had taken over Aruba, allowing the full battalion of the 252nd Garrison artillery to concentrate on Curacao. The gunners had experienced the attacks of Operation Neuland. They were keen and ready, and itching to get their own back. Additionally the refinery had been camouflaged and both aircraft and PCs added to the defence. Kals had the devil's own job evading the patrolling PCs to get into the reef, and even then he couldn't see the refinery. Nevertheless he opened fire. His gun crew managed to get off five rounds of 105mm from his deck gun before the big 155mm cannons of the coast artillery opened up on him. PCs started closing in and aircraft took off from Hato field as though they had been waiting just for him. Kals turned U130 and beat a hasty retreat. He was lucky to get away with the attempt and only did so because the gunners quickly lost their target in the darkness.

The predictable result of this attempt was that the area around Curacao and Aruba became very dangerous for a U-Boat. Kals' five rounds had dropped in the refinery compound, doing some damage, but he was unable to get near another target for the rest of his patrol. His only Caribbean patrol netted just the two ships sunk earlier. The incident however, put Trinidad on the alert for another Achilles-type raid. The defenders were to go through the war waiting for Achilles to return.

In the northern part of the Caribbean, U154 signalled that there was strong air activity in the Mona Passage, and also that San Juan was lit up as if for peacetime. The Caribbean still had not gone onto a war footing, although a storm was approaching. On seventh April U162 under Jurgen Wattenburg had sailed from Lorient for the Trinidad area. Wattenburg had been the navigating officer on the Graf Spee during the battle of the River Plate. Some countries were more neutral than others and he soon found himself back in Germany and in the U-Boat Arm. A popular commander, he was to have two successful patrols around Trinidad.

Five days later the first Type VIIC boats, U69 under Ulric Graf and U588 under Gunther Krech left France, both to be refuelled by U Tanker, then U588 to the Windward Passage and U69 to Trinidad.

On the same day Von Rosensteil sailed from Lorient in his U502 bound for Puerto Rico and then Trinidad. His second cruise to the Caribbean was to be his last. On the following day U103 under Werner Winter, left for the Caribbean and then the Gulf of Mexico. His was the first Type IXB boat to operate in the Caribbean. On the twentieth as U154 cruised through the Bahamas on her way home, U155 under Adolf Piening left Lorient for Trinidad. The following day saw U107, another Type IX B under Harald Gelhaus, leave for the Cuba area.

The day after, Hartenstein left in the U156 on his second of three Caribbean patrols. On this one he was scheduled to operate around Trinidad and the Windward islands. Eight boats were on the way and more to follow. Undoubtedly British code analysis picked up this massive movement of U-Boats towards the Caribbean. Washington must have been informed and they in turn must have warned Admiral Hoover, but absolutely nothing could be done. The resources to meet the threat were just not available, at least not in the Atlantic.

U154 sank the freighter Vineland near Mayaguana island in the Bahamas, while U66 continued to lay the foundation for the carpet of hulks that would cover the sea bed in Trinidad's western fan. On the twenty-sixth they sank the bauxite ship Alcoa Partner, and three days later the tanker Harry G. Seidal followed, eighty miles west of Grenada. The tanker was the seventh largest to be sunk in the Caribbean. Next day attention shifted away from the Western fan to the Atlantic fan, when U162 announced its arrival in the Caribbean. The nine thousand ton tanker Athelempress, was sunk with a combination of torpedoes and gunfire, one hundred and eighty miles east of Barbados. The last day of the month saw U507 on its way to the Gulf of Mexico, sink a tanker only five miles off Cuba's north coast.

April ended with only fourteen vessels sunk, but they were all big ships and accounted for ninety thousand tons. The month of May began with a curious mistake on the part of the Germans. Wattenburg in U162 sighted an armed ship painted grey green, without any flag flying, or so the U-Boat claimed. Wattenburg's suspicion was aroused and he took the boat down to attack from a submerged position. One hundred miles east of Trinidad, he fired a torpedo from his bow tubes and watched as the deadly engine of destruction detonated in the vessel's engine room. Sixty crew members abandoned ship as the old vessel settled lower in the water, but although the ship was going down, her radio operator was still aboard. By this stage, U162 was surfaced and Wattenburg sent another torpedo towards the ship to hasten the vessel's end and stop the radio transmissions.

After the vessel went down, Wattenburg found out that he had sunk the thirty year old Brazilian freighter Parnahyba, which had formerly been the German ship Africa. The seven thousand ton vessel had been on its way to New York with a load of coffee. The Brazilian authorities claimed that the vessel was showing its colours and was sunk without warning. Nevertheless they held an enquiry which penalised the captain for being off his route and in an area where he knew a submarine was operating.

Either way the Parnahyba was the sixth Brazilian ship to be sunk, nudging Brazil further towards war. The German claim that they were not aware that the ship was Brazilian, would be acceptable if they were not aggravating the situation, but while this action was taking place, U128 was off the Brazilian coast, accompanied by two Italian submarines. They were bound to sink more Brazilian ships, which is exactly what happened. It may be that the Germans were aware that Brazil was going to declare war anyway and acted accordingly. Still it seems odd that all the neutral Brazilian ships were armed.

On May first there were three U-Boats in the Trinidad Sector. Zapp and Wattenburg operated U66 and U162 close in to the island's shipping lanes, while Kals hunted around the Dutch islands. U154 was on its way home from the Puerto Rico Sector, having sunk five ships totalling over twenty-eight thousand tons. U125 under Ulrich Folkers and U108 under Scholtz were coming into the Caribbean area from the northeast.

On the second, Richard Zapp sank his last ship in the Caribbean, when he sent the Norwegian tanker Sandar to the bottom, thirty miles northwest from the island of Tobago. On the same day a bauxite carrier, the SS Alcoa Skipper was attacked, but the vessel escaped and reported the attack. At dawn on the following day Zapp had a frustrating experience. He torpedoed the large twelve thousand five hundred ton tanker George W. Knight, thirty miles east of Tobago.

The vessel lay stopped, heavily damaged, but with its radio operator calling for help. Zapp brought U66 in close and opened up with his deck gun. In a short while the tanker was a blazing inferno, but before the U-Boat's gunners could sink it, the B 18s of No. 1 bombardment squadron were on the scene, followed closely by the Royal Navy's MTBs. U66 was forced to back off and watch impotently as the defenders circled the burning ship. They stayed around the vessel until a tug arrived and took the burning tanker in tow. Later that night, the first ship to be saved by the Caribbean's defenders passed through the Dragon's Mouth and on up to Port of Spain. By this stage, the fires had been put out and the vessel would be repaired. On the same day, Folkers in U125 opened his account by sinking the small freighter San Rafael, forty-five miles northwest of Jamaica.

Once again a U-Boat operated on the surface close to Guantanamo Bay and got away with it. The Windward Passage was far too sensitive an area for the US Navy to allow the U-Boats to continue operating with total freedom. It was imperative that Guantanamo be reinforced, but the pressure in an even more sensitive area was about to be increased.

The fourth of May saw the opening of a cunningly timed offensive by the U-Boats. U507 under Schacht sank the tanker Norlindo in the Gulf of Mexico. As the pressure began to ease off the US east coast and the US forces were gearing to transfer urgently needed reinforcements to the hard pressed Caribbean, the U-Boats opened up a new front among the tankers in the Gulf of Mexico.

The Grand Admiral was handling his U-Boats brilliantly. The new offensive was planned to take place at the same time as the number of U-Boats in the Caribbean was dramatically increasing. This gave the Gulf of Mexico offensive the maximum impact, forcing the Allies to make a decision. They could either spread everything they had between both areas, or concentrate on one.

The Gulf of Mexico was the most sensitive, not only because the targets were mainly tankers, but also because it was virtually off the American coast. The US Navy was forced to leave the Caribbean to its fate and concentrate on the Gulf of Mexico. On the fourth of May, the threat in the Gulf was posed by one U-Boat, but Doenitz intended to increase the pressure. Within a week there would be two boats in the area and it escalated until by the end of May, there would be five predators among the tankers.

The fourth of May also saw four ships hit in the Caribbean zone. Soon after midnight, Wattenburg in U162, operating off Georgetown, the capital of British Guiana, sent the bauxite ship, Eastern Sword, to its watery grave off the South American continent. At dawn he came upon the first of the many inter-island schooners. The Florence M. Douglas yielded a large quantity of provisions, as well as a black piglet. After Wattenburg had dispatched the sailing vessel by gunfire, the pig swam to the U-Boat, where it was pounced on eagerly. However, another vessel yielded much more in the way of fresh meat, prompting the crew of U162 to keep the pig as a pet. Eventually, the pig was given the name Douglas and taken back to

France for a ceremonial presentation to the Flotilla commander.

With Wattenburg active off the Guianas, No. 99 bombardment squadron had their work cut out. That afternoon far away to the west, Folkers in U125 sank the five thousand seven hundred ton cargo vessel Tuscaloosa City, forty miles west of Grand Cayman. Administratively this far northwestern corner of the Caribbean was in the Puerto Rico Sector, but the headquarters of the sector on the island of Puerto Rico, was more than a thousand miles to the eastward. The island would never be able to handle operational requirements so far away and responsibility for the area was carried by Guantanamo Bay, but at this stage of the conflict, even Guantanamo was too far away and the area was virtually left on its own. Later in the campaign, the pattern of the U-Boat sinkings forced amendments to the Caribbean's sectors and operationally Puerto Rico controlled only the Mona Passage and the open Atlantic to the northeast of the Caribbean islands. The west would always be the responsibility of Guantanamo Bay.

On the fifth of May U108 raised the tension in the Windward Passage by sinking the freighter Afoundria. U108 was on its way north, and the following day saw the U-Boat sink the four thousand ton Abgard, twenty miles from Great Inagua in the Bahamas. That day U125 sank the two large freighters, Green Island and Empire Buffalo in the Grand Cayman area. All three Caribbean sectors and the Gulf of Mexico were humming with activity and once again the defenders had been swamped by the scale of the onslaught. In the meantime U162 had worked its way up from British Guiana to the Atlantic fan area, northeast of Trinidad. On the way north Wattenburg disposed of two more bauxite carriers by sinking the Mont Louis and the Frank Seamens. Later the seven thousand seven hundred ton tanker Esso Houston, enroute to Montevideo, was sunk east of Trinidad.

The extent to which the US Navy was overstretched can be gathered from what happened to the Mokihana. The vessel had been damaged by Achilles, in what could only be classed as a most spectacular attack. One would have thought that something as dramatic as the attack on Port of Spain, would have called for a searching investigation. In fact Mokihana was temporarily repaired in Port of Spain and left the island under its own power on second of May. On fourth May in mid-Caribbean, the temporary repairs gave way with a loud bank and the Mokihana shuddered to a halt. The ship immediately broadcast a distress signal, saying that it had been torpedoed by a U-Boat, and that it was sinking. The distress signal was picked up in Germany by the B'dienst and caused some confusion in U-Boat headquarters while they tried to figure out which U-Boat was responsible. The US Navy Tugs Partridge and Mankato were immediately dispatched to the scene, to find the Mokihana drifting helplessly, still adamant that they had been torpedoed.

The tugs towed the Mokihana to the Virgin Islands where a temporary patch was affixed, before towing the vessel to San Juan, where more permanent repairs were carried out. The ship arrived in Galveston Texas, for rebuilding on June fifteenth, still with the remains of some of its cargo aboard. It wasn't until June thirtieth, more than five months after the event, that the US office of Naval Intellegience called on the senior USN officer on the ship for a report on the Port of Spain attack.

On the same day that U162 sank the Mont Louis, Folkers in U125 sank the large tanker Calgorolite, fifty miles from Grand Cayman. At eleven thousand nine hundred tons, the Canadian vessel was the third largest to be sunk in the Caribbean. Folkers advised U-Boat headquarters that he intended to operate in the Cayman-Yucatan area where traffic abounded, rather than off the Panama Canal where moonlight made conditions dangerous. Folkers didn't know that there were as yet no serious anti-submarine forces based on the Atlantic side of the Panama Canal.

The next four days were to see a dramatic increase in the number of U-Boats in the Trinidad Sector, signalled by a veritable holocaust of sinkings. The first to strike was Von Rosensteil in U502, on his last cruise. He used torpedoes and his deck gun to sink the five thousand ton British freighter Cape of Good Hope, carrying a cargo of lend-lease armoured cars and ammunition, with broken down aircraft on the hatchcovers. The freighter was enroute from New York to Capetown with equipment for the troops in North Africa. U502 consigned it instead under three miles of water in the Nares Abyssal Plain.

The second new boat to announce its presence was the U69, but before this, she had become involved with the defences in the Mona Passage. The U69 was the first Type VIIC U-Boat to operate in the Caribbean and she became the first U-Boat to be depth-charged by a surface vessel in the Caribbean. On ninth March her commander Ulrich Graf on the way through the Mona Passage, fired at a US Coast Guard cutter and missed. The cutter turned on the U-Boat and with the support of the B 18s of No. 45 squadron, they made Graf work to get out of the Mona Passage. Three days later Graf sank the six thousand eight hundred ton Norwegian tanker Lice, ninety miles north of the Dutch island of Bonaire. Graf had come to replace U130 which hadn't been able to find targets after its abortive bombardment of Curacao.

On the thirteenth the same day that U162 sank the Esso Houston, Werner Hartenstein signalled the arrival of the U156 in the zone, by sinking two freighters with lend-lease material enroute New York to Capetown. Just before midnight on the twelfth he torpedoed the Dutch freighter Koenjet on the eastern edge of Puerto Rico Sector, opposite the island of Dominica. After lunch he used torpedoes and gunfire to dispatch the six thousand six hundred ton British freighter City of Melbourne, a hundred miles closer in. U69 had also found another target and while the SSS had been coming in from the Koenjet, Graf had stopped the American freighter Norlantic, with one torpedo and proceeded to pound the ship into a wreck with his deck gun, thirty miles from La Orchilla Island in Venezuela.

At nine o'clock that night Wattenburg caught the six thousand nine hundred ton tanker British Colony, ninety miles east of Barbados. The tanker which had been trying to make a lone run from Trinidad to Gibraltar, with desperately needed fuel, burned all night. Just before midnight another new boat U155 under the command of Adolf Piening, holder of the Knight's Cross, caught the Belgian freighter, Brabant, eighty miles northwest of the Dragon's Mouth and sent to the bottom the fifth ship in twenty-four hours. It was more than Trinidad's defenders could handle. They were under seige. In the far northwest, the U506 and U507 had sent nine ships to the bottom in the Gulf of Mexico.

Dawn on the fourteenth of May saw five U-Boats, U69, U155, U156, U162 and U502 active in the Trinidad Sector. Up north U130 and U108 were passing through the area north of Hispaniola and a new boat U558, was coming south for the Windward Passage. Another new boat U106, under Hermann Rasch was also closing the north coast of Cuba. Keeping up the tempo U125 sank the Honduran freighter Comayagua, only five miles off the coast of Grand Cayman.

To add to these twelve U-Boats in the Caribbean Theatre, U68 and U159 sailed from Lorient to join U103, U107, U172, U504, U751, U753 and U755 who were already at sea, enroute to the Caribbean. Off the US Coast a full inter-locking convoy system had at last been implemented and sinkings by the U-Boats were dropping off. Most of the U-Boats were now being concentrated in the Caribbean, where there were virtually no defences and a lot of shipping. That night, U156 sent two more freighters, the Norwegian Siljestad and the Yugoslavian Kupa, to join the growing number of ships settling on the bottom, in the Atlantic fan, northeast of Trinidad.

The sixteenth of May saw a large number of signals being sent from and to the U-Boats. U162 advised that they had checked Bridgetown harbour in Barbados and found it empty. They also noted that the southern half of the island was blacked out, but the north was lit as in peacetime. U108 advised that it had been depth-charged by a destroyer. U103 advised that there had been no traffic in the Caicos Passage and it was moving down through the Windward Passage. U155, a boat that was to make three successful Caribbean patrols, advised that Trinidad had strong but careless air patrolling and further recommended that the area was suitable for mining. U507 in the Gulf of Mexico, advised that it had suffered an all day depth-charge attack from a US destroyer.

Then U-Boat headquarters signalled an astonishing order to all boats at sea. The boats were advised that they were now free to attack all South American shipping without warning, with the sole exceptions of Argentinian and Chilean vessels. Apparently Germany had resigned itself to the fact that Brazil and Venezuela would join the Allied camp. There were neutrals and neutrals, and that day U68 was to prove the fact. The boat stopped in at the Spanish port of El Ferrol to repair its exhausts, before resuming its cruise to the Caribbean.

Without any help from the Germans, the Allies were also depleting the Caribbean's scarce resources. MTB 338 exploded and was destroyed alongside its base at HMS Benbow in Port of Spain. Apparently, its temperamental gasolene engines had been at fault. As evening fell on the sixteenth U103 under Winter used its deck gun to destroy the American freighter Ruth Lykes, off the desolate Honduran coastline. Then just before midnight, Piening put two torpedoes into the eight thousand two hundred ton British tanker San Victorio, eighty miles from the Dragon's Mouth. The tanker burned until dawn, before settling into six hundred feet of water, to join the Brabant, which Piening had sunk in the area two days before. Seven hours later he torpedoed the American freighter. Challenger, and watched it sink, fifteen miles off the coast of Grenada.

Just after lunch on the seventeenth, Hartenstein in U156 sent the wreck of the British freighter Barrdale which had been enroute to Basra, to join the other ships he had put down in the eastern fan. When the moon came up, Wattenburg aimed carefully and used his last torpedo to sink the British tanker Beth, one hundred and thirty miles southeast of Barbados. With all its torpedoes gone, U162 turned for home with a very happy crew. They had sunk forty-seven thousand one hundred and sixty-two tons of shipping. In addition the sinking of the Mont Louis on the ninth had netted another two pigs and a number of hens, and the crew were able to enjoy fresh meat.

At midnight, the U125 sank the nine thousand ton American tanker Mercury Sun, one hundred miles south of Cuba's western tip. Just after midnight a new boat, the U558 under the command of Gunther Krech, holder of the Knight's Cross, sank the small Dutch freighter Fauna, twenty miles east of Mayaguana island in the Bahamas. An hour before dawn Hartenstein struck again and the five thousand ton American freighter Quaker City, went down among the bed of wrecks that U156 was laying to the east of the islands.

By this time, the Trinidad command was well aware that there was an almost stationery U-Boat operating five hundred miles out in the Atlantic fan. A destroyer had been dispatched and No. 1 squadron B 18s were quartering the area, so that when Hartenstein struck again, they were ready. At twelve noon U156 fired at the eight thousand ton British tanker San Elismo. One torpedo struck while the other missed. The tanker called for help and continued pounding towards Trinidad at its best speed. Hartenstein chased after it and managed to put another two torpedoes into the giant, but just as the tanker was slowing down and U156 was preparing a gun attack, the destroyer hove into view and the bombers arrived. U156 beat a hasty retreat, leaving the badly damaged tanker to be helped into Port of Spain.

Far away to the northwest Folkers in U125 sank his last ship of the patrol, the small freighter William J. Salman. The U-Boat turned for home, having sunk eight ships of a total tonnage of forty-one thousand nine hundred and fifty-three. The U-Boatmen now wished that their boats could carry more torpedoes, because that seemed to be the only limiting factor on what they could achieve. The boats in the Caribbean were now averaging twenty-five thousand tons of shipping sunk each day. It was very good hunting.

The area encompassed by the Caribbean Zone was so vast and the few defenders stretched so thin, that the U-Boats were seldom troubled by surface escorts, or aircraft and many of the boats that operated in May, did so without ever meeting any opposition. In most cases the boats were able to operate permanently on the surface, watching their victims sink and questioning the survivors about cargoes and destinations. Often they handed over provisions and water and gave directions for survivors to reach the nearest land. There are also cases on record of survivors being scrubbed and put ashore, or placed in positions where they would be quickly rescued. One survivor spent five happy days aboard the U126, before being passed to a Venezuelan vessel. The behaviour of the U-Boat crews in the Caribbean however, did not change the attitude of the merchantmen to them. Allied propaganda was very thorough.

The Caribbean proved to be the most attractive area in which the U-Boats operated throughout the war. Without the cold of the Arctic, or the never ending storms of the North Atlantic, their only problem was to get used to the change in temperature. There were uninhabited islands off the Yucatan Peninsula, in the Bahamas, in the Virgin Islands and in the Grenadines, where boats could rest up and allow their crews ashore. Hunting, fishing and bathing provided a welcome break for the men from their steel coffins and the absence of air patrols in the early days meant that the boats needed only a minimum of camouflage to remain unseen. Nearly all the boats in those golden days, took an occasional day off to rest and recuperate.

Then there were places where the U-Boats could call and buy fresh provisions from natives who didn't understand and didn't care what the war was all about. Some of these visits are reputed to have involved the provision of female company as well. Stories abound in the Caribbean of the daring of U-Boat commanders in some of the more serious war centers. The most bizarre and unlikely of these has never been substantiated, but is widely believed in Trinidad.

The small steamer that plied between Trinidad and Tobago is reputed to have been stopped by a U-Boat off Trinidad's north coast. The U-Boat commander is reputed to have asked the captain of the merchant vessel about his destination, as well as the usual questions about cargo. The U-Boat commander then advised the captain that his vessel was too small to waste a torpedo on, but warned that if the vessel continued to ply between the islands, it would be sunk. The U-Boat commander is then reputed to have produced two ticket stubs and recommended the film then showing at Port of Spain's leading cinema, as very good. Unbelievable — yet it was around this time that the MTBs began escorting the Tobago-bound vessel.

Rumour abounded in the islands and the daily sight of half-starved oil-covered survivors staggering ashore, and the quiet rumble of U-Boat diesels offshore at night, made the sea a place to be avoided. Inter-island schooners moved only at high-noon and the U-Boats reported the passages between the islands deserted at night. Only the merchantmen carrying vital raw material were at sea, and when they had to transit through one of the passages, they frequently hugged the shoreline. Generally, there was great frustration among the military men, over their inability to do something about the situation and an all encompassing fear in the civilians, about where it was all going to end. To the U-Boat crews it was the merry month of May.

At dawn on the nineteenth of the month, Gerhard Bigalk in command of U751, the third Type VIIC boat to arrive, opened his scoring by sinking the freighter, Isabella, seventy miles east of Jamaica, at the southern end of the Windward Passage. The following morning U155 ran into the first convoy. U502 had reported a small convoy of three merchant ships, escorted by the Dutch gunboat Jan Van Brakel, but the collection of ships discovered by U155 was the first large convoy.

The convoy was enroute from New York to Trinidad, with its final destination being Africa. The U-Boat moved towards the ships when they were off Testigos island. Almost as soon as Piening was in position, a US Navy four-funnelled destroyer turned towards him. U155 was forced to dive and trail the convoy. Forty miles from the Dragon's Mouth, Piening saw his chance. Each time he raised his periscope, the USS Upshur, charged in, but he got a quick look and then plotted the range and bearing of the ships by hydrophone data. Firing by sound alone, he loosed four torpedoes. Two of them romped home into the seven thousand eight hundred ton tanker, Sylvan Arrow, and broke the ship's back. On fire, the Sylvan Arrow slowly went down, but Piening could not see this. − In only two hundred and seventy feet of water, he was trying to creep away, as the USS Upshur, and a PC plastered the area with depth-charges. For two hours, until the convoy was close in under the guns of Chacachacare, the destroyer kept the U155 down.

The sinkings in the Caribbean had reached such alarming proportions, that Washington felt that there was a danger of the Vichy French naval vessels in Martinique, sallying forth to join in the destruction of Allied shipping and Admiral Hoover was instructed to blockade the harbour at Fort de France. He dispatched the USS Blakely, the USS Ellis, and a PC to carry out the operation.

All shipping into and out of the port was stopped and checked by the destroyers. The Germans on the other hand, felt that the Vichy French might take the opportunity to add their support to the Americans and British in the Caribbean, at a time when such a move would be most appreciated. Accordingly, first Hartenstein in U156 and then Graf in U69 were ordered to blockade Fort de France and ensure that the Allies could not go into the harbour, or the Vichy French come out. Thus it transpired that both sides were blockading Martinique at the same time, and they got in each other's way. On the way to join U156, the U69 also ran into U155's convoy, but Graf had orders to ignore it and proceed to Martinique.

While U155 was encountering the first signs of the end of total freedom, U103 was completely free at the other end of the Caribbean. Winter sent the two freighters Clare and Elizabeth, down into the underwater Yucatan Basin, off the western tip of Cuba.

At two o'clock next morning, Graf sank the Canadian freighter Torondoc, sixty miles west of Martinique. At midday Krech in U558 sank the British freighter Troisdoc, in the mile-deep waters of the Jamaica Channel, east of the island. The U558 had come down through the Bahamas and was now operating in the Windward Passage. At twelve-thirty Hartenstein sank the small Dominican Republic freighter President Trujillo, ten miles outside the Fort de France harbour. Later that evening U558 attacked the American tanker William Boyce Thompson near the Pedro Bank, south of Jamaica. The tanker was hit by two torpedoes and stopped, but as Krech tried to move in, PCs from Guantanamo arrived and saved their first ship.

On the following day U156 checked the harbour at St. Vincent and reported it empty, while U69 fired at a freighter entering Martinique and missed. The freighter fired back with the ancient cannon mounted on its stern, as it scuttled into the harbour. Further south U155 sank the freighter Watsonville, three miles off the coast of St. Vincent. Far away to the west Winter in U103 sank the six thousand ton tanker Samuel Q Brown, in the Yucatan Channel, and on the following morning sent the Dutch freighter Hector, to join the wrecks in the area.

At nine fifteen on the morning of May twenty-fourth, U502 put two torpedoes into the starboard side of the Brazilian vessel Concalves Diaz. The U-Boat had been having a lean time during the previous ten days and Von Rosensteil must have welcomed the chance to fire at something. He signalled to say that the vessel which was enroute to New Orleans with coffee, did not carry neutrality markings. Six men died in the blast from the torpedoes but the remainder managed to launch their lifeboats. Von Rosensteil questioned them before ensuring that they had adequate provisions. They were picked up the following morning, south of Haiti and taken to Key West.

The morning of the twenty-fifth saw the expected clash off Martinique. U156 saw the destroyer Blakely cruising inshore of the U-Boat's position, and Hartenstein grabbed the opportunity. Two torpedoes hissed away. One passed ahead of the vessel, but the other blew the bows clean off the destroyer. Blakely was brought almost to a standstill and her captain acted promptly to save his ship. The bowless Blakely swung away from the U-Boat, towards Fort de France harbour. When Blakely was safely inside the neutral harbour, Hartenstein signalled U-Boat Headquarters. He advised what he had done and requested permission to enter the harbour and finish off the destroyer. Hartenstein would no doubt have loved to have gone into the familiar harbour and created even greater disturbance than he already had. U-Boat headquarters vetoed the plan.

The Blakely incident however, was to have an adverse effect on the

U-Boats off Martinique. The US Navy had to get the destroyer out of the harbour within the stipulated twenty-four hours, and to do this they threw in all their resources. The destroyers Breckenridge, Greer and Tarbell raced for the island and more importantly, two PBYs of VP-53 moved from San Juan to Chaguaramas and began spending a lot of time over the sea to the west of Martinique. Within two days both U156 and U69 were claiming exhaustion because they were required to stay submerged almost all the time. U156 noted a hundred and twenty-one hours underwater in one week. The full moon ensured that they were attacked constantly by flying boats, so much so, that U156 developed serious cracks in her tanks.

U-Boat headquarters relented and allowed the boats to withdraw to the westward, but before Hartenstein pulled back, he attempted to sink the US destroyer Tarbell. The torpedo missed and U156 withdrew quickly, before the expected counter-attacks developed. At the same time, Göing in command of U755 reported that there was no shipping in the Florida Straits, other than in heavily guarded convoys. The boat was reassigned to the Gulf of Mexico, but the report was an indication of what was going to happen in the Straits of Florida.

The last six days of May saw seven ships sunk. On the same day that the Blakely was hit, U103 sank the five thousand six hundred ton American bauxite ship Alcoa Carrier, between Jamaica and Grand Cayman. Two days later another bauxite cargo was lost, when U502 sank the Alcoa Pilgrim, south of Puerto Rico. That same day, the twenty-eighth, U155 sank the freighter Jack, off the Windward Islands. A little later that morning, U103 sent the six thousand ton American tanker New Jersey, to the bottom in the Cayman Trench, southeast of the island of Grand Cayman. Late that night U156, now operating in safer waters, sixty miles west of Martinique, sank the British freighter Norman Prince.

That same evening Harald Gelhaus in U107 announced his arrival in the Caribbean by sinking the British freighter Western Head, fifty miles east of Guantanamo Bay. The following day another new boat the U504 under Poske marked the start of his second Caribbean visit by sinking the British freighter Allister, near Grand Cayman. The thirtieth of May saw U155 sink the last vessel of the Merry Month of May. Piening torpedoed the Norwegian freighter Baghdad with his last fish, three hundred and ninety miles east of St. Lucia. U155 was going home with a very satisfied crew. They had sunk seven ships, worth thirty-three thousand and eighty-six tons. Piening had sunk nearly all of his targets off the coast of Trinidad and he would be returning to this lucrative area.

During May seven U-Boats, U66, U69, U130, U155, U156, U162 and

U502 operated in the Trinidad Sector. Together they sank eighteen ships and damaged two others. Three boats, the U103, U125 and U504 operated in the northern part of the Guantanamo Sector and the western extremity of the Sector. Together they accounted for fifteen ships sunk. The Puerto Rico Sector was a transit area that boats destined for the Gulf of Mexico, the Panama Sector and the Trinidad Sector, used to reach their respective operating areas. As a result twenty ships were sunk in the sector with two others damaged.

Only four boats, U107, U108, U172 and U558 operated exclusively in the Windward Passage and the Puerto Rico Sector during the month. These figures meant that a total of twenty U-Boats operated in the Caribbean zone during the month. They sank an incredible fifty-three merchant ships and seriously damaged four others. However many of the ships sunk within the Caribbean proper were small vessels, so that the total tonnage added up to only two hundred and forty-six thousand and sixty-three tons during the Merry Month of May. Just a quarter of a million tons.

In the Gulf of Mexico, U106, U506, U507 and U753 operated, with U103 doing a short stint. They sank nineteen ships and seriously damaged six others. When the figures for the Gulf are added to those for the Caribbean zone to get the theatre total, the astonishing figure of seventy-two ships sunk in the month of May emerged. These ships represented a total of three hundred and sixty-four thousand tons for the month. Yet, the Grand Admiral's strategy was more than this.

Doenitz must have guessed that the bigger ships coming from South Africa and South America towards the United States would try to divert around the Caribbean, once the news of the sinkings in the zone got around. This is the reason why U156 and U162 operated well east of the islands for a considerable period of time. They were sitting astride this diversionary route.

But the Grand Admiral devised a much more far-reaching strategy. U593 under Kilbing, U594 under Mumm, U578 under Rewinkel, U588 under Vogel and U404 under Von Bulow, were positioned nine hundred miles north of the Caribbean, in an area from the longitude of the eastern tip of Cuba to the longitude of Antigua. These five boats were a stop-group to catch the ships diverting around the Caribbean, and they all achieved success.

The other part of the overall strategy involved U126 under Bauer, U129 under Ulrich Heyse and U161 under Achilles. These boats came down the central Atlantic to the Equator, then turned west towards Brazil. Once off the South American coast, they spread out into a fan with U161 on the landward side and moved northwards. They acted like a group of shepherd dogs, driving the merchant ships ahead of them. Thus the Grand Admiral's brilliant strategy for May was far greater than just the events within the Caribbean Theatre. The focal point concerns us in a study of May 1942, but the total sinkings for the entire operation were much greater.

The Allies had to do something about the Caribbean.

CHAPTER

5

The Golden West

During the month of May, one hundred and nine merchant ships were sunk by U-Boats. Seventy-eight percent of these were in the Caribbean Theatre. The Grand Admiral's strategy of striking at the weak links was paying off handsomely. In comparison, the merchant ships found the area off the US coast and the notorious North Atlantic relatively quiet.

Appalled at the losses in the Caribbean and unable to reinforce the area quickly enough, the Allies adopted the only short term counter-measure that could be quickly implemented. They changed the merchant shipping routes throughout the region, in the hope that the U-Boats would be left waiting in the old areas while cargoes got through.

In the Caribbean however, the U-Boats enjoyed an extraordinary amount of freedom and many went roaming away from their assigned areas and fate took a hand. Quite by chance, many of the U-Boats discovered the altered routes and reported the intelligence to U-Boat headquarters. The Grand Admiral reacted by transferring to the Caribbean six boats from off the US coast and four boats enroute to that area. The result was that June turned out to be an even more disastrous month for the merchant ships, than May had been. In fact, June would be the high point of the Caribbean war, from the U Boats' point of view.

The month opened with ten boats in the Caribbean Theatre. Three boats the U69, U156 and U502 were operating near Trinidad and the Windward Islands. There were also three boats off Central America. U107 and U504 had cut the shipping route for the Gulf of Mexico, one off Honduras and the other south of Cuba. U158, a new Type IXC under the command of Erich Rostin was also in this area, working his way westwards before entering the Gulf of Mexico.

In the north, U103 and U753 were in the Bahamas, while U68 was nearing the Mona Passage. Another new boat, the Type IXC U172, under the command of Carl Emmermann was north of Puerto Rico, coming south. In addition to these ten, the special hunting group of U128, U126 and U161 were off northern Brazil, moving towards the Caribbean, while six new boats were in mid-Atlantic, enroute to the Caribbean zone.

On the Allied side, the situation didn't look very hopeful and they could only look forward to another bad month, but in the longer term, several developments were emerging which in time would swing the pendulum their way. The first of these was Mexico's declaration of war in June. This auspicious event opened up Mexican air bases to US aircraft, thus allowing greater coverage of the Gulf of Mexico and in time, the Yucatan Passage.

The second advantage accruing to the Allies was a curious signal from U-Boat headquarters to all boats, warning them that they might be attacked at any time by Brazilian forces. From the U-Boat captains' point of view, this automatically meant that Brazilians were hostile, further increasing the tension between the two countries. Then on the twentieth of June, another signal informed the boats of the opening of hostilities against Brazil. In fact Brazil did not declare war on Germany until August. Ironically, it appears that Germany pushed Brazil into the war, without realising what a disastrous effect this would have on the U-Boats.

The third advantage was the establishment of several British and American radio direction-finding stations on the US coast and in the Caribbean. All U-Boats were centrally controlled, they did not just go hunting. Every few days they were required to report their positions and their activities and in return received instructions. This constant radio chatter was to give the Allies in the theatre the opportunity to triangulate the sources of radio traffic and to keep tabs not only on the rough areas where the boats were operating, but sometimes also, home hunters onto them. These stations also gave Allied intelligence the first real chance to assess accurately how many U-Boats they had to contend with.

The final advantage lay in the combination of the Leigh light, carried by RAF coastal command aircraft, with the airborne ASV radar. This allowed the RAF to turn the U-Boats' transit route through the Bay of Biscay, into a death trap. These long term advantages, combined with the gradual reinforcement of the Caribbean, would in time check the ravages of the U-Boats.

Doenitz was fully aware that the rich harvest he was gathering in the Caribbean could not last, and while the going was good, he intended to make the most of it. His boats were astride the area's shipping lanes and to the U-Boat Commanders, the Caribbean was the Golden West. It appeared in June as if the farther west boats operated, the more golden it became.

In this area, Harald Gelhaus in U107 opened the scoring for June. At dawn on this first day of the new month, the boat with the "Four Aces" on the conning tower, crept in close to the shore of the island of Grand Cayman and carefully stalked the cargo ship, SS Bushranger. As the sun peeped over the eastern horizon, two torpedoes leapt out of the bow tubes and buried themselves in the Bushranger's side. The explosions broke the vessel's back and she went down less than five miles offshore, within sight of the startled inhabitants.

That evening, on the other side of the Caribbean, U156 caught the Brazilian freighter Allegrate forty miles from the island of St. Lucia. One torpedo from the U-Boat's bow tubes crashed into the vessel and she began to settle. Before abandoning ship, the master ensured that every light was left burning in the vessel so that even in its death throes, the ship was proclaiming its neutrality. After the four lifeboats with all sixty-four survivors pulled away from the ship, Hartenstein put two more torpedoes into the vessel and then opened up with his deck gun. This six thousand ton vessel's full load of coffee destined for the United States, ended up a mile and a half below, forty miles southwest of St. Lucia. USS Tarbell which was still hunting the U156, picked up one of the lifeboats, while the other three ended up in Port of Spain, Blanguilla island and La Guaira in Venezuela. Hartenstein's explanation that the vessel was painted grey was quite correct, but it didn't really matter in view of the recent signals from U-Boat headquarters.

On the second of June, Rostin in U158 opened his Caribbean account by sinking the American freighter Knoxville City thirty-five miles west of Cuba's Isle of Pines. Late that evening. Emmermann in U172 sent the five thousand four hundred ton American freighter Illinois to the bottom in the underwater Nares Abyssal Plain. northeast of the Caribbean islands.

On this, his only Caribbean cruise, Emmermann was to sink seven of his final total of twenty-seven ships, which put him thirteenth on the list of U-Boat Aces.

At the same time that Emmermann was beginning his successful Caribbean cruise, Von Manstein in U753 operating north of Cuba, and Rasch in U106, operating in the Gulf of Mexico, were both reporting that they had met convoys which they could not penetrate. It was a portent of things to come. In the meantime, the special hunting group was dissolved and the three U-Boats reallocated to the Caribbean. U161 was to move up the South American coast to its own playground around Trinidad, then further west to Central America, while U126 and U128 were to operate east of the Windward Islands.

Hardly had the special group been dissolved before the boats were in among the area's shipping. At dawn on the third of June, Bauer in U126 used two torpedoes to bring the large Norwegian tanker Hoegh Giant, to a halt off French Guiana. The U-Boat then moved in close and shelled the giant ship into a blazing inferno. By the time No. 99 squadron arrived over the area, the eleven thousand ton Hoegh Giant was no more and all they could do was report the position of the survivors.

Further to the north, Hartenstein was at work again, shelling the schooner Lilian into matchwood, twenty-five miles from Barbados. He was out of torpedoes and just setting course for home when he chanced on the little sailing vessel. He was still to sink one more ship, the freighter Willimantic, by gunfire alone, well to the northeast of the islands. He was completing the most successful Caribbean cruise of all the U-Boats, when success is judged by number of ships hit. He and his crew had sunk eleven vessels and damaged two others during this cruise. His total score in the Caribbean during his two patrols in the area was sixteen ships sunk and four damaged. This tally was not equalled by any other U-Boat, either on a single trip or their combined Caribbean totals, but this was a tonnage war and in total tonnage he placed way down the ladder at ninth. Even so, his ships sunk averaged out at over four thousand tons a piece. The boat that started Operation Neuland would be back in the Caribbean on a third cruise, but the only thing U156 would achieve, would be to give a Catalina pilot a most spectacular target.

Two more merchant ships were lost that day. Von Rosensteil was on patrol just to the north of Margarita Island, when the seven thousand ton tanker M.F. Elliot, came over the horizon, heading towards Trinidad. One torpedo fired from the surface caused a giant explosion that tore the ship apart. As the wreck slid down to join the growing fleet on the ocean floor,

U502 picked up a solitary survivor. He was later put into a dinghy under a circling rescue aircraft. U159 under the command of Helmutt Witte, holder of the Knight's Cross, finished off the day by sinking the cargo vessel City of Alma, three hundred miles north of Antigua. This was the U-Boat's first kill on what was going to be a very successful patrol.

The following day was relatively quiet, with only one ship being sunk by U158, but the fifth of June was to see the U-Boats hard at work, shattering the confidence of the defenders.

The first ship to go was the three thousand five hundred ton freighter, Delfina. The vessel was heading northwest, away from Puerto Rico when at eight minutes past midnight, Emmermann in U172, sent it to the bottom. Daylight saw the large Brazilian, sailing schooner Paracury, have an amazing escape. The U-Boats usually stopped these schooners and allowed the crew to abandon ship before they used the twenty millimetre to sink the sailing vessels. Usually, a twenty millimetre shell would make a sizeable hole in the wooden sides and that would be the end of the vessel, but the Paracury actually survived. U159 was a highly efficient boat and it seem unlikely that they left the job unfinished. It is more likely that an army Air Corps bomber from Puerto Rico appeared on the scene, forcing the U-Boat to back off and allowed the heavily damaged Paracury to reach the shores of Puerto Rico, thirty miles away. One hour later, the schooner Sally's luck ran out. No aircraft intervened and the unfortunate vessel's crew watched from their dinghy as Witte finished off the boat.

An hour later and many miles to the south, the tanker L.J. Drake, disappeared in a gigantic fireball as torpedoes from U68 tore into it. There were no survivors from the six thousand seven hundred ton vessel. This was Frigattkapitan Karl Merten, holder of the Knight's Cross with Oakleaves, opening the most successful Caribbean cruise of the tonnage war. Merten had brought the U68 into the Caribbean via the seldom used, Anegada Passage. He found it very quiet and was able to remain on the surface throughout the transit. This entry point into the Caribbean was much smaller and shallower than the larger, better known Galleons, Mona or Windward Passages, but it paid off for a U-Boat commander willing to take the risk, of being caught in restricted water. It would be a very long time before the Anegada Passage would be guarded.

Six hours after the destruction of the L.J. Drake, Merten had the good fortune to see a very large tanker racing past his bow. All three torpedoes hit the thirteen thousand and six ton C.O. Stillman. The explosions opened up the great ship to the sea and a very satisfied Merten watched as the Panamanian-registered ship's stern dipped below the waves, on its way to the underwater Muertos Trough. This was Merten's first trip to the Caribbean and he must have been very surprised at his luck. To sink such a tanker on the North Atlantic route, a U-Boat commander would have to battle his way past the escorts and into the convoy, in the dead of night and take enormous risks. Instead, he could sit on the surface, thirty miles south of the dangerous Mona Passage and in broad daylight, find such a ship unescorted. The C.O. Stillman turned out to be the largest ship sunk in the Caribbean during June and the second largest sunk in the area during the war. Twelve hundred miles to the westward, Rostin in U158 finished off the day by sinking the freighter Velma Lykes, shortly after sunset. This was U158's last sinking in the Caribbean sea, as she moved up the Yucatan Channel to enter the Gulf of Mexico.

Only one ship was sunk on the sixth of June 1942. Gelhaus took U107 northward from the Grand Cayman area to sink the Honduran freighter Castilla, west of Cuba's Isle of Pines. Witte had now brought U159 down from the Mona Passage, past the Dutch islands and into his assigned western Caribbean hunting ground. On the seventh, he sank the freighter Edith, well north of Baranquilla, Colombia. U172 in the meantime had moved close inshore to Hispaniola and at eleven o'clock that night, destroyed the freighter Sicilien, only ten miles from Cabo Beata.

Two days had gone by since the numerous sinkings on the fifth and it was time for the U-Boats to treat the Caribbean Sea Frontier to another one-day spectacular. At one o'clock in the morning on the eighth of June, Poske in U504 sank the four thousand ton Tela, off the Yucatan Peninsula. Two hours later, he used a torpedo and his deck gun to dispose of the freighter Rosenburg, in the same area. At eight o'clock that morning, two thousand miles to the eastward, U128 under the command of Ulrich Heyse achieved his first sinking in the Caribbean zone. The nine thousand, two hundred ton tanker South Africa, went down six hundred miles east of the islands, at the outer edge of Trinidad's Atlantic fan. As night fell, the action switched back to the western Caribbean, as Gelhaus in U107 sent the American freighter Suweid, to the bottom just off Cozumel Island near the entrance to the Gulf of Mexico.

Once again the Caribbean Sea Frontier was reeling from the scale of the attack. Merchant ships were going down too fast for an accurate picture of the U-Boats' movements to be plotted. Added to the problem of lost merchant ships and cargoes, was the problem of survivors. All over the Caribbean there were lifeboats with badly sunburnt scarecrows, all waiting to be rescued. The current in the area generally flows northwest, then northward to join the Gulf stream off Florida. Left alone the survivors would eventually be carried right round the Caribbean and out into the Atlantic. Part of the very scarce resources had to be allocated to rescue duties, and survivor camps had to be established in all the major centers to cater for the half starved, frequently deranged, often injured seamen whom the sea had given up.

For the Allies, the situation was indeed grim, but there was hope on the horizon. The southward shift of the U-Boats had also allowed the southward shift of some of the resources. Ten US Navy destroyers had been added to the forces in the area. Part of the British B-5 escort group and a Canadian group had also been allocated to the Caribbean. In fact, both San Juan and Chaguaramas now each had four destroyers based in their respective sectors. Actually, the sectors now carried very little meaning other than as a quick reference for merchant shipping sinkings, because the escorts had to work according to where the greatest threat existed.

Examples of this included No. 59 squadron in Curacao, who although they were under the command of the Trinidad Sector, were required to patrol westwards, well into the Panama Sector. Another example concerns the situation around Martinique. In theory the island lay in the Puerto Rico Sector, but it was much closer to Trinidad, so all the activities concerning the blockade came under Trinidad control. This same type of situation existed throughout the Caribbean, with forces being allocated as the need arose, but in all cases, the Germans held the initiative.

There were now destroyers working in the Panama Sector, in a vain attempt to stem the tide of sinkings in the far west, but by far the most important change, was that there was a destroyer stationed in the center of the Straits of Florida, round the clock. This meant that at least one of the zone's many entrances was now guarded and it would pay off. The time would come when all the passages would be similarly guarded, but in June 1942 that was only a dream.

Despite the westward shift of the U-Boats to the Panama Sector during June, the Trinidad Sector was still the most important. It was the crossroads of all shipping for North and South America and in accordance with its importance there were more naval resources allocated. The B-5 group and the Canadians operated from Trinidad. The Royal Canadian Navy detached two corvettes and assigned them permanently to the base for work alongside the TRNVR patrol vessels and the Royal Navy's MTBs.

All over the island new defence works were being undertaken. It was at this stage that Trinidad's strategic position was finally recognised. If the Bases Agreement had not been negotiated in 1940, it would have had to be agreed to, in June 1942. In fact, the eventual defeat of the U-Boats in the area can be directly attributed to the existence of the bases. If the Americans had been forced to start base construction in 1942, the U-Boats might well have won the battle of the Atlantic, without fighting the North Atlantic convoys. In May and June 1942, ships were being sunk in the Caribbean at more than double the rate at which they were being built in the great American shipyards.

All the boats in the eastern Caribbean were now reporting the presence of convoys. They were not of the highly disciplined North Atlantic variety, but rather the loose gatherings of groups of ships wishing to cross the Caribbean. The majority of the escorts were not as experienced as the combat veterans in the U-Boats, but it was a start. Admiral Andrews and Hoover in command of the US East coast and the Caribbean Sea Frontier, could see the glimmer of hope on the horizon, and so could the U-Boats.

Shortly after daybreak on the eighth of June, convoy TA-5 left the Dragon's Mouth. To try and protect the ships, the routing had been changed. Merchant shipping leaving Trinidad for the west had always set course west northwest, to pass to seaward of the Los Testigos group of islands, keeping well clear of the shallow water around Margarita Island. The traditional route then ran westwards, passing to the north of Blanquilla Island and the hazardous Los Rogues group, off the Venezuelan coast to the Dutch Islands. TA-5 had been rerouted to pass inshore of the Los Testigos group, closely rounding the northern tip of Margarita, then hugging the Venezuelan coast all the way to Aruba. This routing would avoid the suspected U-Boat concentration to the north of Testigos and Blanquilla. Unfortunately for the convoy, Von Rosensteil had gone exploring.

On June third, U502 had been ordered to move in close to Trinidad to take advantage of the new moon period and U-Boat headquarters confidently expected that U502 was sitting astride the shipping route in the western fan from Trinidad. Instead, Von Rosensteil had come in close to Trinidad and then moved westwards, hugging the shoreline. On the morning of the ninth of June, he was nearly three hundred miles away from his assigned operating area, exploring the inshore shipping routes off Caracas in Venezuela. Disobeying his orders, Von Rosensteil found himself in the right place at the right time.

TA-5 came up over the horizon and Von Rosensteil took U502 down to periscope depth, to await their arrival. The convoy was on a course of two seven zero degrees, moving forward at seven knots, when the first two torpedoes hissed out of the bow tubes. The hydrophone operator confirmed that the eels were running and taking advantage of the excellent attack conditions, Von Rosensteil stayed at periscope depth. As the twin towers of water rose up alongside his first target, he fired the second pair. The Belgian freighter Bruxelles was already dropping back, when the secon pair slammed into the tanker, Franklyn K. Lane.

The convoy slowly pulled ahead, leaving the two stricken vessels to their fate, but an escort destroyer had seen the U-Boat's periscope. U502 went deep, but almost immediately the probing Asdic fingers found them. They could hear the approaching destroyer's propellers. Then the depth-charging started. U502 was severely shaken up and one particularly well placed pair shattered light fittings. The depth-charge attack was well carried out, but it was nothing compared to that which the North Atlantic boats regularly had to endure, to be able to sink two such ships. Attack conditions in the Caribbean were still excellent.

The tenth of June was to be another bad day for merchant shipping in the zone. U68 had made its way westward and was now in its assigned operating area off Panama. Merten announced his presence shortly after midnight, by torpedoing the eight thousand five hundred ton British freighter, Surrey. This was one of the largest freighters sunk in the Caribbean and its cargo of tanks, guns and ammunition went under just to the east of Isla San Andres. Ten minutes later, the five thousand ton freighter, Ardenvohr was in Merten's sights. Two torpedoes sufficed to break the ship's back, but the cargo must have caught fire, because long after the ship had disappeared, U68 was rocked by a gigantic underwater explosion. Both vessels had gone down with their precious cargoes, within a mile of each other.

Five hours later, the long grey hull of the U-Boat was still cruising in the same area, when the British freighter Port Montreal, hove into view. Merten sent the vessel and its cargo down to join the other two lying in the underwater Clark Basin. In a matter of hours, U68 had accounted for twenty thousand tons of Allied shipping.

However the day had hardly begun. Poske in U504 had been in the waters off the Yucatan Peninsula since late May and had sunk four cargo ships, when the Dutch steamer Crijnssen came into sight on a north westerly heading. Seventy miles from Swan Island, a torpedo sent the passenger ship to the bottom. Witte In U159 ended the day by sinking the British-crewed Liberty ship, Fort Good Hope, fifty miles from the Atlantic entrance entrance to the Panama Canal. The day had netted thirty-one thousand tons. In the far west of the Caribbean, there were no convoys, virtually no air patrols and many targets. The wolves were among the sheep and both U172 and U161 were ordered to join the hunting.

U158 had gone up into the Gulf of Mexico, replacing U106 which was now homeward bound. U157, a new boat and U129 under Hans Witt, the original commander of U161, were both on their way to the Gulf of Mexico, as well as the familiar U67. Muller-Stockheim was coming back to collect his fair share of merchant vessels, to make up for all the ill luck that the boat had endured on its first cruise. U67 had had bad luck long before its first Caribbean cruise. It was probably the only submarine which has ever been accidentally rammed by an enemy submarine. Both boats' crew were probably so shocked by the occurrence that there was no thought of offensive action. All that was behind him now and Muller-Stockheim intended that the white painted Chamois on his conning tower would bring the luck he deserved.

The eleventh of June was scarcely less disastrous for the merchant ships. The Type IXC boat U157 under the command of Korvettenkapitan Wolf Henne had received his orders on June ninth, detailing the boat's operating areas in the Gulf of Mexico. Daylight on the eleventh found U157 on the southern edge of the Old Bahama Channel, off the north coast of Cuba. Henne was in his first command and that morning he made his first kill in the new U-Boat. The American tanker Hagen, was torpedoed less than ten miles off the Cuban coast. Undoubtedly, Henne enjoyed the sight of his first ship sinking below the waves and just as well, because he had an appointment to keep with a US Coast Guard cutter. After watching the tanker die, U157, the doomed boat, set off up the Old Bahama Channel. At eleven o'clock that morning, Poske in U504 collected his sixth kill by sending the tanker American, to the bottom, once again in the Swan Island area.

Late on the night of the eleventh, Rostin in U158 carried out a daring attack close to the Mississippi Delta. In less than ten fathoms and less than thirty miles off the Delta, Rostin torpedoed the largest vessel sunk during the war in the west. From the shore, onlookers could see the burning thirteen thousand four hundred and sixty-seven ton tanker, Sheherazade. Eventually, the giant vessel settled into water scarcely deep enough to cover its masts. Rostin continued operating U158 in water too shallow for the boat to dive and sank the eight thousand ton tanker Cities Service Toledo. The second tanker went down less than ten miles offshore, before he turned U158 southward to make his dash to deeper water.

The whole attack, so deep in the Gulf of Mexico was an affront to the US Navy and they would exact a terrible revenge.

While Rostin was making his escape, U-Boat headquarters made another broadcast to all boats about the status of neutral vessels. This one advised that nearly all Swedish vessels were on enemy service. All boats were required to stop and board Swedish vessels, but if the ships were zig-zagging,

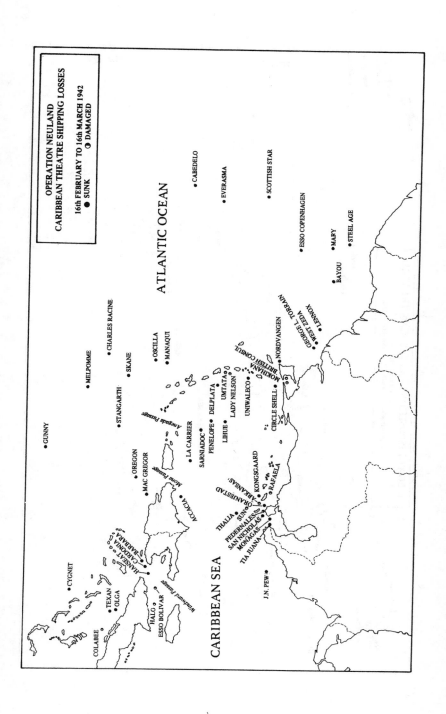

OPERATION NEULAND
CARIBBEAN THEATRE SHIPPING LOSSES
16th FEBRUARY TO 16th MARCH 1942
● SUNK   ◑ DAMAGED

ATLANTIC OCEAN

CARIBBEAN SEA

• CABEDELO
• EVERASMA
• SCOTTISH STAR
• ESSO COPENHAGEN
• BAYOU   • MARY
• STEEL AGE

• GUNNY
• MELPOMME
• CHARLES RACINE
• SKANE
• OSTLLA
• MANAQUI
• STANGARTH
• OREGON
• MAC GREGOR
• LA CARRIER
• SARNIADOC
• PENELOPE
• LHUE
• DELPLATA
• UMTATA
• LADY NELSON
• UNIWALECO
• MOKHANA
• BRITISH CONSUL
• NORDVANGEN
• CIRCLE SHELL
• GEORGE L. TORRAIN
• WEST ZEDA
• LENNOX

Anegada Passage
Mona Passage

• ACCAYA
• CYGNET
• HANSEAT
• CARONIA
• BARBARA

• COLABEE
• TEXAN
• OLGA
• HALO
• ESSO BOLIVAR

Windward Passage

• THALIA
• ORANJESTAD
• KONGSGAARD
• ARKANSAS
• RAFAELA
• PEDERNALES
• SUN
• SAN NICHOLAS
• MONAGAS
• TIA JUANA

• J.N. PEW

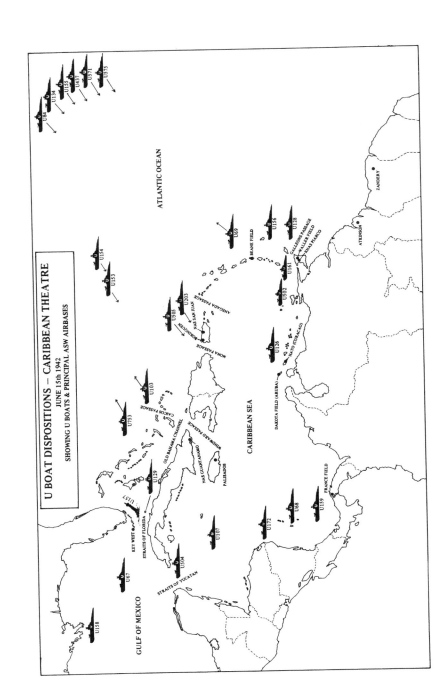

U BOAT DISPOSITIONS – CARIBBEAN THEATRE
JUNE 15th 1942
SHOWING U BOATS & PRINCIPAL ASW AIRBASES

ATLANTIC OCEAN

CARIBBEAN SEA

GULF OF MEXICO

U84
U134
U155
U437
U571
U575
U154
U153
U69
U136
U128
U103
U753
U203
U505
U161
U502
U126
U129
U157
U107
U504
U172
U68
U159
U67
U158

BEANE FIELD
GALLEONS PASSAGE
WALLER FIELD
NAS PIARCO
ATKINSON
ZANDERY
ANEGADA PASSAGE
NAS SAN JUAN
BORINQUEN
MONA PASSAGE
HATO (CURACAO)
DAKOTA FIELD (ARUBA)
FRANCE FIELD
CAICOS PASSAGE
OLD BAHAMA CHANNEL
WINDWARD PASSAGE
NAS GUANTANAMO
PALISADOS
KEY WEST
STRAITS OF FLORIDA
STRAITS OF YUCATAN

they were to be sunk. Portuguese vessels were to be handled in the same manner. Actually, the instruction about Swedish ships was a very prudent precaution. Sweden was officially neutral, but she did trade with the Allies, often delivering vitally-needed machinery.

While the broadcast was being made, the Royal Navy, the US Navy and the TRNVR were completing a joint deep sea exercise off Trinidad's north coast. The exercise lasted for four days and was part of the overall Trinidad defence plan. After the exercise was completed, the joint defence plan was formally accepted. At last, Trinidad had a unified solution to the possibility of a raid. It was almost four months since Achilles had made his raid. The old Governor who had fought so hard against the American bases, had been recalled on June eighth and the new Commander in Chief was Sir Bede Clifford, a man with whom the Americans could live. The common enemy had at last broken down national barriers. British, American and Trinidadian were now working towards a common goal.

The thirteenth was to be a red letter day for the Allies, — for a change. One ship was sunk by U159, operating in the Golfo de los Mosquitos, shortly after midnight and the U-Boat sank another off Panama, after lunch, but between these two events, a U-Boat died. U157 reported the sinking of the Hagen in the Old Bahama Channel and the US Navy were able to get a fix on the transmission.

A U-Boat coming up the Old Bahama Channel could have only one destination and the US forces were waiting. No doubt, Henne had heard the many broadcasts by other boats, warning of the presence of destroyer patrols in the Straits of Florida and this could possibly be the reason why he hugged the northern side of the Straits. He evaded the standing destroyer patrol, but in doing this, he ran into a US Coast Guard cutter. The USS Thetis WPC 115, had been patrolling the northern side of the Straits, when the tiny dot of a radar contact attracted their attention. As the cutter worked up speed towards the radar contact, the U-Boat continued her westward course, unaware of the danger closing in from the north. The U-Boat's lookouts may have been at fault, because it appears that the boat saw the cutter long after the bridge of the cutter had them visual. When U157 finally crash-dived, it was far too late. Thetis raced across the swirl of water and the deadly cans rolled off. U157 was finished. It is more than likely that the depth-charges, going off so close to the U-Boat cracked her pressure hull, or seriously damaged her to the extent that she plummeted out of control. There were no survivors.

No one knew the fate of Wolf Henne and his crew, not even the crew of the Thetis. Certainly, U-Boat headquarters knew nothing and continued to plot the boat's dead reckoning position into the Gulf. It would be only after the boat missed a routine report, that the first suspicion would be aroused. The other U-Boats in the Caribbean, knew nothing of the drama that had been enacted thirty miles from Key West, and they continued slaughtering the merchantmen. Far away to the south, a destroyer attacked U159 off Panama and claimed a kill. As far as the US command was concerned, they had two possibles that day.

The fourteenth of June saw the magnificent Achilles and his U161, once again off Trinidad. Ashore, the defenders continued to wait and guard against his return. On this cruise, Achilles intended another spectacular attack, but not against Trinidad. He was probably well aware that no one could get away with another Trinidad raid.

On this day, U161 intended to attack a convoy. While she cruised westwards along the north coast, Poske in U504, far away to the west, sank his seventh ship, the freighter Regent. Once again it was near Swan Island. An hour later, Emmermann in U172 sank another of the large freighters to be hit in the Caribbean. The eight thousand three hundred ton Lebore, went down eighty miles off San Andres island.

The rising sun found U161 a hundred miles northwest of the Dragon's Mouth. Achilles was on the surface when smoke on the horizon signalled the approach of a ship. A few minutes later, he could tell that it was not a single ship, but a whole convoy. The escorts were aware that they were now in dangerous waters, − Trinidad's western fan, and everyone was cautioned to be extra vigilant. Achilles had taken U161 down to periscope depth to await the arrival of the convoy.

The hydrophone operator reported the convoy closing and U161's periscope slid upwards. Achilles picked out a large freighter in the port outer column. The phalanx of ships would be passing close and Achilles intended to hang onto it, taking out each ship in turn. Firing calculations complete and the target in his sights, he ordered the firing of two torpedoes. The hydrophone operator was barely able to discern the high speed whine of the torpedo propellers, against the great thunder of the propellers of the merchant ships. Achilles stood in the control room hanging onto the periscope controls, with his eyes glued to the eyepiece. He watched as the twin columns of spray rose up alongside the target, to be followed seconds later, by the dull thunder of the explosions.

Unfortunately for Achilles, someone in the Commodore's ship had seen the twin wakes coming in. The signal for an emergency turn to port had been given just too late for the U-Boat commander to see the ships beginning to swing. The eight thousand ton American registered freighter

Scotsburg, was finished, but in dying she was creating confusion. The ship had begun to slow down and settle as soon as the torpedoes detonated and now she wallowed in the middle of a group of ponderously-turning merchant ships. The masters of the merchant ships now had to turn past the drifting hulk and it meant that some had to put on starboard wheel to avoid the Scotsburg. This effectively broke up the convoy. There were now ships going in a variety of directions, with the majority swinging onto a heading towards the hidden U-Boat.

U161 had gone deep to escape the expected counter attack and except for the reports from the hydrophone operator, they had no idea what was happening on the surface. The underwater noise gave the impression that the convoy was breaking up and if this was so, then ideal conditions for another torpedo attack would exist. Achilles ordered the boat up to periscope depth. As U161 levelled off just below the surface, the sound of propellers was loud, but not the high speed variety signalling destroyers. The merchant ships were close. Just as Achilles was about to raise the periscope to take a look, the whole U-Boat shuddered and they could hear a rending of metal. U161 was rolled over to port and they heard the great thrashing of a propeller, very close. U161 had been rammed. As Achilles picked himself up, the stunned crew of the boat instinctively looked upwards, expecting to see the hull caving in. Then the rending sound stopped and the propeller noise receded. There was now no thought of an attack, but rather how badly damaged they were. As soon as it was apparent that the pressure hull had not been punctured, Achilles took U161 deeper. They had been very lucky.

It was a long time before the sound of propellers disappeared completely and the boat was able to come to periscope depth for a look to make sure that the horizon was clear. Then U161 surfaced and Achilles clambered up the ladder to the conning tower, to be greeted by an amazing sight. The starboard side of the conning tower screen had disappeared. Apparently the merchant ship had just hit the conning tower without significantly damaging the boat. The periscope was miraculously undamaged and the boat was functional. With torpedoes and a working periscope, Achilles could continue and as the sun went down, U161 resumed her course towards the far corner of the Caribbean. Behind her, the wreck of the Scotsburg had joined the fleet in the western fan, but there was also another wreck from the convoy. U502 had responded to Achilles' initial sighting report and had been able to take advantage of the confusion U161 had caused. Von Rosensteil sent the five thousand ton freighter Cold Harbour, to join the Scotsburg. The day had seen twenty-five thousand tons of shipping sunk.

U504 was on her way home. She had sunk seven ships and would not be back in the Caribbean theatre. She was leaving a Caribbean where the U-Boats were enjoying their last fling of total freedom and even as she pointed towards the Windward Passage, the boats were busily destroying more vessels. U126 had also worked her way past Trinidad and the fifteenth of June found her northeast of the Dutch Island of Bonaire. That morning, she destroyed the little sailing schooner Nueva Alta Gracia, before turning back east. At one o'clock in the afternoon, U172 operating in the far west caught the freighter Bennestret, off Porto Limon in Costa Rica. The vessel was heading towards Panama when Emmermann intercepted it. Fifteen minutes later U502 still in the western fan from Trinidad, sank its last victim. The six thousand ton freighter West Hardaway was sailing independently when Von Rosensteil caught it. The U-Boat had almost doubled the number of kills that it had achieved on its first cruise. The toll for this cruise had amounted to eight ships totalling forty-six thousand tons. A very happy crew set off on the homeward journey, not aware that time had almost run out for Von Rosensteil.

In the afternoon, U68 continued sinking only big ships. The nine thousand three hundred ton tanker was enroute to the Panama Canal when Merten caught it off the Colombian coast. The Frimaire was a Vichy French ship on charter to the Portuguese, but Merten never found out who she was. The vessel disintegrated in a fire-ball and there were no survivors. At half past four that afternoon, Bauer in U126 caught the seven thousand ton freighter Arkansan west of Grenada, and sent her down in the western fan. An hour later, he also caught the American freighter Kahaku, heading towards Trinidad with a cargo of military equipment which was ultimately destined for North Africa. He sent the vessel down to join the Arkansan, in Trinidad's western fan. U126 had indeed enjoyed a successful day and her sinkings had contributed considerably towards the total of thirty thousand, five hundred tons of shipping that the U-Boats claimed that day.

U159 had enjoyed herself off the Panama Canal, so much so that the boat was now almost out of torpedoes. U-Boat headquarters ordered U161 to rendezvous with U159 mid way between Hispaniola and Aruba. U161 had a lean time on the long central Atlantic/Brazilian run and she had most of her torpedoes still aboard, but she was short on food. The two boats were to meet and exchange torpedoes for food. That way U161 could continue into the western Caribbean and U159 would have a torpedo or two for its return journey. The meeting took place on the twentieth and U161 also received some fuel from U159, but before that meeting both U-Boats still had work to do.

The seventeenth of June found nine U-Boats operating in the theatre. U68, U107, and U172 were in the far west, U159 was moving towards her rendezvous with U161, − while Ul26 and U128 were off the Trinidad area. Up in the Gulf of Mexico, U158 had made good her escape from the Mississippi Delta and was now operating off the coast of Mexico, while U67 was just getting past the dangerous Straits of Florida. U106, U502 and U504 were on their way home, while U129 was coming in from the northeast and U203 and U505 had just been ordered to leave the US coast and head for the Caribbean.

At five thirty that evening Witte took U159 inshore on the western side of Point Gallinas in Colombia, and operating in shoal water, sank his ninth ship, the freighter Flora. Half an hour later, Emmermann in U172 sank the tanker Motorex, just off Isla de Colon near Panama. Early next morning, Gelhaus in U107 probably sank the freighter Tillie Lykes, off the Honduran coastline. Gelhaus did not claim the vessel but the survivors were quite adamant that their vessel had been sunk by a U-Boat and U107 was the only one in the area. At four o'clock that afternoon, Hans Witt in U129 showed his contempt for the defences in the Straits of Florida by sinking the freighter Millinocket, in the Nicholas Channel, north of Cuba. This was his third ship and he hadn't even reached his operational area as yet. The Nicholas Channel was the continuation of the Old Bahama Channel and it virtually led straight into the Straits, but U129 was always a lucky boat.

The next morning, Helmutt Witte in U159 sank the freighter Ante Motkovic, a hundred miles west of Aruba. The boat was completely out of torpedoes at this stage and they sank the Yugoslavian vessel by gunfire alone, in broad daylight. Apparently, No. 59 squadron didn't bother Helmutt Witte at all. After the sinking he turned for his meeting with U161, but Achilles was not sitting by idly. He was on the surface sinking the schooner Chererio, between Isla Mona and Puerto Rico, in the Mona Passage.

Ironically, No. 45 squadron which had done so much to make the Mona Passage a highly dangerous place for U-Boats, had been transferred to France Field in Panama, two days before. The squadron had been moved to try and stop the submarine that was creating havoc off the Canal. In fact, the day the aircraft had arrived in the Canal Zone was the same day that U159 had run out of torpedoes and left the area. After leisurely taking care of the schooner, the daring Achilles turned south and raced for his meeting with U159. U128 finished off the action-packed day by sinking the American freighter West Ira, southeast of Barbados.

By the end of the third week in June, the defenders were once again stretched beyond their limit. Even the experienced No. 45 squadron were beginning to feel the strain. In the two weeks after their arrival at France Field, each pilot flew ninety hours. The situation in that part of the Caribbean was so desperate that they were forced to hand over the vital Mona Passage to an inexperienced squadron. The squadron's commander, Major Gianetti gave the pilots the choice of either flying for half a day, every day, or flying all day, every other day. Precious cargoes were being lost by the score and the havoc in the Caribbean was beginning to affect other theatres of war. Among the lost cargoes was also important equipment for the Caribbean's defenders. It was around this time that the British nine point two inch guns for Claxton Bay and Point Ligoure in the Gulf of Paria were lost. The order for the guns was never repeated and just as well, because they were a waste of effort.

In the First World War and again in the Second, the British concentrated on protecting specific areas within the Gulf of Paria, rather than denying entry into the Gulf. It was the Singapore mentality with the guns facing the wrong way. Those nine point two inch guns with a range of seventeen miles could have been sited more profitably to cover the Dragon's Mouth, denying entry to the vital Gulf of Paria. In view of the American batteries already emplaced in this area, the guns could have been mounted on either side of the Galleons Passage or on Trinidad's north coast. With radar to assist in night firing, these long range cannons could have covered easily the vital traffic junction along the north coast and thereby saved many an important cargo. An enormous amount of energy and material was expended in building the bases and associated facilities for these weapons to cover the area off the refineries, which was already adequately covered by the six inch batteries. A fraction of the resources expended on these projects could have provided the north coast with a measure of protection which might have ensured that it did not become known as Torpedo Junction.

Although the defenders were being worn down and the U-Boats seemed to be having it all their way, there were signs that the situation would change. All the boats were continuing to report contact with convoys in the eastern Caribbean, and in several cases they had been driven off by the escorts. U172 reported a destroyer patrolling off Panama along with several PCs, while No. 59 squadron had carried out the first combined ship and aircraft anti-submarine attack on the nineteenth.

An A20 from Curacao had teamed up with a PC and given U159 a rough ride, but it appeared as if nothing could stop Witte. Half of the success of the Caribbean campaign was due to the daring of some of the U-Boat commanders and U159's commander was among the best. On the twenty-second, he sank his last ship of the cruise. He came upon the nine thousand five hundred ton tanker E.J. Saddler, two hundred miles north of Bonaire. The fact that he didn't have torpedoes was no hindrance to Witte. On the surface, U159 chased the big tanker for some considerable time before managing to get a shell into the vessel's engine room, bringing it to a halt. The gun crew then proceeded to shell the ship for four hours. At the end of that time the ship was virtually a wreck, but it wouldn't sink. Tankers are said to die hard and the E.J. Saddler was proving it. Despite the fact that the vessel had informed the whole Caribbean of the action and an aircraft could appear at any time, Witte dispatched a boarding party. The German sailors climbed down into the burning tanker and placed explosive charges against the hull before beating a hasty retreat. The explosions under the waterline, let the sea in and finally allowed the big tanker to die.

With a very happy crew, Witte finally turned away from his spectacular exploit and set course for home. He had sunk eleven ships and damaged one. Hartenstein in U156 was the only commander to do better than Witte on a single patrol and then only by one damaged ship. These two boats, U156, U159 and another boat were the only U-Boats to sink eleven ships in the Caribbean on a patrol. Witte's tonnage worked out at forty-one thousand, four hundred and eighty. His next combat patrol would be a long one, all the way to the Indian Ocean, where he would once again sink eleven ships. On his return from this cruise, Witte would hand over command and leave the boat. A year after his successful patrol, U159 would return to the Caribbean, but like U156, only to die.

The twenty-third of June would see a number of important events. Just after midnight, Heyse in U128 set fire to the large Norwegian tanker Andrea Brovig, fifty miles from Barbados. At ten thousand and seventy-three tons, she was one of only a dozen such large ships sunk in the zone. The tanker was well alight and the glow could be seen from Barbados, when another torpedo let in the sea and the ship slipped beneath the waves.

U159 was not the only boat leaving the Caribbean. Emmermann in U172 was out of torpedoes and turned for home. North of Aruba, he came upon the tiny schooner Resolute and destroyed it with the twenty millimetre cannon. To the south of U172, Merten was also taking U68 home. He was almost out of torpedoes. Shortly after noon the boat came upon its last vessel of the cruise. The final torpedo sent the two thousand, four hundred and sixty-nine ton tanker Arriaga, to the bottom, one hundred miles west of Aruba. The little ship was so much smaller than the ships Merten specialised in on this cruise, that it seemed almost insignificant. But the Arriaga had the dubious honour of bringing up the one million ton mark.

Since Hartenstein had fired that first torpedo in the early morning of February sixteenth, the U-Boats had accounted for one hundred and sixty ships, in the Caribbean Theatre, totalling one million tons. With the sinking of the Arriaga, Merten also set a record. The little vessel gave him fifty thousand, eight hundred and ninety-eight tons sunk on a single Caribbean cruise. No other U-Boat equalled this formidable total. It had also been achieved with only seven ships sunk. Merten was a specialist in the big ships. In the Gulf of Mexico, U158 used up the last of its torpedoes sinking the freighter Henry Gibbons, a hundred and fifty miles north of the Yucatan Peninsula. This was Rostin's eighth ship and he had come close to the record with a total tonnage of forty-eight thousand, seven hundred and twenty-five tons.

With so many boats out of torpedoes and making their way home, a three day lull developed in the region. But the lack of torpedoes was not the only reason for the lull. The moon was full. The defending pilots had gained immeasurably in experience during the holocaust of sinkings in May and June and they made operating on the surface near any of islands during the full moon period, an extremely hazardous undertaking for a U-Boat. As the nights got brighter, the remaining boats pulled back into the open reaches away from the islands, or moved east of Trinidad.

It had been a very long time since the Caribbean had experienced three days without the frenzied SSS signals from dying men. It gave the defenders a chance to pick up some of the many survivors drifting in the Caribbean and Gulf of Mexico. While the boats were sitting out the moonlight well away from the shipping lanes, U-Boat Headquarters broadcast an ominous warning about the Bay of Biscay. The boats needed to traverse the Bay to get into and out of their bases and RAF coastal command were very active. Actually, the signal cautioned the boats to surface only at night and only for long enough to charge their batteries.

The U-Boat commanders operating around the world's oceans were probably in one respect, the most fortunate of German warriors. They were sheltered from politics. The Grand Admiral was one of a very small core of senior German officers who stood up to Hitler. He never grasped completely the strategy that Doenitz was employing, nor does it appear that he realised the full importance of the battle of the Atlantic. Doentiz was forever fending off Hitler's alternative plans for the employment of the U-Boats. Indeed, approval did not come from Hitler for the offensive off the US coast, until long after the U-Boats could no longer safely operate in that area. June 1942 was no different. When Doenitz had finally achieved a stranglehold on Allied shipping in the Caribbean, Hitler called for U-Boats to be deployed off Madeira, to stop a landing that he imagined the Allies might make. Doentiz fought and luckily the Naval War Staff agreed with his views. The navy as a whole was not a very political organization and this could possibly explain how they came so close to winning the war at sea. The twenty-sixth of June was to see the U-Boats begin to strike again, but not with the same ferocity as in the first three weeks of the month. U203, a boat that was to make only one Caribbean cruise was the first to achieve success. Under the command of Rolf Mutzelburg, Knight's Cross, they sank the Brazilian armed ship Pedrinhas, three hundred miles north of Antigua. The survivors were lucky, they were rescued in three and a half days.

U203 was on her way to operate off Trinidad. The following day seemed more like June. Bauer in U126 started it off by sinking the ten thousand ton Norwegian tanker Leiv Eriksson, eighteen miles west of Barbados. The inhabitants of the peaceful island could see the tanker burning until dawn, when it slipped beneath the waves. Three hours later U128 sank the seven thousand ton freighter Polybius, two hundred miles east of Trinidad.

Up in the Gulf of Mexico, Witt in U129 sank the Mexican tanker Tuxpan and followed it up eight hours later by sinking another Mexican tanker, the Las Choapas. A new boat to the Caribbean ended the day's tally. U153 under Wilfred Reichmann sank the American freighter Potlatch, well northeast of Antigua. The boat was under orders to operate off the Panama Canal. The day had netted the U-Boats thirty-two thousand tons.

The twenty-eighth of June was very little different. U203 caught the American freighter Sam Houston, ninety miles north of Antigua. The cargo ship was loaded with military equipment and on its way to Capetown when Mutzelburg used a torpedo and gunfire to send it to the sea bed, nearly three miles below. At nine o'clock that night Korvettenkapitan Axel-Olaf Loewe in command of the Type IXC boat U505 sank the freighter Sea Thrush, north of the islands. Lowe was on his way to the Panama Sector. Later in the evening Heyse in U128 hit his last Caribbean ship. The American freighter Steel Engineer, was enroute New York/Capetown when one of U128's torpedoes hit amidships. Badly damaged, but still able to run, the freighter turned for Trinidad. June is a month of many rain squalls in the Caribbean and the captain of the Steel Engineer probably used one of these squalls to get away.

The twenty-ninth of June was another terrible day for the merchantmen. An hour after midnight, Muller-Stockheim in U67 made his third kill of the cruise, when he sent the eight thousand ton tanker Empire Mica to the bottom, in the Gulf of Mexico. Before daylight, Bauer in U126 dispatched the Canadian schooner Mona Marie, south of Barbados. Later in the morning, Reichmann in U153 sank the freighter Ruth in the Crooked Passage, near Acklins island in the Bahamas. The vessel's cargo of iron ore, ensured that it didn't linger on the surface. At two o'clock in the afternoon, Lowe in U505 sank the American freighter Thomas McKean, two hundred and forty miles north of Antigua. This last ship of the day was enroute from New York to Trinidad, loaded with war material. No merchantmen died on the last day of June, it was almost as though the entire theatre stopped to witness a spectacle.

After the sinking of the Henry Gibbons that had brought him close to the record for the area, Rostin turned U158 homeward. That same day he reported the sinking to U-Boat Headquarters. The US Navy had been listening to him since the sinking of the Sheherazade, and his reports had given them an accurate plot of the boat's movements. He had used his radio constantly and although the signals were in coded groups of numbers, they could be identified by the frequency used and certain similarities in the start of the coded messages.

On the twenty-fifth, he fired his last two torpedoes at a heavily loaded freighter. Both missed and the long signal he sent gave technical reasons for the failures. He easily evaded the destroyer patrol in the Straits of Florida and then promptly sent off a report on his having done so. On the twenty-eighth he came across what he described as a heavily armed freighter, and explained that he didn't have any torpedoes left, so he couldn't attack. Presumably the freighter had a heavier set of guns than the U-Boat and Rostin prudently refrained from provoking trouble.

The report of his sighting gave the exact position, although in code. He was leaving a line across the ocean which was being plotted by the US Navy. The line gave his course and his rate of progress and allowed them to plot ahead to his projected position for the following day. Undoubtedly, Rostin was a talkative commander. There were U-Boats that operated for days, sinking ships and not reporting, until they had ammassed a report to be sent off in one signal, but Rostin reported every day.

On the twenty-ninth, he came upon the Latvian freighter Everalda, and stopped the vessel with his main gun. The ship sent off a submarine attack report, at which point Rostin sent across a boarding party. The seamen opened the ship's bottom valves as well as placing scuttling charges on the hull. The survivors were set adrift, but the Captain and one Spaniard were taken on board the U-Boat as prisoners, to join another merchantship master already aboard. He then resumed his original course and speed.

He was dealing with a very harassed US Navy, under enormous pressure to do something about the depredations of the U-Boats. They desperately wanted to hit back and here was a U-Boat leaving an almost dead straight line. They listened to his account of the sinking of the Everalda and compared it with the vessel's report. Yes, it was the same U-Boat. They worked out where the U-Boat would be on the following day and orders went out to US Navy Patrol Squadron 74.

VP-74 were one of the first US Navy squadrons to operate the magnificent Martin Mariner flying boat, coded the PBM by the navy. On Tuesday the thirtieth of June, a Mariner was dispatched to a point seven hundred miles equidistant from the US coast and the north coast of Hispaniola. The aircraft was due to arrive in the area shortly before Rostin was scheduled to give his daily broadcast. Dead on time Erich Rostin began his final broadcast. He was not only giving his usual daily report, but repeating the previous day's report of the sinking of the Everalda. The shore stations picked up the start of the broadcast and immediately relayed the frequency to the Mariner. The aircraft was able to pick up the U-Boat's signal and home in on it.

The U-Boat was twenty miles ahead when the Mariner began its attack run and the radio transmission was still going on when the aircraft crossed the U-Boat. The boat was taken completely by surprise and it was only when the depth-charges were on their way down that the lookouts saw the danger. Three depth-charges hit the water and three seconds later, three tall columns of water climbed upwards. The conning tower watch probably saw the depth-charge explosions and heard the tremendous detonations, as they tumbled down the hatch.

It is also probable that Rostin was among them and it is likely that they felt that they had escaped. The Type IXC boat would be well underwater before the aircraft could make another attack. No one looked for the fourth depth-charge. Even the aircraft crew thought that it had failed, but if a member of the conning tower watch had looked at the deck beyond the railings, they could have seen the fourth charge and known the terrible fate which awaited them. The fourth charge had hit the U-Boat squarely. It had burst the wooden deck planking and lodged itself against the steel plating below. It could not roll off, but its hydrostatic fuse would detonate the charge when it got to twenty-five feet. The last man of the conning tower watch slid down the ladder and slammed the hatch shut. U158 was on its way down. There were no survivors.

CHAPTER

6

The third wave

June in the Caribbean had been an experience for all concerned. The ferocity of the attack had shocked the Allies and cost the numbing loss of sixty-four ships sunk and two damaged. The Gulf of Mexico losses added a further twelve sunk and one damaged, to give the combined theatre of operations a total of seventy-six ships lost and three damaged. It had meant the loss of the staggering total of three hundred and seventy-eight thousand tons of shipping, with probably an equal weight of cargoes. Since the start of the campaign in the Caribbean, the U-Boats had sunk one hundred and eighty-one ships and seriously damaged eighteen. But what did this one million and sixty thousand tons of lost shipping represent?

One hundred and thirty-one vessels were sunk around the world's oceans during the month of June. Of this total, sixty percent were in the Caribbean theatre. This zone of operations had taken over from the US coast and was now the single most profitable area for U-Boat operations. The campaign to the end of June had seen sixty-seven of the precious tankers lost and a further dozen out of service in the zone. Added to this, at least a hundred cargo vessels had been destroyed, nearly all of them loaded with vitally needed war material. These losses affected the Caribbean, Britain and America, almost immediately.

The first area to suffer was the Caribbean. The inter-island trade had been seriously curtailed and the inhabitants of the islands would not see certain foodstuffs for many years.

The losses in June also caused the institution of rationing in the United States for the very first time. Sugar and coffee were affected and oil for domestic consumption was cut off.

In Britain, the loss of precious oil was almost catastrophic. Since the commencement of the Caribbean campaign, one hundred and twenty-four tankers had been lost, more than half of them in the Caribbean. The RAF depended on the fuel these lost tankers carried and loss of aluminum also affected both British and American aircraft construction.

At this stage of the war, except for North Africa, the RAF was the service most involved in carrying the war to the Germans. Even the Allied navies began to feel the pinch, as fuel stocks began to drop to the danger level. Lack of adequate reserves of fuel would have far reaching effects, but the loss of the vital war material would have serious consequences on Allied operations, particularly the Russians who were confronting the might of the German armed forces. In this respect, freighters lost in the Caribbean would ultimately affect even the operations around Stalingrad at the end of the year. The Eighth Army's build up to El Alamein was slowed down, and operations even in the Far East had to be curtailed.

Operation Torch had to be postponed, as a direct result of the U-Boats in the west. Most American troops for the invasion of North Africa staged direct from the United States and thus the affected flow of war material to the United States hit at the actual frontline built up. Ultimately, the losses in the Caribbean ensured that all thoughts of a cross Channel invasion in 1942 were cancelled. Too much vital war material had gone to the bottom to allow for the stockpiling of the necessary reserves that were essential to such an undertaking.

The Allies had to defeat the U-Boats before they could consider anything else. In the final analysis, the U-Boats caused delays. Nearly all the projected operations were delayed or cancelled and time is immensely costly. Although it is a generalisation, World War Two cost eighteen thousand lives each day, and this probably is what the Caribbean campaign meant.

Ironically, the U-Boats were just as exhausted as the defenders. There simply were not enough U-Boats to make their breakthrough decisive. The boats in the Caribbean had used up all their torpedoes too quickly for sufficient reinforcements to reach the area and thus keep up the tempo of operations. This meant, that in July shipping losses began to drop, not so much because of more effective defensive measures, but rather because there were not enough U-Boats.

On an average, a U-Boat would take two weeks to reach the Caribbean, and two weeks to return. An average cruise, even with the U tankers to help out with fuel, could last up to nine weeks. The crews needed three to four weeks rest, which meant effectively that a Caribbean cruise for one boat could use up three months. During this period of time the boat might be expected to use up to twenty torpedoes, if it was in a lucrative area. Logistically, Doenitz needed twice the number of boats to keep enough permanently in the Caribbean and effectively cut the shipping lanes. Because of these factors, U-Boats tended to arrive in the Caribbean in waves. This helped the defenders by giving them periods between the waves to reorganise, train and stockpile.

Allied propaganda pictured the U-Boats sinking helpless merchantmen, as butchery. Even today, there are many who would so judge this mode of warfare.

The fact of the matter was that the U-Boats were waging economic warfare. By cutting off the supply of raw materials, they were being more effective than all the battles that have ever been fought. There is no more certain way to bring the fighting services to a halt than by cutting their lines of supply, and this was what the U-Boats were doing. It was and still is, the very core of warfare. They had done this in the first half of 1942 with the loss of only two boats.

The U-Boats also played another role. They could almost be described in the Caribbean context, as "a fleet in being". After the rampage of May and June, there was no question in anyone's mind about the strategic importance of the Caribbean, with the result that an ever increasing flood of Allied reinforcements were dispatched to the zone. Even during the occasional periods when there was only one boat loose in the Caribbean, the defenders remained on guard. It does not take too much imagination to visualise what effect these defensive resources could have had if they had been deployed in other war zones.

During the month of June, a large proportion of the available U-Boats had operated in the far west of the Caribbean. This had caused the area to be heavily reinforced. In fact, the U-Boats were finished with the Panama Sector and the center of gravity now went back to the area off Trinidad, and it would be almost a year before the boats went back to the Panama Sector in strength.

As far as the Allies were concerned, the next wave of U-Boats to arrive would return to the far west and they could not reduce the defences there. Achilles was to reinforce this idea with another of his specials. The first day of July saw U 126 and U161 set off alarm bells both in Trinidad and Panama. At twelve noon, Bauer in U126 hit the seven thousand ton freighter SS Warrior, only three and a half miles off the village of San Souci on Trinidad's north coast. The vessel went down in eighteen fathoms, taking a cargo of leather to the sea bed. The ship had intended to join a convoy in the Gulf of Paria, which would, ultimately, allow it to be escorted in stages, to the Russian port of Murmansk. This sinking triggered a massive anti-submarine reaction because it was so close to the shore of the now heavily defended island. For two weeks the area immediately around Trinidad had been quiet. The sinking of the Warrior was a signal to the Caribbean Sea Frontier that the U-Boats were back close in to the focal point of Trinidad, but Achilles now confused the issue by creating alarm and confusion in the west.

U161 had sailed right across the Caribbean after its meeting with U159, and was now off the coast of Costa Rica. This Central American country shared a common border with the sensitive Panama defence area. U172 had sunk a few ships off Costa Rica's only Caribbean port in June, and this had caused an immediate strengthening of the defences in the mountainous country.

As the sun set on the first day of July, Achilles was moving U161 closer to the Costa Rican coast on a raid that was to upset the balance in the area permanently. When it was fully dark, U161 surfaced and began threading its way between the rocks and sandbars outside Porto Limon. By nine thirty, he was well into the bay, having crept past the PC base on the southern arm and the headland guarding the harbour on the right. Ahead lay the peaceful harbour with one solitary cargo vessel, tied up on the inner dock. At one minute past ten o'clock, two torpedoes left the bow tubes and raced across the enclosed harbour. The twin explosions almost lifted the San Pablo out of the water and deposited it on the dock. The blast of the two torpedoes wrecked the little ship, damaged the wharves and touched a very sensitive American nerve. While absolute confusion reigned ashore in the port city of Limon, Achilles took U161 back out of the harbour, past the protecting moles and into the Bay.

Porto Limon immediately became very important. The attack caused the Americans to lay an extensive, complicated minefield across the entrance to the harbour. Coast defence guns, infantry and more naval vessels arrived, to be followed by the building of an airfield. At the same time the danger to

Colon at the Caribbean entrance to the Panama Canal was recognised and an even greater defensive scheme was laid on for this vital port. Eventually, all the ports along the Central American coastline had to be similarly protected against the return of a certain Albrecht Achilles.

Achilles took U161 across the Caribbean and out through the Windward Passage. His Caribbean adventures were over. Having created alarm and confusion across the area, he was never to return. But thousands of men spent the rest of the war waiting for him. In a war of material, he had certainly justified his existence. Every Caribbean port had to be protected, because U-Boats seemed to like coming in and getting the ships while they were at anchor. It would have been very difficult to convince the defenders that it was the same U-Boat that kept repeating the exploit.

North of the Caribbean, the boat with one side of its conning tower missing, ran into convoy AS 4 from the United States to Sierra Leone. Achilles attacked and sank the cargo vessel Fairport, but ended up being hunted and depth-charged for nine hours. During the course of this encounter, the boat was heavily damaged by the depth-charge hammer blows, but Achilles's skill saved them. Once again he returned to Lorient for a hero's welcome.

In October, the team of Achilles and Bender were separated when Bender left U161 to take command of his own boat, U841. Although neither was to serve in the Caribbean again, they were both connected to the Caribbean story of 1943.

On the following day, Bauer used his last torpedo to hit the American freighter Gulfbelle, twenty miles north of the island of Tobago. B18 bombers from Trinidad were quickly on the scene and he had to leave the vessel drifting, stern down. U126 was also finished with the Caribbean. On this trip, the boat had sunk seven ships totalling forty-one thousand tons. She had sunk fifteen ships in the Caribbean and damaged four others.

As U126 turned homeward, the third wave of U-Boats was beginning to arrive. In the north, U171 and U575 were moving in towards the Cuban coast and the Windward Passage, while U153 and U203 were coming down the island chain, towards the island of Tobago. In the west U129 came out of the Gulf of Mexico into the Yucatan area, leaving U67 and U437 in the Gulf. U66, U154 and U166 were also enroute to the theatre. U66 and U166 had both left Lorient on the same day bound for the Caribbean theatre. Both boats were minelayers, one destined for the Mississippi Delta and the other to upset St. Lucia again.

On the fifth of July, U158 became the first U-Boat to miss a rendezvous with a U tanker and that night Von Rosensteil met his end. U502 was on the last leg of its second Caribbean cruise when the boat was caught by a Wellington bomber of Coastal Commands No. 172 squadron, in the Bay of Biscay. The boat was on the surface, when they were surprised to see a searchlight coming up the wake. The aircraft homed on U502, using its ASV radar and in the last few seconds, used its Leigh light to illuminate the boat. Von Rosensteil and all his crew perished.

The Bay had now become a deathtrap and within two weeks the RAF were to strike at another Caribbean boat. U751 commanded by Gerhard Bigalk sailed from St. Nazaire on the fourteenth of July, bound for his second Caribbean cruise. The Type VIIC boat had taken part in the Caribbean operations in May and was on its way back to the rich hunting grounds, when Whitley bombers of No. 91 and No. 502 squadrons caught it in the Bay of Biscay. The same combination of airborne radar and the Leigh light, ensured that there were no survivors. By this time, the deadly combination had also been reported in the Florida Straits by a lucky U-Boat.

On the sixth of July, Kolle in U154 on his second Caribbean cruise, entered the Caribbean via the Windward Passage. He was enroute to the Gulf of Mexico. The boat sank a schooner off Yucatan and thereafter ran into trouble. The Gulf of Mexico had now become a dangerous operating area and U154 seemed to be constantly dodging escorts or aircraft patrols. On one of these occasions, the boat was surprised by an aircraft and bombed. Kolle got the boat submerged before a second attack could be delivered, but at the expense of leaving one of the bridge watch up above. The sharks probably got the sailor before U154 could return to the area.

From that moment on U154 had a very difficult patrol. Damage to the boat caused a continuous oil leak, which left a telltale smear on the surface. This streak of oil was a sure giveaway and the escorts and aircraft hunted him to the point where he had to request permission to leave the confined Gulf. The boat moved to a safer area north of the Caribbean and later to the east of the islands, but she suffered a number of missed torpedo shots and continuous attacks by aircraft. It turned out to be an unsuccessful patrol.

In the meantime, both U203 and U575 had been scoring. The Type VIIC boat U575 under the command of Gunther Heydemann was making its first and only Caribbean cruise. On the night of the third, Heydemann sank the freighter Norlandia north of Hispaniola, then entered the Windward Passage and sailed southeast to the Trinidad area. By eighth of July, he was off the island of Tobago when he chanced on the British freighter Empire Explorer. Torpedoes and gunfire disposed of the freighter, thirty miles off the island.

On the following day, Rolf Mutzelburg in the Type VIIC boat U203, also on its first and only Caribbean cruise, sank the British seven thousand ton freighter Cape Verde, just north of Tobago and followed this up by stopping the ten thousand ton British tanker Stanvac Palembang only ten miles off the island's eastern tip. U203 shelled the burning hulk for several hours, before it went down on the underwater Tobago ridge. Dawn found the sea around the island of Tobago dotted with liferafts and shocked survivors. Most came ashore on the island and volunteers spent two harrowing days rescuing and caring for badly burned men who had been fished from the sea. It was an experience that brought home rather forcefully the facts about what was taking place in the Caribbean.

Incidents like this confirmed to the civilians that something was very wrong. All through May, June and now July they had to deal with survivors. At night they could hear the throb of the U-Boat diesels off the coasts, punctuated every now and then by the explosions as torpedoes found their targets. Rumour was rife and anyone interested enough could hear tales from the survivors, yet there was official silence.

The Americans had not been involved in the Caribbean before the war and as such had not built up a rapport with the populations of the various territories. For this reason they distrusted many of the locals and were constantly on the lookout for fifth column activity. Yet much of their official correspondence stressed the loyalty of the islanders to the war effort and the Empire. It was a dual approach to public relations that gave the censors the authority to veto any mention of the momentous events taking place.

The British military authorities put little into writing, but it can be assumed that they did not feel strong enough to challenge the American view. Nine-tenths of the servicemen in the islands were American. Traditionally, Englishmen accustomed to colonialism found it easier to blend into their surroundings, unlike the Americans who always remained totally American. This surfaced rather dramatically many years later, in the Viet Nam conflict where a conscious effort had to be made to win the people over to the American view. The whole thing only served to widen the gulf between the civilians and the soldiers.

There were many occasions during the war when Trinidad was put on alert because of German U-Boat activity. The civil defence organisation always reacted, but not once were they told why, — not even to the extent of admitting that there were U-Boats in the Caribbean. To some extent, this also applied to the Volunteers and other local defence forces.

Added to this was the effect of rum on the servicemen. There were always fights between British and American sailors and probably this will always be so, but the Trinidad rum often turned these fights into full scale battles that affected civilians and property. Actually, this blowing off of steam by men who lived very close to danger was quite natural and healthy, and the right public relations attitude could have won over the civilians to be more sympathetic, but the official silence was deafening.

This became worse as the Gulf of Paria assumed a greater strategic importance, which meant that after the war, the area was just as important, or even more so. The result was that the silence continued after the war and the Caribbean story was never told. This was unfair, not only to the civilians, but also to the American serviceman, who had to face the question, why are you here? Much more could have been achieved against the U-Boats, if the censors had allowed the Press to indulge in a campaign to win the active co-operation of all the inhabitants. Even in 1942, there were many successes that could have been played up to the population and the first big one was the sinking of U153.

The first U-Boat to die in the Caribbean was listed at the end of the war as being sunk by No. 59 squadron based in Curacao on the seventh of July, or by the destroyer USS Landsdowne on July thirteenth. No one will ever know for certain how the boat was lost. The Type IXC boat U153 under the command of Korvettenkapitan Wilfred Reichmann, had been accepted into service in July 1941. The boat had been built by A.G. Weser of Bremen and completed its trials in the Baltic, before being assigned to the 10th Flotilla in Lorient. Early in 1942, Reichmann took U153 on its first patrol in the North Atlantic. With the majority of the operational boats busy off the US coast and in the Caribbean, U153 had been almost alone in the wastes of the Atlantic and without convoy sightings to home on, they spent a fruitless month searching.

After a three week rest, U153 left Lorient again on May eighteenth, bound for the Caribbean, as one of the third wave. Reichmann worked his way southwest across the Atlantic until he was roughly on latitude nineteen north, before turning westwards for the Bahamas. On twenty-fifth June, he torpedoed the British cargo vessel Anglo Canadian, eight hundred miles northeast of Antigua. Two days later, the American liberty ship Potlach was sunk eight hundred miles due east of Antigua, as the boat turned westward. On June twenty-ninth, the American cargo vessel Ruth had been sunk in the Bahamas, then U153 seems to have disappeared.

From the few radio reports logged, it appears that Reichmann took his boat through the Windward Passage, then in a southeasterly direction to the area of the Dutch islands, before turning westward to run along the Columbian coast. Reichmann must have been one of the silent U-Boat commanders, the exact opposite of Rostin in U158, because there are very few references to him in the U-Boat command diary. After the sinking of the Ruth, he reported the facts and confirmed that his operating area was to be off Colon in the Panama Canal zone.

According to No. 59 squadron war diary, no attacks on U-Boats took place on July seventh, but two days before on the fifth, Lieutenant Groover flying an A20A from Hato Field in Curacao, sighted and attacked a submarine. The attack took place thirty-six miles north of Cabo de la Vela in Colombia, and the pilot was confident that he sank the U-Boat. No other boat was in this area and it could only have been U153. Yet five days later U-Boat headquarters logged a signal from U153 repeating the details of the sinking of the Ruth. This seems to confirm that U153 was not sunk by 59 squadron, but why would a U-Boat commander repeat a sinking report of an incident that took place eleven days before? Additionally, the signal made no mention of the supposedly damaging attack delivered by the American aircraft. The communication on tenth July is the last recorded contact with U153, if the boat that sent it was U153.

On thirteenth July, the two thousand ton Buchannan class destroyer USS Landsdowne DD486, delivered a punishing depth charge attack on a contact, eighty miles west northwest of Colon, in the Panama zone. Was this then the end of U153? In any case the boat disappeared. Neither No. 59 squadron, nor the USS Landsdowne sighted wreckage or could prove a sinking, although both units were confident that they had sunk a U-Boat. U-Boat headquarters commented on July fifteenth that U153 had failed to reply to numerous signals. On the following day, the boat was removed from the plot and its loss was assumed on first August. Ironically, the first U-Boat to be lost within the Caribbean Sea cannot be pin-pointed. The locations of the two attacks are five hundred miles and eight days apart.

The sixteenth of the month saw the arrival off the north coast of Trinidad of another master of the hunt. Kapitanleutnant Georg Lassen took command of the Bremen built Type IXC boat U160 in October 1941. Early misfortune hit the boat during its work up period near Danzig, when an accidental fire killed seven crewmen and injured another. Lassen had overcome his setback and U160 completed a Paukenschlag patrol, before being assigned to their first Caribbean cruise.

At two o'clock in the morning, Lassen put two torpedoes into the seven thousand ton tanker Beaconlight, just ten miles off the village of Matelot on Trinidad's north coast. From the shore, the watchers could hear the dull thunder of the explosions and see the big tanker ablaze, before she slipped beneath the waves in thirty fathoms. This was the first of Georg

Lassen's many victims which would litter the ocean floor around Trinidad. Two days later, Heydemann in U575 hit the tanker San Gasper with two torpedoes, thirty miles off Manzanilla on Trinidad's east coast. The giant thirteen thousand ton vessel heaved to the twin detonations and oil poured out of her wounded side, but she did not stop. Her cry for help brought the bombers from Waller Field and U575 was forced to back off and allow the great ship to turn and make it back to Port of Spain. Much of her cargo of oil originally destined for the Eighth Army in North Africa ended up congealed on Trinidad's beaches. Heydemann took his revenge on two sailing schooners that he caught before the sun came up.

The attack on the San Gasper brought all Trinidad's anti-submarine aircraft out that morning and the area became extremely hazardous for U-Boats. Heydemann took U575 well east of the island to escape retribution, but the numerous American aircraft did not seem to bother Lassen at all.

At nine o'clock in the morning, he torpedoed the freighter Carmona, only ten miles north of the Army observation post at La Fillete Point, on Trinidad's north coast. Three days later, Lassen was still off the north coast and despite the intense air activity, he attacked again. The British eight thousand two hundred ton tanker Donavania was set on fire at three forty in the morning off Grand Matelot Point. A short while later another torpedo sent the blazing wreck to the sea bed in eighteen fathoms.

While the boats operating off Trinidad were finding targets, Lowe in U505 off Yucatan had ended his short run of luck. On its first cruise off West Africa the boat had done very well and this had been followed by a good start to his first Caribbean cruise, with the sinking of two vessels. Then on July twenty-second Lowe sank the schooner Roamer. It seemed as though this event changed the luck of the U505 for good. Old salts swore that it was bad luck to sink a sailing ship, but if there was anything to this old lore of the sea, then all the Caribbean boats should have had bad luck. In fact nearly all the boats that operated in the Caribbean sank schooners and with good reason.

For hundreds of years, much of the intra-Caribbean trade had been moved by schooners. Whether the U-Boat commanders were aware of it or not, every time they sank a schooner, a vital cargo of food went to the bottom. The result was that the inhabitants of the islands began to feel the effects of the U-Boat campaign and demanded that the Allies do something about the situation. The military forces could not eat as well as they did, while the civilians starved. This forced the Americans to form a schooner pool to control the movements of the former free trading schooners, and in time to escort the larger vessels.

It is doubtful if the U-Boat skippers were fully aware of the disruption they caused by sinking these schooners. They usually stopped the tiny vessels and allowed the crews to get off before sending the schooners to the bottom with gunfire, but no U-Boat commander took the trouble to report these sinkings. They usually made a note in the deck log, while many U-Boats never recorded the sinkings at all. Research that is by no means complete indicates that a large number of these sailing vessels were sunk and not recorded, either by the Germans or the Allies. In fact, roughly double the number of recorded sinkings, actually took place.

In some cases the schooners turned out to be passenger-carrying vessels and the U-Boat commanders understandably made no entries at all about the attacks. Not all the schooners were sunk by U-Boats, drifting mines probably accounted for a high proportion. Nevertheless, the belief persists that the sinking of the Roamer, changed the luck of the U505. After this event, Lowe could not find another target. His boat was transferred to the Trinidad Sector where the others were doing well, but no sooner had they moved their operating area, than Lowe became ill and the boat returned to Lorient. Lowe had to have his appendix removed and was transferred ashore for the rest of the war. A new skipper was appointed to U505 and she would return to the Caribbean in October, for another appointment with destiny, on her long road to immortality.

The situation on the northern side of the Caribbean was in stark contrast to the ease with which Lassen, Heydemann and Mutzelburg had been achieving easy kills around Trinidad. U84 under Horst Uphoff reported that he was unable to get through the Straits of Florida. The boat was repeatedly forced to dive by attacking aircraft and go deep to avoid the escorts. The Straits were no longer protected by a single destroyer. Uphoff was reallocated the areas in the Old Bahama Passage and the Crooked Passage, as an alternative. To make up for being forced to be the first boat to concede defeat in the Straits of Florida, Uphoff sank two ships and damaged another before hastily retiring to the Bahamas.

U129 decided against attempting the Straits and left the Gulf of Mexico via the Yucatan Passage, then up through the Windward Passage. On the twenty-third, Witt sank his last ship of this second Caribbean patrol, in the Old Bahama Channel. When U129 turned for home it had equalled the records set by U156 and U159, sinking eleven ships in a single cruise. Before the end of the year U129 would be back in the Caribbean, on its third cruise.

The last week of July contributed eleven ships hit, but all in widely different circumstances. On the twenty-fourth, Lassen carried out a submerged attack on a group of escorted merchantmen southeast of Trinidad. In the brilliant moonlight, the Dutch freighter Telamon became the unlucky victim, settling into the mud of the Orinoco Delta. Then at ten minutes past two in the morning of July twenty-sixth, Markworth used the same moonlight to sink the Brazilian freighter Tamandare. A torpedo crashed into the ship's engine room, killing the four-man watch and smashing the lifeboats on the port side. The radio operator abandoned ship when he realised that the radio aerial was broken, but the Captain later procured a spare aerial and personally sent out the distress signal. The ship went down forty minutes later, ten miles off Tobago. The SSS alerted the B18s and next morning the forty-eight survivors were picked up by US Navy PC 492.

The subsequent enquiry into the loss of the vessel throws some light on a possible reason for U-Boat Commanders' callous attitude to the sinking of neutral Brazilian ships. The captain of the Tamandare stated that he had obeyed all the instructions of British naval control, given to him in a sealed envelope. The ship had left Recife on 16th July and had not touched land before being sunk. This can be inferred to mean, that there was a British naval-shipping control office in Recife and that they were issuing orders to Brazilian merchant ships. If the Germans were aware of this, then their attitude to Brazilian shipping might be a little easier to understand.

On the following night Markworth, who was operating U66 as successfully as its old commander Zapp, sank the British five thousand ton freighter Weirbank, one hundred miles east of Tobago. Two torpedoes opened up the old vessel's plates and she was gone in a short while. The survivors, nearly all of them injured, came ashore in Tobago, once more inundating the island's slender facilities. Markworth was free to hunt for merchant ships because he had already carried out his primary mission.

On the arrival in the Caribbean, he had gone straight to the island of St. Lucia. The night of July sixteenth had seen U66 creeping into the outer channel of the by now, heavily defended Castries harbour, to lay a dozen mines in the channel. The boat remained undetected and slipped away round the island.

Hardly had U66 cleared the island when one of his mines claimed a victim. A US Coast Guard cutter, leaving the island on an anti-submarine patrol passed over one of the mines and the resulting explosion almost destroyed the ship. The trauma of getting the heavily damaged cutter back into the harbour was nothing compared to the ripples of concern that spread throughout the Caribbean. St. Lucia once again found itself thrust into the limelight and the knowledge that the Germans were now laying mines, once again almost brought shipping to a standstill. It would be almost a year before the U-Boats would lay mines within the Caribbean, but the St. Lucia mining meant that the Caribbean now needed a fleet of minesweepers and every major port had to be regularly swept. Like Achilles, Markworth in U66 was to have a long term effect on the Caribbean.

The last few days of the month saw Lassen in U160 carry out another submerged attack, this time off the mouth of the Waini River in British Guiana. The Canadian bauxite carrier Prescodoc went down in very shallow water, leaving an orange blanket of dust on the sea around it.

This period of time also saw another predator arrive. Adolf Piening in U155 on his second Caribbean cruise brought his boat down the center of the Atlantic, before coming into the Caribbean zone from the east. At one thirty on the morning of July twenty-eight, Piening sent two torpedoes crashing into the side of the Brazilian freighter Barbacena. Seven men died aboard the merchant vessel. The remainder were picked up by three vessels, the Argentine Tacito, the English Elmdale and the St. Fabian.

The sinking of Brazilian vessels hardly called for comment, now that the U-Boats were under orders. Moving from the area, two hundred miles east of Barbados, he had hardly covered ten miles before he came upon a second Brazilian ship, the freighter Piave and used two torpedoes to send it to the bottom, to join the Barbacena. Most of these Brazilian ships were former German vessels built before or during the First World War and they carried mixed cargoes of coffee, nuts and leather.

On the following day, Piening sank the Norwegian freighter Bill. The small ship went down, three hundred and sixty miles east of Trinidad. On the last day of July, he sank the six thousand ton American freighter Cranford, over three hundred miles east of Grenada. The month had seen a shift of the U-Boats away from the Panama area towards the eastern Caribbean and the coming month would see this effort intensified.

The bulk of the U-Boats had now switched back to the North Atlantic, which had been strangely quiet for the first half of 1942. Logistically, it was far easier to keep boats in this area than in the Caribbean where the turnaround time for boats was inordinately long. Although there would be U-Boats operating off the US coast, the offensive in that area was over. The defences were now too strong for the profitable employment of U-Boats in groups, as in the early months of Paukenschlag.

Off West Africa another small group of boats were operating on the shipping lanes to and from Freetown and the Cape. The third wave of boats for the Caribbean had begun arriving in the area in July, and among them there were some outstanding hunters. The group would not be complete until the middle of August, but the first boats of the third wave had achieved successes. Together they sank twenty-four ships and damaged four. However, there were only three tankers lost and this was a direct result of the institution of convoys in the Caribbean.

Trinidad stood at the crossroads of merchant shipping between South and North America, and from the Caribbean to Europe and Africa. The Gulf of Paria provided an ideal convoy assembly area and a safe haven for bunkering. In July, the US Navy set up an elaborate system of convoys with Trinidad as the hub. Ships were convoyed from Trinidad past Aruba, up through the Windward Passage and along the north coast of Cuba to Key West. This series of convoys were lettered WAT or TAW, depending on direction.

From Key West the ships joined the US east coast convoy system to get them up to New York or Halifax and thence across the Atlantic. In September 1942, the designation of these convoys was changed to GAT or TAG. Guantanamo Bay and Aruba were collecting points for merchant ships to join the convoys and the U-Boats would always be found preying on the waiting ships, despite the heavy protection that these areas received.

Convoys also ran from Trinidad to Freetown, designated TF or FT as well as TO or OT for North Africa. TM was reserved for convoys direct from Trinidad to Gibraltar, while CU and UC were the designations for convoys to and from the United Kingdom. Strangely, the bauxite route remained open until the end of 1942 when first TB, BT convoys and later JT and TJ were introduced. The Caribbean also had a special convoy route from Aruba direct to New York, for fast tankers. In time, the Gulf of Mexico and the Panama Sector were also to be included in the regular convoy routings.

Despite the availability of regular convoys either to or passing close to all the major Caribbean ports, we find that roughly fifty percent of all vessels that arrived in Trinidad were sailing independently. This situation continued throughout the war and highlights the difficulty of convincing merchantmen that the Caribbean was as dangerous as the North Atlantic. The very weather that was one of the factors that made the North Atlantic a grimmer theatre of war, also occasionally contributed to hiding the merchant ships. Yet in the Caribbean, where the weather always favoured the U-Boat, they still sailed independently. So much so that on nineteenth July, Doenitz commented that the Gulf of Mexico and Trinidad were his only favourable operating areas. Very shortly, enhanced defences were going to rule out the Gulf, but Trinidad remained favourable to U-Boats throughout the war.

Doenitz was always aware that the extraordinary freedom that his boats enjoyed in the west, could not last. He commented that he was surprised that the Americans allowed him this freedom and wondered why they had not acted more quickly.

The original Paukenschlag attack area was a relatively thin strip of coastal water which would not have taken too much out of the Allies to protect. In the case of the Caribbean, this judgement is even more damning because, they were dealing almost with an enclosed sea. There were no air gaps in the Caribbean, and all the entrances to the area are confined and should have been easily controlled. It might have made for an interesting confrontation if the Allies had concentrated all the aircraft and surface vessels in the Channels into the area at the start of May. It might have worked.

It has often been put forward that the Caribbean was a peripheral campaign that had little bearing on the main fight in the North Atlantic. In fact the U-Boat war started in the narrow seas around Britain, then spread to the wide Atlantic, then the Golden West, then back to the wide ocean, then back to the narrow seas for the finish.

Another point of view frequently expressed is, that the big battle between the U-Boats and the escorts began in the North Atlantic and had to return to that area for the decisive round. On the other hand, it is possible that the return to the North Atlantic was for logistic reasons. In May and June, the sinking rate in the Caribbean was double the ship building rate, and in a tonnage war this could have been decisive. Had Germany enough U-Boats to have kept the Caribbean campaign going with enough reinforcements, it might have been possible to cut the North Atlantic lifeline with a relatively smaller number of boats. Regardless of where ships were sunk, the tonnage was lost and would have to be replaced. Had the Germans been able to keep the Caribbean campaign going, it would have caused a considerable reassignment of Allied escort facilities, both air and sea.

This brings into question, how effective were Allied anti-submarine weapons and particularly, how closely were they cooperating in the fight against the U-Boats? There were always differences in technique between the British and Americans. These differences were so basic that it became necessary in 1942 to establish an Atlantic "Chop-line" at forty-seven degrees west longtitude. The British operated to the east of this line and the Americans to the west, while the adaptable Canadians were able to comfortably operate on either side.

Nowhere is this difference in anti-submarine technique more apparent than in the operation of anti-submarine squadrons. The American approach tended to ensuring that all prospective U-Boat operating areas were covered by anti-submarine squadrons, whether the U-Boats were active in the area or not. This tended to make US Navy anti-submarine squadrons into rather large, relatively immobile organisations. The result of this philosophy was that they established a measure of air control over all the U-Boat operating areas, but seventy percent of these squadrons never got the opportunity to attack a U-Boat.

The differences in technique were very similar to the differences that existed between British and American commanders during the invasion and conquest of Europe. In contrast, British anti-submarine squadrons tended to be relatively mobile organisations, which were required to concentrate at threatened points, according to the U-Boat concentrations. The result of this was that every British anti-submarine squadron carried out at least one attack on a U-Boat. The British method could possibly have been the result of their chronic lack of resources, or it could have evolved from a completely different concept of warfare. Often, there was little common ground between the systems and this showed up early in the Caribbean. This was the only theatre where they fought side by side throughout the war.

The Caribbean conflict resolved itself into a contest between aircraft and submarines, particularly as the American squadrons began to be deployed in significant numbers. The US Navy was not ready with suitable aircraft in time to meet the initial U-Boat thrust into the area, but were able to base scouting squadrons in several areas. These units flew the OS2N, or Kingfisher, as it was more popularly known. This was a twin seat, single engine floatplane originally designed as an artillery spotter for battleships. The machine suffered from limited range and bomb load, with the result that few of the type were able to cause the U-Boats any significant damage. They could however, force a U-Boat to dive and in many instances saved merchant vessels by just being present.

It was not until the arrival of the legendary Catalina, with VP-53, that Navy aircraft were able to present a serious threat to the U-Boats. The Catalina or PBY as the US Navy preferred to call it, was an aircraft that happened to be in the right place at the right time. It was by no means the best flying boat used by the Allies, but it was available and amassed a considerable reputation for reliability, particularly its very long range and ability to take punishment. In July, the second PBY squadron, VP-92 arrived in the Caribbean and took over the Guantanamo Bay air station.

The Army Air Corps used the ungainly Douglas B18, throughout 1942. This little known aircraft spent almost all of its wartime career in the Caribbean. There were several of the type based at Pearl Harbour but the majority were destroyed in the Japanese attack.

The type was then converted to anti-submarine duties and posted to the Caribbean. This slow, vulnerable aircraft dated back to a 1935 specification when the Douglas design surprisingly, beat the Boeing B17. However, when the latter type got over its early troubles, it quickly superseded the B18. The machine was a marriage of the DC-2 tail, wings and powerplants, with a deep-bellied fuselage and a true shark nose. Capable of carrying a six thousand pound weapon load, with a primitive search radar in the nose, the machine took the brunt of the anti-submarine effort. Alongside the B18, No. 59 squadron operated the early A20A which was the first version of the Havoc light bomber. Its range and bomb load were inadequate, but like the B18, it was all that was available to the Caribbean based Sixth Air Force.

In July a US Navy CVE accompanied by some experienced destroyers arrived in the Gulf of Paria to conduct anti-submarine training exercises with the forces based in this area. Part of the problem in the Caribbean was the experience level of the defenders. Doenitz echoed the views of his commanders in a letter to Hitler on July fifteenth, when he wrote that the advantage still lay with the Germans because the American airmen appeared to be blind and the navy did not operate fast enough, nor were they persistent enough.

The British never put such criticisms into writing but it appears that they were convinced that the Americans needed experienced help in the Caribbean. The result was the posting of No. 53 squadron of RAF Coastal Command to Trinidad in mid-August. This squadron flew the reliable Lockheed Hudson. The Hudson was the first anti-submarine aircraft fitted with a reliable anti-submarine bomb distributor, which could space depth charges correctly across a submarine. The squadron, although it arrived in the Caribbean far too late, played a significant part in checking the U-Boats during the second half of 1942.

While the boats of the third wave had sunk ninety thousand tons of shipping in the Caribbean zone, six U-Boats had accounted for thirteen ships sunk in the Gulf of Mexico with four damaged, totalling forty-five thousand tons. Two tankers had been sunk and the four damaged ships had also been tankers. This gave the theatre a total of thirty-seven vessels sunk and eight damaged. The theatre's total tonnage had now risen to one million, two hundred thousand. Actually the month of July was to see the virtual end of the Gulf of Mexico campaign. The defences in this landlocked sea were now far too strong for U-Boats to survive.

CHAPTER

7

Convoys

The first day of August found five U-Boats homeward bound and twelve operating in the Caribbean theatre. Around Trinidad U66, U155, U160, U162 and the Italian boat Tazzoli, formed a wide ranging group preying mainly on this area's independently sailing merchantmen. Three boats U108, U134 and U173 were closing in from the northeast, while U508 and U509 were in the Windward Passage. Two boats U166 and U171 were left in the Gulf of Mexico. U67 and U129 were homeward bound and had left the Gulf a few days before. The rest of the third wave numbering twelve U-Boats were northeast of the Caribbean, moving towards the islands. The boats of the third wave were about to challenge the newly set up Caribbean convoy system.

At one minute past midnight, Piening in U155 opened the month's tally by sinking the Dutch freighter Kentar, one hundred and eighty miles east of Tobago. Later that morning he sent the six thousand ton British freighter Clan MacNaughton to join the Kentar. These two vessels were U155's fifth and sixth victims achieved in five days. By six o'clock in the evening, de Cossato in the Italian Tazzoli had added the Greek freighter Kastor to the day's total, but the Allies had more to celebrate on this first day of August, than did the Germans.

During the course of the day, two transport aircraft landed at Waller Field carrying the advance party of No. 53 squadron, and a freighter arrived in Port of Spain with the first of the Torpex filled depth-charges. These new anti-submarine weapons were one third more powerful than the old Amatol filled charges. These new, more powerful charges could crack a U-Boat's pressure hull at twenty feet. While the charges were being unloaded from the freighter, the first U-Boat died in the Gulf of Mexico.

The brand new Type IXC boat U166, under Oberleutnant Zur See Hans-Gunther Kuhlmann, had been built in 1941 by Seebeckwerft of Bremerhaven and accepted into service in March 1942. The boat had been fitted with minelaying shafts and departed Lorient on June tenth for the Caribbean theatre. The inexperienced crew, under an equally inexperienced commander, had been given the important and dangerous task of mining the Mississippi Delta, in the Gulf of Mexico.

By July eleventh, Kuhlmann was off the north coast of Hispaniola and blooded his crew with the sinking by gunfire of the schooner Carmen. Two days later, they sank the American freighter Oneida in the Bahamas, near the island of Great Inagua. Kuhlmann took U166 past the dangerous Straits of Florida and then turned northwest towards his primary objective. The new boat was doing well and they even took time off to dispatch the small freighter Gertrude once inside the Gulf.

On the night of July twenty-fourth, Kuhlmann edged his boat into the very shallow waters of the Delta and closed the loading jetties on the surface. Soon after midnight he was in position and proceeded to lay his twelve mines in an arc, only six hundred yards from the dock. At this stage Kuhlmann could have turned and sped down into the safety of the Gulf, but the courageous young man decided to stay close to the Delta observing and reporting the traffic that used the Mississippi. He spent three days mostly submerged, with very little water under his keel, despite the intense air and sea activity. It had not taken the Americans very long to discover the presence of mines in such shallow water and they were fully aware that there was a U-Boat in the area.

Kuhlmann stayed too long in the Mississippi Delta area, giving the Americans the opportunity to triangulate the source of his numerous radio reports. Each night he had to surface to charge his batteries, change the air in the boat and transmit his reports and they were hot on his scent. On the last day of July, he sank the five thousand ton freighter Robert E. Lee, not

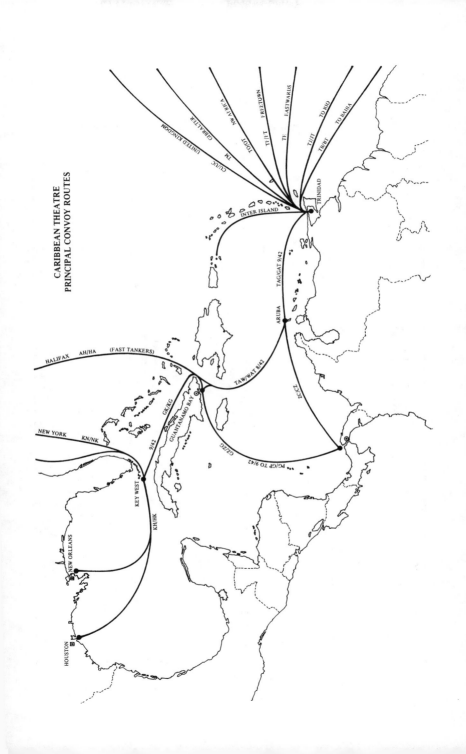

CARIBBEAN THEATRE
PRINCIPAL CONVOY ROUTES

UNITED KINGDOM
GIBRALTAR
CU/UC
NW AFRICA
TO/OT
TJ/JT
FREETOWN
TL
EAST WAR US
TJ/JT
TO RIO
TR/RT
TO BAHIA

TRINIDAD

INTER ISLAND

TAG/GAT 9/42

ARUBA

HALIFAX   AH/HA   (FAST TANKERS)

TAW/WAT 8/42

ZC/CZ

NEW YORK   KN/NK

GK/KG

GUANTANAMO BAY

GZ/ZG

PG/GP TO 9/42

9/42

KEY WEST

KH/HK

NEW ORLEANS

HOUSTON

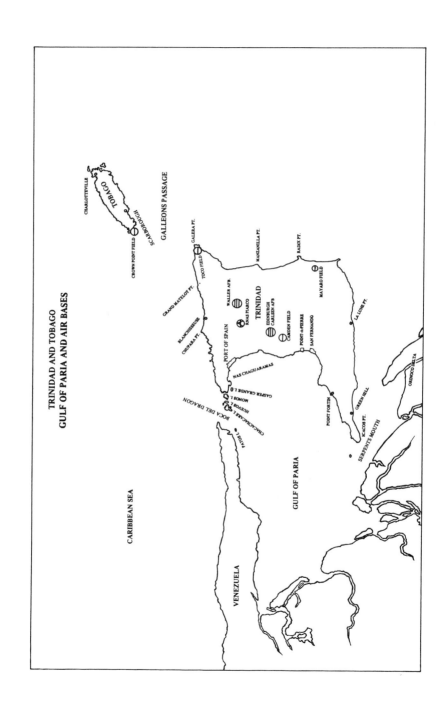

TRINIDAD AND TOBAGO
GULF OF PARIA AND AIR BASES

CARIBBEAN SEA

TOBAGO

CHARLOTTEVILLE

SCARBOROUGH

CROWN POINT FIELD

GALLEONS PASSAGE

GALERA PT.

TOCO FIELD

MANZANILLA PT.

RADIX PT.

MAYARO FIELD

GRAND MATELOT PT.

WALLER AFB.

TRINIDAD

NAS PIARCO

BLANCHISSEUSE

CHUPARA PT.

EDINBURGH
CARLSEN AFB

CARMEN FIELD

LA LUNE PT.

PORT OF SPAIN

POINT-A-PIERRE

SAN FERNANDO

NAS CHAGUARAMAS

GASPER GRANDE I.

MONOS I.

HUEVOS I.

CHACACHACARE I.

GREEN HILL

PATOS I.

BOCA DEL DRAGON

POINT FORTIN

ICACOS PT.

SERPENT'S MOUTH

VENEZUELA

GULF OF PARIA

ORINOCO DELTA

far from Grand Isle. This pinpointed his position and convinced even the most sceptical of his presence. By this time Kuhlmann must have been aware that he was the center of a massive hunt, because no sinking report on the Robert E. Lee was sent. Sooner or later U166 had to surface and the US forces were waiting. The early German U-Boats were basically surface vessels which had the ability to submerge, but they could seldom spend too long underwater. They were limited by the air supply in the boat and the capacity of the batteries. When Kuhlmann brought U166 to the surface on the first of August, the aircraft of Coast Guard squadron 212 were waiting. The wreck of U166 went to the bottom in very shallow water. In water so shallow, the U-Boat's crew should have been able to escape to the surface, but the absence of survivors must indicate that even the boat's escape compartments were shattered.

The sinking rate in the Gulf of Mexico was dropping off and this indicated that the American forces were beginning to take charge of the almost landlocked sea. This allowed the first transfers of anti-submarine forces to help ease the pressure in the Caribbean proper. However, there were still one hundred and thirteen U-Boats operational in the Atlantic as a whole, and the decision to transfer resources out of the Gulf was a calculated risk.

The U-Boats were spread out from the Gulf of Mexico to Africa and from the equator to the icecap, but they could still concentrate in any given area very quickly. Additionally, the Allies had to guard against the unexpected thrust in a weakened area or in a sensitive spot. Before daylight on Sunday second of August just such an emergency arose. Two Royal Navy MTBs attempted to use the main channel into Castries harbour in St. Lucia and both of them activated mines that had been laid by U66. The heavily damaged boats MTB 349 and MTB 342, were probably saved from total destruction by their speed, but both had to be beached to save them from sinking.

At twenty past eleven that morning, Lassen in U160 came upon a group of eight merchant ships being escorted westwards to Trinidad by two B18s of No. 1 USAAF squadron. Lassen carefully lined up his boat on one of the ships and loosed two torpedoes. The five thousand ton British freighter Treminard took both torpedoes and immediately dropped behind. U160 could not launch another attack because one of the B18s spotted her and forced the boat to dive. From a submerged position the hydrophone operator could hear the sound of the Treminard on its way to the sea bed two hundred miles east of Trinidad, and they could also hear the sound of the convoy receding in the distance.

While U160 was sinking the Treminard, the first six Lockheed Hudsons of No. 53 squadron RAF landed at Waller Field. Initially they were to be based at the field named after Major General Alfred J. Waller who had been killed in a 1937 aircraft crash at Langley Field, Virginia. The squadron had two main objectives. The first was to check the U-Boats who appeared to be operating with an extraordinary amount of freedom around Trinidad and secondly, to assist in the training of US airmen in attacking U-Boats. The British objectives were admirable, but like the United States Navy reactions, were lamentably late in being implemented.

By August 1942, the US Navy were at last beginning to get over the early set-backs and create a problem for the U-Boats, as evidenced by the experience of two other boats that day. U509 under the command of Werner Witte, a newcomer to the Caribbean, was caught by a VP-92 PBY operating out of Guantanamo and given such a severe shaking up that the boat was forced to retire north of the Caribbean for repairs. The attack so damaged this boat and demoralised the crew that although it was posted to the area around Trinidad, it failed to sink any ships at all on this patrol.

The other new boat, U134 under Rudolf Schendel attempted to attack a convoy coming down from Key West and was driven off by the three destroyers and aircraft escorting the eight merchant ships. Schendel claimed to have sunk a US destroyer on the following day but there is no Allied loss to relate to his attack. One day later he became ill and had to return from his first Caribbean patrol having failed to sink any merchant ships. The claim on the destroyer however, still managed to win him a Knight's Cross and he would come back to the Caribbean.

On the third of August the boat with the Polar Bear painted on the conning tower U108 under Klaus Scholtz, arrived in the zone for its second cruise. At three in the afternoon Scholtz announced his presence in the area by sinking the six thousand ton British tanker Tricula. The tanker was making a lone run from Trinidad to Gibraltar when U108 caught her two hundred and fifty miles away from the island. At seven fifteen that night, Lassen in U160 caught the Norwegian tanker Havsten, three hundred and fifty miles east of Trinidad. A torpedo stopped the ship and Lassen then gave his gun crew some practice. An hour later, with the tanker burning from end to end and low in the water, U160 turned away and began its homeward journey. The boat had sunk seven ships by its reckoning, but the tanker which they left did not sink. Three days later the Italian boat Tazzoli came upon the wreck of the Havsten still afloat. de Cossato was obliged to use a torpedo to get the much battered ship to give up the fight and sink.

On the following day, Piening in U155 who had been reporting to U-Boat headquarters about the abundance of targets off Trinidad, came upon a dispersed Atlantic convoy five hundred miles east of the island. Two torpedoes dispatched the British freighter Empire Arnold and Piening fished a ship's officer out of the sea, who confirmed that the vessel had carried a cargo of tanks and aircraft. These military stores had been enroute to Alexandria, via Capetown.

On the fifth of August No. 53 Coastal Command squadron received another five Hudson MK III aircraft from the US east coast where they had been operating. Eventually the squadron would build up to a strength of twenty of these radar-equipped submarine hunters. The main base with the bulk of the aircraft was in Trinidad, but they also established detachments at Beane Field in St. Lucia, Atkinson in British Guiana and Zandery in Dutch Guiana. With these dispositions the squadron was able to mount comprehensive anti-submarine coverage of the shipping lanes from north of St. Lucia to the French Guiana/Brazil border. In response to the increased U-Boat concentrations around Trinidad, the Caribbean Sea Frontier also based a detachment of No. 5 bombardment squadron from Borinquen to Beane Field. There were now four anti-submarine squadrons operating between St. Lucia and Zandery and they began to make an impact on the freedom enjoyed by the U-Boats.

On the same day that the additional aircraft arrived for No. 53 squadron, Markworth in U66 reported the increased air activity around Trinidad and added the comment that there was a suspicion that the aircraft were radar-equipped. The two other boats close to Trinidad, U108 and U162 heard the exchange of signals and both commented that something suspicious was going on. Well to the east Piening in U155 was untroubled by aircraft and he sank his eighth ship of the cruise the Dutch coaster Draco. Piening was three hundred and ninety miles east of Trinidad, but he was scheduled to come in closer to the mainland and his time to meet these new aircraft was not far off.

The seventh of August was to see Sholtz in U108 continue his scoring by sinking the Norwegian freighter Brenas east of Trinidad. Three more Hudsons arrived for 53 squadron and U508 got into trouble. This new Type IXC boat under the command of Kapitanleutnant Georg Staats was on its first Caribbean patrol. Staats took U508 along the Cuban coast until he came to Havana harbour and nosed his boat in to see what was inside. There were twenty merchant ships and four destroyers in the harbour, but in obtaining this vital information the U508 was spotted from the shore. Before Staats could get to deep water, US Navy PBYs gave the boat a severe shaking up. Staats retired westwards into the Gulf of Mexico where he could find a quiet spot to carry out repairs.

Probably the most important event of this Friday concerned Harro
Schacht in U507. This was not a boat destined for the Caribbean, but rather
for the central South Atlantic. Schacht signalled U-Boat headquarters and
requested permission to operate off the Brazilian coast. U-Boat command
made a critical mistake when they signalled U507 clearing her to move in.
All the Brazilian vessels sunk so far had been in the Caribbean or well off
the coast. Now U507 was going to change the entire strategic situation in
the west. Piening provided light relief at the end of the day when he signalled to say that he had engaged in a gunfight with a freighter on its way to
Trinidad. The freighter escaped.

Two days later Piening took his revenge on the eight thousand ton
British tanker San Emiliano. Eighty miles off Dutch Guiana he sent the
tanker to the bottom with two well placed torpedoes, that broke the ship's
back. At ten fifteen that night the U510 achieved a well-earned success. The
Type IXC boat under Kapitan Zur See Karl Neitzel had started off a US
coast patrol but found merchant ships few and far between. After sinking
one freighter he was reassigned to the Windward Passage but on arrival
there, Neitzel found that the boat's listening gear had gone dead.

A submarine which cannot hear is like a blind man in a lighted room
full of assailants. Under similar circumstances, many a U-Boat captain would
have started for home. Neitzel however, requested to be allowed to operate
outside of the Caribbean where there was less likelihood of a surprise attack.
Thus U510 virtually had to stay away from busy well-patrolled areas in
order to survive. A week later Neitzel came upon the eight thousand ton
British tanker Alexia, sixty miles east of Guadeloupe. He fired a three torpedo spread and observed all three fish detonate in sequence on the target.
Naturally he assumed that three torpedoes would sink any tanker and
turned away to escape the expected air reaction. However, although badly
damaged the tanker did not sink. Alexia was not only a strong ship she was
also lucky. Barely afloat she was found and towed to safety in Puerto Rico.
In the meantime, U510 had to go well east to escape the destroyer patrols
which saturated the area of the attack.

The tenth of August saw Piening use his deck gun to sink the small
Dutch coaster Strabo, one hundred miles off Dutch Guiana. Unknown to
the crew of U155, this was to be the last vessel sunk on this highly successful patrol. Piening had now accounted for ten ships sunk, but he still had
fuel and torpedoes and intended to continue the hunt.

The RAF and the US Army Air Corp had other ideas and they intended to hound him for the next ten days. On the same day Bernhard Zar-
muhlen in the Type VIIC boat U600 on its only Caribbean patrol, sank the

schooner Vivien P. Smith near the exotic-sounding Caicos Islands. On this date there were still thirteen U-Boats in the Caribbean and Gulf of Mexico, although there had been much changing of places and boats. U508 was with U171 in the Gulf of Mexico. U654 and U509 were near the Windward Passage while U600 made its way there. U217 was through the Mona Passage and heading for Curacao, while eight boats U66, U108, U155, U162, U173, U510, U564 and the Italian Tazzoli were in an arc around the eastern side of Trinidad.

August signalled the return of the Wolf packs to the North Atlantic convoy route with successful attacks against convoys SC94, SL119 and ON127. Paralleling this North Atlantic offensive was a similar push against the Caribbean convoys. Coming in from the Atlantic were U84, U163, U164, U511, U553, U598 and U658. They were going to challenge the new Caribbean convoy system which in theory was highly vulnerable. The geography of the region forced merchant ships to concentrate in selected choke-points, making the location of the convoys a much easier proposition than intercepting the constantly rerouted North Atlantic convoys. These new boats were going to find out that although Caribbean convoys had weaker, less experienced escorts, they were always accompanied by the air-cover that North Atlantic convoys prayed for.

The first U-Boat to intercept a convoy in the Windward Passage choke-point was U658 commanded by Hans Senkel. On the twenty-first of July, U658 had met the tanker U463 in mid Atlantic and then received orders for the Caribbean. The experienced Type VIIC boat arrived in the area off Guantanamo Bay at midday on August twelfth. Twelve hours later and fifty miles east of the American base, Senkel sighted convoy WAT 13 moving southwards through the Windward Passage. The twenty-four merchant ships were on a course which would bring them across the U-Boat's bow and Senkel set up for an immediate attack.

Seven minutes later, two torpedoes hissed out of the bow tubes and began their race for the densely packed columns of ships. Three minutes and fifty-eight seconds later Senkel observed a flash in the convoy followed by the rolling thunder of the torpedoes detonating. A sheet of fire lit up the ships in the convoy as Senkel kept his bow tracking to port. The detonations in the convoy had hardly died down when Senkel fired two more torpedoes from the remaining bow tubes. Down below the sailors began the harassing and difficult task of reloading the bow tubes, as Senkel ordered full speed and began closing on the convoy. Almost immediately a lookout's hail drew Senkel's attention to a bow wave coming towards them. A corvette was following the torpedo wakes and closing fast. Senkel ordered the boat down just in time to avoid the first depth-charge pattern from the corvette. Within minutes a destroyer joined the corvette and the hunt began in earnest.

For three hours the two escorts held U658 down with continuous depth-charge attacks. The U-Boat's crew crept around listening to the scratching sound of the asdic searching for them, followed by the violent shaking up each time a pattern exploded. In the confusion of undersea noise after each pattern Senkel increased speed for a couple of minutes changing position and depth, before the asdic probing began again. Finally the two escorts were satisfied that they had driven off the U-Boat and left to rejoin the convoy.

The situation above was not a little confused. Senkel's first two torpedoes had hit the small Dutch freighter Medea and destroyed the vessel. The ship must have been carrying explosives which caused the flash and tremendous detonation which Senkel had observed. The second pair of torpedoes had missed the ships and passed between the lines of vessels causing confusion among the merchantmen. The boat's attack had almost broken up the formation and the two escorts had been sitting over the U-Boat to give the other escorts time to reform the convoy.

After the departure of the escorts, Senkel brought U658 to the surface to search for the convoy but there was no sight of it. However, the hydrophone operator could hear a great deal of propeller noise to the west of the U-Boat and out of the confusion of other noises, deduced that the merchant ships were moving away from the U-Boat. Senkel turned his boat until his stern was pointing at the source of the noise and fired his remaining torpedo. The convoy was still close to the U-Boat, moving on a westerly course and the torpedo passed right down between the columns of ships. In the convoy they could see the lone torpedo streaking westwards and after its end-run detonation, the escorts raced back eastwards to get the offending U-Boat. Once again Senkel took U658 down to avoid the two escorts racing towards him and this time the hunt lasted for a full eight hours. U658 was subjected to a severe hammering, but the U-Boat's hydrophone operator could hear other noises besides the shattering depth-charge explosions. Someone else was also in trouble.

That night the Windward Passage was a scene of utter confusion. Coming south on the western side of the passage was convoy WAT 13, while going north on the other side of the passage was convoy TAW 12. Ships were detaching from both convoys to join another convoy being formed outside Guantanamo Bay, for the Panama Canal and the far west of the Caribbean. Ships were also leaving in an easterly direction for the ports in the northern Caribbean islands and added to all this were the ships which had been waiting off Guantanamo and Jamaica for both the northbound and southbound convoys. There were ships going in all directions in the confined passage and it was the worst time for a U-Boat to attack, but there were three U-Boats in attendance.

One hour after U658's first attack on WAT 13, Bernhard Zurmuhlen in U600 sighted convoy TAW 12 opposite the Golfe de la Gonaives in Haiti. At one fifty in the morning he had his boat in position to the west of convoy TAW 12 and turned inward to attack. U600 worked its way past the outer escorts and from a position between the convoy and its corvettes, he fired three torpedoes in succession. The torpedoes were aimed at the outer column of ships but all three missed the target ships and passed on into the convoy. Two of the torpedoes detonated after two minutes at the end of their run, but the third ploughed into the Lebanese freighter Everela. The four thousand five hundred ton ship exploded with a six hundred foot tower of flame. Her cargo of ammunition had exploded and the shattered hulk was gone in less than a minute.

For the next ten minutes as the escorts hunted for the attacker and fear mounted in the convoy, U600 crept closer to the lines of ships. The escorts and the circling PBYs were looking for a U-Boat outside the screen not among the myriad radar contacts within the convoy. Zurmuhlen waited until he was right up to the convoy's outer column before he loosed the remaining bow torpedo and turned his boat to bring the stern to bear. The torpedo left the stern tube and followed the first, past the outer column towards the big ships in the inner columns. Both torpedoes hit the convoy commodore's ship, the five thousand ton American freighter Delmundo.

The heavily laden freighter sank within five minutes but Zurmuhlen could not tarry to see the ship go down. Even as the torpedoes hit, the escorts finally located him and U600 crash-dived as a VP-92 PBY came into its attack dive. The boat was hardly down when an escort destroyer alerted by the PBY's attack, was over the spot and the depth-charges started raining down. Both U658 and U600 were being held down while the confusion of merchant ships sorted itself out.

Dawn on Thursday thirteenth found both U-Boats still being hunted by the escorts and the waters of the wreckage strewn Windward Passage being quartered by aircraft from Guantanamo Bay. The two reorganised convoys were drawing apart and the escorts were counting themselves as lucky. Only three ships had been lost, in a night when at times it seemed as if charging merchant ships would help the U-Boats by ramming each other.

The twin convoy action in the Windward Passage had not been the only attack launched by the U-Boats that night. Staats in U508 had completed his repairs in the Gulf of Mexico and come out into the dangerous Florida Straits. He reported to U-Boat headquarters that he had spent most of the night trying to penetrate the screen of a large convoy. The alert escorts had frustrated each attack and U508 could only back off and head eastwards along the Cuban coast in search of easier prey.

Convoy WAT 13 was through the Passage and would reach Trinidad without further loss but TAW 12 was not free yet. Before Zurmuhlen in U600 attacked he sent off a convoy-sighting report.

This report had been picked up by Gottfried Holtorf in U598 as he cruised near the northwest tip of Haiti and the boat moved westwards into the northern exit from the passage. On the morning of the thirteenth, he called for more information on the convoy's position, but both U600 and U658 were fully occupied and could not pass position reports. U-Boat headquarters directed Holtorf to the eastern tip of Cuba and indeed, the convoy had rounded Punta Maisi. It was now convoy TAW 12J, to denote the fact that additional vessels had joined from Jamaica.

At about the time that the escorts finally gave up trying to sink the two U-Boats in the passage and turned to catch up with their respective convoys, U598 set off in pursuit of convoy TAW 12J. All day on the fourteenth the boat from the 6th Flotilla at St. Nazaire chased after the convoy as it made its ponderous way along the Cuban north coast.

In the meantime, U600 and U658 surfaced among the oil and wreckage of the passage and began the delicate job of getting out of the confined waters, while charging their batteries and reporting on the night's activities. By eight o'clock that night U598 had caught up with convoy TAW 12J as it passed between Cuba and Great Inagua Island, and Holtorf began the task of working his boat abeam of the mass of ships. At four fifty the following morning the convoy was thirty miles southwest of Ragged Island in the Bahamas and U598 was in position on the convoy's port side. Holtorf estimated that convoy TAW 12J was on a course of three hundred degrees and progressing at eight knots when he fired two torpedoes from his bow tubes. He was unsure of his firing position and target data and thought that the torpedoes would miss, but both of them smashed into the British freighter Michael Jebson. The two thousand three hundred ton freighter was ripped open by the twin explosions and went down immediately.

Once again the action station alarm sounded and the weary escorts went racing outwards probing for the unseen U-Boat. Holtorf held his position inshore of the convoy and brought his bow to bear on the lead ship in the third column. Two more torpedoes hissed out of the bow tubes and began their journey into the convoy. On the target, the newly appointed Commodore's ship Empire Corporal, they saw the two torpedo wakes pass ahead of the bows. One torpedo went right through the lines of merchant ships and exploded at the end of its run, but the other detonated against the side of the six thousand ton British tanker Standella. The vessel came to an immediate stop, badly damaged. Holtorf was still undetected and he meant to hit his original target. He turned his boat and lined up his stern on the Empire Corporal. A carefully aimed torpedo streaked out of the stern tube and ran true towards the seven thousand ton British ship. The torpedo detonated on the vessel's side, blowing a great hole in the plates and rupturing the bottom plates. The Empire Corporal went down in the mile deep water, west of Cay Santo Domingo.

The U-Boat dropped back to reload its empty torpedo tubes, while the escorts fussed around the tanker Standella. Eventually she was towed to Key West. Throughout the attack Holtorf had remained on the surface and he stayed there watching the Empire Corporal disappear.

When U598 was ready Holtorf set off after the depleted convoy but this time the escorts were ready and they kept him at bay, while the convoy got into the restricted shallow waters of the Old Bahama Channel. The first convoy battle of the month had cost four cargo vessels and a tanker sunk, with one other badly damaged tanker.

Convoy battles were always spectacular and often created an atmosphere of fear among the merchantmen. During August while one wolf pack attacked a North Atlantic convoy three merchant vessels were abandoned by their crews before any of the ships were hit. Nevertheless convoy battles seldom contributed materially to the U-Boats' tonnage war. Up to May 1943, seventy-two percent of the U-Boat losses occurred in these battles. It was much more efficient to hunt the lone merchant ships on the shipping lanes and in August 1942, the most profitable area for doing this was off the Windward Islands and along the South American coast. The boats operating in this area had only one problem to contend with and this was the increasingly aggressive anti-submarine patrols. The aircraft were becoming a problem.

On Saturday fifteenth of August Scholtz in U108 was cruising on the surface one hundred and fifty miles northeast of Georgetown, British Guiana, when Hudson PZ/Z of 53 squadron out of Zandery picked up a radar contact at twelve miles. Squadron Leader Hilditch brought the aircraft round to the east and attacked with four torpex filled depth-charges, spaced thirty feet apart. U108 had just dipped below the surface, when the charges dropped across the swirl and sank to twenty-five feet. The resulting explosions gave the boat a severe jolt, smashing light bulbs and Scholtz later reported the attack. The aircraft crew remained in the area for forty minutes watching the depth charge scum and oil on the surface, confident that they had either sunk the boat or seriously damaged it. This was No. 53 squadron's first attack since their arrival in the Caribbean.

Sunday sixteenth of August was to belong to the aircraft. U654 reported to U-Boat headquarters that the area off Colon was clear of traffic. This was in stark contrast to the situation a month before when U172 and U159 had achieved success in this area. Then U564 advised its base that it was going to concentrate on the area off Trinidad. This boat was coming south along the island chain, but this was not the last signal received from the Caribbean that day. Piening had cruised north from Dutch Guiana and Sunday found him sixty miles east of Martinique with his crew relaxing, but the days when a U-Boat could take a day off and enjoy the Caribbean sunshine were over.

Hudson PZ/W flown by Flt. Sgt. Sillcock with Sgts. Nelson, Miller and Skinner aboard had left Waller Field at nine twelve that morning. At eleven fifty the aeroplane was east of Martinique when the radar gave a contact at twenty-seven miles. At sixteen miles the boat was visible, or at least the wide wake that it was leaving. Sillcock realized that he had a golden opportunity because it was obvious that his aircraft had not been seen. He made a wide detour to get the Hudson upsun of its intended victim before turning onto his attack course and losing height. At thirty feet above the water he was doing two hundred knots and closing the unsuspecting U-Boat fast.

The conning tower watch saw the machine at two miles. There was a mad scramble on the U-Boat's casing as sailors tumbled below in answer to the crash-dive alarm. Hatches slammed shut and air hissed out of ballast tanks to get the boat down fast. With the Hudson at one mile U155 began to go down, but a Type IXC boat took thirty-five seconds to dive under ideal conditions and a Hudson at two hundred knots could cover a mile in less than twenty seconds.

When the Hudson with its open bomb bay crossed the spot U155's conning tower was still visible. Three torpex filled depth bombs spaced thirty feet apart plummetted into the sea. By the time the depth-charges sank to twenty-five feet and their hydrostatic triggers activated them, U155 was underwater almost at the same depth. The hammer blows from the explosions smashed equipment throughout the boat, but Piening was lucky, his pressure hull was still intact except for small leaks. Sillcock remained in the area for fifteen minutes taking photographs before he flew off to St. Lucia. A few hours later Piening brought his battered boat to the surface and after surveying the damaged, he reported to U-Boat headquarters that he had to move away from the islands to see what he could repair.

Two hours later Hudson PZ/H enroute from Guantanamo Bay to San Juan, picked up a radar contact north of the Mona Passage and barrelled into the attack at two hundred knots. U511 under the command of Friedrich Steinholf was just arriving in the Caribbean for his only cruise in the area. As Flt. Sgt. Henderson roared in, the conning tower watch scrambled down the hatch with Stienholf shouting orders for a crash-dive. Once again the aircraft was over the boat before the conning tower disappeared, but this time the depth-charges overshot by sixty feet outside the lethal range. Nevertheless the shock wave caught U511 in the middle of an awkward manoeuvre and the blast helped to unbalance the boat.

When the fountains of water subsided, U511 had her entire after-end sticking out of the water at an angle of thirty degrees, with the propellers clear of the water. The crew of the aircraft must have thought that they had sunk the boat, because they took their time about positioning themselves for another attack and in that short space of time brilliant work by Steinholf saved the boat.

A crash-dive by a U-Boat was an extremely complicated manoeuvre. For the diving planes to work, the boat had to have forward motion and this had to be kept up while the engineers switched off the diesel engines and clutched in the electrical power. At the same time the forward ballast tank had to be flooded to get the bow down to an angle of about ten degrees before the flooding of the aft tank commenced. In the case of the U511 there must have been a delay in the flooding of the aft tanks, probably caused by the fact that the U-Boat had been surprised by the aircraft. The result was that the weight in the bow caused the downward angle to increase beyond ten degrees.

At this stage the stern of the boat would come out of the water and forward motion would cease. More importantly, the open bottoms of the aft ballast tanks would now be clear of the sea and the situation would be aggravated by the ballast water pouring out, further lightening the stern. The boat would eventually get to a critical point where the weight in the bow would cause it to slide deeper until with the boat almost vertical, the propellers would re-enter the water. Power would then drive the boat to destruction as it dived beyond its maximum depth.

Steinholf worked quickly, blowing the forward ballast tanks to bring the bow back to the surface and start the crash-dive again from scratch. This catastrophe sometimes happened to boats with new crews under training, but seldom did a U-Boat escape if it took place with an attacker above. Although Steinholf was not an ace he must have been an exceptional U-Boat commander.

The Hudson eventually got into position for another run but U511 had gone. The aircraft circled the growing stain of oil and depth charge scum for a while before setting course for San Juan. Late that evening as the same Hudson was landing at Waller Field, the machine swerved to the left and was written off, fortunately without injury to the crew.

But No. 53 squadron had not finished Sunday's work. at five o'clock in the afternoon U108, U162 and U173 had an unofficial rendezvous, one hundred and fifty miles off the Dutch French Guiana border. Hudson PZ/H flown by P/O Kennard homed on the group by radar, but with three sets of lookouts on duty the boats were able to pick up the attacking aircraft in good time. The Hudson chose U173, which was the last of the three still visible and the aircraft came in to the attack. The boat had disappeared by the time the aircraft crossed the swirl, but four depth charges still plummetted into the sea. U173 was well down by the time the charges went off, but the underwater shock wave still damaged equipment. The aircraft remained in the area for a while to ensure that the Sunday evening "Social" was not resumed. No. 53 squadron had enjoyed a good day.

That evening U-Boat headquarters reallocated new attack areas in the eastern Caribbean. U155, U108 and U173 were now to operate off the Guianas. U162 and U564 were to close in on Trinidad, with U217 to the west off the Venezuelan coast. U66, U509 and U510 were now to operate within the Caribbean south of Puerto Rico, but for the moment the convoy action still centered around the Windward Passage.

U658 had stayed south of the passage after the WAT 13 escorts had given up their eight hour hunt. Shortly after dusk on Sunday evening, Senkel sighted a convoy coming out of the Jamaica Channel just south of Navassa Island. This was convoy PG 6 on its way from Panama to Guantanamo Bay. U658 trailed the convoy northwards into the Windward Passage, with Senkel working the boat onto the convoy's starboard flank.

At nineteen minutes after midnight, the boat was in an attacking position between the escorts and the convoy and two torpedoes left the forward tubes. Both slammed into the seven thousand ton British freighter Fort La Reine, forty miles from Guantanamo Bay. The big freighter dropped astern immediately and began to go down. One minute later Senkel fired again and a single torpedo sped across the intervening space to bury itself in the side of the four thousand ton Egyptian freighter Samir. The

torpedo split the ship's side and she rolled over and plunged to the bottom
in the deep water off the US base. The fourth torpedo that Senkel fired
from his remaining bow tube crashed into the side of the large British
freighter Laguna. The ship was severely damaged and came to an immediate
stop, while the rest of the convoy pulled away.

Senkel was moving in towards the freighter when he saw an escort
corvette crashing towards him. He quickly turned U658 and fired the stern
torpedo at the onrushing escort. The corvette manoeuvred out of the way of
the torpedo and came on at the U-Boat. U658 was forced to crash-dive and
go deep to escape the first pattern of depth-charges. In between the volleys
of depth-charges, Senkel could hear the sinking noises of the two freighters
on their way to the bottom, but the boat had to endure a punishing search
and series of depth-charge attacks. While Senkel was thus held down, a tug
towed the Laguna to safety.

After the Canadian corvette rejoined its convoy, U658 surfaced and
tried to continue the attack but the PBYs of VP-92 were very active. He
was continually forced to dive as the big flying boats kept up their ceaseless
searching. With the coming of daylight it became impossible for U658 to
continue the convoy action and she retired southwards away from the land.
Senkel spent another five days in the area before beginning his return
journey across the Atlantic on the twenty-first. He had sunk three vessels
and damaged one, all from convoys. U658 was not to operate in the Caribbean again. On its next patrol the boat was caught by an RCAF Canso and
sunk in the Western Atlantic with the loss of all hands. U600 also left the
Caribbean without finding any other target.

While U658 had been attacking PG 6 and No. 53 squadron had been
surprising the U-Boats, Schacht in U507 had been engaged on deadly work.
The U-Boat hit the Brazilian coastal traffic like a whirlwind. Within thirty-
six hours he sent five freighters to the bottom. It was a tremendous feat by
the U-Boat commander, but a major diplomatic blunder by Germany.

The seven Brazilian ships previously sunk had all been in the Caribbean or well out in the Atlantic and their loss had not caused too much
concern among the population and the German Brazilians had been able to
keep reaction to a minimum and influence the Government to stay out of
the war. But U507's savage assault was too close to home. Street riots
erupted and Nazi flags were burned in the streets forcing the Brazilian
Government to act.

On August twenty-second Brazil declared war on Germany, and the
enormous Brazilian coastline was opened up to the basing of American
aircraft and escorts. The U-Boats still sank dozens of ships off Brazil and

indeed they mounted a campaign similar to the Caribbean, off the Brazilian coast, but American concern about the South American threat was now over. The southern flank was secure and the Allies could control the South Atlantic.

Monday August seventeenth was to see another convoy action develop in the Windward Passage but earlier in the day U108 made a kill. The boat was operating one hundred and twenty miles north of French Guiana when at seven thirty in the evening the American tanker Louisiana came into range. The big eight thousand five hundred ton tanker was on course for the Cape of Good Hope with a load of fuel from Trinidad. Scholtz put two torpedoes into the vessel. The explosion destroyed the tanker's engine room and set fire to its volatile cargo. The bombers from Zandery were able to drive off the U-Boat but they were not able to save the Louisiana.

At the other end of the Caribbean zone, U508 and U598 both tried to get at convoy PG 6, but the wary escorts drove off each attack and the merchant ships rounded Cuba's eastern tip for their run to the Straits of Florida.

Convoy TAW 13 consisting of twenty merchant ships with an escort of two destroyers and two corvettes left Trinidad on thirteenth August on its long run to Key West. Because of the strong concentration of U-Boats known to be operating at the southern end of the Windward Passage, the convoy had been rerouted around the western end of Jamaica. At sunset on the evening of Monday seventeenth, U553 picked up convoy TAW 13 between Jamaica and Cuba. The rerouting of the convoy had not saved it from discovery.

The Type VIIC boat under the command of the veteran Korvetten-kapitan Karl Thurmann, holder of the Knight's Cross, was on its only Caribbean cruise when they sighted the columns of ships coming up from the west. Thurmann sent off a sighting report and tucked in behind the convoy.

U508 under Staats had worked its way down from the Florida Straits and was now in the Windward Passage. U163 under Korvettenkapitan Kurt-Eduard Engelmann who had arrived in the area on the previous day, picked up the sighting report and together with U508 set course to intercept the convoy. By ten o'clock that night three U-Boats were in contact with the convoy. U553 was astern while U163 and U508 lay in ambush ahead of it. The detachment from the Royal Navy B 5 escort group had their hands full. When the attack developed the two destroyers ahead of the convoy took on the two U-Boats ahead while the two corvettes astern were respon-sible for keeping U553 out. But Thurmann was a veteran of four successful North Atlantic patrols and an experienced convoy fighter.

Thurmann worked his way slowly up the coast of Jamaica until he was opposite the convoy and then came in from the starboard side. At five minutes past midnight Thurmann saw his chance and two torpedoes hissed out of the boat's bow tubes. Both torpedoes detonated against the side of the little Swedish freighter Blankaholm. The twin explosions opened up the little ship and she went quickly. Ten minutes later Thurmann fired the two remaining bow torpedoes and turning quickly fired the stern torpedo. The first two torpedoes passed right through the convoy, but the stern shot hit the American Liberty ship John Hancock. The torpedo blew in the vessel's side plates and ruptured the adjacent cargo bulkheads. Within minutes the freighter was stopped and sinking fast. Ahead of the convoy the destroyers were depth-charging U163 and U508, while torpedoes ripped into the convoy from an unseen assailant. The merchantmen were well aware that they were approaching the dangerous Windward Passage and it appeared to them as though they were in the center of a U-Boat pack, which they were.

As soon as the first torpedo struck, the corvette HMS Pimpernel turned towards the probable firing position and built up speed, but Thurmann had expected this move and after firing his stern shot, he took U553 southward at her best speed. Thus when Pimpernel arrived at the firing position and commenced her search, the U-Boat had evaded her and was well south. Thurmann kept his boat trimmed down while the crew strove to reload his torpedo tubes.

With three escorts attacking U-Boats, the fourth found it very difficult to keep the panicky merchantmen in check. At this stage the escorts' problem was greatly magnified because there was a delay in the joining merchant ships getting into columns. The convoy first slowed down and then had to come to a complete stop. Because of the number of U-Boats in the area the merchant ships who should have been waiting in the passage had refused to leave the Cuban port of Santiago de Cuba until the convoy was opposite the port. Convoy TAW 13 was obliged to stop and wait for the joining vessels.

The great mass of helpless merchant ships wallowed in the swells with very nervous merchant seamen all on deck. The four escorts did a magnificent job of keeping the convoy in some sort of formation while they waited and kept three U-Boats at bay. They defended the stationary merchant ships by carrying out aggressive attacks on the boats trying to get in. Both U163 and U508 were under constant attack and only U553 was unmolested, but she was reloading.

At three fifteen, Thurmann was ready for another attack and he brought U553 northwards, while the two corvettes were shepherding the new arrivals into position. Thurmann was aware that he was dealing with a highly efficient escort group and realised that if he got too close the corvettes would pin him down. With this in mind he had to fire at long range. Four times in succession the U-Boat shuddered as each bow tube discharged its torpedo towards the distant ships. The fan of four torpedoes sped across the intervening sea just as the convoy began to move again.

Three of the torpedoes raced right through the convoy without hitting anything but their tracks alerted HMS Pimpernel to the position of the elusive U-Boat. The fourth torpedo hit the freighter Empire Bede after a run of one minute six seconds. The explosion opened up a hole in the ship's side and the crew promptly abandoned ship. The ship was not sinking, but the long wait had been too much, so the crew took no chances. By this stage U553 had finally been pinned down by HMS Pimpernel and Thurmann was running silent and deep as he manoeuvred to avoid the shower of depth-charge attacks being delivered by the corvette.

Two hours later while Pimpernel kept U553 down, Staats in U508 finally broke through the screen and got between the destroyers and the convoy. U163 was providing a diversion that had opened up a gap in the screen and Staats seized the chance. Even before Staats could fire, one of the escorting destroyers spotted him and turned to attack. Hurriedly Staats fired two bow torpedoes and crash-dived. The torpedoes missed the ships and detonated after nine minutes, by which time U508 was once again being rocked by underwater explosions.

The corvette and each of the destroyers sat over a U-Boat, keeping them down while the fourth escort vessel led the convoy up past Guantanamo Bay. Daylight brought the PBYs of VP-92 and the escorts could leave their U-Boats and hurry after the convoy. On the way, HMS Pimpernel sank the damaged Empire Bede. VP-92 kept the U-Boats busy all day, giving TAW 13 the chance to round Punta Maisi and start up the channel to Key West.

It had been a rough night and honours were about even. Three ships had been sunk, but the performance of the air and sea escorts had been magnificent. U553 had been the only boat to score, but she had only done so because of the all night attacks being launched by U163 and U508. This was U553's last and only Caribbean action. She operated in the Windward Passage and south of Hispaniola until the end of August before leaving for home. In December the boat made another North Atlantic patrol where she became involved with convoy HX 217 and may possibly have been damaged. One month later she disappeared without trace. No Allied unit attacked her and it is probable that some vital piece of machinery gave out during a dive.

The eighteenth of August saw another convoy action develop, but before that happened U217 woke up the island of Curacao. At seven in the evening Kurt Reichenburg-Klinke in command of the Type VIID boat U217 on its first Caribbean patrol, followed the American tanker Esso Concord through the outer reef around Willemstadt harbour in Curacao. The boat had been stalking the fast tanker all afternoon, but an opportunity to fire did not arise until the tanker was tied up against the jetty. A fan of three torpedoes left the U217's bow tubes and raced across the harbour. Unfortunately all three torpedoes missed the stationary tanker and detonated in succession against the stone harbour mole. The shattering explosions woke up everyone in the tiny island and U217 got out of the reef as fast as was prudent, but the U-Boat had roused up a hornet's nest.

On Tuesday afternoon, while U217 had been stalking the tanker, Wattenburg in U162 observed a group of fourteen merchant ships come out of Trinidad's Third Boca and take up their positions in convoy formation. The patrol vessels of the TRNVR fussed among the merchantmen getting them into the correct order, while the escort of two destroyers and two PCs took up station. Wattenburg had to stay submerged because there were Hudsons and B 18 bombers constantly overhead. As soon as the group of ships moved off to the northwest and the sky cleared for a few minutes, Wattenburg brought U162 to the surface and a sighting report went out. Convoy TAW (S) or Special was on its way.

Initially fourteen ships left the terminus with more to join off Aruba, Guantanamo, Key West and Halifax, until under a completely different designation the same convoy would be crossing the North Atlantic to England. Wattenburg had observed the birth of a giant that would take many lives as it progressed and built. The fuel in the tankers could end up powering a bomber over Berlin, the copper could end up in projectiles and the food would sustain someone in the front line. It is unlikely that Wattenburg realised the full significance of the event he had witnessed as he tucked U162 in behind the convoy.

Wattenburg's sighting report was picked up by U564 under the command of Reinhard Suhren and he turned his Type VIIC boat to intercept. As the sun set that evening U162 began edging its way abeam of the mass of ships as they worked their way northwest to clear the Los Testigos group. At ten o'clock U162 was in position having avoided the strong air escort, and two torpedoes left the U-Boat's bow tubes. Both torpedoes hit the American freighter West Celina. The five thousand seven hundred ton vessel shuddered to a halt and began to go down by the head, as the other ships of the convoy swung wide of the drifting hulk.

Frantic crew members struggled to get the lifeboats down, as Wattenburg lined up on the convoy for his second attack, but TAW (S) had a strong air escort. A shout from a lookout warned Wattenburg of the diving Hudson bomber and he abandoned the attack as the watch tumbled down the hatch. U162 was well down by the time that the depth charges hit the sea, but they signalled the position of the boat to the surface escorts. U162 was running silent and deep by the time the PC was overhead.

Two hours later as Wattenburg was tentatively bringing his boat back to the surface, Reinhard Suhren in U564 sighted the convoy. This boat was commanded by an experienced convoy fighter who had already completed five North Atlantic patrols before operating in the Gulf of Mexico during May 1942. Suhren held the Knight's Cross with Oak Leaves and Swords for his fifteen victories, almost all out of convoys. After his fifth North Atlantic patrol where he was embroiled with convoy OS34, he was directed to rendezvous with the tanker U463, followed by orders to operate off Trinidad. Suhren found that working his boat into position alongside TAW (S) was more difficult than the North Atlantic convoys because of the constant attacks by No. 1 and No. 53 squadrons. U564 was constantly diving to avoid the aircraft who had been thoroughly worked up by U162's attack, but by four o'clock in the morning he was in position to commence his attack.

At seven minutes past four in the morning Suhren fired a salvo of four torpedoes from his bow tubes. The tanker British Consul had been badly damaged by Achilles during his raid on Port of Spain harbour in February and had spent the next six months being repaired. The second torpedo which Achilles had fired, opened up a large hole in the vessel's side and fire did the rest. Now at last British Consul was ready for sea. She had been loaded with a cargo of fuel oil from the Point-a-Pierre refinery and then joined convoy TAW (S), but the tanker did not get very far.

The first three of Suhren's torpedoes detonated in succession against the side of the tanker. The staggering triple blows were too much for the vessel and quite unlike the usual tanker catastrophe, she simply died. The torpedoes opened up her sides and let in the sea, sending the big tanker to the bottom to join the ships in Trinidad's western fan. Fate had not intended the British Consul to leave Trinidad. She lies eighty-five miles northwest of the Grand Boca. Suhren's fourth torpedo found the six thousand ton British freighter Empire Cloud and she dropped astern of the convoy, sinking slowly.

Suhren dropped back to allow his crew to reload the torpedo tubes, joining Wattenburg astern of the convoy. Both boats sailed past the wreck of the Empire Cloud, but in fact the freighter did not sink until the evening of the following day. A corvette stood by the stricken vessel until she went down. At this stage Suhren sent off a sinking report and U-Boat headquarters replied by instructing U217 operating off Curacao and U164 Fechner, to join the hunt for the convoy. By triangulation of the many signals, the U-Boat plotting room in Trinidad was able to estimate the rough position of the boats in contact with TAW (S) and they dispatched additional surface escorts and aircraft to support the convoy.

As U164 and U217 set course for the convoy's position, Suhren began working U564 back to a position abeam of the convoy. Just as dawn was breaking two torpedoes left the boat and began their journey towards the merchant ships, but Suhren was to be disappointed. Both torpedoes detonated prematurely, well short of the targets. This signal brought an escort destroyer racing towards the scene and a Hudson came boring in. Suhren took U564 down fast and stayed deep to avoid the probing fingers of the asdic. For several hours the hunt continued until the convoy was well out of danger. After the destroyer left to rejoin the convoy, aircraft constantly patrolling ensured that Suhren had lost the ships.

U164 and U217 made contact with the convoy that day, but by now TAW (S) was heavily protected and either escort vessels or numerous aircraft frustrated every attempt to break in. Steinholf in U511 had also heard the radio traffic and set course for the position of the convoy. By seven thirty that night Steinholf was in position but before he could fire a torpedo, a PBY of VP-92 was diving at him. In response to the urgent calls for help VP 92 had detached two PBYs from Guantanamo Bay to work with the convoy from Aruba. Steinholf was forced to dive, losing contact with the convoy. Both U164 and U217 unable to penetrate the escort screen, broke off the action and set course for the Curacao area. Only U162 remained in contact and she shadowed the powerful convoy until the following day.

While the five U-Boats had fought with the escorts of TAW (S), Staats in U508 attempted to attack convoy TAW 13 in the Straits of Florida. The boat managed to fire two torpedoes at the twenty merchant ships, but both missed and detonated at the end of their runs. Within minutes Staats was forced to take U508 down fast as aircraft and surface escorts converged on his position.

Two thousand miles to the east U510 with its dead listening gear, fired four torpedoes at a fast freighter but all missed and the vessel outran the U-Boat. U217 took her revenge for the failure with TAW (S) on the schooner Seagull, but paid for it two hours later when Captain Campbell flying a 59th squadron A-20A caught the boat on the surface east of Bonaire.

The bomber crossed the U-Boat and released its depth charges while the watch were still on the conning tower. The pilot was convinced that the men on the conning tower had been killed by the machine gun fire from the bomber, but the damage was done by the depth-charges. When the towers of water fell back U217 was still on the surface heavily damaged. As U217 dived Captain Campbell was sure that he had sunk the boat.

Two hours later U217 surfaced to check the extent of the damage only to find another A20 diving into the attack. Lieutenant Sheddon raked the boat with machine gun fire, but his depth-charges overshot and fell just outside lethal range, and once more U217 was rocked by massive explosions. Richenburg-Klinke was forced to take his boat north, away from the aircraft of No. 59 squadron on Curacao in order to carry out repairs. U510 ended the day by sinking the British freighter Cressington Court almost nine hundred miles east of Trinidad.

In contrast to the first three weeks of August, the twentieth and twenty-first were to be harassing days for the U-Boats, particularly U155. U217 was licking her wounds out in the center of the Caribbean, while U66 attacked a French ship which it claimed to have sunk. However there is no mention of such a ship being hit in the records. U164 complained that it was forced to stay submerged in daylight off Curacao, because of the activities of No. 59 squadron.

In the meantime U511 cruised back up towards the Windward Passage. Once again they found a convoy and were about to attack it when a VP-92 PBY attacked. U511 was forced to crash-dive.

Piening in U155 had not sunk anything for ten days and he was still east of Trinidad, when a B18 of No. 1 Bombardment squadron caught him on the surface. The shout from the lookout was so late that Piening had to leave one of his men still on the conning tower when the boat crash-dived. The crewman was probably killed by the blast of the four depth charges going off as the U-Boat went down. The detonations caused light bulbs and glass fittings to shatter in the boat and severely shook up the crew.

On Thursday twentieth Piening had another bad shock. U155 was on an easterly heading at eight knots when P/O Rickards flying Hudson PZ/C picked it up on radar at fifteen miles. The pilot of the aircraft had the U-Boat visual at eight miles and brought his machine down almost to ten feet above the waves on the run in. At two miles the conning tower watch saw the aeroplane and the crash-dive routine started. To help the U-Boat to dive quickly Piening ordered the crewmen not immediately occupied to run forward to help the bow down-angle, but they had less than a minute. When the Hudson crossed the U-Boat the conning tower was still visible. Four torpex-filled depth charges left the bomb bay, spaced thirty feet apart. The last of the four landed in the water just ahead of the conning tower. The charges sank to twenty-five feet before detonating. The shock wave from the explosions almost crushed U155.

Anything that could move was smashed and the planesmen had to fight to stop the boat from plummetting to the sea bed. Damage control reports flooded in to the control room, with all compartments reporting severe damage. Gingerly Piening kept the boat at sixty feet for an hour, with damage control parties working to stop leaks and repair what they could. In the meantime the 53 squadron machine had gone back to Zandery.

When eventually Piening brought U155 to the surface, he was able to inspect the damage to the boat's hull and signal U-Boat headquarters that his boat was so badly damaged that it could not dive again. U155 was running on the surface at the best speed to try and get out of range of the aircraft. U-Boat headquarters instructed U510 to rendezvous with U155 and escort the boat home. In fact U510 was also a cripple because she was unable to hear.

Piening had completed his second Caribbean cruise having sunk forty-three thousand five hundred and four tons, to bring the boat's Caribbean total to over seventy-six thousand tons in two patrols, but ahead of them lay a hazardous four thousand mile journey to get home. Escorted by U510, Piening had to wait in mid-Atlantic for another boat with spare parts before he could complete the last, most hazardous part of the journey to Lorient. All the way U155 had to stay on the surface with U704 acting as a guard, while they hugged the Spanish coast. Finally on September fifteenth Piening brought his boat into Lorient, arriving on the same day as the also damaged U108.

Piening and Scholtz were able to sit down that night and drink a toast to the damnation of 53 squadron and to their survival. Piening would bring U155 back to the Caribbean in 1943, but without the success that attended his 1942 efforts. However his was one of the lucky boats, surviving the whole war to be surrendered in 1945. U108 was also to be a lucky boat. The boat with the Polar Bear badge never returned to the Caribbean. Her next patrol would be off Casablanca in November, following which U108 was retired from service in March 1943. She was damaged in an American bombing raid on Stetin in April 1944 and scuttled as part of operation Rainbow in May 1945.

CHAPTER

8

Three U-Boats

The boats of the third wave were finding the Caribbean a very different place to the ideal operating area that the previous boats had enjoyed. The targets were still there, but airpower was making any sort of movement very hazardous. This was particularly true for the boats that were trying to break into the convoys. No boat could hope to catch a convoy, or manoeuvre into a firing position while submerged, and only those that happened to be ahead of a convoy stood a chance of getting in.

Even the North Atlantic veterans were now finding the Caribbean convoys particularly trying. In that theatre boats operated either in the air-gap where there were no aircraft, or came in on the surface and took their chances with the occasional aircraft, but Caribbean convoys seemed seldom to have less than four aircraft as air escort. There was no air-gap anywhere. Airborne radar was the key.

With typical boldness, the U-Boat commanders came up with the solution of operating on the surface close to the escorts, where it was difficult for the radar operators to distinguish them as hostile. August was to see this tactic employed successfully by a number of boats, but success was short-lived. Once the aircrew and surface escorts got over their surprise, it became difficult to fool them.

This solution however could not help boats operating away from the convoys. Out in the open ocean even the smaller handier Type VII boats were at a disadvantage. They could dive in twenty-five seconds, ten seconds less than the big Type IXs, but even this slender advantage was not enough. The U-Boat seldom saw the attacking aircraft at more than two to three miles and this gave them less than a minute, not only to dive, but get deep enough to escape the blast. Theirs was a three dimentional problem; they had to move horizontally, laterally and vertically to get out of the depth charges' lethal range. Even the expedient of having the crew run through the boat towards the bow to quicken the dive was not enough.

Seldom did a boat relying on visual warning of an attacker, manage to solve the three dimensional problem in time, and in fact most boats still had their conning tower showing when the attacking aircraft crossed them. This left the boats chances of survival entirely dependent on the accuracy of the attacking pilot's aim. It was a forgone conclusion that experience would ensure that the pilot's aim would get better and better. This was the cause of the loss of the second U-Boat in the Caribbean. They ran up against a squadron which had long experience.

The Type VIIC boat U654 was built in early 1941 by Howaldswerke of Hamburg and accepted into service in July of that year. Korvettenkapitan Hesse handed over command to Kapitanleutnant Ludwig Forster on the second of December 1941. Forster took U654 into a convoy battle around ONS 61 in February 1942 and torpedoed the escort corvette Alysse. One could not ask for a more auspicious way to start a wartime career and Forster was sent back out to the North Atlantic in April, to attempt the feat again. This time he did not find a convoy, but instead three merchant ships totalling eighteen thousand tons.

Forster took U654 out of the 1st Flotilla base at Brest on July ninth and out into the Central Atlantic on its third war patrol. The boat did not find any targets and on July twenty-first, it made a rendezvous with a U-tanker well northeast of the Caribbean. After its refuelling from U463, the boat was ordered to proceed to the Caribbean as part of the third wave. By August third, Forster was bringing U654 down the Caicos Passage and past Great Inagua Island on its way to the Windward Passage. Strangely, U654 passed through the Passage, without being attacked.

In fact, when the boat arrived in its operating area off Colon in the Panama area, it still had not experienced a Caribbean air attack. U654 was alone in the Panama Sector, where it replaced the illfated U153. It was a lonely patrol and Forster found neither merchant ships nor aircraft. For ten days he cruised off the Colon area without seeing anything worth the firing of a torpedo. At first U-Boat command assumed that the lack of targets was the result of a temporary lull in traffic, but when Forster complained on the twentieth about his inactivity, they relented and reallocated U654 to an area further north.

The American command in the Panama Sector were unaware that there was a U-Boat operating in that sector until Forster transmitted on the twentieth. They were able to get a fix on the transmission and plot his approximate position. From that moment on his fate was sealed. Number 45 bombardment squadron was one of the original Caribbean aviation units and during May and June, while based in Puerto Rico, they had picked up considerable experience. The fact that they could not get any definite information on U-Boats in their area since the raid on Puerto Limon, did not daunt them.

The squadron was still on the punishing ninety flying hours per pilot routine, patrolling empty wastes further north around the last reported U-Boat positions of nearly six weeks before. The news that there was a U-Boat closer to their home base at France Field brought forth an extra effort from the already fully stretched unit and it paid off.

On Saturday twenty-second of August, a B18 caught U654 on the surface, one hundred and fifty miles from Colon. At two miles the aircraft observed the U-Boat beginning its crash-dive as the B18 dropped closer to the water. Seven months of frustration went into the attack. The four depth-charges bracketed the diving boat and it simply continued on down to the sea floor, nine thousand feet below. U654 lies not too far from the probable position of the wreck of U153, on the floor of the underwater Clarke Basin. No. 45 squadron had got their U-Boat and continued to operate from France Field until November, when they exchanged their B18s for long-range B24s and transferred to David Field for operations in the Pacific.

On the day after U654 was sunk, Zurmuhlen in U600 was caught in the Windward Passage by a VP-92 PBY, but he was luckier than Forster and the depth-charges only damaged the boat. Several hours later when he was able to surface, Zurmuhlen realised that the damage was much more serious than he at first suspected. The boat was forced to leave the Passage and head for home. U600 was not destined to operate in the Caribbean again. She was destroyed off Gibraltar with all her crew in November 1943 by HMS Bazeley and Blackwood.

On Monday morning, Wattenburg in U162 was east of Barbados when he sighted the Dutch freighter Moena making a lone run across the Atlantic. Two torpedoes sent the nine thousand two hundred and eighty-six ton vessel to the bottom. She turned out to be the largest freighter sunk in the Caribbean campaign. Two days later Wattenburg caught the eight thousand ton Norwegian tanker Thelma coming towards the Caribbean. Two torpedoes did the job. U162 was working up towards another successful cruise.

In August 1940, Herbert Kuppish accepted the Type VIIC boat U94 into service on behalf of the Kriegsmarine. In December he took the Germania Werft built boat to sea on its first war cruise. The boat became involved in the battle around convoy HX 90 and racked up a score of six ships sunk. On its next patrol Kuppish sank seven more vessels in the North Atlantic, to give the boat a total of thirteen ships sunk and win for himself the Knight's Cross.

In May 1941, he handed over command to the twenty-four year old Otto Ites who took the boat on a North Atlantic patrol in September. Ites came back with four ships sunk, three of them out of convoy ON 14. In March 1942, he took the boat to the American coast and claimed another five ships and a Knight's Cross. U94's next patrol was in June and she sank one ship out of convoy ONS 100.

When Ites took U94 out of the 6th Flotilla base at St. Nazaire on August second, he was a popular, successful commander. All U-Boat crews wanted their commanders to have an element of luck and Ites had it. Although very young for a commander, he was affectionately known as Onkel Otto to the crew of his boat. A mid-ocean rendezvous with the tanker U463 was followed by orders for operation in the Windward Passage. By August twentieth he was in position in the vital Passage, waiting for the first convoy sighting report.

Convoy TAW 15, the last of the TAW series before the changeover to TAG, formed up outside the Dragon's Mouth on August twenty-fourth. The TRNVR senior officer handed over the convoy to the escort group commander and the twenty-nine ships set off to the northwest.

The escorting ships comprised the senior officer in the destroyer USS Lea, along with the Canadian corvettes Oakville, Halifax and Snowberry, with the Dutch gunboat Jan Van Brakel and three US Navy PCs. Overhead No. 1 and No. 53 squadrons in their B18s and Hudsons provided continuous aircover.

The ships of the convoy were going to run westward, passing close to Aruba where a group of tankers waited to join. Ships from Panama would be waiting in the Jamaica Channel and ships from the rest of the Caribbean would be waiting to join at Guantanamo Bay. Convoy TAW 15 would end at Key West, where another group of ships would join from the Gulf of Mexico. The combined groups would then become a KN convoy to New York. After this the ships at New York would combine with ships from Halifax and together they would cross the North Atlantic to England as an HX convoy. It was a long and dangerous route and the planning and organisation involved thousands of people.

The Trinidad based escorts would go as far as New York, where they would take over a southbound group of ships on the return route. A convoy could become an administrative monster and so it became with TAW 15. Three days before the main convoy was due, a group of ships was waiting in the Jamaica Channel and a similar group was waiting south of Haiti. To the planners these ships were already part of TAW 15, even though the convoy was a long way away.

Thus when Gunther Krech in U558 on its second Caribbean patrol, sighted the group of ships in the Jamaica Channel, he was officially in contact with convoy TAW 15. At four thirty-seven on the morning of August twenty-fifth, he fired a torpedo at the small British freighter Amakura, aware only that he was attacking a small convoy of war material destined for the Allies. The torpedo slammed into the little ship and opened up its plates. As the Amakura went down Krech was surprised at the violence of the reception awaiting him.

Almost immediately, a PBY was diving at the boat and U558 was forced to crash-dive. Within a short time more aircraft and a PC arrived, driving him away from the remaining ships.

Just after lunch that day, Korvettenkapitan Otto Fechner had a similar experience. U164 came upon a small group of ships south of Haiti. At twelve twenty he fired two torpedoes at the four thousand ton Dutch freighter Stadt Amsterdam. The freighter went down eighty miles off the coast of Haiti, but Fechner was also surprised at how quickly aircraft were overhead. He also was forced to dive and lost contact with the group. Neither of the U-Boats was aware that they had started the battle of TAW 15.

On August twenty-sixth No. 59 squadron took over aircover of the vast assembly of ships known as convoy TAW 15, as they neared Aruba and the PCs shepherded the waiting tankers out to join the passing armada. Shortly afterwards the convoy altered course to the northwest for the long run up to the Windward Passage. That night Otto Ites in U94 sighted the convoy two hundred miles from the passage and took up a shadowing position. His sighting report alerted U164, U511 and U558 that a large convoy was heading for the Windward Passage. At this stage, the long ranged PBYs of VP-92 had taken over aircover of TAW 15 from the shorter ranged A20s based in Curacao.

At the headquarters of the Caribbean Sea Frontier in Puerto Rico, Admiral Hoover's staff moved symbols forward on the plot to indicate the progress of TAW 15. They had picked up the sighting report sent by U94 and the attack reports from U164 and U558. They were aware of the threat facing TAW 15 and an appreciation of the situation was sent out to the convoy commander in USS Lea. By dawn on the twenty-seventh, the USS Lea had taken up position ahead of the convoy. On its starboard flank HMCS Halifax, a USN PC and HMNS Jan Van Brakel were about four miles from the ships. On the port side of the convoy, HMCS Snowberry another PC and HMCS Oakville were also in a similar formation, as TAW 15 neared the dangerous Windward Passage. Trailing astern was a solitary PC.

In the late evening of the twenty-seventh, Steinholf in U511 gained contact with TAW 15 and joined U94 trailing the convoy. Both boats were preparing for a night attack on the convoy despite the moonlight. Steinholf had been having a difficult time with the Allied aircraft and he made his plans accordingly, but Ites had not faced a Caribbean air attack.

Before midnight both boats began working up alongside the convoy so that they could come in from the flanks. U511 was heading for the starboard side, while U94 took the port. The two boats slowly drew ahead of the convoy which was travelling at eight knots on a course of three hundred degrees. Both boats were continually diving to escape the attentions of the convoy's strong flying boat air escort, but eventually they were in position slightly ahead of the escort wings. At midnight they turned inwards to commence the attack.

U94 was barely moving as Ites brought the trimmed-down boat on an easterly course. The escorts were well out from the convoy and he would have to slip past the three vessels before he could get at the merchant ships four miles away. The moonlight glinted on the water as the dark shape of the U-Boat crept past HMCS Snowberry at the head of the port line. Ahead of U94 was the US Navy PC, which Ites ignored. These eighty foot PCs did not carry much of a punch and the U-Boats frequently ignored their presence. Astern of the PC there was the faint bow wave of a corvette and he knew that this type of vessel was dangerous. His attention was probably focussed on HMCS Oakville to the exclusion of all else, because she was the only barrier to the convoy that he needed to negotiate. In doing this, Ites ignored the air.

The VP-92 PBY was on a continuous circuit around TAW 15, when the crew spotted the darker shape of the U-Boat creeping in on the convoy's port side. The pilot did not hesitate and the big flying boat swept down on the intruder like an avenging hawk. The lookouts on U94 were good and Ites had the boat diving long before the aircraft was overhead, but the damage had already been done. The PBY swept over the swirl and four depth-charges left the racks. The four tall columns of water and the dull thunder of the explosions were adequate warning to HMCS Oakville. On the bridge Lt. Cmdr. King ordered full speed ahead and raced for the spot.

As the corvette swept over the disturbed water her asdic operator had a good fix on the boat trying vainly to escape. Two depth-charges left the corvette's throwers and three others rolled off the rails at the stern. The three hundred pound charges bracketed U94, as the noise of the PBY circling overhead filled the air.

The tremendous blast of the five charges going off so close to U94, shattered equipment in the boat, damaging its diving planes and tanks. With water coming in through cracks in the pressure hull, Ites knew that the boat was crippled. He had no alternative but to surface and try to fight it out. Above the PBY kept circling and dropping flares to light up the area of the attack, as U94 came up from the depths.

Throughout World War Two and indeed for many ages past, naval officers have felt a compulsion to ram. It seemed to be the first reaction of escort commanders, despite the fact that the vessel doing the ramming was always seriously damaged. In fact, during this period of time a destroyer was lost in the North Atlantic as a direct result of ramming a U-Boat.

Lieutenant Commander King in Oakville was no different and the sight of U94 surfacing brought on the urge to ram. The glistening U-Boat lay on the surface in a welter of foam, as the corvette under full helm attempted to get around fast enough to ram the long steel cylinder. Oakville did not have enough searoom to turn and the attempt to ram ended with the corvette bumping and scraping its way down the side of the U-Boat. Two rockets soared upwards to keep the boat lit up as Oakville swung away. The corvette's four inch main armament opened fire, along with the twenty millimetre cannons, and soon hits began to register on the U-Boat. The smaller calibre projectiles cut down U94's gun crew as they scrambled to reach their main deck gun.

In August 1941, the Royal Navy captured U570 on the high seas. No word of this capture leaked out and the secret documents on the captured boat were of great assistance to the escorts. The Royal Navy went so far as to recommission the boat and put it into service against its former owners.

Throughout the rest of the war, the other Allied navies all tried to emulate this feat. The Americans finally achieved the capture of one in

1944 and Lt. Cmdr. King was going to make the Canadian Navy's try on U94.

Lieutenant Hal Lawrence was already detailed as the boarding officer and his boarding party stood by, as once again the corvette swung in on another attempt to ram. Otto Ites was not quite ready to be rammed and as Oakville swung towards him he managed to manoeuvre U94 out of the way. This attempt ended with the corvette once again bumping along the U-Boat's side. Oakville was lucky, because the forward diving planes and their associated guards stuck out from the side of the U-Boat in such a fashion that they could have opened up the corvette's side. King intended to get his adversary, and as he crashed down the U-Boat's side, depth-charges rolled off the corvette's stern. Even more lethal to the U-Boat's crew were the empty Coca Cola bottles, that a group of stokers were hurling at the U-Boat's conning tower as the corvette ground past.

As Oakville swept clear, the depth-charges exploded almost under the U-Boat. The explosions damaged machinery and forced U94 to slow down to a crawl. This gave King his chance and Oakville raced in and hit the U-Boat squarely. The corvette impacted just ahead of the conning tower and climbed right up over the boat, smashing the forward part of the structure. The corvette forced U94 under and to a chorus of bumping, crashing and grinding, passed right over the boat.

By this stage, U94 was finished. The pressure hull had been subjected to numerous close range detonations from depth-charges, as well as the hits from four inch and twenty millimetre shells. The ramming had smashed in the front of the conning tower and split the hull where Oakville had torn its way across. In full knowledge that he had won, King brought Oakville alongside the boat once again to let his boarding party get across. In the event, only Lieutenant Lawrence and Petty Officer Powell made it to the U-Boat's deck before the corvette was past.

Once on the U-Boat, Lawrence and Powell confronted the submarine's crew who were frantically trying to abandon ship, shooting some and checking the rush. After checking the deck hatches, they let the crew come up from below. Lawrence then did an extraordinarily brave thing by going into the doomed boat in an effort to close the scuttling valves. While Lawrence was down below, Powell on deck realised that the boat was going. A warning shout down the hatch brought Lawrence struggling back through the darkness and chest deep water to the conning tower ladder. No sooner had they abandoned ship, than the U94 raised its stern and slipped down to its grave. She sank forty miles southwest of Point a Gravois, Haiti, in water more than a mile deep.

The USS Lea arrived while the drama was being enacted on the U-Boat and she was able to rescue many of the men from the sea, including Lawrence and Powell. Meanwhile the heavily damaged Oakville also picked up survivors, including the U-Boat's captain. The U94 had gone down forty-five minutes after the first sighting.

While the escorts on the port side of the convoy had been occupied with U94, Steinholf in U511 had broken through the line of escorts on the starboard side. He was on the surface between the escorts and the merchant ships. At twenty past one in the morning, two torpedoes left the forward tubes of the U-Boat. Three minutes later, the remaining two torpedoes from the bow tubes left the boat and began their run towards the merchant ships. Steinholf's aim had been particularly good. The first pair romped into the British tanker San Fabian. The detonation of the warheads ripped open the sides of the giant tanker and ignited her volatile cargo. A towering flame exploded upwards for many hundreds of feet, as the thirteen thousand and thirty-one ton vessel shuddered to a halt. She was the largest vessel to be sunk in the Caribbean during the war.

Three minutes later the second pair of torpedoes found the nine thousand ton Dutch tanker Rotterdam. The big tanker came to an immediate stop with tongues of flame licking around her tanks. She burned as the fractured hull let in the sea and she began to settle.

Steinholf had turned U511 as the second pair of torpedoes left the boat and as soon as the stern was on target, he loosed the two stern torpedoes at another tanker. Thus before the first torpedo hit the San Fabian, Steinholf had fired all his torpedoes and was able to dive. He had made up for the highly embarassing incident in the Mona Passage where 53 squadron had watched the boat fumble its crash-dive. U511 was almost underwater when the first torpedoes hit and was well down when one of the last pair found a target. The torpedoes smashed into the side of the American tanker Esso Aruba. The big tanker shuddered with the impact of the explosions and slowed down. By now the escorts on the starboard side of the convoy were racing to the probable firing position, but U511 was deep and creeping away.

Officially, TAW 15 had lost four ships totalling twenty-seven thousand seven hundred and sixty-six tons, as well as having one large tanker badly damaged. The loss was counter-balanced by the loss of the U94, but these figures do not include the damage to Oakville. She was out of action for ten days in Guantanamo Bay while temporary repairs were carried out and for a longer period later on while she was properly repaired. It is arguable whether she needed to ram.

Late the following afternoon the convoy was off Guantanamo Bay. Oakville and the Esso Aruba entered the bay along with the survivors. Otto Ites was alive with one leg broken and the other with bullet wounds. Nineteen of the crew of U94 died in the encounter but US Navy intelligence still had twenty-six valuable sources of information to probe. Fifty-nine injured survivors from the two sunken tankers were also brought in. They told.a tale of sharks.

The morning of August twenty-eight left ten U-Boats operating in the Caribbean. This was a sharp drop from the seventeen that had been in the zone a week before. In the Gulf of Mexico, U171 continued its lonely patrol. The Gulf was now regularly patrolled by aircraft and convoys protected the shipping. To all intents and purposes the offensive in this area was now over. What could be described as the battle of the Windward Passage was now also over. The U-Boats had failed to decimate the convoys. Air protection was so strong in the confined passage that the boats could not challenge the convoys in this area again. Independently sailing merchant ships would continue to be attacked in the passage for another two years, but the convoy battles were over.

The offensive against the convoys would now switch to the Trinidad area. U164, U511 and U558 remained south of the passage after the fight around TAW 15, but they would not achieve any further successes. U553 was operating south of the Mona Passage, while U66, U162, U173, U217 and U564 were in the Trinidad area. The Trinidad Sector command was aware of the presence of the five boats and its aircraft were all out hunting. Along the island chain, TRNVR patrol vessels and RN MTBs were also operating. It was a far cry from the early days when the entire naval force in the Caribbean had been two old destroyers.

U173 was now to go through an ordeal at the hands of the Trinidad based airmen. No. 53 squadron did not start off the day very auspiciously. Hudson PZ/B inadvertently attacked a merchant ship southeast of Trinidad. At the last moment a mast and funnel were observed and the pilot momentarily delayed depth-charge release. The charges overshot and went off with a thunderous roar beyond the merchant ship. Not surprisingly, the aircraft crew could not get the ship's master to reply to light signals.

At one forty-five, Hudson PZ/W flown by Flt. Sgt. Sillcock, the pilot who had first damaged U155 east of Martinique on the sixteenth, took off from Waller Field on an anti-submarine sweep. By three thirty in the afternoon, Sillcock was roughly four hundred and fifty miles east southeast of Trinidad, when he picked up a radar contact at eight miles. At six miles Sillcock had a U-Boat visual. The boat was moving very slowly on a course for Trinidad as the Hudson came in at forty-five degrees to the U-Boat's track, on the starboard side. At one mile the U-Boat began to submerge and had almost completely disappeared when the aircraft crossed the still visible stern at thirty feet. Four two hundred and fifty pound torpex-filled depth-charges left the bomb bay. The aim was good and two charges entered the water short of the boat, while the other two went in just beyond the swirl. After the gigantic columns of water had subsided, the crew noted oil and bubbles rising to the surface, with a yellow object floating in the depth-charge scum. About a minute later a long black object rose to the surface beyond the patch and then submerged. On return to base the pilot was credited with a U-Boat damaged, and indeed U173 had been damaged.

Schweichel had been alerted to the presence of the aircraft by the starboard side lookout, just in time. The conning tower watch tumbled down the hatch and landed in a heap in the control room, while the boat was already diving. It was a good fast crash-dive, but the pilot's aim had been very good. U173 had been bracketed by the depth-charges and two had been very close. The explosions shook the boat and damaged a great deal of internal machinery, leaving the pressure hull cracked in several places. The boat stayed at sixty feet for a while, as the crew strove to check the leaks and repair what they could, before Schweichel brought her to the surface to have a look at the outside.

The sight from the conning tower appalled them. The four deck containers with spare torpedoes were smashed and the black object that Sillcock had seen after the attack had been a torpedo. Additionally, five of the six torpedo tubes were out of action and a periscope had been smashed. U173 was virtually useless and Schweichel radioed U-Boat headquarters that he was moving eastwards to open water, to see what he could repair. The operational boats were now down to nine, but the aircraft were not finished with U173.

That afternoon, Markworth in U66 caught the American freighter Topa Topa loaded with cars and aircraft, five hundred miles east of Trinidad. The vessel was on its way to Freetown when U66 sent it to the bottom with two torpedoes and gunfire.

As the sun went down that Friday afternoon, a US Army B18 from No. 1 bombardment squadron at Waller Field caught the U173 again. Schweichel managed another good crash-dive and this time the U-Boat was lucky. The pilot's aim was not as good. The depth-charges shook up the boat, but the damage of earlier in the day was not increased. The pilot claimed to have sunk the boat and so it was logged. That night U173 was ordered home by U-Boat command, but the pilots still had more trouble for the boat.

Next morning U164 attacked a freighter, but the torpedoes missed and No. 59 squadron gave the boat a good shaking up, damaging the feed-water pipe. At eleven fifteen in the morning, Hudson PZ/C of 53 squadron flown by Flt. Sgt. Badger caught U173 on the surface east of Barbados. The four depth-charges straddled the boat and once again U173 was subjected to another severe shaking. This time the crash-dive had not started when the aircraft crossed the submarine's conning tower and the aircraft's machine gunners peppered the exposed crew. The boat had been engaged on the delicate job of cutting away damage from the day before and this time there was no quick crash-dive. After the Hudson had dropped its charges, the boat began its descent. It was probably saved from more serious damage because it was fully surfaced when the charges detonated. Later the aircraft observed a hundred foot oil patch near the depth-charge scum. After this attack, Schweichel decided to wait until he was well out of range of any aircraft before commencing any further repairs.

That evening No. 53 squadron moved their main base to the newly completed Edinburgh Xeres runway complex in central Trinidad. The base was intended orginally as a satellite field for Waller Field, but it developed later into the main anti-submarine base in the island.

Shortly after midnight, the veteran Suhren ended his only Caribbean patrol by sinking the eight thousand ton Norwegian tanker Vardass, only forty miles from Trinidad's Grand Boca. U564 used a torpedo to stop the vessel and then brought the deck gun into action, setting the tanker on fire. The tanker burned all night and into the next day. The glow on the horizon brought anti-submarine aircraft swarming into the area, but Suhren was well out of the way by the time they arrived.

Two hours later Jurgen Wattenburg in U162 sank his last ship, the new Liberty ship Star of Oregon, seventy miles south of Barbados. The American vessel was on course for Trinidad when Wattenburg used two torpedoes to stop it and then his deck gun to pound the wreck.

At three forty-five in the morning, Markworth in U66 caught the Panamanian registered freighter Sir Huon on its way from Australia to Trinidad, via Capetown. Two torpedoes dispatched the six thousand ton vessel east of the island. At one thirty that afternoon U66 struck again east of Trinidad when she sank the five thousand six hundred ton American freighter West Lashaway. On the following day U66 sank the eight thousand six hundred ton British tanker Winamac, three hundred and ninety miles east of Trinidad. The heavily laden tanker was on its way to Gibraltar when Markworth found it on the last day of the month.

August was the high point of the U-Boats' Caribbean campaign.

The third wave of U-Boats was the largest to operate in the area. In the first week of the month, ten U-Boats operated, while in the second week there were thirteen. The third week saw the record established for the war with nineteen U-Boats operating, one in the Gulf of Mexico and eighteen in the Caribbean or the zone around it.

The third wave began thinning out in the last week of the month until on the last day of August there were only nine boats operating. Ten of the fourteen boats making their way back home across the Atlantic had been damaged by air attack, after having been caught on the surface. The experience of these boats, together with similar occurrences in the Bay of Biscay, was to cause the development of the Metox set and Biscay Cross. With this equipment the boats would be able to detect the transmissions of the early Allied airborne radar sets and be able to dive before the aircraft caught them. These developments were to be first used in August, but it was too late for U94, U166 and U654, they would never go home.

The large concentration of U-Boats in the Caribbean during August had not achieved the level of sinkings that Doenitz had hoped for. Forty-one ships had been sunk in the Caribbean zone, with seven others badly damaged, while the Gulf of Mexico accounted for a further three sunk. Forty-four ships sunk by twenty-six U-Boats, although still above the new tonnage construction rate, was not a high enough ratio. The second wave of U-Boats that operated during May and June achieved a better ratio, but there deployment had been checked by logistics.

The third wave of late July and August had not been checked entirely by logistics, although this factor was still very important. Airpower had tipped the balance. The Caribbean campaign was by no means over and indeed many more ships were to be sunk in the months to come, but the balance began to shift in favour of the Allies. From now on the days of easy sinkings in the Caribbean were over, although there were to be a few notable exceptions. To borrow a Churchillian turn of phrase, it was perhaps the end of the beginning. August was the turning point in the battle of the Caribbean.

The third wave had accounted for eighty-one ships of four hundred and fifty-six thousand tons in July and August, bringing the Caribbean theatre totals up to two hundred and sixty-two ships sunk, at just over one and a half million tons. This had been achieved in six and a half months. This gave the Caribbean an average of forty point three ships per month. It cost the Germans five U-Boats sunk in the theatre and two others U158 and U502 lost on the way home.

This meant that Doenitz was losing one U-Boat in the theatre for every fifty-two ships sunk. This was a very favourable rate of exchange and he intended to continue the Caribbean campaign. However, the North Atlantic air-gap still existed and logistically this was an easier area for the U-Boats to operate in. Before the Allies finally closed this air-gap, he intended to try and reap whatever profit he could from the North Atlantic and many of the U-Boats would now be diverted to that zone. The U-Boats would not return to the Caribbean in massive strength until after their defeat in the North Atlantic, but by then it would be too late.

Admiral King was under pressure from Roosevelt and Churchill above, and Admirals Andrews and Hoover from below, to give the Atlantic war against the U-Boats a higher priority. The end of August saw this escalation in priority finally bear fruit.

The results for Trinidad were dramatic indeed. September saw the focal point of the Caribbean war finally achieve the status of two patrol squadrons. VP-53 transferred from San Juan to Chaguaramas and their PBYs were joined shortly afterwards by the VP-74 PBM Mariners. The Mariner was the best flying boat produced by the Americans during the war. It was not as famous as the Catalina, but was adjudged superior both in performance and combat capability. The aircraft was capable of lifting up to eight thousand pounds of bombs as well as absorbing considerable punishment. VP-74 arrived with only four of the type, but the numbers would build and the gull-winged, sea-grey, camouflaged flying-boats would become very familiar in the Caribbean.

Changes also took place at Waller Field, when No. 1 bombardment squadron moved to Edinburgh Field, where together with No. 53 squadron, they formed the 9th Bomber Group. No. 1 squadron's place at Waller Field was taken by the 22nd Pursuit Squadron, equipped with twelve P-39 and four P-40 fighters. These aircraft were not any use from an anti-submarine point of view, but they performed as a Scouting Unit, alongside the US Navy VS-4 and USMC VMS-3, with their longer ranged OS2N Kingfishers at Chaguaramas. Presumably, the fighter element may have had something to do with the threat from South America.

Nevertheless, the island now boasted fighters, bombers and long-range patrol planes. Other Caribbean changes accompanied this reorganisation in Trinidad. VS-62 and VP-92 continued to serve in Guantanamo Bay, but VP-92 now operated a detachment at Coco Solo Naval Air Station, Panama, alongside the B18s of 45th squadron at France Field. The responsibility for continuing the Panama deployment of patrol planes eventually passed to the Trinidad Sector.

No. 59 squadron continued to operate their A20A Havocs from the island of Curacao, covering the tanker terminus for the Caribbean convoys. VP-204 moved in to Naval Air Station San Juan and operated a detachment of PBMs at Antigua. The detachment used the beach opposite the newly completed Coolidge Field as their base, while ashore the 10th bombardment squadron helped to cover the northeast corner of the Caribbean.

No. 5 bombardment squadron with their headquarters at Boringquen, increased their St. Lucia detachment to nine B18s, serving alongside four OS2Ns from VMS 3. Another new unit in the zone was the 430th bombardment squadron which operated B18s alongside the RAF Hudsons at Atkinson Field, British Guiana. In the far south, the RAF Hudsons and 99th squadron B18s continued operating from Zandary Field. The changes were comprehensive and there was now not an area of the Caribbean or adjacent South American coast which was not regularly patrolled.

Trinidad was now firmly established as the Caribbean convoy terminus and its command structure and naval forces reflected this. On seventh September, Rear Admiral Jessie B. Oldendorf took command of the Trinidad Sector. At last there was a naval man in command, to prosecute what was essentially a naval war.

Chaguaramas now boasted a considerable force of naval vessels which included, six USN destroyers, three RN destroyers, four US, one RN and a Dutch gunboat, one submarine, fourteen PCs, nine RN MTBs, two US PTs and the vessels of the TRNVR. The Gulf of Paria was now well protected, indeed over-protected as its minefields were soon to prove, but the stretch of water had not as yet reached its full potential.

It is arguable whether Albrecht Achilles was responsible for this greatly enhanced scale of protection, or whether it would have come naturally because of Trinidad's strategic position. At the very least, he hastened realisation of the magnitude of the threat. In doing this he may also have opened many eyes to Trinidad's potential.

September started very quietly. The number of U-Boats was steadily diminishing and for the first five days there were no merchant-ship sinkings, but during that same period the third U-Boat died. U162 had been building up towards completing another successful cruise and it is probable that if the boat had survived, it may have surpassed the record set by U156, but the forty-one year old Wattenburg was to become the Royal Navy's only Caribbean victim.

The boat had been built by Seebeckwerft of Bremerhaven and accepted into service in September of 1941. Jurgen Wattenburg, late of the Graf Spee, took command and sank his first ship out of convoy ONS 67 in February 1942. The boat's next patrol was its most successful, sinking nine ships in the Caribbean in May and setting a record for tonnage. The boat with the Roman sword on a shield as its personal emblem, left Lorient on July seventh for the second Caribbean cruise.

Fourteen days later Wattenburg was on station off the coast of Trinidad. After attacking convoy TAW (S) on nineteenth of August and shadowing the convoy for two days, he moved eastwards to the area around Barbados and commenced hunting big ships. With his last ship at the end of August, Wattenburg had already reached thirty thousand four hundred and eighty-one tons, with an average of over seven thousand six hundred per ship. On first September, U162 sent off its last radio report to U-Boat headquarters. That evening Wattenburg made a serious mistake. He inadvertently attacked three destroyers.

The three destroyers, HMS Pathfinder, Quentin and Vimy, were enroute to Trinidad to pick up a convoy of tankers to escort back across the Atlantic. Pathfinder was an Onslow class, war-construction destroyer of fifteen hundred tons. She carried four single four inch guns and was fitted with Type 286 radar. Quentin was also one of the war-construction programme destroyers, but of the Q class, with four single four point seven inch guns and the Type 286 radar. The oldest of the trio was the 1917 built V Class destroyer HMS Vimy. Displacing fourteen hundred tons, she had been refitted with two twin four inch high angle turrets and Type 271 surface search radar. All three ships were fitted with asdic and carried depthcharges, both for firing off the launchers and from the rails at the stern.

On the third of September, the three ships were in line-abreast formation with Pathfinder in the center, Quentin to port and Vimy to starboard. They were roughly fifty miles northeast of Tobago. Shortly before six o' clock that evening, Jurgen Wattenburg in U162 sighted a destroyer at ten miles. He had ample time to get out of the way, but working on the principle that only the bold succeed, he decided to attack. Not many U-Boat commanders had sunk destroyers and undoubtedly it would look good if he got one. At this stage, his hydrophone operator should have informed him that there were three sets of propellers on the bearing, but for some unexplained reason, Wattenburg never got this information until it was too late.

U162 dived to periscope depth and waited for the destroyer to come into range. At five past six, HMS Pathfinder obtained an asdic contact to port at twelve hundred yards. The officer of the watch pressed the actionstations alarm and turned the ship to run in and attack.

Almost immediately, the captain arrived on the bridge and countermanded the order. Pathfinder was stopped to give the asdic operator the best possible conditions for sound detection. It was at this moment that

Wattenburg, still thinking that he was attacking a single destroyer, fired a torpedo. The hydrophone operator on Pathfinder picked up the sound of the torpedo and reported it to the bridge. Seconds later the bridge personnel on both Pathfinder and Quentin could see the torpedo. At first it appeared that the torpedo would pass well ahead of Quentin, but it made a wide turn to the right and came straight for Quentin. The destroyer had great difficulty in getting out of the way and there were a few bad moments when it looked as if Quentin could not turn fast enough. The torpedo passed down the starboard side of the still heeling destroyer. From the bridge they could clearly see the whisker type pistol on the torpedo as it continued its erratic course.

By this stage Pathfinder had a firm submarine contact at six hundred yards. The destroyer quickly increased speed to make an attack. On the assumption that the U-Boat would dive deep after having fired the torpedo, the depth-charges were set to go off between one hundred and fifty, and three hundred feet. As soon as he heard the propellers speed up, Wattenburg increased his speed and moved southwards. He had indeed gone deep and as Pathfinder passed over, ten depth-charges rolled off its stern.

The charges sank at the rate of fourteen feet per second, until their hydrostatic triggers caused detonation. It was an accurate attack and the hammer blows from the three hundred pound charges shattered a number of instruments and equipment, including the hydrophone gear. U162 was now virtually blind and in a highly dangerous predicament. The depth-charges had also damaged one of the diving tanks. Up above all three destroyers could hear a loud underwater whistling sound, probably caused by the escape of high pressure air.

Pathfinder quickly regained asdic contact and was about to make another attack, when they saw Quentin gathering speed for an attack. As Quentin passed over the U162, six depth-charges left the ship. Two charges were set to explode at one hundred and fifty feet, two others were set to two fifty and the third pair to three hundred and fifty. U162 was bracketed by the exploding charges and the massive pressure-wave further damaged her diving planes and rudders. Leaks also developed in the U-Boat's engine room and her damage control party had their work cut out, but Wattenburg was a seasoned campaigner and had no intention of giving up as yet. The boat was rigged for silent running and the leaks plugged, as she very slowly crept away.

It was now six thirty and all three destroyers had lost contact with the elusive boat. The wily Wattenburg had managed to give them the slip, but it proved only to be a temporary reprieve. By now the destroyer captains

were aware that they were dealing with a master of the hunt and they
formed up to the westward of the initial attack position and began a syste-
matic search to the east. The senior officer had assumed that the U-Boat
would run to the east to escape towards open water and indeed within
thirty minutes, Vimy had asdic contact.

Both Pathfinder and Quentin had made attacks on U162 and now it
was Vimy's turn. The old destroyer crept right over the U-Boat without
attacking and regained asdic contact astern at eight hundred yards. Down
below, the crew of U162 could hear the destroyer's propellers pass right
over them and they braced for the blast of the depth-charges that never
came. The captain of Vimy was merely making sure that he had the U-Boat
pinpointed and after running out to fourteen hundred yards, he turned to
attack. This time fourteen depth-charges, set to one fifty, three hundred
and three hundred and eighty-five feet, rolled off the destroyer's stern.
Wattenburg had not been fooled by the destroyer's dummy-attack and when
he heard the destroyer running in, he turned towards it and came up to a
shallower depth. The result was that Vimy's charges exploded astern of the
U-Boat and too deep to cripple the already heavily damaged boat. Once
again the hunters lost U162.

The destroyers had no intention of letting the U-Boat get away and
having failed to dispose of it quickly, they now settled down to a comprehensive anti-submarine search of the area that went on until ten o'clock that
night. It was now over four hours since the first contact and two and a half
hours since the last attack. The nerve-wracking scratching of asdic beams
on the U-Boat below and the constant thrashing of destroyer propellers,
were exhausting the crew of U162, but Wattenburg was handling the boat
brilliantly.

It seemed impossible that any U-Boat commander could escape from
three experienced destroyers, particularly with the hydrophone dead, and
the boat badly damaged, but Wattenburg was doing it. By the end of the anti-submarine sweep, the senior officer of Pathfinder was convinced that the
U-Boat had surfaced and made off in an easterly direction. He did not intend to give up either. It was unthinkable that a U-Boat could outguess the
three hunters and they decided that the best course of action would be for
the destroyers to spread out and leave the attack area, conducting radar and
asdic searches to the east. Whether the boat was surfaced or submerged they
would pick him up as he tried for the open Atlantic.

At this stage Graham de Chair in command of Vimy, suggested to the
senior officer that there was a possibility that U162 was to the southeast of
their position. This was based on the fact that during the last attack

made by Vimy, the U-Boat had been plotted moving in that direction. The three destroyers moved off to the southeast conducting asdic searches. Wattenburg was working on only the information that his ears could pick up and as soon as he heard the destroyers move off, he slowly turned onto the opposite heading and slipped behind them. Wattenburg was on a course of three one five degrees and there was a good chance that he would get clean away.

U162 was heading towards the Caribbean islands, exactly opposite to the direction the destroyers guessed he would move on. If U162 had stayed underwater for another hour she would have pulled it off, but the air in the boat was becoming foul and his nerve-wracked crew needed a break. Surfacing would also give them a chance to assess the damage to the boat as well as allowing them to head northwest at nearly three times their submerged speed. Cautiously U162 came up to periscope depth and Wattenburg scanned the sea. The horizon was clear, the destroyers had gone and it was safe to surface. As the boat broke the surface, the hatch was flung open and a cool draught of fresh air swept through the boat. The diesels coughed into life and U162 began her run to safety.

Well to the southeast the three destroyers had completed their asdic sweep. It was now ten fifty and time for the three ships to spread out and carry out their planned sweep to the east. The hunt for U162 was going to be a long one, probably well into the following day. The sweep eastward was scheduled to begin at eleven o'clock and while the three destroyers slowly edged southeast, the senior officer on Pathfinder sat down to study the plot.

The chart was crisscrossed with their tracks, but there was one small cone that appeared not to have been searched. The center of this cone was three one five degrees. The senior officer was a careful man and although it seemed an unlikely direction for the U-Boat to take, he did not intend to leave a stone unturned. As a precaution he delayed the planned sweep to the east and instructed Vimy to carry out a search on three one five degrees. While Vimy was ensuring that the cone was clear, the two other destroyers would steam slowly northwards to the original attack site. When Vimy was finished, she would rejoin and they would carry out the combined sweep to the east. Thus it transpired that Vimy set off along the same course which U162 had taken.

At ten minutes past eleven, Vimy's radar operator reported a contact dead ahead at twenty-eight hundred yards. As soon as the bridge had the contact visual they realised that they had found the illusive U-Boat. The destroyer increased speed and almost immediately, her forward four inch guns opened fire. The gunnery officer thought that he detected a direct hit on the U-Boat conning tower with the second round, but the U-Boat's crew later denied that any shells hit them. In any case, the traditional naval officer's love of ramming now came to the fore and the captain ordered the guns to cease fire. The flashes from the guns were blinding the bridge personnel and obscuring the U-Boat which they intended to ram.

Wattenburg must have realised that there was now very little chance of his damaged boat escaping, but he hadn't given up yet. Quite unexpectedly, two red flares soared upwards from the U-Boat's conning tower. Wattenburg was trying another ruse. Two things happened. By chance, two red flares happened to be the Allied naval recognition signal in force for that night and their appearance confused the destroyer's crew and secondly, the flares were so bright that they blinded the bridge personnel and they lost sight of the U-Boat.

On the eastern horizon, Pathfinder and Quentin were not sure what was going on. The gunfire followed by the flares could mean that Vimy had sunk the U-Boat, or that the boat had sunk Vimy. Both destroyers turned towards the fighting to the west. Vimy in the meantime, was racing at full speed towards a target which she could not see, with her guns silent.

When the U-Boat finally came in sight, Vimy was racing off at a tangent with U162 broad on her port bow. In the destroyer full port wheel was put on and she heeled alarmingly, clawing round to port in her attempt to ram the U-Boat. Just at this moment, the bridge personnel realised that instead of ramming, they were going to be rammed. U162 was also under full helm and coming for Vimy's engine room. The destroyer went from full port wheel to full starboard wheel in her attempt to get away. The U-Boat could easily have ripped its way through the destroyer's thin side plates and de Chair was acting to save his ship. Vimy rolled to port and started clawing her way round to starboard as she fought to get away. Vimy's violent swing away saved her and the U-Boat only hit her a glancing blow that just dented the plates. The damage from the glancing blow was minor, but the aftermath was crippling. The racing destroyer with full starboard wheel on was skidding to port, and the U-Boat ended up sliding along the destroyer's side.

The hardened Krupp steel of the U-Boat's pressure hull came into contact with the destroyer's port propellers. Vimy came to a stop some distance off, minus one of her propellers. At this stage, it is probable that if Wattenburg had steerageway, he could have turned and emptied his torpedo tubes at the destroyer, but he had finally given up. His U-Boat had a damaged pressure hull, diving planes, rudders and no listening gear, with three destroyers in contact. The U-Boat's crew were ordered up onto the casing.

To the watchers on Vimy's bridge, the sight of German sailors on the casing dressed in shorts and swimming trunks looked very suspicious. It was possible that they were giving up, but then there could be others down below who would dive the boat and escape. Vimy decided that what they were witnessing was a ruse and the damaged destroyer gathered way on her single propeller. One is tempted to believe that there was a little annoyance at the fouling up of the ramming. As Vimy steamed past the sinking hull of the U162, a single depth-charge left her launcher and landed in the sea alongside the stricken boat. The blast from the charge going off with its shallow setting, flung all the Germans from the U-Boat's casing into the sea. By the time Vimy manoeuvreing with difficulty, could get close again, only the top of U162's conning tower was visible.

U162 went to her watery grave on the underwater ridge between the Barbados and Tobago Basins. Her chief engineer went with her. He had been responsible for getting U162 going again after the punishing depth-charge attacks, and now his responsibility was to ensure that she sank. He died down below opening the sea cocks when the depth-charge went off. One other sailor was lost, probably during the explosion of the last charge.

Pathfinder and Quentin were now on the scene and the two destroyers picked up forty-nine survivors, including Wattenburg. Then Vimy had to run a series of tests to ensure that she was still seaworthy, before the three proceeded. At seven minutes past two in the morning, eight hours after the first contact, the three destroyers turned for Trinidad and left the scene of the demise of the third U-Boat.

Graham de Chair received a DSC for his part in the action and HMS Vimy went on to team up with HMS Beverley in the sinking of U187, six months later. HMS Pathfinder teamed up with HMS Biters aircraft to sink another U-Boat that had served in the Caribbean. They caught U203 in April 1943 and destroyed her in the North Atlantic. HMS Quentin was not so fortunate. She was unable to dodge the next torpedo fired at her. Three months after the action with U162, she was sunk by an Italian air-dropped torpedo off the island of Galita, north of Algiers.

The survivors from U162 were landed at Port of Spain and taken to the St. James prisoner-of-war camp. A US Army Intelligence officer witnessed their arrival in Trinidad and commented that they were an undisciplined lot, suggesting in his view that they were poor military material. It was probably the same officer who commented that Achilles was a liar. If the battle of the Atlantic proved anything, it was that a sparkling uniform and a clean shave do not necessarily signify efficiency.

After a couple of weeks the U162 crew were flown to the United States, where they ended up picking cotton in Arizona for the next four years. During this period twenty-five Germans escaped from the POW camp. Wattenburg stayed free the longest, thirty-six days.

CHAPTER

9

The Changing of the Guard

The sinking of U162 left only six boats remaining in the theatre and they were all nearing the end of their patrols. U171 continued its lonely Gulf of Mexico deployment, while Steinholf in U511 guarded the Windward Passage. Perhaps guarded may be the wrong word to use, because convoys were passing through without loss. There was no chance for a single boat to challenge the strong escort groups with unlimited air support, that now characterised the area.

U558, U164 and U217 patrolled in an arc from south of Haiti, past Aruba, to the convoy terminus in Trinidad. In the lucrative area east of Trinidad, only U66 was on station. U553 and U564 had left the Caribbean on September first and were both homeward bound. Neither boat would return to the Caribbean. Thurmann in U553 did not have long to live, but U564 would operate in the Atlantic under a new commander until June 1943. Reinhard Suhren handed over U564 to Hans Fiedler on his return and received the Swords to his Knight's Cross. The U-Boat was sunk by a 10th Coastal command squadron Halifax in the Bay of Biscay on the day after it had shot down a similar aircraft. Eighteen of her crew survived and were rescued by U185.

The end of August also signalled the end of the useful Italian participation in the Caribbean campaign. Six Italian submarines, the Torelli, Da Vinci, Finzi, Tazzoli, Morsini and Calvi, operated in the theatre. They usually cruised to the north or the east of the island chain and managed to sink twelve merchant ships within the zone. Torelli was seized by the Japanese, while Da Vinci was sunk in May 1943 near the Azores, by HMS Active and HMS Ness. On Italy's surrender in September 1943, the Finzi was seized by the Germans and renamed UIT-21. She operated as a U-Boat until August 1944, when she was scuttled in Lorient. The Morsini was lost in the Bay of Biscay on eleventh August 1942, cause unknown, while the Tazzoli was sunk in the same area in May 1943 by air attack. The last boat Calvi, was lost in July 1942 to HMS Lulworth.

On the day after U162 was lost, Pfeffer in U171 sank the six thousand five hundred ton tanker Amatlan in the Gulf of Mexico. This was the last ship sunk in the Gulf for a full six months and then only one more ship was to die in these waters. With the shutdown of the U-Boat playground in the Gulf, the United States Navy had finally achieved control of its coastal waters. They had paid an awful price for the prewar neglect.

After the lone sinking, Pfeffer left the Gulf via the Yucatan Channel. His single Gulf patrol had been in marked contrast to the experience of the previous boats and no doubt, he must have wondered often what the area had been like during its hey-day. He made his way eastward and left the Caribbean via the Mona Passage. U171 was not to operate in the Caribbean again, in fact the boat had but a short run to make. On the way home through the Bay of Biscay, she became one of the few U-Boat victims of a mine. It may have been laid by the British, or it might possibly have been a drifting German mine. In either case, U171 became the third U-Boat to be lost on its way home from the Caribbean. Twenty-two of the crew died in the explosion and the remainder were rescued by the Germans. Pfeffer was among the survivors and he went on to command of U548 later in the war.

At twelve forty-five on September sixth, Fechner in U164 achieved his second and last Caribbean success. He sent the Canadian freighter John A. Holloway to the bottom, one hundred and twenty-five miles northwest of Aruba. The boat still had another fruitless week of patrolling to complete before it left the area. On the same day, Schacht in U507 finally left the Brazilian coast and began his return journey.

Rather belatedly, U-Boat command realised the misjudgement which they had made with the Brazilian coastal deployment and ordered all boats to stay at least twenty miles off the coast. This came after the Brazilian declaration of war and was a classic case of closing the barn door long after the horse had bolted. The damage had already been done and Germany now had to face another not inconsiderable foe.

In addition to the basing of US forces, the Brazilian navy was to play an active part in prosecuting the war against the U-Boats. Brazil would also become the only South American nation to commit ground forces to combat in the European theatre. The events of August had also broken German influence in Brazil for good, so that by the end of the war the German community in the country was forced to become truly Brazilian, even to the extent of their language, which at one time had been taught in all schools.

In the first ten days of September, only three merchant ships were sunk in the Caribbean theatre. The first had been U171's tanker in the Gulf of Mexico, the U164 got its freighter and the third belonged to U66.

On the ninth of the month, Markworth sank the neutral Swedish freighter Peiping, northeast of Antigua. This was the last ship of the patrol and indeed, U66 was on its way home from its last Caribbean patrol. This Type IXC boat was one of the Caribbean Aces, coming third in total tonnage sunk. First under Zapp in April, and then under Markworth, the boat had accounted for fourteen ships, of eighty thousand seven hundred and forty-six tons. Added to this U66 had damaged seven other vessels with torpedoes and mines. After a rendezvous with the tanker U460, Markworth took the boat into Lorient on the twenty-ninth.

U66 was to make three more successful North Atlantic patrols. On the third of these patrols, the boat chased a tanker southward into the area north of the Caribbean and was caught on the surface by an American-based Mariner. The crew suffered three killed and eight wounded in the attack. Markworth was one of the critically injured and the boat had to rendezvous with the tanker U117 for a replacement commander to be transferred aboard to take the U-Boat home. On its eighth war patrol, U66 under Frerks was sunk by a homing torpedo while on its way home from the Gulf of Guinea. An Avenger aircraft operating from the USS Bogue finally brought an end to the boat's illustrious career. By this stage, U66 had been responsible for the sinking of twenty-eight ships.

The remnants of the third wave were one by one turning for home and the Caribbean was emptying of U-Boats, but not for long. The first group of boats of the fourth wave, U175, U201, U202, U332, U512, U514, U515 and U516 were taking over. It was the changing of the guard. These boats were all new to the Caribbean and on the same day that Markworth sank the Pieping, U-Boat headquarters gave U514 and U515 freedom to operate anywhere east of Trinidad.

Of these boats U512 would never leave the Caribbean zone and her story starts on the tenth of September. The Type IXC boat began experiencing problems that day, when north of the Caribbean it chased a freighter for fifteen hours. The chase lasted all day and during that time, two attacks were carried out. On both occasions the torpedoes missed the target. Kapitanleutnant Wolfgang Schultz was on his first war patrol in command of a brand new boat, and U-Boat headquarters automatically put down his failure with the torpedo attacks to inexperience.

However, Schultz had other ideas and he signalled to say that he believed that the target ship had anti-torpedo nets rigged, because the hydrophone data for the target and the torpedoes were the same. He felt that he had hit the ship. Possibly because of the excuse he gave, the Staff officers took the unusual step of making a note in the command war diary, to the effect that they did not believe him.

Actually, the Americans did experiment with anti-torpedo nets on a ship and the vessel is reputed to have reached harbour with a torpedo tangled up in its net, but the idea was unworkable and dropped. It is possible that Schultz was the man that tangled up that net, but then it is also possible that the Staff officers were correct and Shultz had simply missed his target. In either case, the exchange of signals soured relations between the boat and its headquarters, starting a chain of misfortunes for U512, which were to run until October.

On Friday eleventh of September, one of the new wave of boats brought the war to the island of Barbados and caused a major flap. Germany started World War Two with just over fifty U-Boats commanded by long and painstakingly trained officers. During the first two years of the conflict, the U-Boat expansion programme was just gaining momentum and there was still time to train the new commanders, not to the standard of the first group, but in the hard school of the North Atlantic convoy battles.

Many of these early Aces were now dead. The original commanders who first set the Caribbean afire, came from the second group of Aces. The men commanding the fourth wave of U-Boats to hit the Caribbean, made up for their lack of experience and hasty training by extreme aggressiveness and a sense of mission. Although they were operating in an environment that was becoming increasingly hostile, their achievements were no less spectacular. Hans-Jurgen Auffermann in command of the Type IXC boat U514 was a good example of the new commanders.

After lunch on the eleventh, a report was received in Trinidad saying that a U-Boat had been sighted off Carlisle Bay in Barbados. At this stage of the war in the Caribbean, people were claiming to see U-Boats all over the area and such reports were being received in Trinidad on a daily basis. The report from Barbados was filed among the volumes of such sightings and not taken too seriously.

In fact Auffermann had been hanging around Barbados for several days. He had not found any worthwhile targets and decided to check the island's harbour to see what sort of trouble he could cause. Since Achilles' time, all the major Caribbean harbours were protected by anti-submarine nets, but the existence of a net seemed only to be a challenge to Auffermann. To be effective, these anti-submarine nets needed to be covered by guns and constant patrols, but Barbados had neither of these.

The island's Volunteer Force manned a number of coast-watching stations and the only Regulars on the island were an RAF signals detachment based at the airport. Their job was to handle RAF signal traffic and assist in the triangulation of U-Boat radio signals. Auffermann was to change the status of the military in Barbados, by employing a very unconventional form of attack.

U514 was on its first patrol under a new commander. Auffermann's previous command experience revolved around a three day stint when his captain in U69 fell ill and he was called upon to act. He intended to make this first patrol worthwhile and the Bridgetown harbour seemed like an excellent place to begin.

At four thirty in the afternoon, U514 came into the outer harbour and nosed its way towards the net defences. Through his periscope, Auffermann was able to see the line of buoys that marked the anti-submarine net and he also noted the absence of surface patrols guarding the obstacle. Five minutes later, the four bow torpedoes erupted from their tubes and sped across the anchorage, towards the net defences. As soon as number four torpedo had left its tube, Auffermann began to turn U514.

The boat had hardly begun to answer the helm before one after the other, the four torpedoes hit the net. Watchers on the shore could see the line of buoys beginning to pitch upwards, long before they heard the shattering detonation of the four six hundred pound warheads going off. Great fountains of water rose upwards and hung over the shattered sections of the net, while the huge two ton buoys were being tossed about as though they were tennis balls. The consternation in the tiny harbour can be imagined. A few clear-sighted individuals probably guessed what the great upheaval in the quiet harbour meant and silently blessed the net, without fully realising just what the unseen U-Boat meant to do. Auffermann continued his turn until the stern of the boat was lined up with the harbour and two more torpedoes leapt out of their tubes and began their race for the torn up net.

The Canadian freighter Cornwallis was anchored in the harbour and by this stage the crew were all on deck, watching the great upheaval taking place around the net. The fifth torpedo also detonated against a section of net and another great explosion tossed water and sections of net skywards, allowing the sixth and final torpedo to sweep through.

The watchers on the Cornwallis were horror-struck to see a torpedo emerge from the chaos of sea, sand and wreckage that had been that net and come charging through the crystal clear water, straight at their ship. They barely had time to get away from the threatened side of the ship, before the engine of destruction entered number three cargo hold. The explosion burst a great hole in the ship's side and shattered the adjacent engine-room bulkhead. The sea rushed in, flooding the boiler room and washing cargo out of the great gash in her side. Cornwallis began settling onto the sand, as Auffermann swept out of Bridgetown harbour, probably immensely satisfied with the work his torpedoes had done. Behind him the whole island was in a state of considerable confusion.

The frantic signals to Trinidad generated an immediate response. Two B18s were scrambled from Edinburgh Field, on one of which there were a number of intelligence officers. It would take the bombers at least an hour to get to Barbados and the island needed quicker reinforcement, even if it was to check the onset of panic. St. Lucia was instructed to dispatch a couple of OS2N Kingfishers. They could reach the island long before the Trinidad based aircraft. RAF bombers on patrol east of Trinidad were diverted and two RN MTBs left the docks at Benbow, crashing westwards to get to the Bocas, before turning northeast for the seven hour trip to Barbados. The American army history of the Caribbean describes the situation with just one word, — SNAFU.

Barbados had always been a holiday resort and no one had imagined that a serious threat existed, but now it looked as though the opening up of the net could be the prelude to a raid on the island. Haunting some of the planners was a German initiative that appears never to have been considered by the Germans themselves.

The German U-Boat campaign was probably one of Germany's most effective methods of waging war, but the U-Boats always operated unsupported. Doenitz's concept of war against the lines of communication was little understood, even within his own navy. There was little coordination or support for the U-Boats from the German surface navy and in fact, they thought only in terms of U-Boats supporting the big ships.

There was virtually no support forthcoming for the U-Boats from either the Luftwaffe or the Wehrmacht, but Auffermann's raid on Barbados highlighted what might have been possible. Barbados had always been staunchly British and there is no question of the Germans ever winning the support or cooperation of the island's population, but this was not important. What was of paramount importance was the strategic position that the island occupied. It lay one hundred miles east of the Caribbean and could have been the bow that shot arrows of destruction at the Caribbean and influenced the whole course of the war.

The German capital ships spent most of World War Two tying down Allied forces, without achieving material destruction. Other than the sinking of the Hood and the losses incured by convoy PQ 17, they were indeed a waste. In this respect Hitler's judgement of their usefulness may have been correct, but if he together with the heirarchy of the Reich had understood what Doenitz was doing, some of these capital ships could have been very usefully employed, supporting the U-Boats in their pivotal role.

Had the Channel dash in February 1942 by the Scharnhorst and Gneisenau been delayed, the two ships could have made their dash in mid 1942, ostensibly to the traditional South Atlantic hunting ground, but in reality with the Caribbean island of Barbados as their destination.

Each ship could have carried a German infantry regiment and been accompanied by their attendant destroyers. A combination of a diversionary sortie by the Tirpitz and other deception methods, along with the massed strength of the U-Boats, would have ensured that they reached the undefended strategically placed island. Blockade runners and the U-tankers could have followed up the two ships or preceded them.

Barbados could have become the Caribbean U-Boat base. The big ships would not have survived. Preferably they could have stayed in Barbados and become anti-aircraft and coastal defensive batteries, as many of them ended up anyway, or they could have landed their troops and supplies and proceeded into the Caribbean on an orgy of destruction, in support of the U-Boats. They would have died gloriously, but the consequences for the Allies would have been catastrophic.

With Barbados as a temporary refuelling and re-arming base, the U-Boats would have denied the use of the Caribbean and its associated zone to all Allied shipping. The existence of a German base even a temporary one, would have brought to reality all the American concerns about South America and the threat to the soft underbelly of the United States. Who knows on what course the Vichy French in Martinique and French Guiana would have embarked? What would the German-dominated South American

Republics have done? Where would have the Caribbean adventure ended?

Yet, all this is not of paramount importance. What is important is the fact that the German Caribbean adventure would have temporarily swung the centre of gravity of World War Two away from Europe. In mid-1942 German arms were triumphant everywhere. The Allies would have been forced to react with immediate and massive reinforcement of the Caribbean. Most of the British Home Fleet would have had to concentrate in the Caribbean, providing of course that the other German capital ships would have permitted such a redeployment.

The whole American Atlantic Feet, possibly with reinforcements from the Pacific, would also have been redeployed. Even elements of RAF bomber command would have had to be diverted from their German offensive to the Caribbean.

At this stage of the war the US Navy Atlantic Fleet and their Army Air Corps were not up to the standard of experience or equipment to have handled this threat alone. While this massive shift of resources was taking place, the U-Boats could have cut the Atlantic lifeline, both in the North Atlantic and between South and North America. With two German infantry regiments in Barbados and U-Boats operating without a logistic problem, many other acts of mischief could have been perpetrated throughout the region.

How long could have this German adventure lasted? The question revolved around how aggressively the other German capital ships were utilised, but the fact is that the whole operation would have been in support of the primary naval weapon, the U-Boat. Assuming that the Allies took three months to eliminate the German threat in Barbados, then the strategic picture would have been permanently altered.

Firstly, the Russian front would have paid the price. The cutting off of Allied supplies and the shift of resources, might have allowed the German troops to reach the river Volga and set up their defensive positions. The battle of Stalingrad would not have been fought in 1942. From a British and American point of view, the battles of Alam Halfa, El Alemain and operation Torch would not have taken place in 1942 with the resultant strategic consequences.

The shift of American Pacific resources would have given Japan a breathing space after the disastrous battle of Midway. On the other hand if the adventure had been mounted early enough, the battle of Midway might not have been fought. All this would have cost Germany only two battle cruisers and two infantry regiments. In the meantime, the U-Boats would have achieved the primary job of cutting the lifeline.

It appears that only one man in the hierachy of the Reich could see what the U-Boats were capable of. By the time Auffermann demonstrated what was possible, it was almost too late for such an adventure, but during May, June or July, the history of World War Two could have been altered.

Saturday twelfth of September is an important date in the history of the war. This is the date on which Hartenstein in U156 sank the liner Laconia. Before this drama was played out, another of the New Guard who would also achieve fame, began his career off Trinidad.

Concern over the situation in Barbados was at its height when U515 moved in towards Trinidad's northeastern tip. The Type IXC boat built by Deutsche Werft of Hamburg was under its young commander Werner Henke. He was on his first patrol in a new boat, which had only recently joined the tenth Flotilla at Lorient. Despite the dire warnings from U-Boat headquarters about the aircraft based in Trinidad, Henke intended to operate close inshore to ensure that he found targets. Midnight on the eleventh found U515 cruising slowly westwards, towards Trinidad's Manzanilla Point. At two o'clock in the morning, he sighted the large Panamanian registered tanker Stanvac Melbourne, on a course of three-one-zero degrees.

The tanker was enroute to Trinidad to join a New York bound convoy, when U515 pulled abeam of it. At three o'clock in the morning, the first torpedo crashed into the side of the ten thousand and thirteen ton tanker. The vessel's volatile cargo caught fire almost immediately, as the great ship staggered to a halt. Henke did not want the vessel to burn and serve as a beacon for anti-submarine aircraft and sent two more torpedoes crashing into the ship. The radio operator barely had time to get off his distress signal, before the ship began breaking up. She went down in fifty fathoms, forty miles off Manzanilla Point. Ironically, she was sunk only seventeen miles from Darien Rock, which the US Army aircraft used as their bombing range.

With the flames from the Stanvac Melbourne quickly extinguished, Henke turned eastwards and began to cruise slowly away from the island. Forty minutes later, the Dutch tanker Woensdrecht came into sight, also heading for Trinidad and Henke manoeuvred his boat into position for an attack. He estimated the vessel at six thousand tons and decided to use two torpedoes. In fact the Woensdrecht was a small ship of only four thousand six hundred and sixty-eight tons, but this made little difference to the outcome. Henke had met a ship he could not sink.

The two torpedoes that Henke fired, both detonated on the tanker's side. Two great holes were blown in the plates and in one case the plates on the other side of the ship were opened up by the blast. The crew lost no time in abandoning ship, but no tanker ever died as hard as the Woensdrecht. The vessel just wallowed in the slight swell and settled a little lower. There was no fire and Henke could not discern any sign that she was going down. The ship's radio operator had managed to get off a distress signal and even as Henke watched, the patrol vessels were leaving the US Navy base for the scene of the attack.

Henke had fired three torpedoes at the previous big tanker and now two more at this stubborn little ship, which left him with only one stern tube still loaded. He fired his stern torpedo at the little ship and watched as the six hundred pound warhead detonated on the little ship's side. When the fountain of water had cleared, the grievously wounded ship still floated. All the torpedo tubes were now empty and still the little ship defied him. Barely an hour before, three torpedoes had broken up a ship more than double the size of the Woensdrecht, but the little Woensdrecht only floated slightly lower in the water.

Henke called on his crew to hurry up reloading the bow tubes, because it was almost dawn and soon the escorts would be on him, − not to mention the dreaded aircraft. It seemed like forever, but eventually his First Watchkeeping officer reported number one tube loaded. Henke brought the boat in close to the little tanker and loosed the torpedo at the ship. Even as the torpedo was charging across the dark water, the lookouts reported aircraft approaching. U515 crash-dived so Henke did not see the final explosion, but his hydrophone operator could hear very well when a torpedo went off that close. Incredibly, the Woensdrecht absorbed the fourth torpedo, without catching fire or breaking up. When Henke could finally take a periscope look at the vessel, it still floated. He could do nothing about it, because there were aircraft overhead and they could hear escort propellers.

At full daylight, the escorts came upon the Woensdrecht. It did not seem possible that she still floated. There were four great holes in her starboard side and she showed very little freeboard, but the game little tanker refused to sink. Her crew were located a few miles away and tentatively a few of them reboarded their ship. Gently, almost tenderly, the escorts took her in tow. The little ship was a hero and they treated her as one. Trinidad's escorts came out in force and surrounded the little ship as she was slowly towed down the island's north coast and into the Boca. Alas, when she finally arrived in Port of Spain harbour, the surveyors reported that the Woensdrecht would never sail the oceans again, but Henke was not to know this. All he knew was that a little ship had taken four of his torpedoes and refused to sink.

Daylight found U515 submerged off Trinidad's east coast, evading the escorts who were hunting for the slayer of the Stanvac Melbourne. While the hunt was concentrated in the east, U558 was submerged off Trinidad's Dragon's Mouth.

After the battle around convoy TAW 15, Gunther Krech had brought his boat down across the Caribbean to the area off Trinidad. He was aware of the Trinidad five-day convoy cycle and he was off the north coast, expecting a convoy. Krech was not disappointed. Shortly after dawn the familiar routine was observed. US Navy PCs and RN MTBs swept out of the Third Boca and spread out, covering the convoy forming-up area. They were followed by the merchant ships, one at a time as they sailed through the Third Boca and were shepherded into formation by the TRNVR vessels. Lastly, the convoy escorts came out to take over from the patrol vessels. Overhead there was the constant roar of aircraft engines as Trinidad's fighters, scouting planes, bombers and patrol planes showed their strength. All Krech could manage was the occasional quick glance through his periscope.

Finally the formalities were over and convoy TAG 5 began moving off to the northwest. Overhead the air cover thinned out somewhat and Krech was able to watch the great assemblage of ships disappear on the northwest horizon. Only then was U558 able to surface and send off a sighting report before taking up a shadowing position.

The convoy ran northwest until they were abeam of the Testigos islands before turning westwards. All day Krech trailed the convoy, being very careful to avoid the flying boat and bomber air escort. Shortly after sunset U558 set off westwards to pull abeam of the convoy. At midnight Krech was inshore of the convoy, forty miles north of Margarita Island.

At twelve twenty, he took U558 into the attack, firing a three torpedo spread from his bow tubes. At twelve twenty-two a torpedo slammed into the Dutch freighter SS Suriname. One minute later the other two torpedoes found the British freighter Empire Lugard. Both ships dropped back sinking, but before Krech could consider another torpedo shot, a flying boat was coming into the attack and his hydrophone operator could hear high speed propellers. As U558 went down, the depth-charges from the aircraft rocked the boat, but they were not within lethal range and Krech was able to get his U-Boat deep, before the destroyer arrived overhead.

For two hours the destroyer stayed over U558, but when dealing with an experienced convoy fighter like Krech, this was not enough. Once the destroyer commander lost contact he raced off to rejoin his convoy, leaving Krech free to surface and renew the attack. In two hours the convoy had only advanced sixteen miles and for a U-Boat this was only an hour's run.

By twenty past two in the morning Krech had U558 once more in an attacking position, with two of his bow tubes reloaded. Eight minutes later the two torpedoes leapt out of their tubes and raced towards the convoy. Before the torpedoes found a target, Krech was forced to crash-dive by another of the air escort. Both torpedoes struck the Dutch freighter Vilja and she dropped out of the convoy and began to go down. This time the escorts seemed to realise that they were dealing with an experienced opponent and they subjected the boat to a long tenacious hunt, ensuring that U558 lost the convoy. The only consolation Krech had was that his hydrophone operator could hear the freighter breaking up on its way to the bottom.

While U558 was engaging TAG 5, Henke was in his favourite area and hard at work. He had spent the daylight hours submerged off the east coast, listening to the escorts searching for him and the rescue operation around the Woensdrecht. After sunset he brought his boat to the surface to charge his batteries and allow fresh air into the craft.

At eight forty, the seven thousand ton British freighter Ocean Vanguard came in sight and once again U515 lined up for an attack. The U-Boat was sitting astride the route from South America and South Africa to Trinidad and there was no shortage of targets. Two torpedoes detonated on the freighter's hull. The first opened up the side of the ship and the second ploughed into the hull a little further aft. The Ocean Vanguard's back was broken and she disappeared within two minutes. No signal went out and all Henke could discover was a collection of floating cargo and hatch covers. The sharks in that area ensured that there were no survivors. The freighter went down in fifty fathoms, forty-five miles off Trinidad's Galera Point. Four hours later and fifteen miles closer to Trinidad, the small Panamanian registered freighter Nimba crossed Henke's bow and one torpedo dispatched the vessel, just as quickly as the Ocean Vanguard. The wreck of the Nimba lies in forty fathoms east of Emerald Shoal.

The twelfth of September had seen a record established. Henke in U515 and Krech in U558 had together accounted for forty-five thousand and thirty-six tons, in a twenty-four hour period. It was the highest daily loss that the Caribbean suffered throughout the whole war and it had been done by just two boats. While this record was being established around Trinidad, Schultz in U512 achieved one of his rare successes by sinking the ten thousand ton tanker Patrick J. Hurley. The sinking took place outside the Caribbean zone. Schultz was making his way southwards towards the islands and either he did not trust his torpedoes or his aim, because he sank the tanker by gunfire alone.

On the other side of the Atlantic, Hartenstein in U156 sank the liner Laconia and found out afterwards that there were two thousand seven hundred passengers on board. This total included eighteen hundred Italian prisoners of war. Hartenstein loaded his boat with as many of the women and children that he could carry and then called for help in English on the international frequencies. The Vichy French in Dakar dispatched two naval vessels as rescue ships and Doenitz responded by ordering U506 and U507 to assist in the rescue operation. However, before the French ships could arrive, an American bomber appeared overhead.

At this stage U156 had more than a hundred and fifty survivors on board. They were down below in the U-Boat hull, on her conning tower, and all over her deck. U506 and U507 were also in a similar position. All three U-Boats were towing strings of overloaded lifeboats and there were dozens of rafts and other floatation devices scattered around. Hartenstein had a large Red Cross flag showing and was continuing his English language distress broadcast.

On the appearance of the bomber U156 transmitted repeated radio messages, none of which were acknowledged. Light signals were tried, while the bomber circled the U-Boats for thirty minutes, but the bomber did not respond to any of the signals and then flew off towards the land. Half an hour later, the bomber was back but this time it roared into an attack. U156 was damaged and some of the bombs dropped among the lifeboats and rafts. Hartenstein was forced to return his survivors to the sea and dive his damaged boat. One female survivor later testified to his anger.

The American pilot is reputed to have explained that there were Allied ships in the area and that he considered the U-Boats a threat. Despite the damage to U156, Doenitz ordered U506 and U507 to continue the rescue operation, but the commanders of these boats were wary of American aircraft and with good reason. Later in the day a flying boat appeared, and U506 took the precaution of diving with the boat packed with survivors. The U-Boat had hardly dipped below the waves before the depth charges went off. On the evening of the thirteenth, the French warships arrived and twelve hundred survivors were rescued.

The attacks on the U-Boats involved were a serious blunder that was to have very far reaching consequences. The anger of the U-Boat commanders was understandable and on their return to France, Doenitz issued his famous Laconia order. He said that in future he did not intend to endanger any of his boats to pick up survivors. At the end of the war, the Grand Admiral was tried for murder, but thankfully acquitted on the grounds that although the Allies had not issued a Laconia Order, their boats also waged unrestricted submarine warfare and seldom if ever, picked up survivors.

The Laconia incident was to sour the battle of the Atlantic even further and cause the death of many would-be survivors. The Laconia Order was to affect many U-Boat captains because they were now forbidden to pick up survivors. None were to be affected quite like Henke. His future was being decided on the other side of the Atlantic, even as he ravaged the shipping off Trinidad.

Fechner in U164 had picked up U558's sighting report on convoy TAG 5 and taken up a position across the convoy's path, but daylight on the thirteenth revealed the U-Boat to a 59th pilot from Curacao. U164 was caught on the surface and the explosion of the four depth-charges ruptured the boat's fuel tanks. Fechner was forced to take his boat northwards away from the land to attempt repairs, but the pilot's aim had been good. The damage to the fuel tanks, combined with the earlier damage that the boat suffered in air attacks, meant that U164 now had to leave the Caribbean. Fechner had worked hard for his two ships sunk. Playing his part in the battles around convoys TAW (S) and TAW 15 had not necessarily meant that he had sunk ships, but often boats had to occupy escorts while others got into the convoys. In addition, he had endured constant harassment from the air, particularly from No. 59 squadron in Curacao. He never returned to the Caribbean, but gained the dubious distinction of being the first U-Boat casualty of 1943, when U164 was sunk by VP-83 off Brazil in January.

Monday fourteenth of September found Henke still off Galera Point in an area that he seemed to be becoming very fond of. It was a lucrative area but very dangerous. He was close to the numerous anti-submarine aircraft based in Trinidad and he was operating in relatively shallow water. Henke was aware of the danger but he was young and ambitious and off Galera Point he was in a merchant ship choke-point. At eight twenty that morning, he carried out a submerged attack on the five thousand four hundred ton British ship SS Harborough. The vessel went down forty miles from the Point, a little to the east of the Delaware Bank, not too far from the wreck of the Nimba.

Sixteen hours later he was still off Galera, despite the intensive hunt in progress for him and sent the Norwegian SS Sorholt to join the Harborough. Henke was no fool and he realised that he had to move U515. He had carried out six attacks on merchant ships in two days and it was only a matter of time before the anti-submarine forces found him. Aircraft and ships from Trinidad were beginning to form hunting groups specifically to get U515 and Henke wisely turned his boat southward for the Guianas.

Some of these commanders of the fourth wave, operated as if Operation. Neuland was still in progress and it may be that their boldness caught the defenders off guard. It was long past the time where Henke in U515 should have been allowed to operate in the fashion that he had and get away with it, but what was even worse was that as soon as Henke left the area, Auffermann moved in.

U514's Barbados attack was unconventional, but not anything as bold as the one he was about to pull off. At three o'clock on the afternoon of September fifteenth, Auffermann brought U514 westwards into the Galleons Passage between Trinidad and Tobago. Close to Tobago he observed the small British freighter Kioto running westwards. Auffermann must have thought that the vessel was much bigger than its three thousand three hundred tons because he attacked it as if it were ten thousand tons.

U514 came down the Passage surfaced and chased the Kioto almost into the shallows. Two torpedoes romped into the tiny ship. Auffermann recorded that the ship had five hatches and indeed the Kioto must have been a strange ship, because she carried a very large crew. Both Auffermann's description of the ship and the number of crew seem to suggest a much bigger vessel, but postwar records indicate that she was just a small freighter.

U514 was only five miles from the town of Scarborough when the attack began and the U-Boat was in full view of the many onlookers on the fort overlooking the harbour. The torpedoes blew out the vessel's engine room. Surprisingly the wreck still floated and Auffermann ordered up his gun crew. From Scarborough onlookers watched fascinated yet terrified, as the U-Boat began to shell the Kioto. It is difficult to believe that U514 was allowed to operate as audaciously as she did in broad daylight.

During July and August, the Trinidad based aircraft had achieved a fearsome reputation, yet in mid-September when there were more aircraft available, first Henke and then Auffermann were allowed to operate with impunity. The records are silent on the reasons and we can only assume that the defenders were caught on the wrong foot. The Kioto was soon on fire. She was now less than five miles from Tobago's airfield and also in sight of the Royal Navy's emergency field at Toco. The site of the attack was only forty miles from the fighter base at Waller Field, fifty miles from the bomber base at Edinburgh Field and sixty miles from the Flying boat base at Chaguaramas.

When U514 finally pulled away from the shallow coastal water and submerged, the Kioto did not look much like a ship, but the wreck still floated. There were big holes in her hull and she was a raging inferno. The wreck of the Kioto drifted ashore on Columbus Point in Tobago still burning. In fact the vessel burned all night. By the time the horribly burnt survivors were rescued and the dead bodies recovered, it was found that the tiny Kioto carried a crew of eighty. The experience gave the islanders another night they could not forget.

While U514 had been horrifying Tobago, Henke in U515 had been running south on the surface. At midnight he came upon the American freighter Mae, sixty miles north of Georgetown in British Guiana. A torpedo sent the ship to the bottom and covered the sea in a spreading orange blanket of bauxite dust.

At four o'clock next morning, the last of the boats of the third wave struck, when Krech in U558 dispatched the American freighter Commercial Trader, forty-five miles east of Manzanilla Point. After the ship had disappeared beneath the waves and the survivors had begun their journey to Trinidad's wreckage-strewn east coast, Krech set course for home. The departure of U558 left only five operational U-Boats in the Caribbean zone and they were all from the new guard. U175 under Bruns was off the Guianas, along with Henke in U515. U514 was off Trinidad's north coast being hunted by the aircraft from the island's airfields, all burning with the desire for revenge. U512 Shultz and U516 Weibe, were coming south along the eastern side of the island chain. All the rest of the Caribbean was empty of U-Boats, for the first time since April.

The last boats of the third wave were all on their way home. U558 had completed her second Caribbean deployment and would not be returning to the area. She was destined to die in the disastrous month of July 1943. Steinholf in U511 had left the Caribbean on the tenth of September. From the boat's embarrassing entry into the Mona Passage in August, Steinholf had been involved in the convoy battles around TAW (S) and TAW 15 and survived numerous air attacks. After No. 53 squadron's triumph in the Mona Passage, Steinholf had got the crew's diving drill so correct, that his was the only U-Boat that the aircraft failed to catch on the surface during the next three weeks.

Actually U511 may have been the world's first missile submarine. Before its Caribbean cruise, Steinholf had operated the boat off Penemunde, where a number of submerged rocket firings had been carried out from forty feet down. The rocket rails had been taken off before the Caribbean cruise. Steinholf and U511 would not see the Caribbean again. He relinquished command in December and survived the war in command of U873. In December, Schneewind took command of U511 and sailed her to the Far East, where the boat was handed over to the Japanese to become the R500. The boat survived the war and was scuttled by the Americans in

1946. U511 had sunk three ships in the Caribbean, but Reichenburg Klinke left the area in U217 having sunk only a solitary schooner. He like Fechner in U164, had become the special target of No. 59 squadron and the boat had been heavily damaged. U217 would also be one of the boats which would not see the Caribbean again, and would die in the traumatic months of June and July 1943.

On the eighteenth of September, U516 under Korvettenkapitan Gerhard Wiebe arrived in the area and began his first action with Trinidad's anti-submarine forces. U516 was to take the special place reserved for the Neuland boats in its association with the Caribbean, making three trips to the zone. Two commanders were to bring the boat to the Caribbean and the first Gerhard Wiebe, was to be a controversial character. U516 had been built in Hamburg and completed one patrol in the Central Atlantic before being assigned to this Caribbean cruise. On his way to the area Wiebe missed the SS Port Jackson with four torpedoes but unlike Schultz, he made no excuses. On the last day of August he achieved his first success, sinking the freighter Jack Carnies, after using six torpedoes and gunfire.

The early morning of the eighteenth found him waiting outside the Dragon's Mouth for the expected convoy. Dead on time, the vessels began to come out of the third Boca, just as Wiebe had been briefed they would, but he was on the surface. Wiebe either did not know or did not believe the stories about the massive aircover which departing Trinidad convoys received. Within minutes a B 18 roared into the attack and U516 was forced to crash-dive. The depth charges overshot, but the boat still received a severe shaking. Unfortunately for Wiebe the aircraft attack was only the start and soon the escort vessels were probing for him. When the U-Boat was finally able to crawl away, Wiebe had learned something about Caribbean convoys and their aircover.

While U516 was receiving a pounding, Henrich Bruns in command of the Type IXC boat U175 was having a curious adventure off Guiana. In the early morning hours he came across the Canadian bauxite carrier Norfolk and used one torpedo to dispose of the ship north of Georgetown. Two hours later Bruns met the SS Sanvangin. He got the impression from the way the freighter was altering course erratically that the vessel might be a Q ship. Bruns decided to take no chances and carried out a submerged attack on the suspicious vessel. He was more suspicious than ever when his two torpedoes appeared to coincide with the ship, but failed to explode.

However, the vessel seemed to alter course almost immediately and increase speed. Bruns curiosity got the better of him and he brought U175 to the surface and chased after the ship. He brought his deck gun into action, but was again puzzled by the fact that he could not observe the fall of shot. The Sanvangin was calling for help on the radio and the prompt appearance of an aircraft convinced the U-Boat commander that he was dealing with a very special vessel. He wasted no time in getting U175 down and away from the Sanvangin.

In fact what Bruns was witnessing was the accumulated psychological effect of the U-Boat campaign on the area's merchantmen. The Sanvangin was a terrified merchantman. All the losses of the previous months combined with the rumours, had affected the vessel's crew and they were on an exaggerated zig-zag when first sighted. The two torpedoes had passed very close to the ship and acted as a trigger for the crew's already nervous condition. The ship promptly turned towards the distant coast and increased to its maximum speed.

U175 could not observe the fall of shot because the shells were detonating deep in the vessel's cargo of bauxite. The appearance of the B 18 from the 430th bombardment squadron had done nothing to calm the vessel's crew, with the result that long after U175 had gone, the Sanvangin was still running at full speed for the shore. Despite signalled pleas from the aircraft the ship ran itself aground, opposite the mouth of the Waini river. The vessel's radio message describing its plight, gave its position at least one hundred miles inland, on the South American continent. The 430th squadron then began the operation of co-ordinating the rescue effort. Luckily for the Sanvangin, U175 did not see the amusing culmination of the drama.

After Wiebe in U516 had escaped from the escorts outside the Dragon's Mouth, he took the boat northwards along the island chain to get away from the Trinidad based bombers, but promptly ran into an inter-island convoy. Once again Wiebe set up for an attack and once again the convoy's air escort caught him. Even the small coastal vessels now had aircraft overhead. There was only one alternative and that was to head east away from the islands. Thus it was that he chanced on the six thousand ton American freighter Wichita and sent it to the seabed in the deep water north of Barbados.

Wiebe had attempted to take on the anti-submarine forces before getting to know the area, with the result that he ended up making a large circle, finally finding success right where he had started. Wiebe however, was a determined man and instead of staying around Barbados, he set course once again for Trinidad. At twelve noon on the following day he was to the north of Tobago, when another small inter-island convoy came into view. Once again Wiebe attacked on the surface and once again the aircraft came roaring in. This time a St. Lucia based B18 of No. 5 squadron planted his depth charges so close that U516 was damaged. This time Wiebe had to turn back east to find a quiet enough area for repairs.

Auffermann was also in trouble. On the day after the sinking of the Kioto he realised that the area off Trinidad's north coast was far too dangerous and he turned U514 eastwards. In the Caribbean the nights just prior to full moon were usually much brighter than the night when the moon was full, and all the boats were now experiencing difficulty. The anti-submarine aircraft were out in force, whether they had radar or not. On the night of the sixteenth, U514 was stalking a fast transport on the surface east of the island, when the boat was caught. A Mariner of VP-74 picked up its wake in the moonlight and delivered an accurate attack. The depth-charge explosions smashed a lot of the boat's internal equipment. The Mariner stayed overhead and vectored a destroyer to the scene.

The pounding which the destroyer delivered put U514 unserviceable. The escorts were taking their revenge for the Kioto and the U-Boat was lucky to escape. As soon as he was able Auffermann turned U514 eastwards and raced for safety. For the next four days his engineers worked ceaselessly to get the boat back into an operational condition. There were now two boats being repaired out of reach of the aircraft. The anti-submarine forces had recovered their balance.

While the boats of the fourth wave were getting into trouble with the aircraft, Shultz in U512 was getting into trouble with authority. At two thirty on the afternoon of the nineteenth he observed a four thousand ton vessel, sixty miles east of the island of Dominica. The ship looked like a neutral, but Shultz decided that she was a camouflaged English ship and attacked with two torpedoes. The two torpedoes buried themselves in the little ship and she went down quickly. Shultz had got his aim correct and his torpedoes had worked, but after checking the survivors he realised to his horror, that he had torpedoed the Spanish ship Monte Gorbea.

There were neutrals and neutrals, but a U-Boat could not torpedo a Spanish ship. Spain was neutral in a very special way, and no U-Boat commander could even cut Spanish fishing nets without getting into serious trouble. Shultz had no alternative but to confess what he had done, but once again he gave a long explanation.

For some undisclosed reason, Shultz had a very poor relationship with the Staff officers. They could easily have waited for Shultz to return and held an enquiry into the affair before condemning him, but they chose instead to make an example of him. They broadcast to all the boats that Shultz's excuse was not good enough and directed that he would face a court martial on his return. We will never know Shultz's reaction to this public humiliation, but it certainly did not help him on his patrol into the hostile Trinidad area.

At three o'clock on the morning of the twentieth, Henke caught the four thousand three hundred ton British freighter Reedpool, on course for Trinidad. Two torpdedoes sent the vessel to the bottom two hundred miles southeast of the island. After the ship had gone down, he took U515 over to the spot and found a group of survivors swimming about in the brilliant moonlight. There had not been time to launch the Reedpool's lifeboats or rafts and these men faced certain death in the shark infested waters. He brought U515 to a stop and despite the danger from aircraft, picked up the oil covered survivors. Down below they were scrubbed clean and given hot food and clothing. This incident is of importance, particularly in the light of what was to happen to Henke.

On the seventeenth, U201 under Rosenberg, U202 under Poser and U332 under Leibe had made a rendezvous with the tanker U460. Present at the mid-ocean meeting had been Steinholf in U511, on his way home. The three outbound commanders were able to get a first hand, up-to-date briefing on the conditions in the Caribbean. Four days later U-Boat headquarters signalled the three boats, giving them a free hand in the waters around Trinidad and the area to the east. The signal also contained a warning about air activity.

The veteran Suhren, on his way home in U564 also picked up the signal and decided to pass on some advice to the young commanders. He advised that in the area one hundred and eighty miles around Trinidad, he had remained submerged during daylight as a matter of principle. He elaborated on the danger from small, fast, land-based aircraft and added that if a U-Boat was sighted, shipping was rerouted around it. He also mentioned that he had not encountered patrols at night, unless he was operating near convoys.

The three captains were being given good advice from a survivor and the point was further driven home when Auffermann signalled to say that U514 was so badly damaged that despite the repairs he had carried out, the boat was no longer capable of operating close to Trinidad. As if to further highlight the danger from aircraft, U203 which had operated around Trinidad in July, signalled U-Boat headquarters to say that its commander Rolf Mutzelburg, had died of concussion and internal injuries, after an air attack. The three captains making their way to the West Indian Islands could not have received more cautioning.

On the night of the full moon, Bruns torpedoed the Yugoslavian freighter Predesnick, while the ship had been running for British Guiana.

U175 was operating on the surface in the brilliant moonlight, but a good hundred and fifty miles southeast of Galeota Point. Although still well within the range of the anti-submarine aircraft, he remained undetected and as soon as the vessel went down, he turned eastwards to put as much distance as possible between his boat and the land.

For the next two days, U512, U514, U515 and U516 joined U175 well east of the land. The moonlight made conditions close to the bases extremely hazardous and the merchant ships were able to sail the bauxite route safely. During this lull, Lassen brought U160 out of the dock at Lorient and turned his bows towards the distant Caribbean. The master hunter was returning.

On the morning of the twenty-third Henke ended his brief association with the Caribbean by sinking two ships. As soon as the moon began to wane, he turned U515 once again towards Trinidad. Shortly after midnight a torpedo put paid to the small Norwegian freighter Lindvangen, seventy-five miles east of Galeota Point. Four hours later he fired his last two torpedoes at the American fruit carrier SS Antinous. Both torpedoes entered the vessel and the crew promptly abandoned ship. Henke turned away believing that the vessel was going down, but in fact Shultz in U512 found the Antinous still afloat but abandoned, some eight hours later and dispatched it with another torpedo.

Henke was taking U515 home, having sunk eight ships on his first cruise. The two additional ships which he damaged were also total losses, because the Woensdrecht would be scrapped, and Shultz got the other. He had accounted for forty-six thousand seven hundred and eighty-two tons. Against this, he had one seaman killed by the accidental discharging of a machine gun, but Henke's first war patrol was only the beginning of his tragic story.

On Henke's return to Lorient with the survivors of the Reedpool aboard, he found out that the days when U-Boat commanders looked after survivors were over. He heard the full story of the Laconia incident from the men who were actually involved and was appraised of the Laconia Order and its implications. No doubt Henke was just as annoyed over the air attacks on the boats involved as all the other U-Boat commanders were, and it is almost certain that he made a vow to obey the Laconia Order to the letter.

After the customary rest, he took U515 to sea again in November. On the night of the seventh of December while operating off West Africa, Henke came across the twenty thousand ton British liner SS Ceramic. It took four torpedoes to break the great ship's back and Henke was under the impression that he had sunk an important troopship. If at this stage he had turned away and continued his patrol in accordance with normal procedure, his life would have been completely different and he might even have survived the war as a highly decorated U-Boat Ace, but Henke wanted to collect proof of what he had done and turned his bows towards the area where the Ceramic had gone down.

The SS Ceramic happened to be one of very few merchant ships which continued on its normal peacetime route during the war. When U515 caught the ship, it was carrying six hundred and fifty passengers. Four hundred of the passengers were military personnel on duty and civil servants on transfer, or official business, but there were also one hundred and fifty women and children aboard. The majority of these people jumped into the sea when the ship had first been hit and as U515 cruised into the area, they realised that the surface of the sea was teeming with survivors. It must have been a shock to Henke, particularly as he heard the cries for help coming from all sides, but Henke was under orders not to save them.

Twice U515 stopped and each time desperate survivors hung onto the boat or scrambled onto the deck. On the first occasion, he ordered his sailors to get the survivors off his boat which they did. On the second occasion he selected one survivor to be a witness to his tonnage claim, who turned out to be Sapper Munday of the Royal Engineers. By the time U515 was ready to move again, there were dozens of people hanging onto the U-Boat and lying on her casing. As the boat gathered way the majority of them lost their hold and were left behind in the darkness, but there were still others lying on her casing. Someone in the conning tower watch drew Henke's attention to the exhausted people lying on the deck. He obeyed his orders to the letter and ordered U515 to dive. That night the sea got up and by next day, the only survivor of the Ceramic was Sapper Munday on board U515.

Henke handed over Sapper Munday to the authorities on his return to Lorient and he eventually passed to Dr. Goebels propaganda ministry. They could not resist combining all the circumstances surrounding the sinking of the Ceramic into a propaganda coup. The broadcast gave the British the first news of the loss of the Ceramic.

Throughout World War Two the British operated a number of propaganda stations aimed at the various sections of the German war machine. The station aimed at the U-Boatmen was called Deutscher Kurzwellenseder Atlantik and one of its signature tunes was the song, "Vicky the sailors' sweetheart". The station broadcast music and an accurate news service mixed with propaganda. The German sailors were forbidden to listen to the station but because they could always get news of their comrades, the men of the U-Boat arm were the station's most ardent fans. They could get news of the loss of a U-Boat and the fate of its crew, long before the U-Boat headquarters would even know that the boat was lost.

Sometime after the German broadcast about Sapper Munday, the British propaganda station is alleged to have made a broadcast about U515. They claimed that they had information that U515 had machine-gunned the helpless survivors from the vessel and that any member of the U515's crew that fell into their hands would be treated as a criminal and hanged. After the war, the British denied all knowledge of this broadcast, but it could not have been as widely discussed among the U-Boatmen unless such a statement had in fact been made. It was probably made by an announcer during one of the news breaks, purely for its propaganda value. In any case the crew of the U-Boat believed the story.

U515 had not machine gunned the survivors of the Ceramic, they had simply obeyed orders, but in doing so it had left a stain on each man's conscience. It is alleged that Henke did lose some sleep over the incident. He could not get the cries of the survivors out of his mind. This must undoubtedly be true, because U515 rescued two groups of survivors during 1943. In March they picked up men from the SS California Star and again in December from the SS Phemius. On both occasions they were acting contrary to the Laconia Order and it would seem that Henke was trying to salve his conscience and make up for the Ceramic. During this period none of the other U-Boats were worrying about survivors.

Henke became an Ace, falling twelfth on the list of Ace U-Boat commanders, with twenty-five ships sunk. He was awarded the Knights Cross with Oak Leaves, but it could not last. On the ninth of April 1944, Rear Admiral Gallery's famous hunting group of the carrier Guadalcanal, with the destroyers Pope, Chatelain and Flaherty, caught up with U515, and an Avenger from VC-58 sent the U-Boat to the bottom. Forty-four survivors, including Henke were rescued. The Americans knew nothing of the threat of hanging haunting the survivors of U515, but they found out from Henke himself, because the thought of death by hanging was not the way for a U-Boat Ace to end his career.

When the Americans realised what they had, they promptly used the threat of handing Henke over to the British to get him to sign a document promising to co-operate with US Navy Intelligence. Henke later claimed that the document was signed under duress and refused to co-operate, but hanging over his head was the constant threat of being handed over to the British. Eventually after the interrogators had got all they could from the

U-Boat's crew, they made arrangements to transfer them to a prison-of-war camp in Canada.

To Henke, this was tantamount to being handed over to the British. On the day before he was due to be transferred, he decided to end the whole thing by climbing the fence of the prisoner-of-war camp. Werner Henke knew that he did not have a chance and in fact he did not start to climb the fence until he was sure that the sentry in the watchtower was looking at him. He deliberately ignored two shouts to stop and ended his life on the wire.

With such an ending it is not surprising that the British claim no knowledge of the broadcast. The Americans had used Henke's own fear of hanging, in a legitimate ruse of war. Some may say that he was cruelly used by the Allies, while others may say that he also cruelly used the Ceramic survivors, but all forget that Henke was the same man who rescued the Reedpool's survivors. The Laconia Order was the instrument which made some men change their habits, while it provided a justification for the actions of others. Was the Laconia Order wrong? Was Doenitz wrong to put into writing what all submarine captains were and are expected to do? It appears that Henke was everybody's pawn.

CHAPTER

10

The veterans' return

Six merchant ships were sunk in the last seven days of September 1942. Heinrich Bruns in U175 was the first to strike, when he sank the American freighter West Chetac, two hundred and fifty miles southeast of Trinidad. He was working his way closer to the island and two days later he caught the Panamanian registered Tambour, one hundred miles southeast of Galeota Point. The little freighter was heading west for the southern Serpent's Mouth entrance to the Gulf of Paria, when the torpedo from U175 ripped it apart.

Just after midnight on September 28th, Gerhard Wiebe inadvertently got himself into trouble. U516 was operating close to the shore of French Guiana when the lookouts detected the outline of a small freighter scuttling along the coast. Wiebe identified it as Brazilian and in fact it was the twelve hundred ton Antonico, loaded with a cargo of cement and asphalt on its way to Brazil. He decided that the vessel was too small to waste a torpedo on and called up his gun-crew to sink it. The gun-crew of the U516 were obviously out of practice, because it took thirty rounds to send the little ship to the bottom and in the process, sixteen crewmen including the captain died.

When the shocked leaderless survivors reached land, six of them were admitted to hospital and the remainder told a tale of a night of terror. They claimed that the U-Boat had used machine guns against them and that many of those who died, had been killed by this fire. In time the Brazilians listed Wiebe as a war criminal who would be dealt with at the appropriate time.

Wiebe and the U516 were destined to survive the war and in the immediate aftermath, serious consideration was given towards extraditing the U-Boat commander to face war crimes charges, but by this time the Antonico survivors had calmed down and before proceedings could get going, Brazil was forced to drop the charges due to lack of evidence.

It is possible that U516 used her machine guns on the survivors, but then it is also possible that the survivors were mistaken. Thirty rounds of 105mm slamming into a small ship or the area around it, in the dead of night, would cause casualties. It is probable that shell splinters did kill some of the crew, while others simply drowned in the confusion. In any case Wiebe was not a popular U-Boat commander as far as the Allies were concerned.

On the twenty-eighth Bruns struck again and sent the five thousand six hundred ton American bauxite carrier Alcoa Mariner to the bottom, ninety miles off Galeota Point. In the meantime U512 was operating well to the east away from the dreaded aircraft, while the engineers attempted repairs on the air compressors. Having been publicly rebuked over the sinking of the Monte Gorbeo and been advised of his impending court martial, Shultz was in no mood to compromise. He decided to play the game by the rule book and set out to embarrass the Staff by dealing with a Spanish ship strictly in accordance with the laid down guidelines.

A shot across the bows brought the Spanish vessel to a halt, following which a heavily armed boarding party left the U-Boat. They gave the Spaniard a thorough search, leaving out most of the usual courtesies normally extended to this particular neutral nation. While the search was being carried out, Shultz allowed the Spanish radio operator to continue transmitting, knowing full well that his headquarters would pick up what was going on. Finally when he was certain that the Spaniard did not carry any contraband cargo, he signalled to tell U-Boat headquarters what he had done.

An embarrassing silence greeted his signal because in fact, he had not contravened any orders. As Shultz must have expected, Spain protested to Germany over the incident and in a few days, Grand Admiral Raeder had to address a signal to all boats, personally laying down the new procedure to be used in handling neutrals. Shultz probably intended to use the new rules as a defence document at his court martial. It is possible that Shultz did not like Spaniards, but it is more probable that he disliked the Staff. At this stage of the war, U512 was definitely not the favourite of the Staff Officers.

On the following day, the three new boats arrived in the Caribbean zone. The first to strike was the Type VIIC boat U332, from the 3rd Flotilla at La Pallice. U332 was under the command of Johannes Liebe and carried the unusual personal emblem of a mermaid painted on the bow. The U-Boat was moving southwest, one hundred and forty miles from Barbados, when the six thousand ton British freighter Registan, came into sight. Liebe lost no time in sending the vessel and its cargo to the bottom.

The second of the boats to strike was the Type VIIC U202, under Gunther Poser. He was on his first patrol as a commander, having taken command of the boat with its experienced crew at the start of September. U202 had operated under Kapitanleutnant Linder during the Paukenschlag offensive and had dropped agents ashore on Long Island during June.

Poser made his way to the area off Trinidad's north coast and promptly attempted an attack on a fast tanker. He fired a four torpedo spread at the vessel, but before he could observe that all the torpedoes had missed, a VP-53 flying boat was diving at him. The four depth-charges rocked U202 as Poser took her down. U202 crept away to a quieter area and reported to U-Boat headquarters that its compressors had been damaged in the attack. This effectively meant that U202 was a cripple, before she had sunk anything and she was ordered to retire and operate east of longitude fifty-two west. In the case of U202, all the warnings had been in vain.

With dramatic suddenness during the month of September, the U-Boats had switched all Caribbean operations to the Trinidad area. Except for three vessels sunk to the northeast all the action had taken place off Trinidad. Despite the problems they experienced with the numerous aircraft, the new guard had done surprisingly well.

Ten U-Boats worked the Caribbean at various times and between them, they accounted for twenty-seven ships and if the tanker Woensdrecht is included, they totalled one hundred and twenty-seven thousand eight hundred tons. The convoys within the Caribbean had cut down drastically on the opportunities for effective U-Boats operations, with the result that the boats were now concentrated where the ships still sailed independently. Doenitz commented at the end of September that the area in the Windward Passage was similar to the area west of Trinidad. In both areas there was a high probability of detecting convoys, but the conditions were difficult for the successful operation of the boats.

Airpower had made both areas highly dangerous. He considered the area east of Trinidad as promising and noted the only difficulty as being the ability to predict the frequent changes in routing which the merchant ships adopted. He commented that radar interception equipment was required to cut down on the comparatively high losses in the Caribbean.

By this statement he was not referring to U-Boats sunk, because the area had accounted for only four boats sunk, with another in the Straits of Florida and one in the Gulf of Mexico. Six U-Boats lost, against the two hundred and eighty-seven merchant ships, was a pretty good rate of exchange. He was referring instead to the surprise attacks which caught the boats on the surface and damaged them. A damaged U-Boat four thousand miles away from home, presented a serious problem and nearly every boat which operated during the previous two months had been damaged. The situation was going to get worse, because there were now ten anti-submarine squadrons operating between Antigua and Dutch Guiana, and the numbers were growing.

October was to see very few merchant ships sunk in the Caribbean zone in comparison to the preceeding months, and the first reason for this was the fact that there were very few U-Boats operating in the zone, but this was only part of the cause. For eight months the Caribbean had virtually been under seige and although the U-Boats had bested the defenders at every turn, the hard pressed anti-submarine forces were learning their trade in the hard school of combat. During October they mounted their first serious challenge to U-Boats hegemony of the Caribbean and the fight was vicious.

Midnight on the last day of September found seven U-Boats in an arc between Barbados and the French-Guiana-Brazil border. One group comprising U175, U202 and U332 were east of Trinidad, while further southeast, U512 and U516, with the damaged U514 well to seaward, formed the second group. All the boats were operating outside the Caribbean Sea, and the area off Trinidad's north coast was clear for the first time since April, but not for long. Support was on the way in the form of two groups of veterans.

The first group comprised U67 and U129 on their third Caribbean patrols and U160 on its second. Behind them U163, U505 and U508 were plodding across the Atlantic, all on their second Caribbean patrols. There was to be no let up in the offensive around Trinidad.

At three forty that morning, Bruns in U175 began the October account by torpedoing the British freighter SS Empire Tennyson, seventy miles southeast of Galeota Point. The small vessel went down quickly in a hundred and fifty feet of water, but even so the radio operator managed to get off an SSS signal. This signal was to cause U175 to have a rough day.

Twice during the morning the boat was forced to crash-dive to escape the B18 bombers of No. 1 squadron. On each occasion the boat managed to get under before the aircraft were overhead, but the crashing explosions of the depth-charges were damaging the boat's sensitive equipment, and damage was accumulating.

The repaired U202 was operating very close to U175 and she received unwanted attention from the defenders. At nine forty that morning Poser had the boat on the surface when a shout from the lookouts drew his attention to the unmistakable shape of a PBY coming in. The watch landed in a heap in the control room with the boat already starting to dive. The conning tower had just disappeared when the VP-53 Catalina swept over and four depth charges hit the water. Poser had got the boat down in time and the explosions did no more than shake them up. An hour later, U202 was on the surface again cruising slowly southeast of Trinidad. At seven thirty that night Poser's chance came. The little Dutch freighter Achilles running from Trinidad to Guyana, came in sight and one torpedo sent it to the bottom.

At one thirty next morning, U201 got her opportunity to open a Caribbean account. This Type VIIC boat had been commissioned in 1941 under the command of Adalbert Schnee, who had the distinction of being one of the very few U-Boat commanders to torpedo a neutral Argentinian vessel. He survived the subsequent exchange of diplomatic notes and eventually joined Doenitz's Staff.

Oberleutnant zur See Gunther Rosenburg took command of U201 on September first just prior to his Caribbean cruise. Like Poser in U202 he was on his first war patrol as a commander. Operating one hundred miles southeast of Galeota Point he was only twenty miles away from U202, when he sent the bauxite carrier Alcoa Transport to the bottom.

Two and a half hours later Bruns in U175 put two torpedoes into the Panamanian registered freighter Aneroid, one hundred and forty miles southeast of Galeota. Bruns watched the twin explosions on the five thousand ton vessel and waited long enough to see the ship begin to settle before turning away. The crew of the Aneroid promptly abandoned ship, but the vessel did not go down. Twelve hours later a 53rd squadron Hudson found the ship abandoned and drifting southeast of Trinidad. Sometime that night the old ship must have given up and slipped beneath the waves, out of sight of any witnesses. But merchant ships were not the only vessels to die that night.

After baiting the Staff officers with his searching of the Spanish ship,

Shultz brought U512 closer inshore, but stayed off the French Guiana coast. Operating this far southeast, Shultz must have believed that he was out of range of the Trinidad based aircraft. It appears that he did not know of the existence of No. 99 bombardment squadron, based at Zandery in Dutch Guiana, because he was scarcely one hundred miles from their base. The squadron had been operating out of Zandery since Clausen cut the bauxite route in March, carrying out numerous patrols and attacks, but without making a kill. In the early morning of the second of October they received their reward.

Lieutenant Lehti took off in his B18 bomber at midnight and flew eastwards to his assigned patrol area along the French Guiana coast. At about four o'clock in the morning the radar operator advised Lehti that he had a contact at twelve miles. He brought the machine down to three hundred feet and began his run in. At a mile he was over a U-Boat's wake, heading northwest. Within seconds U512 was visible. The boat was moving very slowly fully surfaced, and the B18 dropped lower and came boring in. U512 was taken completely by surprise.

The bomber crossed the U-Boat and as the two depth-bombs dropped the crew noticed that two deck-hatches were open, with light showing upwards from them. One six hundred and fifty pound bomb entered the water ahead of the boat with another three hundred and twenty-five pound bomb thirty feet further on. The aim was excellent, because the U-Boat was moving towards the charges as they sank to twenty-five feet. We can assume that the boat was damaged by the blast, but by the time that Lehti could get his aircraft round for a second attack, U512 had disappeared. The radar operator reported his screen clear and the MAD gear gave no indications of a U-Boat in the area.

Lehti was an experienced pilot who had carried out many attacks on U-Boats and he knew that submarines didn't disappear. Either the boat had been sunk or it was still there underwater. He turned his B18 for the shore one hundred and twenty miles distant. Crossing over the prominent Cayenne lighthouse he got a good check on his position. He recrossed the lighthouse on the reciprocal course and flew back towards the scene of the attack.

Nine miles from the position of the previous attack his radar operator advised that he had a contact at the original attack position. Shultz must have thought that his troubles for the night were over, because U512 was once more on the surface. Lehti brought his bomber close to the water and ran in on the radar contact. For the second and last time he caught the U-Boat by surprise. As the B18 crossed the U-Boat, Lehti released two three hundred and twenty-five pound bombs simultaneously. Both bombs plummetted into the water close alongside the U-Boat. After the explosions there was no sign of U512.

With typical understatement Lehti claimed on his arrival back at his base, that he had, "shook up the boat a little". He did not claim a kill, but the squadron intelligence officer knew his man and requested a reconnaissance of the area at dawn. The B18 which crossed the area in daylight, found a large oil patch at the center of which was a man in a lifejacket. They dropped a dinghy to the survivor and watched the exhausted man climb into it. He was the sole survivor of U512. Shultz would not face any court martial.

With U512 gone, the Staff at U-Boat headquarters would not face any problems from wayward commanders, but they did have a problem with Caribbean convoys. The U-Boats in the area were all concentrated off the east side of Trinidad and there were no boats off the Dragon's Mouth. Convoys were moving freely, as the third of October proved.

At nine in the morning convoy TAG 10 departed with seventeen merchant ships on its long journey to England, via its many ports of call. At nine thirty convoy TRIN-15 departed on its coastal run with thirteen merchant ships.

Twelve noon saw the arrival of convoy GAT-9 with eleven merchant ships. This was the final arrival of ships that had started from England under escort, some three to four weeks before. Reinforcements were arriving constantly to match the U-Boats' shift of operations to Trinidad and shortly after the arrival of the convoy, the destroyers Belknap and Eberle steamed into the Bocas to join the Chaguaramas forces.

To end the day a VP-74 Mariner caught U175 on the surface southeast of Trinidad and delivered a good attack. U175 was badly shaken up, but Bruns was not out of action and at five o'clock next morning, he dispatched the American freighter Caribstar, only five miles off the mouth of the Waini river. The ship went down stern first in very shallow water, but the defenders had a much more difficult problem to solve on the morning of October fourth.

At seven thirty that morning the British freighter SS Athelbrae was steaming up the swept channel in the southern Serpent's Mouth, when the ship struck a mine. The captain realised that the Athelbrae was going down and he immediately ordered full starboard wheel to be put on. The dying ship made it to the shallows off the Green Hill batteries and ran aground. She was so badly damaged that the sands off the south coast became her final resting place.

Why was a mine in the center of the channel? The question galvanised naval investigating teams. In fact it was an American mine that had broken loose. Both sides of the southern Serpent's Mouth were mined, but the current running up this channel was too strong for the cables or sinkers. This generated the questions, how many mines had broken loose and how long would the minefield remain effective? The British always maintained that the mines were quite useless, but neither of the Allies had considered the possibility of the current being too strong for the mooring cables. Like the U-Boats, this problem would not go away.

At five fifteen next morning Bruns ended his successful Caribbean patrol by torpedoing the six thousand ton American freighter SS William A. McKenny. The cargo ship had been hugging the South American coastline in order to escape the U-Boats that were known to be operating in the area. Bruns used his last torpedo and hit the vessel, setting it on fire. Much later that day an RAF Hudson found the freighter still burning only ten miles from the coast. Nearby the aircraft noted three overcrowded liferafts drifting towards the shore. Bruns turned away and began his homeward run, but almost immediately a shout from the lookout warned him of danger and indeed a PBY was coming in.

U175 was a highly efficient boat and they were completely underwater by the time the aircraft crossed the spot and delivered its load of depth charges. VP-53 was saying farewell to U175 and probably good riddance. U175 had sunk nine ships in its three weeks off Trinidad, but about half of these ships were small vessels and together his kills only added up to thirty-three thousand four hundred and twenty-six tons. Bruns never got the opportunity to bring U175 back to the Caribbean. The boat was sunk in April 1943 off the US coast by the Coast Guard cutter Spencer. Thirteen of her crew were killed in the final battle.

As U175 began pulling away from the Caribbean, both U201 and U202 also fell back eastwards. The three boats had spent four lucrative days off Trinidad's southeast point and the aircraft were now beginning to target the area. Well to the north Muller-Stockheim spent a full day chasing a tanker. The vessel was on a fast lone run and each time U67 began to pull into a firing position, the tanker's captain seemed to anticipate the move and altered course. The boat eventually gave up and resumed its course for Trinidad.

On October eighth, the sisters U201 and U202 had to combine their talents to sink the seven thousand two hundred ton Liberty ship John Carter Rose. The vessel was technically outside of the Caribbean zone, as it passed nine hundred miles east of Trinidad with a cargo of aircraft, bombs and petrol in drums for Capetown.

Just as dawn was breaking, Rosenburg in U201 caught sight of the cargo ship and manoeuvred into position. One torpedo left the U-Boat and raced across the intervening water. A loud underwater clang told the hydrophone operator that they had fired a dud. The John Carter Rose altered course immediately and U201 set off in pursuit. Two hours later, the vessel came in sight of U202. Poser set up his firing angle and two torpedoes hissed out of the tubes. Both torpedoes hit the freighter and detonated. The John Carter Rose slowed down and finally came to a stop.

During the running battle with U201, the ship's radio operator had carried on a commentary of the action, but now he signed off and joined the crew as they abandoned ship. The freighter was grievously wounded and she wallowed low in the water, but she was not sinking. In deference to the fact that she had been U201's target Poser drew away, leaving Rosenburg to deliver the coup de grace. A torpedo streaked away from U201 and slammed into the side of the ship. The impact caused the hull to ring like a bell, but once again U201's torpedo was a dud. In exasperation Rosenburg ordered up his gun crew and they finished the job.

By the evening of October eighth, there were only three U-Boats still operating from the new guard. U332 had been ordered in to the Trinidad area to replace U175. U514 was off Cayenne in the area where U512 had been lost, and U516 was off British Guiana. Both U201 and U202 had turned for home after the affair with John Carter Rose. Neither boat had done particularly well, sinking a vessel apiece and sharing another between them.

The two Type VIIC boats were not destined to operate in the Caribbean again. U201 met her end in February 1943, when HMS Fame destroyed the boat and its crew, while U202 was to become one of the famous Captain Walker's victims. Just entering the northeast corner of the Caribbean zone were the replacement boats. Muller-Stockheim, Hans Witt and Georg Lassen were coming back.

Leibe brought U332 in to the area southeast of Trinidad in accordance with his instructions, but he now paid for the damage to the area's shipping that Bruns had caused. At eleven thirty on the morning of the ninth, U332 was cruising three hundred miles southeast of Galeota Point when the lookouts spotted an attacking aircraft. The U-Boat dived quickly but the B18 from the 99th squadron was quicker. The conning tower had just dipped below the waves when the three depth charges hit the water. At twenty-five feet they exploded but U332 was also at about the same depth. The shock of the charges going off rocked the U-Boat, shattering equipment and damaging the boat.

An hour later, Leibe brought his boat to the surface to check the damage. The first thing they saw was that the U-Boat's attack periscope was badly bent. There would be no submerged attacks for U332. One hour after they surfaced while the damage was still being checked, a lookout's shout sent the working party and the bridge watch tumbling down the hatch. They did better this time and the conning tower dipped below the waves a good thirty seconds before another B18 roared overhead. The explosions this time were a little further off, although more damage was done to the boat's sensitive equipment.

Wiebe realised that there was no hope of doing any repair work while he was so close to Trinidad and decided to wait for the night. At dusk the shape of the U-Boat rose to the surface and the watch raced up the ladder to scan the horizon. U332 was virtually blind because of her damaged periscope and surfacing was a chancy business. After half an hour of careful scanning of the horizon, the working parties came up from below to begin the task of clearing the mess caused by the depth-charge attacks.

At two o'clock that afternoon, Wing Commander Leggate lifted Hudson PZ/S off the Edinburgh Field runway and began an eight hour anti-submarine patrol. At eight o'clock that night, his radar operator reported a contact at ten miles. Leggate brought his aircraft close to the water and began an attack run. U332 was on a heading of three hundred degrees and barely moving when the aircraft's crew saw it. The conning tower watch saw the Hudson very late and the crash-dive had hardly started when the commanding officer of No. 53 squadron released his four depth-charges. The fact that they were late saved U332. The depth charges fell alongside the boat's conning tower, the nearest about thirty feet away. By the time the aircraft could get round, U332 had disappeared, but down below Wiebe was contemplating the considerable additional damage which had been done. It had been a bad day for the U-Boat.

U-Boat headquarters were acutely aware that convoys were arriving and departing Trinidad quite unmolested and U516 was ordered to move northwards. By the tenth of October Wiebe was in position off the north coast of the island and almost immediately he ran into a convoy. The movement of military equipment from the United States to Brazil was gathering momentum and the ships moved in heavily escorted groups known as TRIN convoys.

Wiebe moved in against convoy TRIN 17, but was almost immediately driven off by the convoy's strong escort of the US destroyers Ellis, Greene, Badger and Osmond Ingram, plus PCs. The convoy's seventeen merchant ships sailed past U516 and the boat could do nothing to interfere with the movement. On the following morning, Wiebe once again moved against another convoy. This time TRIN 18 was departing with only six merchant ships and a much smaller escort, but again Wiebe was thwarted. An OS2N Kingfisher came diving in and U516 was forced down as the fast troop transports slipped away.

On the twelfth Wiebe was still off the north coast, but he found that there were several hunting groups looking for him and the area was becoming decidedly unhealthy. At ten forty-five that morning, the US Coast Guard cutter Crawford cornered him and the boat had to endure a punishing depth-charge attack. The U-Boats were having a rough time at the hands of the escorts, but the scales were still tipped heavily in their favour because of the experience level of many of the escort crews.

While U516 was creeping away from the Crawford, the British freighter SS Pan Gulf struck a drifting mine off Cedros Point, within the Gulf of Paria. The vessel was badly damaged and had to be towed back to Port of Spain. More and more mines were breaking their mooring cables and drifting up into the sensitive Gulf, adding a new dimension to the defensive problem. Aircraft had to be diverted from their vital anti-submarine patrols to look for mines.

At four o'clock that afternoon the damaged U514 made its last Caribbean kill. Auffermann put two torpedoes into the American freighter Steel Scientist, sixty miles off Cayenne. After watching the vessel go down Auffermann turned his bows homeward. The boat had sunk only two ships and damaged one in its three week patrol, but they had made an impact on the area out of all proportion to the tonnage sunk. Auffermann's destiny was also tied up in the battles of July 1943. On the following day, U514 was first sighted by a VP-53 PBY and then attacked by a B18 of the 99th squadron.

But the most important sighting made that day was by a Mariner of VP-74, when the aircraft glimpsed U160 submerging just northeast of Tobago. Lassen had met the tanker U461 in mid-Atlantic on October second before resuming his course for the Caribbean. The Mariner had picked up the U-Boat on its radar and begun tracking towards it, but U160 had also picked up the Mariner. The battle of technology was now in full swing, a conflict within a conflict that would eventually decide the outcome of the battle of the Atlantic.

U160 was the first U-Boat into the Caribbean area to be equipped with the Metox receiver and its cumbersome Biscay Cross aerial. Now the U-Boats could pick up the radar transmissions from the anti-submarine aircraft and the Caribbean pilots would find it a lot more difficult to catch U-Boats

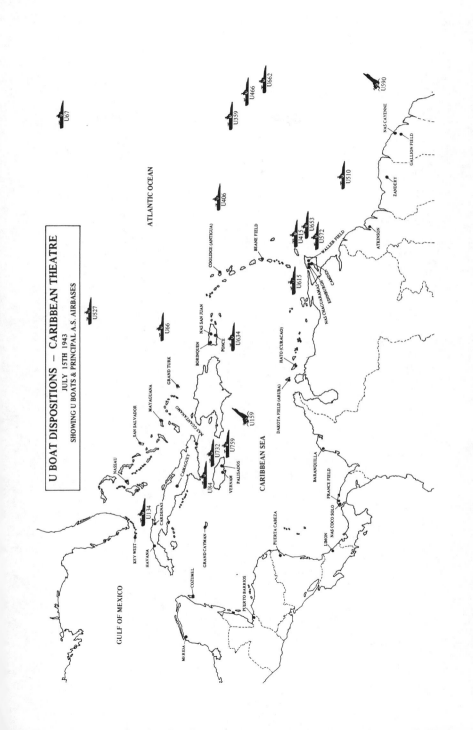

U BOAT DISPOSITIONS – CARIBBEAN THEATRE
JULY 15TH 1943
SHOWING U BOATS & PRINCIPAL A.S. AIRBASES

ATLANTIC OCEAN

GULF OF MEXICO

CARIBBEAN SEA

U67

U527

U359

U466

U662

U590

U510

U406

U415

U653

U572

U615

U66

U634

U159

U732

U759

U84

U134

NAS CAYENNE

GALLION FIELD

ZANDERY

ATKINSON

COOLIDGE (ANTIGUA)

BEANE FIELD

WALLER FIELD

NAS CHAGUARAMAS

EDINBURGH

CARLSEN

NAS SAN JUAN

BORINQUEN

PONCE

HATO (CURACAO)

DAKOTA FIELD (ARUBA)

BARANQUILLA

FRANCE FIELD

NAS COCO SOLO

LIMON

PUERTA CABEZA

PUERTO BARRIOS

COZUMEL

MERIDA

GRAND CAYMAN

KEY WEST

HAVANA

CARDENAS

CAMAGUEY

NASGUANTANAMO

VERNAM

PALISADOS

NASSAU

SAN SALVADOR

MAYAGUANA

GRAND TURK

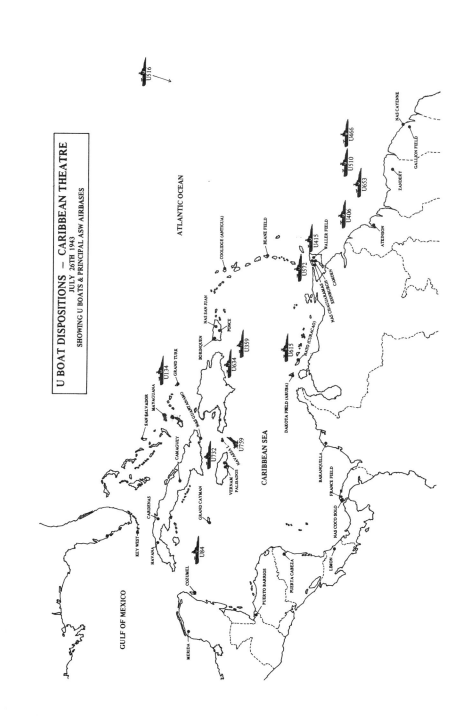

U BOAT DISPOSITIONS – CARIBBEAN THEATRE
JULY 26TH 1943
SHOWING U BOATS & PRINCIPAL ASW AIRBASES

ATLANTIC OCEAN

CARIBBEAN SEA

GULF OF MEXICO

U516

U466
U510
U653
U406
U415
U572
U134
U359
U634
U615
U732
U759
U84

NAS CAYENNE
GALLON FIELD
ZANDERY
ATKINSON
WALLER FIELD
BEANE FIELD
COOLIDGE (ANTIGUA)
CAMDEN
EDINBURGH
NAS CHAGUARAMAS
MATO (CURACAO)
DAKOTA FIELD (ARUBA)
NAS SAN JUAN
PONCE
BORINQUEN
GRAND TURK
SAN SALVADOR
MAYAGUNA
NAS GUANTANAMO
CAMAGUEY
CARDENAS
NAS VERNAM (KINGSTON)
VERNAM
PALISADES
GRAND CAYMAN
KEY WEST
HAVANA
COZUMEL
MERIDA
PUERTO BARRIOS
PUERTA CABEZA
LIMON
NAS COCO SOLO
FRANCE FIELD
BARRANQUILLA

on the surface. The German equipment had one serious fault and this was that the receiver could not give a range reading, which meant that U-Boats were continually diving to escape aircraft that sometimes could be very far away.

For the next two days the sector was relatively quiet. An RAF B24 Liberator on a ferry flight to Brazil and then across the Atlantic, crashed at Waller Field killing all the crew. Off the north coast U516 was once again cornered and depth-charged by two US Navy PCs, but Wiebe was able to successfully evade them. After the attack U516 turned its bows homeward. The boat had managed to sink three ships in the area during its patrol, but U516 would have a lot more to do with the Caribbean.

The departure of U516 left only U332 still operational in the Caribbeen zone, from the original boats of the New Guard, but the veterans had taken over. Georg Lassen in U160 was in his special area off Trinidad's north coast and would soon resume his task of carpeting the area with wrecks.

Muller-Stockheim in U67 was back for the third time and was cruising near Tobago, while Hans Witt was at that time watching the Norwegian motorship Trafalgar go down, seven hundred miles from Antigua.

Dawn on Thursday sixteenth found Lassen waiting expectantly for a convoy off the Dragon's Mouth. At six o'clock while keeping an eye out for aircraft, he observed the first signs of activity. MTBs and PCs came out of the third Boca and began spreading out. Lassen had U160 on the surface waiting, when the Metox equipment warned of approaching aircraft and he took the boat down to periscope depth to watch the performance.

At six-forty-five the fourteen merchant ships of convoy TRIN 19 began steaming out of the Dragon's Mouth and forming up. The TRNVR handed over the convoy to the senior officer in the Dutch gunboat Jan Van Brakel, and TRIN 19 set off eastwards along Trinidad's north coast. The Dutch gunboat took up position at the head of the convoy, while the RN sloop HMS Clarika took post on the convoy's northern seaward side, along with four of TRIN 19's six, one hundred and ten foot long submarine chasers. The other two escorts worked the safe inshore side of the convoy.

As soon as it was safe to do so, Lassen brought U160 to the surface and sent off a convoy sighting report. U67 off Tobago and U332 off the east coast picked up the signal and turned to intercept, as Lassen began working U160 up towards the convoy's flank. All the boats had to be very careful because the convoy was close inshore, with a heavy surface and air escort.

It had been a long time since any U-Boat had attempted to attack a Caribbean convoy in daylight. Directly over the convoy were P-39 fighters and OS2N Kingfishers, while VP-53 PBYs and VP-74 PBMs covered the area ahead and to seaward of the convoy. U67 was running westwards from Tobago to come up on the convoy's seaward side, when at seven twenty a VP-53 PBY spotted the boat and set up an attack.

Muller-Stockheim's metox gave him ample warning and he had the boat well down by the time the aircraft was overhead. The report from the PBY confirmed that there were two U-Boats in contact with the convoy, because an aircraft had picked up U160 off the Bocas before the convoy came out. The escorts were briefed and they were fully prepared to handle the night attack they were sure would develop as soon as the sun set. Similarly No. 53 squadron was holding back as many aircraft as they could, so that they would have Hudsons around the convoy all night. No one thought that U-Boats would attempt a daylight convoy attack that close to Trinidad.

Lassen was continually forced to dive by the non-stop aircraft patrols around the convoy, but he was slowly working his way eastwards alongside the eight knot convoy. By two o'clock that afternoon Lassen was ready. The convoy had progressed eastwards past Chupara Point, into the stretch of water where he had sunk the Beaconlight, Donavania and Carmona, in July. The majority of the escorts and all the patrol planes were concentrating their attention on the seaward flank of the convoy: this was where danger lurked.

At twenty past two a lone P-39 fighter pilot crossing the convoy's starboard side was startled to see torpedo tracks heading towards the ships from the inshore side of the convoy. His shouted radio warning could do nothing to save the vessels. Lassen was not on the open northern side of the convoy, but between the mass of ships and the rocky coastline and he achieved complete tactical surprise. Three torpedoes left the U-Boat's bow tubes and raced across the sparkling water. Two of them slammed into the seven hundred and thirty ton American coaster Castle Harbour. The little ship was split open by the force of the twin explosions and within thirty seconds she was gone.

Seconds after the two torpedoes detonated on the American ship, the third torpedo romped home into the steel sides of the six thousand ton American freighter Winona. The big ship went out of control and began swinging to port, causing chaos. It had been a month since any Caribbean convoy had been attacked and at the convoy briefing on the previous evening, the merchantmen had been told that the possibility of a U-Boat attack on them was remote.

Not only were the merchantmen not expecting an attack, but their attention had been concentrated on the northern side of the convoy. The fact that the torpedoes had come from the south, created a measure of panic among the ships on the convoy's starboard side. They felt completely exposed, because the majority of the escort was on the opposite side of the convoy and the merchant ships of the starboard column began swinging to port, away from the danger.

The damaged Winona was also swinging to port and causing other ships to swing to starboard to avoid her. The inevitable happened and two of the big freighters collided and remained locked together in the center of the mass of swinging ships. At the same time, the Jan Van Brakel and two submarine chasers were racing through this mass of careering merchant ships to get to the threatened side of the convoy.

The very confusion which Lassen's attack caused ensured that he could not get another target. The escorts were closing and time was limited, but none of the ships appeared to be on a steady course. The attack had taken place off the Trinidad north coast village of Sans Souci, but by this stage the convoy was beginning to break up.

When the confusion was at its worst, a VP-53 Catalina detected U67 trimmed down, moving in against the northern side of the convoy. The air-craft swept into an attack, but Muller-Stockhein had the boat down in quick time. Nevertheless, the aircraft released its depth-charges. The explosions alerted HMS Clarika and she turned towards the danger. To the merchant-men, it appeared as if they were hemmed in. U-Boats to the north and at least one U-Boat between them and the shore. The merchant ship captains were by no means certain of the escort's ability to protect them and they appeared to have one of two options. Either increase speed and race ahead to get out of what appeared to be a trap, or turn back. The majority elected to push ahead. Breaking the convoy speed, they individually sought safety ahead.

The fighter pilot above the convoy was carrying on a running com-mentary of the action below which was causing alarm bells to ring, at the airfields and escort bases ashore. At this moment of maximum confusion, a VP-74 Mariner spotted U332 coming in at the head of the convoy. As the big flying boat dived in to attack, Leibe crash-dived.

The depth-charge explosions ahead of the racing ships seemed to signal disaster. Two submarine chasers increased speed and charged ahead to get to the area of the latest attack, while many of the merchant ships began turning back. To them the trap had been closed. U-Boats ahead and on either flank, with very little sea room. There appeared to be depth-charge explosions on all sides. By this time Jan Van Brakel was assiduously hunting U160 and Clarika, assisted by a submarine chaser was attacking U67. The

Mariner ahead was circling the spot where U332 had dived, holding the boat down, while two submarine chasers were racing for the spot. The other submarine chasers were vainly trying to control the charging merchant ships.

The convoy had disintegrated. The merchant ships were now spread between Grand Matelot Point in the east and Chupara Point in the west, and they were all going in different directions. The damaged Winona had come to a stop, with her crew abandoning ship and nearby, the two locked freighters slowly spun in a macabre dance. The fighter pilot reported a growing stain of bauxite dust on the water and survivors splashing about in the sea. The crews of the two locked merchant ships were also adding to the confusion by lowering lifeboats and attempting to get away.

Above this confusion, an OS2N Kingfisher pilot ran out of oil pressure and his engine quit. The pilot attempted to do an emergency landing, but the swell was too high and the aircraft crashed into the waves disintegrating. Leibe in U332 had slipped away from the submarine chasers, but at this stage he suffered a bout of giddiness and had to break off the action and disengage from the convoy. Without a doubt, Leibe had never seen such confusion in a convoy action.

The frantic signals for help coming from the convoy, combined with the running commentary from the fighter pilot, caused a complete reassignment of priorities at the anti-submarine bases in Trinidad. The reserve flying boats at Chaguaramas were being run up prior to take off. Convoy TRIN 19 had to be reassembled quickly. With the ships scattered along the north coast and three U-Boats in contact, there was a distinct possibility that they would all be sunk. No. 53 squadron at Edinburgh Field was bringing forward its programme so that the Hudsons could join the air escort, while destroyers and MTBs were leaving the Bocas to reinforce the surface escort.

Lying doggo on the bottom in fifteen fathoms, Lassen in U160 listened to the utter chaos taking place above. All he had done was sink one tiny coaster and damage a freighter, but the effect had been magnified out of all proportion by the tactics he had employed and the reaction of the startled merchantmen. Convoy TRIN 19 would be reassembled and once again resume its course, minus four ships, but he had struck a tremendous pyschological blow: the master hunter had done it again.

On Friday a VP-74 Mariner attacked U160 off Trinidad's east coast, as the boat trailed the re-formed reinforced convoy, but the Metox warning ensured that Lassen was well down by the time the depth charges hit the water. At the same time, a VP-53 Catalina attacked Auffermann in U514. That evening U67 and U160 broke off trailing the convoy and turned eastwards. Leibe in U332 was also running eastwards. All the boats were putting as much distance as possible between themselves and Trinidad, because this was the night before full moon.

At six thirty on the morning of the nineteenth, Leibe in U332 achieved his second and last Caribbean kill when he sent the British freighter SS Rotherly to the bottom, three hundred miles east of Barbados. After his success over the Trinidad-bound ship Leibe turned for home. He was not to see the Caribbean again, but the Trinidad based aircraft were not quite finished with the U-Boat. On the following day, when they were well east of the islands and supposedly safe from the regular aircraft patrols, a VP-74 Mariner caught the already three times damaged boat and in an accurate attack, further damaged it. One gets the impression that the crew of U332 were quite pleased to see the last of the Caribbean, but in fact they still had one more incident in which to become involved. U332 was being replaced by the ill-fated U505. The boat had operated off the Yucatan area in July and then been forced to return when its commander became ill.

Lowe handed over command to Kapitanleutnant Peter Zschech. This officer had been the first watchkeeping officer of the great Johann Mohr, in the famous U124 and was supposed to be very experienced, but on this patrol, friction began developing between the new commander and the crew of the U-Boat. It was a classic case of an ace second in command becoming an overconfident, unapproachable commander. U505 was not a happy ship under its new commander and this second visit to the Caribbean was to be a traumatic experience, both for U505 and No. 53 squadron.

On Thursday twenty-second of October another of those enigmatic incidents of war occurred. Hans Witt in U129 met the Spanish tanker Campeche, three hundred and ninety miles east of Barbados. The Campeche had picked up the survivors of the SS Rotherly sunk by U332. The U-Boat went alongside the Spanish vessel and Witt went aboard. It is not certain whether this was a chance meeting, or whether it was a planned rendezvous. It could be also that Witt boarded the Spanish ship to interrogate the survivors of the Rotherly. U332 was also in the vicinity of the neutral Spanish tanker and it is possible that Leibe also went aboard.

The Spanish ship was enroute to Aruba and would eventually get there, but three days after picking up the Rotherly survivors, it found itself thirty miles further east. While this tete-a-tete between the U-Boats and the Spaniard was taking place, two independently sailing American merchant ships appeared. It is obvious that the Allied vessels had not been invited to the party and were intruding on a meeting which was supposed to be very private.

The first ship on the scene was the six thousand eight hundred ton SS
Reuben Tipton. The master of the American ship recognized the silhouette
of the U-Boat alongside the Spaniard and immediately altered course and
called for the maximum speed his engines could give. No doubt the appearance of the Reuben Tipton caused the hurried break up of the meeting
on the tanker and Witt reboarded his boat as quickly as possible.

The U-Boat commander was hardly back on board before the American freighter SS Kabot appeared. The master of the second American vessel
also recognized the danger and sheared off. Witt moved U129 away from
the tanker and turned in pursuit of the Reuben Tipton, while Leibe in
U332 set off after the Kabot. At twelve noon as soon as he realised that he
was being chased, the master of the Reuben Tipton signalled Trinidad describing what he had seen. The master of the Kabot followed suit and then
called on his chief engineer for every ounce of speed the old ship could
give.

At four o'clock Witt had finally drawn abeam of the Reuben Tipton
and turned for his attack. Two torpedoes left the U-Boat and raced towards
the freighter, but the old captain was a wily one. The freighter turned away
in time and the torpedoes raced past. U129 was once again astern of the
freighter and Witt began all over again working his way up alongside the
cargo ship.

In the meantime U332 had caught up with the Kabot and worked its
way into an attacking position. Leibe fired two torpedoes but the master of
the old ship also turned away and U332 was once again astern. After a few
hours Leibe gave up the chase and the Kabot escaped towards Trinidad.

The U-Boat now turned for home. U332 was not to return to the
Caribbean and under a new captain, was to become one of the famous
victims of May 1943. In the meantime Witt was racing after the Reuben
Tipton, intent on catching the ship. Darkness gave him the cover he needed
and at eleven thirty he was once again abeam of the freighter. Two torpedoes smashed into the side of the ship and she came to an exhausted stop
east of Martinique. Her journey from Capetown to Trinidad ended that
night in the dark waters east of the islands.

Two days later Muller-Stockheim had an amazing adventure and a
lucky merchant ship escaped his torpedoes. At six forty that morning, the
SS Peter Minuet ran into U67. The merchant ship turned tail and sped off
with the U-Boat chasing. At nine o'clock the merchant ship came in sight of
the Norwegian freighter Primero and a frantic exchange of signals took place
between the two ships. The Peter Minuet was urging the Primero to run also,
but the other vessel was not fast enough. At nine fifteen Muller-Stockheim

turned inwards. The merchant ship and the U-Boat were both running at their best speeds when the U-Boat turned onto a converging course. An electric torpedo hissed out of the U-Boat's bow tube and sliced through the sea towards the old merchant ship.

The Primero's master was aware that the U-Boat had fired, although the electric torpedo was not leaving a prominent wake and he put on full port wheel to avoid the missile. The torpedo had hardly crossed the half way point between the two charging vessels when it suffered a premature explosion. The great fountain of water from the torpedo explosion, hid the merchant ship for a few seconds and during this time, the ship stopped turning and settled down on a new course, ninety degrees to the old.

As soon as Muller-Stockheim could see the ship again, he fired an air-driven torpedo. This time the merchant ship's captain could see the torpedo wake and it was coming straight for him. Once again the old ship heeled to starboard as full port wheel was wound on. The captain rushed to the bridge wing to see if he would avoid the torpedo. His whole attention was focussed on the awesome missile churning its way torwards the ship's side and it was obvious that it was going to hit. The captain backed away from the bridge wing and braced himself for the detonation. The helmsman was completely forgotten, the ship still had full port wheel on, but that fact was academic at that point. The Primero was going to die anyway.

The torpedo slammed into the Primero's side and the ship rang like a bell. The impossible had happened. While the ship's master tried to bring himself back to reality, the Primero continued under full helm. The torpedo pistol failure exasperated Muller-Stockheim, but he didn't have too much time to worry about it. His boat was now in serious trouble. He had relied on the torpedo to stop the ship and now he had a four thousand five hundred ton ship bearing down on him.

U67 put on full starboard wheel to try and escape. By this time the Primero's master was aware that he had a golden opportunity. The U-Boat was almost under his stem. A shouted order eased the helm and the Primero was now on a course to hit U67 amidships. Muller-Stockheim had full starboard helm on the U-Boat and full power on the diesels. He had one chance and he took it. A barked order killed the diesels and the U-Boat slowed immediately, still swinging to starboard. The U-Boat commander's quick thinking saved U67. The Primero hit the U-Boat just forward of the conning tower, but it was a glancing blow. The impact rolled the U-Boat towards the ship and the old vessel's stem raked the Type IXC's deck and storage bins.

As the Primero ground its way down the U-Boat's side, the captain and officers were looking down at one of the famous Atlantic predators and cursing their luck at not having destroyed it. As soon as the Primero was past, Muller-Stockheim brought his diesels back into play and continued his starboard turn. Primero had had her chance and failed, now she had to die. As the U-Boat's stern swung round, two torpedoes romped out of the stern tubes and both slammed into the ship. The old ship came to a stop, already going fast. U67 pulled away as the liferafts splashed into the sea.

U67 was damaged and she had to get away from the area before aircraft arrived. Muller-Stockheim called on his senior engineer to report on the damage and a damage control party climbed down to the U-Boat's deck. The boat's port side, upper deck spare torpedo containers were damaged. They had to be opened to see if the torpedoes had been crushed or not. From the conning tower, Muller-Stockheim felt the blast as an explosion rocked the boat. A sailor had tried opening one of the containers. The old Primero had taken its revenge.

U67 reported to headquarters that it would have to move well east in order to affect repairs, but by an odd quirk of fate, she crossed the Peter Minuet's path. At eight o'clock that night the original target crossed U67's bow and Muller-Stockheim sent a torpedo after the ship. The torpedo missed and once again the Peter Minuet hustled away. U67 had more important considerations than to chase the merchant ship again.

Dawn on October twenty-ninth found the little Panamanian freighter SS Macabi ploughing along Trinidad's south coast, towards the Serpent's Mouth entrance to the Gulf of Paria. The vessel's master was in a hurry and he didn't care too much for the wartime restrictions being imposed on the routes he had travelled for years. At six twenty-two he cut the corner at Icacos Point, intending to round the Point via the inshore channel and found himself in the defensive minefield. There was no way out and when the vessel's bows touched the first Mark IV mine, the explosion opened up the little ship. She settled onto the mud in the shallow water to become a permanent feature of the entrance to the Gulf. A warning to all users of the Serpent's Mouth.

At the Dragon's Mouth entrance, there were no mishaps and the convoys moved freely. At eleven o'clock convoy TAG 17 with twenty-seven merchant ships escorted by five warships, began its long run. Then at one o'clock the USS Ellis came through the Bocas. She was a member of Task Group 23.3, composed of the light cruiser Omaha with the destroyers Davis, Jouett, Badger, Osmond Ingram and Ellis. The powerful Task Group was the escort for convoy BRN-2, which brought its twelve merchant ships through the Bocas at four fifteen that afternoon.

BRN was the designation for the recently introduced Brazilian coastal convoys, many of which used Trinidad as their northern terminus. The Ellis had been detached from the convoy, so that she could arrive early with an important candidate for ONI interrogation. When she docked, signalman Francissek Machon was led down the gangplank by an armed escort. The twenty-four year old German sailor was the sole survivor of U512. He claimed to have escaped from U512 from a depth of fifty meters using a survival lung after the 99th squadron depth charges destroyed the boat on October second.

At five fifteen that afternoon, U129 achieved its second kill of this third Caribbean cruise. The boat was operating four hundred miles east of Martinique, when the five thousand six hundred ton American freighter West Kehar, crossed its path. Witt sent two torpedoes into the big cargo ship and broke her back. As the vessel went down, the crew managed to lower one lifeboat. Twelve days later the thirty-eight sunburned, starved survivors reached Barbados.

The West Kehar had been the thirteenth ship sunk by the U-Boats during October. Added to this was the Macabi, destroyed by the defending minefield and the three ships damaged in the action around convoy TRIN 19. It meant that only fifty-two thousand and thirteen tons of shipping had been lost during the month. Compared to the months before, this was a negligible total, particularly when compared with the ninety-two ships sunk worldwide. In fact, it was roughly what a good U-Boat could have achieved during May or June, but to win this total the U-Boats had fought very hard. Only ten U-Boats operated in the area during October and there were seldom more than four operational at any given time.

The bulk of the U-Boats were back in the North Atlantic enduring the fierce gales that were lashing the area. They were in the mid-Atlantic air-gap, known to the Germans as Das Todtesloch, or the death hole. October in the Caribbean had seen a lull develop in the sinking rate, but Doenitz had been giving the area some consideration. It was his intention to get what he could from the North Atlantic while he could, but he felt that the Caribbean campaign should not be allowed to die out. In October the boats had not penetrated the Caribbean Sea, other than off the Dragon's Mouth and he intended to remedy this in the coming month.

The end of the month found seven experienced veteran U-Boats ready to set the Caribbean defences hopping again. U129 was four hundred miles east and moving in towards Trinidad, with the intention of moving at the Aruba oil terminus once more. Lassen in U160 was just south of Grenada, preparing to move against the convoys and create the usual consternation that he specialised in. Zscheck in U505 was coming down the Windward

Islands towards his operating area off Trinidad. Behind U505 were Engelmann in U163, Staats in U508 and U154 on its third cruise under its new captain, Heinrich Schuch. Five hundred miles east, Muller-Stockheim was repairing the considerable damage inflicted by the old Primero and the subsequent explosion. U67 would be ready in time to play its part in the November actions. It was not a strong force, but they were all experienced and knowledgeable about the Caribbean.

During the lull, the defenders had been steadily building their strength and both the convoy terminus and the naval base had been expanding their activity. Eleven large convoys had arrived in Trinidad with a total of one hundred and thirteen ships, while eighteen convoys had departed with one hundred and ninety merchant vessels. At the naval base, fifty-four warships had arrived and eighty-six departed. There were now more than fifty US Navy and Coast Guard vessels attached to Chaguaramas Naval base, while the Royal Navy and the TRNVR were operating a further twenty-six escort vessels. Additionally, the Canadian corvettes were still based in Trinidad, but by far the most significant new arrivals, were the twenty-three surviving RN anti-submarine trawlers which had now been transferred from the US east coast.

Important changes took place in the aviation community at the end of October. The highly efficient No. 99 bombardment squadron were transferred from Zandery in Dutch Guiana, to Orlando in Florida, for service off the US coast. Their place was taken by the 35th bombardment squadron from Boringquen. The new unit operated a detachment at Atkinson Field, replacing the 430th squadron who moved south to Brazil. No. 1 bombardment squadron, the first Caribbean aviation unit, left Trinidad at the end of the month. They had worked long and hard, without achieving a U-Boat kill but their chance would come in March 1943.

Replacing them at Edinburgh Field, were three units forming the 25th Bomber Group. These were the B18 equipped Numbers 10 and 80 bombardment squadrons and a detachment of the 417th squadron. Edinburgh Field was now operating twenty-eight B18s and twenty Hudsons. The second runway had been completed and the base was now a large sprawling complex of runways, taxiways and dispersals, although much of its accommodation was still tented. In fact, Edinburgh Field had now grown larger than its parent Waller Field and work had commenced on a satellite field at Camden. Waller Field was now used exclusively by fighters and the many aircraft transiting to Brazil.

At the Naval Air Station in Chaguaramas VP-74 had grown to its full complement of thirteen sea-grey camouflaged PBM Mariners. VP-53 had twelve PBY Catalinas camouflaged white, with a detachment in Panama of two aircraft. VS-45 now had a total of seventeen OS2N Kingfishers and the squadron would soon start to base detachments in the river deltas along the South American coast. The air station had grown considerably and the flying boats now continually patrolled the shipping lanes. With these enhanced resources, the defenders awaited the November onslaught.

CHAPTER

11

The death of an escort

At nine o'clock on the morning of November first, convoy TRIN 23 came out of the Bocas and two hours later convoy GAT 17 arrived. The convoy escorts reflected the U-Boat operating patterns in September and October. The inbound convoy, coming through the quiet Caribbean had been escorted by one gunboat, one destroyer and two PCs.

However, TRIN 23 which was going to traverse the area east of Trinidad and the South American coast was heavily escorted. The twelve merchant ships had the light cruisers Omaha, and Marblehead, with the destroyers Davis, Badger, Jouett, Ellis and Osmond Ingram protecting them. No one had informed the convoy routing center that the Grand Admiral had changed his tactics. The U-Boats were returning to the Caribbean. Shortly before the convoy left the Bocas, Witt passed through the Galleons Passage and set course for Aruba. Staats in U508 was not far behind and Lassen in U160, was already in the Caribbean west of Grenada.

At ten o'clock on the following morning, convoy TAG 18 left the Bocas on its long run, with an escort that reflected an outdated appreciation of the U-Boat dispositions. The twenty-two merchant ships in the slow convoy were being escorted by one destroyer the USS Siren, and three one hundred and seventy foot PCs. At five o'clock that afternoon Lassen sighted the great mass of ships moving west and sent off a convoy sighting report. Well ahead of the convoy, Witt in U129 picked up the signal and plotted his course to intercept them near the tanker terminus at Aruba, while Staats in U508 behind the convoy, increased speed to catch up.

By eleven o'clock that night, Lassen had U160 in position for an attack on the convoy's starboard side. Seven minutes later, a torpedo hit the Canadian freighter Christian J. Kampman. The little ship spilled its cargo of sugar into the sea and was gone in a matter of minutes. Lassen dropped back as the starboard escort turned towards him. An hour later Staats in U508 caught up with convoy TAG 18 on the port side and began to work up to an attack position. The little PCs were not a serious threat, provided that the U-Boats did not allow themselves to get caught and Lassen did not intend to be pinned down. He kept U160 astern of the convoy's starboard wing and waited.

At two o'clock in the morning both U-Boats began to come in for attacks on either flank. U508 had not gone far before she was sighted by the air escort and forced to dive. A PC raced out to the port wing and began probing for her, but Lassen had again managed to work his way abeam of the convoy. At twenty-six minutes past two, four torpedoes left the U-Boat and began their run. Two of the missiles passed right through the convoy, but the other two hit the Norwegian tanker Thorshavet. The big eleven thousand and fifteen ton vessel staggered to a halt, as the other ships in her column manoeuvred to avoid the giant vessel. Once more a PC came crashing towards U160 and Lassen employed the same tactics as previously, dropping back into a position astern.

At this stage the senior officer in the USS Siren was aware that he faced a double threat which his escorts could not handle. He sent off a message to Trinidad requesting urgent reinforcement, which generated an immediate response. Two destroyers, USS Biddle and USS Greer were ordered to sea, and both VP-53 and No. 53 squadron at Edinburgh were alerted. The convoy was still only one hundred miles away from Trinidad and this meant that within an hour additional aircraft could be on scene and it would take only four hours before the destroyers were with TAG 18.

For the rest of that night, Staats harassed the convoy's port side and this had the effect of drawing most of the escort away from the starboard side of the convoy. Lassen used the gap created on the quiet side of the convoy and at dawn U160 was in position with her torpedo tubes reloaded.

The solitary PC guarding this side of the convoy was left astern as U160 drew ahead of the starboard column of ships and turned inwards.

It was full daylight by the time Lassen was satisfied with his attack position and he took U160 down to periscope depth to ensure that his attack was not disturbed by the circling aircraft. At seven thirty two torpedoes left the U-Boat and began their journey through the convoy. One torpedo passed right through the columns, but the second found the four thousand ton British freighter, SS Gypsom Express. The old tramp steamer staggered under the impact and began to go down immediately. The starboard side escort turned towards the suspected position of the U-Boat and came into the attack, but Lassen was moving closer to the convoy. The PC began laying a pattern of depth-charges.

Thirteen minutes later, the slender attack periscope slid upwards and Lassen fired two more torpedoes. These engines of destruction raced across the intervening space and buried themselves in the sides of the big Panamanian registered tanker, Leda. The eight thousand five hundred ton vessel came to an abrupt stop veering to port. This time the PC on the starboard side realised that the U-Boat was almost inside the convoy and it came charging into the attack. U160 went silent and deep as the depth charges began detonating.

At roughly the same time Hudson PZ/L flown by P/O Rickards came upon the first of Lassen's victims. The big tanker Thorshavet was still afloat but in a sinking condition. The Spanish tanker Gobeo was standing by near the wreck of the Thorshavet and one of the ship's boats was being lowered. The Allied airmen never trusted Spanish ships and the Hudson immediately signalled the Gobeo instructing the vessel to proceed on course.

There were now five 53 squadron Hudsons working the area immediately astern of the slow moving convoy while the PBYs of VP-53 circled the convoy itself. Fifteen minutes later Hudson PZ/E flown by P/O Puckeridge sighted the Spanish boat making its way towards the sinking Thorshavet. The Hudson came into an attack dive and opened fire at the water ahead of the ship's boat forcing the Spaniards to back off. The Gobeo continued altering course and moving erratically all morning, among the many sinking wrecks and boatloads of survivors behind the convoy. The Hudsons kept driving it away from the scene as a whole host of patrol vessels, tugs and escorts came sweeping out from Trinidad.

By midday the tanker Leda had five vessels from Trinidad surrounding it. On the next day when the Spanish ship entered Port of Spain, British and US Naval Intelligence operatives went on board for a full interrogation of the officers and men of the ship. However, the Spaniards could and did claim that they were only intent on saving lives and the Allies were forced to let the matter drop, but since the incident with the Campeche, the Spanish ships in the area were viewed with deep suspicion.

By eight o'clock that morning the TAG 18 escorts were exasperated. Four ships totalling over twenty-five thousand tons had been taken out of the convoy. Continuous aggressive rushes and depthcharge attacks had not stopped the carefully timed and co-ordinated attacks. Since dawn the area on the starboard side of the convoy had seen numerous depth charge explosions, but the U-Boat was still there and the reports of periscope sightings were continuous. The reinforcing escort destroyers were still an hour away, but in that time the U-Boats could well strike again.

Something had to be done and the senior officer in the USS Siren decided on an unusual tactic. Since the PCs were not capable of pinning down the U-Boat, he ordered them instead to lay a smokescreen along the convoy's starboard flank. The smoke screen proved very effective because Lassen could not see the ships in the convoy. The only counter-tactic that he could employ would be to surface and dash through the screen, but he faced two dangers. The surfaced boat would immediately attract the attention of one of the circling VP-53 flying boats, or the escort's radar would pick him up and they would be ready for him when he emerged from the smoke. Reluctantly, Lassen had to admit defeat and drop back. The escorts' smoke screen was so effective that they were ordered to renew it twenty minutes later.

By this time the giant Thorshavet had gone down, but the heavily damaged Leda was still afloat and Lassen set course for it. In the breathing space that the smokescreen created, the USS Biddle and Greer arrived and took post on either flank of the convoy. U508 was also forced to drop back from the now overwhelmingly powerful air and sea escort of TAG 18.

She had hardly broken off the action before a No. 53 squadron Hudson was diving at her. However, the metox equipment gave ample warning and Staats had the boat down in good time. A No. 53 squadron Hudson also sighted U160 enroute to the damaged Leda, but again the metox gave sufficient warning and U160 was down while the aircraft was still seven miles away.

The escorts and patrol vessels were now out in force, picking up the many survivors from the wreckage-strewn seas behind the convoy. They surrounded the Leda and a tug took the damaged ship in tow, but the vessel was not destined to make it. When she was thirty miles northwest of Trinidad's Grand Boca, the tanker gave up and slipped beneath the waves. Lassen's fourth victim from the convoy was gone.

TAG 18 had now left the two U-Boats behind and all afternoon of the fourth the escorts prowled around the remaining ships, ensuring that no U-Boat could get in. No. 53 squadron had sighted two U-Boats well astern of the ships and the assumption was naturally drawn that TAG 18 was now safe.

No U-Boat had operated near Aruba or across the Caribbean to the Windward Passage for a considerable period of time, but unknown to the convoy, U129 was across their route. The boat had transited the area between Trinidad and Aruba and taken up position at the traditional joining point for the tankers from Aruba. In the late evening of November fourth, PCs escorted the eight joining tankers out of Aruba and co-ordinated their arrival to coincide with the head of convoy TAG 18.

At two o'clock next morning Witt was in position to attack. Three torpedoes left the U-Boat and raced away towards the unsuspecting convoy. One minute and twenty-nine seconds later, the first of the three detonated on the American tanker Meton. In quick succession the other two torpedoes romped into the tanker, bringing it to an immediate and final stop. The vessel's crew abandoned ship, as the tanker's stern slipped below the waves. Within a minute the seven thousand ton tanker had gone.

Witt in the meantime, had turned U129 and now brought his stern tubes to bear. Both stern tubes discharged their deadly cargo and three minutes after the Meton had been hit, the two torpedoes detonated on the tanker Astrel. The seven thousand six hundred ton tanker came to a halt on fire. TAG 18 had lost its sixth ship. The convoy escorts were quick to react and by the glow from the burning Astrel, they converged on the U-Boat. While the angry escorts held U129 down, TAG 18 sailed on and finally entered safe waters.

On the following day Kurt-Edward Engelmann opened his second Caribbean patrol, by sinking the five thousand ton British freighter La Cordillera. The vessel which was travelling from Capetown to Trinidad in ballast, went down into the deep water of the Barbados Basin, south of the island. Staats in U508 stayed north of Margarita, where the fight with TAG 18 had taken place, while Lassen brought U160 back down to the Trinidad north coast.

At two o'clock on November sixth he caught up with the small convoy TRIN 24, with eight merchant ships, escorted by HMS Clarika and the anti-submarine trawlers Artic Explorer and Lady Elsa. From a position eight miles off Trinidad's Galera Point, Lassen fired two torpedoes. One torpedo ran right through the convoy and detonated at the end of its run, but the other buried itself in the British freighter Arica. The stern of the five thousand four hundred ton vessel sank immediately and a P-39 fighter pilot reported only the bow sticking out of the water. The vessel went down in fifty fathoms, halfway across the Galleons Passage between Trinidad and Tobago. After the vessel went down, Lassen worked his boat round Galera Point and lay on the bottom to the southeast to avoid the searching anti-submarine trawlers.

U-Boat headquarters were satisfied with the job being done by the few boats around Trinidad, but they realised that tankers should be the targets for the boats' torpedoes and dispatched U163 to back up U129 off Aruba. It is likely that Staats in U508 had been a friend of Shultz in the U512, or at least he was in sympathy with Shultz's predicament, because that day he signalled U-Boat headquarters requesting permission to sink a Spanish ship. It could have been the tanker Gorbeo which was still hanging around and as far as Staats and the Allies were concerned, was behaving erratically.

U-Boat headquarters sent back a terse signal reminding him of Standing Orders. At seven o'clock that evening Zschech sank his only Caribbean target. On the trip across the Atlantic, he had not endeared himself to his crew and this first Caribbean attack only worsened the situation. U505 was operating sixty miles east of Trinidad's Galera Point when the British freighter Ocean Justice came in sight. Zschech over-estimated the vessel's speed and the first two torpedoes passed well ahead of the target. On the British ship they could not have been keeping a very good lookout, because no one saw the torpedo tracks and the vessel continued on course. On the U-Boat Zschech blamed the First Watchkeeping officer for plotting the wrong target speed instead of taking the blame for the miscalculation.

His second pair of torpedoes hit the forward part of the vessel, showing that even his adjusted estimate of speed had been out, but the twin explosions were enough to send the seven thousand ton vessel to the seabed. The crew expected Zschech to close the stricken vessel and check its name as their previous commander would have done, but probably because they expected it, Zschech did the opposite. He turned U505 and sped off, in the process underestimating by nearly two thousand tons in his attack report.

Saturday seventh of November saw the Allies begin the re-conquest of North Africa, with the much delayed operation Torch. U-Boat command responded by transferring boats from the North Atlantic to the area off Morocco. Thirty-one boats were involved and these included U173 on its way to the Caribbean. This boat had operated in the Caribbean under Schweichel in July and August. The diversion was to spell disaster and U173 was caught on the sixteenth by three US destroyers, the Woolsey, Swanson and Quick and destroyed with all its crew.

The redirection of U-Boats to the coast of Morocco provided the first serious check to the Caribbean offensive because U173 was not the only boat diverted while on its way to the Caribbean. Piening in U155, Henke in U515, Jannsen in U103 and Nietzel in U510 were also redirected, but all of these boats were lucky and survived. Many other boats which had served in the Caribbean took part in operations against the American invasion convoys.

Doenitz was not in agreement with this massive shift of boats into an area that was literally crawling with anti-submarine forces. He would have preferred to allow the boats to continue hitting at the lines of communication leading to the invasion area, but Hitler had his way. The result was that the carefully worked out rota of operations was completely disrupted, and in December there was a marked shortage of U-Boats in all areas. This hit the Caribbean campaign hardest, because Doenitz was planning a year-end gathering of veterans in the sunny Caribbean, instead of pitting them against the winter storms in the North Atlantic.

In the Caribbean the day was marked by several significant events. The first of these was the return of U67. Muller-Stockheim had finally repaired the damage done to the boat by the old Primero and he brought U67 into its operating area off Trinidad's north coast. In July and August U508 had operated against heavily defended convoys off the north coast of Cuba and in the Florida Straits, without success. After this U508 had vainly attacked convoy TAW-13 and created the diversion which had allowed Thurmann in U553 to get in. Against convoy TAG 18, he had provided the diversion for U160 to do the damage and to Staats, it was beginning to seem as if his was a permanent diversion boat, but on the seventh his chance came.

Convoy TAG 19 left the Bocas on Friday sixth of November with seventeen merchant ships. The escort consisted of the senior officer in the old flush-decked destroyer USS Breckenridge, and the corvette USS Surprise on loan from the British, along with five PCs. Soon after its departure, the convoy was sighted by Staats and he brought U508 into a shadowing position, while sending off his sightings report.

At midnight Staats began to work his way up the convoy's seaward flank, diving each time one of the air escort approached too closely. Staats moved carefully and at three forty-five in the morning he was in a good position and ready to attack. Two torpedoes left the tubes and both hit the American freighter Nathaniel Hawthorne. The seven thousand ton Liberty ship came to a halt going down by the head, as its crew frantically began to abandon ship.

Seven minutes later he aimed carefully and discharged two more torpedoes. By this stage the destroyer Breckenridge had picked him up on radar and was closing fast. Staats wasted no time in taking his boat deep, while the two torpedoes romped home into the five thousand four hundred ton British freighter Lindenhall. The vessel yawed out of line and came to a stop not far from the sinking Nathaniel Hawthorne. Within an hour both ships had gone to the seabed, forty miles north of Margarita Island. However, U508 was hunted for the rest of the night by the destroyer and the corvette.

The day ended with U154 on its third Caribbean cruise, sinking the Free French freighter D'entrecasteaux. The seven thousand ton ship went to the bottom one hundred and fifty miles east of Barbados. At dawn next morning, U67 used an electric torpedo to damage the four thousand seven hundred ton freighter Campo Olmo. The British ship was hit when eight miles off the Trinidad north coast village of Blanchisseuse. MTBs were in the area and Muller-Stockheim was forced to pull back, as the heavily damaged vessel slowly made its way down the north coast and into the Gulf.

There were five U-Boats in a ring around Trinidad and all day the anti-submarine forces were busy. VP-74 and No. 53 squadron carried out a number of attacks on U67, U160, U154 and U508, while PCs tried to pin down the boats with depth charge attacks. MTBs rescued twenty-six survivors from the sunken Ocean Justice, and a lifeboat carrying the remainder was washed ashore on Balandra beach. No. 53 squadron also vectored PCs onto liferafts with survivors from convoy TAG 19. At eight o'clock next morning U67 struck again, sinking the Norwegian freighter Nidarland, twenty miles north of Tobago. An hour later U154 hit the British freighter Nurmahal three hundred miles east of Martinique. The crew abandoned ship, but the five thousand five hundred ton vessel remained afloat for the next three days until it quietly disappeared on November eleventh.

Convoy TAG 20 another slow convoy, came out of the Third Boca at nine o'clock on the tenth of November and began its run to Aruba. The thirteen merchant vessels were escorted by the US patrol gunboat USS Eire, the destroyer Biddle, recently returned from its stint with TAG 18 and the corvette USS Spry. Three PCs also accompanied the convoy on its long journey. Shortly after leaving the Boca, TAG 20 crossed the inbound convoy GAT 19, led by the destroyer Upshur and the Coast Guard cutter Guyahoga. Both convoys had heavy aircover in response to the damaging attacks on TAG 18 and 19, and in fact three U-Boats were sighted and forced down.

At one o'clock that afternoon, an RAF Hudson reported a large underwater explosion eight miles off Manzanilla Point, and claimed that bubbles were still rising from the spot twenty-five minutes later. No U-Boat was in this area and it could only have been a mine drifting into the Manzanilla Bank, which at this point, had six fathoms of water over it. Nevertheless, with the increased U-Boat activity around the island, the report had to be investigated. But by far the most important event that day was not seen by Allied eyes and remained a mystery for many years.

At nine forty-five that morning, Flt. Sgt. Sillcock lifted Hudson PZ/L off the runway at Edinburgh Field and set course for the bauxite route. Sillcock was one of No. 53 squadron's top pilots. He was the first squadron pilot to carry out an anti-submarine attack when the squadron had recently arrived in Trinidad during August. The attack had caught U155 east of Martinique and severely damaged Piening's boat. Later that month, he was the pilot who delivered the attack on U173 which almost destroyed the U-Boat, east of Trinidad. On the morning of the tenth, he had the same experienced crew of Sergeants Nelson, Miller and Skinner aboard, when he set course for the area east of Trinidad.

Zschech had spent the previous three days cruising along the Trinidad east coast, one hundred and fifty miles offshore. There had been continuous aircraft alarms from the metox equipment and the boat had spent eighteen hours submerged during that time. On the morning of the tenth Zschech had U505 fully surfaced under clouds that had their bases as low as one thousand feet. It was ideal weather for attacking aircraft. Under such a sky of patchy low clouds, the boat's previous commander Lowe, would have had the boat trimmed down, ready to submerge and the fact that Zschech was fully surfaced worried the crew.

Zschech was still having clashes with his crew, as he sought to assert his authority and his way of doing things, on a crew who had been trained by another man. He was acutely aware that he was not proving to be a lucky commander and that the crew were looking at him critically. This made him obstinate to the point where he was taking chances, which he might not have, if he had not been under pressure to prove himself.

Nervousness overcame the First Watchkeeping officer, and he politely asked if Zschech wanted the lookouts doubled. Apparently irritated by having an obvious precaution pointed out to him, he brushed the suggestion aside, by pointing out that the metox equipment would warn of any approaching aircraft, and the fact that too many lookouts on the conning tower would only cause them to take longer to dive. With U505 fully surfaced under low cloud bases, Zschech patrolled close to the island of Trinidad.

Sillcock and his experienced crew died that morning, and it is almost impossible to say exactly what happened aboard the aircraft. Either the

ASV radar failed, or Sillcock ordered it turned off, because the weather was ideal for hunting. In either case, the metox receiver on U505 gave no warning at all of the approach of the Hudson. It is probable that Sillock picked up the U-Boat visually and worked his way into an ideal attacking position, using the clouds as cover. At any rate, the lookout on U505 did not see the aircraft until it was only five hundred yards away. There was no time to do anything other than scream a warning and duck behind the spray shield. The officer of the watch and the other lookouts whirled in time to see the four deadly objects on their way down from the aircraft. The record will show that when Sillcock attacked a U-Boat he never missed and on this occasion, his aim was too good. It is possible that three depth charges passed over the boat and into the water, but the fourth hit the afterdeck squarely. The charge should have smashed its way through the decking as had happened with U158, but the impact caused it to explode on contact.

If that fourth depth charge had undershot or overshot by six feet, it would have cut U505 into two halves, but exploding on the deck, its blast was directed mainly upwards against the Hudson. There was a blinding flash of flame and a terrific detonation which hurled the conning tower personnel to the deck. The U-Boat pressure hull rang like a giant bell. It was as if U505 had run into a wall. The explosion of the other three depth-charges were minor in comparison to the violence of the blow on the U-Boat. Seconds later the Hudson hit the water in a great ball of flame, one hundred yards ahead of the U-Boat's bow. Sillcock and his crew never had a chance.

The shambles which greeted Zschech as he scrambled up the hatch stunned him. Half the conning tower watch lay in spreading pools of blood, but it was as if a giant hammer had hit the after end of the U-Boat. The anti-aircraft platform was gone and beyond it there was just a shambles of twisted steel. Both engines were dead and the boat stopped moving, close to some of the bodies of the aircraft crew.

At last Zschech found his niche. He was cool and collected as he directed the massive damage control operation that was now required, but the damage had already been done to the crew's morale. At eleven o'clock in the morning U505 began moving again on one engine. It was forty-five minutes since the attack, which meant that Sillcock had attacked the boat shortly after beginning his patrol.

No radio report had been sent prior to the attack, which meant that the Hudson would not be missed until his patrol was due to be over. Zschech had just over eight hours to get away. They tended the wounded, while the engineer's party blanked off the port engine which was completely unserviceable. On deck, parties using blow torches cut away masses of tangled metal, exposing the bare pressure hull below. When the radio was repaired, Zschech reported the attack and called for a doctor. He was vectored to rendezvous with U462, in mid Atlantic. Twice they had close calls when a flying boat passed close to them without sighting the U-Boat. Before U505 got to the rendezvous point with the tanker, they met U105 and received morphine for their wounded and then met U68 for spare parts.

U505 escaped because No. 53 squadron did not know what had happened to Sillcock and in fact they never found out. On the following day aircraft searched Sillcock's patrol area, but there was no sign of wreckage and no clue as to what had happened to the aircraft.

By this stage Zschech had got his badly damaged boat out of the area. In time he got U505 home but as far as his crew were concerned he was useless. The boat never returned to the Caribbean but continued its long tortuous road to immortality. It was as if the ghosts of Sillcock and his crew were haunting Zschech. It took six months to repair the bomb damage to the boat and during that time the war in the Atlantic turned against the U-Boats. Some boats were going out and their commanders were making a name for themselves, while the vast majority were going out, never to come back. Through this time of greatest trial the crew of U505 had to endure being laughed at by their comrades, and their opinion of their commander sank lower.

When in June 1943 U505 was finally handed over, Zschech took her to sea, intent on making up for the enforced inactivity, but he was back alongside in Lorient within twenty-four hours. The boat had a long list of defects still to be corrected. Five times U505 left Lorient and each time she was forced to return before getting out of the Bay of Biscay.

Ships, sailors and superstition traditionally go together and it was not long before some less pragmatic sailors began to find an imaginary umbilical cord of superstition between the boat's bad luck and its Caribbean adventures. Some attributed U505's plight to the spirit of the old sailing ship that Lowe had sunk, while others were certain that it was the ghost of Sillcock and his crew.

In fact it was the work of the French Maquis, but superstition lurks in the corners of every sailor's mind, even the most professional. During all these comings and goings, the crew's morale went to zero and Zschech's self confidence with it. While others died, U505 became known as the boat that would always come back.

Zschech's private nightmare ended on October 24th, 1943. He had finally got U505 out into the Atlantic and almost immediately got pinned down by a destroyer. By this stage Zschech was suffering from acute depression and he had reached the stage where he considered himself to be a failure. During the depth-charge attacks he gave up, and Meyer, his new First Watchkeeping officer was forced to take over the controls. With the destroyer running in for another attack, Zschech became the only U-Boat commander ever to desert his ship when he committed suicide in the control room. Some claimed that from that moment Sillcock's ghost was avenged and Meyer was able to get the boat away from the destroyer and home to Lorient, but the U505 story was not over, it was only working towards its climax.

After Flt. Sgt. Sillcock's attack on U505, the boat was no longer an operational member of the Caribbean team as it ran eastwards for survival. This left U67 close to Tobago, U154 near Barbados and U160 running southeast towards British Guiana. The only boat northwest of Trinidad was U508, but the aircraft had it targeted and convoy TAG 20 was rerouted around the suspected position.

Ahead of them lay U129 and U163 off the Dutch islands. At three o'clock next morning with TAG 20 running easily westwards, Lassen in U160 had arrived off the mouth of Waini river. He had left the Trinidad north coast for the last time, having put nine ships on the bottom in that area. He was thirty miles off the river entrance when the six thousand four hundred ton British freighter City of Ripon, on course for Trinidad, came up over the horizon. Lassen used two torpedoes to send the ship and its precious cargo down to the mud of the delta.

Dawn on the twelfth found convoy TAG 20 running westwards towards the island of Curacao, with its seven escort vessels disposed around the columns of merchant ships. Three of the escorts were equipped with radar and all of them had asdic. Overhead the long range, radar-equipped Catalinas of VP-53 endlessly prowled round the mass of shipping. During the night, aircraft had detected three U-Boat contacts astern of the ships. In fact this had been Staats in U508 searching ceaselessly for a convoy he knew should have passed his way, but the escorts could only assume that there were three U-Boats trailing them.

More important than the contact astern was a report from an A 20 pilot that he had attacked a U-Boat north of Curacao. This was Hans Witt in U129 and he was sitting astride the convoy's route. Despite the overwhelmingly powerful escort surrounding TAG 20, Commander Mack in USS Eric was worried about being caught between two groups of U-Boats and suffering the fate of the two previous convoys.

He decided to confuse the U-Boats with another major rerouting of the convoy. He signalled the other escorts giving an appreciation of the tactical situation and then brought the convoy round to port. The alteration took the whole convoy southward, between Isla Orchilla and the Isla Los Roques group and then westwards. This brilliant move would take TAG 20 south of Bonaire to the area South of Curacao, where the joining tankers from Aruba would meet them. After the rendezvous, the convoy could then proceed northwest between Aruba and Curacao, up to the Windward Passage. The rerouting left U508 searching for a convoy that had side-stepped it and left U129, waiting north of Curacao for a convoy that would never arrive.

Unfortunately Engelmann in U163 was not hunting convoys, he was after unescorted ships and had positioned himself south of Curacao. The boat had not transmitted for four days, so the Allies had no knowledge of his presence astride the new route that the convoy had taken. There was no escape for TAG 20. Whichever route the ships took they were bound to run into one of Doenitz's wolves. U163 had taken part in the all night attack on convoy TAW 13 in August along with U508 and U553. Like U508, Engelmann in U163 created the diversion against the experienced B 5 escort group, which had made the convoy battle a success. She had paid that night by having to endure the continuous depth-charge attacks, while other boats got the opportunity to fire. Engelmann had enough experience of the Caribbean to have a healthy respect for its airpower, and this is the reason he had been able to remain undetected south of Curacao.

The USS Erie was one of only two such ships in the world. She was a patrol gunboat built in 1936, to an outdated specification that was no longer relevant, but she found her niche as an escort leader. At two thousand tons, this graceful ship was much bigger than a destroyer, but her speed was restricted to twenty knots, which meant that she could not steam with the Fleet. She carried a considerable punch with four six inch guns in single turrets and was fitted with radar, asdic and a full load of depth-charges.

She was an excellent escort for the Caribbean convoys and in addition to her other attributes, she carried an aircraft. The attached floatplane was particularly useful in convoy work, especially when there was no shore based aircover. In the Caribbean the floatplane was seldom needed, but it would have been very useful in the North Atlantic. The gunboat carried the necessary equipment for her to function efficiently as a leader and she was used on the Trinidad/Key West run, always in charge of a convoy.

The early afternoon of the twelfth, found the convoy approaching Willemstadt in Curacao with the USS Erie, two miles ahead of the main group of ships. Normal practice during daylight was for convoy escorts to use only passive listening devices and switch to active asdic pinging only at night, but because of the prevalence of U-Boats in the area, all the escorts were instructed to use their asdic during daylight. Each vessel was assigned a hundred and twenty degree search arc, which ensured a considerable overlap. In theory, no U-Boat could get into this convoy undetected.

At five thirty that afternoon the convoy was on course three hundred degrees, a few miles south of Willemstadt. The merchant ships were in six columns with the destroyer USS Biddle and three PCs in an arc across the stern. Off to the right, the Navy tanker Gulf Dawn and another merchant ship had detached and were under PC escort for Willemstadt.

Across the front of the convoy were a PC out to port, the USS Erie in the centre and the corvette USS Spry to starboard. Off the convoy's port bow, was the joining convoy of four tankers with a PC and a submarine chaser as escort. Ahead of the convoy was the powerful Dutch sloop Van Kinsbergen and a detached PC. At this point, there were twelve escorts in the immediate vicinity of the convoy, as well as the patrolling aircraft. No U-Boat could handle that, but Engelmann was inside the convoy screen.

U163 did not survive the war and unfortunately the boat's torpedo log does not coincide with the observer's testimony, but it would indeed be interesting to find out how Engelmann got U163 inside the escort screen undetected. At five thirty U163 was immediately ahead of the columns of merchant ships, facing not at the tempting target behind her, but at the USS Erie. The U-Boat was at periscope depth almost under the stems of the advancing cargo ships, when two torpedoes left her tubes. Seconds later the remaining two bow tubes discharged their deadly missiles. Engelmann then turned U163 until his empty bow tubes were facing the merchant ships and discharged one stern torpedo at the Erie.

The senior escort was five thousand yards ahead of the convoy moving at fifteen knots, when the officer of the Deck noticed what appeared to be two torpedoes porpoising two thousand yards on the starboard side. The torpedoes were throwing up a considerable amount of spray and Erie began to turn to starboard to investigate. The sonar room was given a new bearing to conduct an asdic search, and the ship had just begun to answer the helm. Almost immediately the navigating officer reported another two torpedoes, five hundred yards on the starboard quarter. The order, hard left, was followed almost immediately by a call for full speed. Reports of two torpedoes close in now came streaming in from lookouts, signalmen and gun crews.

The officer of the deck sounded the siren for collision, while dozens of eyes followed the closer pair of torpedoes. They appeared to be running on shallow setting, four to six feet down and occasionally porpoising. The

Erie began swinging to port, but it was too late. The torpedoes were so close that witnesses could see on one of them a copper coloured head and the grease on its body. The torpedoes seemed to be gently curving to the left as they came in to the gunboat's starboard quarter

One torpedo hit the Erie and the other passed ahead of the ship. The torpedo impacted roughly five feet below the waterline, under number four gun turret. The blast from the torpedo warhead opened the hull right up to the main deck and ruptured the fuel tanks. The Admiral's stateroom area and Wardroom were in the immediate vicinity of the explosion and many officers who were in this part of the ship died. Ten seconds after the warhead detonation, a secondary explosion took place as the aviation fuel went off. There was now fuel oil, diesel fuel and aviation gasolene flowing through the ship. The ship lost power and came to a stop, with its starboard propeller shaft cut. The explosion blew open many watertight doors, allowing the spread of fire. This was aggravated by the interior paintwork helping to conduct the fire. The Erie took up a stern-down angle and a starboard list, which slowly increased.

Once the torpedo hit the Erie, the corvette USS Spry surged forward into a depth-charge attack and shortly afterward, both the Spry and the US Navy tanker Gulf Dawn were seen firing at something in the water. It may have been Engelmann's periscope, but this is doubtful because Engelmann would have been very busy making his escape. With a dozen escorts present, he could not have come to periscope depth among them and escaped.

The Erie had been hit no more than four miles from the entrance to Willemstadt harbour and although there was deep water right up to the coast, it was restricted. U163 must have been submerged and creeping southward, away from the area of the action. Once clear of the convoy's area, U163 surfaced and Engelmann sent off an attack report. As was normal in these cases, the German propaganda ministry took over and the radio story turned out to be highly inflated.

With Erie stopped and the fire spreading, the captain ordered all boats lowered and the wounded placed in them. While this operation was in progress, the ship's damage-control parties attempted to handle the fire. The initial explosion had cut the fire main, killing all water pressure and until ancillary power was restored, there was very little that could be done in the area of the fire which had spread across the ship, cutting off those in the aft section.

The Dutch sloop Van Kinsbergen came crashing back from its forward position and commenced an asdic search for the U-Boat, while the USS Spry turned towards the Erie to render assistance. Ten minutes after the initial

Chaguaramas Bay in 1943. A bauxite ship, a liberty ship, and a net tender are visible. *(National Archives)*

Coolidge Field, Antigua. B25s are parked on the second runway and in dispersed bays. In 1942 VP-204 operated its Mariner flying boats from the beach alongside the runway. *(author's collection)*

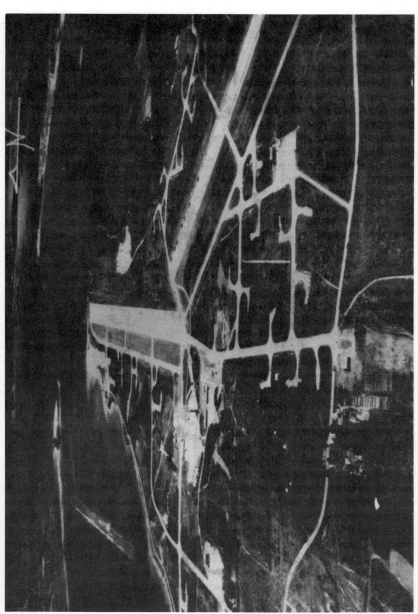

Hato Field, Curacao. U.S. Navy Harpoons are parked at dispersed sites. *Left*, the island's rocky, steeply shelving coastline parallels the airfield. (*U.S. Army photo*)

The Fleet Air Arm's Barracuda torpedo bombers, based at Piarco airfield in Trinidad in 1943. *Inset*, an Albacore antisubmarine aircraft at Piarco. *(author's collection)*

Kapitanleutnant Albrecht Achilles, wearing the Knight's Cross. *(Courtesy Klaus G. Ehrhardt)*

Kapitanleutnant Achilles inspects the crew of *U161* at the Second Flotilla base at Lorient in 1942. *(Courtesy Klaus G. Ehrhardt)*

U161 leaves Lorient. *(Courtesy Oskar Steiner)*

The entrance to Castries Harbor at St. Lucia in 1942. The new antisubmarine net can be seen across the entrance where the channel curves to the right. This photo also shows the shallows on both sides of the channel and the airfield off to the left. *(U.S. Army photo)*

Korvettenkapitan Georg Lassen commanded *U160* for two successful Caribbean patrols in July and October 1942, when he sank fourteen ships primarily off Trinidad. Lassen finished as the sixth-highest U-boat ace of the war. *(author's collection)*

Korvettenkapitan Karl Friedrich Merten commanded *U68* when it established the Caribbean record of over fifty thousand tons sunk on a single patrol in 1942. Merten finished as the fourth-highest U-boat ace of the war. *(author's collection)*

U161 enters Lorient on 7 August 1942 at the end of its second and last Caribbean patrol. Note the damage on the starboard side of the conning tower sustained in a collision with a merchant ship off the Dragons Mouth. (Courtesy Klaus G. Ehrhardt) Inset, A U162 crewman holds the pig, "Douglas," rescued from the sailing ship Florence M. Douglas, which was sunk on 4 May 1942. (Courtesy Alfred Hiller)

The crew of *U162* prior to their last cruise in 1942. (*Courtesy Alfred Hiller*)

Convoy escorts enter the third Boca on 1 October 1942. The photo was taken from the deck of the seaplane tender *Pocomoke* and shows the destroyers ISS *Greene* and *Osmond Ingram*. Almost lost against the background of the Dragons Mouth is an OS2N Kingfisher escorting the ships. (*National Archives*)

The Royal Navy motor launch *Fairmile* in the Gulf of Paria in 1943. *(author's collection)*

Chaguaramas Naval Operating Base, Trinidad, in October 1942. *Foreground,* the corvette USS *Surprise* and the destroyers USS *Goff* and USS *Barney* lie alongside the destroyer tender USS *Altair.* Behind the ships and beyond the small islands, a convoy gathers in the Gulf of Paria. *(National Archives)*

Chaguaramas Naval Air Station, Trinidad, on 29 June 1943. On the ramp are PBYs, Mariners, OS2N Kingfishers, and a Grumman Goose. *(National Archives)*

Blimp K16 of ZP-51 attached to its mooring mast at Carlsen Field in 1943. *(National Archives)*

The blimp facilities at Carlsen Field in 1944. *Top*, a blimp hangar. *(National Archives)*

Landing craft practice for the invasion of Martinique in June 1943. *Left*, the fleet carrier USS *Bunker Hill* operates in the Gulf of Paria. *(National Archives)*

This 1943 photo of Chaguaramas Naval Operating Base shows U.S. Coast Guard cutters, PT boats, and PCs in the escort base. *(National Archives)*

The USS *Missouri* and the light cruiser USS *Vincennes* in the Gulf of Paria fleet anchorage on 25 August 1944. *Background*, note the antisubmarine net and the coastlines of Diego and Gaspar Grande Islands. Achilles traversed this area while surfaced during his escape from the gulf. *(National Archives)*

The battle cruiser USS *Alaska* anchored off Chaguaramas Naval Operating Base, within the antisubmarine net. *Top left*, Chaguaramas Bay and the antisubmarine loop station at Staubles Bay, alongside the first Boca. *(National Archives)*

Commissioning ceremonies for the naval air station on 1 October 1941. British and American army and navy officers are present; the U.S. Navy officer in the center is Capt. Arthur W. Radford. *Inset,* Jesse B. Oldendorf, commander of the Trinidad Sector in 1942. (*U.S. Navy photos*)

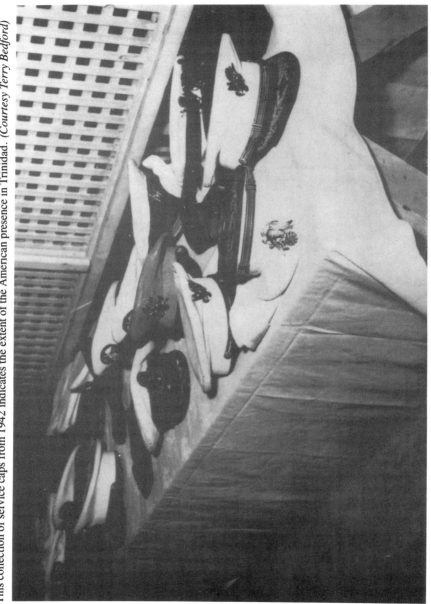

This collection of service caps from 1942 indicates the extent of the American presence in Trinidad. *(Courtesy Terry Bedford)*

U.S. troops arrive in Trinidad in 1942. (*Courtesy Terry Bedford*)

The USS *Essex* runs plane guard duty in the Gulf of Paria, 20 March 1943. The *Essex* was on her shakedown cruise. Note the white stripe around the ship and the call letters atop the pilothouse. *(U.S. Navy photo)*

Brig. Gen. Stokes Roberts, chief of staff of British forces in 1942. *(Courtesy Terry Bedford)*

Top military personnel stationed in Trinidad during the early years of World War II. *Left to right*, Col. W. V. Rutter, CO Fort Read; Col. H. R. Alley, CO Veteran Guard Canada; Lt. Col. O. P. Wren, CO 252d GA; Lt. Col. E. F. Muller, public relations officer; Capt. V. K. R. Bedford, GSO III British HQ. *(Courtesy Terry Bedford)*

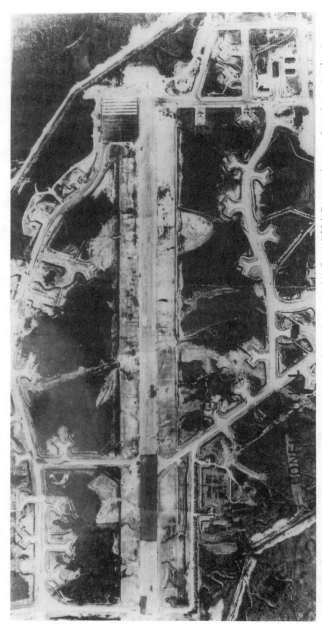

Xeres runway on 15 December 1943, photographed by the U.S. Army Air Corps' 39th Reconnaissance Squadron. *(author's collection)*

The Trinidad memorial. *(author's collection)*

explosion, the engineers working in the smoke-filled engine room, got the port engine going and the Erie started moving. Some water pressure was restored, but it was not enough to make an impression on the fire, with the result that a garden hose had to be hooked up to the galley pipe and a bucket brigade was organised. As the Erie went ahead at seven knots, across the wind to minimise the spread of the fire, the ship's list began to increase and the stern sank lower. The captain decided that the only course of action was to beach the ship and shaped course for Piscadero Point, near Willemstadt.

At this point the corvette Spry came alongisde with her fire hoses rigged, attempting to get water onto the fire aft, but her streams were not long enough. Then the six inch ready-use ammunition began to cook off. The USS Spry had to back off hurriedly and Erie signalled the Gulf Dawn to stand clear. On the fantail, the injured Executive officer and a small party were setting the depth charges to safe, before the flames sweeping aft forced them to jump overboard.

At this stage the ship's boats were following the Erie, picking up the men who had been blown overboard, or jumped from the stern. A party under the gunnery officer had been picking up six inch ammunition and heaving it overboard, but the ready use ammunition cooking off now made the stern of the vessel highly dangerous.

A Dutch PT boat came alongside the slowly moving Erie and advised the captain which beach would be best. Very deep water surrounds most of Curacao and the bottom shelves rapidly. With this in mind the captain had to choose carefully, because on most of these beaches the bow would be held fast and the stern sink into deep water. The captain of the Erie had no intention of beaching his ship hard on the land and abandoning, he wanted to rest her gently on the sand to insure that she would not capsize, and then fight the fire. With the crew valiantly tackling the out-of-control fuel fires, the captain aimed his ship for the little beach beyond the point.

Well out from the land Erie began to slow down, until she grounded at three knots. The gunboat came to a gentle stop and righted itself, still in relatively deep water. The captain then instructed that all power be transferred to fire fighting equipment. He wanted to use every available man to fight the fire on his ship, but it was too late. As soon as the Erie righted itself, tons of burning fuel poured out of her wounded side and spread across the water. Within minutes the only area clear of fire was a patch off the port bow. They realised that soon the ship would be completely surrounded by fire and at that stage there would be no escape for anyone. Sadly, the captain ordered abandon ship, via the port bow. As the crewmen backed away from the raging fires below decks, the depth-charges began to cook off and none too soon, the survivors were on the beach watching their handsome ship gut itself. The USS Erie died that night providing spectacular pyrotechnic displays, as her ammunition went off.

The change of command had been smooth. As Erie dropped out, Van Kinsbergen took over and the convoy proceeded on its way. Convoy escorts could not spare time for those that were hit, their prime responsibility was always to look after those that were still going. That was one of the rules of convoy warfare and none understood it better than the crews of the escorts. U163 trailed TAG 20 well into the following day, but the escort was so strong that the boat could not get near the ships.

On the fourteenth, the Dutch PC Queen Wilhelmena attacked U163 and drove it away from the Aruba area. At the time the Americans toyed with the idea that the attack on the Erie was a planned affair, but this is unlikely. The diversion of TAG 20 to the southern route was not known to the Germans and it is far more likely that Erie was a target of opportunity. She was not just another escort, she was a magnificent looking ship that could easily have passed as a light cruiser. The loss of the Erie galvanised No. 59 squadron and during the next two days they carried out a series of depth-charge attacks on both the U-Boats in the area, ultimately forcing both Witt and Engelmann to set course eastwards for the Trinidad area.

The thirteenth of November also saw an important event take place in Trinidad. Convoy TRIN 3 arrived with the Brazilian PC CS 1 as part of its escort. Brazilian naval ships had now joined the fight against the U-Boats in the Caribbean.

On the fifteenth U67 used four torpedoes to sink the British freighter King Arthur. The first two torpedoes missed the five thousand two hundred ton cargo vessel as it raced for Trinidad, but Muller-Stockheim's second pair finished it off. The vessel went down seventy miles east of Manzanilla Point on Trinidad's each coast.

On the same day U160 turned its bows homeward but U-Boat headquarters signalled Lassen ordering that he stay in the Caribbean zone for another week and promising a U tanker rendezvous to get him home. They were rearranging their schedules in a desperate attempt to keep boats in the Caribbean, while still maintaining a massive presence off Morocco, as ordered by Hitler.

U163 in the meantime was moving past Trinidad as quickly as possible. The boat had suffered a metox breakdown and without that vital piece of equipment, she could not long survive in the hostile Caribbean environment. On the seventeenth of November Staats in U508 came upon the British freighter City of Corinth five miles off the Trinidad north coast village of San Souci. A well-placed torpedo sent the five thousand three hundred ton cargo ship to the bottom in twenty fathoms. The vessel came to rest almost alongside the wreck of the Warrior, which U126 had sent down in July.

On November eighteenth, Schuch in U154 discovered a new shipping route. He was operating at longitude forty-nine west, just outside the range of Trinidad based aircraft, when he chanced on the five thousand ton British freighter Tower Grange. The ship was on the new route from Capetown to New York, which passed beyond the area normally used by shipping and thus out of reach of the U-Boats. Schuch sent the vessel to the bottom and signalled the new route to U-Boat headquarters.

U163 had diverted northwards to pass between the smaller Windward Islands in the hope that it could escape the aircraft, but a Hudson caught it. P/O Barnett in Hudson PZ/C enroute to St. Lucia, caught U163 on the surface in an old style visual attack, no radar, no metox and gave the boat a severe shaking up. On the following day F/O Underhill flying Hudson PZ/U carried out No. 53 squadron's last anti-submarine attack in the Caribbean. Once again it was U163, this time as she came out on the eastern side of the islands. Engelmann got no metox warning and in the old style, he saw the aircraft at two miles. The conning tower was still visible as the Hudson crossed the swirl and the four depth charges plummeted into the sea very close to U163. Equipment was smashed all through the U-Boat, as the charges detonated and hammered the pressure hull.

On the following day No. 53 squadron ceased Caribbean operations and prepared to return to the United Kingdom. The US Navy anti-submarine squadrons were now fully operational and the U-Boats had switched their concentration areas back to the North Atlantic. In accordance with their policy of concentrating to meet the U-Boat movements, the British were recalling their units from the west.

No. 53 had carried out fifteen attacks on submarines and in all cases, the boats had been severely shaken up or badly damaged. The squadron had flown seven hundred and two missions and lost five aircraft and three complete crews. Up to their departure from Trinidad, No. 53 had only damaged U-Boats, they had not sunk one, although in several cases they came very close. The squadron's time was still to come and the end of the war found them with four confirmed U-Boat kills. It is safe to say that their arrival in Trinidad marked a turning point in the Caribbean war, but No. 53 was not the only unit leaving. Far to the west, No. 45 Army Air Corps squadron was also pulling out. They would spend the rest of the war in the Pacific.

On the same day as No. 53 squadron's final attack, Muller-Stockheim sank the four thousand six hundred ton British freighter Tortugas, two hundred and fifty miles east of Barbados. After the vessel went down, U67 turned her bow eastward, leaving the Caribbean. She still had one further ship to hit on this third Caribbean cruise.

Most of the boats had gone eastwards for the full moon period and at four thirty on the morning of the twenty-first Lassen sank his last Caribbean ship. The Dutch freighter Bintang was caught six hundred miles east of Trinidad and sunk. U160 remained in the area until the twenty-ninth, when she turned for her rendezvous with the tanker U118. Neither Lassen nor U160 ever returned to the Caribbean. Early in 1943, the boat made a successful Indian Ocean patrol, following which Lassen was transferred ashore.

His U-Boat ran second in the Caribbean totals, sinking fourteen ships and damaging two others for a total Caribbean tonnage of eighty thousand seven hundred and forty-six. Lassen received the Knight's Cross with Oak Leaves and survived the war. On the formation of the Bundesmarine in 1955, he joined and retired several years later as Kapitan zur See. U160 went on under the command of Pommer-Esche and her fate was tied up in the battles of July 1943.

On the same day as the Bintang was sunk Engelmann in U163, now safely east of the islands, sank the British freighter Empire Starling, one hundred and eighty miles east of Barbados. That day also marked the demise of a U-Boat that might have been. Four hundred miles west of the coast of Spain, the Swordfish aircraft of No. 817 Fleet Air Arm squadron, operating from the Fleet aircraft carrier HMS Victorious, sank the Type IXC boat U517. The boat was enroute to the Caribbean for its first patrol in these waters. On the following day Engelmann in U163 closed his Caribbean account by sinking the Brazilian freighter Apaloide, three hundred miles east of Barbados. The boat had sunk four ships on this second and last Caribbean patrol.

For the next four days the only U-Boat close to the islands was Staats in U508. U67, U129, U160 and U163 were making their way homeward, while U154 cruised off French Guiana. On the twenty-sixth Staats caught the six thousand ton British freighter Clan Mac Fadyen. The vessel went down ninety-five miles southeast of Trinidad's Galeota Point. U508 continued its southeastward run and on the following day sank another British freighter SS Empire Cromwell, one hundred and sixty miles from Galeota Point. Muller-Stockheim ended the month's tally by damaging the British freighter Empire Glade, eight hundred miles east of the islands. He used his last torpedo to hit the ship at dawn on the twenty-eighth. The deck gun was brought into action, but the heavily damaged ship escaped to the west.

During November, eight U-Boats operated in the Caribbean zone. U332 spent only two days and as such she did not contribute to the month's total. Similarly, U505 only managed one ship, which meant that the other six boats managed to sink twenty-four and damage two ships between them. The twenty-four ships lost during this month totalled, one hundred and forty-six thousand, eight hundred and twenty-eight tons of shipping. The figures were much better than for October and they had been sunk by a much smaller group of U-Boats, but it was the end. The Caribbean had now accounted for three hundred and thirty ships sunk, with a couple of dozen out of service due to damage. These lost ships added up to one million eight hundred and forty-two thousand tons.

Operation Torch had drawn off the Caribbean bound boats and the end of November found only two boats on station. Five boats were on their way across the Atlantic to the Caribbean, but the lull in the offensive would prove to be fatal. The Caribbean was still to see its greatest number of U-Boats operating at any one time and it was still to see the incredibly fierce battles that would take place between the boats and the defending forces. But the merchant ship losses were virtually over. Never again would the number of sinkings cross double figures. Just as Doenitz's Caribbean offensive had forced the Allies to spread their available anti-submarine resources over a wide area and thus diluted their power, now Allied offensive operations were to do the same to the U-Boats.

The virtual lull in the Caribbean would give the United States forces in the area a chance to catch their breath, reorganise and train. During this period it would be the exploits of individual boats that would create havoc and not the mass that had saturated the area and brought shipping to a standstill. Had Doenitz's ideas on the employment of his boats against the lines of communication been more thoroughly understood by Hitler and his entourage, the Caribbean might have been the decisive theatre in a total German victory. The pendulum was about to swing the other way.

The Caribbean campaign had caused the massive reinforcement of the area and the end of November found one hundred and ten thousand US soldiers stationed in the islands. A similar number of naval personnel manned the heavily defended naval bases and hundreds of ships and aircraft patrolled constantly. Base construction was going on apace and it is true to say that the American response to the U-Boat, built the Caribbean's postwar aviation infrastructure.

In addition to the bases in the southern Caribbean, auxiliary Air Force bases were being constructed on Eleuthera, San Salvador, Mayaguana, Great

Exuma and Grand Turk, in the Bahamas. To control the northwest, Vernam Field and Portland were being constructed in Jamaica and a large base on Grand Cayman, in addition to bases throughout Central America and the Cuban fields.

In Trinidad, the army garrison had risen to over twenty thousand Americans, in addition to the island's Volunteer forces. The US Army had set up its jungle-warfare training school at Manzanilla and during 1942 there was a constant stream of men going through. Merrill's Marauders who fought in Burma were trained at Manzanilla. Trinidad's east coast was now dotted with gun positions and lookouts posts, similar to the north coast.

At the end of the war a Time magazine report concluded that America had lost its innocence. Nowhere was this more true than in the Intelligence field in the Caribbean and South America. In the case of the British, Dutch and French colonies, there were elements who did not care for colonial repression and considered German brutality in the event of a German victory, as similar to colonialism. In all cases they looked to America as the great leveller who would change the area, but their dreams were not to be fulfilled. The prejudiced behaviour of many of the inexperienced American troops quickly soured relations and there were elements of the populations who ended up not caring which side won the war.

In the British colonies the Americans found a well entrenched, efficient, intelligence service put in by the British and thus they could safely rely on information from this source, but on the South American continent a completely different picture emerged. They lived in an atmosphere of rumour, much of it untrue or deliberately planted by anti-government groups, or the Vichy French. In Dutch Guiana, an amateur intelligence officer picked up vast quantities of information planted on him by elements hostile to the Dutch Governor and involved the US Army in a plot to remove the Governor. This soured relations to the point where the Governor maintained a local army hostile to the Americans, with dire consequences for the broader American-Dutch relations.

Much of the misdirected intelligence and public relations activity took place in direct contravention of Roosevelt's written instructions to the US Army, issued before they moved into the region. He urged commanders to impress on their officers and men that they were moving into areas which had been in existence even before the United States had emerged as a nation. In the South American context this was particularly important and the American field commanders could have tread a lot more warily.

On the other hand, they were operating in an area where German colonies abounded. These German South Americans on the whole remained quiet, particularly when it appeared that Germany was on the defensive. This was because many of them had intermarried in South America and wanted to remain there, but the Americans were well aware that had Germany been triumphant, the Germans would have openly become pro-Nazi.

An example of this concerned the many German motorcycle clubs in Venezuela, whose movements had to be continually tracked. In this case they received the active co-operation of the Venezuelan Government, but rumour also played a significant part in confusing the issue. One case involved allegations from a senior Venezuelan diplomat, that the Vichy French Governor of French Guiana was supplying U-Boats with oil in goat skins. A vast intelligence operation swung into action which proved that the method of supply was impractical, but it uncovered a host of other suspicious accusations and reports of movements in and out of French Guiana. This in turn led to further unending investigations.

The American intelligence operatives found themselves embroiled in literally hundreds of investigations, none of which produced results. They lived in an atmosphere of constant rumour and suspicion of fifth column activity, that made the Caribbean Command an intelligence nightmare. On the credit side, it served to build up an American knowledge of the area and its peoples, as well as helping to entrench the American presence in the zone. It paved the way for the American influence in South America after the war. Much of the problem could be attributed to false or misleading information being planted by Vichy French agents operating out of Martinique and French Guiana and from a military point of view, it meant that these territories could not coexist with the rest of the zone. This in turn meant that America would have to make some hard choices in 1943.

CHAPTER

12

TB˜ 1 and TM˜ 1

On the first of December there were four U-Boats operating in the Caribbean zone. U508 was just southeast of Trinidad while U129, U154 and U163 were in a patrol line off the coast of the Guianas. Of these boats only U508 was going to achieve any further sinkings and she opened her December account at seven twenty-five that night.

At that time of the year it was dark relatively early, and at sunset Staats had his boat running in towards Galeota Point. The British freighter Trevalgan was on course from Brazil to Trinidad and her track ran right to where U508 was waiting. Staats was able to make out her silhouette against the dark horizon and dispatched two torpedoes. Both slammed into the five thousand three hundred ton bulk of the cargo vessel and she came to an exhausted stop, with her radio operator hammering out a distress call. While the vessel settled by the head, the shocked survivors scrambled into their lifeboats and pulled away. Staats watched the old vessel finally give up the unequal struggle and slide down towards the mud of the Orinoco Delta.

U508 was one hundred miles from Galeota Point virtually on the shipping route between South America and Trinidad. They were bound to find

targets on this shipping crossroads, but it was also a highly dangerous place
to operate. The water was only one hundred and fifty feet deep, sufficient
to escape from an air attack, but not enough to ensure survival if a surface
escort caught them. To guard against surprise Staats had extra lookouts
posted and the U-Boat trimmed with its decks awash.

The risk paid off and one hour and twenty minutes later another
target appeared. The five thousand ton City of Bath was also trying for
Trinidad along the inshore route, when the U508's torpedo brought it to
a halt almost over the wreck of the Trevalgan. The shocked survivors soon
discovered that they were not alone and the two groups from the lost merchant ships began their long drift to Trinidad's east coast. Although it was
most satisfying to send two merchant ships to the bottom within such a
short space of time, Staats was well aware that sooner or later Trinidad
would react and he very prudently turned his bows southeast, away from
the danger area.

Two days later when the survivors from the Trevalgan and the City of
Bath reached Trinidad, Staats had U508 three hundred miles southeast of
the island in water that was safer. In the late evening the British freighter
Solon II carrying iron ore from Turkey came in sight. The four thousand
five hundred ton vessel had rounded the Cape of Good Hope and crossed
the South Atlantic on its way to Trinidad to join a convoy, when the torpedo ripped out its plates. The old ship went quickly, taking most of the
crew to its muddy grave off the Guianas. On the same day Engelmann in
U163, operating four hundred miles east of Trinidad, attempted to better
his exploit with the USS Erie, by attacking the cruiser USS Omaha. The
Omaha avoided the three torpedoes and its escort destroyer the USS Jouett
turned on U163. After a punishing depth-charge attack and a prolonged
hunt, the U-Boat escaped eastwards.

All four U-Boats were now nearing the end of their patrols and after
the US Navy ships had ensured that honour was satisfied, the U163 was
allowed to start her run homeward. U129 was also working her way homeward, as Witt took her up the eastern side of the island chain. U154 was
nearing Trinidad's east coast also homeward bound, and U508 was not far
behind, but Staats still had one more blow to strike. On December 7th
U508 came upon the five thousand four hundred ton freighter SS Nigerian,
one hundred and thirty miles southeast of Trinidad. The British vessel was
heading westwards towards Trinidad with a cargo of nuts and palm oil from
Lagos, when Staats carried out his final Caribbean attack. After the vessel
went down, he closed the lifeboats and removed four British officers to
take home as prisoners. U508 now also turned her bows northward to join

the other boats in the area northeast of Antigua, for the long haul back across the Atlantic.

U129 was returning from her third Caribbean cruise, having sunk five ships of thirty-two thousand tons. She had now crossed the one hundred thousand ton mark of shipping sunk in the Caribbean and this proved to be the record. She did not sink as many ships as either U160 or U66, but her tonnage was greater than the other boats. She was not finished with the Caribbean because there was still another patrol for her to complete, but the days of big scores were over. Hans Witt, like Clausen before him, would be awarded the Knight's Cross, but unlike Clausen, he would survive the war. Heinrich Schuch in U154 had completed his only Caribbean patrol with three ships sunk. On his return he would hand over command of U154 which still had two further Caribbean trips to make.

U163 was leaving the Caribbean for the last time. If the attempt on the Omaha had succeeded, Engelmann would indeed have created a record. Notwithstanding this, the destruction of the Erie provided ample propaganda material, but he did not have long to live. On its next patrol in March U163 ran into an ambush. The American submarine USS Herring was in mid Atlantic hunting for the U Tanker that Engelmann was supposed to meet, when instead of the tanker, U163 became the target. The explosion of the torpedoes from the American submarine destroyed the Type IXC boat and killed the entire crew. U508 was also finished with the Caribbean. Two patrols had netted them well over fifty thousand tons of shipping sunk, representing eleven ships lost to the Allies. Georg Staats and his crew died a year later when aircraft from VB 103 sank the boat in the Western Approaches.

While this small group of U-Boats were ending the golden days of the Caribbean U-Boat campaign, drifting mines had begun to cause serious problems to Trinidad's defenders. In theory the mines should have deactivated themselves as soon as their cables parted, but this was not taking place and the Dragon's Mouth area was being rocked by frequent shattering explosions, as some of the mines ran into the rocky shoreline. However, only a small proportion of the drifting mines were hitting the shoreline, the majority were being carried out of the Bocas by the current and up into the Caribbean.

On December 5th two days before the first anniversary of Pearl Harbour, the American freighter Frederick R. Kellog had her bows blown off while sailing independently along the Venezuelan coastline. There were no U-Boats in the area west of Trinidad and it was surmised that she could only have hit a mine. A week later, the inter island schooner Thomas B.

Schall disappeared without trace in the area west of Trinidad and once again, it could only have been one of the drifting mines.

The Americans had to institute regular patrols within the Gulf of Paria to try and locate the mines before they could get out and into the shipping lanes. As the war ground on, this problem escalated, until entire units had to be assigned exclusively to minefield patrol work. Luckily, the onset of this problem with the mines coincided with a relative lull in the Caribbean U-Boat war and search units were available. The diversion of the U-Boats to North Africa had completely disrupted the planned gathering of the veterans for a Caribbean Christmas. Five U-Boats were on the way and there would be a ten day lull before they made their presence felt, but even so all the boats would be handicapped by the intervention of an unexpected ally.

When the first U-Boats moved into Lorient after the fall of France, the Germans had behaved correctly, giving the residents of the formally quiet seaside town little to complain about. Unfortunately for the inhabitants, Lorient not only occupied an important strategic position from which the Germans could fight the battle of the Atlantic, but the port also contained excellent ship repair facilities. Previously, the town of Lorient had always been well away from the traditional centers of European war, but the U-Boat would now catapult it to the front line.

The Germans recognised Lorient's excellent position and they moved in more and more U-Boats and Doenitz moved his headquarters near to the town. This automatically made Lorient a prime target and the RAF set out to destroy the wolves in their lair. The Germans reacted by bringing in massive reinforcement garrisons and anti-aircraft units. Bomb proof shelters were quickly built for the U-Boats, but although the RAF could not penetrate the shelters, they could not call off the bombers. The result was that the houses of the town took the brunt of the British assault.

While that was going on the U-Boat crews began to erode French control of some of their women. The crews of Doenitz's boats were the elite of the German navy and with their pay and privileges they were able to entice a number of French women with life styles that the local Frenchmen could not hope to emulate. Antagonism built up between the two races and very soon German sailors and soldiers were being found in back alleys with their throats slit.

In the wake of the massive military presence and the French reaction, came hordes of collaborators, prostitutes, spies and saboteurs, because by 1942 Lorient was the world's largest submarine base. The once quiet backwater became a place of distrust and violence, leading the original inhabitants to wonder who they hated most, the Germans who by their presence made Lorient a front line town, or the British who bombed everybody.

It was difficult for those of the town's people who wanted to be left in peace to exist, because with British support, the Maquis infiltrated the docks. The idea was to sabotage as many U-Boats as possible, which in turn brought in the Gestapo, whose methods often involved both the guilty and the innocent. This only added another dimension to the hell that life had become for the residents of the town. Nevertheless the saboteurs were remarkably successful. They would add sugar to U-Boat fuel, which would ruin the engines, or they would drill cleverly concealed holes in the top of U-Boat fuel tanks, which would cause the boats to leave a telltale trace of oil when they dived. Sometimes deliberately defective welds would be made on U-Boat pressure hulls, which would collapse when the boats went deep.

If the boat didn't return, then no one would know that sabotage had contributed to its demise, but if a boat survived one of these attempts and returned to Lorient with the evidence, everyone would pay. The Maquis were playing a game with very high stakes and sometimes their efforts would cause the U-Boat crews to literally go through hell. The boats of the replacement wave heading to the Caribbean in December had all been sabotaged and one in particular was to have a rough time, contributing to the saving of many merchant seamen's lives.

Approaching the Caribbean for the first time was the ace U124 under the legendary Johann Mohr. The boat with the eidelweis badge on the conning tower was no ordinary U-Boat. The Type IXB U-Boat had been launched early in 1940 and first commissioned under Wilhelm Schultz, who had achieved considerable success before handing over to Mohr in August 1941. Mohr had ravaged shipping in the North Atlantic and off the American coast during Paukenschlag, but he had missed the hey-day of the Caribbean conflict.

Making its way across the Atlantic on its tenth war cruise, the boat had finally been assigned on a Caribbean patrol, but by this stage targets were much more difficult to find and U124 was suffering from the efforts of a group of very professional French saboteurs. Shortly after leaving Lorient, the boat had been warned by signal that the fuel it had taken on at the base had been sabotaged with an additive that destroyed fuel pumps. All the way across the Atlantic the boat had been plagued with engine breakdowns and indeed, Mohr could easily have turned back to base, but he had not achieved his remarkable reputation by turning his back on difficulty.

In mid Atlantic they had met U118 and received some good fuel, but this was only a small proportion of the total fuel load and Mohr decided to keep his good fuel for emergencies. On December 15th U124 entered the zone east of Trinidad and almost immediately experienced another total breakdown, causing some anxious hours while the engineers once again stripped down the fuel pumps.

While U124 was stopped on the surface the rest of the new wave began arriving. The Type IXB U105 under Jurgen Nissen was like U124, a newcomer to the Caribbean and she approached the middle of the island chain on the same day that U124 had her engine breakdown. The third boat into the the area was U217 under Reichenburg-Klinke and she was coming back to try and avenge the rough handling she had received around Curacao in September. The three boats stayed well to the east because full moon had been on the thirteenth and the area was still bright enough to be dangerous.

On the following day Mohr attacked a Trinidad bound tanker convoy claiming two hits, but the records do not list any ships hit. The convoy recorded the attack and also noted that the escorts HMS Tailford and Tamarisk attacked the U-Boat. That same day U217 intercepted the Swedish ship Etna east of the islands and after a search of the vessel revealed contraband cargo, scuttling charges were placed on her hull.

Well to the south U176 also carried out a similar operation with the Swedish ship Scania. Before the end of the day U217 also attacked U124's convoy, but she was also driven off by the escorts. Both U124 and U217, after being attacked by the escorts, were subjected to air attacks by long range PBYs of VP-53 and Mohr noted that their aim was dangerously accurate.

Further to the northeast, two more boats were also moving in towards the Caribbean. The Type IXB U109 under Joachim Schramm was on course for Antigua and the Type VIID U214 under Gunther Reeder was on course for Trinidad. Both these boats were also coming into the Caribbean for the first time. These five boats were all that was left of Doenitz's plan to concentrate in the Caribbean while the winter storms lashed the North Atlantic.

While this small pack closed in on the Caribbean, a much larger group composed of U126, U128, U135, U159, U161, U164, U174, U176 and the Italian Tazzoli were off Brazil. In response to this threat, VP-74 was transferred from Chaguaramas to the Brazilian base at Aratu. This squadron which had already sunk U158, was to go on to become the second highest scoring US Navy anti-submarine unit, with five U-Boats to its credit by the end of the war. VP-51 and VP-94 also passed through Chaguaramas on their way south to Belem. VP-81 replaced VP-74 in Chaguaramas and for a while the base operated only PBYs. In the meantime a new Mariner equipped squadron VP-204 moved in to NAS San Juan and detached a flight to operate from Antigua. Both the Caribbean and the Brazilian commands were on full alert for the expected blow from the two groups of U-Boats.

After the action with the tanker convoy, Mohr turned his bows towards Trinidad, but it became a very harassing journey because there seemed to be an almost continuous relay of flying boats overhead. VP-53 and VP-81 were making life very difficult for the U-Boat. Mohr was still being plagued by corroded fuel pumps and decided to remain east of the island for Christmas. In mid December there had been a remarkable mid South Atlantic rendezvous when eight U-Boats came together and spent two days visiting each other.

The Christmas season was not to see quite such a large gathering, but Mohr managed to link up with Achilles in U161 and Heyse in U128, to the east of Trinidad. U161 had been heavily damaged off northern Brazil and was making her way home, while U128 was also at the end of her patrol. Both U161 and U128 were still to make a number of patrols but they were both destined to die off Brazil, both at the hands of VP-74. The three boats spent a quiet day out of range of Trinidad's aircraft, before U128 and U161 resumed their homeward journey.

On the following day U-Boat headquarters issued new orders to the boats of the Caribbean group. U109 was allocated the northern Leeward Islands, with U105 among the islands further south. U214 and U217 were required to enter the Caribbean and patrol towards Curacao, while U124 handled the Trinidad area.

On the same day the destroyer HMS Havelock along with the corvettes Godetia, Pimpernel and Saxifrage entered the Gulf of Paria for an important assignment. In the meantime Mohr had brought U124 close in under Trinidad's Galera Point and at four forty-five on the morning of December 28th he found the British freighter Treworlas. The cargo ship was ripped open and went down only nine miles from the point.

At dawn Mohr cautiously turned his bows northward to get away from the deadly aircraft based in Trinidad, but shortly afterwards he was to suffer a devastating setback. Some wily Frenchman had added salt to the distilled water and as soon as the batteries were topped up, the boat filled with deadly chlorine gas. It took twelve hours to ventilate the boat and during this time U124 was stuck on the surface between Trinidad and Tobago. It was only with the greatest luck that the boat was not caught by the predators from Trinidad. Eventually when it was safe to dive, Mohr took her around Tobago looking for targets.

On the following night U124 was back in the Galleons Passage when

Mohr sighted two empty tankers racing for Trinidad. U124 built up speed trying to catch the two vessels before they could enter the Gulf of Paria, but the tankers were too fast and the U-Boat's diesels were not giving of their best. More in an effort to slow them down than anything else, Mohr fired a spread of four torpedoes. All four missed the tankers and detonated with a shattering roar on the rocks of Trinidad's north coast. The noise must have woken up a fair number of people and indeed within minutes there was a PBY approaching.

Mohr knew that if he dived the tankers would escape and decided to stay on the surface and bluff. By an incredible piece of luck on the U-Boat's behalf, the VP-53 PBY roared over the boat in a perfect attack, but the depth-charges hung up. Mohr misread this, believing that the pilot was confused about if the vessel below him really was a U-Boat and decided to stay on the surface as the PBY came round in a wide circle.

By this stage he had cleared the conning tower, while he stood alone watching the large aircraft come back in. Incredibly once again the depth charges failed to release. The PBY pilot must have been in a foul mood as he brought his flying boat round for the third pass. Twice he had passed right over the U-Boat, and twice his release mechanism had failed to work. No doubt he would have been in an even uglier mood had he known who was watching him from the conning tower.

By the time he saw the flying boat lining up for its third pass, Mohr instinctively knew that the game was up. He was never to know that it was not his daring which had saved U124 on the two previous passes and on the third pass, he gave the command hard-a-starboard at just the right moment. The U-Boat's wake curved away from the falling depth charges, just as Mohr slid down the hatch shouting dive, dive, dive. The two charges exploded slightly to port of the U-Boat's wake, just as she began to go down. The roar as the charges detonated smashed equipment in the boat, but she escaped. Mohr by now began to realise that he could no longer fool around with the Trinidad based aircraft and kept U124 submerged for seven hours, while running eastwards. He was going to try his luck off the Guianas.

U214 was running in towards Trinidad and also experienced a miraculous escape, similar to the U124 episode, but this time in daylight. Reeder was new to the Caribbean and despite the many warnings, he was still not aware that the aircraft in the area were deadly.

The boat was running fully surfaced, with all the deck hatches open and sailors sunning themselves on the casing, when without any warning, machine gun splashes began walking across the water towards them. The VP-53 PBY had caught them totally unprepared and the warning shouts were drowned by the noise of the great aircraft sweeping overhead, but once again the depth charges failed to release.

As the pilot fought to get his flying boat round and back over the target, the crew of U214 scrambled below to safety, and the U-Boat dived before the PBY was overhead again. Eventually, VP-53 got the problem with their release gear sorted out, but they had missed two great opportunities. Reeder took his revenge that night by sinking the Polish freighter Paderewski entirely by gunfire, only twenty-eight miles from Galera Point.

The sinking of the Paderewski on December 30th marked the end of merchant ship losses in the Caribbean for 1942. The U-Boats had only sunk six ships during the month of December and to be sure, this was far below the sinking levels in the middle of the year, but the Caribbean had changed. The US Navy were beginning to get the measure of the U-Boats and 1943 would be different, although it was to start disastrously for the Allies.

From February 16th 1942, to the last day of December, the U-Boats had managed to sink three hundred and thirty-seven ships in the Caribbean theatre. The average had been one point zero five ships per day and they added up to one point eight seven million tons. This meant that the Caribbean theatre had accounted for nearly a third of the six and a half million tons lost by the Allies during the year. The campaign had only lasted for three hundred and nineteen days, but the U-Boats had created havoc, forcing the Allies to switch considerable resources to the area.

The campaign had been on a far grander scale than the attack off the US east coast and it had lasted longer. In the long run, the Golden West had been the Caribbean theatre in 1942.

The year 1942 had been the high point of the U-Boat war and one thousand one hundred and sixty ships had been sunk worldwide. This represented more than 1939, 1940 and 1941 put together. It had taken far too long for the primary threat in the Caribbean to be recognised and dealt with and even at the end of 1942, the Americans were still deploying vast resources defending the Panama Canal against a possible carrier strike.

During this period while the Americans had been unwilling to recognise the threat, the cost in human lives had been considerable. It has been calculated that the merchant navy sustained a seventeen percent loss rate during the war as against nine percent for the Navy and Air Force and six percent for the Army. The merchant marine lost a higher proportion of its manpower than the armed services and in the Caribbean it is possible to translate this percentage into approximate figures. The survivors did not face the intense cold and storms of the North Atlantic, but instead they faced the menace of sharks, heatstroke and the same death from exposure.

The Trinidad command kept a fairly accurate survivor count and at the end of 1942, they mustered one thousand one hundred and sixty-seven survivors from thirty-eight merchant ships which had been sunk. These figures are for the period at the end of 1942, when there were rescue ships and aircraft, as well as an efficient set of survivor camps in operation, as opposed to the hey-day of the U-Boat campaign when no one had the time to worry about survivors. If it is assumed that the average ship carried a crew of fifty, thirty of them would die when the ship sank. In broad approximate terms, this means that at least seven thousand merchant seamen died in the Caribbean during the three hundred and nineteen days of 1942 when the U-Boats prowled these tropical seas.

Despite the fact that by the end of 1942 the U-Boat war in the Caribbean had cooled down appreciably, two of the most disastrous convoy actions of 1943 were to originate in Trinidad and make the start of the year a grim experience for all concerned. By the end of 1942, the heavy losses of tankers in the Caribbean theatre and off the US coast were beginning to seriously affect operations in the European theatre. Fuel stocks were dangerously low creating a crisis situation particularly in the Mediterranean, where British and American forces were clearing North Africa.

Churchill and Roosevelt recognised that moving fuel from the Caribbean via the traditional convoy routes to Miami, then New York, Liverpool, and finally to the Mediterranean would take too long, and they looked for an alternative.

The situation was becoming so critical that they agreed to accept the risk and run fast tanker convoys direct from Trinidad to Gibraltar. The projected convoy was code named TM-1, but somehow the importance of the convoy was not recognised at lower levels of command and the escorts allocated were insufficient to ensure its protection. Historians basing their judgement of TM-1's escort group on the comments made in the German war diaries have labelled the group as inexperienced, but nothing could be further from the truth.

HMS Havelock, and the corvettes Godetia, Saxifrage and Pimpernel were part of the experienced B 5 escort group, which had fought convoy TAW 13 through the Windward Passage in August 1942 and also handled countless North Atlantic convoys. They were a hard fighting group, but with convoy TM-1, they were simply swamped by the scale of the assault. At the first indication of trouble, the Admiralty should have dispatched heavy reinforcements to augment the convoy's escort before the assault could build, but instead the four vessels were left to fight it out alone.

The doomed convoy TM-1, with nine fully laden tankers and its pitifully small escort of four warships sailed out of the Boca de Navios at three o'clock in the afternoon of Sunday December 27th 1942. From the very start the convoy was in trouble.

U214 picked up the mass of ships and sent off a sighting report. At this stage the Germans had no idea of the convoy's destination and indeed, it would have been difficult for them to have guessed that the ships were destined for Gibraltar. Nevertheless, the first sighting report awoke interest as to where such an important shipment could be going. U214 continued her westward passage to Curacao and soon U105 further to the north, picked up the convoy and passed on the initial routing and the content. Waiting to the northeast of Antigua was the old Trinidad veteran Hans Jurgen Auffermann in U514.

On January 3rd Auffermann found TM-1 eight hundred miles northeast of Antigua. The ships were on course across the Atlantic and at last the Germans knew where TM-1 was going. Auffermann's sighting report galvanised U-Boat headquarters and they hurriedly began signalling to seven other U-Boats to concentrate across the convoy's route.

The pack was given the code-name Group Delfin and their orders were, stop TM-1. Eventually twelve U-Boats became part of Group Delfin. The four escorts stood little chance. After getting off his sighting report, Auffermann moved in to the attack and at five forty-six that afternoon, he put two torpedoes into the eight thousand ton tanker British Vigilance. The explosion of the torpedoes killed forty of her crew and the survivors abandoned the hulk nine hundred miles from Antigua.

The convoy escorts could not afford to waste time around the wreck, nor could Auffermann, whose job it was to shadow the convoy, in homing the other boats of the group on to it. The wreck of the British Vigilance was left behind to float for twenty-one days, until U105 found it and delivered the coup de grace.

The first attack on TM-1 should have been the warning signal to the Admiralty that TM-1 needed urgent support, but apparently neither the scale of the threat nor the importance of the convoy appear to have been appreciated.

While TM-1 was beginning its trial, another new convoy route was being planned in Trinidad. Convoys were working throughout the Caribbean and they had contributed greatly to the drastic reduction in shipping losses. In response to this protection, the U-Boats had switched the centre of gravity of their operations to the area east of Trinidad, where most of the shipping still sailed independently.

It was time for the Allies to institute regular convoys on the bauxite route and its extension as far as Brazil. The new convoy system was to run from Trinidad to Bahia in Brazil, from where shipping could either enter South American ports or set out across the South Atlantic. The first such convoy was coded TB-1 and scheduled to depart Port of Spain on January 5th.

In the last days of December and into the New Year, convoys arrived and departed from the haven of the Gulf of Paria. From these convoys merchant ships detached and anchored, awaiting the departure of TB-1. Signals went out assigning escorts for the convoy, but this time not only was the escort group too weak, but it was also relatively inexperienced, when compared to the veteran with which they would have to contend.

Finally on the appointed day all was ready and at six o'clock in the evening the merchant ships began weighing anchor and proceeding to the third Boca. The TRNVR vessels were in position to organise the ships into their columns and overhead, the customary massive airpower demonstration took place.

Four vessels failed to make the departure. The SS Murena was unable to complete loading in time, SS Forbin was unable to bunker in time, while the SS Radicome and Siranger were unable to find all their crew. Outside the Boca, the convoy Commodore Lt. D.C. Watson USN in the freighter King James, counted twelve merchant ships forming up. The King James was bound for Bahia, whence it was to proceed to Capetown and finally Alexandria, while some ships were bound for Recife, others for Rio and one for Bombay. There were five tankers and seven freighters in the convoy.

The escort commander Lt. Cmdr. C.E. Weakley in the old flush-decked, four funnelled destroyer USS Goff, watched the other escort vessels take up their stations around the plodding merchant ships. Astern was the Flower class corvette USS Surprise, while on either beam were PC 577 and PC 609. The convoy route had been well chosen.

Instead of running directly along the north coast of Trinidad as was customary, this convoy was routed northeast from the Boca so that it passed north of Tobago. The routing then took it eastwards for a hundred and fifty miles from Tobago's most easterly point, before swinging south towards Guiana.

This brilliant routing avoided Torpedo Junction and would confuse any shadower into thinking that the ships were on course for West Africa. Despite its routing the convoy had two problems to face. The first of these was its speed. It was a very slow convoy averaging only six and a half knots. This would create problems for the escorts, who were not at their best at this slow speed. However there was a contingency plan which would allow the escorts to refuel from tankers in the convoy. The second problem was that convoy TB-1 had no control over events in Trinidad.

It was not until ten o'clock that night that the merchant ships were all in their allotted places and the convoy could start its long trek. Quite unknown to the men in the convoy, the ace hunter Johann Mohr had missed them. The U-Boat had been continually harassed by anti-submarine aircraft off the coast of British Guiana, and another engine breakdown had forced them to spend a tension filled afternoon on the surface.

In exasperation Mohr had turned his boat back towards Trinidad and after rounding Galera Point, had sailed westwards along the Venezuelan coast. He attacked two ships off Caracas but failed to score and then turned back towards the ever fruitful waters around Trinidad.

He would have been in position off the Boca when TB-1 came out if it hadn't been for PBY P-1 of VP-53. This aircraft had caught Mohr on the surface northwest of Trinidad and delivered a very accurate attack on the boat. U124 had been badly shaken up by the well placed depth-charges and Mohr decided to stay submerged until the aircraft lost interest in him. While the PBY was holding U124 down, convoy TB-1 had come out of the Boca, formed up and set off. By the time U124 returned to the surface and got to the Boca, TB-1 had disappeared. Neither party knew of the existence of the other.

By daybreak on the sixth U124 was opposite the Dragon's Mouth and TB-1 was north of Tobago, well out of the U-Boat's way. Later that day U124 had yet another of its interminable engine breakdowns and Mohr edged away from Trinidad's north coast, while repairs were being carried out. At this stage the state of the engines would have driven most other U-Boat commanders to abandon the cruise, but Mohr persisted.

When the boat was servicable again he brought her back in towards the north coast and continued his eastward patrol to Galera Point. By the early hours of 7th January when TB-1 turned southward, U124 was just rounding Galera Point to patrol Trinidad's east coast. The convoy and the U-Boat were well apart and on different courses, but by now attention had switched to a drama that was unfolding in the Gulf of Paria.

At three fourteen on the afternoon of January 7th, the Duty Officer at HMS Benbow reported to US Navy headquarters in Port of Spain that something had crossed number nine detector loop, in the southern Serpent's Mouth entrance to the Gulf of Paria. An immediate alert was instituted and anti-submarine bombers were scrambled from Edinburgh Field. Most of the long range PBYs were either out on patrol or being prepared for other scheduled missions and as such they could not react, but the OS2Ns of

VS45 and the P-39 fighters from Waller Field were scrambled.

The 19th MTB Flotilla dispatched some vessels to join the TRNVR in carrying out an investigation. The report was taken seriously because no one wanted a repeat of Achilles' raid. The investigation was well under-way when it was greatly compounded by a report from Staubles Bay at four forty, that something had crossed number six anti-submarine loop in the northern Dragon's Mouth. One hour and twenty-six minutes separated the two reports and the two detector loops were forty-five miles apart.

If the object that caused the southern alarm had traversed the Gulf and exited at the northern end, it would have had to have done so at a speed well over thirty knots. No submarine could do that and the obvious conclu-sion was drawn that two submarines had entered the Gulf, in what looked suspiciously like a co-ordinated operation. The Gulf of Paria was the Carib-bean convoy centre and unlike early 1942 when Achilles had struck, it was now teeming with merchant ships. A raid on the Gulf in January 1943 would have netted a very large haul. Achilles' legacy took over and Trinidad went on full alert.

Operation Faith, the code name for enemy U-Boats in the Gulf of Paria was declared in effect. This was serious enough for some of the VP-53 and VP-81 long range flying boats on patrol to be recalled. Every available aircraft and vessel was put on immediate alert. Within an hour the island's airfields were resounding to the roar of aircraft taking off and the civil air raid organisation was brought to full readiness.

The coastal gun batteries were manned and the mobile guns began taking up previously prepared firing positions. The American infantry and combat engineer regiments moved out of their bases and took up their defensive stations, where they were joined by the Trinidad Volunteer batta-lions and Home Guard platoons.

Signals were sent out warning all merchant shipping that there was a possibility that they would soon come under attack and the Gulf of Paria became the centre of a vast anti-submarine hunt. It was possible that this suspected raid on the Gulf was part of a bigger strike involving shipping outside the Gulf and signals were sent out warning the convoys to be alert for U-Boats in their path.

Although convoy TB-1 was more than a hundred and fifty miles away, they automatically became involved in the alert. Beside the specific warnings they could pick up the dramatic increase in radio traffic generated by the alert in Trinidad and see the preparations being made on the escorts. The merchant ships were also alarmed at the dramatic decrease in their aircover, caused by the emergency in Trinidad. The cumulative effect of all these measures made the merchantmen and the escorts uneasy and throughout the convoy the tension built.

When U124 rounded Galera Point, Mohr set course southeast for the area east of Trinidad. He was converging on the course of TB-1, but well behind and there was no possibility of his intercepting the convoy, besides which he had no knowledge of its existence.

Sometime in the early evening of January 7th, one of the convoy escorts picked up what they thought was a submarine. U214 was operating around Curacao, where they were attempting to rectify a gyro breakdown caused by a shattering depth-charge attack that had been delivered at the boat.

U105 was operating among the islands of the Greater Antilles and complained to U-Boat headquarters about the fact that they were unable to find targets. The boat was well astern of TB-1 and did not report sighting a convoy. Likewise U217 was operating along the one hundred fathom line, well ahead of TB-1 off the coast of the Guianas. Neither of these three U-Boats was near convoy TB-1.

However, the continual alarm reports coming from Trinidad about Operation Faith had made the convoy escorts very suspicious and they fired starshell to the west, in an attempt to light up the alleged contact. This caused a chain reaction and several merchantmen let off their snow-flake rockets.

Pyrotechnics at night can be seen from a great distance and far to the west Johann Mohr on the conning tower of U124 saw them. Fine on his port bow he could see the glow and concluded correctly that it was a convoy. He had been in enough North Atlantic convoy actions to instantly recognize the firework display. The great hunter altered course towards the glow and called on his engineers for the maximum speed his much abused engines could produce. Optimum speed for a Type IX U Boat was seventeen knots and it would only be a matter of time before he caught the six-knot convoy.

Convoy TB-1's problems began that night when the tanker Motorcarline, carrying navy fuel experienced an engine breakdown. The tanker left the convoy without informing the Commodore and there was much discussion about the lack of discipline displayed by her master. When she did get going again, the tanker could only manage four knots and the ship ended up trailing TB-1, out of visual contact. Strangely, the Motorcarline's engine breakdown may well have saved her because Mohr was not directly behind the convoy, but off on its starboard quarter.

That same night while Mohr chased after TB-1, the first of the Group

Delfin boats intercepted convoy TM-1 and Auffermann in U514 was able to relax. Dawn on January 8th found convoy TB-1 being chased by U124 and convoy TM-1 being shadowed by U514 and U436. For most of that day the two convoys were being followed until the afternoon when U436 moved in to begin the slaughter of TM-1.

At four thirty the U-Boat had worked its way up onto the convoy's flank and three torpedoes left the boat. The first two torpedoes romped into the six thousand four hundred ton tanker Olthena. The explosion of the warheads ignited the cargo and the tanker disintegrated in a gigantic fireball, —marking the passing of TM-1's second tanker. The third torpedo hit the eight thousand ton tanker Albert L. Ellsworth. The ship was heavily damaged and the crew abandoned their vessel. The wreck of the third tanker was sent to the bottom on the following day by U436, as she came back in astern of the convoy. Just at the time that the Olthena was meeting her fiery end Mohr in U124 sighted the smoke on the horizon that marked the position of convoy TB-1.

Mohr brought U124 up abeam of TB-1 on its inshore flank and at eleven o'clock that night he was down at periscope depth, ready to commence his attack. In Trinidad the great excitement which had caused the alarm was dying down. All day the Gulf of Paria had been criss-crossed by searching aircraft and destroyers and they had not located any U-Boats. That night Operation Faith was cancelled. The troops remained in their defensive positions, but the Air Raid all-clear sounded and the intense anti-submarine operation was scaled down. The double loop crossings that triggered the alert were never explained, but whatever had caused it was about to cause death to stalk TB-1.

At eleven thirty-five three torpedoes left U124 and began their race towards convoy TB-1. One passed right through the convoy, but the other two missed their intended target which was a freighter in the convoy's starboard column and hit the tanker SS Broad Arrow, in one of the port columns. The two torpedoes detonated on the forward section of the Rio bound, seven thousand ton tanker, and her cargo ignited. A blinding white light burst forth and a tower of boiling flame climbed upward over the stricken ship, until twelve hundred feet up, it burnt itself out. The whole forward part of the ship was aflame as she came to a shattered halt with twenty-eight of her crew, including her captain, killed in the initial explosion.

Well astern of the convoy, the bridge watch on the tanker Motorcarline noted the fireball in their log. Only the dead sailors on the Broad Arrow could have told the escorts that the torpedoes had come in on the tanker's starboard side. The ship had been on the port side of the convoy and they immediately assumed that the U-Boat was to seaward, where the wreck of the Broad Arrow burned.

The old destroyer's ancient machinery pushed her faster through the water to the suspected position of the U-Boat and starshell burst to seaward. The corvette astern also turned to port, avoiding the burning wreck and heading out to join the Goff. The starboard side PC dropped back towards the appalling catastrophe of the burning tanker.

Tankers die hard and so it was to be with Broad Arrow. Her bow section settled low in the water, but to the intense discomfort of the thousand men in the convoy, she would not sink. Initially the fire ball had lit up the convoy and this illumination had been followed by the snowflake rockets from the startled merchantmen and then the starshell. Now everything was lit up by the blazing inferno which the tanker had become.

While PC 577 was intent on finding the twenty-six survivors from the tanker, who had all jumped into the sea rather than face the flames, U124 silently came to the surface, on the convoy's inshore flank. The escorts were busy to seaward and most of the merchant seamen were mesmerised by the Wagnerian display that was the burning tanker and none of them noticed the grey wolf closing in.

It was a long time since a U-Boat had entered a convoy on the surface, but this was precisely what Mohr was doing. He kept U124 trimmed down with decks awash and moved into position between the lines of ships, where he intended to hide while his torpedo tubes were being reloaded. Eventually one of the escorts detached and searched the area inshore of the convoy, but U124 was not to be found. For an hour Mohr threaded his way on the surface between the plodding lines of ships and despite the glow from the tanker no one recognized the wolf among the fold.

By one o'clock in the morning, the escorts with the exception of PC 577 were back in position around their charges. At this stage Mohr brought U124 out from between the columns on the seaward side of the convoy and lined up for his next attack. Once again three torpedoes left the tubes, this time aimed at the outer vessels in the port column. The Rio bound, six thousand two hundred ton freighter Collingsworth, loaded with a mixed cargo of coal and steel, took one torpedo dead amidships. The American ship came to an immediate halt with the sea gushing into the giant hole in her side. Survivors later claimed that another torpedo crossed only fifteen feet ahead of their bow. Within five minutes the Collingsworth was gone, leaving only her two lifeboats loaded with shocked survivors.

The second torpedo passed right through the convoy, but the third found the six thousand ton Birmingham City. The freighter was carrying a general cargo intended for Recife in Brazil and like the Collingsworth, the

Birmingham city was ripped open by the explosion. She appeared to plow downwards and within minutes she was gone. Three lifeboats and a collection of survivors thrashing about in the water, was all that was left of the two merchant ships.

The sinking of the two ships in quick succession had an electric effect on the convoy. Caribbean convoys had always been protected by the small PCs but among the merchantmen there was great distrust of the ability of these escorts. This was not helped by the fact that the U-Boats often appeared to ignore the presence of the little ships. This meant that most of the merchantmen in TB-1 felt that they only had two capable escorts and they knew that this was not adequate to protect them. Distrusting their escort, the masters reacted by increasing speed and spreading out. It was every man for himself, but by breaking up the convoy formation they were making it impossible for the escorts to protect them and the result was soon evident.

At this stage the escorts were firing starshell to both sides of the convoy in an effort to spot their tormentor. This illumination was greatly increased by the snowflake rockets from the merchantmen and the still bright glow from the burning tanker six miles away. The searchlights from the escorts occasionally lighting up the fleeing merchant ships helped to add to the confusion, but now that the convoy formation was breaking up, the escorts had to use lights in order to distinguish friend from foe.

In 1943 U-Boats very seldom enjoyed the freedom to fire at a convoy and then wait while their tubes were reloaded and fire again, but Mohr had been allowed to do just this. In fact the boat had not been detected at all and the merchant ships can perhaps be forgiven for believing that they were under attack by a wolf pack.

U124 should have been deep underwater avoiding depth-charge attacks or sunk. Instead Mohr was still on the surface and lining up on another ship. Two torpedoes raced away from the stern tubes towards the charging merchant ships. They were aimed at two overlapping freighters, both racing at their best speed to get away. Both torpedoes slammed into the four thousand five hundred ton freighter Minataur. The massive detonation as the two deadly missiles touched her plates, cut the Minataur into two pieces. Her cargo of coal was blown upwards out of her holds and in seconds the two halves of the ship were gone.

The dramatic disappearance of the last ship completed the panic in the convoy and it broke up. The merchant ships scattered leaving the oily sea covered in coal dust and bits of other cargo, with shocked exhausted survivors calling for help.

Ironically now that U124 had empty torpedo tubes, the escorts could have turned the convoy towards the shore and kept the U-Boat at bay, but they had no control over the scramble for safety. The commodore's ship King James, was still close to the escorts, but the commodore had little idea of what had happened. His signal to Trinidad gave the information that the convoy had been attacked, with an estimate of which ships he thought had been hit.

It was at this stage when TB-1 was breaking up, that the USS Goff finally located U124. The destroyer turned towards the U-Boat and built up speed, but the wily Mohr slipped into a concealing rain storm and dived. The Goff soon had asdic contact and crept into the attack, but by the time that the depth-charges were on the way down, U124 was out of the danger zone. In the confusion of underwater noise after the attack, the U-Boat slipped away and the Goff lost contact. Although the crew of the destroyer could smell diesel fuel on the water, U124 had no difficulty getting away and shortly afterwards the boat was back on the surface. Mohr was attempting to catch the fleeing ships while his torpedo ratings once again struggled to reload the tubes.

The merchant ships were heading for the shallow water off Dutch Guiana, but the scene of the attack was still being lit up by the occasional starshell and searchlights. On the horizon the wreck of the Broad Arrow still burned, but by this time PC 577 was moving to the scene of the second attack with its load of injured and burned survivors.

Dawn was not far away and the U-Boat had to parallel the coast for the fear of being caught in water too shallow to dive in at daylight. Nevertheless, Mohr was still hoping to catch a straggler, but the French Maquis had done their job well.

With dramatic suddenness, both of the U-Boat's diesels broke down. It took twelve hours before the boat was fit to run again and in that time the remnants of TB-1 escaped. At dawn the wreck of the Broad Arrow finally slipped below the waves and the exhausted escorts chased after their charges, but by this time all the escorts needed refuelling. Trinidad was aware that something very wrong had happened to convoy TB-1 and they ordered the ships to make their way to the Para river and anchor.

While the scattered remnants of TB-1 sought shelter and support, convoy TM-1 had nowhere to run. U436 had reduced the convoy to six ships on the afternoon of the eighth. Shortly after midnight, while Mohr was ripping apart TB-1, U522 and U575 moved against TM-1. U575 missed with five torpedoes, but U522 hit the six thousand eight hundred ton tanker Minister Wedel, with two torpedoes, bringing the great vessel to a blazing halt, with the surviving crew abandoning ship.

The third torpedo fired by U522 smashed into the ten thousand ton bulk of the tanker Norvik and she also had to be abandoned. HMS Havelock attempted to sink the two wrecks with gunfire, but she had to abandon the attempt and hurry to get back to her convoy, which was now composed of only four tankers. Later in the day U522 finished the job and dispatched the two wrecks.

In the late morning U575 attacked the convoy again, but once more all her torpedoes missed. While U575 had attacked from one side, U422 had come in on the disengaged flank and managed to put a torpedo into the nine thousand eight hundred ton tanker Empire Lytton, bringing her to a halt. The drifting wreck was abandoned and left behind, to be finished off by the same U-Boat.

By this stage, the four escorts were thoroughly harassed and exhausted. Twelve U-Boats were constantly probing the convoy screen to try and get at the three remaining tankers. The U-Boat commanders reported that the convoy escort was inexperienced, based on the fact that none of the U-Boats attacking the the convoy were even damaged, but this is not surprising.

With twelve U-Boats moving against them, no escort could stay over a suspected contact long enough to pin down a U-Boat. There was no convenient river estuary for TM-1 to seek shelter in, and it got to the stage where the stern escort was signalling the U-Boat doing the shadowing, requesting that he go away. The U-Boat replied that he couldn't because he had a job to do. This extraordinary situation at this point was such, that an escort could have a U-Boat visual, but could not leave its station to attack it, because there were other U-Boats waiting for just such a move.

Through the night of the ninth, the probing continued as the U-Boats strove to reduce TM-1 to zero, while the greatly outnumbered escort fought to avoid becoming the only North Atlantic convoy to be totally destroyed. At sunset on the tenth, U622 was the only U-Boat to get into a firing position, but her torpedoes missed. Later that night U522 got past the exhausted screen and put three torpedoes into the six thousand nine hundred ton tanker British Dominion. The vessel was badly torn up by the three torpedoes and she had to be abandoned. The wreck was dispatched on the following day by U620.

Convoy TM-1 had now lost seven of its original nine tankers. Only the British SS Cliona and the Norwegian SS Vanja were still afloat. For the next twenty-four hours the U-Boats launched numerous attacks, but both tankers bore charmed lives. All the torpedoes fired at them missed, until finally long range aircover reached the remnants of convoy TM-1 and Group Delfin were forced to break off the attack. What little remained of TM-1 eventually reached safety, but to bitter recriminations and historical condemnation.

Shallow water and the efforts of the French Maquis gave convoy TB-1 its reprieve and like TM-1, aircover provided its final salvation. VP-83 based in northern Brazil was assigned exclusively to protecting the ships, even to patrolling the approaches to the Para river where TB-1 was hiding. PC 577 had the sad and gruesome task of quartering the area of the nights action, picking up the survivors and consigning the dead to the deep.

When the overloaded vessel put into Paramaribo, there were one hundred and forty-nine shocked survivors aboard and many of them were injured or badly burned. Additional surface escorts were dispatched to the Para river and convoy TB-1 did not leave its sanctuary until January 18th, by which time it had accumulated a heavy air and surface escort.

Later that month the SS King James was sunk, but the delay in the Para river meant that U124 had long gone. The U-Boat hung around the area of the attack for two days, until the British freighter Dalcross came in sight. Mohr turned in pursuit but once again the unknown Frenchmen struck and the U-Boat suffered another engine failure. Mohr tried the desperate expedient of running on the surface on one diesel and one electric motor, in his attempt to catch the freighter. When it became obvious that he was not gaining on the ship, he fired three torpedoes, all of which the steamer was able to avoid, while calling for help. Aircraft arrived on the scene and U124 was forced to dive. With fuel running low, most of his torpedoes used, and his engines in a terrible state, Mohr finally turned for home. The boat entered Lorient on February 13th and he was flown to the Ukraine to receive the Oak Leaves to his Knight's Cross from the hand of the Fuhrer.

This successful Caribbean cruise was the last completed mission for U124. On her next patrol in April, the luck of the U124 finally ran out when she was caught by two experienced submarine hunters off Oporto in Portugal. She went down with all hands under the pounding from the anti-submarine sloop HMS Black Swan and the Flower class corvette HMS Stone Crop. At the end of the war U124 was classed as the third most successful submarine of any nation. During her career she sank, one cruiser, one corvette and forty-seven merchant ships.

The two escort leaders exacted a terrible revenge for their humiliation with TB-1 and TM-1. The USS Goff was transferred from the Caribbean and in October 1943 she was one of the screen for the escort carrier USS Card. She was present on October 4th when the carrier's aircraft sank U422, one of the boats that had ravaged TM-1. On the same day she was present when the Tanker U460 went down to a homing torpedo from one of the carrier's

Avengers. Nine days later she was again present when U402 was destroyed with no survivors and on the last day of October she was part of the group that sent U584 to a watery grave with the loss of all the boat's crew. She saw four U-Boats pay the ultimate price before 1943 was over. HMS Havelock's chance came in June 1944 when she teamed up with the destroyers HMS Fame and HMS Inconstant to sink U767 in the English Channel.

The battles of TM-1 and TB-1 had originated in Port of Spain harbour and they opened 1943 in a most auspicious manner for the U-Boats, but in fact 1943 was to be the year of defeat for the U-Boats. In the Caribbean the signs were already evident and the only U-Boat that achieved much was U124.

On January 11th, U105 sank the schooner C.S. Flight northwest of Grenada and then while waiting with U124 for a U Tanker, she sank the five thousand ton freighter Cape Decision, northeast of Antigua. U124 and U217 carried out a number of attacks particularly on convoys, but both boats were continually harassed by aircraft and surface escorts, with the result that neither boat managed to hit any merchant ships.

U109 did not do very well on its first and only Caribbean cruise. At the end of December the boat signalled to say that its commander was ill and they requested permission to return. U-Boat headquarters replied that the commander was to hand over his boat to the second-in-command and remain on station. Needless to say U109 achieved nothing, but the situation was so desperate that U-Boat headquarters had no option. The full effect of the November diversions was being felt and the Caribbean was emptying of U-Boats and for the first time there were no replacement boats on the way. By January 23rd, only U217 was left in the area and three days later she left on her way home.

The Allies reacted quickly to the disaster of convoy TM-1 and dispatched convoy TM-2 with eight fast tankers by a more southerly route, so that they would pick up aircover from West Africa. Group Delfin reduced to ten boats and refuelled, was left waiting well to the north and only one U-Boat found TM-2. U217 on her way home from the Caribbean attacked, but her torpedoes were porpoising badly and the fast convoy was able to turn. The heavy escort made the U-Boat pay for its attack with aggressive anti-submarine tactics that did not even allow the boat to shadow the convoy.

There was also another portent of things to come. On January 12th the tanker U459 reported that when she arrived in her rendezvous area, there were two destroyers waiting in ambush. U459 escaped, but it indicated that soon the vital tanker U-Boats that made the Caribbean campaign possible, would become the targets.

CHAPTER

13

The death of an Ace

The month of February 1943 opened without a single U-Boat on station off the American coast, in the Caribbean, or off Brazil. This was the measure of the disruption caused by the redeploying of the boats to counter Operation Torch. In the Caribbean, this was in stark contrast to the hey-day of the U-Boats when the Allies had been on the defensive and the month of November 1942 had seen fourteen anti-submarine attacks delivered in one day. In many ways, the crisis caused by Operation Torch brought on the massive battles in the North Atlantic between February and May and indirectly led to the Caribbean battles of June, July and August.

On January thirtieth the nonstop friction between Grand Admiral Raeder and Adolf Hitler came to an end, when Hitler replaced Raeder as commander in chief of the German navy with Karl Doenitz. Although Doenitz was now head of the German navy as a whole, he still personally ran the U-Boat war and in his new position he was able to ensure that the U-Boat Arm got the priority it deserved. But it was far too late. Gone were the golden days when so much more could have been achieved, because Doenitz was now on the threshold of dancing to the tune played by the Allies.

The anti-submarine forces were now far too powerful and still growing. The odds against a U-Boat surviving were growing and there was now no question of the bold tactics of the early war years being employed. It is significant that in the golden days of the U-Boat Caribbean war no acts of sabotage ashore were ever attempted, although many U-Boat crewmen landed on the islands.

In October 1942 Radio Berlin broadcasted a report that a U-Boat commander had landed in Curacao, been served at an American hotel, and even attended the Cinderella theatre, without being recognized. Although unable to be proved, this report was very likely true and it is only one of many such reports. With the extraordinary freedom that the U-Boats enjoyed, they could easily have landed teams of trained saboteurs and commandos and taken them off again. Had these tactics been employed in conjunction with the massive onslaught against shipping between May and September 1942, untold chaos would have been caused in the inadequately defended islands.

The disruption so caused would have greatly amplified the Caribbean campaign and gone far towards helping the U-Boats to achieve a great deal more. By 1943 it was too late. The garrisons were too strong and the anti-submarine forces too numerous for U-Boats to operate close inshore on any of the islands. The fact that no such raids were attempted was a measure of the lack of co-operation between the various arms of the German war-machine. By the time Doenitz took overall command, the U-Boat arm was beginning its death struggle and the first battlefield was to be the North Atlantic, with the Caribbean as a secondary theatre.

The Allies used the lull in the Caribbean to good effect and began to thin down the heavy garrisons of soldiers, replacing them with more anti-submarine forces. In January President Roosevelt, accompanied by Admiral Leahy and General Marshall, arrived at Waller Field. They were just passing through on their way to the first summit meeting with Churchill and Stalin at Casablanca, but their visit provided a tremendous boost for the morale of the defenders, who sometimes felt forgotten. From the early days when they were woefully deficient in both experience and equipment, they were building a magnificent anti-submarine organisation which was to prove itself in the months to come, but it was still a boring theatre of operations for all but the sailors and airmen.

One of the important areas that had shown great improvement was in the field of communications. A vast network of radio stations and teletype facilities now spread outwards from the Admiral's headquarters in Puerto Rico even to the most insignificant island. It was now possible for a submarine sighting to be quickly translated into a positive response with a minimum delay and the headquarters was able to control the disposition of forces, although tactical command remained with the various sector commanders.

Allied to the radio network was a chain of radar stations. The Americans were still tied to a flawed tactical concept in which the air threat to Panama was considered to be the greatest, with the result that the radars were all air search sets. Nevertheless, these sets could and were used for surface search. At La Lune on Trinidad's south coast and at Blanchisseuse Point on the north coast, as well as on a hill overlooking the village of Charlotteville in Tobago, three radar sets gave coverage from the Venezuelan coast to Grenada.

Radar was also sited at both ends of St. Lucia and so on up the island chain, until all entrances to the Caribbean were covered well enough to detect the passage of a surfaced U-Boat. Initially training in the use of the equipment in the surface search mode was inadequate, but by the end of 1943 the new American U-Boat plotting rooms knew precisely when and where each U-Boat passed.

The Americans also took over the running of the major docks in the area, thus dramatically enhancing their capacity and efficiency. This ensured that there was no delay in the handling of vital war material and they followed this up with road building. Particularly in Trinidad, they laid a network of highways and secondary roads that ultimately allowed them to accomplish the tactical movement of defending troops in considerably less time than before. This allowed them to begin reducing the size of the garrisons to smaller mobile units. In Trinidad, they took over the maintenance and re-equipment of the railroads and this allowed the stores that they required to move quickly. This was particularly important with regard to the growing air activity generated by the sector headquarters.

On February tenth, US Navy Airship squadron ZP-51, became the first lighter-than-air unit to operate outside the continental United States, when they commissioned at Edinburgh Field. Initially, the anti-submarine aircraft had become too numerous for Waller Field and they had moved to Edinburgh. Now Edinburgh was becoming overcrowded. A blimp matt and its associated massive hanger were constructed south of Edinburgh Fields' second runway, but even this was not enough. Edinburgh needed a satellite and Camden Field some six miles southwest was constructed to take the overflow.

The K Type Airships could carry depth-charges and MAD gear for the detection of submerged objects and they soon set up two major patrol areas.

The first of these was an area called the Golden Triangle, located north of Trinidad, which covered the merchant ship choke-point into the Caribbean. The second area was along the bauxite route and the U-Boats now had to beware of these slow, but far-ranging blimps.

Some PBYs also arrived at Edinburgh equipped with MAD gear and sonobouys, which were in time to become the ultimate anti-submarine detection device. In the meantime ZP-51 expanded its operations with the basing of detachments in Guantanamo Bay, Atkinson in British Guiana and at Zandery. With the arrival of VP-34, Chaguaramas now operated three PBY squadrons, along with the OS2Ns of VS-45. All told, Trinidad now operated well over a hundred combat aircraft and at RNAS Piarco, the Royal Navy operated more than two hundred machines. This greatly expanded air complement was soon to be tested.

On January sixteenth, the veteran U-Boats U68, U156 and U510 left Lorient for the Caribbean. Since the convoy battles of August 1942, the U-Boats had been concentrated around Trinidad and the Windward Passage had been free of U-Boat activity. Oberleutnant zur See Albert Lauzemis on his first patrol in command of the veteran boat U68 was ordered to again interdict the Windward Passage. The defenders of this area had become bored to tears patrolling the empty wastes vacated by the U-Boats, but the Allies did not dare to reduce the protection of the passage and indeed, it had been increased. January had seen VP-32 equipped with the magnificent Mariner flying boats, move into Guantanamo Bay. They were to make the Windward Passage a highly dangerous place for U-Boats, as Lauzemis was soon to find out.

While U68 turned its bows towards the Windward Passage, the redoubtable Hartenstein in U156 and Korvettenkapitan Karl Neitzel were enroute to Trinidad. By February fifteenth the three boats were in position, U68 in the Windward Passage and Hartenstein and Neitzel off Trinidad's east coast. Hartenstein was an ace of the Caribbean war and no one had yet equalled his eleven ships sunk and two damaged in a single patrol. He was coming back on this third cruise to try and add to his already formidable total.

Neitzel on the other hand had been seriously hampered on his first Caribbean cruise, when U510 had suffered an unserviceable hydrophone set. He was back to make up for not being among the high scorers in August, but once again U510 had a problem. Some clever member of the Maquis had drilled a hole in one of the fuel tanks of the boat and U510 was leaving a telltale trail of oil. No amount of trouble shooting had been able to find the leak and U510 could not enter the Caribbean, but this did not stop Neitzel from achieving a spectacular success.

For the last two weeks of February, the three U-Boats prowled the waters around the islands, but none of them found targets.

In the meantime U155, U183 and U185 were ordered to the northern Caribbean. U183 under Heinrich Schafer was ordered to the Windward Passage, while U185 originally enroute to Cape Hatteras was directed to the same area. Adolf Piening in U155 was on his third voyage to the Caribbean and his orders were to reopen the Gulf of Mexico offensive, – if he could. Lauzemis discovered that his metox equipment was unserviceable and knowing that if he remained in the Windward Passage it would become his grave, he took U68 northwards to the area outside the Bahamas to await spare parts.

He did not know it at the time, but the Allies had aircraft with the new centimetric radar which didn't alarm the metox. The battle of technology was in full swing and the boats of this wave were to find out that there were occasions when the metox was useless. Hartenstein brought U156 along the north coast of Trinidad, enduring almost constant air attacks, without being able to get near to the heavily escorted convoys, while U510 kept well clear of the nonstop air activity near the island.

Although the month of February ended without the sinking of a single vessel in the Caribbean zone, the great North Atlantic battle was going into high gear. The constant winter storms did not save convoy UC-1. This was another desperate measure to get oil from the Caribbean quickly, by sailing empty tankers direct from the United Kingdom to Trinidad.

On February twenty-second, two thousand miles northeast of Antigua, convoy UC-1 ran into a wolf pack composed of U66, U202, U382, U522, U558 and U569. The boats were in position, waiting for a repeat of convoy TM-1. The battle lasted for four days until convoy UC-1 was a thousand miles from Antigua, roughly in the position where the battle of TM-1 had commenced. By this stage, UC-1 had lost four of its fast tankers sunk and had three others badly damaged.

Further north, in the wastes of the North Atlantic a drama similar to the battle of TB-1 was played out, when a merchant ship accidentally fired its snowflake rockets and revealed convoy SC-118 to the waiting wolf pack. The battle that ensued saw twelve merchant ships go down, along with three U-Boats. These two battles marked the start of the grimmest phase of the Battle of the Atlantic. Already in the first two months of the year, the former Caribbean boats U164 and U507 had died off Brazil, while U69, U201 and U553 had perished in the North Atlantic. Additionally Ernst

Bauer, the old commander of U126, died in command of U169. The time of slaughter had begun.

February had been the first month in which the U-Boats had failed to sink any shipping, but March was to be quite different and the action started on the second day of the month. At seven o'clock in the evening, a B18 bomber of the 9th Army Reconnaissance squadron sighted U156 fully surfaced, only seventeen miles north of Trinidad's Grand Boca. Hartenstein was attempting to catch convoy TB-4 which had left Trinidad earlier in the day. The U-Boat dived quickly but the B18 put four depth-charges into the water close to the swirl. The explosions shook up U156 and probably damaged some equipment, but Hartenstein was determined to catch the convoy and did not stay down for very long.

The great hunter was not aware that he was dealing with a strong integrated defence that had been considerably strengthened since his last patrol in the area. The B18 radioed its attack report and aircraft were scrambled to assist it. An hour and a half later, a B18 of the 80th Bomber squadron out of Edinburgh Field picked up a radar contact off the north coast. The pilot crossed the contact, but in the darkness was unable to positively identify it as a submarine and he decided to turn on his landing lights, to either pick out the contact or draw fire. Almost immediately U156 opened fire, forcing the pilot to break off. While the B18 tried to set up an attack run, U156 crash dived.

Hartenstein had not operated in the Caribbean since June 1942 and it appears that he was completely out of touch with what had happened in the area since then. It was a very long time since any U-Boat had operated on the surface off the north coast of Trinidad and Hartenstein was attempting to do just that. Even the great Lassen in October 1942, had spent most of his time off the north coast submerged.

The old Torpedo Junction of 1942, now had an almost continuous relay of anti-submarine aircraft patrolling it and in addition, the Americans had already set up a killer operation to get the U-Boat sighted by the first B18. Hartenstein must have assumed that the B18 pilot was inexperienced and cleared out of the area, because within a short space of time, he was once again bringing U156 to the surface. The B18 pilot had not gone away. He was waiting patiently above, to see if the U-Boat would take the chance of coming back to the surface.

He was aware that the tail of the convoy was not very far away and he relied on this to act as bait. As the long grey shape of the U156 broke the surface, the B18 pilot was ready and roared into the attack. The conning tower watch had probably just opened the upper hatch and begun to climb out, when the shadow of the B18 roared overhead. Four depth charges splashed into the water close to the boat and there probably was a mad scramble as the watch fell back into the control room, to reverse the operation and crash dive. U156 was still on the surface when the charges detonated at twenty-five feet and this is probably what saved her. The gigantic explosions shook the boat, smashing sensitive equipment. The B18 pilot hauled his aircraft round for another attack, but the U-Boat had disappeared.

The twin attacks on U156 had set in train an elaborate anti-submarine operation. The Americans now knew that there was a U-Boat off the north coast and they intended to get it. It is probable that Hartenstein surfaced later that night to charge his batteries, but by this stage he would have realised that the area was saturated with patrolling aircraft and he had to give up the idea of trailing TB-4. U156 was damaged, and Hartenstein probably spent a minimum of time on the surface before submerging to head slowly eastwards, away from the danger area. The boat was still dangerously close to Trinidad, but he was not aware that he was now leaving a long oil slick behind him. The second attack had damaged a fuel tank.

At ten forty-three on the morning of March third, Airship K17 of ZP-51 was on patrol off the northeast coast of Trinidad when the crew sighted an oil slick on the surface running eastwards. The pilot brought the airship down close to the water and slowed down so that he could creep along just above the glistening oil on the water. For two hours, K17 followed the slick eastwards, until at length they came to the head of the trail of oil, but they could get no MAD indication of a submarine.

The airship was part of the hunter killer group set up specifically to get the U-Boat and the pilot knew that the submarine was close. He set up a square search of the area and sure enough, he soon had a MAD contact moving slowly eastwards. The airship pilot positioned himself over the contact and dropped three depth charges. U156 was probably cruising fairly deep and the explosions did not harm the boat, but it alerted Hartenstein to the fact that either he was leaking oil, or the Allies were using a new location device.

In fact, the Magnetic Anomality Gear MAD, was highly secret and only mounted on airships and a few selected aircraft. There are no indications that the Germans ever found out about its use during the course of the war. After the attack by the airship, PBYs from VP-53 and some PCs were vectored to the position, but none of them could obtain contact. In the meantime the naval intelligence tracking room kept a plot of the various attacks and the probable eastward movement of the U-Boat.

Hartenstein must have heard the nonstop propeller noises above him and it is possible that he used his periscope and saw the circling aircraft and airship. U156 crept slowly eastward, away from the angry swarm that was looking for her. By this time Hartenstein must have been well aware that this was not the Caribbean he had left. It was now a highly dangerous place.

Early next morning convoy TE-1 left the Bocas. This was the first of a new series of convoys designed primarily to get merchant ships away from the Caribbean theatre killing ground. Once they were clear, the convoys broke up and the escorts returned to Trinidad, while the merchant ships independently sought their destinations. This first such convoy was a small one, with only four merchant ships, but it had a heavy escort of four destroyers, all of whom had been briefed about the suspected U-Boat that lay in their path.

The USS Nelson, Southampton, Maddox and Glennon were grouped protectively around their charges, when the Nelson picked up a firm asdic contact. The new two thousand ton Buchanon class destroyer left the screen and raced in for an attack. It is unlikely that Hartenstein, with his boat leaving a trail of oil and aware that the area was crawling with anti-submarine forces would attempt to attack the convoy. What is more likely is that the convoy blundered into U156, which was continuing its eastward movement. Nine depth charges tumbled from the stern of the Nelson and sank around U156. After the detonations the Nelson lost contact, but a large oil slick marked the scene of the attack. U156 escaped, but it is likely that she was damaged again.

After clearing the convoy Hartenstein brought U156 to the surface. This was probably to charge batteries and assess the damage to his much battered boat. At two twenty-five that afternoon the conning tower lookouts spotted a bomber on the horizon and Hartenstein crash dived. The metox equipment had not given an alarm. The bomber a B18 from Edinburgh had picked up U156 on its radar and turned to intercept, but the radar contact disappeared before the aircraft could set up an attack. Undaunted the pilot carried out twelve radar runs over the suspected position. No further contact was made, but the U-Boat plotting room had got another fix on the elusive boat.

For the next thirty hours U156 did not reveal her position. Then at ten minutes past eight on the night of the fifth of March, the radio operators at Edinburgh Field picked up a U-Boat radio transmission and plotted the direction. Soon a message came in from Barbados to say that the radio operators at Seawell airport had also plotted the transmission and the Americans had a fix. In fact it was Hartenstein sending his last situtation report to U-Boat headquarters. He had managed to make his way eastwards

272 THE DEATH OF AN ACE

to an area where he felt relatively safe and decided to take the chance of detection in order to get off his report.

U156 had not been attacked for more than a day and Hartenstein had something important to say. He advised that it was impossible to operate in the area between Trinidad and Grenada because of the nonstop air activity and that he intended operating east of the islands. He surmised that the anti-submarine aircraft were using a new location device which could not be picked up by the Metox receiver. He reported that aircraft were making precise night attacks, without the use of searchlights.

This was the last message that Hartenstein sent. At roughly the same time, U333 operating in the Bay of Biscay also signalled to report that they were being attacked by aircraft, without the Metox equipment giving any warning. U-Boat headquarters were now aware that the Allies had come up with a new location device and the battle of technology once again slipped into high gear.

From this point of view Hartenstein's final signal was very important, but it gave the Americans a further fix on his position, which when combined with the other attack positions, allowed them to plot his mean course away from the island. They launched relays of bombers and long range flying boats along the suspected track, but without success. For three days U156 ran eastwards without being located, until at length Hartenstein could consider himself safe. He had managed to put more than three hundred miles between his boat and the island of Trinidad and made the fatal error of relaxing his vigil.

At six o'clock on the morning of March eighth, aircraft P-1 of VP-53 lifted off the water at Chaguaramas Naval Station in Trinidad. Lieutenant John D. Dryden brought the white painted PBY round to the right and out over the Bocas, before setting course eastwards. His aircraft was one of a large number engaged on the hunt for U156. Dryden was an experienced pilot and he had attacked U-Boats before. In January, he had delivered a devastating attack on U124 off the north coast, but since then had not achieved a U-Boat sighting. On this morning he took the aircraft eastwards to his assigned hunting ground, well to the east of Trinidad.

At one o'clock in the afternoon, the PBY's radar operator reported a contact at twenty miles. Dryden immediately took his flying boat higher so that he was flying between the clouds at fifteen hundred feet. Not relying solely on radar, Dryden kept the clouds between himself and the contact while working closer. At seven miles through a gap in the clouds, he had the U-Boat visual and began his stealthy approach. Dryden used the cloud cover to maximum effect and moved his flying boat into an ideal attack position without being detected. He broke cover in a diving attack, when only a quarter mile from the U-Boat.

U156 was cruising slowly eastward, fully surfaced and it can be assumed that the Metox did not give an alarm. It is likely that the first indications that the conning tower watch on U156 had of the attack, were the bullet splashes in the sea, as the fifty caliber shells walked towards them. There was no time for the U-Boat's crew to react, other than to take cover as the big flying boat swept overhead, with its guns spitting death.

Dryden knew that he had caught the boat off guard and he ignored the intervalometer and dropped four MK-44 depth-charges manually, from seventy-five feet. The four torpex filled charges landed in a group, only fifteen feet from the U-Boat's hull. There was no way U156 could survive such an attack and the combined explosions almost lifted the boat clear out of the water. Seconds later, a separate explosion that was probably a torpedo warhead, rocked the mortally hit boat and caused a fifth tower of water to climb upwards.

When the spray finally cleared, the crew of the aircraft could see the two halves of the U-Boat sticking up, some distance apart. U156 had been cut in two and the two pieces quickly disappeared. Dryden circled the large stain of oil and debris, and counted eleven of the U-Boat's crew alive in the water. He came in over them and dropped a liferaft, followed by a survival kit lashed to two lifejackets. Five of the survivors managed to pull themselves into the liferaft, but the other six must have been badly injured because they soon slipped below. Four of the survivors were barebacked, but the fifth may have been an officer in a white shirt.

Dryden signalled Chaguaramas indicating that he had sunk the U-Boat, three hundred and eighty-three miles east-northeast of Trinidad. The aircraft continued to circle the survivors for the next hour and a half, before Dryden wearily turned for Trinidad.

The Trinidad based aircraft had been constantly attacking U-Boats for a full year and they had built a considerable reputation for themselves. Many U-Boats had left the theatre showing terrible scars inflicted by the dreaded Trinidad based aircraft, but Dryden's U-Boat was the first kill. It was also the first U-Boat to be lost in the Caribbean theatre during 1943. It was VP-53's twelfth and last attack on a U-Boat. Shortly afterwards, the squadron was transferred to the Pacific to be replaced at Chaguaramas by the redoubtable VP-204, with its Mariner flying boats.

At four thirty that afternoon, the destroyer USS Barney was dispatched to the scene of the sinking to rescue the survivors. The destroyer was capable of getting to the area in just over twelve hours and there were high hopes that the survivors would be rescued, but US Navy Intelligence were to be disappointed. No trace of the dinghy or the survivors were ever found. Two Spanish tankers, the Alecca Espana and the infamous Gobeo were within a hundred and twenty miles of the scene of the sinking, although both were to the west and heading away. For a while the Americans considered the possibility that one of these vessels had snatched the survivors, but post war records do not support this theory.

It is possible that the dinghy drifted westwards between the islands and disappeared in the wastes of the central Caribbean, but the Americans mounted a comprehensive search in an area that was constantly criss-crossed by aircraft. Another possibility is that the catastrophic destruction of the U-Boat deposited a large number of bodies in the water, causing a shark frenzy. Under such conditions it is probable that the dinghy would not survive. In either case Hartenstein and his gallant crew perished. This ace of the Caribbean war had not managed to add to his score before he died, but then it didn't matter because no one equalled his score anyway. Dryden received a DFC and his crew got Air Medals for a brilliant attack which destroyed a very famous U-Boat.

While the U156 drama was being played out Neitzel, with his boat trailing a smear of oil across the surface, was staying a good five hundred miles away from Trinidad, in an area where he felt relatively safe. Despite the handicap, he was about to shock the Americans out of their complacency over the tenacious hunting and spectacular destruction of U156, by carrying out one of the most devastating single U-Boat attacks against a convoy to take place in World War Two.

After the mauling of TB-1, the Trinidad Bahia convoys should have been heavily escorted, but in the six weeks since Mohr had demonstrated his ability, the convoys had run unmolested and complacency had stepped in. Thus it was that on the day of the sinking of U156, convoy BT-6 was coming north with a pitifully inadequate escort of one old destroyer, a corvette on loan from the Royal Navy and two PCs. They were considered adequate to handle any U-Boat, but BT-6 was going to absorb a very high level of protection before the ships made it to Trinidad.

At sunset that day Karl Neitzel sighted the smudge on the southern horizon that marked the position of convoy BT-6, as it plodded northwest towards Trinidad. The U-Boat was one hundred miles off the coast of French Guiana, when the sighting report was sent off. Almost immediately U-Boat headquarters replied, clearing him to attack at his discretion, without sending off further sighting reports. They were unaware that Werner Hartenstein was dead and went on to explain to Neitzel that the nearest U-

Boat to his position was six hundred miles away. In fact the nearest U-Boat was in the Windward Passage, which was sixteen hundred miles away. He was entirely on his own.

By nine o'clock that night, U510 was in position. Ignoring the escort, Neitzel had worked his way between the PC on the convoy's seaward wing and the lines of patiently plodding merchant ships. He lined up on a heavily laden freighter and at six minutes past nine, the U-Boat lurched as two bow torpedoes left their tubes in succession and began their race for the convoy.

One minute later Neitzel had another target in his sights and the second pair of bow torpedoes left their tubes. With four torpedoes running, he began turning U510 to bring the stern tubes to bear. Even as the boat began its turn the torpedoes struck. One minute and fifty-nine seconds after firing, the first two torpedoes romped home into the three thousand nine hundred ton British freighter Kelvinbank. The shattering double explosions tore the bottom out of the little ship and she went down almost immediately. Before the thunder of the explosions had died down, U510 was round and the boat lurched twice as the two stern torpedoes left their tubes.

All six tubes were now empty and Neitzel began his crash dive. The third bow torpedo ran right through the convoy without finding a target, but the fourth found a berth in the side of the seven thousand ton Liberty ship George Meade. The torpedo detonation blew a great hole in the ship's side and the George Meade's cargo caught fire. The U-Boat was hardly underwater before the torpedoes from the stern tubes found their targets. One torpedo slammed into the Liberty ship Tabitha Brown and the other found the side of another Liberty, the Joseph Rodman Drake.

The hammar blows within the convoy galvanised the escort and both the USS Borie and the corvette Tenacity turned towards the suspected firing position. In the meantime Neitzel had turned onto the convoy's course and was preparing to go deep. Neitzel was under the impression that the convoy was escorted by four destroyers and four PCs, an escort that he could hardly hope to escape from. To counter the supposed heavy escort, he decided that the safest course of action would be to get into the convoy, where the destroyers might not find him.

He turned U510 towards the merchant ships, while his crew strove to reload the torpedo tubes. Up above the escorts were firing off starshell in an attempt to expose the attacker, while the asdic operators probed the depths on the convoy's starboard flank. The burning George Meade lit up a scene of utter chaos as the crews of the three Liberty ships abandoned them. Tension in the convoy was at fever pitch as the ships that were still going frantically avoided the drifting hulks. Four ships taken out of a convoy in such a short time spelled either a very experienced U-Boat commander, or a wolf pack.

For the next three hours the destroyer and the corvette hunted for the offending U-Boat without success. The sea heaved with the eruption of depth charge explosions and searchlights probed the darkness. The first attack had broken up the convoy and the ships had stayed widely separated while the escorts carried out their hunt. The merchant captains felt safer with more room between the columns and two PCs were unable to get them back into a tight mass.

At midnight, the U510 with all her tubes reloaded, was ready for the second round. The escorts were just beginning to quieten down and Neitzel realised that he was not dealing with either a powerful, or experienced group. He had remained unmolested throughout the reloading operation and now once again torpedoes began vomitting from the U-Boats tubes.

At four minutes past the hour, two torpedoes left the bow tubes and began their race for the ships. One minute and twenty-seven seconds later, both torpedoes crashed into the side of the American Liberty ship Mark Hanna. The ship shuddered under the double hammer blows and came to a stop in the convoy's outer starboard column. Once again the escorts raced out of their stations and lit up the starboard, seaward side of the convoy with starshell. It is unlikely that many people realised that the Mark Hanna had been hit on her port side, but even if this fact had been observed, no one would have guessed that the offending U-Boat was inside the convoy. In fact Neitzel had taken his boat into the wide open centre of the convoy and now lay across the convoy's northwestward line of advance.

Three minutes after the first attack, the Liberty ship James Smith on the convoy's port side came into line with the U-Boat's stern and a torpedo hissed out. Almost immediately, the Liberty ship Thomas Ruffin also came into the sights and a second stern torpedo left its tube. After a run of one minute and twenty-three seconds, the first stern torpedo ripped into the seven thousand ton bulk of the James Smith and she began swinging out of line with the sea crashing into a gaping hole in her side. Twenty seconds later it was the turn of the Thomas Ruffin and she came to an exhausted stop.

By this stage, all semblance of a convoy formation had disappeared. The Thomas Ruffin had been the seventh ship in the convoy to be hit and it appeared as if the blows were coming from both sides of the convoy. To the merchant seamen, it appeared as if convoy BT-6 was going to be annihilated. One minute after the strike on the Thomas Ruffin, the Liberty ship James K. Polk, pulling away on the starboard side of the mass of ships, came across the U-Boat's bow and the last two torpedoes leapt out of the tubes and raced away into the darkness. Once again U510 had all her torpedo tubes empty and Neitzel took her down fast, heading eastwards. Even as he began his run to freedom, the two torpedoes smashed into the side of the James K. Polk, the convoy's eighth ship to be hit.

The torpedo detonations on both sides of the convoy helped to add greatly to the confusion and starshell now began falling on the inshore side. The strikes on both sides divided the escort, because it was obvious that there were at least two U-Boats in contact, but it also opened a hole on the seaward side of the convoy for U510 to escape. Neitzel could not afford to let daylight catch him near the convoy or the coastline, because he could not survive in daylight with his telltale oil leak and he intended to put as much distance as possible between himself and the scene of the action. There was no longer a convoy as such, because there were only seven merchant ships still going and they were all seeking safety in different directions. One ship had been sunk, and spread over fifteen miles of sea there were seven seriously damaged and abandoned wrecks, because none of the merchant crews wasted time in getting off.

At one fifteen in the morning, the senior officer of the escort on board the destroyer Borie reported the catastrophe to Trinidad. The Borie's responsibility lay with the ships that were still going and the senior officer did not know that all the Liberty ships were still afloat. They were reported as sunk and the Borie called for urgent support for the remnants of the convoy.

PC-592 had been detached as a rescue ship at the start of the attack and that night she picked up one hundred and thirty survivors out of the sea, or from lifeboats. These were all the survivors from eight merchant ships. It meant that although most of the torpedo hits had not sunk the ships, the majority of the crews had either been killed by the explosions, or died in the sea. Air support was quickly on the scene and the bombers from Zandery and Atkinson set up a formidable barrier, but they were concerned with protecting the remaining ships. The abandoned merchant ships were unknowingly left behind.

By daylight on the ninth, U510 was well to the east of the attack position and in fact she was never detected. Sometime that day, the long range PBYs from Chaguaramas came upon the fleet of drifting Liberty ships and at last Trinidad became aware that they had a massive rescue operation on their hands. Convoy BT-6 was effectively divided into two parts and this knowledge brought forth a fleet of rescue vessels.

All the Liberty ships had been heavily loaded and even if the ships were wrecked, some of the cargoes might be salvaged, providing a prowling

U-Boat did not find the deserted ships first. The Royal Navy corvettes and anti-submarine trawlers HMS Woodruff, Amaranthus, Tamarisk, Milford, Morris Dancer and four US Navy patrol vessels, accompanied five tugs out of the Bocas and began a race for the fleet of ghost ships.

On the twelfth of March, they found the James Smith and the James K. Polk, both of which had been confirmed as sunk. They commenced the tow to Trinidad, while the search went on for the others. On the same day the shattered remains of BT-6 were escorted into the Gulf of Paria, by the Borie and the other exhausted escorts. Eventually all seven Liberty ships, including the burnt out George Meade were located and they were towed to Trinidad, arriving with their nine escorts on March seventeenth.

Some of the cargoes were saved, but it was found that the Thomas Ruffin and James K. Polk were too badly damaged to be repaired. This meant that convoy BT-6 had effectively lost three merchant ships and had five seriously damaged. In the end, the convoy had utilized thirteen escorts and seven tugs, with an untold delay to the cargoes and hulls. It was a remarkable achievement for a single U-Boat and proof positive that the escort of convoy TM-1 had not been inexperienced. Had BT-6 had to face the twelve boats of Group Delfin, not even the escort vessels would have reached Trinidad.

Since the loss of U156, U510 was alone in the eastern part of the Caribbean theatre, but in the northwest the situation was heating up for the first time in six months. Where before the northwest had been clear of U-Boats, four of them now prowled the area. U68 had come back into the Caribbean through the Windward Passage and the boat was now on its way to the area north of Aruba. Heinrich Schafer had brought U183 through the Windward Passage and then turned westward between Jamaica and Cuba. At almost the same time, Maus brought U185 through the passage and took up station near Jamaica.

All the boats in the area of the Windward Passage were subject to nonstop American pressure. The combination of the PBYs of VP-92, the Mariners of VP-32 and the Kingfishers of VS-62, backed up by bombers from the newly commissioned Vernam Field in Jamaica, made the Windward Passage as dangerous for U-Boats as the north coast of Trinidad. Added to these defences were the blimps of ZP51's Guantanamo detachment, along with numerous Royal Navy aircraft based at Palisadoes in Jamaica and indeed U185 was bombed by an airship.

Despite the nonstop air activity and some surface harassment by vessels operating out of Jamaica, Maus managed to achieve success. He moved U185 out into the center of the Windward Passage and at midnight on the ninth, he made contact with convoy KG123. The KG series were military convoys that ran from Key West to Guantanamo Bay and were usually heavily escorted. Maus found six merchant vessels, escorted by four naval vessels, but he was not daunted by the odds and at one thirty in the morning he attacked.

Two torpedoes slammed into the six thousand ton American tanker Virginia Sinclair, setting fire to its volatile cargo. The attack took place only twenty miles from the naval base at Guantanamo and it brought forth a furious reaction from the defenders. For the next four hours, Maus crept cautiously around trying to avoid the aircraft and surface escorts that quartered the area.

At five o'clock in the morning he found himself once again in a favourable position to attack and two more torpedoes left the boat. Both struck the Liberty ship James Sprunt, which was loaded with ammunition. With a spectacular series of explosions lighting up the area, the James Sprunt settled onto the bottom, alongside the Virginia Sinclair, in the mile deep waters of the passage.

By this stage it was almost dawn and Maus had his work cut out to get U185 away from the swarm of aircraft and escorts that converged on him. He managed to get the U-Boat a little further away from the naval base, but he was convinced that the area was rich in targets and did not go far.

At three o'clock that afternoon he was still fairly close to Guantanamo and he was rewarded by the sight of a large convoy of thirty merchant vessels coming out of the bay. Maus began moving U185 back in towards the convoy, but he had U185 on the surface in daylight, in the Windward Passage and it was not long before he was detected. He was trying to manoeuvre his boat into a favourable attack position, when a Mariner flying boat came roaring in on an attack run. Maus was forced to crash dive, but he was hardly down before the escort vessels were overhead. The depth charge attack that followed seriously damaged U185 and Maus was forced to pull back and get away from the passage, to find a quiet area where he could repair his boat.

In the meantime Schafer in U183 had made his way westwards along the south coast of Cuba and on the eleventh of March he caught the small Honduran freighter Olancho, just off the western tip of Cuba. This area was technically in the Gulf of Mexico. It was the first ship to be hit in the area since U171 had left the Gulf in September 1942. Two days after U183's sinking of the freighter, Lauzemis in U68 carried out the last successful attack on the main convoy route between Aruba and Guantanamo. The boat had moved into a position roughly halfway between the two ports when she intercepted convoy GAT-49 coming south. U68 sank two of the convoy's twenty merchant ships. The seven thousand ton American tanker Cities Service Missouri, and the Dutch freighter Ceres, both went to the bottom one hundred and sixty miles from Aruba, but the escort destroyers USS Biddle and Leary forced the U-Boat to break off the action.

While these actions were taking place inside the Caribbean, Piening in U155 moved up the north coast of Cuba and very cautiously crossed the Straits of Florida, before setting course for the centre of the Gulf of Mexico. For the rest of the month Piening avoided the strong defensive forces in the Gulf, while the other three boats endured almost nonstop attacks in the Caribbean. The defences had been thoroughly aroused and aircraft and surface vessels fought off all attempts to approach the numerous convoys.

It was a remarkable demonstration of the new power of the United States Navy. Now that they had not only the equipment, but the experience as well, they were able to challenge the U-Boats and win. Sixteen hundred miles away to the southeast, Neitzel in U510 was well aware that his oil leak would spell doom if he came in close to the coast and although he trailed convoys BT-8 and TB-9 respectively, he could not achieve any further success. Judging by what Neitzel had done to convoy BT-6, the unknown Frenchman who punched the hole in the fuel tank saved a number of Allied lives.

In November 1942, the United States had taken action on the Vichy French problem in the Caribbean and abandoned any further attempts at negotiation. As of that month, they instituted a blockade of French Guiana, Martinique and Guadeloupe. US Navy vessels stopped all ships entering the respective ports and ensured that imports of food were cut off. Vice Admiral Robert in Martinique remained defiant, but the situation in the French penal colony on the mainland began to deteriorate. As hunger increased, it generated unrest among the population who began calling for the abandonment of Vichy. By March 1943, the situation in the colony was almost out of hand and on the nineteenth of the month the Governor was forced to concede defeat.

He cabled General Giraud announcing that French Guiana had left the Vichy cause and joined the Allies. At this time the Free French Forces were divided in their loyalty between two competing Generals. De Gaulle had been the first French Officer to arrive in England and begin to organize the French and as such he automatically assumed leadership, which the British recognized.

In November 1942, after the assassination of Admiral Darlan, Giraud became the leader of the French in North Africa and automatically challenged de Gaulle's leadership. The two men could not agree and for a while two competing French armed forces existed. Both arms of the Free French movement immediately claimed French Guiana and this put the United States in a very difficult position of having to make a choice over which side they supported. Eventually they decided to back General Giraud, falling back on the excuse that Giraud was the senior officer. De Gaulle's representative had to be blocked and this was accomplished in Trinidad where he was detained.

The Giraud representative took control of French Guiana and the Vichy Governor was removed to the United States for his own safety. Giraud's previous connection with Vichy was enough to ensure that he was unable to depose de Gaulle and a little later in the war, the Allies were forced to accept de Gaulle as the only leader. The affair over French Guiana contributed in no small measure to the difficulty that the United States experienced in later years with de Gaulle.

At the time of the surrender of French Guiana, the Americans had two immediate concerns. The first of these was to get to the colony before anyone else could and secure the right to base troops and more importantly, aircraft at the French airfield. This they achieved and by the end of March they had an agreement to base anti-submarine aircraft at Gallion Field. This gave them an unbroken string of bases from the continental United States to the southern border of Brazil. The acquisition gave them an immense strategic advantage, which made life much more difficult for the U-Boats.

The second important consideration was to block any move by Vice Admiral Robert in Martinique, to hamper the Allied takeover of French Guiana. There was a very real danger of the French fleet sailing from Martinique with an invasion force to regain French Guiana for Vichy. The Americans had to put aside their kid glove policy for dealing with the French and they found themselves in the same position that Britian had been in during June 1940.

The American counter-measures were swift and decisive. The majority of the American anti-submarine aircraft were quickly re-armed with bombs and torpedoes for a shipping strike and moved to St. Lucia. They were followed up by the Chaguaramas destroyers and others from the Puerto Rican Sector. A Task Force made up of the brand new fleet carrier USS Essex, the cruiser Omaha, with the destroyers USS Beale, Ringgold and Shroeder came south from the US east coast and took up station to seaward of the Windward Islands. Further south forces stationed in Brazil moved to the northern border with French Guiana, ready to deny the colony to the Vichy fleet. The orders were to destroy the French fleet if any signs of hostile movement were observed.

In time, the threat from Martinique died down, allowing the aircraft and surface vessels to return to their primary anti-submarine task. However, by not attempting to come out, or react to the threatening American dispositions, Admiral Robert kept his fleet intact and thereby maintained the threat of a fleet "in being".

In the meantime, officers in French Guiana loyal to Vichy left the colony in the French ship Couventeur Moutette and sailed to join Admiral Robert in Martinique. The French ship ignored repeated American orders to turn back, indicating that the Vichy French were not aware that they had pushed American patience to the limit and created an intolerable situation. They could no longer allow the powerful Vichy French forces in Martinique to exist within easy reach of their vital but thinly held installations. They could not continue looking over their shoulders at the Vichy fleet in Martinique, while trying to concentrate on defeating the U-Boats. The threat was too great. The kid gloves came off and planning for the invasion of Martinique commenced.

CHAPTER

14

A double-edged sword

During the month of March 1943 six ships had been sunk in the Caribbean theatre, while two others had been so badly damaged that they had to be scrapped. From a Caribbean point of view, March had been notable only for the death of Werner Hartenstein and Neitzel's spectacular lone attack on convoy BT-6. The performance of the U-Boats had been to their usual high standard, but the results achieved had been far below expectations. They had of course pinned down a considerable segment of the available anti-submarine forces, but on the whole honours for March must go to the American forces.

Except for the performance of some of the surface escorts, the American forces had shown a marked improvement in their technique and there were no more comments from U-Boat commanders about inexperienced Americans. But March 1943 in the Caribbean was a minor sideshow compared to what had happened in the wider Battle of the Atlantic.

U-Boat command finally got their sailing schedule back in order after the disruption caused by Operation Torch. Doenitz had decided to abandon the emphasis on operations in the west and throw everything into a decisive clash for control of the North Atlantic shipping lanes. The time was right for such a move, because many of the Allied escorts were still tied up off North Africa and he managed to concentrate forty U-Boats in the North Atlantic, where a large proportion of them trapped convoy SC-122 and convoy HX-229. The fight around the convoys was vicious and the U-Boats pulled off a spectacular success.

In the first ten days of March, forty-one merchant ships were sunk and this was followed up during the second ten days with the sinking of fifty-four more merchant ships. All told, one hundred and eight ships were sunk during the month. For a brief period it almost seemed as if the golden days had returned. To achieve this, they lost fifteen U-Boats, two of whom U130 and U163 were former Caribbean boats. U130 had been in the Caribbean during the Merry month of May and she was lost with all hands when caught by the destroyer USS Champlin. U163 had gone to the torpedoes of the US submarine Heering. The losses were not critical, because at this stage of the war there were five new U-Boats entering service every week, which meant that during March, the U-Boat arm kept growing.

The crippling losses in the North Atlantic during March caused serious repercussions among the Allies. Prior to this it had seemed that they were slowly winning the Battle of the Atlantic, but the scale of losses caused doubts to be expressed, even about the effectiveness of the well-tired convoy system.

At Casablanca in January, the Joint Chiefs of Staff had hammered out the doctrine that the first Allied priority was the defeat of the U-Boats, but even though this principle had been agreed to, not everyone had subscribed to it. Admiral King was still Pacific orientated and it was with reluctance that he finally agreed to close the North Atlantic Air Gap. Considerable friction had also arisen over the different anti-submarine methods of the Allies, but this had been smoothed over to present an image of solidarity.

Two months later, the losses in March had tended to accentuate these differences casting further doubt about whether the convoy system was the best way to fight the U-Boats. During March, the Washington Conference on the anti-submarine war saw these differences of opinion once again come out into the open.

Admiral King withdrew all American escort vessels from North Atlantic convoy duty, on the grounds that he did not feel that mixed anti-submarine groups were effective. It has been suggested that Admiral King did this purely because he did not like the idea of American vessels operating under British control. Nevertheless, March 1943 was not the best time to effect this dramatic re-organization. In the final agreement, the British and Canadians were left solely in charge of the North Atlantic lifeline, with a chop-line at forty-seven degrees west longitude. The US Navy in turn, took control of mid Atlantic convoys, US coastal convoys and all Caribbean and South American operations.

Admiral King is one of the most controversial figures among the Allied leaders of World War Two and many ulterior motives have been attributed to him which probably are not true. It is obvious that he always put a higher priority on Pacific operations than the Battle of the Atlantic, but the basic differences between the British and American approaches were more fundamental.

In the dark days of 1942, the British were appalled at the American lack of enthusiasm for the convoy system and quite rightly so. The naval resources simply did not exist to cater for the American idea of hunting groups, but this did not mean that the hunting group concept was wrong. It was not a practical proposition in 1942, but Admiral King and many other American naval officers were firmly committed to this concept and although forced to fall in line with British convoy concepts, they never forgot their original ideas on the subject.

The fact that two thirds of the ships lost in March 1943 were in convoys, provided the proof that the Americans needed to partially disassociate themselves from the concept of all naval anti-submarine forces being tied exclusively to convoys.

The situation in 1943 was drastically different to the early days of 1942. Naval resources were available, the level of technology was adequate and above all, the vital intelligence information was available. Hunting Groups could never have worked in the vast wastes of the Atlantic without reliable intelligence information on where to find the U-Boats.

In 1943, the information picked up by the British Ultra decoders was being made available to the Americans, although the British were wary of allowing too much action based on this information for fear of compromising the source. Nevertheless, there was sufficient information for the hunting group concept to work. Admiral King was aware of this and also fully aware that he could never get the freedom to try the hunting groups again, while tied to the British controlled North Atlantic convoy system. He needed room and his answer was to get out of the North Atlantic system.

With the new freedom to run his area of responsibility as he saw fit, King reinstated the hunting group concept. His move may have been a little premature, because the Caribbean and Brazilian convoys were still inadequately escorted. What Lassen, Mohr and Neitzel had achieved in lone attacks on convoys should never have happened. It is doubtful if a lone U-Boat could have handled a North Atlantic convoy during 1942, in the manner which Neitzel had just demonstrated, and got away with it, even in the North Atlantic air gap. Escort groups in that area frequently had to handle wolf packs of up to twenty or thirty boats.

Part of the reason for the success of U-Boats against Caribbean convoys, was the limited usefulness of the American PC. As an ocean escort the PC never achieved much success and the U-Boats frequently ignored their presence. Yet all Caribbean and South American convoys had PCs making up at least half of the escort group. The corvette was only slightly better than the PC. It could handle the slow convoys adequately and if a corvette caught a U-Boat, there was a good chance that the U-Boat would go down under the hammering.

But corvettes were frequently assigned to fast convoys. In the case of convoy TM-1 moving at twelve knots, the corvette with its sixteen knot speed could not hope to be effective. If one of the corvettes escorting TM-1 had dropped back to deal with a U-Boat, the escort would have had the devil's own job to catch up with the convoy and of course, the absence of the corvette from its station would have opened the way for the other U-Boats to penetrate the convoy.

Although the PC was faster than the corvette, its lack of radar and an adequate sonar limited its usefulness. From this point of view, some of the vessels assigned to the hunting groups might well have been usefully employed guarding convoys, until the DEs came forward in sufficient numbers. Despite the reservations about the protection of convoys, the hunting groups were almost immediately successful and were to play a decisive part in the Caribbean campaign.

The new hunting groups were based on the Task Group system and organized around an anti-submarine escort aircraft carrier escorted by destroyers. The Task Groups were to operate in mid Atlantic and around the Azores, on information about U-Boat refuelling and rendezvous areas, gleaned from British intelligence sources.

The American hunting groups were so successful that the British introduced a similar system with their Support Groups, although these units operated on a different tactical concept. The British Support Group operated in support of the convoys, augmenting escort groups according to the threat and U-Boat concentrations. In the long run, the British and American concepts dovetailed and when they operated in concert with a solid well organized convoy system, they defeated the U-Boats.

The total system made survival very difficult for the U-Boats. On leaving their French bases, they first had to face the increasingly hazardous crossing of the Bay of Biscay. After this they had to face the hazard presented by the American Task Groups waiting in their refuelling areas and along their mid Atlantic transit routes. If they managed to run the gauntlet of the first two, then they had to face the well organized convoy system, covered by radar equipped aircraft and reinforced by the British Support Groups. On the return, they had to face the same threats in reverse order and from early in 1943, their losses began to mount. It was a total anti-submarine system and it was to be decisive.

One other important conference was held in March and this took place in Miami. The US Navy and the US Army Air Corps sat down to thrash out their differences and establish an operational concept. In the Caribbean the two forces were carrying out the same function, because both had finally recognized the fact that the primary threat to the Caribbean was from the U-Boats. This conference was necessary because there was much duplication of effort and they sometimes got in each other's way.

The core of the problem lay in command and control. It is to General Marshall's credit that he called for the conference, because he recognized that the Caribbean was essentially a naval theatre of operations. In keeping with this concept, he agreed to naval control of the Army's anti-submarine resources and even handed over aircraft and crews to the navy. It was a level headed approach, without the hoarding and jealousy which frequently was the hallmark of many of World War Two's senior officers and it was to transform the Caribbean anti-submarine war.

Since the beginning of the war, the Gulf of Paria had been increasing in importance. The start of the U-Boat offensive in the Caribbean had forced the British and the Americans to upgrade the defences, to the stage where by the end of 1942, it was properly protected. The Gulf was being used as a large secure convoy centre and anti-submarine base.

Late in 1942 it had been allocated as a training area for the new destroyer escorts that were coming down the ways in increasing numbers, adding another dimension to Gulf activities. The British also considered the Gulf for the training of mine-sweepers, but the distances involved proved too great and the idea was dropped. The mine-sweepers thereafter conducted their work-up training off the ports of the Unites States and Canada, where they were being built. The crisis over French Guiana was to be the catalyst that opened up the Gulf of Paria and showed the true potential of the area, allowing it to achieve its ultimate strategic importance.

The new completed fleet carrier USS Essex had been working up its new crew and air group in the hazardous waters off the American coast, when the crisis over French Guiana arose. Regardless to its state of preparedness, the carrier had had to sail for the Caribbean, to be on hand to deal with the French carrier Berne, if need be. The work-up area off the US coast had been hazardous, with the constant threat of U-Boats, and it was by no means certain that the escorts could always foil attempted attacks on the vessel. The same was true of the carrier's operational area off Martinique. The commander of the Task Group had decided that rather than risk the loss of a high value warship to a prowling U-Boat, the carrier could wait at Trinidad and be on call if the crisis escalated. Thus it came about that the fleet carriers discovered the Gulf of Paria.

The carrier arrived in Chaguaramas at two fifteen on the afternoon of March twentieth and the ship's captain was immediately taken up with the enormous possibilities for training that the Gulf offered.

The Gulf of Paria offered more than two thousand square miles of protected water, of which more than fifteen hundred square miles were more than five fathoms deep. This was ample room for the big ships to conduct their shakedown training and on March twenty-sixth, the captain signalled Washington advising that the Gulf of Paria showed excellent potential as a carrier shakedown area.

The Essex left the Gulf on the fourth of April escorted by the destroyers Dyson, Beale and John Rogers, by which time French Guiana had been secured and the threat of a sortie by the Vichy French fleet had diminished, but it was not long before the other carriers began arriving.

April saw the arrival of the CVL Independence. May saw the CVs Lexington and Yorktown, followed by the CVLs Princeton and Belleau Wood in the Gulf. This constant procession of carriers continued right up to May 1945. It was only when Germany surrendered and there was no longer any threat of prowling U-Boats that the carriers forsook the Gulf for the wider reaches of the Caribbean. By this stage, fifteen of the large Essex class carriers and ten of the light fleet carriers, had used the Gulf to perfect the damage control techniques that saved many of them after the Kamikaze strikes in the Pacific. The large number of airfields and aircraft based in Trinidad also allowed the carriers to practice their evolutions and handle air attack.

Initially, the carrier air groups flew off to the Army Air Corps airfields, but the naval aviation activity became so intense that an airbase had to be dedicated to their use. The anti-submarine squadrons left Edinburgh Field, then renamed Carlsen Field, and moved back into Waller Field.

At this stage, the U-Boat threat was diminishing and the flying boats out of Chaguaramas were able to handle most of it. Carlsen Field then thundered to the nonstop simulated carrier landings of the carrier air wings, adding considerably to the already crowded airspace. The one hundred

American combat aircraft and the two hundred Fleet Air Arm machines, were now joined by up to two hundred carrier aircraft, if two carriers were in the Gulf at the same time, to make Trinidad a very busy place.

The Fleet Air Arm based at RNAS Piarco already had comprehensive torpedo, bombing and air to air firing ranges in the Gulf of Paria. It seemed a simple matter to add a naval gunnery range and in August 1943, the USS New Jersey arrived to carry out her shakedown training in the Gulf. The firing range for the battleship's sixteen inch guns was adequate and the New Jersey was followed by a succession of battleships and heavy cruisers, alongside the aircraft carriers.

The range organisation necessary to co-ordinate the movements and practice activities of so many ships and aircraft ensured that the expansion programme at Chaguaramas continued virtually through the entire war. The base had to have comprehensive ship repair and servicing facilities and the Gulf of Paria came close to its maximum capacity. It was the largest protected harbour in the western hemisphere and it was not long before Chaguaramas became one of the largest naval bases in the world.

By mid 1943, the Gulf was handling up to thirty convoys of approximately one thousand merchant ships per month. Alongside this large number of merchantmen, the naval base was logging up to three hundred warship movements into and out of the Gulf. Achilles would not have recognized it, nor is it likely that he could have survived in it. The Gulf of Paria had become the hub of the war in the Caribbean.

Besides its tactical and strategic position in relation to the war in the west, the island of Trinidad was very important from two other aspects. Its oil fields and refinery were vital to the British war effort, as well as providing a readily available supply of oil to its many air and sea clients. Without the locally available oil the Allies would have had to bring oil in to feed the vast war machine that had developed. The refinery's two million gallon storage capacity was sufficient for those using the island, as well as the tankers carrying the oil to the United Kingdom.

The second attribute was, that Trinidad stood at the aviation crossroads of the South American continent. The island became the staging post for aircraft on their way from the United States to the African and European theatres of war. It was one day's flying from the Florida area and became a natural overnight stop.

From Trinidad the combat and transport aircraft flew southward to Brazil and then across the South Atlantic to West Africa, thence northward to their various operational theatres. This meant that hundreds of transiting aircraft would pass through on a monthly basis. This volume of aviation activity demanded a comprehensive support organisation, which also had to be protected, necessitating frequent defence exercises which served to fully integrate the garrisons. The comprehensive civil defence organization was now linked to the Home Guard Platoons and integrated with the local Volunteer infantry and artillery, who worked in harmony with the US Infantry and coast defence gunners. It was a far cry from the days of 1942 when there was a constant squabble over command and control.

Surprisingly, the Germans seemed to have recognized the strategic importance of Trinidad even before the Americans and the island always figured prominently in their wartime political writings. There were always a number of neutral ships calling at Trinidad which were the subject of intense scrutiny by British Intelligence, but despite this there was contact between the crews of these vessels and locally based German sympathizers. Some of these local sympathizers were detained for the duration, but others operated throughout the war without being detected.

This meant that the Germans were always up to date on developments in the island and they were fully aware of the vast infra-structure which the Americans had put in. They were also aware that because the Caribbean conflict was basically an aviation and naval affair, the soldiers were frequently bored and lonely. To take advantage of this, they commissioned a radio station calling itself "Debunk", that broadcast propaganda towards Trinidad, aimed at causing disunity between the troops of the various nationalities and the local population. This forced the Americans to retaliate by commissioning in Trinidad, a branch of their Armed Forces radio network called WVDI, whose primary purpose was to counter German propaganda and help to relieve the boredom of the shore-based personnel and influence the civilians. The radio station could be heard through the southern Caribbean and continued its operations long after World War Two.

Despite the differences of opinion as regards the higher direction of the anti-submarine war that existed at the Joint Chiefs of Staff level, the Caribbean naval and aviation forces worked in a remarkable atmosphere of co-operation. The US Army Air Corps under General Marshall's influence integrated itself fully into the US Navy methods and tactics, while the US Navy under Admiral Hoover's direction worked hand in glove with the Royal Navy and the TRNVR.

One of the senior officers who was directly responsible for the vast improvement in the Trinidad Sector was Rear Admiral Jesse B. Oldendorf. He took command of the naval forces in the Trinidad Sector at the darkest period of the fight against the U-Boats and overseered the long struggle to gain ascendency, but because the Caribbean story was largely untold, as well

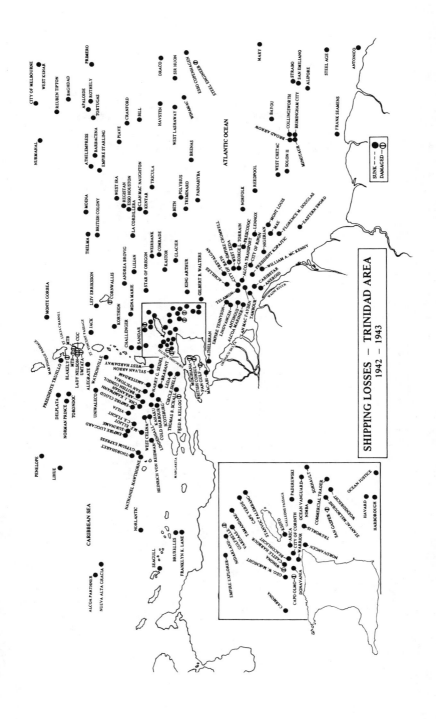

SHIPPING LOSSES — TRINIDAD AREA
1942 – 1943

SUNK — — —
DAMAGED — ①

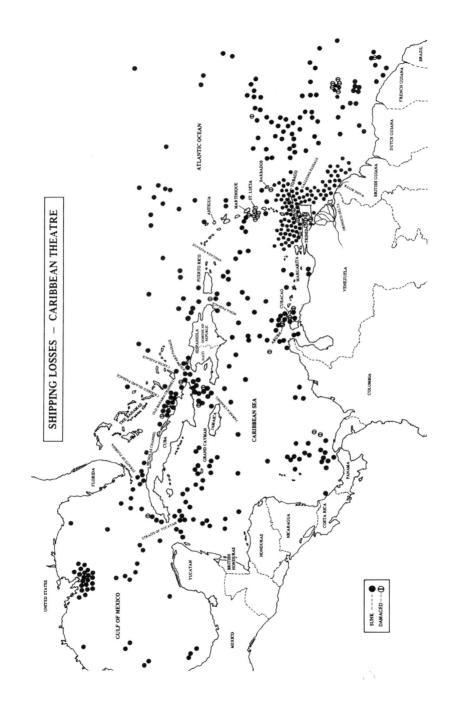

SHIPPING LOSSES – CARIBBEAN THEATRE

as the fact that the Atlantic theatre was not at the top of Admiral King's list of priorities, he never received much credit for his achievement. Oldendorf was not alone.

Many of the naval officers in the Atlantic theatre of operations did a sterling job in the fight against the U-Boats, but few, very few gained recognition. In comparison with their Pacific contemporaries, the US Atlantic naval officers were the poor relations when it came to promotion and recognition. Yet, the Atlantic Theatre where the US Navy fought, was the only US theatre of operations where the Americans never achieved the vast numerical superiority which became their hallmark.

On April twenty-first 1943, Rear Admiral Oldendorf handed over command of the naval forces in the Trinidad Sector to Rear Admiral A. G. Robinson. He handed over a sector that was ready to handle the coming second onslaught of the U-Boats. Oldendorf went on to the Pacific theatre where he saw service in the Marshalls, the Carolinas and the Marianas. Then at Leyte Gulf, he had command of the battleship task force that destroyed the Japanese Southern Force in the Battle of Surigao Strait. He commanded at the last great battleship battle in naval history and was later injured at Okinawa. Despite the fact that at Leyte Oldendorf had command of the only completely successful phase of the battle, the stigma of having served in the Atlantic appears to have remained with him. He started in 1942 in the Caribbean as a rear admiral, and the end of the war saw him in the same rank.

The end of March 1943 found U510 on its way back across the Atlantic, having completed its second Caribbean patrol. The U-Boat had only carried out one successful attack, which had sunk only one merchant ship, but the dramatic quality of its attack on the convoy was out of all proportion to the immediate results achieved. The Trinidad Bahia convoys would not sail inadequately escorted again. Neitzel was not to see the Caribbean again, but under a new commander U510 still had another patrol to make to the area.

U68 was also making its way homeward, if slowly. At the end of the month Lauzemis discovered that his metox equipment was unservicable and he took the boat northwards through the Windward Passage. He spent the next ten days operating in the safer waters north of Puerto Rico. During this period Lauzemis brought U68 southwards to the northern entrance of the Anegada Passage. He found that the once quiet passage was constantly covered by air patrols and surface escorts.

By April fifteenth the U-Boat was well northeast of Antigua, on its way home from its second and final Caribbean patrol. U68 held the Caribbean record for the highest tonnage sunk in a single cruise and it stood for the rest of the war. Under the command of Merten the U-Boat had sunk fifty thousand nine hundred tons during June 1942. In contrast, this patrol under Lauzemis had netted only two ships of just over ten thousand tons, but this was a measure of the change which had come over the Caribbean. U68 met its end a year later in April 1944, when an Avenger operating from the escort carrier Guadalcanal, sent it to the bottom with a homing torpedo. Only one badly injured survivor escaped from the boat.

The departure of U68 and U510 left three boats in the area for a few more days. Heinrich Schafer operated U183 off the western end of Cuba and around Grand Cayman until April eighth, when he started his homeward journey from the boat's first and only Caribbean cruise. Schafer had managed to sink one ship on this cruise. The boat met its end in the Phillipine Sea during April 1945, when it was destroyed by the American submarine USS Besugo.

U185 left the Windward Passage early in April and worked its way up the north coast of Cuba looking for targets, but all shipping in the area was moving in convoys which were all well protected. Maus then took the boat out through the Bahamas, where on April sixth, he achieved his third kill. Twenty miles southwest of Great Inagua Island, he sent the American Liberty ship John Sevier to the bottom. U185, with three ships to its credit was the top scoring boat of the six which came into the Caribbean theatre in March. The U-Boat never returned to the Caribbean and its ultimate fate was bound up with the traumatic battles to come in August.

The last of the U-Boats left in the Caribbean was U155. Piening operated in the Gulf of Mexico until April eighth. During this period he sank the Norwegian freighter Lyseford and then the American tanker Gulfstate, before taking U155 home from the Caribbean theatre for the third and last time. U155 had carried out three successful Caribbean patrols during which Piening had sunk nineteen merchant ships in the theatre, for a total of eighty-four thousand five hundred and sixty-two tons. This made him the top Ace of the Caribbean war. U129 achieved one more ship in the theatre, but this U-Boat had operated under several different commanders, while U155 had been under Piening's command for all of its Caribbean patrols. No other commander came near to Piening's achievement. It is also noteworthy that like U129, Piening never damaged a single ship. Each time he fired, a ship went down. His was also a lucky U-Boat. U155 had been caught several times and badly damaged, particularly when the boat had engaged in its duel with No. 53 Squadron of the RAF, but this U-Boat survived the whole war to be surrendered in 1945 and scuttled in 1946. By this time

U155 had achieved a total of twenty-six ships sunk.

On April sixth, just as the U-Boats in the northwestern part of the Caribbean theatre were completing their patrols, their solitary replacement was leaving Lorient. U176 had been built by A.G. Weser of Bremen and commissioned in December of 1941. The thirty-four year old, Essenhausen born Reiner Dierkson, was appointed in command and the U-Boat left on its first war patrol in July. The boat left the 10th Flotilla base at Lorient, on its third war patrol, with orders for the north coast of Cuba and the hazardous Straits of Florida. For the last three weeks of April, Dierksen slowly plodded his way across the Atlantic and his appointment with destiny. Dierksen had a mid ocean meeting with Piening for a briefing on the northwest Caribbean, but the luck of the U155 failed to rub off.

During March, the North Atlantic U-Boats had used up their torpedoes and fuel so quickly that once again the sailing schedule had been disrupted. The very success of March meant that during April, there would be very few U-Boats on station and the sinkings for the month totalled only fifty-six ships. April was a quiet period for the U-Boats and during this month Doenitz prepared his wolves so that they could fall on the North Atlantic convoys in May. The success which attended their efforts in the North Atlantic in March, served to draw them back. Doenitz hoped to recreate the tactical conditions for a further slaughter of the convoys, but this was a double-edged weapon, because the Germans were returning to an area where the Allies were waiting for them.

During April, while the U-Boats regrouped, the Allies were also regrouping. The majority of the escorts that had been tied up protecting the North African landings were released during April, and May found not only strong escort groups around the convoys, but support groups backing them up. The end of the month also saw the first American carrier task group move out for the mid Atlantic area. The Allies were immensely stronger in May and it was a tactical mistake to attempt to challenge them in the North Atlantic at that time. The air gap had been closed by VLR Liberators operating out of Iceland and this meant that there was no safe haven where the U-Boats were immune from air attack.

To compound this problem, many of the Allied anti-submarine aircraft were now using the new ten centimeter radar, which the German metox equipment could not detect. All the surface escorts were fitted with radar and HF/DF equipment, which allowed them to home-on German U-Boat transmissions. Some of the escorts also carried the new hedgehog forward firing anti-submarine weapon, which vastly improved the escorts' chances of making a kill.

U-Boats were accustomed to hearing the escorts coming in and passing over to drop depth-charges. To counter this, many U-Boat commanders waited until the escort was almost overhead before taking evasive action, but now the escort need never pass the boat. No one knows how many U-Boat commanders died during May, waiting for the escort vessels to pass over. Another advantage of the hedgehog was that the escort did not need to lose asdic contact with the boat it was attacking, which made the attack that much more accurate. The only drawback that the hedgehog suffered was that the bombs were contact fused and actually had to hit the U-Boat for them to explode.

In contrast, the U-Boats went into battle in May with only one new item of equipment and this was the Aphrodite radar decoy. The decoy was useful, if a U-Boat knew that it was being painted, but with the new radar in use by the Allies, the boats were right back at the stage where they had to detect attacking aircraft visually, early enough to crashdive. It is easy to say that Doenitz made a critical blunder by challenging the Allies in May, but he didn't know that the cards were that heavily stacked against his boats. Even if he had known, the boats were available and he had to attack somewhere. The Caribbean would have been a safer bet, but the round trip to and from this area, would have been too long and in the interim he would have lost the initiative in the North Atlantic — the initiative that he thought he had. The stage was now set for the most decisive battle of World War Two.

May was to see the virtual slaughter of the U-Boats and a number of U-Boats that had served in the Caribbean became victims. The first of these was U332. This boat had operated in the Caribbean under Johannes Liebe, during September and October 1942. Eberhard Huttemann took command in January 1943 and was on his way through the Bay of Biscay on the second of May, when he was caught by a Sunderland of No. 461 squadron Royal Australian Air Force. Presumably, the bridge watch saw the Sunderland too late for the U-Boat to dive and Huttemann decided to fight it out on the surface.

The U-Boat did not carry enough firepower to overcome the Sunderland and two series of depth-charge attacks finished it. As the U-Boat with the mermaid painted on the bow finally sank below the waves, the crew of the Sunderland saw a number of Germans in the water, but none survived.

Two days later, it was the turn of Bliedrodt's old boat U109. In January U109 had operated unsuccessfully off the Antilles, while U124 had attacked the shipping off Trinidad. Bliedrodt had relinquished command to Joachim Schramm, who was caught on the surface by a VLR Liberator of No. 86 squadron operating out of Aldergrove in Northern Ireland. One shattering attack destroyed the U-Boat with all hands.

The third of the former Caribbean boats to die was the U125, which had sunk eight ships in the western Caribbean during the Merry Month of May 1942. The twenty-eight year old Ulric Folkers took his boat in against the slow westbound convoy OSN 5, which was protected by the highly efficient B-7 escort group led by Commander Gretton. On May sixth Folkers sank a tanker that was straggling from the convoy, and was operating submerged behind the convoy, when HMS Vidette gained contact. Vidette was an old V and W destroyer, but unknown to Folkers, she was armed with hedgehog. The destroyer was rejoining the convoy when her asdic operator picked up the U-Boat ahead. Folkers probably heard the destroyer and was waiting for it to close, when the end came. Vidette fired only one salvo, but two of the bombs obtained direct hits on the U-Boat. From the surface they could see the underwater flashes as the bombs exploded, puncturing the boat's hull. The operator on the destroyer could hear a great deal of underwater noise, as Folkers fought his last battle, trying to get the mortally wounded boat to the surface, but U125 was never seen again. She was the first former Caribbean boat to succumb to the hedgehog.

The fourth of the former Caribbean boats to die during May was U753. This boat under the command of Korvettenkapitan Alfred Von Manstein had operated at the start of the Gulf of Mexico offensive in May 1942. The U-Boat was last heard from on May eleventh, when two torpedoes were fired at convoy HX 237 in the North Atlantic, after which the U-Boat disappeared without trace. Postwar research has indicated that Von Manstein and his crew probably died after an attack by a Halifax of No. 502 squadron on May fourteenth. The U-Boat did not surface after the attack and the assessment committee credited the pilot with a good attack, but not a kill. It is probable that U753 went out of control and dived to destruction.

On May thirteenth Dierksen had U176 through the Bahamas and was cruising up the north coast of Cuba when he came across the small American tanker Nickeliner. A torpedo sent the tanker to the bottom only five miles offshore. A little later he came upon the small Cuban tanker Mambi and sent her to join the Nickeliner. Dierksen continued slowly up the coast looking for targets, but the coastal waters were clear. The Americans had detected the presence of the boat, although Dierksen had not sent off any signals for more than two weeks. There was an alert in effect and no coastal traffic was moving unless in convoy. In fact Dierksen had been promoted to Korvettenkapitan on May first, but because he had not contacted U-Boat headquarters he did not know of his change of rank.

Cuba declared war on Germany in December 1941, but during 1942 the Americans had expressed doubts about the seriousness of the Cuban armed forces. The Cuban navy was composed of a number of very old patrol vessels and gunboats and with their outdated equipment they could not hope to play a serious part in the anti-submarine war. To attempt to remedy this situation, the United States presented Cuba with seven modern eighty-three foot submarine chasers in April 1943. One month later, three of these vessels were escorting a convoy of two ships up the southern side of the Nicholas Channel, when U176 detected them. The ships were moving from Port Sagus to the town of Cardenas on Cuba's north coast and were still sixty miles away from their destination when U176 moved in.

The boat must have been moving close to the surface because the crew of an OS2N of VS-62 saw the shadow underwater and dropped a smoke float. The pilot then turned towards the convoy which was only a mile and a half distant, flying over the escorts and waggling its wings, before returning to the smoke float. The escort commander in CS 11 instructed CS 13 by radio to investigate why the aircraft had dropped the smoke float and then turned the convoy to port as a precaution. CS 13 left the convoy and began running in towards the smoke float, when at four hundred yards, they gained asdic contact on a submarine.

Dierksen probably did not know that he had been detected until he heard the propellors approaching. When he realized that a patrol vessel was moving in, he probably took the U-Boat down to about two hundred feet but he would not have been worried. None of the U-Boat commanders took the PCs or SCs very seriously, but Dierksen was caught under ideal attack conditions. The asdic operator could hear his propellers very clearly and the Cuban vessel had an excellent contact.

CS 13 ran over the U-Boat's position and dropped a single depth-charge. After the explosion, CS 13 regained contact and came in for a second attack. Three depth-charges set to one hundred, one hundred and fifty and two hundred feet, rolled off the stern of the Cuban vessel. The eighty-three foot submarine chasers were very manoeuvrable craft and the three charges were dropped very accurately. The first two charges exploded normally, but the third charge triggered another underwater explosion. The third charge set to two hundred feet, probably exploded so close to the U-Boat, that it split the hull and caused the detonation of one of the boat's torpedoes.

In March, U-Boat command had decided to remove the deck containers with spare torpedoes from the Type IX U Boats because of the danger of sympathetic detonations during depth-charge attacks. U176 was in dock during March and it is likely that its deck containers were removed during this period. This can only mean that the depth-charge must have been very close to the U-Boat's hull to trigger the explosion of a torpedo inside the vessel. In any case U176 was finished.

The Cuban vessel regained asdic contact, but the target was not moving. As a precaution two more depth-charges were dropped, but by this stage .the shattered hull of U176 must have been well on its way to the bottom, in five hundred feet of water. An oil slick, three hundred yards across marked the passing of Reiner Dierksen and his crew. Up above, the observer in the OS2N opened his cockpit and clasped his hands over his head in congratulation.

The Cuban Navy had proved itself by sinking the twenty-first U-Boat to be lost in May 1943, but May was only halfway through. U176 was the second U-Boat to be lost in the Caribbean during 1943, in a month that was the exact opposite of what it had been like in the Merry Month of May 1942, but U176 was not the most important U-Boat lost that day.

In the late evening, the crew of a No. 58 squadron Halifax operating at the outer limits of the Bay of Biscay, picked up a U-Boat visually and roared into the attack. The U-Boat turned out to be the Type XIV U Tanker U463, commanded by the First World War veteran Leo Wolfbauer. The Halifax dropped six depth-charges at least two of which exploded under the U-Boat. Two minutes after the attack, with the bow sticking vertically upwards, U463 went to the bottom with all her crew. U463 had refuelled dozens of Caribbean-bound boats and was one of a group of tankers which made the campaign in the west possible. The loss of a U Tanker was disastrous, but it was only the beginning of the onslaught on the tankers.

U-Boat command were not aware of the loss of the U176 until several days later when they tried repeatedly to contact her, but they were aware that only one U-Boat was assigned to the Caribbean. This was the first time that the area had received such a low priority and on the same day that U176 was lost they took steps to remedy the situation. Orders went out to U67 and U527 to make for the Caribbean where both boats would operate in concert with U176.

Gunther Muller-Stockheim was an old Caribbean veteran, having been on hand in U67 for the opening of Operation Neuland, then again in the golden days of June and July 1942, followed up by operations off Trinidad, in October November. When Muller-Stockheim turned his bows towards the Caribbean on the fifteenth, it was for his fourth war patrol in the area. Destiny was catching up with U67, because this was to be her final Caribbean patrol, — one from which she would not return.

On the same day the Type IXC boat U527, under the command of Herbert Uhlig also turned towards the Caribbean. During March Uhlig had carried out his first patrol as commander of the new U-Boat against convoy HX 229 in the North Atlantic. This Caribbean trip was U527's second and last war patrol, because she was also destined not to make it back home. These two boats that turned towards the Caribbean in the middle of May, were the first, tentative advance guard of a renewed Caribbean offensive.

While the first moves in the crisis of the Caribbean war were being made, the month of the lost U-Boats continued with no let up in the sinking rate. On May seventeenth another former Caribbean boat died. U128 had operated under Ulric Heyse in the Caribbean during June 1942, when she was part of the group composed of U126 and U161, which had come unto the area from the south. She was now under the command of Hermann Steinert and after leaving Lorient on the same day as U176, she had turned her bows towards the Brazilian coast.

The boat was suffering from the attention of the French Maquis, who had put sand down her periscope tube. Nevertheless, Steinert continued his patrol until the seventeenth, when he ran up against a US Navy combined operation. In the early afternoon, the bridge lookouts had detected an attacking Mariner flying boat. The U-Boat crash-dived and its conning tower had been underwater for fifteen seconds before the VP-74 aircraft piloted by Lt. Davis, crossed the swirl. Six MK 44 depth-charges went down and unluckily for U128, they sank right along the boat's projected underwater track. The detonations damaged the U-Boat, forcing Steinert to surface. He probably thought that he could fight off the Mariner while hurried repairs were carried out, but he was unaware that there were now two Mariners circling above.

As U128 surfaced, the second Mariner flown by Lt. Carey, was overhead and another six depth-charges came down. This time the explosions bracketed the boat and the damage was considerably increased. Steinert now had no option but to stay on the surface and fight it out, but both aircraft were now carrying out co-ordinated straffing runs, making the conning tower untenable. Aware that the game was all but up, a few crewmen tried to surrender, but at that moment the US destroyers Moffet and Jouet appeared on the horizon and opened fire. After four direct hits U128 went down. Surprisingly, fifty-one survivors were rescued.

The sixth and last former Caribbean U-Boat to die in May 1943 was the U755. Under the command of Walter Going, the boat had operated in the Gulf of Mexico during May 1942. In August 1942, Going had taken the boat through the Gibraltar Straits and joined the Mediterranean Flotilla. On

May twenty-eighth U755 was caught on the surface by a Hudson of No. 608 squadron and sunk with strikes by twenty pound armour piercing rocket projectiles. This relatively rare but devastating anti-submarine weapon, ripped the U-Boat's hull open. U755 was the last but one U-Boat sunk in the month of May.

In one month the whole Battle of the Atlantic had turned around. The incredible total of forty-one German U-Boats had been sunk. Added to this were four Italian and two Japanese submarines. It was a shattering blow from which the U-Boats never recovered. U-Boat command were not aware of the full extent of the tragedy for some time, but by the third week of May they were aware that something had gone very wrong in the North Atlantic. Enough boats had failed to answer radio call-ups and those that did gave reports of new weapons in widespread use, to the extent that on May twenty-fourth Doenitz made a decision to pull back his boats.

This was the first time that the U-Boats had ever had to retreat and it seriously undermined the morale of the U-Boat crews. The Battle of the Atlantic had see-sawed between the antagonists for more than two years, with each side gaining ascendency according to the concentration achieved and the current state of technology, but never before had the U-Boats been forced to back down. The decision to pull back from the North Atlantic was a courageous one and shows the level of commitment that Doenitz had for his U-Boat crews, as well as the strength of the Grand Admiral's personality.

In the history of the Third Reich, there are not many instances of senior officers carrying out a planned withdrawal against Hitler's attack at all costs and stand fast oriented philosophy. But Doenitz had very little choice in the matter. His U-Boat commanders were being intimidated by the overwhelming Allied technological superiority and there were signs of U-Boat commanders losing heart and failing to press home attacks, even when they had a tactical advantage. Had Doenitz continued his assault on the North Atlantic convoys, it could well have meant the destruction of the U-Boat arm.

Throughout World War Two, the German armed forces enjoyed a qualitative superiority in weapons over the Allies. German weapons of all types were adjudged better than equivalent Allied models. There was a vigorous scientific programme throughout the war. The proof of this lies in the number of modern weapon systems of today which had their genesis in the experiments conducted by the Third Reich.

This makes it difficult to understand how in 1943 the U-Boats managed to fall so far behind Allied anti-submarine technology. It could have been that Germany was primarily a continental military power and as such, her navy carried a low priority. Yet without a naval victory in the Battle of the Atlantic, there could be no continental victory. Doenitz's pull back from the North Atlantic was not intended as a permanent withdrawal, or in any way a concession of defeat in the North Atlantic, because he intended to return as soon as the technological balance swung in his favour.

He was waiting for a radar receiver which would allow the boats to pick up centimetric radar transmissions, an acoustic torpedo to use against the escorts, and the schnorkel device, which would allow the boats to remain submerged while running on their diesels. All these advances came, but although the U-Boats returned to the North Atlantic in the autumn, they never regained the initiative. In the meantime, another ominous development was taking place which would alter the entire character of the U-Boat war.

Since the advent of the centimetric radar, the U-Boats had been unable to gain sufficient warning of approaching aircraft to dive in good time. This meant that they were entirely at the mercy of the aircraft and their survival depended on the accuracy of the pilot's aim. The anti-submarine aircraft could detect the U-Boats and manoeuvre into the most favourable attack position, revealing themselves only when they were close enough to be sure of surprising the U-Boat. The U-Boat depended on the keenness of the lookout's eyesight and the prevailing weather conditions and there were many occasions when detection of the attacking aircraft came too late for the boat to dive safely. If at this stage a U-Boat commander decided on the standard formula and crash-dived, the attacking pilot was usually presented with a U-Boat that was almost totally helpless, while carrying out a highly complex evolution.

Many U-Boat commanders recognized the fact that when an attacking aircraft was detected too late, it was safer to stay on the surface and attempt to manoeuvre out of the way. The drawback in this case was the fact that attacking aircraft usually raked the U-Boat's conning tower with machine gun or cannon fire, which frequently made the bridge untenable for the commander. One answer was for the U-Boat's anti aircraft gunners to try to neutralize the fire from the attacking aircraft, but this automatically meant that with more personnel on the conning tower, it would take longer for the U-Boat to dive, when a favourable moment presented itself. Nevertheless the idea of fighting back began to appeal to many of the commanders.

Despite the fact that at this stage of the war, U-Boats only carried a single exposed twenty millimeter cannon which was hardly a match for the numerous weapons of the big anti-submarine aircraft, Emmermann in the U172 managed more than just survival on April sixth 1943. His boat fought off an attacking Sunderland flying boat and escaped. On the following day

Pich in command of U168, managed to do the same. The Sunderland was considered one of the most heavily armed anti-submarine aircraft, and indeed it was nicknamed "the porcupine" by the U-Boat commanders. By May nineteenth U666 managed to go one better and shoot down an attacking Sunderland.

In the meantime the Germans had developed U441 into the first Flak Trap U-Boat with multiple anti-aircraft guns and on the nineteenth of May, she shot down an attacking aircraft. Although U441 was damaged in the encounter, the concept was judged to be successful and on May twenty-seventh, U-Boat command published its famous, "Fight Back Order".

No longer would U-Boats attempt to dive under impossible conditions, − now they would fight back on the surface. Hand in glove with this order came a programme to drastically upgrade the anti-aircraft armament of all the U-Boats. In many cases they went so far as to remove the traditional deck gun and replace it by a thirty-seven millimeter automatic weapon. The wintergarden, aft of the periscope standards, spouted first multiple single twenty millimeter cannon, followed by twin cannon mounts and ultimately by a quad twenty millimetre mounting. The Fight Back Order remained in force for ninety-four days, during which time some of the fiercest clashes took place between the U-Boats and the aircraft.

There was one serious flaw in the fight back concept. It left the aircraft with the option to refuse battle and call for reinforcement. If while the aircraft waited the U-Boat commander decided to dive, then the aircraft could safely attack when the conning tower had been cleared. Surprisingly, very few aircraft commanders adopted this safe foolproof method and particularly in the Caribbean, they usually called for reinforcement while actually attacking. The result was some bloody encounters. It was this tactical flaw in the concept that eventually caused the cancellation of the Fight Back Order to be replaced by an optional fight back concept, where the U-Boat commander made the decision.

Historians have dated the winning of the Battle of the Atlantic to the month of May 1943. This is based on the fact that during this month, the Allies won the first clear cut victory over a German U-Boat offensive and this is true, but it gives the impression that Doenitz pulled back his boats and kept them in port, until he was ready to come back out in the autumn. In fact, he merely switched them away from the North Atlantic to an area where he thought they would have a better chance of success. The area that he chose was the Caribbean.

U67 and U527 were the forerunners of nearly fifty U-Boats which were redirected to the sunny Caribbean and the north coast of Brazil. This brought on another giant clash, made much more fierce by the fact that the U-Boats now intended to fight it out on the surface. This time the US Navy was ready and the battle was not only confined to the Caribbean. It stretched from the Bay of Biscay, where the RAF was waiting, out into mid Atlantic, where the US Navy carrier Task Groups were in position, down to the furthest reaches of the Caribbean. It encompassed the vital tanker U-Boats, whose existence made operations in the far west possible and in cases, the entire route to and from Lorient. The stage was set for the second big clash. The double-edged weapon, forged by the very success of the U-Boats in the Caribbean in 1942, was about to cut them.

CHAPTER

15

The wolves gather

June started with the loss of the former Caribbean boat U202. The U-Boat had operated off Trinidad in October 1942 in company with its sister U-Boat U201. In the North Atlantic during February U201 had met its end, but U202 survived until June. The twenty-seven year old Gunther Poser was bringing U202 back home across the Atlantic, when at ten o'clock on the morning of the first of June, a Petty Officer acting as officer of the watch reported a convoy on the horizon. It has been surmised that Poser was a lazy individual, because instead of dashing to the conning tower, he gave orders for the boat to close the convoy and remained lying in his bunk.

When eventually Poser came up to have a look he was horrified. The U-Boat was not approaching a convoy, but rather the anti-submarine sloops of Captain Walker's famous Second Support Group. Their mastheads had been mistaken for merchant ships. The Group was operating independently in the approaches to the Bay of Biscay. The vessels were the new anti-submarine sloops which were a vast improvement on the previous corvettes. At thirteen hundred tons, they were better sea boats and in addition they were capable of working up to twenty knots.

Poser acted quickly to try and snatch survival out of the jaws of disaster, by crash-diving and going deep to five hundred feet, but it was all in vain, because the sloops gained asdic contact almost immediately. The first attack by HMS Starling set the pattern for a long struggle. Above, the tenacious Captain Walker was pitted against the equally determined Gunther Poser who intended fighting to the very end. Repeated attacks on the U-Boat convinced Poser that survival lay in taking his boat very deep. Against the protests of both his watchkeeping officer and the boat's engineer, he took U202 to the unprecedented depth of eight hundred and twenty feet,— well beyond the U-Boat's maximum diving depth.

The tactic worked, because the Allies did not have a depth-charge capable of being set to such a great depth. As the depth-charges thundered harmlessly above them, Poser fired SAT asdic decoys and manoeuvred as silently as possible to try and lose the attackers, but Walker had the U-Boat in continuous asdic contact. The Group tried their famous depth-charge barrage, which consisted of several vessels attacking simultaneously, dropping single charges continuously, in what has been described as the naval equivalent of an artillery barrage. All day the battle continued as Poser fought to escape, but Walker had unlimited time and intended to use it. By eight o'clock that night the sloops had dropped over a hundred depth-charges and Poser had used seventy-six decoys, all to no avail.

Finally the air in the boat ran out. Poser had reached the stage where he had to surface. He didn't have a hope and his crew's nerves were shattered by the all day battle, but he intended to go down fighting. U202 came up from the depths and crashed into view between the waiting sloops. The U-Boat's gun crew tried to make it to the mounting, but with all six anti-submarine sloops firing at it, the boat was quickly reduced to a sinking wreck. With the U-Boat riddled by shell holes and settling, Poser finally gave the long overdue order to abandon ship. He intended to take his own life and go down with the vessel, but two of his officers had not waited to be told to abandon ship and Poser changed his mind, specifically, to some day court martial the pair.

Fifteen of the crew died in the encounter. Curiously, the survivors were refused rescue on the direct orders of Captain Walker, until they gave the name of their captain and the U-Boat's number. Eventually one sailor unable to take the cold any longer gave the required information and the shivering survivors were allowed on deck. Effective,—but the Laconia Order comes immediately to mind. There has been much written on the ruthlessness of the U-Boat commanders.

On the same day, the US Navy U-Boat plotting room gave a tactical appreciation which said that there were no U-Boats in the Caribbean. This was the first time that such a statement had been issued and it was also the first time that it was true. Unfortunately, within twenty-four hours the situation had changed. On June second U67 and U527 entered the area north of Puerto Rico, enroute to their assigned areas. Muller-Stockheim was under orders to take U67 into the Windward Passage and operate in the same area as U185 had covered in April. Herbert Uhlig on the other hand, was required to traverse the Windward Passage and then turn westward for the area off Cuba's western tip, where U183 had operated.

In the meantime U154, which had originally been assigned to the area off Northern Brazil, had its operational area extended northwards to include the sea approaches off French Guiana. Oscar Kusch had taken command of U154 from Schuch in January and he was now bringing the veteran U-Boat into the Caribbean theatre for the fourth time. U154 was the first U-Boat to carry out four patrols in the area, to be closely followed by U67 and much later by U129.

Off northern Brazil Kusch had experienced some success, although beginning with an annoying failure. On May eighth, he fired a spread of torpedoes at a tanker and watched them all hit, but fail to explode. The tanker turned out to be the SS Motorcarline, the same vessel that had missed the Battle of TB-1, but been fortunate enought to witness the whole thing from its safe position astern. Once again, the Motorcarline's luck held good and the dud torpedoes did no harm. By the time Kusch had worked U154 into a position to attack again, the tanker's cries for help had brought the Brazilian based aircraft to her rescue.

However, Kusch got his revenge late in the month of May when he attacked convoy BT-14 off northern Brazil. He fired six torpedoes into the convoy and two of them sent the eight thousand ton American tanker John Worthington, to the bottom. Two torpedoes also romped into the eight thousand five hundred ton American tanker Florida and damaged it so severely, that the destroyer USS Saucy was forced to detach from the escort and tow the shattered hulk into nearby Forteleza. Another of his torpedoes smashed into the seven thousand ton freighter Cardinal Gibbons and brought it to a halt. The freighter was dead in the water, with a large hole in its engine room. The escort commander could not afford to detach any further escort vessels and detailed one of the merchant ships to tow the Cardinal Gibbons. The pair arrived in Port of Spain on June fifth.

During the month of May the first troop and equipment movements began in preparation for the invasion of Martinique. The US Army 33rd Infantry regiment and the 135th combat engineers moved into Chaguaramas to begin their amphibious training. Attack transports arrived in the Gulf and in a short while the bays were being criss-crossed by dozens of landing craft carrying the men ashore on innumerable training exercises.

Further north in Puerto Rico, the 13th Marine regiment and the 501st airborne regiment of the 101st Airborne division, began similar training exercises. While the troops sweated in the tropical sunshine, the planners got down to fine tuning the invasion plan, because it had to work. The United States could not afford to pull troops back from Africa, Europe or the Pacific just to deal with the small island of Martinique and as a result the assault forces were not going to outnumber the Vichy French defenders by any great amount. To this end both the airborne troops and the combat engineers were going to be used as assault infantry, across the beaches.

By this stage of the war, the first tentative efforts were being made to strengthen the escort groups for Caribbean and Brazilian convoys. Frequently there were now four destroyers and up to four PCs with each convoy and Chaguaramas now had seven destroyers based there. Surprisingly, the powerful Fletcher Class destroyers were now operating in the Caribbean, showing the higher priority now being attached to operations in the area.

The TRNVR had increased its strength and the Royal Navy anti-submarine trawlers were still operating from Trinidad. The 19th MTB Flotilla had now gone, to be replaced by two much more useful units. The 30th ML Flotilla, with twelve Fairmile D motor launches was one of the replacements. The Fairmile D craft were one hundred and fifteen feet long, carrying a heavy armament and twelve depth-charges. They were far more useful than the MTBs and even with all the equipment they carried, they were still capable of working up an open-sea speed of twenty knots. These vessels were able to hunt submarines and were used to escort the inter-island convoys. They were not ocean escorts and they were never used as such. They were complimented by the 118th ML Flotilla with the smaller Harbour Defence Motor Launches, HDMLs. Both Flotillas were manned by a mixture of RN and TRNVR officers and men, and by the end of the war many of the vessels were commanded by Trinidadians.

Bad luck was to haunt U67 throughout this cruise and it started on June second. Both U67 and U527 were just entering the Bahamas area, when Muller-Stockheim discovered that his metox equipment was unserviceable. He was directed to operate in the area north of Puerto Rico, where there was less chance of his having to face air attacks. U-Boat headquarters advised him that U758 was on its way with spare parts and that the boat would arrive in two weeks. Muller-Stockheim was destined to spend all his time in the area off Puerto Rico because U758 would not get through. She became the first of the U-Boats from this second big assault on the Caribbean to be turned back by the Task Groups operating along the U-Boats' transit route.

U758 managed to fight off no less than eight carrier aircraft, but in the process she was damaged to such an extent that there was no question of her continuing. She turned back to make her way once again through the hazardous Bay of Biscay to Bordeaux.

In the meantime, U527 moved on alone through the Bahamas and into the Windward Passage, where almost immediately she came under air attack. On June seventh Uhlig took her in against a convoy, but was forced to retreat by the strong aggressive convoy escort. He was hardly clear of the escort before he ran afoul of a hunter-killer group and was forced to endure another punishing depth-charge attack. The Americans had two destroyers operating independently in the Windward Passage and Uhlig had his work cut out to escape their attentions. Unlike convoy escorts, they had unlimited time to hunt U-Boats.

Well to the southeast Kusch off French Guiana found himself under air attack without any warning from the metox equipment. The set was unserviceable and U-Boat command ordered him to take U154 eastwards to longitude thirty west, where he would be safe from air attack. Kusch did not go that far east, preferring instead to take a chance in the hope that he would come upon a target. He took U154 straight north, through the eastern extremity of the Trinidad Sector, then up through the Puerto Rico Sector, to join Muller-Stockheim off the northern islands.

In the meantime, U527 had moved westwards between Jamaica and Cuba, to its operational area off western Cuba. On June thirteenth, Uhlig moved in against another convoy, but once again he was chased off and depth-charged by a destroyer. When the convoy and its escorts moved on, he found himself embroiled with another independent hunter-killer group, this one made up of three PCs.

In fact, throughout the Caribbean the defenders were bracing themselves for the onslaught. Convoy escorts were being beefed up and anti-submarine squadrons were moving into position to cover the likely U-Boat concentration areas, because the Americans were aware that the U-Boats were coming. British intelligence was monitoring the departures from the French bases and the extensive signal traffic.

The Germans had an elaborate deception plan in operation. Four U-Boats had been stationed in the North Atlantic, with orders to transmit continuous broadcasts on different frequencies using different codes and call signs. The idea was to give the impression of a great concentration of boats in that area. Had it not been for a little known act of extraordinary bravery, the British would have been fooled into believing that the U-Boats were planning another massive blow against the North Atlantic convoys.

In February 1942, the Germans introduced a new Enigma coding machine for their U-Boats. Almost overnight the British were unable to read the German signals to their U-Boats. After warning the Americans about the start of operation Paukenschlag, the source of intelligence information almost dried up and the Germans achieved their spectacular 1942 successes. At one time there were more than four hundred people operating a massive code breaking machine, but with little success. The new German naval codes remained a secret.

The breakthrough came in October 1942. A Sunderland flying boat spotted U559 in the Meditterranean, seventy miles north of the Nile Delta. That night a group of destroyers joined the hunt and forced U559 to the surface. Faced by overwhelming odds and certain destruction, the Germans opened the U-Boat's sea cocks and abandoned the boat. One of the destroyers was HMS Petard and in an enterprising move they lowered a whaler, as soon as it was obvious that the U-Boat had given up. The whaler approached the sinking U-Boat and naturally, the German survivors swam towards it. While the whaler was still sixty yards from the U-Boat, a lieutenant and an able seaman stripped off their clothes and dived in.

U559 was going fast and at this stage only the top of the conning tower was visible above the waves. By the time they got to the U-Boat, they were surprised to find that they had been joined by the sixteen year old Naafi canteen assistant, who was acting entirely on his own initiative. Knowing full well the extreme hazard they were placing themselves in, the Lieutenant and the Able Seaman went down into the sinking U-Boat. Inside the control room, they grabbed hold of one of the new Enigma coding machines and the U-Boat's code books, and quickly passed these up to the young man on the conning tower above. By this time the whaler had come alongside and the machine and code books were handed across, but it was far too late for the party in the control room. U559 went quickly, taking the lieutenant and the able seaman with it, but the precious machine and the vital code books were in Allied hands.

Within a short time, the British were once again able to read the German U-Boat signals and the pendulum began to swing against the boats. The victory in the North Atlantic in May and the detection of the coming offensive against the Caribbean, were direct results of the raid on U559.

By mid June, the British knew the U-Boat sailing order, and from the Bay of Biscay to the Panama Canal, the defenders were ready. On June second the Type VIIC boat U572 under the command of Kapitanleutnant Heinz Kummetat, sailed from Lorient for its first and last Caribbean patrol. On the following day, the veteran U510 sailed. On June seventh, the new Type VIIC boat U759 on its second patrol, sailed from Lorient under the command of Kapitanleutnant Rudolf Friedrich. On the following day, the Type VIIC U590 from the 6th Flotilla at St. Nazaire, sailed under the command of Werner Kruer. This boat was on its first Caribbean patrol, but it had been involved in the battle around convoy HX 229 in March. Unlike U124, U590 had been formed to return to base with severely corroded fuel pumps.

On June tenth, four Type VII U-Boats sailed. U84 under the command of Horst Uphoff and U732 under Klaus Peter Carlsen sailed from Brest. Uphoff had brought U84 to the Caribbean in June of 1942, but had been unable to penetrate the Straits of Florida. U84 was one of the boats that was not going to return home, but U732 would be a survivor. U134 and U653 sailed on the same day from La Pallice. The boats were under the command of Hans-Gunther Brosin and Gerhard Feiler respectively. Both were experienced boats, having been engaged in the battle around convoy HX 229. In fact, U653 had been the shadower that had vectored twenty-one U-Boats onto the convoy.

On June twelfth, six more U-Boats left their French bases for the Caribbean. From La Pallice came Kapitanleutnant Kurt Neide in the Type VIIC U415, on its first Caribbean cruise. Two boats from the 9th Flotilla at Brest, U615 under Rolf Kapitsky and U634 under Eberhard Dalhous, left for their first and only war patrols of the Caribbean. Neither boat would make it back and Kapitsky in particular would die an heroic death in a history-making action.

On the same day, Lorient contributed three more boats to join the Caribbean bound armada. The veteran U68 under Lauzemis, on what was intended to be the boat's third war patrol to the area. The veteran Piening in his gallant U155, was trying for a fourth Caribbean patrol and U159, now under the command of Kapitanleutnant Beckmann, who was bringing the U-Boat back to the Caribbean for its second cruise of the area. U159 had served in the Caribbean during May and June 1942 under Helmut Witte, where the boat sank eleven ships and damaged one other on its cruise. Only U156 under Hartenstein, bettered this score on a single patrol. After the Caribbean operation, Witte had taken the boat to the Indian Ocean where another eleven vessels fell to its torpedoes, before handing over to Beckmann.

Two more boats are of interest to the first wave for this second Caribbean assault and they were both from Bordeaux. On June ninth U564 under Kapitanleutnant Feidler, and U185 under Maus, left Bordeaux. U564 was under orders for the Caribbean and U185 for the coast of Brazil. The veteran Korvettenkapitan Reinhard Suhren had operated U564 against shipping in the Gulf of Mexico during May 1942, and then in the Caribbean in August, when he had successfully attacked convoy TAW(S). He had been promoted out of the boat at the end of 1942 and Feidler had taken over. He brought the veteran U-Boat out hoping to play a significant role in this coming Caribbean offensive, but Feidler would never see the Caribbean. There were now fourteen U-Boats making their way out across the Bay of Biscay and together with U758 and the three boats already in the area, they made up the first wave.

Through the first half of June, the U-Boats proceeded across the Bay of Biscay on the surface. They travelled in groups, relying on their anti-aircraft armament as a defence against the expected air attacks. They were under orders to fight their way through. Their metox sets were not much use and rather than attempting to dive at the last moment and in so doing expose their boats to certain destruction, they were going to stay on the surface and try and cross the Bay of Biscay as quickly as possible. RAF Coastal Command was being appraised of this massive movement of boats across the Bay and its aircraft were out in force.

On June twelfth the first big clash took place. A Halifax bomber of the 10th Coastal Command squadron came upon U185 and U564 as they raced for the open Atlantic. The aircraft called for support and waited for the other bombers to join before initiating a series of co-ordinated attacks against the U-Boats.

The German gunners fought fiercely, but they were overwhelmed by weight of numbers. Several depth-charges landed in the water close to U564 and shattered equipment in the boat. Her hull was also damaged by bomb splinters and near misses. By nightfall, when the two boats slipped away in the concealing darkness, they both had a considerable number of dead and wounded crewmen. U564 was so badly damaged that she could not dive and U-Boat Command ordered her to return, escorted by U185. U564 had become the second boat of the first wave to be turned back.

Two days later on June fourteenth, another major action took place between U-Boats in transit and the Coastal Command bombers. U257 under Rache, with U600 under Zurmuhlen and U615 Kapitsky, were transiting the Bay on the surface, relying on the mutual protection of their combined anti-aircraft guns for survival, when Coastal Command fell on them.

The attack by Whitley bombers lasted several hours, during the course of which one aircraft was shot down. But when the bombers drew off, all the boats had suffered killed and wounded crew, as well as damage to their hulls. A stick of bombs had damaged U257's rudder, but Rache decided to continue.

In the lull after the attacks, the three commanders conferred on the best course of action. They decided to separate and bury their dead independently, while continuing their transit across the Bay. They intended to spend as much time as possible submerged. This was a very prudent precaution. The trio had only survived because there were combats taking place all across the Bay. Coastal Command were attacking several groups of U-Boats at the same time. Nevertheless, they realized that it was only a matter of time before the bombers returned and they knew that with enough bombers to launch co-ordinated attacks, the aircraft would eventually get through.

While the Whitleys had fought with the trio, another group of aircraft had hurled themselves at the two boats from La Pallice. U134 and U415 fought off waves of attackers and suffered dead and wounded crew, but neither boat had been seriously damaged. At the same time a little further in the Bay, U68, U155 and U159 were under nonstop attack. Coastal Command Sunderlands, and Halifax bombers roared in against the three boats. The waves of attackers hardly gave the U-Boat gunners time to rest between each bombing run, and the strafing was taking its toll of the anti-aircraft gunners. Losses were heavy on both sides, but by evening neither U68 nor U155 could continue.

Both boats were heavily damaged by the sticks of bombs that had hit close aboard and there were large numbers of wounded on all the boats. Lauzemis and Piening were forced to turn their battered U-Boats and begin the long trek back to Lorient. They had to fight the whole way, but both damaged boats managed to make it home, leaving U159 to continue alone. U68 and U155 became the third and fourth boats of the first wave to be forced to turn back.

While the three groups of U-Boats were under attack, U564 was fighting for her life. On the previous day, RAF Coastal Command had made strenuous efforts to destroy the crippled U-Boat and its escort, but U564 had managed to shoot down one of its tormentors. On the fourteenth the fight against U564 and U185 was renewed, but by this time the U-Boat was so heavily damaged that only strenuous efforts by the engineers were keeping it afloat. Waves of bombers came in again and although the U-Boat gunners fought gallantly, U564 finally succumbed to the concussion of near misses. The U-Boat settled below the waves and U185 ran in to rescue the eighteen survivors. The rest of the crew had died under the strafing of the aircraft. U564 became the first boat of this Caribbean offensive to be lost. U185 turned once again to continue her lone run to the mid Atlantic rendezvous with the tanker, where she could hand over the survivors.

That night U-Boat Command received the results of the previous two days of battle in the Bay of Biscay and decided that it was proving to be far too costly. The fight back order was rescinded for the Bay of Biscay and outbound boats were instructed to traverse as much as possible of the Bay submerged. The returning boats were required to pair-up, so that they supported each other, with double the number of lookouts. During the course of the day another more serious problem began to unfold. U172 reported that when it arrived at the rendezvous area with the tanker U118, an American aircraft carrier was waiting. U-Boat command sent out a signal to the tanker advising that it move one hundred miles further south, but by then it was too late.

While the Caribbean offensive gathered way, the Allied anti-submarine forces were taking a steady toll of U-Boats. Ten boats were sunk in the first half of June, of which five were former Caribbean veterans.

On the day after U202 had gone down to the pounding by the 2nd Support Group, U105 was lost off West Africa. Nissen had operated off the Antilles in January, where he had helped to dispatch one of the TM-1 tankers. His boat was destroyed with the loss of all its crew by the Free French 144th anti-submarine squadron, in the Gulf of Guinea. Two days later the veteran Mumm, met his end when U594 was sunk trying to penetrate the Straits of Gibraltar.

The American hunting groups were now operating in mid Atlantic and beginning to convert the U-Boats safe refuelling and rendezvous areas into a deathtrap. Each escort carrier operated what was known as a composite squadron, made up of a small number of fighters, alongside the excellent Grumman Avenger torpedo bombers, fitted for anti-submarine work. The designation of these squadrons was VC and the Avengers either carried depth-charges, or later in the war an acoustic homing torpedo.

By mid June the USS Bogue was in position, with VC-9 embarked. They turned back U758 and on June fifth they found U217. Richenburg-Klinke had operated in the Caribbean during September 1942 and again in December alongside U124. The U-Boat was far from its Caribbean operating area around Curacao, when the Avengers caught it in mid Atlantic and sent it down with all hands.

While the fight was at its height in the Bay of Biscay, the USS Bogue was hunting important game. When U172 reported the presence of the carrier, neither they nor U-Boat Command knew that the carrier was the USS Bogue and that the Avengers from VC-9 had already sunk the tanker U118. The loss of this first tanker of the offensive was catastrophic. Two days previously, U118 had refuelled U510 and U572, bidding them good hunting as they set course for the Caribbean, but there were a large number of other U-Boats who were scheduled for refuelling before they could begin their long run to the far west.

U-Boat Command were forced to improvise and reorganize their refuelling schedule. The operational Type IXC boat U530 was ordered to refuel the Caribbean bound U759, so that the immediate need for fuel was met with minimum delay. After refuelling, U530 returned to her French base.

The tanker U487 was now required to take over all the refuelling assignments previously planned for U118. In order to do this, the operational boats U170, U535 and U536 were forced to abandon their assigned missions and transfer their fuel to U487. The organisation also meant that the previous practice of refuelling boats when they were outbound and again when they were inbound, to allow them to spend the maximum time in their operational areas, had to be curtailed.

Some boats would have to cut short their deployments, holding back enough fuel to get them home. U67 was one of these boats and she was advised that there would not be a refuelling stop on the way home. Of necessity, it was the larger Type IXC boats who had to cut short their deployments, because the smaller boats had to have tanker support to operate in the west. The tankers were the heart of the Caribbean and Brazilian campaigns and the loss of U118 left only U119 and U487 to handle the refuelling for the first part of the campaign, which was already underway.

U-Boat Command had so far committed nineteen boats to the Caribbean operation. Of these, one had sunk, three had been forced to turn back, twelve were on their way across the Atlantic, two were on station in the Caribbean theatre and one was beginning its homeward journey.

In addition to the major Caribbean thrust, boats were being committed to subsidiary operations off Brazil and West Africa, as well as a long range deployment to the Indian Ocean by some of the larger boats, known as the Monsoon group.

The only group that could carry out their operations without support were the boats destined for West Africa, but they were in a minority. All the other boats needed tankers and this was particularly important for the boats which had already remained in their operational areas and passed the time where they could make it home without tanker support. This ushered in an important phase of the operation which involved not only finding enough tankers, but also protecting them. The outbound passage through Biscay was becoming deadly and in mid Atlantic, the American carriers were massing.

There were now four escort carrier groups operating around the

Azores. In addition to the USS Bogue, the USS Santee with VC-29 embarked, the USS Core with VC-13 embarked and the USS Card with VC-1 embarked, were cruising in the U Tankers' previously safe haven. Each of these Task Groups was escorted by three or four destroyers, making up formidable hunter killer combinations. It was under these conditions of extreme hazard that the first wave approached their tanker hookups and the second wave of U-Boats sailed from their French bases.

On June twenty-sixth, U270, U406, U598 and U662 sailed from St. Nazaire. Of these four, U406 under the command of Horst Dietrich and U662 under Kapitanleutnant Heinz-Eberhard Muller, were destined for Caribbean operations. The type VIIC U406 had operated in the area north of Puerto Rico while on its way home from a US coastal operation in September 1942. The boat had been rammed by U600 at the beginning of May 1943 and thus been fortunate to miss the slaughter in the North Atlantic during that month. U406 was now repaired and on its way to the sunny Caribbean, where the crew would have little time to enjoy the climate.

U270 was scheduled for West Africa, but U598 was on its way to the Brazilian theatre of operations, from which it would never return. U662 was an experienced North Atlantic convoy fighter, but she had never faced a Caribbean air attack.

Two days later the veteran U160 and the tanker U462 sailed from Bordeaux. U160 was now under the command of Oberleutnant Zur See Von Pommer Esche and scheduled for the Caribbean, where its new commander no doubt expected to equal the exploits of his famous forbear Georg Lassen. Unfortunately, Von Pommer Esche was destined never to see the Caribbean and in fact, he was never to see his home again. Likewise U160's companion the tanker U462, was destined to do battle with the American carriers in mid Atlantic with traumatic results.

On the last day of June, five U-Boats left the French bases. The ill-fated U359 under the command of Heinz Forster was accompanied by U386 out of St. Nazaire. The Type VIIC U359 was destined to stay in the Caribbean forever, after suffering the same disastrous fate as U158 in 1942.

U466 sailed alone from La Pallice under Kapitanleutnant Hagenskotter, under orders for the dangerous area east of Trinidad. On the same day the veteran Adolf Piening took his newly repaired U155 to sea alongside the Type IXC U188. Piening sailed from Lorient hoping to resume his interrupted Caribbean journey, but he was fated to spend his time in mid Atlantic dodging the American carriers.

On July first, Brest contributed the two Type VIIC boats U628 and U648, under the command of Heinrich Hasenschar and Oberleutnant Zur

See Stahl, respectively. These two boats were scheduled to carry out their first Caribbean patrols, but neither of them would see the far west. In fact U628 had a very short journey to make.

Two days later, six Type IXC boats sailed out of Lorient. U168, U183, U505, U509, U514 and U532 made their way out into the Bay of Biscay, but only one the U514 under Auffermann, was under orders for the Caribbean. This was Auffermann's last journey and it was not to be a long one.

On July tenth, the last sailing of the second wave took place when U607, U613 and U445 left St. Nazaire. U445 was destined for West Africa, but the other two boats were scheduled for special operations in the west.

As well as being a merchant ship collection point, Kingston harbour in Jamaica was also a haven for Royal Navy fleet carriers in the west. Most of the Fleet Air Arm aircraft based at Palisadoes were flown off from these carriers and U-Boat Command intended to restrict the use of the harbour. U607 was fitted as a minelayer and given a comprehensive set of orders for the mining of the approaches to Kingston, between Port Royal and the mainland. In the event U607 did not get very far. U613 was also scheduled for mining operations, but her target was to be Jacksonville on the Florida coast. A further ten boats were now committed to the Caribbean operation bringing the total to twenty-nine, with more to follow.

While this second group was beginning its journey through the Bay of Biscay with all its attendant hazards, the survivors of the first wave were arriving on station in the Caribbean. They had all had to fight their way through and nearly every boat had handed over wounded crewmen to the U Tankers in mid Atlantic.

The first to arrive was the veteran Type IXC U510, now under the command of Oberleutnant Zur See Alfred Eick. The boat arrived on station off the coast of Dutch Guiana on June twenty-fifth. On the same day Muller-Stockheim in U67, operating northeast of the island of Antigua, attacked a vessel with a four torpedo spread. All the torpedoes proved to be defective and one of them exploded only a hundred metres from the U-Boat's bows.

Four days later U67 met U572 and received the long awaited parts for her metox equipment. With her set once more in operation, she was able to move in much closer to the islands.

New orders had been issued to U572 and U759 on June twenty-sixth, which directed that U572 operate off Trinidad and U759 in the Windward Passage. By June thirtieth, U572 was in position, having come south along the eastern side of the islands. On the same date U759 was north of Puerto

Rico and reported that they had sunk an unidentified sailing vessel, while making their way to the heavily patrolled passage.

In the meantime, U590 had come into position off French Guiana and U159 had been chased off by a US battlegroup northeast of the islands. U159 had attempted to penetrate the screen around an American battleship and been roughly treated, as the U-Boat made its way towards the Mona Passage.

Uhlig in U527 had worked his way up into the Gulf of Mexico and on July second reported strong air activity and continuous surface patrols. But during these last few days of June, several disasters had befallen the U-Boats, not the least of which was the loss of another tanker.

On June twenty-fourth, the Second Support Group led by the sloop Starling, with Captain Walker in command, surprised U Tanker U119 near her rendezvous area. The Group was working independently in a similar fashion to the American hunting groups, when the Starling established asdic contact at a thousand yards. The sloop ran in and delivered a depth-charge attack, with the charges set to between one fifty and three hundred feet. The ten charge attack was remarkably accurate and damaged the U Tanker to the point where she had to surface immediately.

The tanker U-Boats did not carry a deck mounted main gun and Von Kameke could do nothing other than surface and try to run from his attackers. U119 promptly came up right among the sloops of the escort group, startling the hunters by its sudden appearance. Every ship in the group opened fire and the U-Boat's hull glowed from the continuous strikes of the four inch shells burying themselves inside and exploding. U119 was finished and all that was required at this stage was for the escorts to keep pumping shells into the hull until they destroyed it. In any case, the shells exploding in the confines of the U-Boat were probably destroying it and killing the crew.

Alternatively, one of the group could have steamed past the hulk and destroyed it using depth-charges, but again the illogical naval officer's desire to ram overruled good tactical thinking and Walker ordered all ships to cease fire while he manoeuvred.

It was patently obvious that in such an encounter, the precious sloop was going to be damaged. The sloop was the ultimate development of the World War Two escort vessels and at this stage there were not enough of them around to hazard a hull unnecessarily. Walker was easily the Allies' greatest anti-submarine commander, but even he could not resist the temptation to ram.

Starling came running in, but at the last moment a wave lifted the bow so that she did not so much ram, as drop her forefoot onto the U-Boat's hull. The sloop smashed her way across, while U119 rolled upside down, bumping and grinding her way along the escort's bottom. To compound the problem, a pattern of depth-charges with shallow settings were rolled off the sloop's stern, just before the escort's propellers came into contact with the Krupp steel of the U-Boat's hull.

By the time Starling was across, the shattered hull of the U119 was already going down. The sloop was not clear when the depth-charges went off and she received her share of additional damage with every light fitting in the ship smashed. U119 was finished. The four-inch shells had punctured her pressure hull, while the ramming had split her open. The depth-charges disintegratred what was left. There were no survivors, but Starling was no longer an operational member of the hunting group. Her stem had been bent and her hull holed. The forward magazine was flooded and she had lost her asdic dome, as well as damaged her propellers. She was a wreck and had to be sent back to base.

The destruction of this second U Tanker threw all the carefully calculated schedules out and put many U-Boat operations in jeopardy, specifically the Caribbean offensive. It had been intended that the maximum number of U-Boats would be committed to the area so that the American defences would be saturated. Caribbean convoys seldom had ever been attacked by a wolf pack of more than three boats, simply because there were never enough U-Boats in the area at any given time.

Even when the Caribbean boats numbered more than twenty, they were spread out over such a vast area, that a decisive concentration was never achieved. July was meant to be the critical period when U-Boat Command would throw everything they had at the Caribbean and achieve the concentration required to stop all shipping in the area, but this was not to be.

The end of June, saw the virtual end of the U-Boat sailings for the renewed Caribbean offensive. There were two factors which killed the expansion of the Caribbean deployment. The first of these was the loss of the tankers U118 and U119. Without these support vessels, the great deployment was simply not possible. U-Boat Command had to consider the possible loss of more tankers and assess what these projected losses would do to the operation. The presence of the American carriers in mid Atlantic, pointed to future losses of these tanker U-Boats and planning was now centred around ensuring that sufficient tankers could be found to support the boats that were out.

The second factor that affected the continued deployment was the havoc being created among the departing boats by the aircraft of RAF Coastal Command, operating over the Bay of Biscay.

During the month of June, U440, U418, U564, U194 and U200 had been lost in the Bay to aircraft attack. In addition, nearly every boat that had transited the area had been damaged and all the crews had suffered casualties. Doenitz realized that the losses to the boats in transit were too high. He was losing a large proportion of his force before they could get to their operational areas. On the last day of the month, the Grand Admiral acted to stop the losses in the Bay by suspending all sailings until the boats were fitted with the quadruple twenty millimetre anti-aircraft mounting. This order affected all the follow up boats that had been earmarked for the Caribbean offensive. In the long run, the decision was to prove critical to the survivial of the U-Boats as a viable force, because the Germans were going to have enough difficulty handling the requirements of the boats that were already at sea.

Doenitz could have continued the sailings and accepted the losses for the opportunity to saturate the American defences in the Caribbean. However, based on what happened to the boats which ran the gauntlet of the Bay of Biscay, the conclusion can be drawn that further reinforcement would not have enhanced the chance of success.

The prime purpose of the U-Boats was the sinking of merchant vessels and not combat against defending aircraft, into which the Caribbean offensive had degenerated. Like the decision to stop the sailings in May, the curtailment of the sailings at the end of June probably saved the U-Boat arm from total destruction. Despite this, the Caribbean offensive was the last big fling of the U-Boats.

Doenitz's order allowed the boats with the heavy anti-aircraft armament to proceed with their sailing schedule. This was based on the mistaken idea that the boats could win these air-sea combats. Once the U-Boat gave the aircraft the initiative by staying on the surface, it would only be a matter of time before the boat was destroyed. The quadruple twenty millimetre mounting was a fearsome weapon, greatly feared by the pilots, but it could only zero in on one aircraft at a time. Multiple co-ordinated attacks could defeat it, even when boats were paired off for mutual support.

The last four boats of the second wave all sailed with the heavier anti-aircraft armament, but it did not save them. The U628, U648, U514 and U607 all fought titanic battles against aircraft attack, but despite their armament and the fact that they were all supported, only one of them made it out of the Bay of Biscay. This result was to be repeated time after time in the months to come and even the specially equipped flak boats took heavy damage. The answer to the dilemma presented by Allied air superiority over the Bay of Biscay, lay not with heavy anti aircraft armament, but the U-Boats were to go through a veritable cauldron of combat and losses, before they admitted this.

U-Boat Command were aware that even though the Caribbean sailings had been curtailed, there were still a large number of boats making their way across the Atlantic and that a major clash was about to take place. They now had the job of supporting these boats and ensuring that they had maximum back up. This meant shielding the tankers and ensuring that replacements were available. It also meant giving these boats full moral and tactical support in their coming battle. The Staff had done all they could with tactical briefings, based on the experiences of all the boats that had operated in the Caribbean before. Doenitz was well known as a father figure to his men and as a general issues his message to his troops before battle, he issued a communique to the boats ploughing across the Atlantic to their destiny. The message was sent out on the first of July and read as follows:-

"Caribbean boats are instructed that due to intense air activity, especially at focal points of traffic and through passages, stationary operation alone is possible. During waiting periods in operational areas, all safety precautions are to be closely observed, collect experiences and remain unseen. Commanding officers have full freedom of operation, they can therefore of their own accord move into less patrolled areas according to the anti-submarine situation, either into the inner Caribbean, or towards the Atlantic, for instance, during the full moon period. If the enemy is sighted, try to force a success by a well considered, but keen attack. According to boats which have returned from the Caribbean, enemy surface escort vessels with convoys there are untrained and not to be compared to Atlantic escorts. A convoy gives you a big chance, which must be fully exploited, it can mean the success of the whole patrol."

It was a unique before battle message with no frills, that reflected the character of the Grand Admiral. It was a comprehensive set of instructions with good advice, but the comments on the surface escorts were somewhat out of date. They related to the experiences of the 1942 boats, reinforced by Mohr in January and Neitzel with convoy BT-6.

Since these operations, the escorts had been beefed up and the boats of July were to find that it was just as difficult to penetrate a Caribbean convoy, as it was in the North Atlantic.

On the eve of the epic month of July 1943, the US Navy effected an administrative change with far-reaching consequences that reflected the new awareness in the theatre. The Caribbean Sea Frontier now came under the command of the US Navy Tenth Fleet, which was a purely anti-submarine

organisation. This reflected the higher priority being given to the war against
the German U-Boats by the US Navy. Vice Admiral John Hoover remained
in command, and he was to see the Caribbean through its coming trial of
strength before moving on in August.

The month of June had also seen much shifting round of anti-
submarine squadrons, with new powerful units covering the likely U-Boat
concentration areas. New aircraft were also evident in the theatre with the
advent of PV-1 Venturas, B-25 MItchells and B-24 Liberators. The Ventura
was a naval development of the Lockhead Hudson, with more powerful
engines and four forward firing machine guns. As an anti-submarine aircraft
it was to prove a vast improvement on the old B18s.

The Windward Passage had a comprehensive air defense and anti-submarine organization centered on Guantanamo Bay. VS-62, VP-92 and VP-32
with their Mariners, operated alongside the Airship detachment from ZP-51.

Further south in the Passage, the Royal Navy No. 703 squadron
operated Kingfishers out of Palisadoes along with Hellcats, Corsairs and
Avengers disembarked from fleet carriers undergoing maintenance and
repair in US navy yards. At Vernam Field, US Army B18s covered the
southern approaches, with detachments at Grand Cayman. In the far west,
NAS Coco Solo in the Panama Zone operated a detachment of Mariners
from VP-204, while numerous US Army bomber squadrons operated out of
France Field and throughout Central America.

From NAS San Juan in Puerto Rico, a detachment of VP-32 Mariners operated alongside the PBYs of VP-81. US Navy bomber squadron
VB-141 with PV-1 Venturas operated out of Borinquen, from where they
controlled the Mona and Anegada Passages. The US Army 5th bomber
squadron with its B18s still operated out of St. Lucia, alongside the OS2Ns
of VMS 3, but they also had a detachment in Antigua and were responsible
for the island chain. In Curacao and Aruba the picture had completely
changed. The 8th US Army anti-submarine squadron with B-24 Liberators
now resided at the twin fields, where they had been joined by the P-40
fighters of the 32nd fighter squadron.

Important changes had taken place in Trinidad's air organisation. The
end of June saw the departure of the 22nd fighter squadron and they were
replaced by the A-20 bombers of the 39th Reconnaisance squadron. As the
battle developed, a detachment of B-24 Liberators from Curacao was also to
move into this base. At Edinburgh Field, the new arrivals were the PV-1
Venturas of US Navy bomber squadron VB-130, as well as the B25s of the
US Army 7th anti-submarine squadron. The 59th Bomber squadron had
moved from Curacao to Edinburgh and been re-equipped with the powerful

B-25 Mitchell. Also at the field were the B18s of the US Army 10th Bomber squadron and the 23rd anti-submarine squadron. It was quite an array, compared to the height of the first U-Boat offensive when the 1st bombardment squadron stood alone. Over all, the lumbering airships of ZP-51 floated.

Along the bauxite route, there had also been changes. The 35th Bomber squadron was still based at Zandery, but the squadron had been re-equipped with B24 Liberators and the squadron still operated detachments at Atkinson. The US Army 417th squadron operated a detachment of B18s out of Gallion Field in French Guiana, at the southern extremity of the Trinidad Sector. ZP-51 Airships still operated out of Atkinson and Zandery, alongside the fixed wing aircraft.

Chaguaramas had seen a complete changeover. On June 1st VP-53 had gone to the Pacific and VP-81 to San Juan. They had been replaced by the sea grey camouflaged Martin Mariners of VP-204 and VP-205. As well as their detachment in Panama, the two squadrons contributed to basing detachments with the seaplane, tender USS Pelican, anchored in the Cayenne river. Immediately to the south of the Trinidad Sector, the northernmost squadron of the Brazilian theatre was VP-94, operating PBYs out of Belem. They were to play a part in the Caribbean theatre during the month of July.

Caribbean air power in July 1943 was indeed formidable and they were all geared up for the coming offensive.

Both sides were to display extraordinary courage in the next six weeks, when the U-Boats took on the aircraft. Long before the arrival of the U-Boats, tension was at fever pitch. This was caused by the disappearance of Mariner P-7 of VP-205, while on an anti-submarine patrol on June eleventh. The aircraft suffered mechanical failure and disappeared without trace, but no one could convince the defenders that it wasn't a U-Boat. Thus two weeks before the first U-Boat came into the area, the squadrons were out looking for them.

CHAPTER

16

U~Tankers

The crisis in the Bay of Biscay was causing grave concern to U-Boat Command and the situation became more critical as the month of July 1943 opened. Valuable experienced U-Boats were being lost at an alarming rate, before they could get near to their operating areas. The same was happening to tired crews on their way home after their gruelling combat patrols. July opened with the loss of one such boat.

Siegfried Kietz in command of Bauer's old Caribbean veteran U126, had completed a patrol in the Gulf of Guinea, where he had managed to sink two ships. While under Bauer's command this had been the first U-Boat to prowl the waters of the Windward Passage, sinking eight ships and damaging three others during its highly successful Neuland patrol. Later during the golden days of June 1942, Bauer had managed to add another seven ships to his total. He handed over command to Kietz early in 1943 and went on to his destiny in command of U169.

While Kietz brought U126 up from West Africa, Kusch was also bringing U154 across the Atlantic, from its fourth visit to the Caribbean area.

U-Boat Command were pairing off the incoming boats so that they could give each other support on the run through the Bay of Biscay. Thus it came about that these two Caribbean veterans were brought together for the final dash to Lorient.

All day on July second the two boats ran on the surface with lookouts scanning the horizon for the telltale black dots that would signal the arrival of the dreaded aircraft. The anti-aircraft gunners lounged near their mountings, ready to put up a wall of twenty millimetre cannon shells at any aircraft that came in range, but by late evening the RAF had still not put in an appearance.

With the coming of darkness the gunners still could not relax, because the RAF did not need daylight to find or attack them. The two boats huddled together, offering each other a measure of protection, but the evening continued without a sight of a hostile aeroplane, lulling the gunners into a false sense of security. They came soon after midnight. The two boats hardly had any warning at all. The Metox sets gave no indication and it was only when the attacking Wellington bomber switched on its Leigh light that the gunners knew that the time had come.

The aircraft of No. 172 squadron selected U126 as its target and came roaring in with its bow guns spitting death. It was a good attack and the streams of tracer had hardly started to leave the anti-aircraft guns, before the bomber was overhead and the depth charges were on their way down. U154 manoeuvred to keep her guns bearing on the attacker, while U126 disappeared behind the towers of water that marked the depth charge explosions. While blazing away at the Wellington, which was turning for another attack, the lookouts on U154 realized that the fire from U126 had ceased very abruptly. By the time they had beaten off the attack on their boat, and U154 turned towards its sister U-Boat, U126 was nowhere to be seen. The depth-charge attack had been accurate and U126 went quickly, with no survivors. U154 could do nothing more and turned its bows toward Lorient, continuing its now lone dash to safety.

Dawn found U154 inbound and eleven U-Boats on their way outbound. Among these eleven boats, U155, U160, U628 and U648 were bound for the Caribbean. That same morning U514 sailed from Lorient with the large contingent of Monsoon boats and turned its bows towards the Atlantic. As the day developed a series of violent clashes took place between the racing boats and the aircraft. The RAF pilots were equally intent that they should not get through. The battle of the Bay of Biscay had now developed into the most violent clash of the Battle of the Atlantic and its outcome was crucial to the wider struggle.

In recognition of this, the US Navy had based VP-84 in England and assigned it to the Biscay patrols. Before the end of the war the squadron was to become the top US Navy unit, with eight U-Boats to its credit. Now that French North Africa was secured, squadrons also moved into this area to close the air-gap between Biscay and the American carriers in mid Atlantic.

But the battle of Biscay was basically an RAF affair and they flung themselves at the U-Boats, almost without regard for casualties. Before the end of the day Heinrich Hasenschar in U628 found that even with the support of his companion U648, aircraft could and did get through. A Liberator of No. 224 squadron operated out of St. Eval, braved the withering combined anti-aircraft fire of the two boats and planted its depth-charges right around the U-Boat's hull.

When the towers of water cleared, U628 was gone. There were no survivors from this second of the Caribbean bound boats to be sunk enroute. Stahl in U648 reported the loss and continued on his lone passage towards the distant Caribbean. Further out in the Bay, Forster and Hagenskotter in U359 and U466 were more fortunate. They managed to beat off the attacks and bring down one of their tormentors.

For the next four days, combats continued in the Bay of Biscay during the course of which U535 and U951 were sunk, but the Caribbean bound boats did not suffer again until July eighth. The six Type IXC boats U168, U183, U505, U509, U514 and U532 were discovered in a great gaggle on the surface, and Coastal Command threw in all they had. The boats fought well and held off the attackers for as long as they could, but eventually a 224 squadron Liberator broke through and by chance picked out the Caribbean bound boat. The depth-charges landed accurately around the hull of the veteran U514 and detonated.

Hans Jurgen Auffermann of the Cornwallis in Barbados, the Kioto off Tobago and the trailing of convoy TM-1, died that day. The boat went down just four days after leaving Lorient to become the third loss of the Caribbean offensive. The six Type IXC boats had been subjected to nonstop attacks with guns, armour piercing rockets, depth-charges and an acoustic torpedo and they were lucky only to lose U514. No. 224 squadron had accounted for two of the first three U-Boats to die and they would kill again before July was through.

While Auffermann fought his last battle, the surviving U-Boats were beginning their deployment around the Caribbean theatre. Six of the first wave were in position alongside the two that were already in the theatre. Kruer in U590 was close inshore off the French Guiana/Brazil border, while further northwest Eick in U510 patrolled off Dutch Guiana. The two boats were close in, sitting on the bauxite route.

After his rendezvous with U67, Kummetat in U572 sailed down the Windward side of the island chain and entered the Caribbean sea through the Grenadines. Northeast of Antigua, Muller-Stockheim held his position, because he had no tanker hookup for the homeward run and could not spare the fuel to come into the Caribbean Sea.

During the first week of July, Beckmann in U159 and Freidrich in U759 passed U67's area going westward towards the Windward Passage. Both boats came down into the Passage and almost immediately U759 scored. Freidrich caught the three thousand five hundred ton American freighter Maltran and sent it to the bottom twenty miles west of Haiti. This was the first sinking in this area in nearly two months and it brought forth a furious anti-submarine reaction. The Passage was constantly patrolled by aircraft and surface vessels and the boats had to remain submerged almost continuously.

Beckmann in U159 was under orders for the area off Colon in the Panama zone and he could easily have followed these orders and cleared out of the heavily defended passage. But it seems that Beckmann was in no hurry to take post in the lonely southwest corner of the theatre and while U-Boat Command continued a dead reckoning plot towards Colon, U159 hung around the Windward Passage.

In the far northwest, Uhlig was almost finished with his Gulf of Mexico deployment and turned his bows towards the Straits of Florida. He had not been successful in the Gulf and his numerous situation reports had described an area that was heavily patrolled. Each of his attacks on the convoys in the area had been frustrated by the ever vigilant convoy escorts. It was obvious that the Gulf was no longer a favourable U-Boat operating area.

The primary purpose of the U-Boats was the sinking of merchant ships and from this aspect, the first week was not encouraging. U-Boat Command commented on the fact that not one of the Caribbean bound boats had managed to claim a merchant ship while on passage. It meant that in the Atlantic, independently sailing merchant ships had been cut to the barest minimum. In fact the Allies had been fully aware of the great westward movement of U-Boats, and sailings had probably been deliberately curtailed, because the central Atlantic normally would have been crawling with shipping.

The situation in the Caribbean was not much different. The sinking of the Maltran was the only bright spot in an otherwise rather gloomy week for the U-Boats. In the past, as many as eight boats in the Caribbean had usually meant a good harvest of sunken ships. Now all that U-Boat Command was getting were complaints from the U-Boat commanders about the nonstop air activity. This went so far that a comment was entered in the War Diary expressing concern about the effect of the climate on the crews operating in the Caribbean.

The average U-Boat crew consisted of the commander and two watch-keeping officers, backed up by seven Petty Officers, two of whom were the navigators, with thirty-nine to forty ratings running the vessel. When the boat was not in action or in a quiet area, the crew could work three watches and some relaxation was possible. But when they were operating in a hostile aviation environment like the Caribbean had become, it could be very trying for the crew. In the good old days, commanders often let the crew come up from below and spend their off duty hours literally in the sunny Caribbean but in 1943, when men went off watch, they were not allowed to go anywhere but down into the steel cylinder. When the boat was on the surface in this area, the temperature inside the virtually closed steel cylinder could soar to great heights, dehydrating the fifty men confined in its blistering interior. Only the watchkeepers and guncrews got a chance to breathe fresh air for a short while.

In addition, on these long cruises to the Caribbean, the interior of the U-Boats would be more cramped than usual, because of the great quantity of food, ammunition and torpedoes that had to be stored inside. To carry enough food, items would have to be stocked and hung throughout the length of the boat, adding considerably to the smell of oil and stale bilge water that normally permeated a U-Boat.

In the North Atlantic, U-Boat crews had to endure the cold and wet conditions, but in the tropics heat could rob a man of his will to fight just as effectively. The only area which compared to the level of air activity in the Caribbean was the Bay of Biscay, but Biscay was just a transit, five or six days that had to be endured, while the Caribbean was every day, all day. The golden west had become a place of extreme discomfort, fear and death.

The second week of July saw first U67, then U527 start their home-ward journeys. U510 and U590 began the week in the same position off the Guianas, but further north more boats were coming in. Kandler in U653 and Neide in U415 had moved in to the area east of Trinidad, while U572 had come south to the Trinidad north coast, after cruising up to the southern entrance to Anegada. To the west, Uphoff in U84 and Carlsen in U732 had moved into the Windward Passage, to join U759 and U159, while Brosin in U134 was coming in through the Bahamas for the Straits of Florida. There were now eleven boats in the theatre, with a further ten on the way to the

Caribbean and two on the way home.

The TB series of convoys had been running between Trinidad and Bahia since January 1943, but the large concentration of U-Boats operating off the Brazilian coast was causing significant merchant shipping losses, beyond the convoy terminus at Bahia.

To counter this, a new series of convoys was instituted to replace the TB route. These new convoys were instituted to run from Trinidad to Rio de Janiero and afford protection to merchant shipping for three thousand miles along the South American coast. The new convoys were coded TJ and the first one sailed from Trinidad on the third of July.

Since the debacle with convoy BT-14, the convoys along the South American coast had been escorted by powerful groups of warships and remained relatively unmolested, but for some reason two convoys in the first week of July reverted to the old style and both paid dearly. Convoy TJ-1 with twenty merchant ships sailed out of the Bocas with an escort of one old destroyer, the USS Somers, accompanied by five of the ineffective PCs. At the same time, the last of the BT convoys coded BT-18, left Bahia for Trinidad, escorted by two corvettes and two PCs. This same inadequate escort combination had contributed to the disasters which befell convoys TB-1, BT-6 and BT-14 and by the late evening of July seventh, Eick in U510 and Maus in U185 were in contact with the convoys.

For the last two months, the Caribbean U-Boats had been striving to penetrate well escorted convoys and failing, when the record was spoilt and these two opportunities were presented to the boats.

By midnight on July seventh, Eick was moving U510 in against convoy TJ-1, one hundred miles off French Guiana. Twelve hundred miles further along the route off Fortaleza, Maus was moving U185 in against convoy BT-18.

At twenty minutes after midnight Eick fired three torpedoes in sequence and dived to watch the result. The first two torpedoes romped into the ten thousand three hundred ton Norwegian tanker B.P. Newton and the third struck the freighter Everaga. The detonations on the tanker immediately ignited her volatile cargo and again the South American convoy route was witness to the appalling catastrophe of a burning tanker. The freighter Everaga was luckier and the single torpedo that hit her only blew out the engine room plates. The freighter was stopped and abandoned by her crew. Later the hulk was towed back to Trinidad. The tanker however, burned all night and helped to dramatise the plight of the convoy. Once more a U-Boat commander took his boat into a South American convoy and watched as the escorts lit up the area to seaward.

While Eick in U510 was thus engaged, Maus in U185 sank a tanker and damaged another out of convoy BT-18 off Fortaleza. He followed this up by sinking two freighters, while the inadequate escort tried desperately to locate him. At twenty past one in the morning, Eick attacked TJ-1 again and this time his torpedoes sank the six thousand nine hundred ton freighter Eldena. Both convoys had been lit up by burning tankers and by the time that the B.P. Newtown went down at dawn both U-Boats were clear of the convoys. It remained for the aircraft based in French Guiana and Brazil to chase the U-Boats away from the vulnerable convoy routes.

The night's work cost the Allies two large tankers sunk and another damaged, along with three freighters sunk and one damaged. The signals from the respective convoy escorts caused both the Trinidad Sector and the northern Brazilian Sector to dispatch additional surface escorts to beef up the convoys. The strengthening of these convoy escorts should have been done much earlier, but it was caused by a curious miscalculation on the part of Naval Intelligence.

They were aware that the U-Boats were making their way to the Caribbean and Brazilian theatres, but they underestimated the speed at which the boats would cross the Atlantic, with the result that their anti-submarine plots were lagging well behind the actual build up of U-Boats. The shock of having two convoys savaged in one night, caused every command from Trinidad to Fortaleza to go on full alert. Along eighteen hundred miles of coastline troops began moving out and coast defence gunners peered seawards, but U185 and U510 were well offshore.

The activities of U185 and U510 caused U590 to pay the ultimate price. The Blom and Voss built Type VIIC U-Boat had been commissioned early in 1942 under the command of Heinrich Muller-Edzards, who had operated the boat up to March 1943, when Werner Kruer took command.

Kruer had brought U590 in to the Brazilian coast on July third and sunk the Brazilian freighter Pelotasloide, just south of the equator, on the following day. After the sinking, Kruer began working his way up the coast to the Caribbean theatre, while sending off his last report to U-Boat headquarters on the fifth.

By the morning of July ninth U590 was one hundred and fifty miles east of the Brazil/French Guiana border, when it got caught up in the greatly enhanced air activity caused by the double convoy action. The U-Boat was attacked on the surface by a white camouflaged PBY of VP-94 operating out of Belem. The aircraft achieved complete tactical surprise and after the depth-charge explosions, the aircraft crew could see the wreck of U590 slipping below the waves. There were no survivors from this first

U-Boat to be sunk within the Caribbean theatre during the month of July. The defenders had claimed their first victim and it almost made up for the losses in the convoys.

After the convoy battle, Eick had moved U510 away from the coast-line so that the avenging PBYs, Liberators and B18s had missed him entire-ly. While U590 was being made to pay for his impudence, Eick was well off-shore watching the wreck of the Swedish ship Scandinavia go to the bottom. He came upon the vessel six hundred miles southeast of Trinidad and sank it with scuttling charges, in accordance with the Prize Regulations. The sur-vivors set off in their lifeboats for the long drift to Trinidad, thankful that they had all been able to get safely off the vessel.

Saturday tenth of July saw the Allies undertake the invasion of Sicily in the Mediterranean, but the day also marked a further escalation of ten-sion in the Caribbean theatre. Friedrich in U759 moved in against convoy TAG-70, south of the Windward Passage and fired a spread of torpedoes. The convoy had left Trinidad on July third with eleven merchant ships. The escort initially was led by the destroyer USS Biddle, with five PCs in atten-dance. Once again with an inadequate escort, but this time with a heavy air component.

Off Aruba another eight ships and a destroyer had joined for the run up to Guantanamo Bay. Nearing the Windward Passage, the convoy came under the air escort of VP-92 and the Mariners of VP-32, along with the independent hunting groups working the area. U759's torpedoes missed the convoy but the end run detonation of one of them convinced Friedrich that he had hit, and he later reported that he had sunk a tanker.

Friedrich carried out a daylight attack at periscope depth, hoping that this would give him a measure of protection, but the torpedoes were hardly running before a stick of bombs detonated on the surface above him. This was the signal for the hunting group, which was working in the British fashion, providing close escort to the convoy, to move in. It was seven nerve-wrecking hours later before Friedrich was able to ease U759 out of the dangerous area. Further southeast off Trinidad, the pace was also quickening up.

At five eighteen that afternoon, a thousand miles to the southeast of the action in the Windward Passage, the duty staff at the harbour master's entry control post in the Dragon's Mouth hit the alarm bells. The Americans had planted sonobouys across Trinidad's Dragon's Mouth entrance to the Gulf of Paria and the operators had picked up propeller noises.

Messages flashed to the Royal Navy headquarters at HMS Benbow and thence to the nearby US Navy headquarters. For eight minutes the operators could hear the sound of the propellers, while the loop operators in Staubles Bay closely watched their equipment to detect a loop crossing, but there were no indications. Trinidad was still on full alert after the convoy action and it wasn't long before PCs and MLs and a destroyer were on their way to the threatened area. The Gulf was full of its usual quota of merchant ships, but in addition, the area was packed with amphibious shipping for the invasion of Martinique, including a fleet carrier and heavy cruisers of the bombardment force.

The disturbance was caused by Heinz Kummetat in U572. The U-Boat had cruised up to the Anegada Passage area and then turned southward. July tenth had found U572 off Trinidad's north coast and Kummetat decided to take a look at the entrance to the Bocas. He brought the U-Boat right in close to the Third Boca and cruised around submerged, before heading back out. He did not cross the anti-submarine loops, but he was close enough for his propeller noise to be picked up.

The defenders could be pretty sure that they were hearing a U-Boat because the horizon was clear, but they had a peculiar restriction to contend with resulting from the nature of the defences in the area. The PCs and MLs commenced asdic searches, but because of the presence of the defending minefields, a large proportion of the area was forbidden to them.

Additionally, they could not carry out depth-charge attacks for fear of damaging the sonobuoys and the magnetic detector cables, as well as the possibility of setting off their own mines. In the interim a large number of aircraft had been scrambled and these commenced a massive anti-submarine search of the Gulf and the waters outside. Some of the MLs and PCs slipped out of the Bocas and commenced a comprehensive sweep of the surrounding waters. A US Coast Guard cutter obtained an asdic contact and carried out a series of depth-charge attacks off the north coast, but the U-Boat slipped away. Kummetat had awakened the comprehensive anti-submarine defences of the area and the hunt lasted for several days. That night the Port of Spain harbour was blacked out and the full civil defence organization joined the alert.

Kummetat's excursion came at a bad time, because the Trinidad Command was fully geared for the final round in the Martinique situation. Martinique was the most explosive crisis of the Caribbean war. As far back as June 1940, Britain had come down strongly against the Vichy French and there was no question of contact between the two sides. However, in December 1942, right after the United States came into the war they opened negotiations with the military Governor and Commander in Chief.

Vice Admiral Robert, acting for the Vichy French and Rear Admiral

F.J. Horne acting for the United States Government concluded an Agreement, which included a proviso that Vichy French warships, with the exception of the auxilliary Barfleur, would give the United States four days warning of any movement. The Barfleur was excluded because this vessel was to be the primary link between French Guiana, Guadeloupe and Martinique, and as such only required to give two days notice of movement. The Vichy French military aircraft were not allowed to leave Martinique, nor were the French gold reserves, which were kept deep underground at Fort Desaix, allowed to be removed.

Shortly after the agreement was signed, intelligence sources indicated that Admiral Robert had no intention of keeping his side of the bargain and Vichy provocation began. When U156 landed its injured officer in February 1942, he had his leg amputated at the French Military hospital. After his convalescence, this officer became a staunch supporter of Vice Admiral Robert and began to take an active part in the affairs of the island. His influence increased dramatically and he contributed in no small measure to Admiral Robert's defiance of the Americans. Up to the surrender of French Guiana, Vichy naval vessels were moving freely in the Caribbean, defying the Americans to use force against them, leading to the crisis in June.

All through June the American amphibious forces had practised the invasion plan. The assault forces were divided into two Task Forces. The western Task Force was to land the 33rd infantry and the 135th combat engineers, on the beaches immediately to the south of the town of Fort de France. Their objective was the French Fort Desaix which was the military headquarters. The fort was a massive structure and considered to be almost inpregnable.

It was garrisoned by a French Colonial infantry regiment, along with an artillery regiment. The 501st parachute infantry were to be landed on the beaches to the north of the town and they were tasked with the capture of Lamentin airport, after which they would assist with the reduction of the fort.

The Western Task Force was to be under the command of Brigadier General Summers, working under Major General J.L. Collins, who was to assume command of all ground forces, once ashore. The Eastern Task Force under the command of Colonel Simmonds was to land at Le Robert on the island's east coast.

The assault forces were the 13th Marines, the 295th infantry regiment and the 78th combat engineers. Their task was to cut the island in half, linking up with the Western Task Force, before moving north to take care of the outlying infantry and artillery regimental garrisons.

If the French fought, it was going to be a formidable task because the geography of the island favoured defence. Virtually the whole island is mountainous, are as most of the islands of the eastern Caribbean. The Americans were confident that their troops would handle any defence that the French could put up, with the exception of Fort Desaix and the French Fleet. The taking of the fort would ultimately be a straight-forward siege, in which they expected to sustain casualties. The US Navy would provide shore bombardment for all operations,—after they had taken care of the Vichy Fleet, and herein lay the problem.

The French Navy were always the most militantly independent of all the Vichy forces and the Martinique contingent was formidable. In addition to the aircraft carrier Berne, with its combat aircraft, there were the heavy thirty-seven knot cruisers Emile Bertin and Jeanne D'arc. The ultra heavy destroyer or torpedo ship Le Terrible, led a Flotilla of smaller destroyers, patrol craft and the armed auxilliary Barfleur. It was a powerful squadron capable of considerable mischief and to counter it, the Americans moved many of their destroyers and patrol craft and based them in St. Lucia, where they would be close to Martinique. This may be the reason for the poorly escorted convoys of early July.

The brand new fleet carrier USS Bunker Hill, and the CVL USS Cowpens moved into the Gulf of Paria, ostensibly to conduct their shake-down training, but in reality to be available to deal with the Vichy fleet. The same applied to the new battleship USS New Jersey and the heavy cruisers Baltimore and Chester who were also in the Gulf. In the meantime, the military situation in Martinique began to deteriorate dramatically.

The Americans were using a combination of threats and deception to help undermine the resolve of the Vichy defenders and it worked remarkably well. They fed a great deal of information about the coming invasion to the Vichy French and greatly inflated the forces involved, while stressing the resolve of the American Government to carry out the operation. Many of the French initially could not believe that their long time ally America, would actually take up arms against them, but hunger caused by the blockade served to convince them and undermine the will to resist. This was particularly evident among the civil population, many of whom had little love for their Vichy military masters.

Discipline began to break down among the French troops at the thought of the slaughter to come and even Admiral Robert's senior officers began trying to influence him to consider asking for the Allied terms. In the meantime some of the soldiers mutined, sparking off street riots.

Martinique was in a state of chaos and Admiral Robert began to doubt the resolve of his troops to defend the island. Only the navy appeared to stand behind him, but even here there were groups of officers agitating about abandoning Vichy and sailing to join the Free French. It was at this stage that the desertions began. Admiral Robert's prestige suffered as first his infantry commander and then the commander of his artillery escaped from the island and joined the Allies. Then Joel Nicol, the son of the civil Governor escaped and arrived in Trinidad. The desertion of these senior officers greatly affected the Vichy cause, but the flight of Admiral Robert's second-in-command hurt the most.

Rear Admiral Batet escaped to Trinidad and joined the Allies. This last desertion by his trusted senior naval officer finally broke Admiral Robert and on June thirtieth, in an exploratory gesture, he asked the United Nations what terms they offered.

Negotiations began and D. Day for the invasion was delayed to the second half of July. It had originally been timed to coincide with the invasion of Sicily. By July fourteenth, Admiral Hoover was fairly sure that further pressure would succeed in forcing Admiral Robert to give up and he agreed to hand over Martinique to the Free French as soon as the problem was resolved. Generals de Gaulle and Giraud had by this stage come to an understanding and the Americans were no longer forced to choose a French champion. The situation in Martinique was much worse than even the Americans realized and Admiral Robert was under intense pressure from his fellow Frenchmen.

On July fifteenth he finally bowed to the pressure, admitting that his plan to defend the island against the Americans was hopeless. Along with a large party of his closest senior officers, advisers and Vichy supporters he left the island. They sailed to Puerto Rico to give themselves up, rather than face the humiliation of seeing the Americans invade and their troops run away or desert to the enemy. This effectively ended the Vichy French problem in the Caribbean theatre and the invasion was cancelled. The French in Martinique were quick to join the Allies, including elements of the Vichy navy, which had at one time been the backbone of resistance.

The takeover of Martinique did not end the alert in Trinidad because the American command expected a German reaction to the Martinique surrender. They were waiting for a fresh blow from the U-Boats, specifically around the island, but the U-Boats were not primarily interested in Martinique, they wanted to sink merchant ships. Instead, they were under extreme pressure and the emphasis had once more switched back to the Bay of Biscay and mid Atlantic.

In the early morning of July thirteenth, Oberleutnant Zur See Jeschonnek in command of U607 was crossing the Bay of Biscay in company

with U445, when his boat became the fourth Caribbean bound U-Boat to be
lost in the Bay. He was caught by a Sunderland flying boat from No. 224
squadron RAF and the plan to mine Kingston harbour in Jamaica ended up
on the seabed. U607 had completed four North Atlantic patrols before
being assigned to the Caribbean mining operation, but all its experience did
not save it from the Sunderland's depth-charges. Forty-five of its crew
perished leaving only seven survivors to be rescued by U445. The plan to
mine Kingston harbour was dead, but so was the mining of Jacksonville.

U613 which had sailed from La Pallice at the same time as U607
and U445 had left St. Nazaire, also had an appointment with destiny. She
made it out of the Bay of Biscay but was caught at the mid Atlantic rendezvous on July twenty-third. She was sunk thirteen days after sailing, by the
USS Badger and sent to the bottom of the Atlantic, with all her crew. The
destroyer USS Badger had spent all of 1942 as a Caribbean escort based in
Trinidad. In July 1943, she was one of the carrier escorts in mid Atlantic,
working with the Task Group led by the USS Core.

Later that afternoon, U-Boat Command suffered another crippling
disaster. The only tanker at sea was the Type XIV U487 under the command of Oberleutnant Zur See Metz. Since the disaster to U118 and U119,
Metz had been responsible for all the boats coming into the mid Atlantic's
rendezvous point. The tanker was scheduled to refuel U160 and U648, both
scheduled for the Caribbean, as well as U527 returning from that area. U130
and U183 outbound to other operational areas were also scheduled to refuel.

Her rendezvous area was being patrolled by the Avengers of VC-13,
operating from the carrier USS Core, but Metz knew nothing of this, expecting that as usual, the mid Atlantic meeting would be well away from the
enemy. It probably came as a complete surprise to the conning tower watch
when they spotted the attacking aircraft. The Avengers planted their depth-
charges around the hull of the U-Boat, defying the heavy anti aircraft fire
spitting from the conning tower. After the attack, the large hull of the
tanker upended and slowly slipped below the waves. The carrier's escorting
destroyers picked up the few survivors. U-Boat Command were quite
unaware that they now had a major crisis on their hands, although this
crisis had its genesis in events in the Bay of Biscay eleven days before.

On June twenty-eight the U Tanker U462 sailed from Bordeaux
escorted by Von Pommer Esche in U160. The two U-Boats stuck close
together as they made their way through the hazardous Bay. On July second
disaster struck. RAF Coastal Command picked them up and the bombers
came roaring in. The Coastal Command pilots were well aware of the importance of the U Tanker and pressed home their attacks ruthlessly. Finally a

high explosive bomb hit the forward casing of the U462. There was no hope of the tanker continuing and Vowe was forced to turn his bows back to Bordeaux. Once Vowe was out of the danger area, Von Pommer Esche again turned U160's bows towards the Atlantic. The damage to U462 could be repaired but it would take a few days, thus upsetting the already precarious refuelling schedule.

U160 made it back out of the Bay of Biscay without serious damage, but the boat was now in dire need of refuelling, if it was going to reach the Caribbean and operate there. U-Boat Command directed Von Pommer Esche to rendezvous with the only tanker at sea, the U487 off the Azores. The refuelling was scheduled for July fourteenth, in the safe haven that the U-Boats had been using for a year, but U487 was sunk on July thirteenth.

None of the captains hunting for the tanker knew of the existence of the American carrier Task Forces operating in their mid Atlantic link-up area. Thus it came about that the Avengers of VC-29 operating from the carrier USS Santee, found U160 hunting for its lost tanker. The depth-charges ripped open the pressure hull and Georg Lassen's old boat went to the bottom of the Atlantic with all its crew. U160, that had once been the terror of Trinidad's north coast was gone. It was the fifth U-Boat to be destroyed on passage to the Caribbean and the sixth of the offensive.

On the same day that U160 went down Kummetat in U572, after having thoroughly upset the Trinidad defenders was moving down the island's east coast, when he came across the schooner Havard, forty miles from Galeota Point. The schooner's crew were rescued from their dinghy by a US Army transport on its way to Georgetown and they were able to radio news of the sinking to Trinidad. This added another U-Boat to the Naval Intelligence plot, but they were still lagging far behind the actual developments.

By this stage at the start of the third week in July, there were eleven U-Boats in the theatre, with five more closing in from the east. U134 was cruising slowly around in the Straits of Florida, as yet avoiding trouble, while U84, U732 and U759 hung around the Windward Passage. Beckmann in U159 was still well off station. He was south of Haiti, when in fact he should have been off the Panama Canal, and he was soon to pay dearly for being out of position. Dalhous in U634 was south of the Mona Passage and to the east of him Kapitsky in U615 had just safely traversed the Anegada Passage. Three U-Boats, U415, U572 and U653 were patrolling immediately east of Trinidad, while U510 covered the area off the Guianas.

The wolves were gathering, but they were not yet all in position. Like U159, there was another U-Boat that was way out of its operating area.

Markworth in U66 was supposed to be operating off the US east coast, but in reality he was chasing a tanker which was heading for Puerto Rico. He didn't want to let the tanker get away and this drew him into the Caribbean theatre, north of Puerto Rico, adding a twelfth U-Boat to the group in the area. Immediately to the east of the theatre four U-Boats, U359, U406, U466 and U662 were closing in to bring the numbers up to sixteen, but before this group could join another U-Boat would die.

On July fourteenth the US Navy issued a warning to all pilots operating in the Caribbean theatre about the fact that the U-Boats were now staying on the surface to fight it out with aircraft. Unfortunately, the warning did not say anything about not attacking until the pilot had the tactical advantage. This meant that the pilots were just told that they would have to fight the U-Boats. This was a pity because if there was one area where the pilots could easily call for support, it was the Caribbean.

The entire area was now ringed by airfields and there were hundreds of aeroplanes dedicated to anti-submarine work. However the pilots of ZP-51 were also warned that they were excluded from the coming battle, because their airships were far too slow to attempt combat against the heavy U-Boat armament. None of the pilots in the Caribbean theatre had as yet come upon a U-Boat that would put up a good fight and the warning was not taken too seriously. This was unfortunately reinforced by the ease with which the first attack was carried out. The U-Boat was the U159 and the squadron was VP-32, operating out of Guantanamo Bay.

Beckmann must have been aware that the last couple of U-Boats that operated off the Panama area had drawn a blank, and he wanted to hang around the central Caribbean for a while, to see if he could sink some ships out of the frequent convoys. But he was not aware that the Americans knew where he was. Since July twelfth, U159 had been sighted and this had been confirmed by several other observers as well as regular radar contact. He was targeted and VP-32 began flying regular anti-submarine sweeps of the area south of Haiti.

On July fifteenth the sea in the northern Caribbean was rough, with a heavy haze reducing visibility to six miles, when Mariner P-10 piloted by Lt. R.C. Mayo took off from Guantanamo. Mayo was an experienced pilot, who had already carried out a good attack on U527 on June twenty-third. He took his sea grey camouflaged aircraft up to three thousand feet and in five tenths cloud began his patrol. Shortly after takeoff, the aircraft's radar went unserviceable and Mayo continued on a visual search.

At twelve fourteen Lt. jg. W.J. Zepp, the aircrafts co-pilot, drew Mayo's attention to an object off the aircraft's starboard bow. The pilot dipped the nose of the machine for a better view and saw the long shape of the U-Boat battling through the heavy seas, about four miles away. Mayo immediately rolled the big flying boat to the right, while calling for full mixture. The aircraft commenced a steep diving attack and the pilot called for the bomb bay doors to be opened, while he unlocked the racks from the cockpit. Almost immediately U159 opened fire and anti-aircraft shells began exploding ahead of the starboard engine. At one thousand feet, the pilot eased his steep rate of descent and began his run in. The U-Boat's anti-aircraft shells began passing over the machine, as the gunners under-estimated the rate of descent and the aircraft's speed. At eight hundred yards, the aircraft's bow gunner opened fire and raked the U-Boat all the way in, but the U-Boat's return fire continued to pass over the Mariner. When the aircraft was two hundred yards from the boat, the anti-aircraft fire ceased and the Mariner bored in unopposed.

Aircraft P-10 was at fifty feet and doing nearly two hundred knots when it passed directly over the U-Boat's conning tower. The aircraft was so low that the pilot looked downwards and distinctly made out the shape of the Biscay Cross aerial on the conning tower. The tail gunner called out the fall of the depth-charges so that the pilot could assess his attack. The first and second charges were short on the U-Boat's port side, while the third charge actually hit the deck and bounced overboard. The fourth landed just off the boat's starboard bow. Seconds later, the charges began detonating, throwing huge columns of water upwards that totally obscured the U-Boat.

Mayo began hauling his aircraft round to the left, intending to carry out a straffing run, but by the time the spray cleared, they could see the U-Boat going down stern first. By the time the big Mariner could get back to the scene, only the depth-charge scum was visible. It is probable that the third depth-charge opened up the pressure hull just aft of the conning tower and the fourth finished off the vessel. There were no survivors from U159 and as the wreck sank into two thousand three hundred fathoms, those still alive would have been crushed, long before the boat reached the bottom. U159 had come back to the area of its greatest triumph to die.

Bubbles kept coming to the surface for an hour after the U-Boat sank and Mayo stayed in the area one hundred and twenty miles south of Point a Gravois Haiti, for the next seven hours. Surprisingly, he was censured for remaining over the scene of the sinking too long. The Staff felt that in the absence of wreckage, the pilot should have used gambit tactics. There was no mention of the fact that a PC was operating only sixty miles away. The PC could have been called in to help, or other aircraft from Guantanamo

could have been called in, but the attack on U159 had been out of the textbook and they were not to know at this stage that no other U-Boat in the
Caribbean would die as quickly or as cleanly as U159. When P-10 turned for
home there wasn't a single bullet hole in the aircraft.

As a very poor consolation for the loss of U159, Kummetat in U572
sank the schooner Gilbert B. Walters, seventy miles southeast of Galeota
Point in Trinidad. His signal to U-Boat Command could not dispel the
gloom, because the radio traffic concerning the sinking of U159 had been
picked up in Germany. There was however some consolation, because just
as Trinidad was beginning to settle down, Kapitsky upset the defenders
again.

He brought U615 down from the area of the Anegada Passage and
came snooping along Trinidad's north coast. When he came to the Third
Boca, Kapitsky turned U615 inwards. First the operators ashore picked up
the propeller noises from the sonobuoys and then HMS Benbow reported
a loop crossing. Kapitsky had brought U615 in through the Boca. He was
merely having a look at the inner harbour and within a few minutes he had
turned and moved out again, but the fat was really in the fire. The harbour
was still packed with invasion shipping and the defenders reacted vigorously.
The flap caused by U572's visit had not died down as yet and Trinidad was
still on the full alert caused by the double convoy action of a week before.

Every patrol vessel and aircraft was involved in the search of the Gulf
of Paria that followed. For the first time in more than a year, the Royal
Navy stopped training at Piarco and allocated its aircraft to the search. The
situation was not eased by a report that came in from a VP-205 Mariner at
five twenty that afternoon.

P-10 of VP-32 had used up all the luck and when the VP-205 Mariner
attacked U415 northeast of Trinidad, the aircraft got a hot reception.
Similar to the VP-32 attack, the pilot of the VP-205 Mariner had barrelled
into the attack as soon as he saw the U-Boat. The gunners on U415 were
better and they held their fire until the Mariner was only three hundred
yards away and then subjected it to a storm of twenty millimetre shells.
The aircraft continued its attack, but the anti-aircraft fire was too heavy for
an accurate run and the depth-charges exploded out of lethal range. Each
time the pilot tried to set up another attack, he was greeted by very accurate fire that damaged the machine. At this stage it was too late to call for
help, because the Mariner could not remain in the area in its heavily damaged condition. As the pilot eased his badly damaged machine homeward,
Neide took U415 away from the scene of the action.

July fifteenth had been an action packed day in the Caribbean theatre, but once again the emphasis was swinging back to the mid Atlantic. Friday sixteenth was to see the death of one of the Caribbean Aces. Muller-Stockheim had left his station northeast of Antigua on the eleventh and begun his long run homeward. Five days later he was approaching the area where the U Tankers normally carried out their operations. He had been told that they would not be able to refuel his boat on the way home, but no U-Boat commander could pass up the chance to rendezvous with a U Tanker, even for news.

He had no idea what a deadly trap the area had become and was just as surprised as all the other unfortunate commanders, when U67's lookouts picked up the approaching Avengers. The aircraft were from VC-13 operating off the carrier USS Core. An Avenger flown by Lt. Robert Williams dropped one of the new anti-submarine homing torpedoes which followed U67 as it crash-dived. They were very lucky to get the wreck back to the surface where it came under attack by the other aircraft. Only three of the U-Boats crew survived the destruction of the Caribbean veteran. Muller-Stockheim died that day, on his way home from his fourth Caribbean cruise. His total tonnage still stood at seventy-two thousand seven hundred and thirty-seven, because he had not been able to add to it on this final cruise. His was also the eighth operational U-Boat to be lost in this Caribbean assault.

By the following day, U-Boat Command were still not aware that the tanker U487 had been sunk, but they were beginning to suspect that something was very wrong. U130, U133, U188, U527 and U648, had been searching for U487 for four days without success and the situation was getting desperate. U188 and U648 were outbound boats that needed fuel to get to their operational areas, but the other three were all on their way home and they were short of fuel. They had all stayed in their operating areas as long as possible, secure in the knowledge that fuel was available at the mid Atlantic rendezvous to get them home. U-Boat Command could not wait too long, but they decided to hang on for a further twenty-four hours, in the hope that during that time the tanker would call up.

On Sunday eighteenth, the time was up and U-Boat Command were forced to make a decision. The tanker U487 had not shown up or answered any of the numerous radio calls. The first signal that went out announced that neither the Type IX nor the Type VII boats could expect refuelling outbound. This decision effectively spelled the end of the build up for the Caribbean offensive. It meant that only the Type VII boats that had already refuelled could continue with their Caribbean deployment.

The great plan to switch the combined weight of the U-Boat offensive to the Caribbean instead of the hazardous North Atlantic, virtually died before it had a chance to begin, but worse was to come. The second signal that went out cancelled the operational orders for U155, U160 and U648 and called on these boats to become tankers, to get the others home. They were unaware that U160 had been sunk four days previously, but the fact that the U-Boat did not acknowledge the signal, was an indication that she had also gone. At one stroke, not only had the Caribbean deployment been stopped, but the three boats of the reinforcement wave who were already at sea, were diverted from the operation to become tankers. Actually, there wasn't very much else that could be done. The U Tankers were critical to the Caribbean, Brazilian and South African operations and the loss of three tankers in quick succession was bound to spell disaster.

The task of finding and getting U527 home from the Caribbean was given to Stahl in U648. Uhlig was coming across the Atlantic with the bare minimum fuel to get him to the tanker rendezvous and it was essential that someone meet him. Piening in U155 was given the task of bringing the other boats home. Relief would come in time, because as soon as U462 was repaired she would try the Bay of Biscay again. Additionally U117, U459 and U461 were hurriedly being replenished so that they could be brought out, but none of the replacement tankers would be ready in time to bring home the operational boats waiting in mid Atlantic. The boats that were in the Caribbean were now on their own.

CHAPTER

17

Caribbean crisis

Up to the middle of the month of July 1943, thirty U-Boats had been committed to the Caribbean offensive, of which eight had already been sunk and four had been turned back through damage or conversion to emergency tankers. Many other boats that had been earmarked for the Caribbean had also been scratched from the battle order by the various restrictions imposed on U-Boats sailings, because of the Biscay crisis. This left only eighteen U-Boats to continue the task originally intended for the many. Their job had been to bring shipping in the Caribbean to a standstill, but this was not happening.

On July sixteenth, Uphoff in U84 had worked his way well west of Jamaica and up into the entrance to the Gulf of Mexico, where he fired at a merchant ship. He claimed a hit and is said to have left the vessel burning, but no vessel is reported to have been hit in this area.

Two days later Kummetat in U572 was operating one hundred miles southeast of Galeota, when he attacked two freighters. He also claimed both ships as sunk, but there is no record of such losses. Three days later Uphoff once again attacked with U84. By this time he was well up into the Gulf of Mexico, but again no kill is recorded. Neither boat survived and as such it is impossible to determine what happened, but these were the only claims submitted for all the boats in the theatre. Instead of the merchant ship sinkings that U-Boat Command wanted, the U-Boats were becoming entangled in some fearsome battles against the defending aircraft.

The first boat to get itself into serious trouble was U134, operating in the Florida Straits under Brosin's command. As darkness fell on the evening of July eighteenth, the US Navy airship K74 picked up the U-Boat and ran in to attack. The pilot of the airship Commander Nelson R. Grills, ignored all the warnings to airship crew about their slow ungainly craft not being able to survive against U-Boats that were fighting back, and took his airship over U134 in a bombing run.

At the critical moment the bombs failed to release, making it even easier for the U-Boat's anti-aircraft gunners. K74 was ripped apart by the twenty millimetre fire and one of the crew was killed when it crashed into the sea. But the airship had called for help before attacking.

A short while later, a land-based bomber came boring in, but the U-Boat's gunners were still flushed with success and they easily drove the aircraft off with heavy accurate anti-aircraft fire. Brosin should have taken U134 down after his double success, but he stayed on the surface and as the elation wore off, the lookouts relaxed.

Without any visual warning or alarm from the metox, an aircraft was on them. The Navy Ventura planted three depth-charges under the U-Boat's bow and was gone before the gunners could react. The explosions rocked the U-Boat and the shock wave did a considerable amount of damage. When Brosin got the full damage report, he realized that the batteries had been cracked by the great hammering that his boat had sustained. He signalled U-Boat headquarters to say that he would have to pull back through the Bahamas for repairs.

The following day provided a number of shocks for both the U-Boats and the defending pilots. Except for the K74 experience in the far northwest, and the attack by the solitary Mariner on U415, the pilots of the Caribbean anti-submarine squadrons looked to the sinking of U159 as their model attack and still thought in terms of catching U-Boats in the act of diving. The nineteenth of July was to change these ideas completely.

At ten minutes past ten in the morning, a B24 Liberator of the 35th bomber squadron operating out of Zandery, spotted a U-Boat on the surface two hundred and twenty miles east of Cayenne. The pilot immediately rolled the machine into an attack dive, racing to get to the boat before it could disappear underwater.

On U662, the gunners were ready and the aircraft pilot was shocked to see a veritable wall of tracer coming at him. He broke off the attack and circled, waiting for the U-Boat to dive, but U662 remained on the surface. For thirty mintues the B24 pilot tried various combinations of attack to try and force the boat to dive, but each time the long streams of tracer blocked his moves. Eventually, he decided to ignore the anti-aircraft fire and go in.

The B24 planted four Mk-44 depth-charges in the sea short of the U-Boat, but the anti-aircraft fire tore it apart. As the pilot pulled out of his attack dive he was aware that even though the B24 could take heavy punishment, his craft did not feel fully serviceable. One engine was on fire and all the propellers had been damaged. The controls to the tail felt very sluggish and in fact the tail of the aircraft had taken a considerable beating. The B24 pilot was forced to abandon his efforts and head for home.

The depth-charge explosions had not harmed U662 and the only problem they noticed was that the boat was leaving a slight trace of oil. This was the second occasion that a U-Boat had stayed on the surface to fight with the aircraft and it shocked the aircrew, but more was to come.

Three hours later a B18 bomber of the 417th squadron operating out of Gallion Field in French Guiana, came upon the same U-Boat, in roughly the same position. The B18 pilot immediately went barrelling in for a depth-charge attack, but again U662 was ready. The aeroplane was greeted by intense anti-aircraft fire and after taking some strikes on the machine, the pilot was forced to sheer off.

The B18 began to circle the U-Boat, trying to get it at an angle where the spread of depth-charges would do most good. Eventually the bomber pilot found himself committed to an attack run, with the U-Boat in an unfavourable position. Five depth-charges went down, but none of them were near enough to the U-Boat to do any damage, − not so the aircraft.

While the pilot fought to keep his crippled machine airborne, Muller chose his moment and U662 crash-dived. Even if Muller had kept his boat on the surface, there wasn't much that the pilot could have done because all his attention was concentrated on getting his heavily damaged machine home. But Monday the nineteenth of July was not yet over.

VP-205 had already experienced its baptism in the attack on U415. Now it was the turn of its sister squadron VP-204. This was the only Caribbean anti-submarine squadron whose aircraft were equipped with the Leigh Light for precision night attacks.

At nine fifteen that evening, Lt.jg. John M. Erskine picked up a radar contact two hundred and ten miles east of Tobago. Erskine ran in towards the target and sighted a U-Boat visually, but the boat also had the aircraft visual and crash-dived before the Mariner could get into position. Erskine turned his Mariner away from the scene of the attack and commenced gambit tactics, which were designed to give the impression that he had left the area.

At five minutes past ten, he again had a radar contact and the Mariner swept back in. This time Erskine came upon the U-Boat on the surface, running with its decks awash. The U-Boat was Kummetat's U572 and the U-Boat commander had no intention of diving a second time. As the Mariner swept down towards the U-Boat the crew were startled at the volume of anti-aircraft fire that rose to greet them. Erskine sheered off to avoid the lines of tracer that were converging on his machine. Despite its deep sea grey camouflage, the U-Boat's gunners appeared to have no difficulty in tracking the big flying boat, and even as Erskine circled the boat, tracer kept curling up at him.

The pilot was eager to get this U-Boat and after five minutes of sparring, he turned his Mariner in for an attack run. Erskine gallantly held his course and speed, despite the deadly twenty millimetre shells that were now converging on him, but when the explosive rounds began hammering the aircraft, it threw his aim off.

The three Mk-44 Torpex filled depth-charges fell away towards the sea, but Kummetat had increased speed and altered course to starboard. With the U-Boat's stern facing the aircraft, the boat's gunners were able to hammer the flying boat all the way in and through its attack run.

The charges exploded harmlessly to the left of the boat and U572 was safe, but the Mariner was in trouble. There were holes in the flying boat's hull and some explosive shells had buried themselves in the wing root. Shell splinters riddled the tanks in the aircraft's starboard wing and fuel began pouring out. There was a distinct possibility of fire and the pilot had to jettison the remaining depth-charges and shut down the starboard engine, as the Mariner set course for Chaguaramas.

These three incidents in one day provided a considerable shock for the aircrew in the Trinidad Sector. The sinking of U159 had been made to look so easy that the crews had been lulled into a false sense of security, believing that this new fight-back tactic by the U-Boats was only an added nuisance which could easily be overcome.

For a very long time anti-submarine crews had looked on themselves as hunters of wily game, but now they were hunting ferocious wild animals who could hurt them. Now they were truly combat pilots, but in reality the U-Boat gunners had the advantage.

The big flying boats were not fast agile machines and they presented excellent targets to the gunners, as they steadied on their run in. The enhanced twenty millimetre armament of the U-Boats was more than a match for the machines and this changed the nature of anti-submarine warfare. In fairness to the American pilots, they got over the initial shock quickly and modified their tactics.

Few of them took the safe sensible course of declining combat and calling for support, but they modified their attack procedure, so that they could take evasive action on the run in. There wasn't too much that a large flying-boat could do in the way of violent manoeuvres, but the pilots did skid and jink their aircraft out of the streams of glowing tracer and used considerable stealth while stalking the U-Boats. Choosing the right moment to attack became an art and the pilots learned to spar with the U-Boats until they achieved the tactical advantage. The aircrew braced themselves for a bitter struggle and prepared to take casualties in order to get the U-Boats. They did not have long to wait for the next trial of strength, but once more the boldness of a U-Boat commander shocked them.

At eight forty-five on the night of July twentieth Lt. Cmdr. Morgan in command of a VP-204 Mariner, was on patrol two hundred miles east southeast of Barbados, when his radar picked up a contact close to a tanker. Kurt Neide in command of U415 was stalking the American tanker SS Schenectady on the surface, when his lookouts detected the aircraft coming in. The U-Boat commander had enough time to dive safely and get away from the area, but this would have meant an intolerable delay in catching up with the tanker. Instead he decided to bluff.

A number of lights were hurriedly brought up to the conning tower and turned on with crewmen also showing lights at the bow and stern. For a while the pilot was fooled into believing that what he was seeing was in reality two merchant ships instead of a U-Boat stalking a tanker. He eased out of his attack run and circled the area, but he was puzzled because the second group of lights appeared to be very low on the water.

After circling for a few minutes, Morgan decided to climb up and drop a flare. In the glare of the brightly burning pyrotechnic, he recognized the shape of a U-Boat playing possum and immediately rolled his machine into an attack dive. To his astonishment, he was illuminated by a searchlight and saw streams of tracer arcing upwards. The pilot twisted his machine out of the glare of the light and broke away to get his aeroplane into a more favourable attacking position.

Neide probably used a signal lamp or some such device as his improvised searchlight and as soon as he had forced the Mariner to break off, he took U415 down. Eventually Morgan got the flying boat back over the position where the U-Boat had disappeared and dropped a single depth-charge, but U415 was well away and deep. Many hours later the aircraft picked up a disappearing radar contact in the same area. On his return to Chaguaramas Morgan was able to ask the question, who said that U-Boats don't carry searchlights? His experiences that night were able to add another fascinating tale to VP-204's growing dictionary of U-Boat tactics. A spin off of the night's activity was that Neide did not get the tanker.

While Kurt Neide outfoxed VP-204, five hundred miles to the southeast Muller in U662 was engaging in a deadly duel with the PBYs of VP-94, — a conflict that the flying boat squadron would win. Muller had taken his boat southwards and was operating one hundred and fifty miles off the French Guiana Brazil border, in the same area where U590 had been lost ten days before.

At eleven o'clock on the night of the twentieth a white camouflaged PBY of VP-94, operating out of the Northern Brazilian base of Belem picked up U662 on radar. The pilot had no hesitation in swinging straight into an attack, and Muller in command of the boat had no qualms about his ability to beat off the aircraft. He had proved it twice already against the 35th and 417th bomber squadrons and this PBY made an even bigger target. But the pilot of the Catalina had no intention of being clawed out of the sky.

As soon as the anti-aircraft fire started coming up at him, he sheered off and began circling the U-Boat. He kept this up for one hour, making feint attacks and drawing fire before pulling away. The U-Boat's guns spat defiance putting up a deadly wall of fire, but the PBY pilot kept evading it.

Eventually, when the pilot figured he had exhausted the gunners' patience and worn them out, he converted a feint into a serious attack. On the run in, the flying boat's bow machine gunner kept up a steady fire at the U-Boat's conning tower and he was joined by the waist gunners as the range closed. The U-Boat gunners knew instinctively that they had to beat off this attack, regardless of how worn out they were.

Twenty millimetre cannon shells were hitting the aircraft, but the pilot held his course and kept boring in. The depth-charges went in just ahead of the U-Boat's bows. While the pilot fought his damaged machine away from the boat, the depth-charges exploded. The explosions were almost under the U-Boat's bows and damage was extensive, but at this stage the damage was not important because the U-Boat was still operational.

The exhausted PBY pilot turned his damaged machine for VP-94's home base at Belem, nearly five hundred miles away. Some of his crew were wounded and his main concern now was to get them home. He was disappointed that he had failed to sink the U-Boat, but he had no idea just how hard he had hit U662, nor did he know that he had exposed a fatal flaw in the U-Boat's fight back concept. In fact he had prepared U662 for destruction.

The PBY's radio signal describing his attack generated an immediate reaction at Belem. Another PBY from VP-94 was quickly scrambled with orders to go straight to the reported attack position. VP-94 wanted that U-Boat. U662 was now targeted.

Muller's radio signal to U-Boat headquarters, dispatched right after the flying boat set off for home, was almost a cry of panic. The depth-charge damage was negligible, but the machine gun fire from the PBY had destroyed the metox equipment on the conning tower. He could no longer pick up the vital radar transmissions of the hunters, but even this was not important.

What really worried Muller was the fact that U662 had used up nearly all of its anti-aircraft ammunition. In the 1943 Caribbean environment anti-aircraft ammunition was vital. Near the end of his duel with the PBY, he had been forced to allow the attacking machine to get very close before opening fire. Without the metox to warn of approaching aircraft he could not safely dive in time, which automatically meant that he would have to fight. But without enough ammunition, he could not hope to keep the aircraft at bay.

The already overcrowded U-Boats could carry only so much anti-aircraft ammunition and no more. The automatic anti-aircraft weapons on the U-Boats used up phenomenal quantities of ammunition and in fact, the boats could not carry enough to keep the weapons fed. This meant that they could fight back, but only for a limited time. U662 had fought three long duels and won all of them, but now she was virtually defenceless.

The reply from U-Boat headquarters was almost a censure. In the first place U662 was ordered to move north immediately into its proper operating area. Muller had strayed too far south and he had U662 almost in the Brazilian theatre of operations. The fact that he had been attacked by aircraft operating from Brazil was proof of this.

As a longer term solution to U662's plight, the boat was ordered to rendezvous with U516, at the eastern extremity of the Caribbean theatre opposite Trinidad. The rendezvous was fixed for July thirtieth and U516 would hand over a metox set and twelve hundred rounds of twenty millimetre ammunition. The Type IXC U516 was under its new commander Hans Rutger Tillessen and outbound for its operating area off South Africa.

U-Boat Command ordered the boat to refuel and then make for the rendez-vous point. After the transfer, U516 was to return home, while U662 was to move back into its operating area off Trinidad.

The attack by the PBY was causing considerable disruption. When it is realized that each barrel on U662 fired at the rate of six hundred rounds per minute and the boat had four weapons, then twelve hundred rounds was indeed a paltry amount, but U516 had to go home through the Bay of Biscay. However, U662 did not make that rendezvous and this caused U516 to be drawn into the Caribbean theatre to become the thirty-first U-Boat committed to the operation.

In the early hours of Wednesday twenty-first of July, Heinz Muller turned U662 northward and set off at his best speed to get away from the land and its dreaded aircraft. U662 had a lot of time to stay out of trouble between when it set off and the thirtieth of the month. Muller was unaware that at that moment doom was approaching in the form of another PBY from VP-94.

At four minutes past five in the morning, just as the first glow of dawn was lightening the eastern sky, the second PBY from VP-94 found U662. The boat was racing north, but it had only covered about sixty miles from the site of its last duel with the first PBY. The conning tower watch probably picked up the flying-boat against the dark background in the west, but there was not much they could do. It was too late to dive safely, yet they didn't have enough ammunition to make this aircraft keep its distance.

Muller was on the conning tower and he ordered the gunners to hold their fire until the last possible moment and use what little anti-aircraft ammunition they had to throw the pilot off his aim. The PBY came in fast and at the last moment the U-Boat's gunners put up a withering hail of shells, but the pilot held his course. Three Mk-44 depth-charges left the underwing racks and plummeted into the sea right alongside U662's pressure hull. As the pilot hauled his damaged flying boat upwards, the charges detonated and U662 was finished. The end came swiftly and the aircraft crew could see the U-Boat's bow pointing straight upwards as it sank below the waves.

After the Hamburg built boat had slipped out of sight, the pilot of the PBY came in over the spot and sighted three survivors swimming among the debris. A liferaft was dropped to them and the aircraft crew watched as the three shocked survivors hauled themselves in. After this the PBY turned for its distant base, because there were wounded crew aboard who needed urgent medical attention. VP-94 had killed its second U-Boat of the offensive and U662 was the ninth to be lost in this Caribbean venture.

The wreck of U662 sank into almost twelve thousand feet of water and death must have come quickly to the crew members trapped aboard. Long before it reached the seabed the hull would have been crushed, but there was to be no quick end for the survivors. The fire from the PBY and the blast of the depth-charges going off close aboard had killed most of the conning tower watch and the gunners. Kapitanleutnant Muller, a Petty Officer and one of the lookouts were hurled into the sea and it was these three who crawled into the liferaft.

Had the Caribbean Theatre been relatively quiet, strenuous efforts would have been made to rescue them, if only for the intelligence information that the US Navy could have gleaned, but the Caribbean was not quiet.

The U-Boats were out in force and every unit was occupied in fighting them off. The battle between the U-Boats and the defending forces was building towards its climax and the survivors had to fend for themselves. They started off nearly eight hundred miles from Trinidad, with the current slowly carrying them northwest. Eleven days later a Liberator from Zandery sighted the survivors and radioed the report to Trinidad.

The destroyer USS Abbot was dispatched from Chaguaramas to try and find them, but the ship returned empty-handed. The dinghy was not very far offshore, but both wind and current were keeping it roughly the same distance off the South American land mass. They had neither water nor food and it became an epic of endurance. Rain water from the frequent thunderstorms in that area no doubt helped, but it became an epic of survival.

Then on August sixth a Liberator of the 8th anti-submarine squadron escorting convoy TJ-4, sighted the raft three hundred miles southeast of Trinidad. The destroyer USS Siren was detached and shortly afterwards she reached the area. The two survivors were too weak to stand and had to be lifted out of the raft. The young seaman had died many days before and been buried from the raft. The remaining two had survived seventeen days in an open raft, while it drifted for five hundred miles. According to the peculiar usage of war, Muller now had to be clothed, fed and brought back to good health, before being ground down again under interrogation.

At the start of the third week of July there were fifteen U-Boats in the Caribbean theatre. Brosin had U134 just outside the Bahamas, where his engineers were trying to repair the damage caused by the Ventura. He never did go back into the dangerous Straits of Florida. Uphoff had U84 off the western end of Cuba, preparing to try conclusions with the well escorted convoys of the Gulf of Mexico. Carlsen in U732 and Freidrich in U759, were trying vainly to penetrate the heavily escorted convoys in the Windward Passage. Both boats were being constantly harassed from the air and reporting that they could detect nonstop radar transmissions from the land.

Dalhous in U634 had been having a rough time in his position south of Puerto Rico. He also reported continuous radar transmission from the land. He was forced to ignore them, but in fact these were the air search sets in the Mona Passage being used for surface search and they were tracking his movements. Within a few days the air activity was such that he was forced to move U634 westwards to the area south of Hispaniola. Even in this area, he had to be constantly on guard against the PBYs of VP-81 and the Venturas of VB-141, working out of Puerto Rico.

North of the islands Markworth was chasing the American tanker Cherry Blossom which he caught on the twenty-second, only to be surprised two days later by the US based Mariner. With heavy casualties he was forced to turn away from the theatre and make a run for the tanker where a doctor would be available.

Kapitsky had now brought U615 westwards into its operating area off Aruba and Curacao. He was to spend most of his patrol in this area and only achieve one kill, because airpower ensured that he could not get near the convoys that passed through. The Liberators of the 8th bomber squadron based in the twin islands were almost always overhead and the surface escorts were extra vigilant.

The aircraft of the 5th bomber squadron based at Coolidge Field, were checking on a report of a U-Boat east of Antigua and indeed, Forster in U359 was three hundred miles out. He was coming in on the latitude of Antigua, intending to slip through the seldom used passage between Antigua and Guadeloupe, to reach his operating area south of the Mona Passage.

Further south Kurt Neide in U415 and Kummetat in U572 were surviving off Trinidad. The two boats were operating in the dangerous waters off Trinidad's north and east coasts. They were forced to remain submerged almost all the time, surfacing only for short periods at night to charge their batteries. They were not achieving any success at all, because the merchant shipping in the area was heavily escorted and there was nonstop air activity.

Additionally, there were a number of US Navy and TRNVR hunter-killer groups operating independently around Trinidad. There were simply not enough U-Boats to spread the anti-submarine forces out, so that any sighting or radar contact was exhaustively investigated.

Further southeast Horst Dietrichs in U406 had moved into the area off the coast of British Guiana. Alongside him Albrecht Kandler was working U653 off the coast of Dutch Guiana and Hagenskotter in U466 was off the French Guiana coast. These three boats lay across the inshore bauxite route to Trinidad, while Eick in U510 sat further offshore where he was on the route that ran along the hundred fathom line.

Coming south down the central Atlantic was Tillesen in U516 racing for his rendezvous with U662, the boat which no longer existed. The entire strip from Trinidad to the French Guiana Brazil border was aflame with vicious air sea combats. It was an exciting time for the defenders, but a grim experience for the U-Boats. The only thing that they were achieving was the tying down of anti-submarine resources, but at a terrible cost.

Beyond the border of French Guiana, there were eight U-Boats assigned to the enormous length of the Brazilian coastline. U172, U185, U193, U199, U513, U591, U598 and U604 were in combat with the many defenders of the coastline of this large South American Republic. They were being hunted relentlessly and indeed the first one had already died. On July nineteenth the redoubtable VP-74 had caught U513 at the latitude of Rio de Janeiro and sent it to the bottom. Very few of the Brazilian boats were going to survive the traumatic months of July and August.

Throughout the second half of July and into August, U-Boat Command was suffering from a lack of reliable intelligence information. The period was characterised by numerous signals going out to boats that no longer existed. They had no way of knowing what was taking place in the Bay of Biscay, in mid Atlantic, in the Caribbean and off Brazil. They could only assume that the boats were surviving and like a general who could not see the battlefield, operate in an environment that was sometimes weeks out of date.

On July twenty-first, they finally found out about the American carriers operating off the Azores. Only then were they able to make some assumptions about the fate of the boats which were not answering. The report came from Spain, where a merchant ship docked and reported that they had seen the carriers in the Azores. This was confirmed by a U-Boat report that came in on the twenty-fourth.

In the meantime they sent out a signal to all boats warning them to avoid an area that stretched from the Canary Islands in the south, out to the Azores and in on the latitude of northern Spain. This considerable area lay right across the normal U-Boat transit route and they were now re-routing the boats around the western side of the Azores. Boats that had to use the restricted area were warned to exercise extreme caution, but it was already too late for some.

Uhlig was coming northeast across the Atlantic and was right in the danger area when the signal went out. Two days later he was caught by the Avengers of VC-9 operating off the USS Bogue and the tenth U-Boat to be lost in the Caribbean offensive went down to the ocean floor, just south of the Azores.

U527 joined U67 as the first two boats to be lost on their way home from the Caribbean offensive of July 1943. This meant that both the U-Boats that U648 had been tasked to bring home had been sunk, even before they could find their tanker escort. U648 was wasted. She might have achieved something if she had continued to the Caribbean.

The American carrier groups in mid Atlantic were lending considerable tangible support to the defenders in the Caribbean area. Up to July twenty-third they had turned back U758 and forced U155 and U648 to be removed from the battle order. Additionally, they had sunk U67, U160 and U527. These six extra boats might well have helped the Germans to achieve the concentration they needed to break through the convoy escorts in the Caribbean. But their contribution was by no means over, because many of the fifteen boats actually in the Caribbean theatre had to go home and the carriers would be waiting.

Further north, U-Boat Command was striving to find a solution to the chaotic tanker situation, caused in part by the relentless RAF pressure in the Bay of Biscay and the American carriers in mid Atlantic. There were a large number of U-Boats operating in the North and South Atlantic who would start coming home at the end of July. These boats had to have tanker support, which meant that U-Boat Command had to find a way to get their U Tankers out of the Bay of Biscay and then into new safe havens in the Atlantic.

The first attempt was made on July twenty-second when three tankers, the U117, U459 and U461 sailed out of Bordeaux, escorted not by the usual minesweepers, but a powerful force of destroyers. It was intended to fight these tankers through the Bay. However the destroyers could only accompany the U-Boats for a part of the way, otherwise British surface forces would move in behind them and cut them off from their bases. The RAF could operate right out to the limits of the Bay of Biscay.

The problems started almost as soon as the operation began. The tanker U461 was leaving a trail of oil from a cracked fuel tank and it was impossible for the boat to remain undetected in the hostile Atlantic environment. Vowe had no alternative but to turn back and this left just U117 and U459 to make the dash. It wasn't long before the RAF detected the two tankers and their destroyer escort and they held back, waiting to see how far out the destroyers would go. The destroyers escorted the two boats out to their safe limit and bidding the boats good luck, turned to race back to their bases. Three days after sailing, on the night of July twenty-fourth the

RAF came at the U Tankers, four hundred miles from their base.

Wellington Q of No. 172 squadron came in against U459. This was the same squadron which had destroyed Bauer's old boat U126. The U tankers carried a heavier than usual anti-aircraft armament and as soon as the attacking bomber was detected, the gunners put up a deadly barrage of twenty millimetre shells. The Wellington was mortally hit, but in a most unusual circumstance, it crashed onto the U tanker. The wreck of the aircraft smashed the U-Boat's anti-aircraft gunners platform and came to rest on fire, along the U-Boat's deck. The only survivor of the aircraft's crew was the tail gunner, who was rescued from the inferno by the U-Boat's crew.

They set to work putting out the fire, which they succeeded in doing but then made a chilling discovery. Two of the aircraft's depth-charges were lying on the U-Boat's deck and both were armed. The charges were set to explode at a depth of twenty-five feet, as were all aircraft depth-charges. They could not be simply rolled off the deck because they would destroy the boat.

The U tanker's crew embarked on the highly dangerous procedure of rolling the charges to the stern and then letting them slide off, while the U-Boat was going as fast as it could. In theory, a Type XIV U Tanker at twelve knots could progress forty feet away from the charges before they reached their operating depth. Again in theory, the U-Boat should be out of lethal range at this distance.

It didn't work that way for U459. Either the charges were not at the extreme stern when they were rolled off, or one of the charges exploded prematurely. The tanker was crippled and unable to dive. Von Willamowitz Mollendorf knew that he was too far out in the Bay to attempt the run back in with a damaged boat which was unable to dive, and there was no survival in the Atlantic.

The old warrior decided to scuttle the boat. U459 had been the original U tanker that began operations with its refuelling of U108 for the Caribbean in 1942. The crew and the survivors from the aircraft paddled away from the U Tanker, watching the old commander waving farewell to them from the conning tower. He personally set the scuttling charges and went down with the boat. Of the three U tankers that set out only U117 got out of the Bay of Biscay, but this was enough to provide some relief.

While Mollendorf was ending a U-Boat career that spanned two world wars in a dramatic fashion, another U-Boat commander of a much younger generation was finally acknowledging that the United States forces had come of age and indeed, he conceded defeat.

Hagenskotter in U466 arrived off the French Guiana coast on July

twentieth and since that time he had been constantly harassed by the aircraft based at Gallion Field and Zandery. He was considerably put out by
having to dive constantly to escape patrolling aircraft which effectively
stopped him from getting near to the coastal traffic. After four days of this,
he decided to stay on the surface and fight the aircraft. This decision
coincided with the arrival off French Guiana of another of VP-94's PBYs
operating far from its base in the hope of finding targets.

The flying boat pilot sighted U466 one hundred and twenty miles off
the coast. He did not spar with the U-Boat but swung straight into an attack
run. The U-Boat gunners put up the usual fearsome barrage, but the pilot
pressed home his attack. Despite repeated strikes on his aircraft he managed
to place his four depth-charges close to the U-Boat. Hagenskotter altered
course at the last moment and the boat curved away from the tall towers
that marked the exploding charges, but the underwater shock wave damaged
the U-Boat. The PBY pilot circled the U-Boat for a few minutes, but the
condition of his aircraft forced him to break off the action and head for his
home base six hundred miles away.

Hagenskotter had experienced co-ordinated air attacks in the Bay of
Biscay and he knew that under those conditions, pilots would sometimes
face the combined fire of his anti-aircraft battery, but it shocked him to see
a lone aircraft ignore the power of his guns and keep on coming. He was
probably contemplating this while his engineers worked on the damage
caused by the flying-boat.

It was only three hours since the first attack, but enough for U466 to
be targeted in the sector plotting room. Minutes later a shout from the
lookout drew his attention to a black dot on the horizon, that marked
another aircraft coming in. This time he decided to follow the standard
formula and dive.   He had time and he didn't want to take the risk of
another daredevil PBY getting him. The diving alarm sounded and U466
began to go down. The conning tower dipped below the waves a good thirty
seconds before the B18 bomber, out of Zandery crossed.

This was an experienced pilot and he tracked ahead of the swirl in the
direction that U466 had dived and planted his four charges on a dead reckoning position. The U-Boat was directly under the charges when they detonated. The shock was tremendous, smashing equipment and damaging the
hull of the boat. Up above, the B18 pilot noted a large blob of oil rise to
the surface and spread out. Hagenskotter waited until long after darkness
had cloaked the sea before bringing his boat back to the surface.

Throughout that night and into the next morning, the U-Boat's
engineers worked to repair the damage. Hagenskotter was worried because

he was stuck on the surface while these repairs were being carried out and his boat was very vulnerable in a very hostile environment.

It was two thirty in the afternoon when his lookouts detected another air attack developing. As usual, the metox gave no warning, because the Allied pilots had taken to using their radar only for short burst transmissions. There was no time to dive on this occasion and the anti-aircraft gunners began tracking the bomber and bringing up more ammunition.

The machine was a B24 Liberator from the 35th squadron operating out of Zandery and the pilot found U466 right where he had been briefed that it was operating. The U-Boat gunners were not as confident of beating off the attack as they had been on the previous day, but this attack had to be stopped. The pilot of the Liberator was just as determined that his attack should succeed but he was surprised at the volume of Flak coming at him.

He noticed that Hagenskotter had turned U466 broadside on to the attacking aircraft, so that the boat presented the smallest possible target and the gunners had the best field of fire. The pilot pressed on into the teeth of the anti-aircraft fire and he heard his gunners open up with their fifty calibres. When the B24 was almost on the U-Boat, the pilot heard a terrific crash up front and within seconds there was a gale of slipstream blasting past him. Twenty millimetre fire had opened up the nose of the bomber and the shock to the machine had caused the premature release of the depth-charges, but all the aircraft's surviving gunners were hitting back.

The pilot hauled his damaged aircraft upwards and looked back to see the depth-charge explosions just outside lethal range of the U-Boats stern. The aircraft's port outer engine was on fire and there appeared to be a great many holes in the fuselage. After he had feathered the port outer and checked that the wounded crew were being given First Aid, the pilot had another look at the U-Boat. U466 was diving. When last seen the B24 had been on fire and staggering along obviously badly damaged, and that meant that the U-Boat had time to dive.

The B24 pilot saw his chance and while the crew were busy fighting a small fire in the cabin and attending to the wounded, he turned his bomber, with the nose missing, back towards the now defenceless U-Boat. The boat had disappeared by the time he was over the spot, but for good measure he planted a single depth-charge beyond the swirl. The heavily damaged B24 turned for home, with a disappointed pilot at the controls. It would have done him a power of good to be able to see into the control room of U466 and read the signal that was shortly to be sent.

For a while there was mass confusion in the U-Boat's control room as the damage control reports came in and they tended the wounded. The signal that went out to U-Boat headquarters describes the plight of U466. — Quote — "On the twenty-fourth a Liberator fought off in square EP 4327, one engine and tail on fire, — Four bombs on stern, — First Watchkeeping officer and one Rating badly wounded, — Commander, Second Watchkeeping officer and Warrant Quartermaster slightly wounded. — Returning home quickly, — Air activity as in the Bay of Biscay, Day and Night." unquote. No greater compliment could have been paid to the Caribbean aircrews because Biscay was the most dangerous place that the U-Boat crews knew and Hagenskotter did turn U466 homeward. He had been on station in the Caribbean theatre for just four days.

The commander of U466 was not the only one to suffer air attack that day. Nearly every U-Boat in the theatre was forced under or suffered a depth-charge attack, but occasionally there were flashes of extraordinary daring on the part of selected commanders.

Such was the case with Kurt Neide in U415 when he attempted to attack convoy JT-2. The convoy with its ten merchant ships was coming northeast towards Trinidad with an exceptionally heavy escort. Four PCs provided the close in escort with the corvettes USS Courage, Tenacity and the converted anti-submarine yacht Carnelian, working about four miles out from the ships. About ten miles from the convoy a hunting group of four destroyers worked the outer screen. Overhead two Mariners from VP-204 and two from VP-205 covered the four quadrants. What was extraordinary was that Neide should attempt penetrating such a heavy screen, but he was doing it on the surface.

At ten twenty-one that night Mariner P-12 of VP-204, flown by Lt. jg. John Dresbach homed on a contact and discovered U415 on the surface. The boat was running at about fifteen knots and turning sharply to starboard when Dresbach sighted it. He took the Mariner over the U-Boat to draw fire, but U415 did not rise to the bait. Dresbach then took his Mariner outwards in a wide circuit and turned inward for his attack.

The Mariner pilot was shocked by the fact that the U-Boat fired starshell to light him up. Usually it was the aircraft which did the lighting up, but here was a U-Boat commander operating in a very hostile environment, using starshell! By the illumination of the pyrotechnic, the U-Boat's anti-aircraft gunners opened up a fearsome barrage and the Mariner was hit several times. Dresbach held on, but the U-Boat was manoeuvreing at speed and his three depth-charges landed just outside lethal range.

Neide was operating only thirty-eight miles off Galera Point, in water that was only fifty fathoms deep and fighting off a Mariner on the surface. Mariner P-2 also of VP-204 was operating not too far away and they saw the starshell and burst of gunfire, but couldn't home on the U-Boat because of a defective radar. By the time Dresbach and the other Mariner could get back over the area of the attack, U415 had disappeared. The destroyer's hunting group also saw the pyrotechnics and moved in but they could not gain a contact. In lieu of an attack they patrolled the area for the next twenty-four hours, ensuring that Neide could not get near the ships of JT-2.

Throughout the length and breath of the theatre, anti-submarine squadrons were battling with the U-Boats. Aircraft were coming back damaged and with badly wounded crewmen to be rushed to the military hospitals, but not so VP-32. They had destroyed U159 in textbook fashion without harm to either aircraft or crew. On July twenty-sixth they were going to demonstrate the procedure once again in another masterful display of guile and perfect technique, although a confused U-Boat commander was going to help them.

The Type VIIC boat U759 was built by Wilhemshaven Navy Yard during 1942 and handed over to Kapitanleutnant Rudolf Freidrich in August of that year. In March he operated the boat in the North Atlantic without success, following which he was assigned to his second war patrol in the Caribbean. Freidrich had managed to sink a sailing ship and the freighter Maltran, but since then had been constantly under harassment from the air. The US Navy was aware that at least two U-Boats were operating in the Windward Passage and there were four squadrons constantly quartering the area.

In the early morning hours of July twenty-sixth Mariner P-12 of VP-32 took off from Guantanamo Bay piloted by Lt. Ralph Rawson. The aircraft's mission was to conduct an anti-submarine sweep of the Jamaica Channel to clear the zone for convoy TAG-74, which would be entering that area at daylight.

It was a wild night, with a steady thirty knot wind blowing from the east, whipping the sea into a frenzy of white horses. Looking eastwards into a faint quarter moon, the aircraft crew estimated that they could see about three miles, but in all other quadrants the visibility was down to half a mile. It was a very poor night for visual work and even the radar was not at its best with the sea in that condition.

At twelve minutes past three in the morning, the radar operator picked up a contact twenty miles directly south of Navassa Island, and Rawson turned westward to investigate. He did not want to alarm the U-Boat until he was sure of its course and speed and set his course to pass three miles to the north. In an effort to fool the U-Boat he switched his radar to standby, when still five miles from the contact. The Mariner flew past the estimated position of the contact, but none of the crew were able to see it visually.

Rawson took his aircraft westwards and then turned into the faint moonlight, descending to his attack height and commenced a radar guided approach. At eight miles the target disappeared in the clutter, and when overhead the estimated position there was no sign of the U-Boat. Operating close to the sea the radar was picking up the sea returns yet operating high up, it was too wild a night to see the U-Boat visually.

For the next thirty minutes Rawson carried out a series of radar guided runs but each time, he lost the contact when closing in. He decided that the only hope of finding the U-Boat was to use a flare as close as possible to the U-Boat's estimated position. He brought the Mariner up to a height of thirteen hundred feet and commenced a radar guided run. With the radar showing the target one mile distant, there was a shout from a crewman and there below was a broad flat wake, easily discernible against the shorter waves. Rawson released a MK.V. flare upwind of the target and there below was the U-Boat running southeast very fast, leaving its telltale wake.

Down below Freidrich must have been completely fooled. He was depending on the heavy sea to hide him from the air and the movements of the aircraft had probably convinced him that he had not been spotted. First the aircraft had flown right past to the northward. Then on several occasions the aircraft passed right over the boat but no attack was made. Freidrich must have been so confident that he did not apparently consider slowing down, so that his boat did not leave such a prominent wake. Even when the flare ignited above him, he still did not realize that he had been seen and made the critical mistake of diving. This put the U-Boat into its most vulnerable manoeuvre, under a flare with an aircraft attacking.

Rawson could see the U-Boat begin to slow down for its dive and he brought the big blue and grey Mariner round in a descending one eighty degree turn, to get to his attack height. On the run in the U-Boat was going down, but its conning tower was still visible when the Mariner crossed it forty seconds after the start of the attack. It was a perfect run and the four Mk-44 depth-charges straddled the U-Boat at an angle. U759 kept on diving, right down to one thousand fathoms, as in every submariner's nightmare.

The U-Boat left no wreckage and Rawson was only credited with a U-Boat probably damaged, but U759 was the eleventh to be sunk on this renewed offensive. Once again the VP-32 Mariner was untouched. No bullet holes, no wounded crew. The squadron were showing up everyone else.

They were now neck and neck with VP-94, each unit claiming two destroyed. It remained to be seen whether the PBYs or the Mariners would come out on top.

CHAPTER

18

Airpower

The question regarding which was the top anti-submarine squadron operating in the theatre was not left long in doubt. Within two days VP-32 would achieve a remarkable hat trick, but they could not keep up their record of not having an aircraft damaged. They were about to go up against an opponent who could shoot.

U359 had been built during 1942 by Flensburger Schiffsbau and accepted into service with the Kriegsmarine in October of that year. Kapitanleutnant Heinz Forster was appointed its first commanding officer and he took the Type VIIC boat through its exhaustive trials and workup period in the Baltic, after which he sailed to join the 7th Flotilla in St. Nazaire. With the raging bull emblem of the Flotilla painted on his conning tower, Forster took the boat out of St. Nazaire in February 1943 and got involved in the great North Atlantic battle of March. His was one of six U-Boats attacking convoy HX228, but he was not credited with a hit, although he heard detonations and observed a sinking ship.

When U359 departed St. Nazaire at the end of June, it was on its third war patrol, with orders for the sunny Caribbean, where it was expected to play a significant role in the offensive. Heinz Forster was one of the few U-Boat commanders among the boats of July 1943 who was given total freedom of action. He served in the Caribbean as a cadet and was credited with a good knowledge of the area and its merchant shipping. He brought his boat into the Caribbean through the channel between Antigua and Guadeloupe and then set course for the area south of Puerto Rico. No one knows which area of the Caribbean Forster intended to operate in, because he was given little time to put his specialized knowledge of the area to use.

Throughout the previous two weeks Dalhous in U634 had upset the defenders of Puerto Rico by his continuous presence south of the Mona Passage. The anti-submarine squadrons saturated the area with patrols and although they were unable to sink the boat, they forced Dalhous to move westwards to the area south of Hispaniola, so that his crew could get a break from the nerve-wracking tension.

Unknowingly, Forster brought U359 into the area that U634 had vacated and received the hot reception which had been prepared for the other boat. In reply to the continued presence of a U-Boat south of the Mona Passage, VP-32 had moved a detachment from Guantanamo Bay to Naval Air Station San Juan. The PBYs of VP-81 concentrated on patrolling the Anegada Passage and the vast area of water to the north of the island, while the Mariners took over the Mona Passage and its approaches. It was one of these aircraft which caught U359.

At four fifty-two on the evening of July twenty-eighth, Lieutenant junior grade, D.C. Pinholster USNR lifted Mariner P-1 of VP-32 off the waters at NAS San Juan, for an anti-submarine search of the area south of the Mona Passage. He had been briefed that there was a U-Boat in the area, but the radar operators had lost its position during the last few days and they were not able to pin-point where in Pinholster's vast patrol area he might expect to find it.

Pinholster began his search of the area in hazy rough conditions. Two hours later the blue and grey camouflaged flying boat was one hundred and twenty miles south of the Mona Passage, when the radar operator picked up a contact five miles away on the aircraft's port side. Almost at once Pinholster saw the broad wake of a U-Boat running along at the edge of a rain shower.

This was the Caribbean wet season and there were frequent waves of such showers throughout the area, sometimes reducing visibility to zero. The pilot immediately shoved his throttles to full power and as the twin radials built up to their full power, he swung his aircraft into a tight diving left turn to begin an attack. The U-Boat was running at about fifteen knots on an easterly course when the big machine with its pronounced tail dihedral began its diving attack. Fifteen seconds later the U-Boat opened fire. It was almost as if the U-Boat gunners had been waiting for the Mariner to appear.

As soon as the tracer from the U-Boat began to come up, the Mariner's bow machine gunner opened fire, but the range was three miles and the bow guns fell silent when the gunner saw his rounds dropping short. He fired in an automatic reaction to the Flak coming up from the U-Boat. The bow gunner opened up again with his twin fifties, when the range was down to three quarters of a mile and he hosed his rounds onto the U-Boat's conning tower. The port machine gun failed three times on the run in and couldn't be cleared on the third stoppage, but the starboard fifty calibre fired its full belt.

All through the attack run the U-Boat's gunners were firing at the Mariner, but most of the tracer was going over the top of the aircraft. The same thing happened during the attack on U159 and it could be that VP-32's turning diving attack threw the gunners off their aim. Most other anti-submarine squadrons attacked from a long flat run in and they always took considerable punishment from the U-Boats' gunners. On the other hand it could have been the state of the sea that was causing U359's gunners to miss. It was very rough.

Just as Pinholster was approaching his release point, U359 began to turn. She began swinging to port as Forster tried vainly to evade the depth-charges. In fact this last minute turn was helping the pilot rather than the U-Boat. Pinholster had swept straight in to the attack without any sparring or jockeying for position, with the result that he was coming at the U-Boat broadside on. Forster's turn brought the U-Boat round so that the aircraft was going to cross at an angle of thirty degrees, which was much more favourable for the spread of the depth-charges. Pinholster had the flying boat at its maximum speed and crossed the U-Boat only twenty-five feet from its deck. As the four depth-charges left the nacelle bomb bays of the Mariner, Forster reversed his turn, in an effort to get the U-Boat's stern away from the impact point.

At the moment of release Pinholster hauled the big machine upwards in a steep climbing left turn, and looked back over his shoulder to see how the depth-charges were placed. His tail gunner had taken up the fight and he could feel the aircraft vibrating as the twin fifties zeroed in on the U-Boat. The charges detonated and he was intensely disappointed to see only two columns of water climb upwards on the starboard side of the U-Boat. Only two explosions, and they were both outside lethal range. This meant that two of his depth-charges had been duds. What was worse was the fact that the two columns of water were well short of the U-Boat and this could only mean that the two charges that landed close to the boat were the duds.

When the spray cleared he could see the U-Boat running as before, with its guns spitting defiance. As the machine drew out of range the fire from the tail turret ceased and Pinholster was faced with the fact that to him, the attack had been an utter failure. The only thought in his mind was the fact that he desperately wanted to get even. His had been an excellent attack run and the U-Boat had only been able to hit him once or twice, without seriously affecting the aircraft, yet his depth-charges had let him down.

Although his depth-charge racks were empty, he decided to do a straffing run on the U-Boat by circling it to port, so that all his turrets could bear. By this stage U359 was dead in the water, having slowed down very quickly. The sea was very rough and as they circled, they could see the water streaming off the U-Boat's casing, while at other times only the conning tower was visible. Both the nose and tail turrets were hammering away as the big flying boat circled to the left, but the fifty calibre machine guns on the aircraft were outranged by the heavier weapons on the U-Boat.

Up to this time the U-Boat's gunners on the heaving conning tower had not been able to zero in on the Mariner and Pinholster thought that the U-Boat had been stopped to give them a more stable firing platform. Shortly after completing its first full circuit of the U-Boat, the German gunners found the range. Thirty-seven and twenty millimetre shells began hammering the Mariner. Shells hit nearly every part of the aircraft and both the tail gunner and then the starboard waist gunner were badly wounded. Big holes began appearing in the Mariner's fuselage and Pinholster prudently decided to open the range.

With the aircraft severely damaged, all the depth-charges expended, two of the three turrets out of action and two men wounded, Pinholster decided to get the aircraft home, while he still could. The severely damaged Mariner turned northward for its base in Puerto Rico and in the heavy haze that reduced visibility to six miles, the aircraft was soon out of sight of the wallowing U-Boat.

But as the machine sped away, a photographer in the waist hatch was staring back at the submarine and just before the boat disappeared in the haze, he saw a depth-charge explosion hide the U-Boat's conning tower. He yelled into the microphone to get the pilot to turn back, but all the aircraft's interphone systems had been shot out. The Mariner thundered northwards with the pilots trying to assess the damage to the machine, oblivious to the drama being enacted around the U-Boat. By the time the photographer glanced back at the U-Boat's position, it had been lost in the haze.

There were wounded to be attended to and the aircraft had to be prepared for its landing at San Juan, which was only a short distance away and there was no time to speak to the pilot. Only when Pinholster put his severely damaged aircraft down on the waters of San Juan bay and hastily taxied it to the seaplane ramp, did he find out what the photographer had witnessed.

The photographer had not seen U359 sink and he wasn't exactly sure of what he had witnessed, but sink she surely did. All next day aircraft were over the attack position, but all they could see was a large oil slick. The Americans mounted barrier patrols across the Mona and Anegada Passage in case the U-Boat was damaged and trying to get out of the Caribbean. Based on the evidence of the photographer, the pilot was credited with probably damaging the U-Boat and censured for attacking the U-Boat with only his guns and thus endangering the aeroplane to no good purpose. It was felt that he would have done a better job if after his depth-charge attack, he had sheered off and called for help. But in fact everything that Pinholster did, contributed to the end of U359.

It is highly probable that one of the four depth-charges was a dud and never went off, but the other charge more than likely hit the U-Boat's casing and lodged there. One of the two things could have happened, either of which could have destroyed the submarine. Forster could have taken the U-Boat down and when she reached twenty-five feet the charge would have gone off and destroyed the boat. However, it does not seem likely that Forster would have crash-dived, having just defeated the aircraft. In any case the aircraft's waist photographer saw an explosion.

What is more likely is that the crew of the U-Boat saw the depth-charge hit the deck. There was the normal compliment of commander, watchkeepers, and lookouts as well as the twenty millimetre gun crews on the conning tower. Additionally U359 was one of the U-Boats which had been fitted with the enhanced anti-aircraft armament. In place of the normal deck gun she had a thirty-seven millmetre semi automatic cannon, a weapon that took a considerable gun crew to keep it fed.

It is hardly likely that men working on the deck around the conning tower would not have heard and seen the depth-charge on the casing near them. In the case of the attack on U158 during June 1942 by the VP-74 Mariner, the U-Boat's guns had not been manned and as such there would have been very few actually on the conning tower. In that case there were no personnel on the deck at all and it was easy for them to miss the depth-charge lodged in the casing.

In the case of U359 the opposite is likely. If it is that the crew saw the depth-charge rolling about in the heavy sea that was washing the casing, this would explain why U359 stopped so suddenly. If the Mariner had not circled the U-Boat on its straffing attack and kept the gunners on the casing working full time, as well as sweeping the casing with machine gun fire, the U-Boat's crew would have had a lot more time to deal with the menace posed by the armed depth-charge.

There must have been a few minutes of absolute terror on that U-Boat. Firstly watching the charge on the deck being buffeted by the waves that were washing over it, but being unable to deal with it because of the fire from the aircraft. Then when the aircraft finally departed there would have been a mad scramble on the heaving deck to secure the monster. The crew of the U-Boat lost that race and it is probable that while they were wrestling with the charge it was washed overboard. Two seconds of sheer terror must have followed this event as men flung themselves behind cover. The charge would have taken just two seconds to sink to its operating depth. U359 was stopped and she didn't have a hope. She took her entire crew to the fifteen thousand foot depths of the underwater Muertos Trench.

VP-32 had got its third U-Boat and all within a two week period. They became the top anti-submarine squadron of the Caribbean theatre and its adjacent waters. But aircraft P-1 paid the price for the other two kills. There were one hundred and seventy-three holes in the machine and it is a wonder that Pinholster kept it afloat long enough to get it onto the ramp in San Juan. U359 was the fifth U-Boat to be lost in the Caribbean theatre during the month of July 1943.

The Caribbean radio operators had a busy day on the twenty-eighth, because while U359 was being destroyed in dramatic fashion, nearly all of the remaining eleven U-Boats were sending their situation reports.

They were all describing the week's activity and in all cases they were describing combats against aircraft. The Allied radio operators were triangulating the transmissions and plotting the probable positions of the boats, while the U-Boats chatted away to their headquarters. The Caribbean offensive was failing because none of the boats were describing the sinking of merchant ships although that day U615 managed one tanker.

As evening drew on Kandler in U653 came under attack off the Dutch Guiana coast. A B18 out of Zandery picked him up on radar ninety miles north of Paramaribo and roared into an attack. Kandler handled U653 well and his anti-aircraft gunners forced the B18 to break off the attack. As soon as the machine turned away he took U653 down, so that by the time the B18 could set up another run, the U-Boat was long gone.

Two and a half hours later the same B18 picked up U653 again on radar, but could not get the boat visual. The pilot decided to drop a flare and took his machine up to two thousand feet. In the light of the flare he saw the U-Boat submerging. Not having enough time to carry out an orthodox attack, the B18 pilot dropped his depth-charges from fifteen hundred feet! U653 was well away from the explosions, but later that evening Kandler asked U-Boat command if he could move away from that area. He was not sinking merchant ships and the aircraft were making life very difficult. He got permission and took his boat a little further off the coast. However Dietrichs in U406 moved into the dangerous area off Zandery almost immediately.

All the signals from the U-Boats carried bad news, but none quite as disturbing as a signal which came in from U404. She had found American carrier borne aircraft in the central Atlantic, on the same latitude as Miami. This was much further south than any U-Boat had come across them and meant that the Task Groups were hunting the U-Tankers wherever they moved. From now on it became a game of cat and mouse, with the Germans constantly moving the U-Boat rendezvous positions and the Americans following up.

On the night of the twenty-ninth of July Kurt Neide once again set the Trinidad defences a tingling. During the day he was sighted close inshore from Grand Matelot Point. This had caused a flurry among the anti-submarine forces and they raced to the area. For some days, two US Navy and two Royal Navy and TRNVR hunter-killer groups had been working the waters around Trinidad, in response to the large number of U-Boat sightings and radio transmissions.

Additionally, a witch hunt was in progress for spies in the island. A disturbing incident had taken place on the night of the twenty-fifth, when the lookout posts had seen lights flashing morse code from the east coast. Then again on the twenty-ninth, the lights were seen, but this time there were answering signals from seaward. The occurrence caused a major flap, with troops moving out to cordon off the area of the Manzanilla beach. No one was ever caught nor were the signals ever explained, but it is known that U415 was in the area.

Much further north another plan was in operation, intended to upset Trinidad even further. That day U218 and U383 sailed from Brest. Klaus Becker in command of U218 was charged with a special mission. His Type VIIC boat was a minelayer and he was under orders to lay his mines in the

Third Boca. This was the only unmined exit from the Gulf of Paria and all shipping used it. The mission did not succeed on this occasion because when the two boats were one day out from their bases, the RAF caught them.

Both boats were bombed and damaged, but U383 was so badly hit that she could not dive. She turned back to Brest and U218 was ordered to escort her in. Thus three days after leaving the port, U218 was back in and under dockyard hands repairing the damage. She was the thirty-second U-Boat committed to the Caribbean offensive and the fifth to be turned back.

She had been preceded by U525 under the command of Hans Joachim Drewitz, who had sailed from Bordeaux on the twenty-seventh in company with U129. Drewitz was under orders for the Caribbean, but he would never get there.

Both boats, U218 and U525 were rearmed with the heavier anti-aircraft armament and met the stringent departure requirements then in force. They were to be the last boats committed to the great Caribbean offensive.

By this stage U-Boat Command was aware that the Caribbean idea was not working. The offensive was bogged down because of difficulties in getting across Biscay, safe-guarding the tankers and the extremely heavy air activity in the Caribbean. It had been an inspired plan but undertaken far too late. Still it was not finished by any means, because at this stage there were still fourteen U-Boats at sea committed to the Caribbean offensive. These boats had to be brought home and this was going to prove even more difficult than getting out.

July thirtieth was to prove no less hectic than the days before. The Caribbean defenders were aware now that they were winning and they threw themselves at the remaining U-Boats with renewed vigour.

Dietrichs had brought U406 southeast to the coast off Dutch Guiana and was operating only fifteen miles offshore when No. 35 squadron discovered him. The bomber passed over the U-Boat twice, but failed to identify it and on the third run the pilot dropped flares. As soon as the flares ignited U406 was lit up and as though Dietrichs were waiting for this moment, his anti-aircraft guns spat defiance.

The B18 pilot did not hesitate. He brought his aircraft in through the fierce barrage and planted his five depth-charges all around the U-Boat. None of the charges were in lethal range and the U-Boat's gunners riddled the machine as it pulled out. While the pilot fought his aircraft with both wings damaged, Dietrichs took U406 down, but his presence so close offshore caused some concern. It was immediately assumed that he was a minelayer and that the entrance to Paramaribo harbour had been mined. A number of minesweepers were immediately dispatched from Trinidad and the heavy air activity was further increased.

At ten minutes to eleven on the following night Lt. L.D. Crockett in Mariner P-11 of VP-204 homed on U406, one hundred and twenty miles north of Paramaribo. Dietrichs had moved offshore to avoid the hornet's nest he had stirred up. Crockett was unable to visually identify the U-Boat and decided to use flares.

Once again, as the flare ignited, Dietrich's gunners opened fire. Crockett was not in a favourable position to attack and sheered off to position himself for a better run in. The big Mariner began its bomb run and almost immediately the U-Boat's gunners began hitting. A twenty millimetre shell entered the nose of the aircraft and hit the co-pilot Lt. jg. J.G.R. Hershey in the stomach, causing the attack to be broken off.

As they pulled the dying co-pilot out of the cockpit, Crockett took the Mariner back up over the U-Boat and dropped two more flares. Dietrich had all the opportunity he desired to dive, but he was convinced that he could beat this aircraft and stayed to fight. He was right, P-11 eventually ran in making a bow attack and dropped four depth-charges, but none of them were within lethal range. As his co-pilot died in the back of the aircraft, Crockett turned for Chaguaramas. He left the area with a white hot anger eager for revenge and before long some U-Boat would pay. A B18 from Zandery took his place, but by this time U406 had disappeared.

In the Bay of Biscay the U-Boats had experienced a disastrous day. The school of thought who believed that crossing the Bay in groups, relying on the boats' mutual anti-aircraft protection still predominated and in fact, now that U Tankers were in such short supply, their argument was even stronger. The faster the boats could cross the Bay, the longer they could stay in their operational areas and naturally, the more opportunities they would have for sinking Allied shipping. The attempts to cross the Bay on the surface continued and on July thirtieth, the U-Boats' cause was grievously wounded.

On the same day that U525 had sailed, three large U-Boats sailed from Bordeaux in company. Louis in command of U504 escorted the tankers U461 under Stiebler and U462 under Vowe, out of the base and began their ill-fated dash across Biscay. U504 had visited the Caribbean under the command of Poske in March 1942 and then again in May and June where the boat had done rather well. The two Type XIV U tankers had been commissioned in mid 1942 and played a significant role in backing the Caribbean U-Boats in their rampage of the area. It was essential that these U tankers get through, because there were a large number of boats in the Caribbean and in the South Atlantic which would need their services to get home.

On July thirtieth the attempt came to an end when a Liberator of Coastal Command found them ninety miles off Cape Ortegal. The three boats were confident of their ability to make short work of the aircraft, but the pilot declined combat and shadowed them while calling for reinforcements. Soon a Coastal Command Sunderland joined, followed by a Catalina and then by an American Liberator.

Captain Walker's Second Support Group of anti-submarine sloops was operating independently not too far away and the Catalina called on them for support. By this stage the U-Boat commanders were not as confident as before and they radioed for fighter support, but it would be a long time before the JU88s could get to the area. While Walker hoisted his famous signal for a general chase and the sloops crashed through the sea to get to the area in time, the battle began between the U-Boats and the aircraft.

The aircraft came in mutually supporting waves, but the heavy anti-aircraft armament of the U-Boats drove them off. Three times they came in and three times the gunners drove them off, until the pilot of the American Liberator did an extraordinarily brave thing.

He dove his heavy bomber down at the U-Boats and flew right across in front of them. While all three U-Boats concentrated their fire on the Liberator, a Sunderland slipped in and took out U461. By a curious coincidence, the Sunderland that got U461 was from No. 461 squadron RAAF and the aircraft's call sign was U/461. The pilot had never attacked a U-Boat before but he managed to place a depth-charge almost under the U tanker. The explosion nearly lifted the boat out of the water. Only Stiebler and fourteen of his crew of sixty survived the sinking of the boat.

Meanwhile, the American Liberator which had made the strike possible, was badly shot up and the pilot nursed his ailing machine to the nearest land. He pulled off a lucky crash landing in Portugal and all the crew survived.

At this stage, the sloops were racing in and Luis in U504 realized that it was madness to stay on the surface. U504 crash-dived to leave U462 alone to face the remaining aircraft and sloops. Before the sloops could get to U462, a Halifax of No. 502 squadron which had joined the fray, placed its depth-charges under U462 and crippled the boat. Bruno Vowe had no alternative but to scuttle his U-Boat.

Luis in the meantime was very deep, trying to creep away when Walker's indomitable sloops gained asdic contact. The hunt was long but eventually a considerable amount of wreckage came to the surface to mark the passing of the old Caribbean veteran.

The German long range fighter cover never did materialize. The loss of the two U tankers, brought to five the number of supply boats that had been lost in the past five weeks and it simply spelled the end of the Caribbean offensive.

There was no way that U117 alone could handle all the U-Boats which needed a tanker and U-Boat command had to act. They still were not aware of the loss of U67, U527 and U459 and indeed U648 was still searching for its two lost charges, but the double loss in Biscay meant that boats had to be pulled back from the Caribbean before their patrols were completed. On the following day Uphoff in U84, Brosin in U134 and Kummetat in U572 were ordered to leave the Caribbean and start for home.

The last day of July was to see three U-Boats attacked by aircraft in the Caribbean theatre. Dalhaus brought U634 out from his safe haven south of Hispaniola and moved eastward to the Anegada Passage, but the boat was caught on the surface by a VP-81 Catalina and bombed. Dalhaus was forced away from the Passage southward into the Caribbean.

Carlsen had brought U732 out of the dangerous Windward Passage into the the area south of Haiti, to give his crew a break from the nonstop tension, but no sooner had they arrived, than a PBY of VP-92 discovered them and placed its depth-charges just outside lethal range. Carlsen had done remarkably well and in the three weeks since he had arrived in the area, U732 had not been damaged. He managed to keep up his good record and eventually he was to be the only captain of the thirty-two committed to the operation, who finished it with an undamaged U-Boat. The same could not be said for U572, which was just starting its homeward journey.

The recall signal to U572 had found the boat close to the island of Tobago, dodging the hunter-killer groups, but for some reason Kummetat did not immediately start for home. He had faced his first attack on July first, while coming into the area north of Puerto Rico. Since then U572 had taken on virtually every anti-submarine squadron in the Trinidad Sector and beaten them all, although with some damage to the boat. His continued presence near to Trinidad had alerted the defenders and each time he fought a duel or sent off a signal, they plotted in the new position. All the anti-submarine forces that were out were specifically tasked with the destruction of U415 and U572, the two boats which were operating audaciously close to Trinidad. Kummetat left the dangerous inshore area reluctantly and began a very slow protracted return, which VP-205 took advantage of.

At ten past eleven on the night of July thirty-first Mariner P-2 of VP-205 out of Chaguaramas, picked up a radar contact one hundred and eighty miles east of Trinidad. The aircraft climbed upwards and dropped a flare over the estimated position of the contact. U572 was illuminated running eastwards on the surface. The U-Boat's gunners opened up an immediate barrage and watched satisfied as the aircraft turned away. A short while later they heard the aircraft coming back in, but once again it was high. The Mariner pilot was trying a different tactic and with his aircraft at fourteen hundred feet, he dropped two high explosive bombs.

Right through the attack the U-Boat gunners kept up a steady accurate fire, which was returned by the aircraft's machine gunners. Kummetat no doubt thought that the machine was going to drop another flare and he was probably very surprised to be bombed, in what in the anti-submarine context, would be considered a high level bombing attack. The two bombs burst on the surface with a tremendous amount of noise and flying splinters, but they were too far away from the U-Boat to do any damage.

In the bright flash of the two bombs the pilot of the Mariner lost sight of the U-Boat and decided to use gambit tactics. As the machine flew off into the darkness, Kummetat must have been congratulating his gunners on on a job well done. Obviously the U-Boat's anti-aircraft fire had frightened off the pilot, causing him to make the high level attack and then disappear.

Always after a successful engagement men relax and undoubtedly this was true of U572's gunners. No one on the conning tower suspected that the Mariner was coming back. In fact the Mariner pilot was waiting to the westward of the U-Boat and two hours later he began stalking his prey. He lined up the radar contact with the U-Boat's previous course and began a low level approach. Some distance behind the U-Boat he picked up the wake and commenced his final run in at one hundred and twenty feet.

U572 was caught completely by surprise and the anti-aircraft fire only started when the Mariner was almost over the boat. Four MK-44 depth-charges plummeted into the sea around the boat as the Mariner's engines thundered overhead. Even as the depth-charges went off, the Mariner was taking fire from the U-Boat and the pilot twisted his way out of the cone of tracer that had zeroed in on him.

When he could bring the damaged machine back over the spot, all that was visible were the four marker lights that showed where the charges had entered the water. The Mariner was very difficult to control and both the navigator and one of the gunners were injured. The pilot turned for Chaguaramas not knowing what had happened to the U-Boat. There was no wreckage on the sea and the pilot could not tell whether U572 had survived.

U572 survived, but the boat was damaged in the attack. Kummetat did not take this as a warning. He still ambled along almost as though he didn't want to leave the Caribbean. VP-205 had left a calling card and they intended to leave another very shortly. The squadron was reluctant to lose the U-Boat and before that night was out, two more Mariners from Chagua-ramas were vectored to the scene of the attack.

July had definitely not been a good month for the U-Boats. Thirty-seven of them had been sunk during the month, eleven of which had been operational boats for the Caribbean, plus the four tankers which were supporting them.

The RAF had turned the Bay of Biscay into a disaster area for the U-Boats, sinking nineteen of them in a six week period. To achieve this they had lost fifty-seven aircraft which was not too high a price to pay, when balanced against what a U-Boat was capable of. The losses were caused primarily because of the insistence on crossing the Bay surfaced. As soon as this tactic was dropped in August, the losses in the Bay came to an end. It took far longer to cross the Bay submerged, but it was infinitely safer.

In the Caribbean the U-Boats had clashed with the defending aircraft in a traumatic battle that had left both sides shocked at the violence. During the month there had been more than three dozen clashes and in nearly all cases the aircraft were severely damaged. Similarly, nearly all the U-Boats had also been damaged, but they had the additional problem of the wounded. The aircraft had usually been able to rush their wounded crew-men back to base hospitals, but not so the U-Boats.

A call had been made early in the month for each U-Boat to carry a doctor, but at the time there were only sixteen at sea. For a U-Boat to find a doctor, they had to rendezvous with a U tanker, – but where were the tankers? The result was that wounded U-Boat crewmen faced a four thou-sand mile trip back across the Atlantic before they could receive proper medical attention. Most of them died and were buried in the wastes of the Atlantic.

During the month the defending aircraft had sunk five of the U-Boats which had come into the area. This was almost more than in the whole of 1942. Additionally, a further five U-Boats had been sunk on their way to the Caribbean and so far two more had been sunk on their way home from the theatre. This meant that the Caribbean offensive in July had cost twelve operational U-Boats, but fifteen boats still had to attempt to get back home. Nevertheless, what did these boats achieve?

The offensive had been a failure. Twenty-two U-Boats operated in the area including the transiting U66, and U516 which was still searching for the nonexistent U662. The damaged aircraft must be ignored because the U-Boats had not been sent to the Caribbean to fight aircraft. Their purpose had been primarily to sink merchant ships. Between them they sank three tankers, two freighters and two schooners. They also damaged two freighters and these must be added to the total. It was a very poor return on the investment. The failure had been caused by a flawed tactical approach to the Caribbean theatre.

This vast area called the Caribbean theatre extended from the far corners of the Gulf of Mexico for three thousand two hundred miles to the French Guiana/Brazil border. It was longer than the North Atlantic convoy route and in places the theatre was over a thousand miles wide. In the early days of 1942, the U-Boats had spread themselves along this entire enormous area and because the defences were weak, they had set the whole thing afire.

This had led to a Staff attitude to the Caribbean that could almost be summarized as, "a hunting we will go." It worked well because the Americans had not been able to cope with the scale of the assault, but by the dark days of 1943, it was the wrong approach.

The initial German successes in 1942 had forced the Americans to spread themselves out and defend the whole area. In 1943, the Germans should have concentrated and hit at one area at a time. Since the days of Operation Neuland the U-Boats had been spread out and never once had they ever been concentrated. In 1943 this was disastrous, because in every area there were anti-submarine resources to spare. It allowed the U-Boats to be defeated in detail.

The Staff sent the U-Boats off to the Caribbean, assigned them to various spread-out operational areas and then forgot about them. Had they taken a quarter of the effort lavished on a wolf pack attacking a single North Atlantic convoy and dedicated it to concentrating the Caribbean boats for a single strike, they would have brought the Caribbean to a standstill.

Regardless of how strong the defences were, the twenty-two boats which operated in the theatre could have been much better utilized. If this pack had been concentrated in the Gulf of Mexico, in the area between Aruba and the Windward Passage, around Trinidad, or across the bauxite route, they would have decisively defeated the defenders of that specific area and brought shipping to a halt.

This would have caused the Americans to switch forces hurriedly to meet the onslaught, providing of course that they could have managed this. In most places the infra-structure was geared to handling only a limited number of units. Once they detected a strengthening of the defences the pack could have been moved. The initiative rested with the Germans. They could strike when and where they liked, but they gave it up to the Americans. It was most unlike German Staff work.

The result of this July failure was that the Allied ship building programme finally overtook the tonnage lost and never slipped behind again. The victory over the U-Boats in the Caribbean theatre in July was also a superb achievement of American arms. The Mariner flying boat and the B24 Liberator played a decisive role, alongside the untiring surface escorts, but it was more the change in the American attitude to the theatre that was decisive.

At last the ideas about an Atlantic threat to the Panama canal by aircraft based in South America and paratroopers was put aside. They recognized that the threat was the U-Boats and everything was geared to defeating them. It showed clearly how far the US Navy had come since the dark days of 1942, when they danced to a tune played by the U-Boats. They had turned the Caribbean around and it was no longer a favourable U-Boat operating area. July had been a victory for them, but the battle was by no means over and the greatest fight of all was still to take place.

Boats going to, returning from and fighting in, the Caribbean were being sunk, but so were some old Caribbean veterans who were not directly involved in the July offensive against the old battleground. The loss of U126 and U504 has already been recorded, but there were four others.

The first to go had been Wurdemann in U506. This boat had operated in the Gulf of Mexico during May 1942 and then within the Caribbean Sea in October. It was sunk off the coast of Spain by none other than the 1st Bombardment squadron, which had been based in Trinidad through most of 1942. They were now renamed the 1st Anti-Submarine Squadron and flying VLR Liberators.

The second boat to go down was U509. Werner Witte had operated this Type IXC boat in the Caribbean during July and August of 1942. He died on July fifteenth, when the Avengers of VC-29 operating off the USS Santee sent his boat to the bottom off the Azores. There were no survivors. The third boat was sent to the bottom in the Bay of Biscay on July twentieth.

U558 had been under the command of Gunther Krech during the convoy battles of August 1942 in the Caribbean. He was sunk in the Bay by US Army No. 9 anti-submarine squadron. The fourth boat died off Brazil on July twenty-third. VP-74 had already sunk U513 off the South American continent when the Venturas of VB-107 sent U598 to the bottom. Holtorf had operated this boat in the Windward Passage during August 1942 and had taken part in the battle around convoy TAW-12, on the same night that U600 and U658 had attacked in the Passage. U598 was the second of four U-Boats to be lost off Brazil during July. The third was U591 on the thirtieth when she went down to the Venturas of VB-127. The fourth U-Boat lost was U199. This boat was the fourth U-Boat to be sunk by VP-74.

Just north of the Brazilian Theatre a U-Boat had almost lain idle for the last two weeks of July. Eick in U510 had managed to stay out of trouble during this period, but it irked him. His had been the only U-Boat in the theatre which had not experienced an air attack. Part of the reason for this was the fact that Eick was under orders to stay on the one hundred fathom line off the Guianas. The Staff was convinced that traffic would use this route, which in 1942 had been popular, but in 1943 most of the convoys were hugging the coastline where they could gain maximum protection from the nearby shore based airpower. The shallow water also restricted the freedom with which the U-Boat could operate.

Eick had been pleading with headquarters to allow him to move but they had been adamant. At this stage events had caused a shift in the attitude of the Staff. First U590 had been sunk on the inshore route. Then U662 had been sunk. After this U466 had got itself embroiled with the aircraft operating in the area and forced to run for home. Kandler had taken the place of U466, but it wasn't long before U653 was damaged and forced to move to seaward. His place had been taken by Dietrichs in U406, who had thoroughly worked up the area's defenders and in turn had been forced to pull back by the aircraft. In three weeks the bauxite route had used up five U-Boats in succession, now it was finally open for U510 to move in. U-Boat Command relented and Eick took his boat inshore.

Unlike the boats before it, U510 avoided the aircraft. On August first Eick picked up the heavily escorted convoy JT-2 on its way from Rio de Janeiro to Trinidad and began stalking it. Late on August first he began moving in on the surface, but at twenty past six in the evening his conning tower was sighted and the destroyer USS Soames turned towards him. Eick took U510 down, but the destroyer soon had asdic contact. The U-Boat was only thirty miles north of Paramaribo in very shallow water, but Eick managed to slip away from the thunderous depth-charge explosions. When the convoy was well away from the area, the USS Soames turned away from the elusive U-Boat and steamed to rejoin her convoy. She signalled to say that the U-Boat had been left well behind, but Eick was a very persistent man.

Seven hours later, at one o'clock in the morning, one of the convoy's escorts picked up a contact closing fast from astern. Once again the USS Soames left her charges and steamed south to deal with the intruder. Again U510 was subjected to a vicious depth-charge attack and once more Eick managed to escape, despite the shallow water. This time the destroyer stayed longer over the asdic contact, but she couldn't stay too long because the convoy was moving into the waters around Trinidad, where a couple of very elusive U-Boats were known to be operating.

At nine o'clock in the morning the USS Soames received a report that there was a U-Boat astern. Eick was trying again. The Corvette USS Surprise was detached to deal with the intruder. Before she could get to the position, that marked the site of the attack, U510 was as deep as she could get and Eick slowly edged away from the PC. The commander of the little patrol boat was convinced that he had either damaged the U-Boat or chased it away, but the senior officer in the destroyer was beginning to believe that he had a very tenacious U-Boat in contact with his convoy. He ordered the corvette to remain well astern and be on the alert.

One hour later they were astonished to see the USS Surprise rushing in for an attack. Eick was at it again. The corvette plastered the area with depth-charges and even brought mud to the surface but again, the elusive U-Boat slipped away.

The corvette kept up the hunt for several hours but could not regain the contact. Within minutes of the corvette rejoining the convoy another report came in, the U-Boat was once again coming up from astern. The senior officer in the destroyer was utterly fed up with this U-Boat and again the escort leader raced south to deal with him once and for all. Eick took U510 back to the mud of the Orinoco Delta and counted the nonstop depth-charge explosions. Finally the destroyer left the area quite convinced that pieces of the U-Boat were scattered all over the bottom.

This time it took Eick a little longer to get going, but at nine twenty on the night of August second he made his sixth attack on the convoy. The incredulous escorts once again raced south and automatically plastered the area around the U-Boat. After this attack, they called on the air escort to stay permanently astern to guard against the mad U-Boat commander. At no time during the two days when Eick chased JT-2 did an aircraft get a sight of him. It showed the calibre of the U-Boat commander and what might have been achieved if he had not been attacking alone.

The aircraft did not save convoy JT-2 from being attacked again, — it was U-Boat Command reacting to the chaos caused by the loss of the tankers. It is very likely that eventually Eick would have got in a torpedo attack on the ships of the convoy, particularly if Neide in U415 had joined him near Trinidad.

Decisions were being made and signals being sent out from U-Boat Command that affected all the U-Boats. With U461 and U462 sunk, there was no hope of continuing the far-flung deployments and the first signal recalled U68, U123, U505 and U523. These boats had sailed from Lorient on August first, fitted out with heavier anti-aircraft armament, with orders to fight their way through the Bay of Biscay, but the penny had finally dropped.

The next signal ordered boats to abandon all attempts to cross the Bay of Biscay on the surface. All further crossings would be by boats operating alone and submerged. They were to surface only at night and then only long enough to charge their batteries. This one decision ended the Battle of the Bay of Biscay. The U-Boats would take a lot longer to get where they were going, but at least they stood a chance of surviving the crossing.

The third signal ordered Piening in U155, and Stahl in U648 along with U309 and U190 to return immediately. They were to return on the surface and cross the Bay of Biscay by hugging the Spanish coastline, regardless of territorial waters! This was a drastic step indeed, but the situation called for drastic measures. Hope had finally been given up for Muller-Stockheim in U67 and Uhlig in U527.

The fourth signal ordered Eick in U510, Kummetat in U572 and Kandler in U653 to leave the Caribbean immediately for a rendezvous with the tanker U117.

The first signal to the Caribbean recalled three of the boats which had been longest in the area and who would all be short of fuel, but there were others also running critical. On the following day Neide in U415, who had proved to be one of the most audacious of the Caribbean commanders, signalled to say that he was short on fuel and had to leave the area. U-Boat Command responded by directing a signal to all the U-Boats, saying that all boats were to return to base immediately. It went on to say that refuelling would be available only for boats that were critically short of fuel.

This signal was the first admission of total defeat. It was the trumpet blowing the retreat for the U-Boats, but it was not the end of the fighting. There is an ancient military rule that says that you suffer more casualties when you turn your back in retreat than when you are fighting, and it was to be so for the U-Boats. Many would pay the supreme price as they fought to get home.

The first U-Boat to die in the retreat was Kummetat's U572. Kummetat was ambling his way homeward from what by July 1943 standards, was a successful patrol. Before he had got the Hamburg built Type VIIC boat to the Caribbean, Kummetat had managed to sink the tanker SS Lot in the North Atlantic. He had followed this up by sinking the schooners Havard and Gibbert B. Walters. He had driven the Trinidad defenders to distraction. He had entered the Dragon's Mouth and caused a major flap at the start of his patrol. Then he had been detected visually on nine separate occasions, but escaped each time. The Americans had plotted his position while he sent off his radio reports on seven occasions, but failed to pin him down. He had fooled VP-204 with his lights while following the tanker

AIRPOWER

and again got away with it. He had survived six serious air attacks, during the course of which he had seriously damaged five aircraft and wounded the crewmen in each one. And finally he had escaped from a VP-205 attack, after being taken completely by surprise. The Trinidad defenders wanted U572 badly.

Knowing this Kummetat still lingered on his return. It was as though he did not want to leave and it became so glaring that U-Boat Command eventually found a job for him to do on his way home. Dietrichs in U406 had been having a rough time off the coast of the Guianas, during the course of which he had used up too much anti-aircraft ammunition. Because U572 was still in the area, they instructed Kummetat to rendezvous with Dietrichs and hand over some ammunition and gun grease. The meeting was to take place six hundred miles east-northeast of Trinidad. This now gave Kummetat a valid reason for lingering.

Late in the evening of August second, Mariner P-6 of VP-205 took off from Chaguaramas Naval Air Station on an anti-submarine patrol of the area east of Trinidad. The aircraft was under the command of Lieutenant junior grade, C.C. Cox and there were three officers and eight enlisted men aboard. They had been briefed that there was a U-Boat operating some three hundred miles off Trinidad, the same wily one that had escaped from the squadron three nights previously.

At twenty-five minutes past midnight on Tuesday the third of August, a plain language message was received in Trinidad from Mariner P-6 saying, "Sighted submarine, – making attack, – 11.35N 54.05W." Repeated attempts were made to contact P-6, but without success.

At daybreak Mariners from the squadron were over the spot three hundred and ninety miles east northeast of Trinidad. They searched for days, but no sign of that Mariner was ever found. Dietrichs in U406 arrived at the rendezvous point, but U572 never made it.

The aircraft could find no sign of wreckage and they assumed that the U-Boat had destroyed the Mariner. U-Boat Command tried for days to contact U572, but Kummetat never spoke on the radio again. In fact, in what must have been a titanic clash, Mariner P-6 and U572 had destroyed each other. Kummetat had lingered a little too long.

CHAPTER

19

The greatest battle

The recall signal found four U-Boats actually within the Caribbean Sea. Carlsen was south of Navassa Island preparing to take his lucky U-Boat home via the Windward Passage. Kurt Neide was homeward bound off the north coast of Trinidad, where he attempted to penetrate the screen of convoy TJ-4 and was heavily depth-charged. Two boats, U634 under Dalhaus and U615 under Kapitsky were in the area northeast of Curacao.

These latter boats had moved into this quiet area to give their nerve-wracked crews a break from the strain of operating for so long in the hostile aviation environment. At the recall signal all four boats began their perilous journey home. Dalhous started U634 northwards to try the Mona Passage and Kapitsky turned eastwards for the Galleons Passage.

The Type VIIC boat U615 had been accepted by Kapitanleutnant Rolf Kapitsky from its builders Blom and Voss of Hamburg, in March 1942. Kapitsky was a pre-war naval officer, having joined the Kriegsmarine in 1935. In 1937 he was seconded to the Luftwaffe for a two year period before volunteering for U-Boats. As a Midshipman he served in a number of

U-Boats during 1939 and 1940, before being promoted to Oberleutnant early in 1941 and appointed to U93. Here he served as First Watchkeeping officer under Kapitanleutnant Claus Korth. He saw service in the North Atlantic before being appointed to U615 as its commander designate early in 1942. After the boat's trials in the Baltic, it sailed for La Pallice where it was assigned to the Third Flotilla.

Kapitsky's first patrol which brought him from Kiel to La Pallice had been uneventful but on his second, in the North Atlantic, he was assigned to a wolf pack code-named Group Tiger, which became embroiled with convoy ONS 136. In the subsequent battle, he sank the freighter El Lago and captured two of the ship's officers. Later in the month of October 1942 he sank the very large twelve thousand six hundred ton freighter Empire Star.

His third war patrol found Kapitsky in March 1943 embroiled in the battle around convoy HX 229 in the North Atlantic. He succeeded in sinking the Liberty ship Edward B. Dudley out of the convoy, but he really established himself with his excellent shadowing of the convoy. Through the ferocious battle, he held onto the convoy and kept the wolf pack informed of all its changes of course, which ultimately made the U-Boats' successes possible.

However, U615 did not escape unscathed. The destroyers HMS Anemone and HMS Harvester eventually gained contact with the U-Boat that was shadowing the convoy and U615 had to endure seven separate depth-charge attacks within a ninety minute period.

The damage inflicted by the attacks took some time to repair and Kapitsky was fortunate to miss the slaughter of the U-Boats in May 1943. While it was in dockyard hands, U615 was one of the boats that had its armament modified to suit the requirements of the new fight-back order. The old deck gun was removed and replaced by a semi-automatic thirty-seven millimetre cannon. In addition the anti-aircraft gun platform at the after end of the conning tower was extended and two twin twenty millimetre cannons replaced the single mount which had previously been fitted. This enhanced anti-aircraft armament, made U615 ready for Biscay and the Caribbean.

The Caribbean trip had not been uneventful. During the fight against the Whitley bombers in the Bay of Biscay, U615 had managed to bring down one of the aircraft, but Bootsmart Wilke had bled to death on the conning tower from wounds received when the aircraft straffed the U-Boat. The problems did not end with the successful crossing of the Bay, because U615 was one of the boats which suffered as a result of the sinking of the tanker U119.

The tanker U487 found itself alone off the Azores with a large number of U-Boats requiring fuel. As has already been related, three operational boats were required to hand over their fuel to U487. This operation was taking so long that U615 was ordered to take fuel direct from U535. This itself was a tedious operation because it required the slow transfer of twenty tons of fuel using only a small firehose. It was made doubly dangerous by the presence of the American carriers, who were hunting the nearby U487.

After the refuelling, U615 set course for the Caribbean while U535 turned for home. The emergency tanker U535 was not destined to make it through the Bay of Biscay. The boat was caught by No. 53 squadron RAF Coastal Command on July fifth, and sunk with all hands. No. 53 squadron had operated Hudsons from Trinidad during 1942, before being re-equipped with Liberators to operate from RAF Thorny Island in 1943.

In the meantime, U615 entered the Caribbean through the Anegada Passage and Kapitsky brought it down to Trinidad to have a look into the Dragon's Mouth, before moving westward to his operating area off Curacao.

For most of the last two weeks of July 1943 Kapitsky kept U615 close to Curacao, but although he sighted a considerable amount of tanker traffic, he was powerless to interfere because of the strong surface escorts. The Liberators of the 8th Bomber Squadron also made any sort of attack on the shipping impossible and Kapitsky was forced to spend all day every day submerged. At night he would surface for brief periods to charge his batteries and ventilate the boat, but he could pick up almost continuous radar transmissions from the land and knew that he was being constantly plotted. Finally on July twenty-eight an opportunity presented itself and Kapitsky caught the three thousand ton Dutch tanker Rosalia, ten miles south of Willemstadt harbour. Two torpedoes opened up the ship and she went down in the deep water south of the island.

The sinking of the Rosalia was sufficiently important for the Allies to take a special interest in the U-Boat which had perpetrated the deed. Not many ships were sunk during July and when one did go down, it usually generated a furious reaction from the defenders.

Kapitsky had managed to escape attack for the two weeks prior to the sinking, but on the day after he had to face a Liberator. He was caught sixty miles northwest of Curacao and the four depth-charges were close enough to give the boat a severe shaking up. On August second he found convoy GAT-77 in the area east of the Dutch Islands and tried to attack the ships. His periscope was sighted and he found himself under depth-charge attack by a PC. After this Kapitsky moved northeast for a brief rest and rendezvous before commencing his homeward treck.

The attempt on convoy GAT-77 was sufficient for the Allies to begin a serious anti-submarine hunt for the boat known to be operating between Curacao and Trinidad, and the area was under constant surveillance by the long-range flying boats operating out of Chaguaramas. As Kapitsky moved closer to Trinidad, the air activity became even more intense and he found that he barely had time to ventilate the boat before aircraft would home in on him. In fact, the Americans were looking specifically for U615, and they kept at it until at last they found the U-Boat.

At five o'clock on the afternoon of August fifth the destroyer USS Biddle, operating independently in the area northwest of Trinidad, obtained an asdic contact and ran in to attack. While the destroyer was coming in, Kapitsky fired a decoy and slipped away. After the first depth-charge pattern, the destroyer was unable to regain contact, although it hunted for more than an hour. Prior to attacking, the Biddle had radioed its position to Trinidad and it was not long before a flying boat was on the way.

Just before dusk that evening Lt. J.M. Erskine received orders for an all night anti-submarine hunt in the area northwest of Trinidad, where the destroyer had attacked a contact. Erskine was the pilot who had had his Mariner mauled by the guns of U572 on July nineteenth at the start of the great clash between the defenders and the U-Boats.

On this evening he took Mariner P-6 of VP-204 and set course northwest. Four hours later he obtained a radar contact forty miles northwest of Blanquilla island. Erskine took his Mariner up to three thousand feet and ran in over the contact, releasing two flares. By the light of the pyrotechnic he could see a U-Boat running eastwards with its decks awash.

U615 was making six knots so that there would be no appreciable wake to give away its position. Erskine rolled his Mariner into a descending one hundred and eighty degree turn and came out at sixteen hundred feet over the U-Boat. He released two high explosive bombs, which plummeted to the sea below, – exploding with a bright flash. After the detonations, Erskine saw the U-Boat unharmed, and began losing height for another attack.

On the conning tower of the U-Boat Kapitsky was gambling. The demolition bombs had landed some distance from the boat and he was hoping that when the flares went out, the pilot would lose him. It was a very dark rainy night and there was a good chance that he would get away with it, but Erskine wanted this U-Boat. When the pilot had his Mariner close to the sea, he began his run in.

Kapitsky was still on the surface believing that the aircraft had lost him, when to his intense discomfort, the Mariner appeared. U615 was taken completely by surprise and not an anti-aircraft weapon was ready. Erskine held the aircraft steady and passed right over the U-Boat's conning tower, but a mechanical fault, caused three of his four depth-charges to hang up. The single depth-charge that did release, hit the water one hundred and fifty yards from the U-Boat's bow. Kapitsky had U615 swinging to starboard and while the depth-charge was going down he hit the crash-dive alarm. Those members of the crew who were not immediately concerned with the crash diving, ran through the U-Boat to help it to go down quicker.

Erskine pulled his Mariner around, cursing the mechanical contrivance which had spoiled a good attack and came back in for another run. All that was visible was the swirl created by the conning tower as it dipped below the waves, but the pilot still dropped one depth-charge thirty yards ahead of it. The explosion shook up U615, but they were well clear. Kapitsky could congratulate himself on a narrow escape, but above the Americans were jubilant. They had found U615 again.

Erskine's signal to the Naval Station generated an instant response. Mariner P-5 of VP-204 took off immediately and turned for the area to the northwest to back up P-6. At the scene of the attack Erskine began using gambit tactics to induce U615 to surface and Kapitsky obliged, but not quite in the manner the American wanted. Mariner P-5 took about an hour to reach the scene of the attack, but unfortunately suffered a radar breakdown on the way. Nevertheless, the two Mariners set up a criss-crossing grid of tracks, covering the whole area that was designed to pick up the U-Boat as soon as it surfaced.

Two hours after the initial attack Mariner P-6 picked up a radar contact more or less where he expected the U-Boat to be operating. This had to be the same U-Boat and Erskine swung his machine into an immediate attack. In the darkness he could not see the target and dropped his three depth-charges around a dark shadow on the surface that corresponded with the radar position. He pulled the aircraft upwards and began climbing to a height where he could release a flare. The aircraft crossed the target higher up and released two flares.

To the horror of the crew instead of a broken U-Boat, they saw a two masted inter-island schooner rocking in the waves created by the explosions. Fortunately the schooner did not appear to be sinking but the crew must have been absolutely terrified.

Kapitsky had seen the schooner through his periscope and surfaced using it as a decoy. The trimmed down U-Boat remained in the radar shadow created by the schooner and again escaped. But the US Navy had smelt blood and from now on they remorselessly hunted the U-Boat.

The Trinidad Command quickly caught on to what Kapitsky had done and it only served to increase their desire for revenge. Despite all their other committments in the busy area, they began dispatching relays of aircraft to the area. The first was a Ventura of VB-130. This aircraft was a fast navalized variant of the Army Ventura, which the navy called the Harpoon. It had been optimised for anti-submarine warfare and proved to be particularly useful. Its speed was its greatest attribute and on the same day that Kapitsky began his duel with the Trinidad forces, Harpoons based in Brazil accounted for U604 off the coast of Brazil. The U-Boat was caught by Harpoons from VB-107 and VB-127, who were eventually backed up by the destroyer USS Moffet. By the time these forces were finished with U604, Holtring, her commander had no option but to scuttle the boat. She was so badly damaged that there was no hope of taking her back across the Atlantic. At the time of the sinking, U604 was also responding to the clarion call of retreat.

The Harpoon from VB-130 took less than an hour to reach the scene of the search for U615, where she joined Mariners P-5 and P-6 of VP-204 in their protracted hunt. Before the Harpoon reached the area northwest of Trinidad, two B18 bombers of the 7th US Army anti-submarine squadron took off from Edinburgh to join the hunt. With these five aircraft from Trinidad quartering the area, U615 could not surface again that night.

Throughout the Caribbean theatre the defenders sensed this gradual withdrawal of the U-Boats that was taking place, and the anti-submarine squadrons poised to take advantage of it. The radio operators triangulating the signals that the boats sent off were the first to show tangible proof of the withdrawal. For weeks they had plotted these U-Boats' transmissions, usually emanating from the same general areas and had almost come to know the individual boats by their frequencies and method of sending their coded reports.

Now these operating areas were changing and all appeared to be moving away. In the Windward Passage VP-32 were assiduously searching for Carlsen in U732 as he slipped northwards towards the Bahamas having attacked a convoy on the way. Upholf in U84 had preceeded him and the aircraft based in the Bahamas were making his getaway difficult.

From Puerto Rico, the PBYs of VP-81 were all hunting northwards, following up Brosin in U134, as he took his boat ever further from the dreaded Caribbean.

From Antigua in the north to Zandery in the south the squadrons were out. They could sense that something was taking place and in fact, the remnants of the great offensive were drawing off. Hagenskotter in U466 had long gone and Tillesen in U516 had hardly entered the area before turning back. Closer in Eick in U510, Dietrichs in U406 and Kandler in U653 were all pulling back. Even the audacious Neide in U415 had signalled U-Boat Command and advised that his fuel would not allow him to stay any longer.

They were leaving behind the ghosts of U590, U159, U662, U759 and U359, but there were still two U-Boats in the Caribbean Sea. Kapitsky in U615 and Dalhaus in U634. Dalhaus was as yet undetected, but Kapitsky was in trouble.

At dawn on Friday sixth of August Mariner P-4 of VP-205 lifted off from Chaguaramas and set course to the northwest. At the controls of the Mark III C Mariner was Lt. A.R. Mantuski. He had on board two other officers and eight enlisted crewmen and their job was to take over from the aircraft that had carried out the all night hold-down operation over U615. It was a tactical mistake to send out only one Mariner to carry out the functions which had occupied aircraft from three squadrons during the previous night, but the Trinidad Command was very busy. On top of following up the receding U-Boats the convoys in the area also needed their usual aircover.

That day four major convoys were operating close to Trinidad. Convoy JT-2 which had been trailed and harassed so tenaciously by Eick in U510, was due to arrive at the Dragon's Mouth but before it gained the safety of the Gulf, convoy TJ-4 was due to depart on its long trek to Rio de Janeiro.

Convoy GAT-77 which had experienced a brief encounter with U615 was due to arrive at the Dragon's Mouth after being diverted north of its route to avoid the U-Boat. On the same day convoy TAG-76 was due to depart on its long run to Guantanamo and ultimately to New York. This convoy's route lay right through the area where the aircraft were conducting the hold-down operation on U615 and a new routing well to the north of the danger area had to be implemented.

In addition to these major movements, several smaller convoys plying between the islands and escorted by the TRNVR had to be covered, as well as the fast troop convoys which normally traversed the area.

Even with its seemingly vast aviation resources Trinidad's aircover was beginning to wear a little thin. During the last two weeks of July, a large number of aircraft had been badly damaged and some even had to be written off after the combats with the U-Boats. Added to this was the normal attrition due to crashes and the requirements of the maintenance schedules, which of necessity had escalated with the vastly increased workload.

To help to counter the decline in operational machines, the US Army

23rd anti-submarine squadron with sixteen B25 Mitchells had been transferred to Edinburgh Field as a temporary measure to help cope with the crisis.

Trinidad was easily the most powerful anti-submarine base in the Caribbean theatre, yet the U-Boat offensive had worn it down. It is significant that only just over half of the U-Boats assigned to the Caribbean operation reached their operational area, and of these only a portion were operating in the Trinidad Sector. Yet even these few with their aggressive tactics, had managed to stretch the aviation resources. It shows what might have been achieved.

The departure of the five aircraft in the early morning and their replacement by the solitary Mariner, gave Kapitsky the break he needed. The Mariner had conducted a preliminary sweep of the area when it had first arrived and found the area clear of radar contacts. Mantuski had then settled down to a methodical search of the area. The Mariner crew were gambling on the fact that the U-Boat had to surface sooner or later. Kapitsky watched Mariner P-4 conduct its initial search through his periscope and then the aircraft disappeared westwards, to start its coverage working towards Trinidad. As soon as the aircraft was out of sight, Kapitsky brought U615 to the surface and sped off to the northeast.

Kapitsky had handled U615 very well during the previous night and managed to remain undetected as the five aircraft swept his area, but the strain was beginning to tell on the crew. He had to charge his batteries, ventilate the boat and give his crew a breath of fresh air before the Mariner returned. The fact that they had survived made them a little over confident and they made a critical mistake.

Kapitsky did a rough plot of where he figured the aircraft would go and worked out an approximate time that he could safely stay on the surface. He was not far out in his calculations, just fractions of a minute, but enough to spell the doom of U615. After the alloted time Kapitsky sent his crewmen below and prepared to dive, so that when the aircraft returned in a few minutes, U615 would be safely underwater. He must have lingered for a minute too long and in the easy atmosphere of a precautionary dive, no one saw the Mariner on the horizon. The conning tower hatch closed and U615 began to go down.

It was one thirty in the afternoon, when the pilot of Mariner P-4 sighted the U-Boat on the surface and decided to attack immediately. Mantuski may have used the existing cloud cover to get close before revealing his aircraft, but by this stage U615 was going down and there was no one on the conning tower to see him. The Mariner swept over the conning tower and four depth-charges left the nacelle bomb bays for the sea. They bracketed the U-Boat and the resulting explosions mortally wounded U615.

Mantuski pulled his Mariner upwards and reported to Chaguaramas that he had attacked the submarine and damaged it. He said that the submarine was down by the stern and proceeding very slowly. Then he went into another attack. Eight minutes after the first message, Chaguaramas picked up a second cryptic radio message saying, "P-4 damaged, − damaged − Fire," then an ominous silence.

That was the last message ever sent by Mariner P-4. Many days later, a Mariner on patrol well to the west, sighted a broken wingtip float, an uninflated aircraft dinghy and a waterlogged cardboard box. This was all that was left of Mariner P-4, Mantuski and his ten other crew members. This was the third Mariner that VP-205 had lost without trace in the previous month.

The four depth-charges had ruined U615's chances of ever leaving the Caribbean. The blast had severely damaged the boat. Both electric motors and the port diesel were put out of action. The lubricating oil gravity tank split and the oil ran down into the bilges. High pressure air lines were broken by the shock and water poured in through the stern glands. Without electric motors U615 could not proceed underwater and Kapitsky had no alternative but to blow his ballast tanks and surface.

U615 shot to the surface and with no other option, the gun crews raced up the hatch. Since the fight in the Bay of Biscay, Kapitsky had avoided combat with aircraft but now it was inevitable. He directed the fire of his formidable anti-aircraft battery and they clawed Mariner P-4 out of the sky when it made its second attack.

The two radio reports received from Mariner P-4 generated an immediate response from Chaguaramas. VP-204 was the duty squadron for that sector, but they didn't have a single aircraft on the ground that was not damaged or undergoing maintenance. Their duty crew led by Lt. L.D. Crockett were forced to borrow Mariner P-11 from VP-205. This was the only undamaged machine available and Crockett and his crew were scrambled in the borrowed machine.

At two thirty in the afternoon, after a hurried briefing, the Mariner lifted off the waters of Carenage Bay and turned northwest. As the thunder of the Mariner's engines drifted over the naval base, the operations room personnel began to recall aircraft and reassign missions and priorities, in order to find the back up required to handle the crisis which was developing to the northwest.

At three twenty-three Mariner P-11 arrived at the last attack position, one hundred and eighty miles northwest of the Dragon's Mouth and began a search for the U-Boat and Mariner P-4. Fourteen minutes later they picked up a contact, twelve miles to the west. At seven miles they had U615 visual and the long drawn out final drama began.

Crockett was the same pilot with the burning desire for revenge. He was the pilot who sat beside Hershey as he died, with a cannon shell in his stomach fired by U406, but he did not rush into an attack. He kept P-11 at three thousand feet and began circling the U-Boat three miles out. To the surprise of the aircraft's crew, the U-Boat's deck gun opened up a rapid accurate fire. Anti-aircraft shells began bursting immediately behind the Mariner and Crockett opened the range. Crockett did not know that a U-Boat could hit him that far out and here was a clue as to what happened to P-4.

At three forty-five having circled the U-Boat twice at a respectable distance and passed a full appreciation of the situation to Chaguaramas, Crockett decided to attack. U615 was crawling along with her stern low in the water and a blue cloud of diesel smoke hanging over her wake. He brought the Mariner down to fifteen hundred feet and turned inwards towards the apparently crippled submarine.

Over the target he released two MK-17 high explosive bombs with contact fuses. By this stage the U-Boat had turned onto a course of three four zero degrees and the Mariner attacked from the south. The demolition bombs exploded with gigantic bangs off the U-Boat's port quarter and the blast wave rocked the gun crews on the boat, but the U-Boat's gunners had not been idle. The Mariner's bow guns had raked the U-Boat all the way in, but a flying boat at fifteen hundred feet presented a considerable target. The U-Boat's gunners had also raked the aircraft all the way in. Cannon shells smashed into the machine and one of them opened up a great rip in the starboard wing root, rupturing the fuel lines. Fire blazed and the aircraft rapidly filled with smoke as it passed over the submarine.

Crockett realized that his aircraft was in danger of exploding and with remarkable calmness, decided to attack the U-Boat again before they were all consumed. He had no wish to go the way of P-4 but if it was that they were to die, then the U-Boat also had to die.

The large sea grey camouflaged flying boat trailing smoke and flames, turned sharply to starboard and round towards its target. Crockett put the crippled machine into an attack dive and came boring in, but the U-Boat's conning tower and deck were a mass of flashes as U615's heavy anti-aircraft armament opened up at the death and destruction hurtling towards them.

In the steeply diving aircraft's cabin another drama was unfolding. Navy machinist A.S. Croider grabbed hold of a spare shirt and two small fire extinguishers, stumbling through the smoke to the source of the fire. Quite oblivious to the fact that the machine could disintegrate in a fireball at any minute and the repeated strikes of German cannon shells, he hauled himself up into the wing root, to the source of the fire.

As the Mariner came out of its dive, two hundred feet from the waves, the U-Boat was turning to starboard until it ended up heading almost south. The Mariner was shuddering under the impact of the cannon shells, as the German gunners bracketed it, but Crockett held on. He swept the great bird trailing fire and smoke, right over the U-Boat and released four MK-44 depth-charges. Past the U-Boat, Crockett hauled the now heavily damaged machine round to the left, in time to see the U-Boat surrounded by the sub-siding water of the depth-charge explosions.

In U615 the roar of the explosions was ringing in the ears of its stunned crew as they fought to contain the water pouring into the boat from the numerous cracks that had been opened in its pressure hull. All lighting had gone and the men were knee deep in water, but they fought on. On the conning tower, Kapitsky looked aft and realized that the whole stern of the U-Boat was underwater and the bow was sticking out of the sea. The waves were breaking on the after end of the conning tower and the gunners were slipping on the canting deck, while they continued to track the Mariner, now moving away from them.

Kapitsky knew that this was the end. His U-Boat would never dive again. His maximum speed was two knots and the rudder was jammed hard a starboard. Trinidad was only one hour's flying time away and soon the sky would be full of aircraft.

Many a U-Boat had scuttled and some had even surrendered when faced with Kapitsky's situation, but he was now to show that he was one of the elite. He was a warrior. His shocked crew went to work with a will and soon they had restored some of the boat's trim, raising the stern by pumping out most of the water. Other crew members brought up ammunition to the conning tower and piled them in miniature mountains around the guns. They were going to fight to the finish. They intended to see how many of their tormentors they could eliminate before sheer weight of numbers crushed them. The scene was set for an epic struggle.

In the meantime, A.S. Croider was working in the confines of the Mariner's wing root and he managed to do the impossible by putting out a fuel fire. He used the shirt and the two fire extinguishers and managed it even though the front of the wing root was missing. The smoke was rapidly clearing as they pulled the badly burnt crewman out of the still hot wing root. Now that P-11 was not going to disintegrate, Crockett took the

Mariner out to the extreme range of the U-Boat's guns and circled while waiting for reinforcements.

Despite the many holes in the fuselage and the fact that he could no longer transfer fuel, the Mariner was still flyable. At eight minutes past four, he reported to Chaguaramas that the fire was under control and that he was remaining within sight of the German submarine to guide other attackers.

While Crockett's attack had been in progress, the operations room in Chaguaramas had been filling up. Senior officers of the base command had all come in to watch the plot and listen to the running commentary from Crockett.

At the Sector Headquarters in Port of Spain, there was also a considerable gathering. Seldom had a battle against a U-Boat been as protracted as this one and never before had they been able to listen to a blow by blow acccount. The reserve Harpoon from VB-130 at Edinburgh Field had been allocated to the mission and within a few minutes they could hear the roar of its engines as it passed over Chaguaramas. The Staff were also thinning out some of the customary heavy escorts that the convoys received and reassigning Mariners to the distant battle in the northwest.

At four thirty the VB-130 Harpoon arrived on the scene and Crockett in his much battered P-11 assumed command of the operation. This was Crockett's U-Boat. He set up a co-ordinated attack with Harpoon B5 attacking from astern of the U-Boat, while he brought Mariner P-11 back in to attack on the starboard side. The Harpoon would make the major attack, dropping depth-charges, while Crockett did a straffing run and tried to draw the U-Boat's fire onto himself. At Crockett's signal the attack began.

The Harpoon pilot pushed his throttles full forward, allowing his twin two thousand horsepower engines to build to their full capability and the machine began to run in. The fixed nose guns opened up, to be joined by the turrets, as the Harpoon stormed towards the U-Boat.

On the starboard side, the damaged Mariner strove to keep up, but the Harpoon was capable of two hundred and eighty knots and began outdistancing the flying boat. Nevertheless the flying boat's fifty calibre machine guns were hammering the U-Boat all the way in.

The U-Boat's gunners were not fooled and although fire from the Mariner was hitting them, they ignored it and concentrated on the Harpoon. However the Harpoon was so fast, that it accidentally passed right through the streams of tracer from the Mariner without being hit and left the heavy Flak from the U-Boat well behind.

The pilot delivered a beautiful low level attack and bracketed the U-Boat with four depth-charges. It was later evaluated that if the U-Boat had been underwater or in the act of diving, the Harpoon's attack would have destroyed it. The four depth-charges exploded around the submarine just as the Mariner was in a climbing turn above it. The Mariner was rocked by the blast, which also blew the U-Boat underwater.

The force of the explosions was such that it rammed U615 underwater for a full fifteen seconds. Inside the U-Boat, the hammer blows stunned the German sailors throwing them off their feet. Pipes were fractured and all the boat's remaining instruments and sensitive equipment were smashed.

When the U-Boat was forced under, the gunners on her deck were swept overboard and many of those on the conning tower found themselves in the sea. Surprisingly, U615 rose again and the shocked gunners scrambled back aboard and gallantly manned their weapons, ready for the next onslaught.

But the straffing by the aircraft had taken a toll. Rolf Kapitsky had taken a fifty calibre bullet through his thigh. He lay in a corner of the conning tower, with copious quantities of blood flowing out of his lacerated leg. Also lying on the conning tower grating, was the seriously wounded Peter Dittmar, the boat's senior Petty Officer.

The U-Boat's First Watchkeeping Officer Oberleutnant Zur See Herbert Schlipper, only twenty-two years old, rushed to the aid of the two wounded men. He tried to have the two carried below, but both refused. He applied tourniquets to stop the bleeding and accepted his commander's orders.

Kapitsky intended to fight his boat, even if he had to do it lying down. The boat's senior Petty Officer also had no intention of not being a part of this final battle. It is surprising that only these two men were hit, by the combined machine gun fire from the two aircraft.

Crockett could see that the U-Boat had received a terrific hammering and assuming that she was finished, he hauled his Mariner round to deliver the coup de grace, with his one remaining depth-charge. Incredibly, he was met by a withering wall of fire from the crippled U-Boat and he quickly swung his already heavily damaged Mariner away from the danger.

On board U615, the crew again strove to restore the boat's trim, although all they could do was creep around in a continuous circle. That they still fought their boat was a considerable indication of Kapitsky's ability as a leader. On the conning tower, they watched the Mariner and the Harpoon circling out of range and wondered how many more shattering depth-charge attacks they could survive. The U-Boat had been under almost continuous attack for four hours. They had survived four depth-charge attacks, one bombing attack and considerable straffing.

Crockett kept up his running commentary to the base, constantly pleading for more reinforcements, while he and the pilot of the Harpoon warily circled out of reach of this U-Boat that refused to die.

By this stage, the military in Trinidad were in a considerable state of excitement, but there was a certain amount of scepticism. How could a U-Boat take such a concentrated pounding and yet not give up. Each depth-charge attack had been good, and many depth-charges had fallen within what was considered to be lethal range, – still U615 kept on fighting. At this stage the U-Boat was little more than a floating gun platform, but a dangerous one. There was a saying among U-Boat crews, that Hamburg built boats were the strongest, but even for a Hamburg boat, U615 was proving to be something else.

At Edinburgh Field and in Chaguaramas pilots waited impatiently, while mechanics and armourers strove to hoist munitions up to the racks, while from all over the Trinidad Sector, aircraft that had been released from convoy duty raced to get in for the kill. Men who had spent months quartering the endless wastes of the Caribbean, searching vainly for the dreaded U-Boats, now saw an opportunity to see one and be in for the kill. But U615 was not going to die that easily.

Three submarine chasers had been dispatched from Grenada and one from Chaguaramas, but it would be many hours before any of these vessels got to the scene of the action. All Trinidad's destroyers were out, either on convoy duty, or hunter-killer missions off the east coast. For the moment, all that could be spared was the small craft.

The next reinforcement to arrive on the scene was Mariner P-8 of VP-204, flown by Lt. j.g. J.W. Dresbach. He was the pilot who had attacked U415 on July twenty-fourth and been illuminated by starshell. He brought his Mariner into the area after being released from convoy escort duty.

Crockett could see the VP-204 squadron badge of an Indian peeping over a cloud, holding a lantern and a flat nosed depth-charge. Once again Crockett set up a co-ordinated attack. This time the Harpoon from VB-130 was to attack on the starboard side, with his battered P-11 on the port side, while Dresbach brought P-8 in from the south. The two straffing aircraft on the flanks would go in slightly ahead of Dresbach, to clear the way for him, by drawing fire and straffing. Dresbach in P-8 would make the depth-charge attack.

At six fifteen the three aircraft began their attack on U615. The U-Boat had taken such a terrific battering that the pilots were convinced that this was the final run. She couldn't survive this one. The diversion failed.

Although both Mariner P-11 and the Harpoon B-5 crossed the U-Boat carrying out telling straffing attacks on the conning tower, Kapitsky had kept his eyes on the new arrival and was able to distinguish which Mariner was the most threatening.

The gunners ignored P-11 and B-5 and concentrated their full fire on P-8, coming in from astern. Dresbach brought his Mariner down low and barrelled into his attack dive intending to finish off the troublesome U-Boat once and for all.

Down below, the German gunners sighted their weapons, ignoring the American fire hitting the U-Boat and opened fire. The tracer converged on P-8 and when the flying boat was close the streams found the nose of the Mariner. Dresbach was mortally wounded in the chest and shoulder by twenty millimetre shells. His last conscious act was to release the depth-charges.

The co-pilot, Lt. j.g. Oran Christian grabbed the control yoke out of the hands of the dying pilot and hauled the Mariner out of its attack dive just in time. As he eased the damaged Mariner upwards, the four depth-charges exploded. They had been dropped fractionally early and the last of the stick of four exploded thirty feet astern of the U-Boat. Although just out of lethal range, the blast from the last depth-charge kicked the stern of the U-Boat clean out of the water, smashing the rudder and aft diving planes. More cracks opened in the U-Boat's pressure hull and the after end was almost untenable, but U615 still lived.

Inside the flying boat there was chaos. The cockpit was a mess of blood and Christian had to hold Dresbach's body with one hand to stop it slumping onto the control column, while he flew the Mariner with the other. The crew pulled Dresbach out of the cockpit, while Christian strove to control his anger. Eventually it got the better of him and Crockett watched helplessly as he took Mariner P-8 back in for another attack. The Mariner crossed U615 at fifteen hundred feet and two high explosive bombs fell away.

These exploded three hundred feet off the U-Boat's port side. Throughout the second attack, the U-Boat's gunners concentrated their fire at P-8, repeatedly hitting the aircraft. At this stage, Crocket ordered P-8 to return to base.

On board, the pilot was dying and four other crew members were seriously wounded. There was blood all over the inside of the aircraft and the wind whistled through great holes punctured in the machine. Crockett's report was received in Chaguaramas with dismay. Surely this U-Boat did not intend to fight forever. Nevertheless the cradle was readied, because P-8 would not float for long after landing. On the ramp, ambulances were waiting for the dead and wounded and the naval hospital prepared to receive casualties. They had been dealing with this sort of situation right through July and now into August. It looked like it would go on forever.

While the last attack by P-8 had been in progress, Mariner P-2 from VP-205 arrived on the scene, flown by Lt. Cmdr. Hull. He was told to hold off until P-8 finished its attack. A problem of command and control now developed. Crockett was only a Lieutenant and although he was a very experienced pilot, the captain of Mariner P-2 was his senior. Not only was Hull senior, but he was also from a different squadron. Despite this Crockett considered that this was his show, regardless of rank. U615 was his and he gave the orders. When the fountains of water cleared, Crockett shrugged off the disappointment and set up the next co-ordinated attack.

Once more Crockett in P-11 and the Harpoon would attempt to beat down the U-Boat's gunners, while Mariner P-2 came in for the depth-charge attack. In the glow of sunset, the next attack went in and once again it failed.

The U-Boat's gunners again ignored the two diversionary aircraft and concentrated on the newcomer. The lines of tracer converged on P-2, but fate also took a hand. Through a mechanical failure, the depth-charges were released when the nacelle bomb doors opened. They exploded with gigantic fountains of water, six hundred feet short of the U-Boat. In exasperation the pilot of P-2 continued boring in towards the submarine using his turret guns, despite the withering defensive fire being put up by the U-Boat's gunners.

A despairing Crockett tried vainly to order his senior officer to break off the attack, while Kapitsky's gunners made good practice. The result was another heavily damaged Mariner with wounded crew.

Again Crocket tried to coax the Mariner to hold off, but Lt. Cmdr. Hull was somewhat annoyed at that U-Boat. He took Mariner P-2 upwards to fifteen hundred feet and attempted a bombing attack by eye. The Mariner carried neither a bomb sight, nor did it have a good bomb aimer's position and these high level attacks stood little chance of success. The two high explosive bombs landed five hundred feet from the U-Boat and exploded with a spectacular bang, but U615 still lived.

At six forty, the pilot of the Harpoon advised that he was running low on fuel and had to leave. Crockett was sorry to see him go and the Harpoon pilot reluctantly turned for his base at Edinburgh Field. So far, his was the only aircraft that had not received serious damage, although there were holes all over the skin. The weary gun crews on the U-Boat watched the Harpoon leave, thankful that the very fast land based machine was finally leaving. The Harpoon was a difficult machine to hit and on top of this, it carried a heavy forward firing battery. They were also thankful that night was fast approaching, in the hope that darkness would give them a respite. The crew were absolutely worn out, both with fighting off the aircraft and keeping the U-Boat afloat.

At this stage, the heavily damaged U-Boat had withstood twelve depth-charges and bombing attacks from six different aircraft. She was in a terrible condition, but she had spat defiance all day and would continue to do so.

Out of range of the U-Boat's guns her chief tormentor Mariner P-11, with Crockett at the controls circled endlessly. After the deparure of the Harpoon and then the damaged VP-205 Mariner, Crockett was alone again for a few minutes with his enemy. Kapitsky had no way of knowing about the death of Crockett's co-pilot in the fight against U406 and he must have wondered at the dogged persistence of the pilot in the battered Mariner. He appeared to be directing the others, yet taking all the risks with each new attack. On one side a courageous U-Boat commander, with his leg a mass of blood, leaned on the edge of the conning tower spray shield. On the other, a tired pilot nursing a crippled Mariner flying boat, circled endlessly. They stared at each other's craft. One wracking his brains to find a way to finish the U-Boat. The other trying to figure out why this man wanted him so badly. Kapitsky knew that soon the Mariner would be forced to give up and leave, but for him, this was the end of the line. It is unlikely that he was bitter.

Back in Chaguaramas there was disbelief that one U-Boat could resist the attacks of so many aircraft and still live. They ordered more aircraft into the fray in the hope that this was the solution. One of these was the US Navy K Type airship K68 from ZP-51. The Blimp was commanded by Lt. j.g. Wallace Wydean and had been almost at the end of a golden triangle patrol, when the pilot had picked up the urgent calls for help coming from the northwest. Despite the fact that he was low on fuel, the young pilot did not hesitate.

K68 turned westward at its maximum plodding speed of seventy-five knots. The great silver grey envelope of the airship hove into view only minutes after the damaged Mariner P-2 and the Harpoon B-5 left the scene. No doubt the arrival of the giant airship broke Kapitsky's wary concentration of the lone Mariner, but he must have rubbed his hands with glee. There was nothing his gunners would have enjoyed more than having a go at the enormous slow moving target.

Chafing at the bit Wydean begged to be allowed to attack, but wisely Crockett refused permission. He was fully aware that the blimp was no match for the U-Boat's guns, and this U-Boat had proved time and again that its gunners were good. Crockett had no intention of giving Kapitsky a present. A very disappointed airship pilot took up station where he could see the crippled U-Boat, but remain out of reach of its fearsome anti-aircraft battery. No one realized that Wydean intended to play his part to the full, — and more.

The month of August is the height of the Caribbean wet season and all afternoon as the fight around U615 raged, the weather had been deteriorating. It was now almost seven o'clock in the evening and the frontal edge of an easterly wave was moving into the area. To Crockett the onset of low clouds and rain showers spelled disaster, but unsupported there was nothing he could do but wait. On the other hand Kapitsky looked on the deteriorating weather as a blessing in disguise. It would help him to buy time.

Just at the end of twilight the next supporting aircraft arrived on the scene of this epic struggle. An Army B-18 bomber of the 10th Bomber squadron from Edinburgh came racing into the area. This aircraft was from the fifth squadron to become embroiled in the fight against U615. Once again the weary Crockett took command and set up an attack run.

The B-18 pilot was impatient to get at this U-Boat which the navy appeared unable to sink. He wanted to go in alone, but he could not see the U-Boat. By this stage, the line of thunderstorms had reached the area and reduced visibility almost to zero. Crockett gave the pilot of the bomber the course to steer and pulled his Mariner up alongside as they began their attack. But U615 had disappeared. The astonished pilots roared over the area where U615 was last seen, but there was no U-Boat in sight. The frustration of the attackers was beyond description.

The two aircraft set up a series of runs across the area dropping flares to light up the sea below, but this didn't help. They kept up the hunt for one full hour, but still no sighting of U615 was made. Barely able to move and slowly sinking, the battered U-Boat had eased out of the way of her tormentors. Kapitsky was using the cover of the rain showers to hide his crippled boat and buy time.

At eight o'clock the pilots had still not located U615 and the weather was beginning to seriously hamper the search. Low clouds and rain made it almost impossible for the aircraft to get high enough to drop flares. This meant that a number of aircraft were operating close to the water, flitting into and out of rain showers in very low visibility, and the hazard of flying into each other was hampering the operation. It was frustrating to the pilots, but particularly to Crockett, who had worked long and hard for this U-Boat.

His aircraft was running low on fuel and with a heavy heart, he was forced to relinquish command of the operation to Lt. Cmdr. Joster flying Mariner P-15 of VP-205. The new Mariner arrived on the scene while Crockett and the Army pilot had been trying to drop flares in the bad weather. As more fresh Mariners arrived on the scene, Crockett was ordered to take his much battered machine home. He was intensely disappointed, but he knew that he had left the operation in capable hands and had no doubt that they would get U615.

Crockett was a pilot of considerable ability and this was proved by the fact that he was able to get P-11 home. The aircraft had nearly all of its instrument panel shot away and for some considerable time he had been flying by feel alone.

Even worse was the fact that not one compass was working. How he had managed to stay with the hunt under these conditions was a marvel. As the big Mariner swung away from the area, his crew were able to relax from their guns for the first time in six hours. They were all utterly worn out but even then care had to be exercised by the crew moving about within the aircraft because the hull was full of holes.

The machine had been badly battered in its continual clash with the U-Boat. From the great gash in its wing root to the tail, there were great holes with the wind whistling through them. Without a compass Crockett had to head south in the bad weather, hoping to see the mountains of Venezuela in time, before turning east for his run to Trinidad. At Chaguaramas the cradle was made ready because P-11 would not float for long. On the ramp ambulances stood by for the injured crew.

While Crockett was bringing his aircraft home, the operations department in Chaguaramas had finally got a surface vessel released and the brand new Fletcher class destroyer USS Walker, eased out of the Third Boca and began working up to full speed. She set course for the scene of the action but it would be many hours before she could get there. The destroyer was not one of the Chaguaramas based escorts. She was on her shakedown cruise, with a new crew working up alongside the fleet carrier Bunker Hill. She was released from the carrier group for this specific operation.

Meanwhile at the scene of the action, the weather was such that the aeroplanes were having a difficult time keeping the sea in sight and at last the airship came into its own. Just as the U-Boat was slipping from rain shower to rain shower, the airship shrugging off the bad weather and keeping to the cover of the clouds, hunted her.

At nine fifteen that night Wydean found U615. The U-Boat was lying dead in the water having finally broken down. Wydean kept the airship concealed in the low clouds and vectored the B-18 bomber into an attack run.

Once again and for the last time, depth-charges plummeted down around the U-Boat. The U-Boat's gunners put up their last barrage, but the B-18 flew through it without serious damage although it was hit in several places. The depth-charge explosions slammed into the U-Boat's hull and again the great hammer blows increased the damage. Then abruptly the clouds closed in and hid the stricken U-Boat from the eyes of her tormentors.

The airship had made the final attack possible and at last Wydean considered turning for home. No one had sought to ask the young pilot whether he had fuel. He had not considered fuel to get home as important as playing a part in the destruction of the U-Boat and in fact, K68 was almost out of fuel. There was no way he could make the one hundred and eighty miles to Trinidad's north coast and he turned instead for the uninhabited Venezuelaland island of Blanquilla. The airship just made it to the island, but there wasn't enough fuel to attempt a proper mooring operation and the great craft was wrecked. U615 had claimed its last victim. The entire crew were rescued by a launch sent from Trinidad.

On the casing of the battered U-Boat the final drama was being played out. The U615 was a shambles. Everything that could be smashed was in pieces. The hull was dented and cracked and inside the boat the water was rising. For the last two hours men had worked inside the hull in water that was sometimes up to their waists and some of the compartments were completely flooded and had to be sealed. The starboard engine was the only one that had worked after the first attack, slowly pushing them ever northward, away from the land. Then this engine had packed up leaving them dead in the water.

Still the damage control operation continued as they vainly strove to plug leaks and attempted to bring some sense of order to the wreck that was U615. Finally the pumps failed and the U-Boat's engineer ended his heroic efforts.

The decks were awash as she slowly settled and the crew forced their way through the water and tomblike atmosphere inside the hull to the hatches and up onto the casing. Only the gunners still manned their mountings. It was at this stage, with the waves crashing over the casing and only the guns and conning tower out of the water, that the B-18 carried out its last attack. Still they fought.

After the attack and the final shock waves had slammed into the hull, the clouds had thankfully closed in and hidden them again. Then they gathered around their gallant commander. Kapitsky had fought all day, propped against the periscope standard, but he had been bleeding to death. At last his time came and in an intensely moving and dramatic scene, he bade them all farewell. He died with his back propped against the conning tower and the crew knew that the time had come to leave U615.

At four fifty in the morning U615 finally died. She went down quietly, away from the prying eyes of her enemies. In the words of one of the survivors, "she sank under us." In the last few moments the only life-raft was swept away and seaman Richard Sura died while trying to recover it. When the Hamburg built boat finally slipped below the waves, she carried the body of her gallant commander with her while the sea claimed Sura's body.

Forty-four of her crew slid into the water in their lifejackets. They had fought the enemy, they had fought to keep their U-Boat afloat, now they had to fight the sea to stay alive.

Overhead the great engines of the attackers thundered and flares burst continually, lighting up patches of the sea. They were hunting for their prey, not knowing that she no longer existed. She was resting on the bottom nearly ten thousand feet below, just to the west of the underwater Aves ridge. She lies sixty-four miles north of Blanquilla island. She died two hundred and seventeen miles from the great anti-submarine bases in Trinidad.

CHAPTER

20

The retreat

Kapitsky's U615 had been the second U-Boat to die in the retreat from the Caribbean, but in the early hours of Saturday seventh of August the Americans were by no means sure. Some of the pilots who had returned from yesterday's combat were insistent that the U-Boat was too badly damaged to have lasted the night, but there was doubt. Many times the hunters had left U-Boats for dead and the boats had escaped. During the night Mariners had searched ceaselessly, but the boat seemed to have disappeared.

Below all this activity, Kapitsky's men bobbed in tight little groups, trying to keep each other awake as they waited for the dawn. The water was warm compared to what it would have been like in the North Atlantic, but the thought of sharks wasn't far from the men's minds. They knew that with the coming of daylight they would either be seen, or at least see what was going to kill them. Quite unkown to them there was some doubt about who would rescue them.

Shortly after the first attack when Kapitsky realized that there was going to be little chance of escape for U615, he had sent off a situation report. Unknown even to Kapitsky, Eberhard Dalhaus in U634 had picked up the signal and decided to see if he could help. U634 was only a short distance to the north and during the night they set course for the area of Kapitsky's battle. The U-Boat arrived in the area in the early morning hours and commenced a hopeless search for either U615, or the survivors. Now there was another U-Boat in the area and this was going to greatly confuse the hunters.

As dawn flooded the Caribbean the powerful Fletcher class destroyer USS Walker came racing into the area. She had run all night through the heavy seas to get to the area of the great battle, which had been fought on the previous afternoon. As she came into the area, her lookouts scanned the horizon for the first sight of this crippled U-Boat. The Walker would make short work of the U-Boat.

In her radar room, the operators stared at the plot, waiting for the blip that would announce that they had found her. Suddenly, a report came down from the gunnery director, — a U-Boat was seen submerging dead ahead, range sixteen thousand yards. It was extremely long range to pick up a U-Boat's conning tower visually, but there is a possibility that the men in the destroyer did see U634 submerging. The U-Boat was in the area. It took the destroyer fifteen minutes to cover the distance to the area where the conning tower was seen, but when she got there she could not find a contact. The horizon was clear, the asdic room was reporting the range clear and there was no propeller noise. The Walker began a search for a U-Boat with all her sensors alert. Then quite suddenly, they found the U615 survivors.

There were forty-three of them and one corpse still strapped in its lifejacket. The badly wounded Petty Officer Peter Dittmar had died of his terrible injuries. This find created a problem. If the survivors in the water were from the U-Boat that had been attacked all the previous day, then what did the lookouts in the gunnery director see? Were there two U-Boats? If there were more U-Boats cruising around, then these were hazardous waters for the destroyer to stop to rescue survivors. The destroyer's captain decided to take a chance and brought his ship to a stop opposite the groups of survivors and the difficult task began. The sea was very rough and it would take some time. Already it was ten past six and full daylight.

Meanwhile all over Trinidad engines were being warmed up as dozens of aircraft were armed and made ready for the day's activity. There were four Mariners in the vicinity of yesterday's action, but the Americans intended to assign everything that was available to the hunt. U615 must not escape. Never before had a U-Boat defied five anti-submarine squadrons, for what was virtually a whole day, and survived. The pilots were anxious to have a go at this audacious U-Boat and the lineup was impressive. There were OS2Ns and Mariners from Chaguaramas, B18s, B25s, Harpoons and airships from Edinburgh and the big B24 Liberators from Waller Field. Additionally San Juan and St. Lucia were running barrier patrols across all the Channels and passages out of the Caribbean.

While these feverish preparations were in progress, the USS Walker was stopped, as her crew hauled the exhausted groups of survivors up the scaling nets hanging down the destroyer's steel sides.

On her bridge, the anxious captain watched the time consuming operation. The destroyer could not afford to remain stopped for too long, she presented too good a target. The sonar operators were listening intently for the sound of propellers and her radar operators were carefully studying their scopes.

At six fifty-five, the captain's worst fears were realized. The metallic voice of the bridge speaker broke into life. Mariner P-9 of VP-205 reported seeing a U-Boat to the west of the destroyer. The rescue operation had to end immediately. Those who were still in the water had to stay there, and to shouted commands from the bridge, the scaling nets were hauled up, as the destroyer's propellers began pushing her through the sea. The depth-charge crews closed up, because the Mariner had reported that the U-Boat had dived.

Within a short space of time the Walker was approaching the spot where the Mariner was circling. The asdic operators were picking up a contact and she raced in to attack. Twice the destroyer ran over the position and the deadly cans rolled off her stern but by this time, the asdic operators had lost the contact. It is probable that the U-Boat down below was U634 and that Dalhaus used a decoy to get away from the destroyer.

After another fruitless half an hour of searching, the destroyer turned back towards the surprised survivors in the sea. After the ship moved away, none of them expected to be rescued. The Walker completed the rescue including bringing Dittmar's body aboard for a proper burial.

The radioed reports to Trinidad had convinced the command that although the survivors from U615 were aboard the destroyer, there was another U-Boat in the area. More and more aircraft were arriving over the site of the depth-charge attack and spreading out in a gigantic anti-submarine search. By this time PCs were arriving on the scene and the Walker got caught up in the massive operation. If it was Dalhaus in U634 in this area, he did a magnificent job to get away, because it was many days before that operation ended.

While the hunt intensified for the unknown U-Boat northwest of Trinidad, a drama was unfolding in mid Atlantic that was going to turn the retreat into a rout. On July twenty-eighth U404 had reported the presence of a carrier much further south than expected. Where previously the American Task Groups had been concentrated near the Azores, they had now spread out and, although the original area was well covered, one of their number was on station in the new U-Boat refuelling area.

U-Boat Command's staff must have assumed that the reported carrier was simply transiting through the area and not specifically there for a purpose. They went ahead and arranged the new rendezvous position in square DF-2, which lay on the latitude of Florida.

U66 was racing away from the Caribbean theatre with Markworth and seven other crew members seriously wounded, heading for the rendezvous position. On the same morning that U615's survivors were rescued, U66 linked up with the tanker U117 and the more seriously wounded were transferred to the larger boat. The doctor was working on these cases while the refuelling operation took place.

Suddenly the Avengers were overhead. Hurriedly the hoses were disconnected and abandoned, while the two boats separated and dived. A short while later the crew of U66 could hear depth-charge explosions and then silence. The Avengers of VC-1 operating from the USS Card, had destroyed the only tanker at sea. There were no survivors.

Three days before in the area southeast of Iceland, the new tanker U489 had been destroyed by the Royal Canadian Air Force, while it was on its way out from Kiel. There were thirty-five U-Boats on the way home, among whom were U66, U84, U134, U415, U510, U634 and U753 from the Caribbean, who all needed a tanker. U466 had already received fuel and U516 did not need a tanker.

Once again the entire schedule was going to be upset, although at this stage U-Boat Command was not yet aware of the loss of the two tankers. Actually, Dalhaus in U634 was not out of the Caribbean as yet and he had an extremely difficult transit of the Mona Passage to undertake.

The only boat which was going to continue operating in the Caribbean theatre was U406. U-Boat Command cancelled the order for his return and appointed Dietrichs as the rear-guard. They informed him that he would have to operate without the extra ammunition and gun grease which U572 had failed to deliver. Dietrichs was supposed to keep the defenders occupied while the other boats escaped. Although it was not put as dramatically as this, — that was the role reserved for U406.

Dietrichs was fully aware that being the only U-Boat near Trinidad, he would have to face the full weight of the anti-submarine forces operating from that island. He was short of ammunition and knew that he could not face the concentrated attacks that would be thrown at him, and he very prudently kept U406 at least three hundred miles from the land.

The rear-guard role was played first by U615 and then unintentionally by U634. These two boats between them drew nearly all of Trinidad's anti-submarine resources to the westward. This allowed the other boats operating to the east of the theatre to surface and get out of range of the aircraft. The U-Boats could never have got out of the area submerged, and the rear-guard role was vital.

After escaping from the USS Walker, Dalhaus sped away from the area and before the anti-submarine operation was well into its stride, he was making for the Mona Passage. He was sighted once but escaped northwards and through the passage, leaving behind him a gigantic hunt.

To the northwest Carlsen in U732 had played a similar role. By attacking the southbound convoy GAT-79 on August fifth he provoked a massive anti-submarine reaction in the Windward Passage, which had moved southward with the convoy, allowing him to slip away northwards.

By August tenth all the boats were out of the Caribbean with the exception of U406, now well out of range of the aircraft. At this stage, the hunt northwest of Trinidad and the one south of the Windward Passage was dying down.

The destroyer USS Walker was not released from the hunt until the afternoon of August eighth, when she turned for Chaguaramas. When she docked at the Naval Base there was quite a crowd on hand to view the survivors of the greatest battle, as they were led down the destroyer's gangplank to the waiting vehicles. They held their heads high, because they were aware that their's had been an epic fight.

At no time during World War Two did a U-Boat take on five anti-submarine squadrons, virtually at the same time, and put up such a gallant fight. The forty-three survivors were given a preliminary interrogation in Trinidad, before the nine most senior were flown to the United States for a more detailed grilling. This was one fight about which the US Navy wanted to hear the other side.

The other thirty-four were transferred to the prisoner of war cage at St. James, in Port of Spain. At this stage, the Americans were experienced in the anti-submarine war and fully aware that a starched uniform and a clean shave was no indication of military ability. They were struck by the high morale of the survivors and their love for their dead commander. What was also astonishing was the fact that the average age of the crew was nineteen.

The second week of August also saw changes in the American forces in the theatre. Vice Admiral John Hoover was transferred from command of the theatre and the Tenth Fleet, to be replaced by Vice Admiral A.B. Cooke. Hoover had steered the Caribbean through its greatest peril and could leave satisfied that he had done an excellent job.

The Royal Navy also corrected the previous anomaly and replaced Admiral Hodges in Trinidad by Vice Admiral T. Carties. Prior to this, Hodges as a full Admiral had outranked everyone, yet was subordinate to the American commander of the Caribbean Sea Frontier.

General Jessy of the Free French forces took command of Martinique and integrated the island's resources with the rest of the Caribbean command.

Squadrons also changed around again. The 8th anti-submarine squadron were recalled to the American east coast and they took their long range Liberators northward from Curacao and Waller Field at the end of the month.

VB-130 also moved their Harpoons from Edinburgh Field to Zandery in Dutch Guiana and all Army anti-submarine squadrons were transferred to the US Navy.

Fleet Airship Wing Five was commissioned to command the vast airship network that now stretched from Guantanamo Bay to Zandery. More and more modern aircraft and vessels were being transferred to the Caribbean and Brazilian commands, ensuring that never again would the U-Boats operate unchecked in this vital area.

U-Boat Command had received a report from U66 which suggested that U117 was sunk and they began to make preliminary moves to counter the crisis. Orders went out to Drewitz in U525 to turn back from the Caribbean as well as Von Harpe in U129, to standby as emergency tankers. These boats had been on course for a refuelling rendezvous with U117.

The Type VIIC boat U760 under the command of Oberleutnant Zur See Blum also had its operational orders cancelled and was warned to standby for duty as a tanker. These preliminary moves were vital, if the Caribbean boats were to make it back to their bases, but in one case, it was already too late.

Kapitanleutnant Hans Joachim Drewitz in the Type IXC U525 was on course for his rendezvous with the tanker U117 prior to resuming his patrol to the Caribbean when he ran afoul of the same carrier that had sunk the tanker. The U-Boat had safely traversed the Bay of Biscay, but Drewitz did not expect carrier borne aircraft at the new rendezvous point. The new area had been chosen specifically to avoid the previous deathtrap which the area near the Azores had become.

The Avengers of VC-1 made short work of U525 and like the tanker U117, there were no survivors. This happened on August eleventh even before U-Boat Command sent out the signal warning Drewitz about his role as an emergency tanker.

Shortly after this U-Boat Command warned all boats to attack aircraft carriers wherever they were found. Although there were a number of these carriers operating in the Atlantic, they were always backed up by destroyers and it would be an extremely hazardous undertaking trying to get them. The result was that not many U-Boats took on carriers during the war.

On August twelfth Dietrichs sent off his situation report. He claimed that there had been no traffic coming through his area during the previous six days and very little air activity. This is not surprising because he was operating so far offshore that he hadn't a hope of getting near the traffic.

In 1942, to try and avoid the U-Boats, shipping had experimented with routes that were well offshore from the Caribbean, but in 1943 they were all using inshore routes. Close to the islands they could take advantage of the aircover that the Caribbean was becoming famous for. The Caribbean based aircraft did not need to operate far offshore, because there was nothing out there to protect. Nevertheless Dietrichs' signal was triangulated and within a short while his quiet area was being regularly visited by the flying boats.

There were no U-Boats in the Caribbean or along the bauxite route. Nevertheless there were a lot of submarine contacts. The events of July and early August had thoroughly worked up the defenders. This caused a rash of erroneous sightings and reports of U-Boat activity. It is surprising how many definite asdic contacts were made and depth-charge attacks carried out. As in all modern warfare, the whales paid the price. The Caribbean had always been a rich whaling ground, but after World War Two there were precious few remaining.

On August thirteenth U415 and U653 arrived at the rendezvous where they were due to meet U525. By the following day when the emergency tanker had not shown up, they informed U-Boat Command. Once again another reorganisation had to be carried out.

The long range Type IXD boat U849 on its way to the South Atlantic and then the Indian Ocean, had its orders cancelled and became an emergency tanker. The boat was under the command of Heinz Otto Schultze and eventually he had to supply U415 and U653 from the Caribbean as well as three other U-Boats. By the time he had finished all he could do was take his boat back to France. On his next try for the Indian Ocean in November, the boat was sunk with all hands by the Harpoons of VB-107 operating from Ascension Island in the South Atlantic.

In the new reorganisation Von Harpe in U129 was tasked with getting Dalhaus in U634 home. On August fifteenth the two boats met and U634 received her fuel to get home, although Dalhaus was not going to need it.

Blum in U760 was tasked to get Upholf in U84 home, but when the emergency tanker reached the rendezvous point on the seventeenth, they could hear depth-charge explosions and they quietly slunk away.

Upholf was under attack. He managed to slip away and a new rendezvous was set up. In the meantime a number of boats had managed to get back home.

The first to arrive was the veteran Piening in U155. After completing his emergency tanker duties, Piening had obeyed his orders to the letter and sailed home on the surface, inside Spanish territorial waters. No one had interferred with his movement and he had a very successful trip. This made Piening into something of a celebrity and the route was christened after him. On August nineteenth, U-Boat Command addressed a signal to all boats, recommending that they use the "Piening Route." For the next ten days, U-Boats successfully used the Piening route and got home safely, but it could not last.

British code breakers deciphered the signals and although they could not pin-point the route, they made a good guess where it lay. Coastal Command checked it out and found the U-Boats moving in Spanish territorial waters. Within a short time RAF Coastal Command aircraft were over the Piening route and the Royal Navy vessels were poised just outside territorial waters. If Spain allowed the U-Boats the use of that route, then the British would sink them in Spanish waters. Within ten days the Spanish Government knew that they had an intolerable crisis on their hands. They had walked a precarious neutral road that had tended towards sympathy with the Germans, but by 1943 German arms were no longer triumphant everywhere and Spain had to look to the future. If she did not act, the Battle of the Atlantic would move into her waters and it would not be long before one or the other of the contestants started to covet Spanish bases.

German U-Boats based in Spain would have relegated the Bay of Biscay to the status of a quiet backwater. In 1943 such a development would have opened up the Battle of the Atlantic again. On the other hand Allied forces based in Spain would have closed the Bay of Biscay with an iron door, virtually killing the U-Boat offensive. Spain would have been immensely useful to either of the parties. Although the possibility of Spain being invaded was remote, the Spanish could not take the chance. Within a short time the Germans had got the message and U-Boat Command was forced to signal all boats, instructing them to discontinue the use of the Piening route. In the meantime a number of U-Boats had successfully used the route and made it home.

By August fifteenth Stahl brought U648 into St. Nazaire and Hagenskotter brought the damaged U466 into La Pallice with his wounded crewmen. Hagenskotter had not enjoyed his only Caribbean patrol and Stahl had not got near to the theatre. Neither of these Type VII U-Boats were ever committed to the Caribbean again and indeed, except for the minelayers, the Caribbean would see only the large Type IX boats in the future. Without the tankers the smaller boats could not be usefully employed so far away from their bases.

Hagenskotter took U466 into the Mediterranean in March 1944 and the boat ended up being destroyed by the Germans in Toulon during August. It had to be scuttled to avoid falling into Allied hands.

Late in September, Stahl took U648 out for a North Atlantic patrol but he died there, when his boat was caught by the Royal Navy frigates HMS Bazely and Blackwood.

On August twenty-third Tillessen brought the Type IXC U516 into Lorient. He had only touched the fringes of the Caribbean theatre in his search for U662, but he was destined to go back to the area on his next patrol. In fact U516 was to carry out two more Caribbean deployments before the war ended.

Even as the great Caribbean thrust was dying out, U-Boat Command was preparing to keep the area alive. It was obvious that the Caribbean was no longer a favourable area and it was also obvious that there would never be another golden time in the west. Nevertheless, the Americans had stationed vast anti-submarine forces in the area and if the U-Boats abandoned the "theatre", these forces would be freed to make conditions even more difficult in other areas. For this reason, the U-Boats were bound to keep going back to the Caribbean.

During the month of August three such boats left the French bases for the far west. The first of these was the famous U123 now commanded by Oberleutnant Zur See Von Schroeter. The Type IXC U-Boat sailed from Lorient on the sixteenth for Trinidad and the bauxite route.

Two days later the Type IXC U518 sailed from Bordeaux on its first cruise to the Caribbean theatre. The boat was under the command of Oberleutnant Zur See Hans Offermann and he was under orders for the Straits of Florida and Gulf of Mexico.

Four days later one of the rare Type VII U-Boats left Brest for the Caribbean. U214 was a D model boat fitted as a minelayer and it was under the command of Oberleutnant Zur See Ruprecht Stock. The three boats were all new to the Caribbean, but U214 had special minelaying orders.

The entrance to the Panama Canal at Cristobal was a critical area and the Americans had extensively mined the approaches to the harbour, but the mines were giving a certain amount of trouble. They were moored mines, which like the mines in the Gulf of Paria, were continually breaking loose. In addition to the moored mines, they had liberally sown the area with seabed-laid influence mines and these were continually being armed out of sequence. In August the Panamanian registered Tug Chagros had been accidentally sunk, and merchant ships were continually being damaged. Stock's orders were to lay his mines in the swept channel into the harbour, to further the confusion.

As usual the tanker problems in mid Atlantic affected U-Boat operations worldwide. All the U-Boats' operational schedules had to be rearranged and this affected the only boat in the Caribbean theatre. If U117 had not been sunk, Dietrichs would have kept U406 in the theatre until the arrival of Von Schroeter, Offermann and Stock in the three new boats. This would have given a measure of continuity to operations in the area, but without a tanker to back him up, Dietrichs had to get out while he still had enough fuel to get home.

He began his homeward journey on August fifteenth and one suspects that he did not regret leaving the area. The Americans had realized that his was the only boat left in the area and they were concentrating on him. Dietrichs got U406 home to St. Nazaire on September fifteenth, but not without problems. A week after he started his homeward run he was caught on the surface by the Wildcat fighters of VC-1, operating off the USS Card.

Dietrichs fought them off, although he was short of ammunition, but at the cost of two killed and three seriously wounded. He dived and got the boat away from the area before the Avengers could move in. He was lucky and refuelled from U849, and then successfully ran the gauntlet of the Bay. He had been at sea for seven weeks and this was a measure of the time it took to complete an average Caribbean patrol. Having completed two Caribbean patrols, the boat never returned to the area and was lost in the North Atlantic to the depth-charges of HMS Spey, during February 1944.

During July the four American Task Groups operated around the Azores and turned the traditional tanker rendezvous area into a trap. U-Boat Command had responded by moving the refuelling area further southeast, but the carriers had followed up. By mid August, the refuelling area was in mid Atlantic on the latitude between Florida and the Canary Islands. The Americans had responded by splitting up the Task Group so that all the area was covered.

Up north around the Azores, they kept the USS Bogue and the USS Santee, with their attendant destroyers.

Further southwest in the new rendezvous area the carrier USS Core and USS Card operated with their destroyer escorts. It was in this latter area that Dietrichs had his clash with the fighters.

Brosin on the other hand, safely traversed the southern danger area and linked up with U849 between the two. After this he entered the northern area and had almost passed right through it when he had a clash with the aircraft from the northern Task Force. He came under air attack, but managed to get U134 safely out of the area, only to fall into the final trap.

Brosin brought U134 in towards the coast of Spain intending to use the Piening route to get his boat back to La Pallice, but had not quite made it to the route when the RAF found him. A Wellington of No. 179 squadron Coastal Command, operating to the outer limits of the Bay of Biscay caught the boat on the surface and delivered a shattering depth-charge attack. U134 went down and took its entire crew to a watery grave off the coast of Spain. Brosin's boat was the fourth U-Boat to die in the retreat.

In the meantime the new Type IXD long range boat U847 under Kapitanleutnant Kuppish had its operational orders cancelled. Like its sister U849, it was on its first cruise down through the South Atlantic and ultimately to the Indian Ocean, when orders came through allocating it to emergency tanker status, to help the Caribbean and Brazilian boats home. U847 was directed to the new and recently dangerous southern rendezvous area, where the USS Core and USS Card were operating.

The mid Atlantic emergency tanker U-Boats were now U129 under Von Harpe, U760 under Blum, U847 under Kuppish and U849 under Schultze. On August twenty-fifth Blum signalled that he had U760 at the new rendezvous point chosen for U84, but that the U-Boat had not shown up. This refuelling point had been located well to the west of the Azores, on the same longtitude as Belem in Brazil, but on the nineteenth of August there had been no sight of the boat.

This was the third rendezvous set up for Upholf, because on the eighteenth both he and Blum in U760 had been ambushed by destroyers at the second rendezvous area. By a curious coincidence, the destroyers that attacked the two boats were the USS Greene, Belknap and Goldsborough. These three old four stackers had been the original destroyers attached to Chaguaramas during 1942. They had served as Caribbean convoy escorts for the whole of that year and into the early part of 1943.

These destroyers were escorting the USS Core. The carrier was on her second Atlantic cruise, the first having been in June when she escorted a mid Atlantic convoy to Gibraltar. This second cruise was to be her best ever. She started off by sinking the tanker U487 in mid July and thereby precipitating the crisis in mid Atlantic. This was followed up by the destruction of Muller-Stockheim's U67, while he was on his way from the Caribbean.

On August twenty-fourth her pilots were going to add to her tally by destroying two U-Boats. The first of these was the veteran U185. Maus had operated the boat in the Windward Passage during March and April, where he had been able to sink three ships. In June Maus had been the escort for the veteran U564 after she had been mauled by aircraft and he ended up picking up the survivors. After the battle in the Bay, Maus took U185 down to the Brazilian theatre where he carried out the daring attack on convoy BT-18. He followed this up with one freighter, before leaving the area in the great retreat. The Avengers of VC-13 caught Maus on the surface in the new southern rendezvous and sank the sixth U-Boat to be lost from the Brazilian Group.

When Blum sent off his signal to U-Boat Command on the twenty-fifth, he already had an inkling that U84 may have been sunk. He had waited six days in the hope that he could effect another rendezvous with the boat, but Upholf was dead. Soon after catching U185, the Avengers of VC-13 caught Upholf on the surface. He had fought to get his U-Boat back to the 1st Flotilla base at Brest and escaped from two ambushes, but failed at the third. When U84 went down taking her entire crew, she was the seventeenth U-Boat to be lost in the Caribbean venture.

The Core's stable mate USS Card was doing just as well. She started off on August seventh with the sinking of the tanker U117. Two days later the Avengers had disposed of U664. On August fifteenth VC-1 caught Drewitz in U525. Then on the same day that USS Core got her double kills, the Card got the emergency tanker U847. The Type IXD boat had already refuelled U415, U634 and U653 from the Caribbean theatre, as well as three other U-Boats. There were no survivors from the boat after the Avengers of VC-1 were finished. The two anti-submarine carriers had now accounted for eight U-Boats in the retreat.

The veteran U510 arrived in Lorient on August twenty-ninth. Eick was one of the last commanders to use the Piening route successfully. After completing three war patrols to the Caribbean, U510 was not to operate in the area again. In the new year U510 undertook an extensive Far East patrol that did not bring it back to Germany until early in 1945. U510 was surrendered to the Allies in May 1945.

Two days later the gallant Carlsen brought U732 into Brest. He had been one of the rear-guard and then made his way safely back across the Atlantic, avoiding the deadly ambush set up by the American carriers. Carlsen was not to see the Caribbean again and in fact the boat was lost on its next patrol. U732 was sunk on October thirty-first by the destroyer HMS Douglas and the trawler HMS Imperialist. At the time Carlsen was striving to get the boat past the Straits of Gibraltar for the Mediterranean. Thirty-two of the crew died and the destroyers picked up the other eighteen survivors.

While U732 was successfully completing its passage the last operational U-Boat to be lost from the Caribbean group was destroyed. Dalhaus who had played such a sterling role in attempting to rescue the U615 survivors and thereby playing such an important rear-guard role, had made it safely to the mid Atlantic refuelling rendezvous. Beyond this point U634 appears to have got into trouble.

On August twenty-ninth Dalhaus signalled U-Boat headquarters to report that he had been hunted by a corvette while traversing between the Azores and Portugal. This was the last message received from the U-Boat, and may have been the transmission which the hunters used to home on him again.

On the following day U634 was caught by the anti-submarine sloop HMS Stork and the corvette HMS Stonecrop. The corvette in particular, was the same one that got the great Johann Mohr in U124. Dalhaus and his crew of U634 died under the pounding by the two experienced submarine hunters. U634 was the fifth boat to be lost in the retreat from the Caribbean and the eighteenth operational U-Boat assigned to the Caribbean to be lost in the venture.

The end of August found three U-Boats still on their way home from the Caribbean. These were U406, U415 and U653. These three boats all arrived safely in their French ports during the first two weeks of September. None of the three ever operated in the Caribbean again. U406 had completed two Caribbean war patrols and went on to her fate, as already described.

U415 still had almost a year to go before she too perished, but during that time she was to achieve a number of successes. The audacious Kurt Neide went on to sink the British destroyer HMS Hurricane in December and followed this up by shooting down two aircraft inside Brest harbour. The U-Boat U415 struck a mine right outside the bomb proof pens of Brest on 14th July 1944. She was moved into the pens but was found to be too badly damaged and scrapped.

Kandler in U653 did not last long. In March 1944 U653 was alone in the North Atlantic, transmitting weather reports for the Germans, when the British triangulated the boat's position. Capt Walker's Second Support Group, now operating with the aircraft carrier Vindex, was tasked to destroy the U-Boat. It was an almost impossible job until Kandler, unaware that he was being hunted, transmitted again and allowed the Group to pin down his position. An aircraft from the carrier found him and the anti-submarine sloops did the rest. There were no survivors.

Dalhaus in U634 was the last operational boat to be sunk in the Caribbean venture, but another U-Boat still had to be lost before the operation was finally over. The emergency tanker U760 had done sterling service to help get the boats home, but on September eighth her turn came. She was so badly damaged in an attack by No. 179 Squadron that she barely made it to a Spanish port. With the British looking over their shoulder the Spanish Government was forced to impose the requirements of international law and U760 was interned for the rest of the conflict. This final sacrifice of another U-Boat, at last ended the July offensive.

The final tally came to six operational boats U160, U514, U525, U564, U607 and U628, lost on their way to the Caribbean. Seven U-Boats U159, U359, U572, U590, U615, U662 and U759 lost in the theatre of operations, and five boats U67, U84, U134, U527 and U634 lost on the way home. Eighteen U-Boats lost for five merchant ships and two schooners sunk. Of the thirty-two boats involved only U648 and U732 came through undamaged. Eighteen out of thirty-two boats was a fifty-six percent loss rate. To give an idea of how bad it was, we need to consider the equivalent figures for the year 1942.

During the whole year, seventy different U-Boats were committed to exactly one hundred Caribbean patrols. Twelve of these boats were lost in transit to and from the Caribbean or operating in the theatre, for a loss rate of twelve percent. But these figures for the operational boats tell only a part of the story.

U-Boats could only operate efficiently in the Caribbean if they had tanker support. Therefore the tankers must be counted an indispensible part of the whole operation.

The first U-Boats to be committed to the July offensive were U67 and U527 who sailed on May tenth and needed tanker support. The last boats to receive tanker support were U415 and U653 in the first week of September. Between these two periods the tankers U117, U118, U119, U459, U461, U462 and U487 were sunk, either while refuelling Caribbean boats, or transitting specifically to refuel Caribbean boats. The emergency tankers U760 and U847 were also lost while tasked with supporting the Caribbean boats. This brings to nine the number of tankers lost in the offensive.

The only tanker that survived was U460 which sailed from Bordeaux on July thirtieth, and the emergency tankers U129 and U849. This brings to twelve, the number of dedicated and emergency tankers which took part in the operation. When added to the operational boats, we find forty-four U-Boats committed to the operation, of which twenty-seven, or sixty-one percent were lost. It was a greater battle than the North Atlantic in May. It may have been the greatest Allied victory at sea in World War Two.

Shortly after Hagenskotter in U466 arrived at La Pallice on August sixteenth, U-Boat Command put down several reasons for the failure of the offensive. These were probably based on the numerous situation reports and a debriefing of Hagenskotter and his officers.

U-Boat Command acknowledged the tremendous part played in the failure of the offensive by the Allied airpower. The U-Boats had to face the RAF in the Bay of Biscay before they had even covered the first five hundred miles of their approximately fifteen thousand mile round trips. In fact nine of the twenty-seven boats lost, went down in the Bay of Biscay.

But the U-Boats only had to face this tremendous hurdle because of their insistence on crossing the Bay surfaced. Nearly all these losses could have been avoided. After the Bay, they had to face the ambush set up by the American carriers in mid Atlantic, and in this area they lost a further nine boats. These losses were unavoidable.

The Germans simply did not have the intelligence information which would have allowed them to move their tankers in time, but U-Boat Command's concern was with what they considered to be the overwhelming airpower in the Caribbean. The boats were under almost continuous aircraft surveillance throughout the theatre, but this airpower was only overwhelming in certain areas. These were along the coasts in the Gulf of Mexico, in the Straits of Florida, in the Windward Passage and around Trinidad. Yet these were the areas where the U-Boats operated and where they achieved small loose groupings. In other words, they attacked the strongest areas.

The U-Boats avoided totally, the wide five hundred mile long convoy route between Aruba and the Windward Passage. In this area aircover for the convoys would have been reduced to the long range aircraft only providing conditions similar to what obtained in the North Atlantic. Aruba and Curacao were probably the weakest airpower centres in the theatre, yet all the convoys had to go through this area. A worthwhile concentration there, combined with the fact that the boats were willing to fight the aircraft, might well have achieved some success.

The same applies to the lower bauxite route. There were airbases all along the route, but in each location only one squadron or part of one operated. The U-Boats moved into this area in sequence and were defeated one after the other. Again, a worthwhile concentration may have achieved success. There were places throughout the theatre where the Americans were spread very thin and these could have been exploited.

Once again comments were made about the weak, inexperienced surface escorts for the convoys. References were made to the successful battles with convoy TJ-1 and BT-18 and the ease with which the single boats penetrated. But these convoy successes were not repeated. U-Boat Command stated that this was because the convoys stayed close inshore where they could receive the maximum aircover. They also cited the almost continuous surveillance provided by shore based radar stations.

The statements about the Caribbean surface escorts were quite true, because generally the convoys were very poorly escorted. What appears not to have been realized was the fact that these convoys were part of an integrated defence system utilizing shallow inshore routes, constant radar surveillance, continuous aerial coverage and independent hunter-killer groups. Under these conditions the surface escorts were almost superfluous.

However, these same convoys were very vulnerable in the places where there was no shallow water, no radar coverage, no hunter-killer groups and a reduced air escort. These places existed but at no time in July 1943 were they exploited. The U-Boats came to the Caribbean prepared to fight and picked the areas where the defences were strongest. The result was a foregone conclusion.

They also commented on the time restrictions imposed on the boats by the loss of the U Tankers in mid Atlantic. This reduced the time on station to three weeks or less, and according to U-Boat Command, allowed only one opportunity per boat for a convoy attack.

Northbound convoys from Trinidad in 1943 were working on a six day cycle. In between each departure, a southbound convoy arrived. This meant that a convoy could be expected every three days.

The southbound convoys to Brazil also operated on the same cycle and in between there were the inter-island convoys and those that crossed the Atlantic to and from Trinidad. This meant that there was at least one convoy every day to or from Trinidad. The opportunities for attacks on these convoys existed nearly every day, but not in the shadow of Trinidad. However, this must not be allowed to detract from the fact that the defeat of the tankers drastically reduced the effectiveness of the Caribbean boats. When the tankers were defeated, the Caribbean boats were defeated.

Lastly, U-Boat Command mentioned the effect of the climate on the

U-Boat crews. This is crucial because few of the U-Boats operated with the dash of the 1942 veterans.

Kurt Neide in U415, Eick in U510, Kummetat in U572, and Kapitsky in U615 deserve special mention as outstanding audacious commanders, who were prepared to carry the fight to the enemy. But the majority seem to have succumbed to the apathy brought on by the heat in their steel coffins. In this the continuous hostile airpower played a big part. It is not really fair to judge them against the 1942 commanders, who had been painstakingly trained and operated in an environment that was favourable. But by 1943 the 1939 class of naval officers were achieving command of U-Boats and this could hardly compare with the rigorous earlier requirements.

The great venture ended with the loss of twenty-seven boats out of the forty-four committed to, or supporting the operation. Many historians have tended to lump the Caribbean 1943 attack with the Brazilian attack of the same time and refer to it as the South American attack. If this is the judgement of history, then what took place off Brazil must be included in the whole.

Eight boats were assigned to the Brazilian theatre. Of these six were lost. The Brazilian boats used and depended on the same tankers which the Caribbean boats used, but the Brazilian venture was definitely a subsidiary operation. Nevertheless if they are added, the final figures would be thirty-three boats lost, out of fifty-two committed.

This means that the total loss was sixty-four percent. No force could sustain losses at this level and henceforth, both the Caribbean and Brazilian theatres became minor sideshows, where U-Boats continued to operate but only to tie down anti-submarine forces.

CHAPTER

21

U.S. Navy triumphant

During September 1943 the U-Boats returned to the North Atlantic. They took with them the new T-5 Acoustic torpedo, with the express intention of attacking the convoy escorts. The fight back order encouraging the U-Boats to fight the aircraft was at last cancelled and in its place was the much more realistic, fight the escorts order. Once again the battle in the North Atlantic escalated, but this time the Caribbean was not included. The area had gone back to its 1943 status as a secondary theatre where solitary U-Boats had a long hard slug against overwhelming odds.

Von Schroeter received his orders allocating U123 to the four hundred mile wide coastal zone, on the eastern side of the theatre. Previously this had been the province of nine U-Boats and the anti-submarine resources were geared to handling many more enemies.

Following the excitement of the last three months, the defenders were keyed up and indeed they detected U123 long before it arrived in the theatre. On September eighth they triangulated the boat's signals and one suspects that they also received intelligence information from the British.

By September eleventh they had confirmation when the freighter SS Jared Ingersol reported a U-Boat on the surface two hundred and twenty miles east of Trinidad. The freighter set off for Trinidad with the U-Boat in pursuit, but not for long. Within an hour Mariners were coming in and Von Schroeter had to give up the chase and see to his own survival.

The victory over U615, although it had been hard won, still gave the defenders a tremendous boost and since the departure of U406 they had been prowling the Caribbean looking for the next U-Boat to enter their area. Von Schroeter was well in advance of the other three boats of his wave and he was hunted mercilessly. For the next two weeks, he kept well away from the shallow coastal water, but eventually he had to attack.

He chose convoy TJ-9 going southward as it passed off French Guiana and fired several torpedoes. Although he heard detonations, none of the ships in the convoy were hit, but the staggering anti-submarine reaction sent him scuttling northward.

On the following day he found out exactly what it meant to have total superiority. The TRNVR anti-submarine vessel HMS Black Bear gained asdic contact on U123 and attacked with depth-charges but lost the contact after the first attack. Immediately an airship, on OS2N, and a Mariner, were vectored to the scene to assist the four aircraft normally assigned to the convoy, but this was only part of the reaction. The US Navy were so confident that U123 was the only boat in the area that the convoy's surface escorts were ordered to stay with the contact, while the air escort took the convoy to the Dragon's Mouth. However, by this stage some support was arriving in the theatre, if far away from U123.

On September twenty-first Offermann brought U518 into the Bahamas enroute to the north coast of Cuba. On the following day Ruprecht Stock arrived in the area northeast of Antigua, on his way to mine the Panama area.

Curiously, the Caribbean Command had been warned about U-Boats on minelaying missions in the area since September eleventh. This information could only have come from Ultra intercepts.

On September nineteenth Claus Becker once more brought U218 out of Brest, on his mission to mine the Dragon's Mouth and again, a warning signal was sent to the Caribbean Command.

By this stage of the war, British code breakers were reading every signal that referred to the U-Boats. Undoubtedly they read the signal that was sent to all boats on September twelfth warning them that for overwhelming political reasons, Argentinian ships were not to be searched.

One can only guess at the political reasons, but it is known that at this

time Britain was putting pressure on Spain about U-Boats calling at her
ports, and Germany may have been trying to arrange a similar haven in the
South Atlantic. A port which could be used like El Ferrol, situated in
Argentina, would have been invaluable to Germany.

In the meantime the US Army Air Corps was getting out of the Caribbean theatre. By the end of September all their combat aeroplanes, with the
exception of the 23rd anti-submarine squadron, moved northwards to the
United States, or crossed the South Atlantic for the European theatre.

Army aircraft had made a considerable contribution towards defeating
the U-Boats and this had been particularly important in the first year of the
assault on the Caribbean. In the Trinidad Sector alone, their aircraft had
completed thirty thousand flying hours. They were being replaced in the
theatre by navy bomber squadrons' flying Harpoons, some of which were
soon to be equipped with anti-shipping rockets.

The Army Air Corps retained Waller Field and a number of other airbases throughout the theatre, but most of them were now dedicated to
transport aircraft, or the ferrying of combat aircraft to and from Africa.
The defence of the Caribbean theatre against the U-Boats was now a pure
naval responsibility. But probably the most significant event of August
1943, was the death of Albrecht Achilles.

The Caribbean veteran U-Boat U161 departed Lorient on August
eighth for its sixth war patrol, which would take Achilles and his men to
the Brazilian theatre. Two weeks after sailing they had a mid Atlantic rendezvous with a Japanese submarine on its way to France, following which
Achilles took up his post off Brazil. He sank two ships, but as in the Caribbean theatre, the Americans were able to track his progress and were hunting specifically for him.

On the morning of September twenty-seventh Mariner P-2 of VP-74
flown by Lt. Harry Patterson, detected U161 on radar, at a range of thirty-
eight miles. At eighteen miles they had the U-Boat visual and commenced
an attack run. It was a clear cloudless day and Achilles must have seen the
Mariner coming in from a long way off and decided to fight on the surface.
The U-Boat opened fire when the aircraft was still eight miles away which
was extremely long range for the small calibre guns.

The U-Boat's anti-aircraft fire was extremely accurate and the Mariner
took considerable punishment on the run in, but Patterson held on and
placed six MK-44 depth-charges into the water. Most of the charges went in
on the U-Boat's starboard side and the pilot noticed no apparent damage
to the boat. Despite the damage to the aircraft, Patterson decided to go in
for a second attack. Again, the fire from the boat was very accurate and

several of the crew were seriously wounded, but Patterson held on and put his last two depth-charges close to the U-Boat's hull. While fighting to keep his now heavily damaged Mariner airborne, Patterson noticed that U161 had slowed down considerably and for a short while the boat was manoeuvring erratically. Then he saw U161 straighten up its course and dive.

A short while later, a US Navy Harpoon arrived on the scene but saw no sign of the U-Boat. No one ever saw U161 again. It is unlikely that she had a depth-charge lodged on her deck, because the crew of the Mariner would have seen the explosion. It is probable that the depth-charge attack seriously damaged the U-Boat, but that Achilles did not realize how badly his boat was hurt. He had nothing to fear from Mariner P-2, but he must have known that it would not be long before there would be other aircraft on the scene. If this is the case then the occupants of U161 must have died under nightmare circumstances, diving deeper and deeper, with the boat out of control, until the sea finally claimed them. U161 probably lies two hundred and fifty miles south of the Brazilian city of Recife, under more than two miles of water. U161 was VP-74's fifth U-Boat victim.

Achilles was an extremely popular commander and when the boat went down, it took most of the original crew who had served on it during the Trinidad attack in 1942. However Werner Bender was not aboard. The First Watchkeeping Officer who went through all those daring attacks with Achilles, now had his own boat.

In October of 1942, he had completed his commander's course and took command of the new Type IXC boat, U841. He did not long survive his mentor, but died in the U161 tradition. On October seventeenth just a few weeks after the loss of U161, he was attacking convoy ONS 20 in the North Atlantic, when U841 was caught by the first of the Captain class frigates HMS Byard.

A depth-charge attack damaged the boat so badly that Bender was forced to surface where he engaged in a gunnery duel with the frigate. The first round from the frigate hit the U-Boat at the base of the conning tower and time after time, fire from the escort wiped out the sailors around the guns. But the crew of U841 fought on, until finally their boat virtually sank under them. It seems that for once, good sense prevailed and the captain of the frigate declined to ram. One officer, five Petty Officers and twenty-seven seamen were picked up, but Bender went down with his boat.

At this stage of the war anti-submarine technology was well ahead of the design of the boats which were actually in service, but the month of September 1943 saw a swing in the opposite direction, when the first schnorkel went to sea. This device allowed the submarine to run on its diesels while the boat remained just under the surface. In time this was one of the developments that was to revolutionize the submarine, making it an undersea vessel which could also surface, rather than the other way round. However, it was still to be some time before the schnorkel was seen in the Caribbean. The boats that operated in the area for the rest of 1943 were all tied to the surface and thus prey to the flying boats.

The start of October found U123 patiently awaiting a chance to strike, off Trinidad, but the combined air-sea hunter-killer groups that were looking specifically for her, made it difficult to survive, far less attack anything.

By this stage, Offermann in U518 had worked his way through the Bahamas, up the Nicholas channel and through the Straits of Florida. He was operating U518 just inside the Gulf of Mexico close to Key West. He was in a highly dangerous area but one where he was likely to meet much of the traffic for the Gulf.

Ruprecht Stock brought U214 through the Mona Passage at the end of September and turned towards Panama. With the drastic shortage of tanker U-Boats caused by the losses in the Caribbean offensive, Type VII boats like U214 could not afford to tarry and Stock found himself off Colon by October eighth.

Stock had received a comprehensive briefing on Cristobal harbour but it was still difficult to believe that the place was dangerous, because the lights ashore were on as in peacetime. No U-Boat had operated off Panama for more than a year and the only concession to the war was a powerful searchlight that periodically lit up the harbour entrance. Appearances could be deceiving because Cristobal was heavily defended.

Besides the minefields, the entire area was covered by numerous coast defence batteries. However, the area was short of destroyers and anti-submarine aircraft. The last U-Boat in the zone had been U654, which had been sunk on August twenty-second 1942.

This lack of activity had led to the gradual reduction in the anti-submarine coverage. Stock eased U214 carefully through the outer reaches of the harbour and laid twelve of his mines in the channels. They were laid in relatively shallow water and when he was finished, he took U214 northwards and signalled U-Boat Command about the completion of his mission. They instructed him to lay the remainder of his mines in the outer reaches. He turned eastwards and laid the remaining mines close to Point Mazanillo. Once this final part of the operation was complete, U214 turned for the Mona Passage.

Two mornings later a German mine was discovered in the shallow water off the point. Naturally there was a certain amount of panic. U214's success signal had been only a coded four letter transmission and there had not been time to triangulate such a short signal, with the result that the defenders were still unaware of U214's mission.

However, the mine was obviously newly laid and this necessitated an immediate minesweeping operation. Cristobal was an extremely sensitive area because it was the entrance to the Panama Canal, called by some the Achilles heel of America. Even with the combined resources of the area it was not declared safe until the end of the month.

By the middle of October Becker had U218 east of Antigua, on his way down the island chain to Trinidad. On the following day a signal warned the Trinidad Command to expect him, — on a minelaying mission! The available minesweepers were spread out among the harbours of the area and patrols were increased. This did not stop Becker from accomplishing his mission on the night of October twenty-seventh. He laid twelve mines in the area outside the Third Boca.

Becker had been fully briefed on the strong defences in the area and he made sure to carry out his operation on a moonless night without being detected. The mines were laid in water that varied between fifty to a hundred fathoms and four hundred yards apart. As a concession to the strong current in the area, each mine had a six hundred yard long mooring cable. Becker then moved well to the northeast and sent off his code letters AFKP, as a signal that he had completed the mission.

US Navy records do not indicate that they were aware of the mission, or that they ever conducted minesweeping operations to clear these mines. They were having enough trouble with their own mines. Additionally, since Markworth's mining of Castries in 1942, the approaches to the Bocas were routinely swept, but there is no record of German mines being swept. But Becker's mines were never heard of again.

It appears that the Germans took an optimistic view of minelaying in this area, much the same as the Americans. In this matter only the Royal Navy seemed to appreciate the fact that the current in the Dragon's Mouth was far too strong for minelaying. The German mines probably lay so far underwater that no one suspected their presence and eventually they either broke away, or became waterlogged and sank, much like the American mines.

Becker took his boat along Trinidad's north coast and then to the southeast, where on November first he recorded that he sank a schooner by gunfire. Again no record exists of this vessel's name or of the loss, but too many schooners went down unrecorded, not to credit him with the sinking.

In this area they were accustomed to the loss of schooners and it was not until 1944, that records of all these losses began to be accurately kept. After the sinking of the schooner he took his boat safely back across the Atlantic.

In the meantime, the second and much more successful wave of U-Boats were entering the Caribbean. The first into the area was the veteran Kusch in the well tried U154, on its fifth patrol into the Caribbean theatre. He came into position off Cayenne on November third, replacing the unsuccessful U123. Von Schreoter left the area having only experienced a succession of air attacks and harassment. The boat never returned to the Caribbean, but was one of the lucky U-Boats to be surrendered in 1945.

The second new U-Boat into the area was Rutger Tillessen's U516. This time he was not just passing through but bringing U516 down the island chain to pass between Grenada and Tobago for a cruise to the far west.

Behind these first two, Von Harpe was bringing the veteran U129 to the Caribbean, for its fourth war patrol in the area. Not far behind U129 was Korvettenkapitan Hans Paukstadt in the new Type IXC U193. The fifth boat of this new wave was the new Hamburg built Type IXC U530, commanded by Kapitanleutnant Kurt Lange. This boat was destined to make three Caribbean visits, the third of which would be under the strangest circumstances.

Offermann in U518 had spent most of the month of October in the Gulf of Mexico but he had not been able to penetrate the heavily escorted tanker convoys. In fact he was operating so close to Key West that it was surprising that the boat survived. The U-Boats of September and October had not managed to sink any merchant shipping, although U214 claimed to have made an attack in the Panama Sector. It is probable that other than U218's schooner off Trinidad, nothing else was hit. The US Navy had a tight hold on the theatre and it would take an audacious U-Boat commander to loosen it. Such a commander arrived in November.

Tillessen took U516 westwards past Trinidad's north coast and then along the coast of Venezuela, to the Colombian coast. On November eighth a Harpoon of VB-133 attacked the boat west of Curacao. The U-Boat's gunners put up a terrific amount of anti-aircraft fire and just before the aircraft reached its release point they got the range. The Harpoon was damaged and it was only with the greatest difficulty that the pilot held to his attack run and dropped his six depth-charges. However, all the charges overshot and exploded harmlessly beyond the boat.

The pilot got his damaged aircraft and wounded crew home to Curacao and was able to report the presence of the U-Boat. The anti-submarine squadrons had been waiting for just such an occurrence and within a short while most of VB-133's Harpoons were out looking for the U-Boat. They were joined by a surface hunter-killer group, based on the destroyer USS Hurst and the Dutch anti-submarine vessel Queen Willomena. Night and day coverage was afforded to the area, but the bold Tillessen slipped away westwards.

On Thursday eleventh he torpedoed the Panamanian registered freighter Pompoon, right outside Blanquilla harbour. Shock and outrage greeted this attack. It was three months since Kapitsky had sunk the tanker Rosalia. During this time the belief had grown that the Caribbean was totally safe. The U-Boats were beaten and there was no question of one of them breaking through. Furthermore, the sinking took place in the Panama Sector and no U-Boat had successfully torpedoed a vessel in this area, since Achilles' attack on the San Pablo in July of 1942. The sinking of the Pompoon woke up the entire Panama Sector and it was just as well because Tillessen was by no means finished.

On the same day that U516 carried out its audacious attack, Edinburgh Field in Trinidad was renamed Carlsen Field. It was named in honour of Captain Kenneth V. Carlsen of the 35th Bombardment squadron, who had been killed in a B18 on the night of December fourteenth 1942. Carlsen had been operating out of Zandery on an anti-submarine patrol when the aircraft suffered a double engine failure. He held the bomber steady as it fell towards the sea so that his crew could bale out. The unreliability of aircraft engines was still giving trouble and the Harpoons in particular were experiencing a number of engine failures, causing several fatal crashes. This got so bad that VB-130 had to be grounded for a month while engineers did their trouble shooting. In the meantime on the last day of October, a B25 out of Puerto Rico collided with ZP-51's airship K94. The airship exploded, killing all aboard.

Kusch in U154 like Von Schroeter before him, was the only U-Boat operating along the bauxite route and he was subjected to the same non-stop interference from the air. He was unable to get near to the numerous convoys transiting the area. In the far north, Von Harpe brought U129 through the Bahamas and into the highly dangerous Florida Straits area. Pankstadt in U193 came in via the same route but continued on into the Gulf of Mexico. Lange brought U530 through the Mona Passage on the nineteenth. He then turned eastwards and made a long circuit of the western side of the islands passing Anegada then Martinique, before turning for the far west.

Kurt Lange was a pre-war merchant navy captain aged thirty-nine. He was the second oldest U-Boat commander on operational service and had developed a reputation for survival. He had no intention of getting killed uselessly and U530 was considered a safe U-Boat, − one that would always come home.

This instinct for survival had been considerably strengthened by his experience when he attacked convoy HX-229 in March. Lange had been caught by the destroyer HMS Beverley and had to take U530 down to seven hundred and ninety feet in order to escape. This was one hundred and thirty feet deeper than the boat's maximum operational depth of six hundred and sixty feet. Even at that depth he had experienced a narrow escape.

The Allies had developed a one thousand pound killer depth-charge, designed to get the really deep boats and the Beverley had dropped one of these, but fortunately for Lange, its firing mechanism failed. Kurt Lange did not attack until he had all odds on his side. He came to the Caribbean not intending to provoke trouble, but his operational area was in the Panama Sector, where Tillessen was raising a hornet's nest.

After the sinking of the Pompoon, Tillessen had slipped away from the hunt and moved deeper into the sector. On November seventeenth he sank the schooner Ruby, using only his guns, with the U-Boat on the surface, just north of Colon. By the time that the schooner's crew in their dinghy reached the shore, the Americans were aware that they had trouble in the Panama Sector.

The whole hunt moved from off the Colombian coast to the area off Colon, following up the U-Boat commander who did not seem to understand that the war in the Caribbean was over. Despite the presence of two destroyer hunter-killer groups and numerous aircraft transferred from Curacao, Tillessen struck again. At eleven o'clock on the night of November twenty-third he torpedoed the seven thousand ton Liberty ship Melville E. Stone, one hundred and fifty miles north of Colon airbase. The freighter's call for help was picked up all the way in Germany. As the aircraft and hunter-killer groups converged on the area, Tillessen moved closer to the land.

Five hours later U516 was only seventy-five miles from the Colon airbase, when the five thousand two hundred ton tanker Elizabeth Kellog came in sight. Two torpedoes romped into the tanker and she burned. The glow from the burning tanker could be seen from a considerable distance and it was dawn before U516 turned northwards to escape. Daylight found aircraft circling the sinking tanker and Tillessen submerged, a long way from the scene.

The tanker had been his fourth ship. Not since Mohr had decimated convoy TB-1 in January, had a U-Boat in the Caribbean theatre managed to sink four ships, but Tillessen was not finished with the area. That morning the US Navy cancelled the barrier patrols in the Windward, Mona and Anegada Passages. After the attack by the Harpoons on the eighth, they had instituted these patrols because they were sure that the damaged U-Boat would try to get out of the Caribbean. It was now obvious that this U-Boat was no cripple.

For the rest of the month of November Tillessen kept out of the way of the numerous air-sea hunter-killer groups that were looking for him. In fact the only U-Boat of the five in the theatre, which was not being hunted was Lange in U530. He was staying submerged during daylight, not transmitting at all and not attacking anything. Convoys were out, because there was little chance of him escaping. He brought the boat across the Caribbean biding his time. Sooner or later a target would present itself that would allow him to attack and stay alive. Towards the end of the month he joined Tillessen in the Panama Sector.

At the start of December 1943 two additional U-Boats joined the five in the theatre. Gunther Pfeffer in the Type IXC U170 came up past Cayenne from the Brazilian theatre. He sailed right up through the eastern side of the Caribbean theatre and then spent a week on station off the north coast of Puerto Rico. This was the same Pfeffer who had operated U171 in the Gulf of Mexico during September 1942 and had lost his boat to a mine while on the way home.

The second U-Boat also came up from the Brazilian theatre. Max Wintermeyer brought U190 up past Cayenne to the area off British Guiana and for a short while U154 had company. Both the newcomers were detected by their radio transmissions and then they were both sighted. There were now seven U-Boats in the Caribbean theatre and ships were being sunk. It was almost like old times, but for how long? Every available anti-submarine unit was out and the Americans were showing how tightly they controlled the area.

Only Tillessen would not conform and he was soon joined by Paukstadt and Von Harpe.

On December third Paukstadt ended the Gulf of Mexico campaign in fine style. He put three torpedoes into the ten thousand one hundred and seventy-two ton American tanker Touchet. Since Pfeffer had operated in the Gulf of Mexico, only three ships had been sunk in the area and the Touchet was to be the last for the war. After the sinking Paukstadt was hunted relentlessly and he did not get another opportunity to attack.

On the following day Von Harpe brought the northern Caribbean awake by sinking the Cuban freighter Libertad, twenty-five miles south of San Salvador. He also found that the anti-submarine forces in the area concentrated on him. Gone were the days when U-Boat commanders racked up impressive scores. To be fortunate enough to sink one on a patrol was good going. All except Tillessen!

The centre of gravity of the Caribbean war had swung back to the far west, after more than a year around Trinidad. VB-133 had first transferred to Curacao, then to Blanquilla and now it was operating in the Panama Sector. This did not deter Tillessen, and on December eighth he sank the Panamanian registered freighter Colombia only twenty miles north of San Blas Point. Once again a U-Boat was operating dangerously close to the Panama Canal and it generated an immediate response.

The 23rd anti-submarine squadron had detachments operating over the Windward Passage right across the theatre to French Guiana. The powerful B25s were spread out so that each area could benefit, but in December Panama needed them more than anyone else and the entire squadron was transferred to France Field.

The move of the B25 squadron coincided with Tillessen's wish to move on, and just as massive forces were building up to deal with him, the U-Boat swung eastwards. Two days later U516 was nosing around the oil terminal at Aruba. On Thursday sixteenth he shattered the peace of the Dutch islands by sinking the ten thousand ton American tanker McDowell. He used T-5 Acoustic torpedoes to dispose of the giant, only thirty miles from the island of Curacao. This pleased him so much that he decided to hang around the Dutch islands for a while longer, in the hope that more targets would present themselves.

Two days previously Von Harpe had attacked a convoy in the Bahamas, but his torpedoes missed and the escorting destroyers shook him up with some accurate depth-charge attacks. Aircraft frustrated any further moves he attempted to make against the convoy, to the extent that he signalled U-Boat headquarters commenting on the strength of the airpower in this once quiet segment of the theatre.

All the auxiliary flying fields in the Bahamas were now operational and the clear shallow base of the Bermuda Triangle had now become a very dangerous place. By this stage Kusch had taken U154 away from the theatre. Both he and Von Schroeter had found out what any of the U-Boat commanders from July would have told them, that Trinidad was now a most unprofitable area for U-Boats.

Pfeffer in U170 had also turned for home, having failed to achieve anything in the area north of Puerto Rico. This left just Paukstadt in the

Gulf of Mexico, Von Harpe in the Bahamas, Wintermeyer off Guiana, Tillessen off Curacao and Lange in the Panama area.

The sinking of the McDowell forced further reinforcement of the Curacao area and VP-204 moved a detachment from Chaguaramas to the Dutch islands. Almost as soon as the Mariners arrived in the area, they were in action. At nine fifteen on the night of the eighteenth, Mariner P-4 found U516 on the surface to the north of Curacao. The Mariner pilot brought his large aircraft in against the U-Boat, while Tillessen urged on his gunners. He had decided to stay and fight.

The U-Boat put up a fearsome barrage and the Mariner was repeatedly hit, but the pilot held on and placed his six depth-charges right across the U-Boat. U516 came to an immediate stop and on seeing this, the Mariner pilot swung back into another attack run. The U-Boat did not contest the second attack, but the Mariner's racks were empty and all that could be done was the straffing of the conning tower. At this stage, U516 got going again and it crash-dived. The damage in the U-Boat was so extensive that they had to begin their homeward run immediately.

One week later when U516 was safely out of the Mona Passage, Lange was tempted. He fired three torpedoes at the ten thousand ton American tanker Chapultec. Two of the torpedoes romped into the giant vessel bringing it to a dramatic stop. The tanker's SSS was picked up in Germany and before Lange could get U530 into a position to finish it off, the B25s were overhead. He had attacked the tanker only sixty miles from San Blas Point, within easy reach of the defenders. As they began to concentrate on the area, Lange took U530 well north to get out of the way.

The attack on the Chapultec caused consternation ashore. Lange had not used his radio at all and no one knew that there was still a U-Boat in the Panama Sector. The discovery kept both the Panama and Curacao areas humming for the next two weeks, but long before this Lange took his boat northeast for the Mona Passage.

In fact by the first week of January, all the U-Boats were homeward bound. Surprisingly, Lange had kept his operating area off Panama secret from the Americans, but he could not hide his retreat. A detachment of VP-204 picked him up as he came out of the Caribbean and they harrassed him continuously until he was five hundred miles from Antigua.

In the meantime, Tillessen was telling U-Boat Command that he felt the Americans were using his radio transmissions to home in on him while in the Caribbean theatre. Actually, this had been going on since June 1942, but for some reason the U-Boats had continued their regular broadcasts. It reached the stage in 1943 where the anti-submarine forces were able to plot each boat throughout its cruise.

Of all the boats going back across the Atlantic only U516 was seriously damaged but it was also the only one that had been really successful. How did Tillessen in U516 manage to sink two large tankers, three freighters and a schooner in the Caribbean theatre? It was more than twenty-two U-Boats had managed to do in July. Could it be that U516 had simply picked the right area? When U615 sank the tanker Rosalia off Curacao in July, it had caused considerable agitation among the military and civil authorities in the Dutch islands, who it appears did not know that there were still U-Boats in the Caribbean in 1943.

The days when each island had boom town survivor camps were over, and with it the awareness that there was a war in the Caribbean. In November and December, the consternation in Panama was even greater than it had been in the Dutch islands in July.

When there had been survivors to talk to, the civil population of the territories around the Caribbean theatre had been keeping themselves up to date, but now they knew nothing. This meant that the pilots were facing greater hazards in 1943 than ever before, yet they were operating in an environment without understanding from the civilians or even many of the shore bound military personnel.

This was bound to lead to friction. A friction that was to plague the Americans in the area after the war. July had been a great victory for them but not one news item was released telling the population what was going on, or even what had gone on. Very sketchy details of the fight against U615 were released in November.

It was a serious propaganda failure on the part of the Americans and a serious planning failure on the part of the Germans. The mere fact that Tillessen was able to achieve what he did, is a condemnation of what went on before. Even the ultra conservative Lange had been able to hit a large tanker. The shocked reactions of the civilians says that the German planners had allowed several areas in the Caribbean to remain unmolested for a very long time. July could have been very different.

At the end of 1943, U-Boat Command could not look back on the year in the Caribbean with any great sense of accomplishment. The contrast with 1942 was staggering. During the year forty different U-Boats had reached the Caribbean and managed forty-five patrols. During the course of these operations they had managed to sink only thirty-one ships and damage seven others. This was the sort of total that 1942 would yield in a average month.

Tonnage was no longer important because the Allies had managed by the end of the year to vastly outstrip the sinking rate and stockpile so much material, that there was little hope of the U-Boats causing a serious setback. Even if the Caribbean boats had destroyed entire convoys, it would not have seriously affected Allied operations.

Ultimately this means that the purpose of the U-Boats in the Caribbean during 1943 had simply been to tie down anti-submarine forces. From this point of view their 1943 operations did achieve some success, because if the combined Caribbean theatre resources had been deployed elsewhere, they certainly would have hastened Germany's defeat.

The U-Boats' 1943 operations have often been judged by historians as a gigantic failure, but in fact it was a successful defensive, or rear-guard operation. Nowhere was this more apparent than in the Caribbean. There were at least two dozen anti-submarine squadrons operating between the Gulf of Mexico and French Guiana. Large army and navy bases with hundreds of thousands of men were the shore based element. At sea, two fully fledged fleets operated, one in the Gulf of Mexico and one in the Caribbean proper. All this to stop forty U-Boats. The Americans stopped them, but only at the cost of tying down considerable forces to a virtual backwater, very far away from the front lines in Europe.

Actually, these same arguments are valid for the whole U-Boat offensive in the west. The anti-submarine forces were on guard from northern Canada through the length of the American East coast. Then throughout the three thousand miles of the Caribbean theatre and finally, three thousand miles off the Brazilian theatre. Together they accounted for well over a million men tied to the anti-submarine war in the west. This is the reason for the U-Boats coming back to the west.

But to a large extent the level of operational committment by the Allies to the west, depended on the level of loss being suffered. In the North Atlantic the U-Boats had done all they could do, but this was not so in the Caribbean. Tillessen proved this, but because the combined 1943 loss in the Caribbean theatre was so negligible, the Americans were about to start cutting back on their forces assigned to the area.

It can be said that 1943 was a victory for both sides in the Caribbean. For the Americans because they defeated the great July offensive, and for the Germans because by their efforts they kept the American forces tied to the area.

The year 1944 was not to be like that at all. U-Boats in the Caribbean in the coming year would operate purely for nuisance value. The bulk of their strength was committed to the North Atlantic where they were slowly being forced back to the narrow seas. Consequently the Americans began their cutback in the west.

The first to suffer was regular convoy coverage. In January 1944, they instituted a system whereby the combat aeroplanes would fly only when there were U-Boats in the area. The flying boats would carry out dawn and dusk patrols in each area, but there would not be any coverage of convoys unless a threat existed.

They began transferring navy bomber squadrons out of the area to the Pacific and flying boats assumed the bulk of the workload. A separate anti-submarine Sector was created around Curacao and Aruba, but it was a sector virtually without aircraft. When these were required they would be supplied by Trinidad.

The amphibian PBYs of VP-92 moved into Zandery airfield with responsibility for the bauxite route. This allowed the decommissioning of the Cayenne and Essequibo stations and the transfer of the flying boat tenders to the Pacific.

The Chaguaramas based flying boat squadrons now operated detachments in Panama, in the Bahamas, in San Juan and Antigua. The St. Lucia base was closed and Carlsen Field in Trinidad was handed over to the navy to be used exclusively for carrier landing practice. These changes were possible because of the greatly improved intelligence network which the Americans now enjoyed and this was shown most dramatically in the handling of the next wave of U-Boats.

Early in February 1944 a U-Boat was detected approaching the Caribbean. It was Offermann in U518. The Americans were listening to his transmissions as he moved closer and plotting his position. On February thirteenth, he confirmed his presence by attacking a US seaplane tender with acoustic torpedoes, while still one thousand miles northeast of Antigua.

After the attack he transmitted on 6795 Kcs with a sixty-two group coded message. They were able to pinpoint his position and a Task Force moved up to Antigua to meet him. It was composed of six Mariners, three each from VP-204 and VP-205, along with six Harpoons from VB-141, now based at Waller Field.

But by the twenty-eighth, Offermann was through and the US Navy cancelled the barrier patrols. They were fully aware of when and where he passed, and while a part of the Task Force tracked him the rest got ready to meet the next arrival.

Five days later they detected the presence of another U-Boat coming in from northeast of Antigua. This was the veteran boat U154 coming back to the Caribbean for its sixth patrol of the area. Kusch had handed over command of the boat to Kapitanleutant Gemeiner. Once again barrier patrols were set up and U154 was tracked right in. The third boat was U218 with Claus Becker still in command, for his second mining operation in the Caribbean theatre.

To handle the three boats the Caribbean Defence Command switched around its squadrons. VP-204 was transferred out of Chaguaramas to operate in the Bahamas with detachments at San Juan and Antigua. They would now be responsible for the northern flank and were the welcoming committee for all new U-Boats. VP-212 moved their Mariners into Chaguaramas to replace VP-204, while VP-205 moved a detachment to Curacao. VP-215 brought its Mariners down from the US east coast to NAS Coco Solo in Panama.

These deployments were possible because of a change in the way the US Navy constituted their anti-submarine squadrons. They had now been made much more mobile, along the lines of the British model, so that they were able to move quickly to new operating bases. The Gulf of Paria had also been declared the work up area for all the new destroyer escorts coming off the ways, and these superb anti-submarine vessels were now always available as back-up for the Caribbean forces.

This deployment to meet incoming boats was still a project which was in the experimental stage and on this first occasion there was a slip. The squadrons had hardly settled in to their new areas when Offermann struck. In fact the flying boats had lost him.

At nine forty on the night of March sixth he sank the three thousand four hundred ton tanker Valeria, one hundred miles north of Blanquilla, Colombia. VP-205 were quickly on the scene and Offermann was forced to move westward to the open reaches of the Panama Sector, where VP-215 took up the hunt.

In the meantime Gemeiner had moved nearer to Trinidad, being closely tracked by VP-212. On March ninth he moved against convoy JT-24 as it sailed down the bauxite route. The senior officer of the escort in the destroyer escort USS Reynolds, had been briefed on the U-Boat's position and at the appropriate time the Reynolds and the corvette Surprise carried out a devastating series of depth-charge and hedgehog attacks. Gemeiner was forced to take U154 well offshore to escape.

While the larger Type IX U-Boats were attempting to sink merchant ships, Becker brought U218 in to mine San Juan harbour in Puerto Rico. Unlike the Dragon's Mouth, San Juan provided excellent conditions for mining. However, an unexplained occurrence further south was to frustrate his efforts.

On March twentieth the minesweeper YMS-3 was carrying out a routine sweep of Castries harbour in St. Lucia when a mine exploded which had been laid by Markworth in U66 during July 1942. The harbour had been swept on numerous occasions since Markworth had carried out his operation and declared clear of mines. In fact the mines laid by U66 should have de-activated themselves after three months.

The discovery caused the closure of Castries harbour and a squadron of minsweepers moved into the area. Four days later two more mines were activated and it was automatically assumed that a U-Boat had laid a new minefield without anyone being aware. These discoveries had a ripple effect and minesweeping operatings were immediately ordered for all Caribbean harbours. Thus it transpired that as soon as Becker laid his mines in San Juan, the Navy discovered them. They were swept as part of a much larger operation.

Becker remained north of Puerto Rico into early April when he was joined by Offermann on his way home. Both boats had been constantly shadowed by aircraft and opportunities for attacking shipping had not come their way. Nevertheless on April second U518 fired acoustic torpedoes at a tanker while the two boats were well north of the islands. The tanker man-aged to evade and shortly afterwards U218 and U518 were joined by U154 for the homeward journey across the Atlantic.

None of these three boats was to see the Caribbean again. Becker con-tinued his minelaying activities and achieved some success in the English Channel later in the war. His boat survived to surrender in May 1945. U154 was finally finished with the Caribbean after six completed trips to the area. The U-Boat had never been a high scorer, but somehow it had managed to survive, which in itself was an achievement. However, the luck of the U154 must have been connected to the Caribbean and Brazilian theatres, because on its very next trip it was sunk. All hands perished when the Chaguaramas trained destroyer escorts USS Inch and Frost caught U154 off the US East coast.

U518 was one of the unlucky U-Boats. Offermann successfully operated the U-Boat right through the remainder of 1944 and into 1945, only to die a few days before the end of the war, when he was caught in the North Atlantic on April twenty-second by the destroyer escorts USS Carter and Neil A. Scott.

As the war in the Caribbean entered its final phase, the headquarters of the Caribbean Defence Command moved to Trinidad and Vice Admiral Robert C. Giffon took command. With the war entering its final year and the Allies in the ascendent, they could afford to take punitive action against neutral nations which had been sympathetic to Germany.

Spanish tankers had always operated in the Caribbean according to their own dictates, much to the annoyance of the Allies. The Gobeo had

caused trouble in 1942 along with the Campeche in their known rendezvous with the U-Boats. Undoubtedly many others made link ups with the U-
Boats in the Caribbean, out of sight of the defenders. In November 1942,
the Gerona refused to obey the orders of an escorting aircraft and stay away
from a convoy. This same tanker later attempted to obtain six tons of lubricating oil from a Venezuelan port.

This shipment could only have been for the U-Boats and the oil was
refused. All through 1943 the defenders of the area had problems with
Spanish tankers and in April of 1944 they retaliated. The Spanish tanker
Cantabrio was seized in Port of Spain harbour, for sailing outside of established neutral shipping lanes. All Spanish tankers did this, but the Allies had
to wait until they were strong enough before they could act.

Throughout World War Two Spain had trod a precarious neutral road
that tended towards the Germans. This no doubt had its genesis in the con-
nections wrought during the Spanish Civil War. It was quite open and the
Allies were comfortable with Spain, because they knew that by 1944 they
could put on pressure whenever they wanted, without any real deterioration
of the relationship. They were bad anyway, so the Allies were free to take
any action they saw fit to suit the situation, but dealings with Spanish
speaking South American Republics were another matter entirely. America
in particular had to tread warily, but near the end of the war two incidents
took place in the Gulf of Paria which hurt Venezuelan-American post-war
relations.

The Gulf of Paria was enclosed by Trinidad and Venezuela. Trinidad
was at war with Germany while Venezuela was neutral, but tending to
sympathise with the Americans. The Venezuelans kept a low profile over
control of their side of the Gulf, allowing the Allies to fortify the enclosed
sea and establish stringent control over access.

In the meantime, the Americans had established a coast defence
battery of 155mm guns on the island of Patos as part of the defences of
the Gulf of Paria. There had been a long standing dispute over ownership of
the island and in 1942, the British decided to cede the island to Venezuela.
This left American troops manning batteries on Venezuelan soil. An agreement was concluded which would allow the Venezuelans to take control of
the guns on the island in 1943. At the due date the American troops moved
off the island, leaving behind them all guns, ammunition and equipment. The
island of Patos was then integrated into the defence plan, but under Venezuelan control. This boiled down to virtually an undeclared state of war
between Venezuela and Germany, because the Venezuelans were expected
to help in the defence of the Gulf. It was an anomaly, but the area was so

far from Europe, that it could work. There would be no German invasion in 1943 and it was unlikely that the arrangement would cause a diplomatic incident, however it led to problems between the Venezuelan and American forces.

In May 1944 the eight hundred ton Venezuelan gunboat, General Soublet, attempted to enter the Grand Boca in the Dragon's Mouth, without identifying itself or requesting prior permission. Technically, the vessel was in its own territorial waters and the Venezuelan naval officer felt that he did not need to identify himself, or seek permission to sail in his own waters. The vessel was visually identified by the British officers on duty at the harbour control post on the island of Chacachacare, who passed its identity to the American headquarters in Port of Spain.

However, the duty officer decided that the vessel had to comply with the wartime regulations and ordered the American coast defence guns to open fire. Fortunately the General Soublet was not hit, but the incident triggered off a serious diplomatic incident. The Venezuelan vessel was clearly wrong, according to the wartime regulations, but they felt that the Americans could easily have intercepted the vessel with one of the numerous PTs in the area, without opening fire. On the other hand, the Americans acted as though Venezuela was just another neutral, ignoring the fact that Venezuela technically owned half of the Gulf, as well as the fact that Venezuela was party to a special relationship with the United States.

Relations between the two countries were not helped by the incident, but one month later another much more serious incident took place. The aircraft carrier Hancock was in the Gulf of Paria carrying out its shakedown training during the month of June 1944. Its aircraft were using Carlsen Field to practice carrier deck landings and using the numerous bombing, torpedo and gunnery ranges in the Gulf.

On the last day of the month, the carrier's dive-bomber squadron attacked the island of Patos. The pilots had grown bored of bombing the shape of ships marked out in the Gulf and thought that Patos would be a much more realistic target. They claimed that they did not know that the island was garrisoned and a full squadron attack took place. The Venezuelan casualties were a source of much heated discussion and the incident brought to the fore, the thorny question of who really owned the Gulf of Paria.

One month before the incident in the Gulf of Paria, Kapitanleutnant Hans Jurgen Lauterbach-Emden brought the new Type IXC U539 into the Caribbean. It was three months since Offermann had sunk the tanker off Colombia and there had been further reductions in base personnel and anti-submarine squadrons, but VP-204 were ready. On the first evening in June they attacked U539, one hundred and fifty miles east of Puerto Rico. Lauterbach-Emden had sought to enter the Caribbean via the Anegada Passage, hoping that this minor passage would be unguarded. And so it was, except for the VP-204 Mariner. U539 dived quickly and although the attack was good, the boat escaped. However, a message was quickly passed to Puerto Rico and another Mariner was on the way.

Just before the dawn on June second, Lt. J.G. Tomkins USN moved in against U539 in a surprise attack. The U-Boat was caught on the surface and had to stay and fight. The pilot dropped his depth-charges, but the anti-aircraft fire from the U-Boat damaged the aircraft and while Tomkins fought to get his Mariner round for another run, U539 dived. At this point VP-204 lost track of the boat, and they moved a number of aircraft down from the Bahamas to carry out an intensive hunt.

Three days later, Lauterbach-Emden announced his presence by torpedoeing the Panamanian freighter Pillory, only thirty miles south of the Mona Passage. After this he found that VP-204 were tracking his every move and U539 was forced away from the vital Mona Passage.

VP-204 followed up the U-Boat and guessing that the boat's destination would be Curacao, they dispatched a group of Mariners to work from the area around the Dutch islands. In the early morning hours of June eleventh Lauterbach-Emden closed in on the tanker Casandra, as it sailed north of Curacao. He fired two T-5 Acoustic torpedoes, one of which was porpoising badly and the tanker managed to avoid the missiles. At this stage, U539 surfaced and attempted to use its guns on the fleeing tanker.

The U-Boats no longer carried big anti-shipping guns and they found that the anti-aircraft weapons that they carried could damage the tanker, but not stop the ship. The tanker's crew replied gamely with machine guns, while calling for help on the radio. While Lauterbach-Emden manoeuvred to try and get another shot at the tanker, a VP-204 Mariner appeared on the scene. It was too late for U539 to dive and while the aircraft and the U-Boat sparred for position, the tanker escaped towards Curacao.

The Mariner stood little chance against the massive firepower of the U-Boat and when the pilot did decide to attack, it was into a hail of anti-aircraft fire. When the aircraft pulled away, it was all the pilot could do to nurse his heavily damaged machine back to Curacao, while U539 dived. Later that morning, U539 attacked again, but once again the tanker that was the target saw the torpedoes and manoeuvred out of the way.

At this stage, all the Mariners from Trinidad were involved in the hunt, as well as the Harpoons of VB-147 with their anti-shipping rockets. But while the Caribbean squadrons had been hunting their lone U-Boat, another U-Boat was attempting the impossible and the US Navy took their revenge.

In mid Atlantic, the time was right and a U-Boat commander decided that it was his honour to avenge the many boats which had suffered at the hands of the American escort carriers. On May twenty-ninth Kapitanleutnant Detlef Krankenhagen in command of the new Hamburg built Type IXC U549, moved in against the carrier task group led by the USS Block Island.

The carrier was operating in the southern rendezvous area where on May sixth, the aircraft of VC-55 sank the old Caribbean miner U66, with the loss of all hands. Seehausen was in command of Marworth's old boat and U66 had been the carrier's fifth U-Boat kill. Krankenhagen avenged the five lost U-Boats by putting two torpedoes into the USS Block Island and sent her to the bottom to join numerous U-Boats lying on the seabed in mid-Atlantic. He also fired two T-5 Acoustic torpedoes at the destroyer escorts Eugene E. Elmore and the USS Barr. The former managed to evade, but one of the torpedoes seriously damaged USS Barr.

At last a carrier had been sunk, but the revenge was swift and terrible. The destroyer escorts Eugene E. Elmore and Ahrens pounced on the U-Boat and hammered it to destruction. U549 sank with all hands to join the carrier and the numerous other U-Boat wrecks in that area. Krankenhagen did not even have time to let U-Boat command know what he had done. But the revenge of the escorts was minor, compared to the catastophe that was about to befall another U-Boat.

Captain Dan Gallery in command of the carrier USS Guadalcanal with VC-8 embarked, accompanied by the destroyer escorts Pillsbury, Jenks, Pope and Chatelaine were in mid-Atlantic. In April the Task Group had disposed of the two Caribbean veterans, Lauzemis in U68 and Henke in U515, but Gallery wanted to capture a U-Boat. He had briefed his captains on the possibility of actually capturing one, rather than sinking it.

They had been hunting a U-Boat for many days and on Sunday June fourth, they finally cornered it in mid-Atlantic. The destroyer escorts delivered a shattering depth-charge attack that forced the boat to surface. Fifty-nine of the crew abandoned the U-Boat, after opening the sea cocks. With the U-Boat running in a continuous circle at six knots and going down by the stern, the Pillsbury quickly launched a motor whaleboat, which caught the submarine. A boarding party got on board and tossing aside all thought of the extreme hazard involved, they climbed down into the sinking U-Boat. In the dark cavern of the flooding control rooms, they managed to locate and shut off the right valves and the U-Boat was theirs.

The U-Boat's commander was Oberleutnant Zur See Harald Lange and the U-Boat was none other than the old Caribbean veteran U505. This had been Lowe's boat, then Czhech's boat, then Lange's boat and now the US Navy's U-Boat.

Two days later, the Allies invaded France on D Day, but to the US Navy fighters in the Atlantic, the capture of U505 carried much greater significance. After all the bitter experiences and mistakes, they were finally triumphant.

CHAPTER

22

Caribbean Finale

The combined air sea anti-submarine operation off Curacao and Aruba in the last two weeks of June 1944, drove Lauterbach-Emden away from the islands and forced U539 westwards into the Panama Sector. While Lauterbach-Emden was changing his position, Rutger Tillessen slipped through the Mona Passage with U516. The U-Boat was on its third Caribbean cruise, but this time Tillessen was commanding a boat that would be very difficult to detect. While on his last Caribbean patrol at the end of 1943, he had been convinced that the Allies were plotting his position using his radio transmissions, and although he had no official support for this theory, he did not intend to use his radio while in the Caribbean. In addition, U516 was now fitted with a schnorkel. He could cruise submerged while using his diesels. As a result U516 entered the Caribbean without being detected by the land based radar covering the passage.

The Type VII and IX U-Boats were purely fighting machines. This meant that there was very little room within their cramped pressure hulls for recreation of any kind and unfortunately, the schnorkel only made this

aspect worse. In between schnorkelling operations, the crews would need
to conserve the air in the boat by just lying in their bunks. When once again
the schnorkel mast was raised and the diesels began to pull fresh air through
the boats, there would be a mad rush to do some exercise, or get vital maintenance work completed. This led to an unnatural existence which drastically reduced the crews' effectiveness.

However, despite their lowered efficiency, the crew could rely on the
fact that they were virtually immune from attack. The types of radar in use
in the Caribbean could detect a schnorkelling operation only under the most
favourable circumstances; the Caribbean theatre was now right back where
it started, when U-Boats could be detected only visually. There were numerous sightings and anti-submarine attacks, but against driftwood, wreckage,
whitecaps and of course on whales. It was very frustrating because the
Americans could not attack the U-Boats until they detected them and they
could only detect them after they attacked something. Even then, the U-
Boats were difficult to pick up as Lauterbach-Emden proved.

On the fourth of July U539 was operating only thirty miles from San
Blas point in Panama, when Lauterbach-Emden took the boat in against a
tanker convoy. He fired a spread of six torpedoes and heard all six detonate,
but only two found their targets. One hit the ten thousand ton American
tanker Kittang, while the other hit the tanker Hollywood. Both ships were
severely damaged and the hulks had to be towed to Cristobal, but by the
time the escorts converged on the suspected attack position, U539 was well
to the north and the U-Boat escaped.

Two days later Tillessen struck in the northern Caribbean. Remaining
submerged he fired an acoustic torpedo at the nine thousand, nine hundred
ton tanker Harrisburg. The torpedo romped into the tanker's engine room
and brought the vessel to a dramatic halt. Three conventional torpedoes
were then used to tear the big tanker apart and send it to the bottom,
seventy-five miles southwest of Beata Point in Haiti. On the following day
he attacked the American tanker Point Breeze in almost the same position,
but the vessel evaded the three conventional torpedoes fired at it and
followed this up by escaping from a T-5.

These were the last attacks carried out against shipping in the Caribbean Sea, because both the U-Boats operating in the area revealed their positions and anti-submarine forces made conditions impossible. The stalemate
had now reached the Caribbean. The Americans could not pinpoint the U-
Boats to attack them, but the U-Boats could not attack anything without
bringing the anti-submarine forces down on their positions. Thus the Harrisburg was the last of a long line of merchant ships to be hit by a U-Boat in

the area. Both the U-Boats remained in their operational areas for a while longer and indeed, U539 was depth-charged by the USS Biddle, but the days of success were over. However, there was still one more U-Boat destined to operate in the Caribbean.

In the middle of July Kurt Lange brought U530 down into the central Atlantic, where he had a rendezvous with a Japanese submarine. The object of the meeting was to pass on secret equipment for transmission to Japan. After the mid ocean rendezvous, Lange turned his schnorkel-equipped U-Boat for the Caribbean.

Before Lange had a schnorkel, the Allies in the Caribbean could not locate him, – now it was impossible. He was virtually invulnerable and operated U530 all along Trinidad's north coast, in an area that few of the U-Boats had dared approach during the previous year. Not since the days of the great Lassen, had a U-Boat cruised the north coast of Trinidad, in relative comfort.

Lange cruised down the bauxite route then back up to Trinidad and westwards to Curacao but no one knew he was there. There were no radio transmissions and the coastal radar stations reported the passages clear. The flying boats operated their regular anti-submarine patrols, but there were no U-Boats sightings, visual or otherwise.

For a short while there were three U-Boats in the Caribbean. but the conditions were quite impossible. The U-Boats remained undetected, but they could not attack anything and soon afterwards, Lauterbach-Emden and Tillessen took U539 and U516 homeward.

Lange was the last U-Boat commander to operate in the Caribbean and for a full month he remained in the Trinidad area without being detected. Late in August, he turned his bows homeward and the Caribbean campaign would have ended at this point, if the Americans had not made a decision that was long overdue.

In July 1944, just as the last U-Boats were leaving the area, the US Navy extended the area of responsibility of the Caribbean Defence Command to a distance of fifteen hundred miles from the eastern islands. This now made the Caribbean responsible for half the width of the Atlantic. Previously, this vast area east of the islands had been the responsibility of whoever was passing through it at the time. Over the years this had turned this part of the Atlantic into a virtual U-Boat rest area.

These changes that affected the Caribbean and Brazilian theatres, were part of a much larger series of moves that were tightening the Allied noose around the U-Boats, drastically reducing their freedom in the Atlantic.

In January 1944. the US Navy joined the British in the Azores and long range anti-submarine aircraft began regular patrols of the area formally controlled by the carrier Task Groups. This freed the carriers to move southward and concentrate on more inaccessbile areas of the central Atlantic. With aircraft flying from Bermuda and the Caribbean in the west, and the Azores and French West Africa in the east, and carriers loose in the middle, control of the central Atlantic passed to the Allies.

In the south, a similar development occurred when the US Navy based anti-submarine aircraft on Ascension Island. There were aircraft based in Sierra Leone, the Gold Coast, Nigeria and the Cameroons, who were able to cover the Gulf of Guinea as well as operate westwards towards Ascension.

In the west, aircraft based in Recife and along the Brazilian coast operated eastwards to meet the Ascension based aircraft, closing much of the South Atlantic air gap. In the meantime, the British had clapped an iron hand of control on the North Atlantic, to the point where no U-Boat could consider itself in safe waters, from Iceland in the north, to well past Ascension Island. It was a far cry from 1942 and 1943, when vast stretches of the Atlantic were totally free from Allied airpower.

This new area of responsibility for the Caribbean Command almost doubled the size of the theatre, but the move coincided with the virtual departure of the U-Boats from the Caribbean. This freed some of the Caribbean escort groups to operate eastwards from the island chain and the aircraft backed them up by flying to the limit of their endurance.

What took place in the central Atlantic was now of great importance to the Caribbean Command, where before the events in this area were only of passing interest. The reorganisation brought many of the US Navy patrol squadrons back into the theatre. In fact, the western side of the Atlantic was now lined with bases filled with these anti-submarine aircraft.

In the Brazilian theatre, VP-74, VP-94, VP-203 and VP-211 were the long range element, working eastwards across the South Atlantic. In the Caribbean theatre, VP-92 continued operating its long range PBYs out across the Atlantic from Zandery. VP-204 moved its Mariners back into Chaguaramas to operate alongside VP-212. Both squadrons were now tasked with daily patrols out into the central Atlantic.

VP-205 moved from Chaguaramas to Guantanamo Bay, relieving the crack VP-32 who took up residence at NAS San Juan, from where they could sweep well out into the Atlantic. But the flying boat squadrons found little to attack out in the central Atlantic, because the U-Boat war had moved back into the narrow seas.

In August Allied troops advancing out of the Normandy bridgehead cut off the U-Boat Atlantic bases on the French coast. Doenitz was forced to order his U-Boats to sail for German and Norwegian ports. Two Caribbean veterans, U123 and U129 were caught in Lorient without sufficient batteries and both boats were abandoned in the harbour. The schnorkel allowed most of the other U-Boats to make the journey around the British Isles without being detected, but this virtually ended the Caribbean campaign. Sailing from these northern ports added over three thousand miles to a Caribbean patrol and combined with the virtual destructions of the tankers, the Caribbean was now simply too far away. These developments made Kurt Lange in U530, the last commander to sail the true golden west.

The war with the U-Boats had now almost reached a stalemate. The Allies had their very long range aircraft, combined with centimetric radar, asdic, sonar buoys, aerial acoustic torpedoes, depth-charges, hedgehog, the new squid mortars, and the Germans still seemed to be unaware that the U-Boats were being tracked by radio direction finding equipment, both shore and sea based.

The U-Boats on the other hand had their asdic decoys, radar decoys, up to date radar detectors, schnorkels and acoustic torpedoes that could beat the Allied countermeasures. But the tactical picture was the wrong way round. The Allied units carried the offensive equipment, while all the U-Boats equipment was defensive. The U-Boats could avoid detection, or even after they had been detected, they could still fool the hunters and escape, but they could not attack anything.

The Type VII and IX U-Boats had now evolved into defensive weapon systems. Once a U-Boat revealed its position by attacking a target, it was relentlessly hunted to destruction. Occasionally, expert tactics would allow them to fool the hunters and escape. Ernst Cordes in command of U763 pulled off such a daring escape in the English Channel during July, when he was cornered by a group of destroyers.

The U-Boat was hunted for thirty hours and the crew counted five hundred and fifty depth-charge explosions! When Cordes had finally thrown off the pursuit, he found that he was in the Royal Navy's anchorage in Spithead! His escape showed what was possible, but the whole exercise had been defensive. The U-Boats were pinning down considerable anti-submarine resources, but not achieving merchant ship sinkings. They were almost marking time; waiting for an offensive weapon that would once again give them supremacy.

In the Caribbean, the Americans knew that the loss of the French bases spelled the end of their problems with the U-Boats and they began to dismantle the elaborate defensive system. Firstly, they eliminated ships capable of ten knots from their convoys. These were allowed to sail independently.

By October the decision had been taken to restore all navigation lights and buoys, and in December they de-activated the Airship squadron ZP-51. By this stage the blimps had flown thirty-five thousand hours of convoy protection.

The problem of the drifting mines still existed and many of the navy combat aircraft were concentrated on this duty, although there was still a considerable search and rescue commitment.

In August, while U530 was still in the theatre, the two masted schooner Island Queen went missing with a party of seventy-five people aboard. Lange did not claim the vessel and it can only be assumed that it struck one of the drifting mines. For thirteen days, the flying boats and airships kept up a relentless search, but no trace of the Island Queen was ever found. It remains a Caribbean mystery.

Despite the fact that there were no U-Boats in the Caribbean, the theatre was humming with activity. Training for the Pacific war was in full swing and the Gulf of Paria in particular was a very busy place. There were dozens of the new destroyer escorts being trained in anti-submarine warfare, while cruisers and battleships worked up their crews. The carriers were making the Gulf very crowded. At one time in November there were three of them working up at the same time. The USS Randolph, the USS Shangrila and the Bennington manoeuvred out of each others way, while their air wings thundered into Carlsen Field and ceaselessly bombed the targets around the island. Now that there were no U-Boats to worry about, the Gulf could achieve its full potential as the training ground for the Pacific war.

Outside of the Gulf, the flying boat squadrons patrolled the sea lanes, ensuring that they were clear and looking for mines. In fact the Americans were now so confident that on December seventeenth, the carrier USS Randolph left the Gulf for its run to the Panama Canal, completely unescorted. This had never happened before. No high value warship had ever exited the Gulf without the full air and sea escort of which Trinidad boasted.

Few realised how close run a thing the Battle of the Atlantic still was and the reductions continued. Suspected U-Boat contacts were still being made, both by sea and air, but in most cases they were evaluated as doubtful, — which indeed they were. By February 1945, some of the Royal Navy ships began leaving and in March the TJ-JT series of convoys was suspended. In the same month the last Essex carrier to use the Gulf, the USS Antietam arrived. Then on March fourteenth a U-Boat struck.

Korvettenkapitan Ottoheinrich Junker in command of the Type IXC U-Boat U532, sailed out of a Norwegian Fjord and using his schnorkel, skirted the British Isles for the central Atlantic. He did not use his radio, remaining submerged all the time and consequently the Allies had no indication of his presence. On March tenth he sank the freighter Baron Jedburgh, five hundred miles off the Brazilian coast. No signal went out from the doomed ship and the Allies remained in ignorance of his presence.

Then on March twenty-ninth, he caught the American tanker Oklahoma, one thousand miles east of Trinidad and also sent her to the bottom. Again no signal went out and the Americans remained unaware that a ship had been sunk in the Caribbean theatre. Previously, the sinking would not have concerned the Caribbean, but the area one thousand miles out was well within their new boundaries. Junker continued his slow careful cruise which would end when Germany surrendered.

On April fourteenth 1945, a VP-213 Mariner on patrol out of Chaguaramas sighted a lifeboat northwest of the Dragon's Mouth and passed a report to Trinidad. The SS Delaware had just left the Boca and the Trinidad Command diverted the freighter to check. They found the lifeboat from the tanker Oklahoma and aboard were twenty-two scarecrows, all that was left of the crew. They had been drifting for eighteen days and watched many of their number die of a combination of thirst, heat and exhaustion. Consternation greeted the news of this sinking. The U-Boats were supposed to be bottled up in the far north and the Caribbean and South Atlantic were supposed to be completely safe. They were safe, but only just.

Doenitz had been waiting for his new wonder U-Boats and indeed they had arrived, but just too late. Two of them were at sea when Germany surrendered, U2511 under Adalbert Schnee and U3008 under Helmut Mansech. Additionally, ninety other new boats were at sea, either undergoing training or trials, but Germany fell apart around them. The advance of the Allied armies ended German resistance, before these new Type XXI boats could come to the Caribbean, and that they surely would have done.

The Type XXI at last put Germany ahead in the race for supremacy at sea. They had all the defensive devices of the last group of Type IXs and more, − but they were the offensive weapon that would have broken the deadlock. They utilised the elegant highly streamlined hull of the planned Walther Type XVII boats and used instead, triple the battery capacity of the old boats. They were able to run silently for long periods at five or six knots and then work up to an underwater speed of eighteen knots. At this speed they could outrun most of the escort vessels while remaining submerged! They pioneered the long range sonar that led to today's concept of the submarine as the ultimate anti-submarine weapon.

With their new equipment and sensors, they could fire blind from a depth of one hundred and fifty feet. They carried six forward firing torpedo tubes, as well as twelve broadside tubes, giving them eighteen torpedo tubes, with a warload of twenty-four torpedoes. In short, they could dive deeper, run faster and range further than anything seen before. There was nothing in the Allied inventory that could detect, catch and hold a Type XXI U-Boat. The Allies had no answer to the boat and its performance astounded them. The Type XXI served as the basis for all modern submarine design. If these boats had been available a year earlier, it is more than likely that they would have cut the Atlantic lifeline. But why would the Type XXIs have come to the Caribbean?

Doenitz policy had always been to send his boats to the areas where they were most likely to achieve success at the least cost. What then were the final figures for the Caribbean campaign? The Allies lost two thousand six hundred and three merchant ships, as well as one hundred and seventy-five warships in the war against the U-Boats. The Caribbean campaign started in 1942 and only continued at full strength until November of that year, when Operation Torch altered the strategic balance and relegated the Caribbean to the status of a subsidiary operation. Despite this, the Allies lost exactly four hundred merchant ships in the Caribbean theatre. An additional fifty-six were damaged. This meant that the Caribbean theatre accounted for fifteen and a half percent of the total merchant ship losses, which was not very high for a major theatre of war. But what did these four hundred ships cost the Germans?

Only seventeen U-Boats were lost within the theatre during the whole war. This is only two percent of the total U-Boat losses! It also means that Germany achieved twenty-three point five merchant ships sunk, for each U-Boat lost in the Caribbean. This probably makes the Caribbean, the most cost effective campaign that the Germans fought throughout the war. And the Type XXI could operate for a month in the South Atlantic, — without tanker support. The lure of the Caribbean would have been irresistable.

Regardless of how the final figures for the Caribbean are worked out, it still remains the most attractive theatre of war for the U-Boats. Ninety-seven German U-Boats carried out one hundred and forty-five war cruises in the Caribbean theatre. They were assisted by six Italian submarines, which carried out seven patrols, to bring the total figures up to one hundred and two boats carrying out one hundred and fifty-two patrols. (See appendix one). This works out at almost four ships per U-Boat, or two point six ships sunk per patrol. The Type XXI would have dispensed with the extreme hazard of the transit to and from the area that cost so many U-Boats, and the Caribbean would once again have been set aflame.

But none of this happened. On May eighth 1945, the whole edifice that was the Third Reich fell in ruins. The German Army was beaten and being destroyed between the Allied juggernauts. The Luftwaffe was paralysed, Germany was split in two and only the U-Boats were in a position to continue the struggle. But the surrender on May eighth, left them without a Germany to fight for.

To the very end, their morale was superb, even though they had suffered higher losses than any other element of the German armed forces. During the war, the Germans built one thousand one hundred and sixty-two U-Boats. Of this total seven hundred and eighty-four were lost. Of a total strength for the U-Boat Arm of forty thousand sailors, thirty-two thousand lost their lives in battle. Yet despite these appalling losses, they were more than willing to carry the fight to the Allies with the new Type XXI U-Boats. But it seems that even without the new boats they would still have fought, because never once did a U-Boat fail to sail on its assignment.

When Doenitz surrendered Germany, he gave the Allies an assurance that his U-Boats would surrender. A signal went out to those at sea, ordering them to surface and hoist blue or white flags and proceed to Allied ports. Those in German and Norwegian ports were to remain in harbour and surrender when the Allies arrived.

But Doenitz temporarily forgot that he had instilled tremendous spirit into the U-Boat Arm. He must have forgotten the pride that he had instilled and the quality of the weapon he had forged. He refused to sanction the destruction of the U-Boats and in fact forbade it, but his crews took the matter into their own hands.

One hundred and fifty-six U-Boats obeyed their orders and sailed to Allied ports to surrender. It hurt them to meekly submit to the enemy, but they were in the minority. The majority of the U-Boat officers and men refused to believe that their trusted Grand Admiral would just hand over the U-Boats, unless of course he was under pressure to do so. They felt it was a violation of their code of honour to hand over their boats. They were still undefeated.

In great secrecy, the code word "Regenbogen" (Rainbow), was whispered by radio among the boats. One by one the U-Boats slipped out of the harbours, until there was an enormous fleet of them at sea. Then the explosions started echoing around the Baltic and the North Sea, as the Sea Wolves destroyed themselves.

In all, two hundred and twenty-one U-Boats were destroyed by their crews. The commanders of these boats were fully prepared to face the displeasure of the Grand Admiral and ready to accept the expected courts martial. Korvettenkapitan Peter Cremer in command of the Type XXI

U2519, gave orders for his boat to be scuttled along with the rest and describes how they opened the main vents and the hatches and just let the boat go down. He, like the other commanders expected a German court martial as well as reprisals from the Allies, but he was with Doenitz when the results of Regenbogen were reported to him. He wrote that at first, Doenitz looked very surprised, then disapproving and finally a little smile crossed his face. Had Doenitz been one of the commanders, undoubtedly he would have done the same thing. He was proud of his U-Boats. There was no reaction from the Allies either, but for a completely different reason. Few U-Boat commanders realised the fear and awe in which they were held. The Allies were secretly relieved that the U-Boats were at the bottom of the sea.

The surrender finally ended the war in the west. All convoys were discontinued. Merchant vessels ceased their incessant zig-zags and burned their lights. Combat units began leaving the Caribbean bases for reassignment to the Pacific. Chaguaramas was reduced to a single flying boat squadron, carrying responsibility for the area from Panama to French Guiana. The wartime blackout, censorship, rationing and movement restrictions were lifted and all the host of other war regulations were cancelled.

The TRNVR was disbanded and all the remaining Royal Navy vessels left the theatre to return to England. In fact, there was a great switching around of ships as the British returned their lend-lease vessels and the US Navy returned the anti-submarine corvettes. The majority of TRNVR vessels had been converted American and Canadian yachts, with a few minesweepers thrown in. With the disbandment of the unit these vessels scattered to their home ports. Some of the Fairmile D boats of the 30th Flotilla were decommissioned and sold commercially. For many years after the war they could be seen plying the routes between the islands.

The anti-submarine cables across the Dragon's and Serpent's Mouths were lifted and the extensive net defences throughout the Caribbean were removed. The numerous coast defence guns and anti-aircraft batteries were removed and the infantry garrisons thinned down to the bare minimum in the few bases that were to be retained. In each of the islands the local volunteer forces were disbanded or shrunk to very small cadres.

The Caribbean as a whole attempted to return to its prewar tranquility, but it was quite useless. The entire area, its people, its customs and in some cases even the very physical shape of the islands, had been altered. Great earthmoving, filling and dredging works had been undertaken that permanently altered the maps.

But the way the people of the islands thought, had undergone the greatest change. They had been exposed to different lifestyles and values and there was no turning back. World War Two had launched the islands onto the wider world stage.

The mammoth task of clearing the dozens of defensive minefields was probably the most difficult of all. Much of the Caribbean is washed by very strong currents that sweep in from the Atlantic to join the start of the Gulf-stream and in a surprisingly large number of areas, the mines had simply been swept away. Probably the most difficult area for the minesweepers was the Dragon's and Serpent's Mouth entrances to the Gulf of Paria. In these areas none of the mines laid in 1942 were found and only ten percent of the later lays were in existence. They had all been swept away and it is possible that today many of them still exist, in the hundreds of miles of mangrove swamp that borders the Gulf of Paria and the Central American coastline. Many others were probably swept right out of the Caribbean. Post war charts of the Gulf showed the extent to which the area had been used as a training base, with many unexploded depth-charges, bombs and mines marked as hazardous.

Chaguaramas continued as a major naval facility, but gone were the battleships, cruisers and aircraft carriers that once made it the hub of the Caribbean war. Even before the war ended, many of its facilities began closing, some for transfer to the Pacific. In the late forties, the base and its associated Trinidad Sector, now renamed the Antilles command, assumed an important role as the outer defence ring for the Panama Canal. It was commanded for a number of years by Rear Admiral Gallery and this was fitting, because Chaguaramas was first and foremost an anti-submarine base.

When Trinidad became an independent country in 1962, its local defence forces took over areas of the base and fittingly, its navy took control of the old TRNVR anti-submarine loop station at Staubles Bay.

In 1966, the United States Navy deactivated the entire base, although retaining title to a part of it for the remainder of the ninety-nine year lease. Most of the training activity switched to Puerto Rico and Guantanamo Bay, but neither of these areas possessed the potential of Chaguaramas and the associated Gulf of Paria.

Throughout the theatre airbases were deactivated. They had all been built specifically to handle the threat of the U-Boats and now the reason for their existence was no longer valid. Many decades later these airbases with the exception of the ones that were converted for civil use, could still be seen abandoned and slowly decaying. All that was left were weed covered runways and tarmacs, where the ghosts of airmen and the echo of gallant deeds long past might be remembered. But their story was never told, so that to most of the inhabitants of the islands they were an anachronism.

Piarco and Palisados were both deactivated and handed back to the civil authorities to become international airports. The Royal Navy used many of their escort carriers to return the Fleet Air Arm aircraft to England. Waller Field also had its moment of glory. The massive movement of troops from Europe to the continental United States and ultimately to the Pacific, was routed through Waller Field, in an operation code named Project Green. At that time it was the largest airlift ever attempted, and by June 1945 two hundred and sixty Dakotas had been assigned to this single base. Just as Chaguaramas in 1943, had become one of the largest naval bases in the world, Waller Field now became the world's largest airbase. For much of World War Two, Waller Field had been eclipsed by its satellite Edinburgh, but during this time it made up for the neglect. The operation did not last for long, but it became a model for the later Berlin airlift. By the end of 1945, although not abandoned, Waller Field was almost deserted. By 1949, the field was closed and began to decay like all the other Caribbean airbases. But both Chaguaramas and Waller Field outlasted most of the U-Boats.

At the end of the war, the British and the Americans conducted an exercise called Operation Deadlight. The surrendered U-Boats were towed out into the Atlantic and ignominiously scuttled. It was an orgy of destruction, fuelled by fear and hatred, which dictated that the entire German war machine had to be destroyed. The feeling uppermost was that twice in one century they had almost been brought to their knees by these U-Boats and all trace of them must be wiped out. This view took little cognisance of the world that the war had created. The violent century was only halfway through. There were many other solutions as to what to do with the surrendered U-Boats, not the least of which was to let them be broken up in the German Shipyards. It would have provided some work in war-torn Germany and possibly cut down on the amount of aid that had to be injected into the defeated country. Even the steel was useful, but not at the bottom of the Atlantic.

Operation Deadlight took care of more than a hundred U-Boats, but there were very few Caribbean veterans around to destroy. These boats which had set the Caribbean aflame had all been in the thick of the fighting and precious few remained when it was over. Of the ninety-seven German U-Boats and six Italian submarines, only ten were still afloat at the time of the surrender. Piening's old U155, along with U170, U218, U516, U532 and U539 surrendered in Germany and Norway, along with U510 in St. Nazaire. U530 was on a special mission, while U511 and the Italian Torelli had been handed over to the Japanese. Of these ten, only one escaped being sent to the bottom. However, in a strange twist of fate three Caribbean veterans survived.

The first was Hardegen's famous U123. This Type IXB U-Boat was the one that had opened Operation Pankenschlag and begun the war in the west. She visited the Caribbean only for a single patrol in the aftermath of the failed July 1943 offensive, and ended up being abandoned in Lorient. The Allies found her high and dry in the massive bomb-proof pen K3 at Lorient. Unlike U129 which had been scuttled just outside of the protective pens and was so badly damaged that she had to be scrapped, U123 was in a repairable condition and the French ensured that she was not destroyed. They repaired her and she joined the French Navy under the name Blaison and served until 1953, when she was finally scrapped.

The second survivor was Neitzel's U510. This Type IXC boat had carried out three war patrols to the Caribbean. Neitzel's classic attack on convoy BT-6 in March 1943, followed by Eick's aggressive tailing of convoy JT-2 in July 1943, ensured that U510 would be listed among the great U-Boats of the Caribbean war.

She was on an extended patrol to the Far East during the last few months of the war and did not arrive in St. Nazaire until the end of April 1945. St. Nazaire had been surrounded since August of the previous year, when both U-Boat Flotillas had moved out. When the base finally surrendered on May eighth 1945, the Allies found U510 in Pen 4, where she was docked for repairs. Once again the French Navy moved in and U510 was incorporated into their navy. She was renamed Bouam and carried the pennant number S 612 for thirteen years, before finally being broken up in 1963.

The Third Caribbean veteran to survive was none other than U505. She was saved from the orgy of destruction because of the fact that she had been captured and not surrendered. For nine years she lay abandoned until in 1954, when she was acquired by the Chicago Museum of Science and Industry. The U-Boat was moved bodily to the museum site and today she is on view to the public. U505 finally gained immortality and today she is one of only two surviving U-Boats, of the great fleet that went to war. Why did U505 survive, where so many of her sisters perished? Was it that U505 was jinxed from the moment that Lowe sank the sailing ship, or was she haunted by Sillcock's dead crew? Do sailors' superstitions carry any weight? Was she a victim of Zschech's suicide? Did his ghost haunt that control room, or was it simply Lange's misfortune? The Old Salts talk and whisper the lore of the sea, but she is in Chicago because she came up against the cream of the United States Navy. And it is fitting that one of the only surviving U-Boats should be a Caribbean veteran.

The Germans had gone to considerable lengths to make their French

U-Boat bases almost impregnable. Each base was fitted with huge bomb
proof bunkers where in many cases, the boats could be taken out of the
water and drydocked. Allied bombs had done little to harm the U-Boats in
their bases, but when American armoured formations had broken out and
raced across southern France in August of 1944, most of these bases had
been cut off, which forced the abandonment of U-Boat operations. The
boats that were able to move were transferred to Germany and Norway but
this did not mean that the bases were abandoned. In fact, most of these
U-Boat bases were transformed into strongholds that in some cases were
impregnable. The base at Bordeaux was abandoned by the Germans, which
allowed the Allies to enter in September 1944. In contrast, Brest also fell in
September, but only after a one month battle. The other three, Lorient, La
Pallice and St. Nazaire were too strong to be taken by assault and all three
held out until Germany was defeated in May 1945. Fittingly, the last U-
Boat to escape from the great complex of Lorient, was Piening's U155.

Of course, the Type XXI U-Boats were not destroyed. They were far
too valuable to throw away. It shows that although the Navies were willing
to take part in the Deadlight propaganda exercise, they knew when to stop.
Some of these Type XXI U-Boats, including the scuttled U2540 which was
raised and rebuilt for the Federal German Navy, served for many years as
testbeds.

Even though the older Type VII and IX U-Boats were destroyed, the
Allies immediately set about modifying their wartime boats to German
standard, and all new construction was based on the Type XXI, as well as
the German research done on the Walther boats. Curiously, it was the German Type XXI U-Boat which finally gave recognition to the science of anti-
submarine warfare in the United States Navy.

The Russians captured a number of prefabricated sections in the
eastern shipyards of Germany and received some others from the Allies in
the immediate post-war climate of co-operation. They proceeded to commission four Type XXIs into their navy and constructed more than a hundred of their Whiskey Class as a direct copy.

As the east-west political climate deteriorated, it became increasingly
important to find out what a Type XXI could do, to ensure that they could
defend against them and their progeny. Had the Germans not developed the
Type XXI, it is conceivable that the post-war US Navy might have been an
even more carrier dominated service, to the exclusion of all else. Even with
the new awareness brought out by the German boats, followed by the
American nuclear boats, the emphasis was still on the carrier. When U505
was dedicated as a memorial, Admiral Halsey gave the address. Halsey was

an exclusively Pacific carrier Admiral. Why couldn't it have been Admirals Hoover, or Andrews, or Oldendorf? The men who fought the U-Boats.

Two other German U-Boats delayed the hangman for a while. On May ninth 1945, Kurt Lange's U530 now under the command of Otto Wehrmuth, and U977 under Heinz Schaffer, disobeyed the surrender order, and the Regenbogen code. Both commanders acting independently, decided to look for an alternative to the prison camp. Neither relished the thought of hoisting a white flag and later trying to survive in war-torn Germany. Both U-Boats decided to try for Argentina, where they expected a more friendly reception. Argentina had rather belatedly declared war on Germany in March 1945. For most of the war Argentina had been neutral, with a strong pro German element within her population. The two U-Boat commanders felt that if they handed over their boats to the Argentine Navy they would be welcomed, and both set out on a long adventurous passage.

Wehrmuth had left his home port for the Atlantic some time before the end of the war and this put U530 much closer to the South Atlantic than U977 which started its epic journey from the coast of Norway. Both the boats avoided detection. U977 achieved this by staying submerged for sixty-six days, which showed the dramatic difference that a schnorkel made. It was a world record for submarines although it has never been recognised as such. Wehrmuth arrived in Mar del Plata in July 1945, while U977 arrived in August, after a harrowing three month journey. As expected, both boats in turn were welcomed and the crews were accommodated on the old cruiser Belgrano, but in each case the welcome was short lived.

The war had put the United States into the position of the dominant superpower in South America and Argentina had to survive in the post-war world. The crews and the U-Boats were handed over to the Americans and the U-Boat crews ended up as prisoners of war anyway. Sensational newspaper reporting destroyed even the hope of a quiet surrender.

An Argentine daily ran a story to the effect that, U530 and U977 had been part of a ghost convoy which had brought Hitler, Eva Braun and Martin Borman, plus Nazi treasure to Patagonia and put them ashore before surrendering the boats. The Russians were keeping very quiet about what they had found in Berlin, with the result that British and American intelligence took the story seriously. Wehrmuth and Schaffer found themselves very important prisoners indeed.

On August third 1945, the crew of U530 found themselves in Trinidad. They arrived on four transport aircraft that landed at Waller Field. Under heavy guard they were accommodated overnight. Just one year previously they had been cruising off the coast of Trinidad, as predators.

Doubtless they noted the irony of their situation. A month later the crew of U977 also overnighted at Waller Field. They were the subject of considerable curiosity, because it was believed that they were the ones who had brought Hitler to South America. In time after much special interrogation they were cleared and returned to Germany.

From the earliest beginnings of the Battle of the Atlantic, the British were aware that it was a life and death struggle and there was never any doubt as to the importance of anti-submarine warfare. Their anti-submarine specialists were naval heroes. The same cannot be said about the American naval establishment. As important and dramatic as the great carrier battles in the Pacific were, they paled in comparison to the consequences of a German victory in the Battle of the Atlantic. But the US Navy was divided down the middle by the two oceans, both physically and in the way they thought. The best example of this concerns U505.

The gallant capture of U505 although it was overshadowed by the invasion of Normandy, marked the ultimate achievement of the United States Navy in the Battle of the Atlantic. They came in late, making every mistake in the book and progressed to the capture of a U-Boat. There was at the time a pressing need to keep the capture secret but even so, the achievement never received the acclaim which it deserved.

The first nine man boarding party from the destroyer escort Pillsbury, did an extraordinary job in securing the boat, but the man who really made it possible to bring U505 home as a prize of war was the engineer Commander E. Trosino. With the bow of the U-Boat almost out and the stern twenty-five feet underwater, Trosino boarded the U-Boat. The situation was so critical that the conning tower hatch had to be kept closed to stop the waves from swamping the boat. U505 was already at neutral buoyancy and one slip could have sent her to the bottom.

Trosino had never seen the inside of a submarine before, but working under the plates in the boat's bilges, he was able to trace the maze of piping and gain sufficient knowledge to raise the stern and restore her trim. Unless this had been done, U505 could not have been brought home.

After the operation Trosino was recommended for a Navy Cross. The pro carrier establishment downgraded this to a Legion of Merit. To quote Admiral Gallery, "he did it in the wrong ocean."

Virtually the same downgrading took place with respect to the Caribbean war. It was vital that the U-Boats be defeated in the Caribbean because this was the terminus of the trans-Atlantic convoys. Both the British and American forces in the area initially worked under severe handicaps. When the situation became critical, the area received massive reinforcement, yet in the post-war period the part played by the Caribbean anti-submarine forces was downgraded and very few know of its importance.

The Caribbean still represents the soft underbelly of the United States and for the last twenty to thirty years it has been wide open to the same exploitation as practised by the U-Boats. It is often said that defence establishments spend their time preparing for the last war. In the case of the Caribbean, the past should be remembered because the future may depend on it.

CHAPTER

23

Warriors meet

In the crisp morning air of Tuesday October second 1945, there was a considerable gathering of military personnel on the piers of the US Naval Station in Chaguaramas. They represented air, land and sea elements and came from every command in the Caribbean theatre. Along with American, British and local military men, there were Brazilians speaking Portuguese, Venezuelans and some from central America speaking Spanish, Free French representatives from the French territories, and Dutch personnel from Curacao and Aruba. It was an international gathering of those who fought in the Caribbean.

Near the end of the pier, a small group of important military people were gathered around their host, Commodore Courtlant Baughmann, commander of the US Naval Station Chaguaramas. This group clustered near the commodore came from three navies, and for the moment they were the centre of attention.

Captain W. Christiansen was the official representative of the United States Navy. Standing near him were the Royal Navy team, made up of Captain J.H. Breals, with Chief Petty Officer L. King and Mr. C. Penwell from the Admiralty Board of Naval Constructors.

English, French, Portuguese, Spanish and Dutch were the normal languages of the Caribbean theatre, but on this morning there was an addition. Standing in the group and occasionally exchanging comments in their native tongue were Captain Kadov and Captain Favarov of the Russian Navy. This multinational group were known as the Allied Tripartite Committee and they represented the tail end of wartime co-operation, which would soon degenerate into the twentieth century Cold war. However, on this particular morning, they were together on the pier awaiting the arrival of US Navy Task Group 21.4.

The conflicts in both the Atlantic and the Pacific were over and the world was winding down from the high tension of a World War, but for the Caribbean this was a very special morning.

Several Mariner flying boats from VP-213 were airborne, escorting Task Group 21.4 to Trinidad, while the remainder of the pilots from the squadron were on the pier. To the officers and men of the Caribbean Command, the arrival of the Task Group would be the culmination of their war and not many of them would have missed it.

Precisely at five minutes to seven, the bows of the flagship of Task Group 21.4 appeared, thrusting through the Third Boca. She was the twelve hundred ton ocean going tug, USS Cherokee. She was specially equipped with salvage equipment and carried a crew of experienced technicians. The two hundred and ten foot long tug cleared the Boca and turned to starboard, to allow her charges to take centre stage and a suppressed ripple of excitement greeted the bows of the second vessel of Task Group 21.4, as it slid through the dark water. U530 had returned to the Caribbean, – for her third visit.

The long grey forward casing crept into view, glistening with spray in the early morning sunshine. Overhead, the engines of the Mariner thundered, as its arch enemy became the second U-Boat to enter the Gulf of Paria. Then the conning tower was visible, followed by the after casing, with white water foaming at its stern. Her new American passage crew were on deck, as she turned towards the piers and the waiting crowd.

But she had hardly cleared the Boca, before the bows of a second U-Boat appeared. Following closely behind the Caribbean veteran U530 came the Type VIIC U977. As this second U-Boat entered the Gulf, a second Mariner flying boat swept over the ships of Task Group 21.4 and turned south. The Mariners had escorted the Task Group along Trinidad's north coast and now their job was complete.

The U-Boats had come from Buenos Aires, where they had been handed over to American crews by the Argentine navy. The U-Boats' original crews were far away in a prison camp and the two former commanders, Otto Wehrmuth and Heinz Schaffer were still undergoing special interrogation in connection with their alleged involvement with the ghost convoy.

Neither commander had any idea that their U-Boats were in Trinidad, but undoubtedly they would have been pleased at the reception their boats were receiving. It was not rapturous. These denzins of the deep were never greeted with elation. There was more of an awed silence and although these were tame U-Boats, there was still the element of fear. The atmosphere was charged with emotion, and the hatred had not as yet begun to cool.

As the two U-Boats drew closer to the piers, the watchers could make out the wicked looking forest of automatic cannon on the after end of the conning towers. No doubt many of the airmen on the piers had faced these deadly weapons and indeed, many of their comrades had been clawed out of the sky by the heavy anti-aircraft armament carried by the boats. The seamen present, probably concentrated their attention on the hidden menace of the torpedo tubes, invisible from the surface, but there. The majority of the spectators that morning had been engaged in the great battle against the U-Boats, but very few of them had actually seen one, with the result that they were intensely curious about these two. To the Caribbean fighters, these were the Sea Wolves.

The members of the Tripartite Team were also curious about these two U-Boats, but for a different set of reasons. They had already inspected dozens of surrendered U-Boats, right up to the Type XXIs, but these two rusty specimens were different and indeed the Team had been flown to Trinidad specifically to check these two boats.

These boats had surrendered so far from their home bases that there had to be something special about them. In addition to the purely technical aspects, there was the question of this ghost convoy that had dropped Hitler and party off in Patagonia. Although quite unsubstantiated, the rumour was around and everything about these boats had to be thoroughly checked.

For the next four days the two U-Boats lay alongside the pier in Chaguaramas, whilst the Tripartite Team climbed all over them. They found that they were inspecting two quite ordinary U-Boats, similar to those that had already been checked. They found the U977 was similar to U570 which had been captured by the Royal Navy and U530 was similar to U505 captured by the US Navy. The only difference was that these two boats were up to date with the latest torpedoes and sensors. They found the well-known air driven torpedoes, as well as the LUT and FAT electric models; one with a five thousand yard range at thirty knots and the other designed to go through a convoy before turning back to pass back through. They found that the T-5 acoustic torpedoes were the advanced type, designed to ignore the 272 Allied foxers and find the escorts' propellers. They also noted that all the various types of torpedoes could be programmed to run straight, curved or even zig-zag courses, but most of this the Allies already knew.

Both boats were equipped with the schnorkel and they noted that the head of the schnorkel was covered in a rubberised material, with a waffle iron pattern on it, designed to absorb radar pulses and give the equipment a smaller radar signature. Attached to the schnorkel head was a Borkum GSR radar detector, designed to pick up the Allied long wave radar signals. The U-Boats carried portable detector masts for the conning tower, with the Tunis aerial, along with the Mucke and Fliege receivers. This equipment gave them adequate warning of Allied three and ten centimetre radar pulses. Not all the U-Boats equipment was passive and in a large housing on the conning tower they found a radar housing. Fitted snugly inside was the mattress type aerial of the Hohentweil radar, which could be raised and lowered on a hydraulic mast. When tested, it was found that this radar scanner could detect a corvette at five miles and an aircraft at fifteen.

The age of electronic warfare was well underway and the U-Boats had caught up, but probably the most perplexing piece of equipment mounted on the conning towers was a simple direction finder. The U-Boats used this gear to pick up shore stations when returning from patrol, but its chief function was to home on radio signals sent out by a U-Boat shadowing a convoy. This equipment was in use for most of the war, and it deepens the mystery. Surely if the U-Boats had this capability, the Allies would have it. Yet throughout the war they believed that the Allies were incapable of homing on their short wave radio transmissions.

On board the U-Boats, they found sealed cans of Pillenwerfers, designed to be fired from a gun, located near the heads. The Allies called these SBTs or submarine bubble targets, while the Germans referred to them as Bolds, which was an abbreviation of Kobold, meaning an imp or goblin. Both boats carried a large circular hydrophone array under the bows with forty-eight cells, while U530 also had two directional hydrophones mounted at deck level, near the bows. This equipment was capable of an impressive performance and indeed, Lange in U505 is reported to have picked up a depth-charge attack taking place five hundred miles away.

The diving performance of these U-Boats was also very impressive.

Both the Type VIIC and the Type IXC boats were designed to go to sixty fathoms, or three hundred and sixty feet. In practice the U-Boats exceeded these depths by considerable margins. The Type VII U618 went down to eight hundred and eighty-five feet. This was five hundred and twenty-five feet beyond its diving limit. The Type IXs went even further and the deepest dive recorded was to one thousand and twenty feet. This was almost three times deeper than it was designed to go. The new Type XXIs were designed for four hundred and forty feet, but given the actual performance of the earlier boats, it is almost certain that they could get down to twelve hundred feet, if they needed to.

In fact, the two old boats inspected at Chaguaramas in October of 1945, only needed the streamlined hull and vastly increased power of the Type XXIs, to be the weapon that Germany waited so long for. The Tripartite Team knew this, but one suspects that they were not primarily interested in the technical aspects, or the performance of the two boats in Chaguaramas, but rather something to indicate whether Hitler did travel in one of them or not. What they found were simply two standard examples of the Sea Wolves.

At the end of the inspection, the team allowed interested military observers from the Caribbean Command to inspect the boats.

The men who had fought the U-Boats in the theatre lost no time in getting aboard, but they were all horrified. Was it possible that men could fight so well, while being cooped up in these steel coffins? Pilots in particular found the confines of a U-Boat's hull almost claustrophobic. Accustomed to the freedom of the skies, they could not see themselves performing in these floating tombs. What manner of man could continue to go to sea, knowing that each day the odds against coming home were growing.

The first tiny glimmer of understanding was the result of these visits and it was the same wherever U-Boats were inspected. The intense hatred and fear began to be replaced by admiration, that would in the fullness of time allow the U-Boat story to be told. Although there were no German crewmen on these U-Boats, the Allied warriors were meeting the warriors of the U-Boat arm. Their boats spoke for them.

At one thirty-four on the afternoon of Friday fifth of October, U530, U977 and their escort of the USS Cherokee, pulled away from the piers in Chaguaramas. Task Group 21.4 formed up and slowly left through the Third Boca for their trip to the submarine base in New London, Connecticut. They crossed the central Caribbean and exited the sea via the so often used Mona Passage, escorted all the way by the angry sounding Mariners.

Later, both boats were destroyed at sea in a most spectacular fashion. The Sea Wolves had made their final Caribbean call.

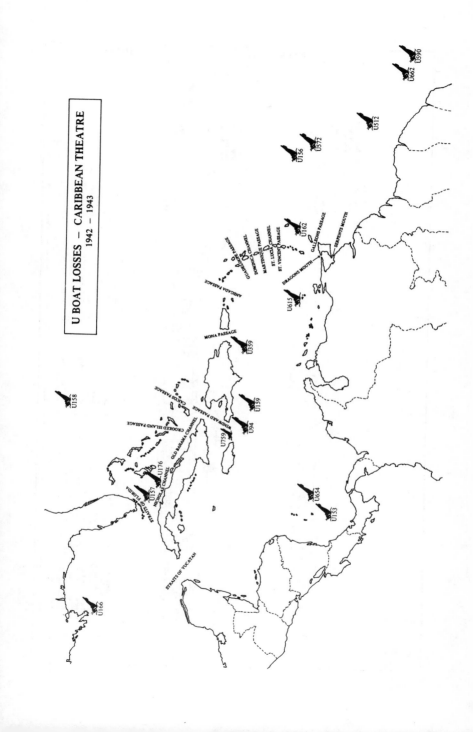

U BOAT LOSSES — CARIBBEAN THEATRE
1942 — 1943

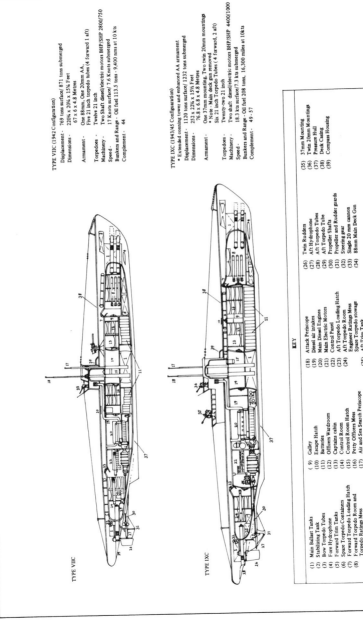

TYPE VIIC (1942 Configuration)

Displacement - 769 tons surface/ 871 tons submerged
Dimensions - 220¼ x 20¼ x 15¾ Feet
            67.4 x 6 x 4.8 Metres
Armament - One 88mm, One 20mm AA,
           Five 21 inch torpedo tubes (4 forward 1 aft)
Torpedoes - Twelve 21 inch
Machinery - Two Shaft diesel/electric motors BHP/SHP 2800/750
Speed - 17 Knots surface/ 7.6 Knots submerged
Bunkers and Range - Oil fuel 113.5 tons - 9,400 nms at 10 kts
Complement - 44

TYPE IXC (1943/45 Configuration)

* Extended conning tower and enhanced AA armament
Displacement - 1120 tons surface/ 1232 tons submerged
Dimensions - 252 x 22¾ x 15¾ Feet
            76.8 x 6.8 x 4.8 Metres
Armament - One 37mm mounting, Two twin 20mm mountings
           • Note - Main deck gun removed
           Six 21 inch Torpedo Tubes (4 forward, 2 aft)
Torpedoes - Twenty-two 21 inch
Machinery - Two shaft diesel/electric motors BHP/SHP 4400/1000
Speed - 18.3 kts surface/7.3 kts submerged
Bunkers and Range - Oil fuel 208 tons, 16,300 miles at 10kts
Complement - 49 - 57

TYPE VIIC

TYPE IXC

KEY

(1) Main Ballast Tanks	(9) Galley	(18) Attack Periscope	(26) Twin Rudders	(35) 37mm Mounting
(2) Stabilizing Tank	(10) Escape Hatch	(19) Diesel air intakes	(27) Aft Hydrophone	(36) Twin 20mm Mountings
(3) Bow Torpedo Tubes	(11) Batteries	(20) Main Diesel Engines	(28) Aft Torpedo Tubes	(37) Pressure Hull
(4) Fore Hydrophone	(12) Officers Wardroom	(21) Main Electric Motors	(29) Aft Torpedo Tube	(38) Deck Casing
(5) Forward Trim Tanks	(13) Captains cabin	(22) Control Panel	(30) Propeller Shafts	(39) Compass Housing
(6) Spare Torpedo Containers	(14) Control Room	(23) Aft Torpedo Loading Hatch	(31) Propeller and Rudder guards	
(7) Forward Torpedo Loading Hatch	(15) Control Room Hatch	(24) Aft Torpedo Room	(32) Steering gear	
(8) Forward Torpedo Room and	(16) Petty Officers Mess	Engineer Ratings Mess	(33) Single 20 mm cannon	
Torpedo Ratings Mess	(17) Aft and Sea Search Periscope	Spare Torpedo stowage	(34) 88mm Main Deck Gun	
Spare Torpedoes		(25) Aft Trim Tank		

CARIBBEAN U-BOATS

U-Boat	Type	Caribbean Patrols	Fate
U66	IXC	(Apr/May 42) - (Jul/Aug/Sep 42) - (Jul 43)	Lost 6/5/44
U67	IXC	(Feb/Mar 42) - (Jun/Jul 42) - (Oct/Nov 42) - (Jun/Jul 43 SUNK)	16/7/43)
U68	IXC	(Jul 42) - (Feb/Mar 43)	Lost 10/4/44
U69	VIIC	(May/Jun 42)	Lost 17/2/43 *
U84	VIIB	(Jun 42) - (Jul/Aug 43 SUNK)	24/8/43 *
U86	VIIB	(Sep 42)	Lost 29/11/43 *
U94	VIIC	(Aug 42 SUNK)	28/8/42
U103	IXB	(May/Jun 42)	Lost 15/4/45
U105	IXB	(Dec 42/Jan 43)	Lost 2/6/43 *
U106	IXB	(May 42)	Lost 2/8/43
U107	IXB	(May/Jun 42) - (Sep 42)	Lost 18/8/44 *
U108	IXB	(May 42) - (Aug 42)	Decomm. 4/44 Rainbow 5/45
U109	IXB	(Dec 42/Jan 43)	Lost 4/5/43 *
U123	IXB	(Sep/Oct 43)	Scuttled 8/44 - Raised Renamed
U124	IXB	(Dec 42/Jan 43)	Lost 2/4/43 *
U125	IXC	(May 42)	Lost 6/5/43 *
U126	IXC	(Mar 42) - (May/Jun/Jul 42)	Lost 3/7/43 *
U128	IXC	(Jun 42)	Lost 17/5/43
U129	IXC	(Feb/Mar 42) - (Jun/Jul/Aug 42) - (Oct/Nov/Dec 42) - (Dec 43/Jan 44)	Scuttled 8/44 Raised Scrapped
U130	IXC	(Apr/May 42)	Lost 12/3/43 *
U134	VIIC	(Jul/Aug 42) - (Jul/Aug 43 SUNK)	24/8/43 *
U153	IXC	(Jun/Jul 42 SUNK)	13/7/42 *
U154	IXC	(Apr 42) - (Jun/Jul/Aug 42) - (Nov/Dec 42) - (Jun 43) - (Nov 43) - (Mar 44)	Lost 3/7/44 *
U155	IXC	(May 42) - (Jul/Aug 42) - (Mar/Apr 43)	Surr 5/45 - Operation Deadlight
U156	IXC	(Feb 42) - (May/Jun 42) - (Feb/Mar 43 SUNK)	8/3/43 *
U157	IXC	(Jun 42 SUNK)	13/6/42 *

U-Boat	Type	Caribbean Patrols	Fate
U158	IXC	(May/Jun 42 SUNK)	30/6/42 *
U159	IXC	(Jun 42) - (Sep 42) - (Jun/Jul 43 SUNK)	15/7/43 *
U160	IXC	(Jul/Aug 42) - (Oct/Nov 42)	Lost 14/7/43 *
U161	IXC	(Feb/Mar 42) - (Jun/Jul 42)	Lost 27/9/43 *
U162	IXC	(Apr/May 42) -	
		(Jul/Aug/Sep 42 SUNK)	3/9/42
U163	IXC	(Aug/Sep 42) - (Nov/Dec 42)	Lost 21/3/43 *
U164	IXC	(Aug/Sep 42)	Lost 6/1/43
U166	IXC	(Jul/Aug 42 SUNK)	1/8/42 *
U168	IXC	(Jun 42)	Lost 5/10/44
U170	IXC	(Dec 43)	Surr 5/45 - Operation Deadlight
U171	IXC	(Jul/Aug/Sep 42 SUNK)	9/10/42
U172	IXC	(Jun 42)	Lost 13/12/43
U173	IXC	(Jul/Aug 42)	Lost 16/11/43
U174	IXC	(Oct 42)	Lost 27/4/43
U175	IXC	(Sep/Oct 42)	Lost 17/4/43
U176	IXC	(May 43 SUNK)	15/5/43 *
U183	IXCs	(Feb/Mar/Apr 43)	Lost 20/4/45 *
U185	IXCs	(Mar/Apr 43)	Lost 24/8/43
U190	IXCs	(Dec 43)	Surr. 5/45 - Operation Deadlight
U193	IXCs	(Dec 43/Jan 44)	Lost 28/4/44 *
U201	VIIC	(Sep/Oct 42)	Lost 17/2/43 *
U202	VIIC	(Sep/Oct 42)	Lost 1/6/43
U203	VIIC	(Jun/Jul 42)	Lost 25/4/43
U214	VIID	(Dec 42/Jan 43) - (Sep/Oct 43)	Lost 26/7/44 *
U217	VIID	(Aug/Sep 42) - (Dec 42/Jan 43)	Lost 5/6/43 *
U218	VIID	(Sep/Oct 43) - (Mar/Apr 44)	Surr. 5/45 - Operation Deadlight
U332	VIIC	(Sep/Oct 42)	Lost 2/5/43 *
U359	VIIC	(Jul 43 SUNK)	28/7/43 *
U406	VIIC	(Sep 42) - (Jul/Aug 43)	Lost 18/2/44
U415	VIIC	(Jul/Aug 42)	Lost 14/7/44
U437	VIIC	(Jul/Aug 42)	Lost 4/10/44
U466	VIIC	(Jul 43)	Scuttled 8/44 - Raised Scrapped
U502	IXC	(Feb 42) - (May/Jun 42 SUNK)	5/7/42 *

U-Boat	Type	Caribbean Patrols	Fate
U504	IXC	(Mar 42) - (May/Jun 42)	Lost 30/7/43 *
U505	IXC	(Jun/Jul/Aug 42) - (Nov 42)	Captured 4/6/44
U506	IXC	(Oct 42) - (May/Jun 42)	Lost 12/7/43
U507	IXC	(Apr/May 42)	Lost 13/1/43 *
U508	IXC	(Aug 42) - (Nov/Dec 42)	Lost 12/11/43 *
U509	IXC	(Jul/Aug 42)	Lost 15/7/43 *
U510	IXC	(Aug 42) - (Feb/Mar 43) - (Jun/Jul 43)	Surr. 5/45 — Renamed
U511	IXC	(Aug/Sep 42)	To Japan 1943 — Renamed RO500
U512	IXC	(Sep/Oct 42 SUNK)	2/10/42
U514	IXC	(Sep 42)	Lost 8/7/43 *
U515	IXC	(Sep 42)	Lost 9/4/44
U516	IXC	(Sep/Oct 42) - (Jul 43) - (Nov/Dec 43) - (Jun/Jul 44)	Surr. 5/45 - Operation Deadlight
U518	IXC	(Sep/Oct 43) - (Feb/Mar/Apr 44)	Lost 22/4/45 *
U527	IXCs	(Jun/Jul 43 SUNK)	23/7/43
U530	IXCs	(Dec 43/Jan 44) - (Jul/Aug 44) - (Ret. USN Crew)	Surr. 5/45 - Destroyed by USN 46
U532	IXCs	(Apr 45) *East of the Caribbean	Surr. 5/45 - Operation Deadlight
U539	IXCs	(May/Jun/Jul 44)	Surr. 5/45 - Operation Deadlight
U553	VIIC	(Aug 42)	Lost 28/1/43 *
U558	VIIC	(May 42) - (Aug/Sep 42)	Lost 20/7/43
U564	VIIC	(May 42) - (Aug/Sep 42)	Lost 14/6/43
U571	VIIC	(Jul 42)	Lost 28/1/44
U572	VIIC	(Jun/Jul/Aug 43 SUNK)	3/8/43 *
U575	VIIC	(Jul 42)	Lost 13/3/44
U590	VIIC	(Jun/Jul 43 SUNK)	9/7/43 *
U594	VIIC	(Sep 42)	Lost 4/6/43 *
U598	VIIC	(Aug 42)	Lost 23/7/43
U600	VIIC	(Aug 42)	Lost 25/11/43 *
U615	VIIC	(Jul/Aug 43 SUNK)	Lost 7/8/43
U634	VIIC	(Jul/Aug 43 SUNK)	30/8/43 *
U653	VIIC	(Jul/Aug 43)	Lost 25/3/44 *
U654	VIIC	(Aug 42 SUNK)	22/8/42 *

U-Boats	Type	Caribbean Patrols	Fate
U658	VIIC	(Aug 42)	Lost 30/10/42 *
U662	VIIC	(Jul 43 SUNK)	21/7/43
U732	VIIC	(Jul/Aug 43)	Lost 31/10/43
U751	VIIC	(May 42)	Lost 17/7/42 *
U753	VIIC	(May/Jun 42)	Lost 13/5/43 *
U755	VIIC	(Apr/May 42)	Lost 28/5/43
U759	VIIC	(Jun/Jul 43 SUNK)	26/7/43 *

Italian Submarines

Enrico Tazzoli	(May 42) - (Aug 42)	Lost 16/5/43 *
Guiseppe Finzi	(May 42)	Siezed 9/43 - Became UIT21 - Scuttled 8/44
Leonardo da Vinci	(Feb 42)	Lost 23/5/43 *
Luigi Torelli	(Feb 42)	Siezed 9/43 - Became UIT25 - To Japan as RO504
Morsini	(May 42)	Lost 11/8/42 *
Pietro Calvi	(Mar/Apr 42)	Lost 15/7/42 *

Note   U-Boats marked SUNK were lost in the Caribbean or on their way home from the area

Boats marked Scuttled were sunk in the French ports by their German crews.

Operation Deadlight was the British operation to sink all surrendered U-Boats in the North Atlantic.

Operation Rainbow was the scuttling of U-Boats by the German crews to stop them falling into the hands of the Allies.

*   Denotes no survivors

IXCs   Denotes an improved Type IXC U-Boat

APPENDIX TWO

TOP TWENTY-FIVE U-BOATS – CARIBBEAN THEATRE

By Total Tonnage Sunk

U-Boat	Tonnage Sunk	Ships Sunk	Ships Damaged	Commanders/Patrols
U129	107,235	23	Nil	Clausen 1/Witt 2/Von Harpe 1
U155	84,563	19	Nil	Piening 3
U66	80,746	12	5 @	Zapp 1/Markworth 2
U162 *	77,643	13	Nil	Wattenburg 2
U126	74,705	15	4	Bauer 2
U160	74,106	14	2	Lassen 2
U67 *	72,737	11	5	Muller-Stockheim 2
U502	71,272	13	1	Von Rosensteil 2
U156 *	67,529	16	7	Hartenstein 3
U68	60,439	9	Nil	Merten 1/Lauzemis 1
U516	53,108	11	1	Weibe 1/Tillessen 2
U508	52,905	11	Nil	Staats 2
U515	46,782	8	2 #	Henke 1
U154	46,716	10	2	Kolle 2/Schuch 1/Kusch 2/Gemeiner 1
U158 *	44,717	9	Nil	Rostin
U507	44,027	8	Nil	Schacht 1
U159 *	41,480	11	1	Witte 1/Beckmann 1
U161	39,403	8	5	Achilles 2
U558	39,129	10	1	Krech 2
U125	33,060	7	Nil	Folkers 1

APPENDIX TWO CONTINUED

U-Boat	Tonnage Sunk	Ships Sunk	Ships Damaged	Commanders/Patrols
U103	32,831	7	Nil	Winter 1
U510	31,352	5	8 **	Neitzel 2/Eick 1
U175	30,834	8	Nil	Bruns 1
U124	28,259	5	Nil	Mohr 1
U506	27,858	5	3	Wurdemann 2

Notes

*	Sunk in the Caribbean or on the way home
@	Three ships to mines laid by U66
#	One damaged ship subsequently scrapped
**	Two damaged ships subsequently scrapped

APPENDIX THREE

TOP SCORING CARIBBEAN U-BOAT PATROLS

Tonnage Sunk on a Single Patrol

U-Boat	Commander	Patrol	Tonnage	Ships Sunk	Ships Damaged
U68	Karl Freidrich Merten	June 42	50,898 tons	7	Nil
U508	George Staats	Nov/Dec 42	50,195 tons	9	Nil
U162	Jurgen Wattenburg	Apr/May 42	47,162 tons	9	Nil
U515	Werner Henke	Sept 42	46,782 tons	8	2
U502 *	Jurgen von Rosensteil	May/Jun 42	46,044 tons	8	Nil
U160	Georg Lassen	Oct/Nov 42	44,865 tons	8	1
U156	Werner Hartenstein	May/Jun 42	44,806 tons	11	2
U158 *	Erich Rostin	May/Jun 42	44,717 tons	9	Nil
U507	Harro Schacht	Apr/May 42	44,027 tons	8	Nil
U66	Richard Zapp	Apr/May 42	43,957 tons	6	1
U129	Hans Witt	Jun/Jul 42	43,571 tons	11	Nil
U155	Adolf Piening	Jul/Aug 42	43,504 tons	10	Nil
U66	Freidrich Markworth	Aug/Sep 42	43,152 tons	7	3
U126	Ernst Bauer	Jun/Jul 42	41,750 tons	7	1
U159	Helmut Witte	May/Jun 42	41,480 tons	11	1
U155	Adolf Piening	May 42	33,086 tons	7	Nil
U125	Ulrich Folkers	May 42	33,060 tons	7	Nil
U126	Ernst Bauer	May 42	32,955 tons	8	3
U103	Werner Winter	May/Jun 42	32,831 tons	7	Nil
U129	Hans Witt	Oct/Nov 42	32,613 tons	5	Nil

APPENDIX THREE CONTINUED

U-Boat	Commander	Patrol	Tonnage	Ships Sunk	Ships Damaged
U175	Heinrich Bruns	Sep/Oct 42	30,834 tons	8	Nil
U161	Albrecht Achilles	Feb/Mar 42	27,997 tons	5	4
U67	Gunther Muller-Stockheim	Jun/Jul 42	27,795 tons	5	2
U558	Gunther Krech	Aug/Sep 42	26,421 tons	5	Nil
U129	Nicolai Clausen	Feb/Mar 42	25,610 tons	7	Nil
U516	Hans Rutger Tillessen	Nov/Dec 43	24,831 tons	6	Nil

Note   *   Sunk on the way home from the Caribbean

APPENDIX FOUR

TOP U-BOAT COMMANDERS

Caribbean Theatre

Commander	U-Boat	Tonnage	Sunk	Damaged	Patrols	Notes
Adolf Piening	U155	84,562 tons	19	Nil	3	
Jurgen Wattenburg	U162	77,643 tons	13	Nil	2	Captured POW
Hans Witt	U129	76,184 tons	16	Nil	2	
Ernst Bauer	U126	74,705 tons	15	4	2	Killed in U169
Georg Lassen	U160	74,106 tons	14	2	2	
Gunther Muller-Stockheim	U67	72,731 tons	11	5	4	Killed in U67
Jurgen Von Rosensteil	U502	71,272 tons	13	1	2	Killed in U502
Werner Hartenstein	U156	67,529 tons	16	7	2	Killed in U156
Karl Fredrich Merten	U68	50,898 tons	7	Nil	1	
Georgr Staats	U508	50,195 tons	11	Nil	2	Killed in U508
Werner Henke	U515	46,782 tons	8	2	1	Captured. Died as POW.
Erich Rostin	U158	44,717 tons	9	Nil	1	Killed in U1588
Harro Schacht	U507	44,027 tons	8	Nil	1	Killed in U507
Richard Zapp	U66	43,957 tons	6	1	1	
Freidrich Markworth	U66	43,152 tons	7	4	2	
Helmut Witte	U159	41,480 tons	11	1	1	
Albrecht Achilles	U161	39,403 tons	8	5	2	Killed in U161
Gunther Krech	U558	39,129 tons	10	1	2	
Hans Rutger Tillessen	U516	34,718 tons	7	Nil	2	
Ulric Folkers	U125	33,060 tons	7	Nil	1	

U-Boats Bases and Flotillas

BORDEAUX   — Initially an Italian submarine base. to October 42.
              12th Flotilla — Command by Klaus Scholtz - ex U108
                          — Disbanded 12th August 1944
                             Base captured 24th August 1944

BREST   — 1st U Flotilla "Weddigen"
                 Commanded in 1943 by Werner Winter ex U103
                 Disbanded August 1944
                 9th U Flotilla, Formed November 1941
                 Disbanded August 1944
                 Base captured on 18th September 1944.

LA PALLICE   — 3rd U Flotilla "Lohs"
                 Commanded by Richard Zapp, ex U66
                 Transferred to Norway August 1944
                 Base surrendered 8th May 1945.

LORIENT   — 2nd U Flotilla, "Saltzwedel"
                 Transferred to Norway August 1944
                 10th U Flotilla — Commanded in 1943 by Ernst Kals ex
                 U130
                 Disbanded October 1944
                 Base surrendered 8th May 1945

SAINT NAZAIRE 7th U Flotilla "Wegener"
                 Transferred to Norway August 1944
                 6th U Flotilla "Hindius"
                 Disbanded August 1944
                 Base surrendered May 8th 1945.

TOP ANTI SUBMARINE SQUADRONS

Associated with the Caribbean Theatre —
Showing U-Boats sank and Data

USN

VB – 107	–	U598 7/43, U148 8/43, U848 11/43, U849 11/43, U177 2/44, U863 9/44
VP – 74	–	U158 6/42, U128 5/43 (S), U199 7/43 (S), U513 7/43, U161 9/43
VP – 32	–	U159 7/43, U759 7/43, U359 7/43
VB – 127	–	U591 7/43, U604 7/43 (S), U761 9/43 (S)
VP – 94	–	U590 7/43, U662 7/43
VP – 83	–	U164 1/43, U507 1/43
VP – 205	–	U572 8/43, U615 8/43 (S)
VP – 204	–	U572 8/43 (S)
VB – 130	–	U615 8/43 (S)
VP – 92	–	U94 8/43 (S)
VP – 53	–	U156 3/43
VB – 129	–	U604 8/43 (S)
VS – 62	–	U176 5/43 (S)
USCG – 212	–	U166 8/42

USAAF

59th Sqn – U844 10/43
45th Sqn – U654 8/43,
99th Sqn – U512 10/42,
10th Sqn – U615 8/43 (S)

RAF

53rd Sqn – U535 7/43, U391 12/43, U608 8/44, U618 8/44

Notes
(1)   S. – Shared –
(2)   **VP-84 – Sank 8 U-Boats in the North Atlantic and Western Approaches.**

MID ATLANTIC

TOP ESCORT CARRIER, GROUPS

USS BOGUE — VC-9/VC-19/VC-95/VC-42 — embarked with escort destroyers U569 5/43, U217 6/43, U118 (T) 6/43, U527 7/43, U86 11/43, U172 12/43, U850 12/43, U575 3/44, U1229 8/44

Total 9 U-Boats — (4 Caribbean veterans).

USS CARD — VC-1/VC-9 embarked, with escort destroyers U117 (T) 8/43, U664 8/43, U525 8/43, U847 8/43, U422 10/43, U460 (T) 10/43, U402 10/43, U584 10/43, U233 7/44

Total 9 U-Boats (

USS CORE — VC-13 embarked, with escort destroyers U487 (T) 7/43, U67 7/43, U185 8/43, U84 8/43, U378 10/43, U172 12/43

Total 6 U-Boats (4 Caribbean veterans).

USS BLOCK ISLAND — VC-6/VC-55 embarked with escort destroyers U220 (T) 10/43, U392 3/44, U801 3/44, U1059 4/44, U66 5/44

Total 4 U-Boats, (1 Caribbean veteran).

Carrier SUNK by U549 5/44: The U-Boat was then sunk by the Escorting destroyers.

USS GUADALCANAL — VC-58 embarked with escort destroyers U554 1/44, U515 4/44, U68 4/44, U505 CAPTURED 6/44

Total 4 U-Boats, (3 Caribbean veterans).

USS SANTEE — VC-29 embarked with escort destroyers U160 7/43.

NOTE — (1) (T) Represents a U Tanker. Eq. U118 (T)
(2) USN CVE' Groups were responsible for sinking 40 U-Boats in mid Atlantic.

TABLE OF EQUIVALENT RANKS

Kriegsmarine	United States Navy	Royal Navy
Grossadmiral	—	—
Generaladmiral	Fleet Admiral	Admiral of the Fleet
Admiral	Admiral	Admiral
Vizeadmiral	Vice Admiral	Vice-Admiral
Konteradmiral	Rear Admiral	Rear-Admiral
Kommodore	Commodore	Commodore
Kapitan zur See	Captain	Captain
Fregattenkapitan	Commander	Commander
Korvettenkapitan	Lieutenant Commander	Lieutenant Commander
Kapitanleutnant	Lieutenant	Lieutenant
Oberleutnant zur See	Lieutenant, Junior Grade	—
Leutnant zur See	Ensign	Sub-Lieutenant
Oberfahnrich zur See	—	—
Fahnrich zur See	Midshipman	Midshipman
—	—	Cadet
Stabsoberbootsmann*	Chief Warrant officer	—
Oberbootsmann*	Warrant Officer (W-3)	Warrant Officer
Stabsbootsmann*	Warrant Officer (W-2)	—
Bootsmann*	Warrant Officer (W-1)	—
—	Master Chief Petty Officer	—
—	Senior Chief Petty Officer	—
Oberbootsmannsmaat*	Chief Petty Officer	Chief Petty Officer
Bootsmannsmaat*	Petty Officer 1st Class	Petty Officer
Matrosenstabsobergefreiter	Petty Officer 2nd Class	—
Matrosenstabsgefreiter	Petty Officer 3rd Class	Leading Seaman
Matrosenhauptgefreiter	Seaman	Able Seaman
Matrosenobergefreiter	—	—
Matrosengefreiter	Seaman Apprentice	Ordinary Seaman
Matrose	Seaman Recruit	—

*Bootsmann designates the rating or specialty of petty officers and warrant officers.

The suffix maat designates a senior petty officer. A title without a suffix designates a warrant officer. Other ratings are substituted as appropriate. For Example: Maschinenmaat, Obersignalmaat, Oberartilleriemechankiker, Stabsoberbootsmann.

SOURCES

PUBLISHED

A Bloody War — Harald Lawrence, McMillan NAL, Ontario, Canada, 1979

A Marinha do Brazil, No Segunda Guerre Mundial, — Arthur Oscar Saldanha de Gama, Grafica, Brazil, 1982

Autumn of the U-Boats — Geoffrey Jones, William Kimber Ltd, London, 1984

Axis Submarines — Anthony J. Watts, Arco Publishing, New York, 1977

Axis Submarine Successes — Jurgen Rohwer, US Naval Institute, Annapolis, 1983

British Warship Losses in World War Two — H.T. Lenton & J.J. Colledge, Ian Allen London 1976

Building the Navy's Bases in World War Two, — US Govt. Printing Office, 1947

Convoy — Martin Middlebrook, Ian Allen, London, 1976

Dynamite for Hire — A.V. Sellwood — Panther Books, London, 1958

Encyclopedia of World War Two — Editor John Keegan, Hamlyn, London, 1977

Encyclopedia of World War Two — Editor Thomas Parrish, Secker & Warberg, London, 1978

Grey Wolf, Grey Sea — E.B. Gassaway, Futura Books, London, 1972

History of the Second World War — Winston Churchill, Cassell, London, 1959

Janes Fighting Ships 1939/40 — Janes Fighting Ships Publishing Co. Ltd., London

Janes Fighting Ships 1945/46 — Janes Fighting Ships Publishing Co. Ltd., London

The Battle of the Atlantic — Donald Macintyre, Pan Books, London, 1961

The Battle of the Atlantic — Barrie Pitt, Time Life Books, New York, 1977

The Battle of the Atlantic — HMSO, London, 1946

The Deadly Stroke — Warren Tute, Pan Books, London, 1976

The Month of the Lost U-Boats — Geoffrey Jones, William Kimber Ltd., London, 1977

The Sea Wolves — Wolfgang Frank, Ballantyne, New York, 1955

The Squadrons of the Royal Air Force — James J. Halley, Air Britain, 1980

The Squadrons of the Fleet Air Arm — R. Sturtivant

The War at Sea — S.W. Roskill, HMSO, London, 1956

They Were Dependable, The History of US Navy Airship Operations in World War Two, US Navy 1946

U-Boat — David Mason, Purnell, London, 1968

U-Boat 333 — Peter Cremer, Grafton Books, London 1983

U-Boat 977 — Heinz Schaffer, Tandem Books, London, 1952

U-Boats in the Atlantic — Paul Beaver, Patrick Stephens Ltd, London, 1979

US Navy Aircraft Since 1911 — Gordon Swansborough & Peter Bowers, Funk & Wagnals, New York
Walker RN. — Terrence Robertson, Pan Books, London, 1956
We Captured a U-Boat — Admiral Gallery, Landsborough Publications, London, 1957

PROFESSIONAL JOURNALS

US Navy Proceedings — US Naval Institute, Annapolis, Maryland, — Issues 1954 to 1986
Warship — Conway Maritime Press Limited, London, Issues Nos. 1 to 20

UNPUBLISHED DOCUMENTS

Scholarly Resources Ltd., Willmington, Delawave, The War Diaries of the German Submarine Command, 1942-43-44
US Naval Historical Centre, — Operational Archives, Branch, Washington — War Diaries, — USN Trinidad Sector, Chaguaramas Naval Air Station, 1942-45, Chaguaramas Naval Operating Base 1943-45, Unit Returns — Caribbean Theatre, US Naval Station Trinidad, Command History File.
Squadron War Diaries — USN VP-32, VP-53, VP-74, VP-94, VP-204, ZP-51, USN Fleet Airship Wing Five, FASRON 105, Hedron 71
Reports — Convoy Signal File TB-1 USN, Convoy Signal File BT-6 USN, Report on the loss of the USS Eire USN, US Submarine Losses, U-Boat Section
National Archives Administration, Washington, War Diaries, — U161, U156, War Diary Summaries, All Caribbean U-Boats
Department of the Air Force, — Albert F. Simpson Historical Research Centre, Maxwell AFB. Ala. History of the US Army and Air Corps in the Caribbean theatre 1940-45, History of the US Army in the South American theatre 1942-45, History of the US Army in the Trinidad Sector 1940-45, G-2 Intelligence Reports, Caribbean Command, War Diary Summaries — US Army Air Corps 45th, 59th, and 99th squadrons
RN Naval Historical Division, — MOD London, Selected — RN Anti-submarine Summaries, World War Two, Merchant Ship Losses Caribbean 1942, German and Italian U-Boat Losses, 1939-45
Public Records Office London — War Diary Attack Reports — No. 53 Sgn. RAF, War Diary, RN Trinidad Command 1942-45, TRNVR Command History File — 1940-45
Directorate of History, National Defence Headquarters, Ottawa Canada,

RCN Anti-submarine Summaries 1941-45

In addition to information from published and unpublished sources the author wishes to thank the following individuals who greatly assisted in providing information and answering my many queries on the U-Boat War:-

Prof. Dr. Jurgen Rohwer — Stuttgart, West Germany
C. Clout — Imperial War Museum, London
G. Jones — London
D.C. Allard — USN Naval Historical Centre, Washington
Hal Lawrence — Lt. Cmdr. RCN, Canada
R.M. Coppock — Naval Historical Branch, MOD London
Horst Bredow — U-Boat Archiv Moltenort, West Germany
Timothy P. Mulligan — Modern Military Archives Branch, Washington
Klaus G. Erhardt — Hamburg, West Germany
Dr. Hoffman — Bundarchiv, Koblenz, West Germany
T.R. Padfield — Public Records Office, London
F.J. Kemp — Imperial War Museum, London
Sandy Fell-Smith — Lt. Cmdr. TRNVR Ret. Trinidad
Cesar de Wint Lavendier — Rear Adm. Ret. Dominican Navy
Arthur Oscar Saldanha de Game — Vice Adm. Ret, Brazilian Navy
Alfred Hiller — Hamm, West Germany
Axel Niestle — U-Boat Archiv Moltenort, West Germany
L.F. Lovell — Fleet Air Arm Museum, England
Col. W. Stanick — USAF Historical Research Centre, Maxwell AFB USA
W.A.B. Douglas — National Defence Headquarters, Ottawa Canada
Major Lester A. Sliter — USAF Historical Research Centre, Maxwell AFB USA
Ralph J. Kelshall — Trinidad

Notes

Chapter 1   If You Want Peace, Prepare for War

Much of this chapter is based on the following records: History of the Trinidad Sector, vols. 1–5 (microfilm, nos. 32951, 32952, and 32954), and G-2 periodic reports, HQ Trinidad Sector (microfilm, no. A4190), Albert F. Simpson Historical Center, Maxwell AFB, Ala.; war diaries of the Caribbean Sea frontier, the Trinidad Sector, and the Chaguaramas Naval Operating Base and Naval Air Station (microfilm, no. A6693), U.S. Naval Historical Center, Washington, D.C.

2   Two German photographs, 86 MW 4285/3 and 32, show *U69* and *U107* being refueled by the American tanker *Prairie* in the mid-Atlantic. The caption states that four American tankers were waiting to refuel the *Bismark*. See Paul Beaver, *U-Boats in the Atlantic: A Selection of German Wartime Photographs from the Bundesarchiv, Koblenz* (Cambridge: Patrick Stephens, 1979).

11   The defensive stance of U.S. forces in the Caribbean theatre is described in the preamble to History of the Trinidad Sector (no. 32951).

13   The escorts available were three Eagle boats, one large and six small Coast Guard cutters, three patrol gunboats, four yard craft, and four sub chasers. Admiral Andrews reported this return of his available forces to Admiral King in January 1942 along with the status of his 108 available aircraft. In his summary Andrews stated, "Should the enemy submarines operate off this coast, this command has no forces available to take adequate action against them, either offensive or defensive." See Comdr. C. Alphonso Smith, "Battle of the Caribbean," U.S. Naval Institute *Proceedings* 80 (1954): 976–82; Lt. (jg) T. J. Belke, " 'Roll of Drums,' " U.S. Naval Institute *Proceedings* 109

(1983): 58–64; war diary of the eastern sea frontier, 1941–42, chap. 2 (microfilm, nos. 1–3). On U.S. Navy convoy and escort policy, see Donald G. F. W. Macintyre, *The Battle of the Atlantic* (New York: Macmillan, 1961), 126–35.

16 On destroyer basing policy, see Belke, " 'Roll of Drums.' "

17 On U.S. Navy escort vessels and convoy considerations, see eastern sea frontier command history file, vol. 1, chap. 2 (microfilm, no. 1).

18 On reinforcements for the 434th Infantry Regiment at Fort Reid, see History of the Trinidad Sector, vol. 1, chap. 1 (no. 32952). This section deals with the state of readiness of the reinforcements and the methods adopted to begin their training.

Chapter 2   Operation Neuland Begins

26 The meeting in Lorient of U-boat commanders destined for the Caribbean is described in the 1942 war diary of the German Submarine Command, 30302–14B (microfilm, no. 2), available from Scholarly Resources Inc., Washington, D.C.

Interestingly, the notion that Albrecht Achilles had sailed in Trinidad is a long-standing belief among TRNVR veterans and local people involved in the war. According to a biographical sketch of Achilles issued by the German Submarine Association of Lubeck (based on the book *Marine Offizier Vereinigung,* published in Bonn), his first appointment was as a watchkeeping officer aboard the battle cruiser *Gneisenau* from February 1939 to April 1940. However, it is possible that he was on a German Navy sail training ship that visited Trinidad before the war.

28 Attack reports and descriptions of firing sequence come from Jurgen Rohwer, *Axis Submarine Successes, 1939–1945* (Annapolis, Md.: Naval Institute Press, 1983). Conditions ashore, troop dispositions, and defensive arrangements are found in the U.S. Army command history file, Trinidad Sector, DOD, DIR (microfilm, no. 52009).

33 The 1942 war diary of the German Submarine Command lists the orders for *U156* and *U67* but do not indicate that *U502* was supposed to head toward the Dutch Islands after its first attacks in the Gulf of Maracaibo. For claims of attacks on U-boats by the 59th Squadron,

based in Curacao, see the squadron's war diary summary, available from Maxwell AFB, Ala.

34 On the confusion in Trinidad over the command structure, the differences of opinion between the British and American commands, and the chaos that followed *U161*'s attack on Port-of-Spain, see U.S. Army command history file; war diary of the Caribbean Sea frontier, nos. 1901–90; TRNVR war diary, PRO, London.

35 This description of Achilles' attack on Port-of-Spain harbor is based on a report on Radio Berlin monitored by Allied sources and quoted verbatim in the U.S. Army command history file. Although the report was considered propaganda and was widely disbelieved at the time, its details are corroborated by the log of *U161*, now held by the Bundesarchiv, Koblenz. In addition, former U-boatman Oscar Steiner, who was on *U161* at the time, confirms the procedure for entry, attack, and exit as well as the story that a local fisherman was taken aboard the U-boat to prevent him from raising the alarm. Naval reaction to the attack was supplied by interviews with Lt. Cmdr. C. Geofrey and Lt. Allan Lawrence, executive officer and navigating officer, respectively, of HMS *Dorothy Duke*. The response of Civil Defence was described by Ralph Kelshall, who was deputy area authority of the San Fernando district during World War II.

43 John Colville, one of Churchill's secretaries, recalls being told by Harry Hopkins that that nation's resolve in dealing with the French Fleet convinced President Roosevelt that Britain intended to fight on—alone, if need be. See Colville's introduction to Warren Tute, *The Deadly Stroke* (New York: Pan Books, 1976).

On the mutinies by crews of the shallow-draft tankers traveling between Maracaibo and the Dutch Islands, see Smith, "Battle of the Caribbean."

Chapter 3   The Second Half of Neuland

The general outline of this chapter is based on records compiled in Rohwer, *Axis Submarine Successes;* war diary of the German Submarine Command, 30302–14B; and interviews with TRNVR veterans.

47 The *Nordvangen* is not listed on the 1946 merchant shipping list issued by the Admiralty and available from the Navy History Division in London. The Norwegian shipping registry subsequently showed the *Nordvangen* as missing in World War II. Rohwer, *Axis Submarine Successes*, 79 n. 16, states that wreckage from the ship was found in the area, presumably by *U129*. Unfortunately, the Trinidad harbormaster's office was destroyed in a fire in the 1960s, and all of the records from World War II were lost.

51 This account of the sinking of the *Circle Shell* is taken from the survivor report written by Lieutenant Burch, USN, and addressed to the CNO, 28 April 1942, file OP-16–B5, U.S. Naval Historical Center, Washington, D.C.

52 Admiral Hoover's reports appear in the U.S. Navy war diary of the Trinidad Sector (microfilm, nos. 1901–90). Additional material comes from the war diary of the eastern sea frontier.

60 *U161*'s attack on St. Lucia harbor was aired by Radio Berlin. This broadcast was monitored by Allied sources and quoted verbatim in the war diary of the Trinidad Sector. The war diary of *U161* confirms the accuracy of the Radio Berlin account, as do residents of St. Lucia in 1942. For a lengthy description of the confusion caused by lack of experience and inadequate fire orders for garrison troops in the Caribbean theatre, see U.S. Army command history file, vol. 2 (no. B15218).

Chapter 4   The Merry Month of May

This and subsequent chapters are based on the author's Caribbean combined operations war diary, which is an amalgam of the following records: war diaries of the Chaguaramas Naval Operating Base and Naval Air Station, and the Caribbean Sea frontier; war diary of the German Submarine Command; and squadron war diaries as appropriate.

73 For a history of mining operations in the Bocas and the Royal Navy's objections to them, see war diary of the Chaguaramas Naval Operating Base. TRNVR veteran Lt. Cmdr. Sandy Fell-Smith, who commanded a Royal Navy ML on Gulf of Paria patrols and interisland escort missions, told the author in 1984 that he was not aware of any mining operations in the Bocas; he knew only that three of the four islands were out of bounds. On 31 March 1942 the B'dienst warned its U-boats that the Bocas were mined.

79   The story of the sinking of the *Douglas* and the piglet that swam to the U-boat was related by survivors of *U162*.

80   The *Mokihana* incident is described in a memorandum for file written by Lt. Thomas A. Courtney, USNR, and addressed to the CNO, 30 June 1942, U.S. Naval Historical Center, Washington, D.C. The war diaries of both the Chaguaramas Naval Operating Base and the German Submarine Command record the ship's distress call on 4 May 1942.

   On the behavior of U-boat crews toward survivors, see Barrie Pitt, *The Battle of the Atlantic* (Alexandria, Va.: Time-Life Books, 1977), 176. This account documents the experiences of survivors from the *Kahaku* (sunk by *U126*), the *Esso Houston* (sunk by *U162*), and the *MF Elliot* (sunk by *U502*).

85   The author is still unable to verify this tale, which allegedly originated with Captain Boden, commander of the interisland ship. But the story even reached Parliament and entered official government records.

Chapter 5   The Golden West

92   U-boats never operated in packs in the Caribbean and did not need to attack convoys at this stage because of the large number of independently sailing merchant ships. This made it extremely difficult for escorts—operating either with convoys or independently as hunting groups—to catch and sink U-boats. As a result, during the first half of 1942 the Caribbean was a very difficult antisubmarine command. The ultimate solution involved not just heavily escorted convoys as in the North Atlantic but also up-to-date intelligence and round-the-clock surveillance of the open waters near shipping routes. It would be 1943 before the sector received the aviation resources necessary to this winning combination.

96   Survivors' camps were established on all of the major islands of the Caribbean to handle the flood of merchant seamen plucked from the sea. Taking part in this humanitarian effort became a serious social obligation for islanders, and many of the volunteers (who were mostly women) still carry vivid memories of their experiences in the camps and the state of some of the survivors. For their part, the survivors spoke of their terror of sharks and of what they had seen sharks do.

100   *U67* was rammed off Gibraltar on 28 September 1941 by a Royal Navy submarine, HMS *Clyde;* both boats returned to their respective bases. See Records Relating to U-Boat Warfare, 1939–45, p. 38, National Archives and Records Administration, Washington, D.C.; John Winton, *ULTRA at Sea: How Breaking the Nazi Code Affected Allied Naval Strategy during World War II* (New York: Morrow, 1988), 100.

101   The message about Swedish and Portuguese ships was sent out on 12 June 1942. See the war diary of the German Submarine Command.

103   The collision of *U161* and a merchant ship is mentioned in the boat's war diary, p. 143. Seaman Oscar Steiner, who transferred out of the boat before its final patrol in 1943, confirms that the impact rolled *U161* over to port and that some damage was done to the pressure hull, causing water to leak into the vessel.

105   The list of shipping losses issued by the Admiralty does not name the *Tillie Lykes* as a casualty of World War II. The war diary of the Trinidad Sector mentions the receipt of an SOS from the ship on 7 June 1942, while Rohwer, *Axis Submarine Successes,* reports that the ship was listed as missing on 18 June. When he was rescued, one of the survivors claimed that the ship was sunk by a U-boat. *U107* was the U-boat closest to the Honduran coast at that time, but that boat did not report an attack on the *Tillie Lykes.* The ship could have moved northward into the area occupied by *U502* and *U158* and been sunk at a later date; but neither U-boat survived the cruise, and neither claimed the *Tillie Lykes* in their radio reports. The evidence suggests that *U158* reported on its actions meticulously, and the absence of any mention of the *Tillie Lykes* or of being off the Honduran coast between 7 and 18 June would seem to rule out this boat as the attacker. *U502,* on the other hand, was operating well to the east and did not move into the Panama Sector at all, according to its radio reports.

The author has credited *U107* with the kill because it was the only boat in the area where the 2,572-ton *Tillie Lykes* went down. However, it is possible that the ship struck a drifting mine, and that the crew mistook this for a torpedo hit.

110   The end of *U158* is described in Beaver, *U-Boats in the Atlantic,* 9.

Chapter 6   The Third Wave

115   The SS *Warrior* lies in shallow water, despite being on the open sea. As a result of numerous diving expeditions, many Trinidad residents possess items of her cargo as mementos.

On the layout and defenses of Porto Limon, the effect of Achilles' attack, and the U.S. defensive stance in the Panama Sector, see History of the Trinidad Sector, vol. 3.

122   Many tales are told in the Caribbean about U-boats chasing and sinking schooners. Eyewitness accounts of these attacks exist, from both crew members and shore-based observers. The names of vessels sunk and the precise dates of such attacks are matters of local record and do not appear in Allied or German archives. Presumably the Germans considered the small two- or three-masted vessels not important enough to record, and the Allied command simply never heard about the individual episodes. Based on numerous interviews, the author estimates that at least three times as many schooners were sunk as can be verified in official sources. Cases in which schooners escaped would by themselves provide sufficient material for another book.

U84 sank the 7,166-ton *William Cullen Bryant* and hit a 12,000-ton President Line tanker. On 23 July 1942 *U129* sank the 2,310-ton SS *Onandago* in the Old Bahama Channel.

123   The report on the sinking of the *Tamandare* appears in war diary of the Chaguaramas Naval Operating Base, 26 July 1942.

125   Convoys' routes and designations are detailed in war diary of the Chaguaramas Naval Operating Base, July 1942.

126   Doenitz's comments about the Caribbean theatre and his letter to Hitler are contained in war diary of the German Submarine Command, 19 July 1942.

Chapter 7   Convoys

130   See war diary of RAF Squadron No. 53, PRO, London.

135   This and subsequent descriptions of attacks on convoys in this chapter are based on U-boat firing data in Rohwer, *Axis Submarine Successes;*

war diary of the German Submarine Command; U.S. Navy war diary
of the Trinidad Sector; war diary of RAF Squadron No. 53.

139   According to David Mason, three merchant ships were abandoned by
their crews in the North Atlantic in August 1942. See Mason, *U-Boat:
The Secret Menace* (New York: Ballantine, 1968), 90.

143   On Brazil's declaration of war, see Pitt, *Battle of the Atlantic,* 179.

Chapter 8   Three U-Boats

155   In addition to the war diaries, see Samuel Eliot Morison, *History of
United States Naval Operations in World War II* (Boston: Little,
Brown, 1947–63), 1:346; Hal Lawrence, *A Bloody War: One Man's
Memories of the Canadian Navy, 1939–1945* (Toronto: Macmillan,
1979), 103–15; Royal Canadian Navy antisubmarine summaries,
Directorate of History, National Defence Headquarters, Ottawa.

165   On Admiral King, see Winston Churchill, *The Second World War*
(Boston: Houghton Mifflin, 1948–53), 3:303, 342, 346, 395–96,
484, 606; Macintyre, *Battle of the Atlantic,* 130. It is debatable
whether U.S. antisubmarine resources in 1942 were insufficient or
simply misused. Captain Macintyre states that in 1939 Britain faced
the U-boat threat and instituted convoys with 112 surface vessels and
45 aircraft; an antisubmarine summary issued by the U.S. fleet in
1945 claims that the navy had 173 surface vessels and 268 aircraft in
the Atlantic in January 1942. See monthly summaries, war diary of
the Chaguaramas Naval Operating Base.

167   Capt. Lloyd Clarke, U.S. Army, reports that while in Clarke's cus-
tody as a POW, Jurgen Wattenburg said he did not know that he was
attacking three destroyers; he thought there was only one present.
Other survivors of *U162* confirm Wattenburg's account. In addition to
the standard Caribbean references, see the narrative Sinking of *U162*
by HM Ships *Vimy, Pathfinder,* and *Quentin,* p. 26, in Royal Navy
antisubmarine summaries, file ADM 199/2059, PRO, London.

Chapter 9   The Changing of the Guard

179   The account of *U514*'s attack on the *Cornwallis* is based on TRNVR
war diary, 11 September 1942; war diary of the Chaguaramas Naval

Operating Base, 11 September 1942; History of the Trinidad Sector, vol. 2.

180   This depiction of the disruptive consequences of the establishment of a German base on Barbados is purely speculative. Its purpose is to highlight how important the U-boat arm might have been against the Allied lifeline—particularly in the first half of 1942. This is not to say that Germany could have won the war in that year.

183   The attack on the *Woensdrecht* is recorded in the war diaries of the Chaguaramas Naval Operating Base and the German Submarine Command, 12 September 1942.

186   On the *Laconia* incident, see Pitt, *Battle of the Atlantic,* 155; war diary of the German Submarine Command, 16 September 1942.

192   The air attack on *U514* is mentioned in war diary of VP-74, 16 September 1942.

193   The account of *U515*'s attack on the *Reedpool* is based on war diary of the German Submarine Command, 20 September 1942.

195   On the encounter between *U515* and the *Ceramic,* see Daniel V. Gallery, *We Captured a U-Boat* (London: Sidgwick & Jackson, 1957), 142–46.

Chapter 10   The Veterans' Return

199   The war at sea was relatively free of war crimes, probably because the vast majority of seamen saw the sea as their common enemy. The Hague Convention, which all the major powers had signed, stated that a submarine did not have to pick up survivors but could not hinder their survival, regardless of whether they were civilians or combatants. Most seamen obeyed both these rules and what is called the law of the sea. However, there were exceptions. The crew of *U852,* for example, killed the survivors of a 1944 attack. As a result the captain, Heinz Eck, and one of his watch officers were executed after the war. On the other side, the commander of the Royal Navy submarine HMS *Torbay* machine-gunned a number of German survivors in the Aegean in 1941. The Admiralty, unwilling to remove one of its top-scoring commanders, simply issued a letter of censure; the officer later won the Victoria Cross, promotion to admiral, and a knighthood. The war in the Pacific was more vicious. There are unsubstantiated allegations that both American and Japanese commanders machine-gunned survivors, but no one was ever punished.

203   See History of the Trinidad Sector, vol. 3; war diary of the Chaguaramas Naval Operating Base, 2 October 1942.

205   The wreck of the *Athelbran* is still visible off the southern coast of Trinidad.
          Photos of the loss of *U175* appear in Pitt, *Battle of the Atlantic*, 84–93.

213   The rendezvous between the *Campeche* and U-boats *U129* and *U332* is not mentioned in the war diary of the German Submarine Command, but the war diary of the Chaguaramas Naval Operating Base records the radio signals as well as crew reports from the *Reuben Tipton* and the *Kabot*. Crew members from the Spanish ship were later questioned by British intelligence in Port-of-Spain. The author has not seen the interrogation report but has interviewed persons who were present.

215   The war diaries of the Chaguaramas Naval Operating Base and the German Submarine Command, 25 October 1942, give brief outlines of the incident involving *U67* and the *Primero*. The author has reconstructed the course changes necessary by both vessels for the encounter to have occurred.

Chapter 11   The Death of an Escort

221   Details about convoy TAG 18 are assembled from U-boat firing data in Rohwer, *Axis Submarine Successes;* war diary of RAF Squadron No. 53; war diary of the German Submarine Command; war diary of the Chaguaramas Naval Operating Base, 2–4 November 1942.

225   The outline of *U505*'s second Caribbean cruise is contained in war diary of the German Submarine Command, 19 October–12 December 1942. The difficulties experienced by the captain and crew on this cruise are described in Gallery, *We Captured a U-Boat*, 95–107.

228   The attack by Squadron No. 53 against *U505* is detailed in the signals sent by the boat to headquarters and recorded in war diary of the German Submarine Command. On the fate of Sergeant Silcock's aircraft and what transpired aboard the U-boat, see Gallery, *We Captured a U-Boat,* 100–107, 121–34.

231 The loss of the USS *Erie* is described in a declassified confidential report from the ship's commanding officer to the secretary of the navy, 9 December 1942, document PG50/A16-3/L1-1, U.S. Naval Historical Center, Operational Archives Branch, Washington, D.C.

237 See war diary of RAF Squadron No. 53.

238 On 26 November 1992 K. M. Maclean of the Isle of Benbecula, Scotland, held a memorial service in Trinidad for his father and the other seamen who died when the *Clan Mac Fadyen* was lost. A wreath was dropped over the spot where the ship went down, one hundred miles southeast of Trinidad. This was the first memorial for the merchant marine ever held in the Caribbean. On the *Clan Mac Fadyen* and other ships of the Clan Line in World War II, see Gordon Holman, *In Danger's Hour* (London: Hodder & Stoughton, 1948).

The *Empire Glade* was badly holed and taking terrible punishment from *U67*'s gun. The captain tried to ram the boat, as the *Primero* had done; but unable to get at his assailant, he used smoke floats to cover his escape. See Bernard Edwards, *Grey Widow Maker* (n.p.: Robert Hale, n.d.).

240 Intelligence summary derived from G-2 periodic reports, August 1942–April 1944 (microfilm, no. 2266).

Chapter 12   TB-1 and TM-1

This chapter is based on U-boat firing data in Rohwer, *Axis Submarine Successes;* war diary of the Chaguaramas Naval Operating Base; war diary of the German Submarine Command; war diary of VP-53.

245 On Lorient, see Gallery, *We Captured a U-Boat,* 111–16.

246 The Caribbean patrol of *U124* is outlined in E. B. Gasaway, *Grey Wolf, Grey Sea* (n.p.: Future Books, n.d.), 224–36.

249 See war diary of VP-204, 24 December 1942.

252 For the sighting reports of *U214* and *U514,* see war diary of the German Submarine Command, 27 December 1942 and 3 January 1943.

255 Operation Faith is recorded in war diary of the Chaguaramas Naval Operating Base and TRNVR war diary, 7 January 1943.

256 See the convoy signal file for TB-1, document NCR 2243, U.S. Naval Historical Center, Washington, D.C., as well as the attached letters to the commander in chief U.S. Navy, and commander South Atlantic, document A14-/96/yg, regarding the tanker *Motorcarline*.

260 For the full story of convoy TM-1, see Winton, *ULTRA at Sea,* 110–12. Additionally, John Terraine reports that all of the convoy's escorts experienced simultaneous surface radar failures. See Terraine, *Business in Great Waters: The U-Boat Wars, 1916–1945* (London: Leo Cooper, 1989), 514–15.

Chapter 13   The Death of an Ace

265 The Radio Berlin report appears in History of the Trinidad Sector, vol. 1.

266 See war diary of ZP-51, 24 January 1943.

270 On the loss of *U156,* see ibid., 3–8 March; war diary of the Chaguaramas Naval Air Station, 3–8 March 1943; war diary of the German Submarine Command, 6 March 1943; war diary of VP-53, 8 March.

274 Convoy BT-6 is discussed in war diary of the Chaguaramas Naval Operating Base. See also U-boat firing data in Rohwer, *Axis Submarine Successes.*

278 For details on the bombing of *U185,* see war diary of ZP-51, 26 March 1943; war diary of the German Submarine Command, 30 March 1943.

280 On the surrender of Vichy French Guiana, see G-2 periodic reports; war diaries of the Chaguaramas Naval Operating Base and Naval Air Station, 19 March 1943; History of the Trinidad Sector, vol. 2.

Chapter 14   A Double-Edged Sword

284 On merchant ship losses in March 1943 and the doubts they raised about the convoy system, see Stephen Wentworth Roskill, *The Navy* *at War, 1939–1945* (London: Collins, 1960), 273–74; Terraine, *Business in Great Waters*, 536, 543, 569, 570; Pitt, *Battle of the Atlantic*, 182–86.

287 Material on the Miami conference comes from U.S. Army command history file, vol. 4; and U.S. Navy war diary of the Trinidad Sector, March 1943.

289 See U.S. Navy war diary of the Trinidad Sector.

290 In the St. James area of Port-of-Spain, a large holding camp was built. This camp remained in operation throughout the war. Part of the camp housed Jews awaiting resettlement in the United States; another section held detainees, mostly Trinidadians thought to favor the Axis cause as well as citizens of such nominally Axis nations as Finland. The remainder of the camp served as a prisoner-of-war facility where the captured U-boatmen were held.

291 Oldendorf had command of the battle line (composed of seven old battleships from the Seventh Fleet) that defeated Admirals Nishimura and Shima's southern support force in the night action in Surigao Strait. This marked the last time that battleships fought one another directly, and it was also the only decisive victory that either side could claim in the Battle of Leyte Gulf.

294 On U-boat losses in May 1943, see Geoffrey Patrick Jones, *The Month of Lost U-Boats* (n.p., n.d.), 15–17 (*U332*), 21–27 (*U109*), 54–55 (*U125*), 100–103 (*U750*), 114–15 (*U176*), 128–32 (*U128*), 181–82 (*U755*).

Chapter 15   The Wolves Gather

The basic source documents for this chapter are History of the Trinidad Sector, vol. 2; U.S. Navy war diary of the Trinidad Sector; war diary of the German Submarine Command.

303 On the sinking of *U202*, see Terence Robertson, *Walker, R.N.: The Story of Captain Frederic John Walker* (London: Great Pan Books, n.d.), 94–101.

305 Dispositions for the proposed invasion of Martinique are found in History of the Trinidad Sector, vol. 3.

308 The matter of the codes seized from *U559* is addressed in Winton, *ULTRA at Sea*, 119.

316 On the sinking of *U119*, see Robertson, *Walker, R.N.*, 105–7.

Chapter 16   U-Tankers

Much of this chapter is based on the war diaries of VP-32, VP-204, VP-205, ZP-51, Chaguaramas Naval Operating Base and Naval Air Station, and the German Submarine Command for July 1943.

326 Survivors from *U162* and *U615* have told the author that in the Caribbean the temperature inside a U-boat could go as high as 120 degrees Fahrenheit.

328 On the loss of *U590*, see war diary of the Chaguaramas Naval Air Station, 9 July 1943.

331 For details of the Martinique invasion plan, see History of the Trinidad Sector, vol. 3.

334 On the sinking of *U487*, see Geoffrey Patrick Jones, *Autumn of the U-Boats* (n.p., n.d.), 146.

336 The warning to U.S. Navy pilots is recorded in war diary of the Chaguaramas Naval Air Station, 14 July 1943. On the sinking of *U159*, see war diary of VP-32, 15 July 1943; VP-32 attack report, narrative document, FF1/A16-3 (18), U.S. Naval Historical Center, Operational Archives Branch, Washington, D.C.

339 On the sinking of *U67*, see Jones, *Autumn of the U-Boats*, 146.

Chapter 17   Caribbean Crisis

Much of this chapter is based on the war diaries of VP-32, VP-204, VP-205, ZP-51, Chaguaramas Naval Operating Base and Naval Air Station, and the German Submarine Command for July 1943.

342 The loss of airship K74 is described in war diary of ZP-51, 18 July 1943. The attacks on *U662* are recorded in U.S. Navy war diary of the Trinidad Sector, 19 July 1943.

344 The attacks on *U572* and *U415* are recorded in war diary of VP-204, 19–20 July 1943.

347 The signal from *U662* appears in war diary of the German Submarine Command, 21 July 1943.

348 On the sinking of *U662,* see war diary of the Chaguaramas Naval Air Station, 21 July 1943.

353 On the sinking of *U459,* see Jones, *Autumn of the U-Boats,* 70.

354 The attacks on *U466* are recorded in the war diaries of the Chaguaramas Naval Air Station and the German Submarine Command, 24 July 1943.

356 See war diary of VP-204, 24 July 1943.

357 On the sinking of *U759,* see war diary of VP-32, 26 July 1943; VP-32 attack report, U.S. Atlantic Fleet, document no. 8144.

Chapter 18   Airpower

360 On the sinking of *U359,* see war diary of VP-32, 28 July 1943; VP-53 attack report, U.S. Atlantic Fleet, document no. 8463.

366 Reports of fifth-column activity are from U.S. Army intelligence reports, Trinidad Sector, 24 July 1943.

367 The attacks on *U406* are recorded in war diary of the Chaguaramas Naval Air Station, 30 July 1943; war diary of VP-204, 31 July 1943.

368 On the sinking of *U461, U462,* and *U504,* see Robertson, *Walker, R.N.,* 119–20.

370 The attacks on *U572* are recorded in the war diaries of VP-205 and Chaguaramas Naval Air Station, 31 July 1943.

373 At no time did the German Submarine Command set up a patrol line across a convoy or shipping route in the Caribbean, or establish a wolfpack to harry a particular convoy. When boats did concentrate in 1942, it was usually the result of a sighting report and actions by individual U-boat commanders.

375   The activities of convoy JT-2 are described in war diary of the Cha-
        guaramas Naval Operating Base, 1–2 August 1943.

376   On the recall signals, see war diary of the German Submarine Com-
        mand, 31 July–4 August 1943. On the sinking of *U572*, see the war
        diaries of VP-205 and Chaguaramas Naval Air Station, 2 August
        1943.

Chapter 19   The Greatest Battle

This chapter is based on the following records: war diaries of the Trinidad
Sector (U.S. Navy), Chaguaramas Naval Operating Base and Naval Air
Station, VP-24, VP-205, and ZP-51, 7 August 1943; report on the interroga-
tion of survivors from *U615*, 22 September 1943, declassified document
ON1 250/9, serial no. 21; and the author's conversations with *U615*
survivors.

380   Survivors from *U615* described to the author the difficulty of crossing
        the Bay of Biscay. The boat had to remain underwater most of the
        time, with the body of Bootsmart Wilkes laid out on a bunk for four
        days.

Chapter 20   The Retreat

401   This account of the final moments of *U615* is based on interrogation
        reports. However, one of the survivors, Seaman Josef Faus, assured
        the author in 1992 that *U615* did not sink during the night. He claimed
        that the crew put Kapitsky's body into a hammock and gave him a
        proper naval burial from the boat. Further, he stated that on the morn-
        ing of 8 August the crew scuttled the boat when they saw the topmasts
        of a warship on the horizon. This would mean the U-boat that the USS
        Walker saw sinking may have been *U615* and not *U634*, as the author
        suggests. Perhaps the survivors told their captors what they thought
        the Americans wanted to hear; because *U634* did not survive this
        cruise, it may never be possible to reconstruct accurately the sequence
        of events that preceded the boat's demise. For *U615* 's last signal and
        the progress of the U-boats' retreat, see war diary of the German
        Submarine Command, August 1943.
          U117 aborted a minelaying mission off New York in order to
        refuel *U66, U129,* and *U525.* The boat was lost on 7 August 1943.

411 On the loss of *U84*, see Jones, *Autumn of the U-Boats,* 147.

414 Reasons for the failure of the Caribbean offensive are discussed in war diary of the German Submarine Command, 23 August 1943.

Chapter 21   U.S. Navy Triumphant

418 The activities of convoy TJ-9 are described in war diary of the Chaguaramas Naval Operating Base, 21–22 September 1943.

419 On the loss of *U161* and *U841*, see war diary of VP-74, 27 September 1943; Jones, *Autumn of the U-Boats,* 19–22, 134–35.

424 The airship K94 was piloted by Lt. (jg) Wallace Wydeen, who was involved in the attack on *U615*.

428 The attack on *U516* is recorded in war diary of VP-204, 18 December 1943.

431 This change in operating procedure by U.S. naval aviation indicates that it was being kept informed of U-boat movements by the British, with their ULTRA intercepts. The British began to release more information by 1944, as the chance that the Germans might discover the intercepts diminished. See war diary of Chaguaramas Naval Air Station, 13 February 1944.

432 The deployment of antisubmarine squadrons, the coverage of convoy JT-24, and the mining of San Juan are described in war diary of the Chaguaramas Naval Operating Base, March 1944.

434 The seizure of the *Cantabrio* is mentioned in TRNVR war diary, 15 April 1944.

435 On the *General Soublet* incident, see war diary of the Chaguaramas Naval Operating Base, 18 May 1944; TRNVR war diary, 18 May 1944. The USS *Hancock* 's attack on Patos Island is noted in war diary of the Chaguaramas Naval Operating Base, 31 May 1944.

436 The attack on the tanker *Cassandra* by *U539* and the subsequent air attack against the U-boat are recorded in war diary of VP-204, 2 June 1944.

437 The capture of *U505* is detailed in Gallery, *We Captured a U-Boat,* 193–204.

Chapter 22   Caribbean Finale

440   On the disadvantages of schnorkelling, see Mason, *U-Boat*, 143–44.

441   The extension of the Caribbean theatre is discussed in U.S. Navy war diary of the Trinidad Sector, 1 July 1944.

443   On the escape of *U763* at Spithead, see Roskill, *The Navy at War*, 392; Mason, *U-Boat*, 143. The dismantling of the convoy system is outlined in U.S. Navy war diary of the Trinidad Sector, December 1944 summary.

444   The loss of the *Island Queen* on 5 August 1944 remains a mystery. The log of *U530* does not mention the vessel—and in any case, the U-boat was nowhere near the spot where the ship disappeared.

445   On Type XXI U-boats, see Mason, *U-Boat*, 151.

447   On the code word "Regenbogen," see ibid., 154.

449   The mines in the Gulf of Paria are mentioned in war diary of the Chaguaramas Naval Operating Base, June 1945 summary.

453   On the arrival of *U530* and *U977* in Argentina, see Heinz Schaeffer, *U-Boat 977* (n.p.: Tandem Books, n.d.), 149–90.

454   Admiral Gallery's assessment of Commander Trosino's achievement is found in *We Captured a U-Boat*, 196.

Chapter 23   Warriors Meet

This chapter is based on war diary of the Chaguaramas Naval Operating Base, 2 October 1945, plus interviews with veterans who were present that day in Chaguaramas and local civilians who witnessed the event.

SHIP INDEX

Abbott USS 349.
Abgard 80.
Accacia USS 66.
Active HMS 175.
Achilles 202.
Afoundria 80.
Ahrens 437.
Albert L. Ellsworth 257.
Alcoa Carrier 88.
Alcoa Mariner 199.
Alcoa Partner 77.
Alcoa Pilgrim 88.
Alcoa Skipper 78.
Alcoa Transport 202.
Alecca Espana 274.
Alexia 134.
Allegrate 93.
Allister 88.
Alysse F.F. 153.
Amakura 155.
Amaranthus HMS 278.
Amatlan 175.
American 100.
Amsterdam 76.
Andrea Brovig 107.
Anemone HMS 380.
Anglo Canadian 119.
Antietam, USS CV 444.
Anti Motkovic 105.
Antinous 194.
Antonico 198, 199.
Apaloide 238.
Ardenvoir 99.
Arica 224.
Arkansan 104.
Arkansas 30, 32.
Arriaga 107.
Artic Explorer HMS 224.
Astrel 224.
Athelbrae 204.

Athelempress 77.
Badger USS 204, 334.
Baghdad 88.
Baltimore USS 332.
Barbacena 124.
Barbara 58.
Barfleur 331, 332.
Barney USS 35, 42, 273.
Baron Jedburgh 445.
Barr USS 437.
Barrdale 83.
Bayou 57.
Bazeley HMS 154, 408.
Beaconlight 120, 210.
Beale USS 281, 288.
Belknap USS 204, 410.
Belleau Wood USS 288.
Bennestret 104.
Bennington USS 444.
Berne 42, 288, 332.
Bessugo USS 292.
Beth 83.
Beverley HMS 172, 425.
Biddle USS 221, 223, 227, 233, 280, 329, 381, 441.
Bill 124.
Bintang 238.
Biter HMS 172.
Birmingham City 258, 259.
Black Bear HMS 418.
Black Swan HMS 262.
Blackwood HMS 154, 408.
Blaison ex U123 451.
Blakeley USS 35, 42, 86-88.
Blankaholm 145.
Block Island USS 437.
Bogue USS 176, 312, 314, 351, 410.
Borie USS 275-278.
B.P. Newton 327, 328.
Bouam ex U510 451.

INDEX

A20A 128.

Achilles, Albrecht 26, 35-43, 49-55, 59, 66, 71, 72, 76, 89, 101-105, 115, 116, 124, 166, 172, 178, 248, 255, 289, 419, 420, 424.

Acoustic Torpedo 200, 417.

Airships K. Type 266.

Allied Tripartite Team 456-460.

Amazon Plain 7, 9.

American, Preparedness; 17, 18, 100, Attitude to; 118, 241.

Andrews, Adolphus; Admiral 17, 98, 164, 453.

Anegada Passage 10, 59, 95, 291.

Antigua; Bases 4, 6.

Anti Submarine; System 286, 287, Differences in technique 126, 127, 284, 432, Weapons 443, Sloops 303, Trawlers 70.

Aphrodite; Radar Decoy 294.

Aratu Base 247.

Argentina 11, 83, 202, 453.

Aruba; Bases 8, 9, 18, 22, Attack on; 27-34, AS Base; 49-54, 217.

Ascension Island Base 442.

ASV Radar 92, Centimetric sets 268, 298.

Auffermann, Hans-Jurgen 177, 178, 188, 192, 193, 208, 252, 256, 315, 324.

Azores, Bases 441, 442.

B-18 Bomber 127, 128.

Badger, Flt. Sgt. RAF. 163.

Bahamas 4, 10, 57, 58.

Barbados Attack on; 178, 179, Strategic position; 179, U-Boat base; 179, 182.

Barnett P/O RAF 237.

Bases Agreement 3-5, 97, 98.

Batet, Rear Adm. 333.

Battle of the Atlantic, Importance of; 18, 113, New Phase; 230, Grim Phase 268, Battle of Technology, 208, 268, 272, 294, 298, 300, Crisis in, 292-297, 299, U-Boat Losses in; 284, 297, 298, MV Losses in; 284, Close run thing; 444.

Battle of the Bay of Biscay 310-318, 322, 323, 335, 352, 353, 368-370, 372, 377, 414.

Bauer, Ernst 52, 58-60, 65-71, 75, 89, 94, 104, 109, 110, 115, 116,269. 322.

Baughmann, Cmdr. USN 456.

Bauxite Route, Killing ground, 75, 267.

Beane Field 61.

Becker, Klaus 366, 422, 431-433.

Beckmann K/L 309, 324, 335, 336.

Bede Clifford, Sir 101.

B'dienst, German radio monitoring service 55, 80.

Belem 346.

Benbow HMS 21, 36, 39, 82, 254, 329, 338.

Bender, Werner 35-38, 55, 60-63, 116, 420.

Bermuda 4, 8.

Bigalk, Gerhard 85, 117.

Biscay Cross, Development 164, First Use 208.

Bliedrodt, Heinrich 294.

Blum Oblt Z.S. 405, 407, 410, 411.

Bormann Martin 453.

Braun, Eva 453.

Brazil 10, 11, 56, 78, 85, 92, Coastal Assault, 134, 143, Declaration of War; 143, 144, 176, 199, U-Boats attitude to; 123, 124.

Brazilian Theatre 10, 247, 252, Move-

About the Author

Gaylord T.M. Kelshall was born in San Fernando in 1940. He was educated at St. Peters College Pointe-a-Pierre, before becoming an Airline Operations Officer in 1958. In 1964 he was commissioned into the Trinidad and Tobago Coast Guard. He received training in England with the Royal Navy during 1965 while completing a combat survival instructors course with the Royal Air Force, as well as attending the commando course and amphibious warfare course with the Royal Marines. In 1966 he received further training with both the United States Air Force and the United States Coast Guard.

During his twelve years of military service, he was an operational search and rescue pilot and founder of the Trinidad and Tobago Coast Guard Air Wing, while continuing duty as a seaman executive branch officer.

In 1968, he founded the Coast Guard Commando Unit and led this Special Forces group throughout the 1970 disturbances, with specific responsibility for tactical demolition, while being commander of the nation's first political prison.

Gaylord T.M. Kelshall – 1987.

In 1972, he became Executive Officer of the Coast Guard and followed this up with an appointment as Air Staff Officer at Defence Force Headquarters.

His last military appointment before retiring in 1976 was as founder of the Defence Force helicopter division, before attending Embry Riddle Aeronautical University.

After retiring from the navy, he became a Corporate Airline captain and flew extensively throughout the Americas.

In 1980, following specialist training by the United Kingdom Ministry of Defence he became an aviation security specialist. He subsequently formed a military and aviation consultancy company.

Today he is chairman of the Airports Authority of Trinidad and Tobago. He is collector of militaria and a keen model builder, as well as being a military history consultant.

He is on the executive of a number of prominent Clubs and Associations and contributes regularly to military and historical journals, as well as being the author of the History of Aviation in Trinidad and Tobago.